MANAGEMENT BY MENU

Lendal H. Kotschevar, Ph.D.

MANAGEMENT BY MENU

A NIFI Textbook

Published by the
National Institute for the Foodservice Industry

Illustrations by Egon Ungar

Typographic design by Fred Schiesser

Special typography courtesy
Monarch Printing Corporation, Chicago

© 1975 by the NATIONAL INSTITUTE
FOR THE FOODSERVICE INDUSTRY
    120 S. Riverside Plaza, Chicago, Ill. 60606
All rights reserved. Printed in the United States of America
by Worzalla Publishing Company, Stevens Point, Wisconsin.

LIBRARY OF CONGRESS CATALOGING IN PUBLICATION DATA
Kotschevar, Lendal Henry, 1908-
    Management by menu.
    Includes bibliographical references and index.
    1. Food service management. I. Title.
TX943.K66   642'.5   75-5732
ISBN 0-915452-20-0

This book is dedicated to
ROBERT W. LANNAN
and
SAUL E. RYKOFF

leaders of our industry
in whose name a memorial grant
to the Institute has been subscribed
by their associates in the
North American Food Service Corporation.

Foreword

"No one ever *said* a textbook should be dull — it just seems to be traditional."

In thinking about textbooks and how they should be written, I can't help recalling this observation by a favorite professor of mine. After making it he would always proceed to tell about the label he once saw on a bottle of meat sauce in Australia which proclaimed: HUNGER IS THE GREATEST OF ALL SAUCES. THIS IS NEXT BEST. WE THINK YOU WILL PREFER THIS.

The analogy never quite came across until a number of years later when all those beautiful school books, simply written and wonderfully illustrated, started coming off the press. Textbooks designed for the *student*. Then I got the message. Obviously a lot of people had.

Appetizing educational fare is especially appropriate in career education, where the student must have authentic and complete information in the most digestible form. Without laboring the question of liberal arts versus "bread and butter" education, let us recognize that a community college student or the restaurant manager often has less interest in and little time for the classical approach.

We are pleased to offer a book on foodservice management conceived and executed in the new tradition. Len Kotschevar is its "natural" author, having taught and written on the subject for years. Admitting a measure of prejudice, we would call it a synthesis of his best works to date and a wealth of new material, with a refreshing new perspective.

Why the emphasis on the menu? It is not uncommon to hear a restaurateur say, "Start with the menu" — a byword of the trade. What *is* new is that this valuable idea has now been incorporated in an authoritative book on the subject. In fact, Dr. Kotschevar goes that familiar prescription one better. He not only starts with the menu; he never lets it go. In a very readable and richly documented text he shows the menu to be an indispensable management tool in planning a foodservice enterprise and in every phase of its operation.

This book gives a clear answer to questions facing today's foodservice executive, whether he be concerned with making a profit or getting the most out of an institutional budget. While it consistently emphasizes financial stability and good business practice, it never short-shrifts the manager's professional obligation to his guests.

The National Institute for the Foodservice Industry is firmly committed to the principle that consumer interests are paramount, and that these interests are most effectively served by advancing management standards in every way possible. Such a program inevitably means more and better education and all this entails in the way of improved curricula, meaningful courses, competent instruction, and scholarship incentives.

Course development is clearly a major part of the Institute's comprehensive educational mission. Updated materials are urgently needed to satisfy the growing demand for career-oriented courses in schools and industry, and to support our commitment to train more than 25,000 new managers and supervisors each year.

It is our hope that *Management By Menu* and other publications in the NIFI series will make life easier for educators and operators engaged in that formidable task.

> Chester G. Hall Jr., Ph.D.
> Executive Vice President
> National Institute
>   for the Foodservice Industry

Contents

Preface

Menu is the dominant character in this play entitled *Management By Menu,* a work written in prose with little plot but dealing with a very important, highly interesting subject around the theme: "How to write a menu which satisfies the needs of management as well as those of the individual who eats the food Menu offers."

Management By Menu is somewhat different from today's offerings on Broadway, but it is also much in keeping with the times. First of all, as in old Greek plays and in some modern dramas, there is a prologue. This serves as an introduction to the main part of the play and should help the reader understand a bit more about the dramatic problems of the foodservice industry and how it operates. Perhaps it is romanced a bit in certain areas, but this is to be a happy play and not a tragedy. The reader will encounter in the first two chapters a number of basic facts about the foodservice industry in which Menu lives and works. For those who know the industry, this part may be only a review. For those who do not, it should set the stage for Menu's actions in the second part and provide a backdrop for all that follows.

There are other characters in this play, but Menu pretty much predominates. He becomes a very much analyzed individual in the second act. Such an analysis is in keeping with modern theater. The object is to study the character of the principal actors and discover what really makes them "tick". We also want to know how Menu influences other characters and how he is influenced by them. There are many sides to Menu's nature, each facet of which is examined from its own special angle in the chapters of Part II. To wit: How he is basically constructed (**Menu Planning**). What the limitations are in his make-up (**Constraints in Menu Planning**). What his tangible worth is (**Menu Analysis and Pricing**), his physical structure (**Menu Mechanics**). And we may even observe how he carries his liquor (**The Liquor Menu**), and what he does to benefit his fellow beings (**Nutrition**). The purpose is to show the spectator how he might himself create such a central character that would perform satisfactorily in a foodservice drama of which he was the playwright.

Our drama is concerned with the powerful effect the menu has in the evolution of the basic functions of a foodservice. It is more than a treatise on how to plan and write a menu, and how to design an attractive menu card. We examine the menu as the central document influencing most of the other functions of the operation. We seek to show how it can be made the most effective tool for management in controlling and directing the entire enterprise. A good menu must meet the immediate needs of communicating between an enterprise and its patrons, but it must also serve to give continuity to the various functions of the establishment and bring them all together in a common goal.

Perhaps the most dramatic scenes of the play are to be found in the third act. This part tells how Menu should relate to other important characters in the foodservice drama, such as Financial Management, Personnel Management, and Food Production, Purchasing and Service. While these characters play seemingly minor roles compared to the predominant part played by Menu, they are extremely important because they influence greatly the action Menu must take in this play to bring it to a happy conclusion.

Lastly, there is an epilogue dealing with the foodservice enterprise as an investment venture. This has been included because a character such as portrayed here in Menu must certainly relate to the basic capital investment and operating costs of a foodservice. If he does not, the play becomes a tragedy.

This is a deep play, not one to be skimmed over lightly. The reader should move slowly through it, giving each scene careful study and thought. But it will all be worth it; for, unless one does master the content of this drama, he cannot set up a character like Menu who will perform successfully. Therefore, Reader, read on. Enjoy the drama. Forget the plot. And remember: "The play's the thing."

Lendal H. Kotschevar, Ph.D.
Adjunct Professor,
College of Hotel Administration
University of Nevada at Las Vegas

6 February 1974
Las Vegas, Nevada 89154

Author's Acknowledgement

No one ever writes a book alone, least of all a book like this. It started as an idea by Chet Hall in one of his intriguing "Do you suppose? . . ." proposals that so often get things going. But once the idea was planted, it grew. No one had ever tried to conceptualize the menu before as a central document by which management can exert control over almost every department in a foodservice organization, and it took a lot of reading, study, discussion and thought to round out the idea, define its scope and put boundaries on it. While its development was rather blind and haphazard at first, our idea did reach manuscript form, and it was then that the editors, Jack and Mary Ryan, tore the thing to pieces asking blunt and direct questions as to what was meant here, how much we should say there, etc. They also corrected misspelled words, punctuation errors and other literary indiscretions. After some rewrite the manuscript got into Floyd Greene's hands at NIFI, where he and Chet Hall recognized that we had a book, but what about this and this and this? The manuscript was kicked around, read by several competent authorities and then came back for a final rewrite which Floyd Greene assisted in mightily. It was he who smoothed out jerky writing and rephrased material so that parts blended into one another and readers would be led smoothly from one major topic to the next./

While an author wrties a book, a publisher has to put it together. The book has to take form and shape. Illustrations and tables have to be fitted into the text. Art work must be done and readied for the engraver. All of this is no small job, and to Floyd Greene must go additionally the credit for bringing a manuscript to life and making it a living book.

Thus, while this book will carry the name of the author on its cover and title page, other names are there — if only implicitly — of these and others not mentioned who contributed ideas and information and gave so much to its content and final form.

L.H.K.

PART ONE

THE FOODSERVICE INDUSTRY

THE story of man and his food is the story of life itself, and would ultimately lead us back to the one-cell organism metabolizing nutrients in some warm, shallow sea untold millions of years ago. Our account is a little less ambitious. Here we seek only to trace the history and development of the human tradition of group feeding. And, even more particular than that, we confine our study to community feeding outside the home — to commercial and institutional food-serving operations.

Food has been a basic article of commerce from earliest times. Organized traffic in ready-to-eat food dates perhaps from times less remote. But that is where we pick up the story, and even there it turns our attention as far back as classical Greece and Rome and the ancient civilizations of Asia. Mass-feeding enterprises were not then so industrialized, but today — supported by advancing technologies in food production and processing — they easily merit the designation of an industry.

This industry has grown from the modest roadside inn and tavern of another day to the burgeoning complex that now hires more people and has more places of business than any other industry in the United States, and represents a considerable part of our gross national product. As of the mid-1970s it serves more than one fourth of the meals eaten in this country, and by the mid-1980s can be expected to serve one half the meals consumed, according to official estimates.

It is against this impressive backdrop, and with this imposing prospect, that we examine the science and art of managing a modern foodservice, and consider the oportunities and responsibilities that confront the enlightened professional pursuing a foodservice career.

In citing the competencies required of foodservice personnel it is important to recognize the value of knowing the job. Anyone who undertakes to do a job must possess adequate knowledge and skills. Some jobs may not require much of either; others require a great amount of both. A worker who knows what to do and how to do it assures himself of being able to function satisfactorily and to meet the expectations of his employer. Such a worker is more apt to be satisfied with the job and stay on it.

However, for best job satisfaction and performance it is not enough just to function adequately. An individual needs to know more than *how to do* a job. He needs to know as much as he can about the enterprise of which his job is a part, and how his job fits into the total system. If he does not, he is hardly more than a bundle of protoplasm responding to stimuli from the work environment. On the other hand, when a person is competent to do a job and understands *why he does it*, the job becomes more meaningful and gives greater satisfaction to all concerned. He then does not work for the job, but makes the job work for him.

To grasp fully the principles of managing a foodservice, one must reach beyond the workings of a particular establishment, which is itself part of an extensive industrial system. Every enterprise is subject to powerful influences exerted by its parent system, just as the earth is affected by the sun, and the solar system in its turn is affected by the still greater galactic system in which it moves. With this in mind the prologue of this book presents background information on the industry and its history.

If one takes an optical lens he can concentrate enough of the sun's energy at one point to kindle a fire. Similarly, the menu planner must collect a broad knowledge of the industry and of his particular establishment, and focus that knowledge at a single point — into his menu.

Since this text revolves around the menu and the many roles it plays in operating a foodservice, it is advisable to attempt a formal definition: *A menu is a list of food items served in a foodservice establishment. It is usually in written form and includes the prices of the items, or groups of items, listed.* As we move more deeply into the subject we will enlarge on this definition. Like the tip of the iceberg, which shows only one tenth of the huge mass that lies below the surface, the menu represents a great deal more than immediately meets the eye. Later on we will see the menu as a means of communication among operating personnel of the establishment as well as to its patrons. And finally we will identify it as an indispensable tool of management in planning and controlling the entire operation.

CHAPTER 1

A Short History of Foodservice

Ancient Foodservices

The foodservice industry is both old and new. It is new in that it has changed considerably in the past 150 years and it is old in that man has prepared food and consumed it in large amounts from earliest times. There is evidence that before 10,000 B.C. tribes in Denmark and the Orkney Islands cooked food in large kitchens and ate together in large groups. Swiss lake dwellers left records of the same kind around 5000 B.C. Pictorial evidence in the tombs and temples of the ancient Egyptians also show that man knew how to prepare and serve food for large groups. There is also evidence in these pictures that prepared food was sold in market places just as might be purchased today in ours. Vendors also sold foods in the streets and elsewhere the same as a mobile unit might do today.

Chinese records long before Christ indicate that travelers and others ate and stayed in roadside inns. In large urban cities, restaurants existed in which foods, rice wine and other items were sold. In India the operation of roadside inns, taverns and foodservices was so prevalent that ancient laws were passed to control them.

The Bible gives many accounts of a mass feeding industry. For instance, accounts tell of Xerxes giving a banquet that lasted 180 days and of Solomon butchering 22,000 oxen for a public feast. Sardanapalus, the Assyrian king, was a patron of the art of eating and loved huge feasts. He organized a cooking contest at which the top professional cooks vied for honors much as they do today at the Culinary Olympics held in Frankfurt, Germany every four years.

In ancient Mohenjo-Daro, recently excavated in West Pakistan, we find evidence that people ate in restaurant-type facilities equipped with stone ovens and stoves for the preparation of food in quantity.

The ancient Greeks had a high level of public dining and much of their social lives took place around foods either in banquets at home or at public feasts. Inns and foodservices existed. The land of Epicurus was Greece, the symbol of good eating and good living. The Grecians went all out for their feasts. The Bacchanal feast in honor of the god of wine, Bacchus, was a lavish outlay of food, drink and revelry. Professional cooks in Greece were honored people and had important parts in plays where they declaimed their most famous recipes. It was even possible in ancient Greece to copyright a recipe.

The Romans also loved feasting. In fact, several of the emperors were so fond of banquets they bankrupted the nation. Emperor Lucullus loved lavish banquets and today whenever the word "Lucullan" is used is means lavish and luxurious dining. A special rich sauce used to grace meat is called Lucullus Sauce. It is perhaps one of the richest sauces used and has in addition a garnish of cock's combs. Mark Antony was so pleased with the efforts of Cleopatra's cook that he presented him with a whole city. Tabernas* from which we get the word "tavern" were small restaurants in ancient Rome where one could get wine and food. We can see one almost intact in Pompeii. It had a large service counter where huge urns of wine were kept. In the back area a huge brick oven and other cooking equipment still stand. These small tabernas were the forerunners of the *trattorias* or small community

*Probably an Etruscan word meaning hut or inn; Etruscan was a civilization that existed near Rome before the Roman Empire.

restaurants of Italy today. The first cookbook we know of was written by a Roman named Apicius and some of its recipes are used today in the famous Forum of the Four Caesars restaurant in New York City. Apicius is reported to have committed suicide in remorse when he found himself bankrupt after giving a lavish banquet. The Romans had a number of laws regulating the sale of foods and the operation of foodservices.

Foodservices in the Middle Ages

Public eating pretty much went "underground" in the Dark Ages. Some inns functioned along the most protected and traveled highways. We can read about these in the tales of the Crusaders. But quantity foodservice in its highest form was practiced in the monasteries and abbeys. They considerably advanced the knowledge of baking, wine and beer making, and cooking. Many of the master craftsmen who later formed the various foodservice guilds gained much of their knowledge in these religious communities. Some recipes originated in those times still are used today, such as pound cake and many meat dishes. It was during that time that Benedictine, Cointreau, Grand Marnier, Chartreuse and other famous liqueurs were developed. These are still made by formulas held secret by the makers. Chaucer's *Canterbury Tales* are rich with accounts of the food and drink served at inns of the time.

About this time various guilds took over the preparation of food in quantity. The Chaine de Rotissières (Guild of Roasters) was chartered in the 12th century. This charter is owned today by the gourmet society of that name. A guild had a monopoly on the production of its specialties and could stop others in their manufacture. The guilds started the development of a professional culinary group that was to be the forerunner of the chef and his entourage. Also at that time many of the professional standards and traditions that are in existence today were begun. It was at that time that the chef's tall hat, the *toque*, became the symbol of the master craftsman, and the round white hat the symbol of the apprentice. It was not until some time later that the black hat came into existence. This was the mark of a master chef voted by his peers as having the right to wear it. The hat was a small, round one made of black silk and could be worn only by chefs elected to wear it. Black in medieval times was the color indicating nobility.

France has not always been a country of fine food. In medieval times, its food was coarse and plain. However, with the marriage in 1547 of Henry II of France to Catherine de Medici of Florence, Italy, France started toward its ascendancy as the country of *haut cuisine*. The Medicis were great patrons of the arts and in their households fine food and drink were served. When Catherine came to France she brought Medici household cooks and servants with her and established herself with them as the dictator of Henry's household and court. Soon foods never before known to the French appeared on the king's table, much to the delight of Henry and his nobility. Catherine in-

troduced ice cream* and many other unusual dishes to the French which we still enjoy. All this started the French on their way toward a great improvement in the quality of foods appearing on the tables of the court and elsewhere. Besides fine food, Catherine taught the French to eat with knives, forks and spoons, instead of their fingers, by bringing these utensils from Florence and introducing them at her table. Soon it became a custom for guests to carry their own eating utensils when they went elsewhere to eat.

Fortunately, Henry's nephew Henry of Navarre, who soon became Henry IV after his uncle's death, visited the court frequently and became quite fond of a good table. When he became king, he continued to encourage the service of fine foods and soon many of the more wealthy households in France began to do the same. Henry IV became known as a great gourmet and today we have a famous soup named after him, Henry IV Soup, which is dished in a large tureen and has a whole chicken in it.

France, however, did not have a monopoly on fine food at the court. Spain's Philip II, son of Charles V, who

---

*Our earliest record of ice cream is that it was made for the Persian kings by freezing cream, honey and delicate flavorings in snow in the high mountains. It was then packed in snow and taken by runners down the mountain to the king's court. The Carthaginians learned how to make ice cream from the Persians and carried the knowledge to the Sicilians who in turn brought it to Florence. Franklin, when he was ambassador to the French court, liked it so much that he brought the recipe to the United States where both Martha Washington and Dolly Madison made history by serving it at the White House.

launched the Armada against England (1588) also loved good food and required a fine table. After he later abandoned Mary, his English queen, she returned to England with a number of the best Spanish cooks and began to undo the harm the glutton Henry VIII had done to English traditions of cooking. Her Spanish cooks taught the English to make sponge cake which the English think was an original product of the English cuisine.

Thus, largely through the royal courts, the production of good food, the art of eating and an interest in gastronomy grew. About 1600 another important development came about which would influence the foodservice industry. The first coffee houses (cafés) began to appear and their spread was rapid over the great cities of Europe. Not much food was served, only coffee and other beverages and they were largely places where people could go and get the latest news and gossip, discuss matters of interest and partake of the latest beverage of the time—coffee. This establishment of the coffee house was later to become a significant factor in restaurant growth.

France, however, continued to take the lead in promoting the production of fine foods and also became a sort of cultural center from which advancements in food and service spread to other areas of the world. The courts of the Bourbons, Louis XIII to Louis XV in the 1600's, continued to develop a knowledge of cuisine and to encourage the training of top chefs and others. Louis XIV was very active in the development of good schools where chefs and cooks could be trained. One of his nobles also became famous as a gourmet and did much to promote the art of eating. This was Count Bechamel, after whom the famous white sauce is named although his chef developed it. Maria Leszczynska, wife of Louis XV, the daughter of the famous Polish king Stanislaus II who himself was a gourmet and also a top cook, emphasized food at the court functions. In addition Louis XV's mistresses, Madame Pompadour and Madame du Barry, were not only lovers of good food but proficient cooks and today we have many fine dishes named after them. Madame du Barry was considered by the king such an excellent cook that he had her awarded the Cordon Bleu, an award given only to the best chefs.

About this time Peter the Great of Russia (1682-1725) was spending much of his youth in Paris at the court and he picked up the French love for food. When he later returned to Russia to become its Czar, he brought with him some of the best French chefs who introduced the hearty-eating Russians to the art of fine cuisine. But Russian gourmets imprinted their own stamp of culture on the art and soon had a very distinct style of food and food customs that differed in many ways from those of the French. A part of this was built upon the rich resources they had in animals, game, fish, vegetables and fruits. It was not long before Russia was returning its debt to the French in fine dishes such as Stroganoff (originated in Poland), caviar, borsch, etc.

While the French Revolution ended the reign of the Bourbons in 1799, it did not stop the French love of food and its dominance in the art of fine eating and dining. Now, instead of nobility and royalty, commoners such as Brillat-Savarin, who wrote *The Physiology of Taste,* Grimod de la Reynière, editor of the world's first gourmet magazine, Alexander Dumas, compiler of the *Grand Dictionnaire de Cuisine,* and Vicomte de Chateaubriand, after whom the steak was named, practiced the art of fine eating and became famous gourmets of their time. Also, many of the impoverished French nobility now threw open their Paris homes as restaurants, still retaining their retinue of servants and chefs, and began to sell dinners and meals. Some of these became the forerunners of the fine restaurants of Paris.

Le Restorante

Another important event occurred during the reign of Louis XV (1760) which considerably influenced the direction of the foodservice industry. A man named Boulanger opened an eating place which served highly nourishing soups. He called these health restorers *(restaurers)* and the enterprise in which they were served a *restorante*. The Chaine de Rotissières and Chaine de Traiteurs ("caterers"—from the French verb *traiter* "to treat") took exception to his doing this in an area in which they should have sole jurisdiction. They brought Boulanger into court to stop him. The case gained wide notoriety and soon the leading gourmets, the French legislature, the king and other influential individuals got into the controversy. The decision of the court presaged events to come and the breakdown of entrenched power of the guilds when Boulanger won his case. He now enlarged his menu and included a much wider list of foods which met with great success. Other restaurants followed and within 30 years Paris had over 500 restaurants. Many coffee houses now changed over to become restaurants, and these were a ready medium to serve as a base upon which to build the restaurant industry.

The Golden Age of Cuisine

The century of the golden age of cookery began around 1800 with the rise of Carême who was perhaps one of the world's most famous chefs. The century ended with Escoffier, another chef of equal eminence, who died in 1935. Carême during his lifetime worked as chef for Talleyrand, Czar Alexander I*, the famous gourmet, and Count Rothschild, the wealthiest man in Europe. Carême wanted to become an architect but never was able to. His father apprenticed him as a small boy to Carême's uncle who operated a small restaurant. Here Carême learned the basic rudiments of cooking.

In his teens Carême traveled to Paris where he quickly progressed through the various food production sections to become a chef. He soon attained a position of prominence and was sought by the leading gourmets of the time to prepare foods for them. With them Carême developed many of the basic concepts

---

*Alexander finally died of eating a dish of poisonous mushrooms several years after Carême left him to go to the Count Rothschild household.

for the progression of courses in a dinner and the sequence of the proper wines to accompany them to improve taste sensations. Carême perfected the very delicate soup, consommé, which took its name from the word "consummate" which means "to bring to completion, perfection or fulfillment." After he introduced it at a dinner as a first course, Grimod de la Reynière exclaimed in his approval, "A soup served as the first course of a meal is like the overture to the opera or the porch to the house; it should be a proper introduction to that which is to follow." Carême also developed many fine French sauces and other fine dishes. He also originated *pièces montées* such as ice carvings, tallow pieces and highly decorated foods which were used as displays, evidently working out his love of architecture. However, Carême's greatest claim to fame, and perhaps his greatest contribution to food preparation, was that he trained a large number of famous chefs who became his disciples and followed him in holding some of the most prominent positions in the world in clubs, restaurants and hotels. Two of them, Soyer and Fracatelli, were the chefs du cuisine of the famous Reform Club of London. Carême also gave a considerable period of his time to writing, and today we still have a rich legacy of his ideas on foods. Undoubtedly, Brillat-Savarin and other great gourmets of the time were considerably influenced by him.

Escoffier, like Carême, was an innovator of fine foods. Peach Melba which he made for Nellie Melba, the famous singer, and many other dishes remain today in the repertoire of many chefs. Escoffier was also sought by royalty and leaders of the time as their chef and at one time was the executive chef of the Reform Club. Later in his life, to spread his talents, he became the supervising chef of a number of the leading hotels and clubs in London.

It was Escoffier who perfected the classical or continental organization of workers in the kitchen and defined precisely the responsibility of each one. Escoffier was first to use a food checker and to establish the close coordination that an executive chef must have with the chief steward. Escoffier insisted that his men dress neatly, never swear, and work quietly and with decorum and gentlemanliness. To reduce the amount of noise and talking in his kitchen he introduced the *abbayeur* (announcer) who took orders from service personnel and in a clear, loud voice called out the foods ordered to the various production centers. He wrote many articles and several books, one of which is a cookbook used over the world today both in homes and institutions.

Escoffier was a true scientist, giving careful observation to the reactions of foods in his kitchen and from these developing sound rules for the preparation of food. He teamed up with the famous hostelier, Cesar Ritz, to operate many of Europe's finest hotels, Escoffier running the back of the house while Ritz tended to the front area. Perhaps at no other time has the level of dining and living been raised so high as under these two men. Even today the word "ritzy" means "elegant, ostentatious, fancy or fashionable." It was the highly social Prince of Wales, the playboy of Victorian England, who remarked "Where Mr.

Ritz goes, there I go." The leaders of culture, society, politics, the arts and sciences became the patrons of these two men. When Ritz and Escoffier died, an era died with them. However, a new order was ready to take over and this one belonged more to the common man who was beginning to emerge as an important figure in society because of the wages he could earn. Coupled with this was the fact that his wages now were sufficient not only to satisfy his and his family's basic needs but left him a surplus which he could use to purchase foods formerly only available to others much higher in society.

The United States

The early development of the foodservice industry in this country was little different from that of Europe. Perhaps because it was a newer country and had fewer cultural traditions, many phases developed much later. In fact, until about 20 years ago any foodservice that wanted a good chef searched for one trained in Europe. Some operations still seek those who have had good European training in spite of the fact that American trained chefs and cooks have equivalent training. This is attested by their success in competitions at the Culinary Olympics and other international competitive meetings.

For a considerable period of time, wayfarers in horse-drawn coaches were cared for at roadside inns some of which still exist as famous eating places. Coffee houses also existed in New York, Philadelphia, Boston and other large cities. Taverns and "eateries" ("beaneries" in Boston) also served food. Some clubs existed which served a fairly high standard of food usually of a local character. As the country became more affluent and resources of food and craftsmen became more plentiful, better and better food was served. In the early 1800's the first hotels were started and these soon began to serve very adequate food. The Astor House in New York City was probably one of the first and also the most luxurious. In 1818 New York had eight hotels but in the next 28 years there were more than 100. By 1850 Chicago had 150 hotels. As the railroads grew and spread over the country, hotels followed them. Soon hotels of considerable luxury were to be found in most large cities. Some, like the Brown Palace in Denver catering to the successful silver magnates and ranchers of the west, were as elegant and fashionable as any operated by Ritz and Escoffier. Many of these hotels became the cultural and social centers of the city.

Fine restaurants also came into being. Lorenzo Delmonico (1818 to 1881) started in the Wall Street area the famous Delmonico restaurant which soon earned an international reputation. He and his brothers also started several other restaurants in New York City beginning what was probably one of the first restaurant chains. However, the era of the common man also was rapidly approaching in this country and with it came a need for a type of foodservice suited more to him than to the elegant and fashionable society that would patronize an establishment such as Delmonico's.

At the turn of the century people began to leave their homes to work in factories, office buildings, stores, hospitals, schools and commercial centers. They needed food and many coffee shops and restaurants sprang up to meet this need. Most of these plainer restaurants were in the downtown areas where there was a high concentration of population. The customers were not wealthy and could not afford to pay much, but because there were large numbers, it became feasible and profitable to serve them. It was at this time that Schrafft's, Childs and others in New York City, the Henrici restaurants in Chicago, and chains in other large cities became highly profitable.

CHAPTER 2

Profile of the Industry

More than 25 per cent of the meals eaten in this country are consumed away from home in restaurants, hospitals, schools, airplanes, bars, department stores, drive-ins, hotels and other places. This is about 150 million meals per day, or almost 55 billion per year. Approximately 55 per cent of these are eaten in restaurants, 15 per cent in schools and hospitals, five per cent in factories and office buildings, and the remaining 25 per cent in hotels, motels, etc. About 7.4 per cent of our disposable income is thus spent for food eaten away from home.

The foodservice industry serving these meals is the fourth largest in retail sales. It is first in number of units—with over 550,000 establishments. In 1972 these foodservices did $48.6 billion worth of business, accounting for more than five per cent of the gross national product. (See Table 2-1.)

The foodservice industry not only has the largest number of places of business but employs more people than any other industry in the United States—estimated to be about 3.7 million as of 1974. This number represents about 22.7 per cent of the total number of workers employed in service industries. And employment has been rising rapidly. From October 1972 to October 1973 the labor force increased seven per cent. Between 1970 and 1980 the work force is expected to increase 25 per cent in commercial operations, compared with a 21 per cent increase in the nation's overall work force. About 250,000 new foodservice employees are required each year to take new jobs or replace people leaving the

Table 2-1

Foodservice Sales in 1972

Commercial foodservices	$40,027,046,000
Institutional foodservices (non-catered)	8,130,236,000
Government feeding	449,336,000
TOTAL	$48,606,618,000

(Data abstracted from National Restaurant Association publications)

industry. Wages and salaries are also increasing rapidly and the industry is no longer one of the lowest paying. The average wage paid in 1972 was $2.16 per hour not counting tips, which can be substantial in some job categories.

This huge group of eating places called the foodservice industry was not always as large nor as important as it is today. In 1900 the industry was relatively small and did not grow much until the 1920s and 1930s when people began to work away from home in much larger numbers. Previously the country had been largely agrarian. People either ate at home or carried their meals with them.

After World War II the industry grew rapidly, having an expansion rate in dollar sales of more than 10 per cent per year, and far outstripped the growth of many other retail industries. While it has never again reached such a rapid growth, its growth has been substantial and in some years has exceeded 10 per cent.

The type of financial organization of foodservice enterprises has also changed gradually. Some are classified as proprietorships (individually owned, family owned or otherwise owned as proprietorships), some as partnerships and some as corporations. Only a short time ago more than 80 per cent of the establishments in the industry were classified as proprietorships. Today the number has dropped to 74 per cent, with partnerships amounting to nine per cent and corporations 17 per cent. From 1960, the number of corporations almost doubled, the number of proprietorships remained about the same, and the number of partnerships declined by about 10,000 units.

Table 2-2
Monthly Eating and Drinking Place Sales

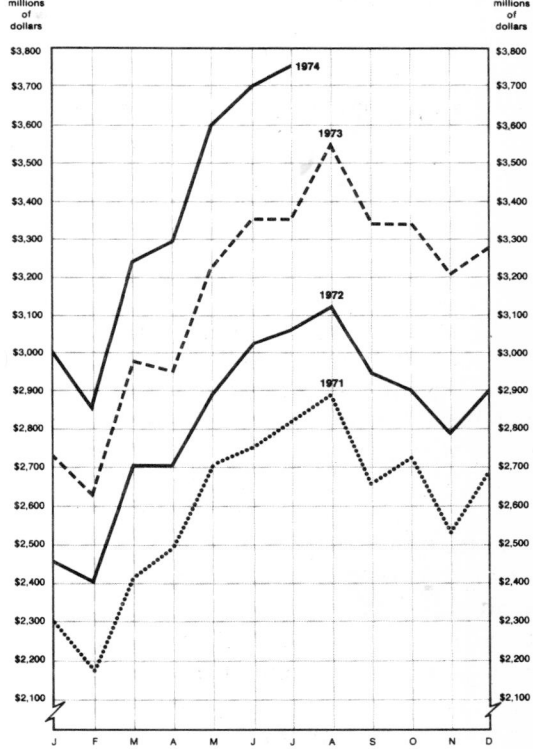

Source: *Current Business Reports,* **Bureau of the Census. Data represent only the commercial portion of the foodservice industry and are unadjusted for seasonal variations. Chart courtesy** *NRA Washington Report)*

In 1969 proprietorships did about $11.4 billion in sales, partnerships $2.5 billion and corporations $16.3 billion. Thus, corporations, only one fourth as numerous as proprietorships, did almost $5 billion more business. We can expect this trend to continue at an even faster pace.

The average daily income per unit in the industry is not large, being around $200 a day or $73,000 a year. The average yearly income for proprietorships in 1969 was about $39,500; for partnerships $70,800 and for corporations $218,000.

The industry is also not as profitable as some others. Dun and Bradstreet in 1967 indicated that more than half the restaurants in the country had no taxable profit. The average net income for corporations in 1969 was 1.9 per cent. The average net income for proprietorships that same year was 8.9 per cent, and for partnerships 10.4 per cent, but one must remember that these net profits do not show the salary of either the proprietors or the partners. This comes out as a part of the profit. If a proprietorship averaged $40,000 in sales (the average for this type of operation in 1969) and made nine per cent profit (also about the average), the proprietorship would make only $3,600 for the year as a salary. For a partnership with an average of $71,000 in sales and a profit of 10½ per cent, the profit would be $7,455. A corporation takes the salaries of management out of expenses before calculating profit. Thus, a 1.9 per cent

Table 2-3

Profits for Eating and Drinking Proprietorships, Partnerships and Corporations[1]

	Proprietorships	Partnerships	Corporations
Sales	100.0%	100.0%	100.0%
Cost of goods sold	53.3	49.1	44.0
Gross profit	46.7	50.9	56.0
Salaries & wages	13.4	16.9	37.8[2]
Payments to partners		1.4	
Rent	3.7	3.4	4.3
Advertising & promotion			1.4
Administrative & general			4.2
Interest	.7	.6	.9
Bad Debts	.03	.03	.07
Taxes	3.5	3.6	3.3
Repairs & maintenance	1.2	1.1	1.1
Depreciation & amortization	2.5	2.3	2.6
Insurance	1.1		
Legal fees	.4		
Other deductions	8.2		.1
Net profit before income tax[3]	11.9	13.2	5.4

[1] Data summarized from 1969 income tax returns to the Internal Revenue Service by foodservices *with* a profit, and do not therefore represent the entire industry. Thus, if we include corporations *with* and *without* net income, the average net profit for the year is 1.9 per cent; for proprietorships it would be 8.9 per cent, and for partnerships, 10.4 per cent.

[2] Includes salaries to officers, casualty losses and some administrative expenses.

[3] Proprietorships and partnerships show a higher net profit because no salary is paid to them as is paid out to officers in corporations.

profit average is perhaps not low compared with the other ownership categories. On the average sales in 1969 for corporations, the net profit at this rate would be $2,834 per unit. The reason for this low profitability has been assigned by Dun and Bradstreet to (a) lack of industry experience, (b) lack of good managerial experience, (c) unbalanced experience—e.g., the manager knows finance or merchandising but does not know food production or service— (d) incompetent management, and (e) lack of capital. It should be noted, however, that the level of profit in many industries has been dropping and is low. For instance, supermarkets make less than one per cent profit on their sales.

The industry has also been characterized by considerable instability. Fewer than half the operations started survive for five years or more. Each year the industry accounts for about 20 per cent of retail failures. Most failures or discontinuances occur in the second year of business, leaving an average of almost $50,000 in liabilities. This instability is changing, however. There is a downward trend in failures of foodservice enterprises, probably the result of improved operational know-how, better management and better financing.

The fact that its units for the most part are small and widely dispersed has prevented the industry from improving efficiency by mass production—combining a number of units in one central area—as some small-unit industries like the garment industry have been able to do. Compared to industries such as steel, coal and automobiles, the foodservice industry does not show the same ratios of efficiency in the use of labor hours. The fact that it must sell a highly perishable product has made it difficult to manufacture and stockpile items as other industries do. Most of the food must be produced and sold immediately upon demand. A steak cannot be broiled and put on a shelf to await the customer's selection. It must be cooked after the customer arrives and orders it. Furthermore, it is not mass-produced by machine. Most of the operations are by hand. This makes a vast difference in how the foodservice industry must operate, and precludes a conventional approach to efficiency through automation.

The industry has also had many problems connected with rapid growth and fast-rising labor and food costs. It has not always been able to pass these costs on in its prices. Instead, it has had to take less profit or seek economies through improved operating efficiency and increased volume. Today there are many operations in the industry doing double the volume they did 10 years ago that are not making more dollars in profit.

In spite of these negative factors, the foodservice industry is a growing, viable, dynamic, vigorous entity making good progress and enjoying fairly good health. It is aware of the need to improve the productivity of its labor, and has done a remarkable job in achieving results in other areas despite inherent difficulties. It is becoming a much more stable industry. Its management is also improving in educational background and ability. The industry is much more professionally minded. More and more, its people realize that they must belong

Table 2-4

Operating Data for Commercial Foodservices

Operating Ratios	Restaurants No-Alcohol	Restaurants Alcohol	Quick Service Restaurant	Cafeteria	Drive-Ins Curb	Drive-Ins Self-Service	Drive-Ins Takeout
	%	%	%	%	%	%	%
Sales	100.00	100.00	100.00	100.00	100.00	100.00	100.00
Cost of food and beverage*	39.90	39.23	36.21	37.32	38.23	42.07	46.95
Gross profit	60.10	60.77	63.79	62.68	61.77	57.93	53.05
Controllable expenses:							
Payroll & employee benefits	29.37	28.87	30.70	30.68	26.72	20.82	17.27
Direct operating expenses	4.82	6.05	6.80	6.29	6.49	6.09	6.00
Music & entertainment	.43	1.28	.50	.25	.09	.24	.00
Advertising & promotion	1.61	1.74	1.40	1.07	1.87	2.53	4.07
Utilities	2.50	1.79	2.30	2.30	2.34	2.30	1.36
Administrative & general	2.83	3.20	3.80	3.79	2.75	5.10	4.54
Repairs and maintenance	1.62	1.62	1.80	1.44	1.72	1.41	1.04
Bookkeeping	1.04	1.12	1.00	1.54	.62	1.73	.84
Computer expenses	.46	.47	1.20	.30	.00	.40	.00
Occupancy costs:							
Rent	4.43	4.90	5.40	5.39	4.59	5.81	3.03
Property taxes	.97	.91	.80	1.44	1.09	.67	.75
Property insurance	.83	.95	.80	.68	.82	1.06	.26
Int. & principal on mort.	2.50	3.32	2.90	3.81	3.19	3.53	2.94
Depreciation	2.12	2.55	2.90	2.12	1.86	2.25	.91
	4.57	2.00	2.29	1.58	7.62	3.99	10.04
Balance							
Average sales/year	$522,000	$243,000	$269,000	$503,000	$219,000	$206,000	$192,000
Seat turnover/day	2.3	3.5	8.0	8.00	10.0	15.4	
Sales/employee/year	$8,208	$10,229	$9,459	$10,482	$8,815	$11,134	$21,125
Sales/seat or stall/year	$1,476	$2,028	$2,271	$1,685	$3,680	$4,263	
Sales/labor hour/year	$4	$5	$4.6	$5.1	$4.3	$5.4	$10.3

*Before employee meal credit

(Data adapted from the NRA Washington Report, Vol. 11, 1968)

to professional organizations which represent the interests of the industry. Unstable units in the industry are gradually being replaced by much stronger ones which will remain as contributing members to the best interests of the industry. The fact that the foodservice industry shows, each year, significant growth patterns over other industries in the retail group, also is proof of its viability and endurance. The industry is of tremendous importance to our economy not only because it hires so many people and contributes so many dollars to it but because it supports many other economic units. Without it, individuals could not leave their homes for long periods of time. When one has to carry along his own food he is considerably hampered in his freedom of action. Our schools, hospitals and transportation systems would not be able to function as they do without adequate foodservice. The importance of an efficient and smoothly functioning foodservice industry can be seen when one visits a developing country and sees how efforts to further its economic growth are hampered by a lack of an adequate mass-feeding industry.

An adequate foodservice industry is also needed to promote the world economy, global trade and commerce. It is essential to world tourism which has become a major industry in our time. In some countries it contributes more to the gross national product than manufacturing, agriculture or commerce. In recent years, tourism and travel have been growing twice as fast as world income. From 1961 to 1970 tourist arrivals throughout the world increased from 71 to 169 million. In Europe in this period the rise was from 50 to 126 million. While this rate of growth is slowing, the growth will continue to be substantial and will require a strong, efficient and growing foodservice industry to support it.

TYPES OF FOODSERVICES

The foodservice industry is a huge conglomerate of different kinds of operations. An individual who would seek to know how this industry is made up and what makes it work should be aware of the nature of these different units and how they are related. Basically, there are two kinds of foodservices to serve two broad markets. The first is composed of those serving food which meets the requirements of necessity or convenience more than elegance or relaxation. The emphasis is on meeting the physical needs of the human body. This in no way implies that the food is of lesser quality, acceptability or appeal. The food must be satisfying and good even though it is plain. But, food is also pleasurable to eat and can be helpful in satisfying social, psychological and emotional needs. A second group of foodservices emphasizes this part of food's role. Food in such operations is accompanied by a pleasing décor and atmosphere, fine service and sometimes entertainment. In fact, the food and service themselves may possess entertainment factors. Besides satisfying physiological needs they now do other things. The eating must be an "occasion." We frequently refer to this second group as "luxury" type operations to differentiate them from the "necessity" type. These two types cater to very different markets and require different modes of opera-

THE GLORY OF CONEY ISLAND

Continued from page 1

"The Steeplechase," "The Thrilling Parachute Jump" and "The Wonder Wheel" and countless others hurtled and still thrill whole generations of screaming riders.

Coney Island has the largest beach and boardwalk in the world. It has the new Coney Island Aquarium and in the fall of 1969 will have an ultra modern Indoor Ice Skating Rink and Convention Hall with a Nathan's Restaurant and Snack Bar.

When was the last time you visited Coney Island? Come on down and visit the Original Nathan's.

Sights that welcomed generations of thrill-seekers . . . the gateways to Luna Park and George C. Tilyou's "Steeplechase . . . The Funny Place."

**INVITE NATHAN'S
TO YOUR NEXT PARTY**
. . . and be a guest yourself!

Be sure to find out about Nathan's Party-at-Home packages . . . for five people or five hundred! Each features Nathan's famous foods.

Ask for our
HOME CATERING
brochure for sure!

NATHAN'S OPENS
AND AN ERA BEGINS

continued from page 1

Near the corner of Surf and Stillwell Avenues, however a different kind of history was being made, as young Nathan Handwerker and his bride-to-be, Ida, made last-minute preparations to open their new hot dog stand.

Nathan and Ida Handwerker

That modest stand represented the realization of a dream for Nathan Handwerker. From 1912-1916, after his arrival in America from Poland, Nathan worked for Feltman's, a nearby hot dog emporium, as a roll slicer and delivery boy. Among his customers were two Coney Island singing waiters, Eddie Cantor and Jimmy Durante. They objected to the ten-cent price of the hot dogs, and suggested to Nathan that he open his own place and sell red hots for a nickel.

Scrimping and saving, Nathan Handwerker managed to save $300.00, enough to rent a small stand which is today the site of the hot dog counter of Nathan's Coney Island. The original stand has been enlarged many times to include the corners of Surf and Stillwell Avenues.

FIG. 2-1
The back of a menu of the Nathan restaurants in New York City. These restaurants are seated-service, delicatessen-type places that cater to family trade. Note the material especially directed to family groups and their entertainment. (Courtesy Nathan's Restaurants)

tion, menus, service and food. It is usually not possible to include both types in a single operation, although in a few cases this can be done.

Public Eating and Drinking Places

By far the largest group in the food-service industry is composed of what the federal government defines as "public eating and drinking places." These operate largely to make a profit, and may also be called "commercial" operations. Institutional foodservices such as those in schools, factories and hospitals are not included in this commercial group although some do operate to make a profit.

The National Restaurant Association classifies commercial operations as (1) seated-service restaurants, no alcohol, (2) seated-service restaurants, alcohol, (3) quick-service restaurants, (4) cafeterias, (5) drive-ins, curb service, (6) drive-ins, self service and (7) take-outs. Two other categories, vending and catering enterprises, could be added. Roughly, 75 per cent of these units are independently or family owned.

SEATED-SERVICE RESTAURANT, NO ALCOHOL. A restaurant of this type may be either a necessity or luxury type, catering principally to family groups and the general public rather than to the "expense account" trade. It seldom will have entertainment offered with the food. This type makes low dollar sales per labor hour used and low income per seat per year. Few are specialty restaurants. They usually are located in or near suburban residential areas where the average family income is sufficient for their support. A favored spot for some new units is a large shopping center.

The menu in this type is apt to feature simple table d'hôte meals and à la carte foods popular with family groups. The food will be "home style" rather than elaborate, gourmet or unusual.

SEATED-SERVICE RESTAURANT, ALCOHOL. Restaurants serving alcohol usually have a more elaborate menu than those not serving alcohol. They also have a larger check and a much better income per labor hour and per seat per year. They also have a better seat turnover rate, the average being 3.5 seats per day compared to 2.3 seats per day. Restaurants with alcohol frequently emphasize "occasion" dining and may have entertainment, especially in the bar. Night and expense account trade may be sought. The menu usually features steaks, lobsters, roasts and other well-liked but more expensive and unusual foods. The foods will be more elegantly dressed with sauces and garnishes. Service will also be more elaborate. However, some may attempt to draw a family trade as well, and will feature foods and service to attract it. The menu in this case may be a combination that seeks to satisfy both needs.

QUICK-SERVICE RESTAURANT. Quick-service units have a limited menu featuring fast foods. They are largely necessity types. A large part of the income may come from sandwiches, coffee, pie, cake and other snacks or partial meals. A "blue-plate special" and a few simple table d'hôte meals may be featured. The service is usually by waitresses who work quickly to move trade in and out. The cooks will know how to fry many orders

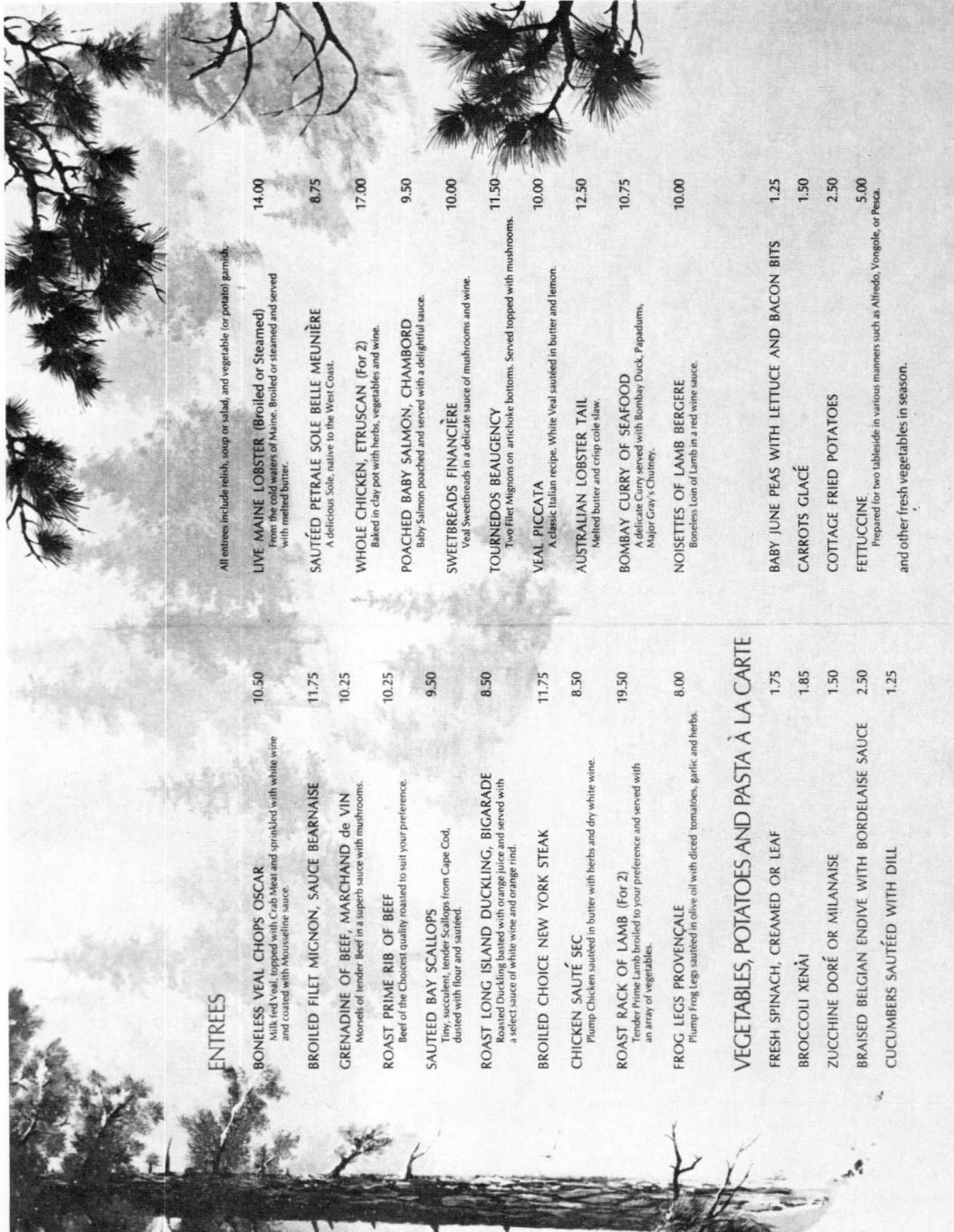

ENTREES

All entrees include relish, soup or salad, and vegetable (or potato) garnish.

LIVE MAINE LOBSTER (Broiled or Steamed)	14.00
From the cold waters of Maine. Broiled or steamed and served with melted butter.	
SAUTÉED PETRALE SOLE BELLE MEUNIÈRE	8.75
A delicious Sole, native to the West Coast.	
WHOLE CHICKEN, ETRUSCAN (For 2)	17.00
Baked in clay pot with herbs, vegetables and wine.	
POACHED BABY SALMON, CHAMBORD	9.50
Baby Salmon poached and served with a delightful sauce.	
SWEETBREADS FINANCIÈRE	10.00
Veal Sweetbreads in a delicate sauce of mushrooms and wine.	
TOURNEDOS BEAUGENCY	11.50
Two Filet Mignons on artichoke bottoms. Served topped with mushrooms.	
VEAL PICCATA	10.00
A classic Italian recipe. White Veal sautéed in butter and lemon.	
AUSTRALIAN LOBSTER TAIL	12.50
Melted butter and crisp cole slaw.	
BOMBAY CURRY OF SEAFOOD	10.75
A delicate Curry served with Bombay Duck, Papadums, Major Gray's Chutney.	
NOISETTES OF LAMB BERGERE	10.00
Boneless Loin of Lamb in a red wine sauce.	

BONELESS VEAL CHOPS OSCAR	10.50
Milk fed Veal, topped with Crab Meat and sprinkled with white wine and coated with Mousseline sauce.	
BROILED FILET MIGNON, SAUCE BEARNAISE	11.75
GRENADINE OF BEEF, MARCHAND de VIN	10.25
Morsels of tender Beef in a superb sauce with mushrooms.	
ROAST PRIME RIB OF BEEF	10.25
Beef of the Choicest quality roasted to suit your preference.	
SAUTEED BAY SCALLOPS	9.50
Tiny, succulent, tender Scallops from Cape Cod, dusted with flour and sautéed.	
ROAST LONG ISLAND DUCKLING, BIGARADE	8.50
Roasted Duckling basted with orange juice and served with a select sauce of white wine and orange rind.	
BROILED CHOICE NEW YORK STEAK	11.75
CHICKEN SAUTÉ SEC	8.50
Plump Chicken sautéed in butter with herbs and dry white wine.	
ROAST RACK OF LAMB (For 2)	19.50
Tender Prime Lamb broiled to your preference and served with an array of vegetables.	
FROG LEGS PROVENÇALE	8.00
Plump Frog Legs sautéed in olive oil with diced tomatoes, garlic and herbs.	

VEGETABLES, POTATOES AND PASTA À LA CARTE

FRESH SPINACH, CREAMED OR LEAF	1.75
BROCCOLI XENÀI	1.85
ZUCCHINE DORÉ OR MILANAISE	1.50
BRAISED BELGIAN ENDIVE WITH BORDELAISE SAUCE	2.50
CUCUMBERS SAUTÉED WITH DILL	1.25
BABY JUNE PEAS WITH LETTUCE AND BACON BITS	1.25
CARROTS GLACÉ	1.50
COTTAGE FRIED POTATOES	2.50
FETTUCCINE	5.00
Prepared for two tableside in various manners such as Alfredo, Vongole, or Pesca.	

and other fresh vegetables in season.

of food and prepare simple soups and other foods. The food is good but plain. Seat turnover may be fairly high, being around eight customers per day per seat. Sales per seat per year will reflect a lower check average but be fairly high because of the better than average volume.

Quick-service units are apt to be located in dense urban areas where many people pass by. A large number are owned by corporations, only 59 per cent being independently owned, compared to about 80 per cent of the two types previously discussed. The California menu is often used, allowing a patron to select a snack, partial meal, breakfast, lunch or dinner any time of the day. Thus, in such an operation one might find patrons eating hot cakes while others are having a steak sandwich. Some attempt to emphasize fountain items.

COMMERCIAL CAFETERIA. Per unit, commercial cafeterias have one of the highest incomes among public eating and drinking places. They have a low average check and a low income per seat because foods are not high priced, but they show a good average dollar sale per labor hour. The seat turnover is high, about equal to that of quick-service restaurants. Food and labor costs are fairly high and the operator must depend upon volume to make a profit. Cafeteria menus are usually planned to meet a specific market, usually one that wants food at a modest price, although some family-type cafeterias may offer foods that rank in cost with restaurants serving no alcohol. The menu should offer a fairly large number of items including snacks, partial meals and complete meals. Foods permitting fast turnover are needed so that customers may immediately find what they wish and wait only a short time for it. In addition to à la carte items, food combinations and complete meals should be offered. The foods need to be filling, satisfying and not high in cost.

Some commercial cafeterias are located in office areas where workers can obtain food at moderate prices. Some may cater to shoppers. Coffee break and lunch periods are often the busiest. At night the patronage can be expected to drop severely as shoppers and workers return home.

←——————————————————————

FIG. 2-2   The inside pages of a four-page menu for Harrah's of Tahoe. This menu is done with elegance and good taste, and is not difficult to read even though the number of entrées, vegetables, etc., shown is large. Thanks to excellent presentation. Printed on linenized paper and beautifully illustrated with soft browns and greens, it is designed to give the patron a feeling of haute cuisine. The original, much reduced here, is nine by fourteen inches folded. (Courtesy Harrah's of Tahoe)

DRIVE-IN, CURB SERVICE. Drive-ins with curb service are usually located in dense urban areas.* About 46 per cent are independently owned. They have a good food and labor cost ratio and profit. Income per seat or car space is high but the check average is low. This indicates a high turnover which runs an average of 10 customers per day per seat or car space. The menu should feature foods easily bussed and prepared. A good cash accounting system is required, and the foods should allow good control and accountability. Menu offerings must be limited. Most drive-ins feature items such as hamburgers, French fries, carbonated beverages, hot dogs, chicken, chili, tacos and other quick-service items. Some may serve specialty foods such as Mexican dishes, chicken, fish and chips, etc. Some menu items should have a good profit margin while others may be sold as "leaders" at low profit. Inventories should be held to only a few days' required supplies. Most foods are prepared upon demand. These should be quickly done and be easily controlled from the standpoint of cost, quality and quantity. Good portion control is essential.

DRIVE-IN, SELF-SERVICE. Drive-in self-service units differ from curb operations in that customers leave their cars and go to a window or drive up to a window to obtain their food. They can eat in the car, at outside tables, or drive away and eat elsewhere. Most of these drive-ins are located in dense urban areas. Only 22 per cent are independently owned.

The turnover rate is high. Sales per unit, either by car space or seat, is the highest among commercial units. Food and labor costs are low and the units are the most profitable among commercial groups. There are also specialty units that feature foods much the same as curb service drive-ins. Since workers are usually young and relatively inexperienced, rather tight controls must be used.

TAKE-OUTS. Take-outs sell food to be consumed off the premises. They usually are specialty type operations and sell a limited number of menu items. Take-outs are increasing at a rather rapid rate because most are profitable. They should be located in areas of high population density or where a large number of potential customers pass by. The foods must be a very popular kind and not too unusual, although Chinese food or other specialty types may be quite successful. Since some foods must be held for long periods, they should be able to stand the delay and still hold quality. Or they should be quickly prepared upon demand. They must lend themselves to packaging and this should not be too expensive. Since some must be reheated or otherwise processed later, they should be of the correct type. For instance, mashed potatoes might not be a good item to have on the menu. Other foods, at home or elsewhere, usually are added to make a complete meal and the menu items should lend themselves to this kind of use. If the take-out unit also serves food to customers on the premises, the take-out section is best limited to a few specialty items. Particular care should be taken to see that perishable foods are properly refrigerated.

---

*In 1967 a *Drive-In Management* survey showed the division of drive-ins as: car hostess (curb) service 33.4 per cent, inside seating 17.6 per cent, take-out 33.1 per cent and self-service 16.9 per cent.

FIG. 2-3 Menu for a fast-service type of operation. This menu is designed to give a patron anything from a snack to a full meal. It seeks to promote quick-turnover trade. (Courtesy of the Patio Room, a Milton D. Faber enterprise, Chicago)

VENDING. Vending is a significant factor in the foodservice industry, with more than 6,000 companies and over $4½ billion in annual sales. About 25 per cent operate their own commissaries. Many do catering in addition. Some provide cafeteria or other kinds of service.

A recent *Vend* magazine study showed production percentages in central commissaries for vending as follows: sandwiches 60, pastry 28, casserole and platter foods 7, and salads 5 per cent. A central commissary should produce not less than 600 to 700 units per day to be efficient. If this volume is not achieved, purchase from outside units is usually best. Foods can also be obtained from purveyors, wholesalers or from other vending operations.

Over 20 per cent of in-plant feeding services are operated completely from vending machines. For in-plant needs, the food must be substantial and popular with workers. Thus, a ham and Swiss cheese, or lettuce, tomato and bacon sandwich may be more popular than a sardine and rye sandwich, but some types of clientele may prefer the latter. Food products should be available from vending units at high, fresh quality.

Vended foods may require a substantial investment in machines and distribution equipment. A simple candy, pastry or other machine needing little or no refrigeration may cost $700 or $800, and one that dispenses hot beverages or soup, or that refrigerates or holds frozen foods may cost twice as much or more. Attendants appreciably raise costs. Normally, from five to eight years are required to recover the cost of a machine. Food costs may be as high as 65 per cent and labor and commissions 21 per cent. Sanitation is an important factor in the selection, preparation and holding of the foods.

If a vending operation, or any other foodservice, transports food across state lines, the place where these foods are processed must meet federal standards for food production facilities and the standards established for them in sanitation.

CATERING. Catering operations may be classified as industrial, mobile and private. Industrial catering is a relatively new development in the foodservice industry but it has grown rapidly in the last 20 or 30 years. Such catering is actually the management of a foodservice operation by an outside company for some account such as a factory, school, hospital, convention center, office building, nursing home or other business. The company may even operate a commercial restaurant in a shopping center. Contracts for operation are usually awarded on a bid basis and the space, equipment and furnishings are usually

The National Automatic Merchandising Association in 1966 indicated the following average operating ratios for vending companies:

Sales	100.00%
Cost of Sales	51.38*
Gross Profit	48.62
Operating Expenses:	
Service salaries commissions	9.71
Maintenance labor, machines	1.57
Other salaries, wages, etc.	9.82
Total Payroll	21.10
Maintenance cost, machines	.84
Commissions to locations	8.17
Machine depreciation or rental	4.02
Other depreciation (less buildings)	.86
Truck and automobile expense	.91
Sales tax	1.29
Other taxes	1.49
Insurance	.63
Building and garage rental	.71
Other expenses	4.93
Total Operating Expense	44.95
Operating Profit	3.67
Other Income	.85
Profit before Income Taxes	4.52
Sales per employee on payroll	$37,408

*Includes packaging costs which may sometimes be from 10 per cent to 25 per cent of the cost of the item.

provided by the client, the contractor providing management and workers. Usually the contractor charges a fee for his service and any profit goes to the client. Most clients are happy to break even or have a small loss. In some cases, the contractor may take a part or all of the profit as his fee.

The advantage of having a contractor is that he can usually provide better professional management and operation know-how than the client. The client is also spared the problem of managing something he usually knows little about.

Private catering can be quite varied, running the gamut of small side-line units to full-service enterprises capable of serving a banquet to several thousand individuals in a convention center. At times, caterers may even furnish some food to commercial or other foodservices. Some caterers may restrict their activities to small parties, serving tea, hors d'oeuvres or simple buffet dinners, while others may perform almost any kind of food and beverage service. The unit must be located where a good market study indicates there is sufficient demand for the products and services.

A sales program must be established to work out catering arrangements with clients, and it is usually wise to have pre-planned menus listing services offered and prices. Other factors for special arrangements should also be listed. Since the need for service may be spasmodic but may cover an extremely wide range, a considerable stock of equipment may be necessary, even if it is used only occasionally. Therefore, the mark-up must be higher than that of a regular foodservice. The products offered must be suitable for preparation, holding packaging and transporting. They must be attractive and simple to serve. Because most catering is done to order, over-production or waste is small.

A caterer may provide food that is delivered, or customers may call for orders. Some caterers furnish and deliver the food, provide the service personnel and do the serving, clean up, etc. Equip-ment for complete service may have to be provided. Some restaurants, delicatessens and bakeries may do catering in conjunction with regular business. Some caterers make arrangements with party-oriented retail units, such as liquor stores, bakeries, delicatessens or others, to seek out business and turn it over to the catering company. The commission paid for this is usually five to 10 per cent of the price.

Close control of costs must be maintained, since they can increase rapidly and get out of hand. Transportation can be a sizable expense. Efficiency is needed in getting food prepared, delivered and served, and in cleaning up and returning equipment. Guest guarantees should not allow more than five to 10 per cent over or under numbers stated. Some use sliding scales for guarantees, allowing a larger per cent of leeway as the numbers increase.

Large industrial caterers may operate catering divisions. Many will take contracts to provide the catering needs of convention centers, sports areas, etc. They usually have an office located at the place where service is required and operate from there. This, then, becomes much like a normal catering service. Snack foods, beverages, hot dogs, peanuts, pop and other items may be offered. In many, service personnel circulate in the stands and sell items to customers. Counters will also be located where patrons can purchase items they want. If a dinner or other meal must be catered, this company does it. They may purchase foods from a restaurant or other foodservice, if they lack complete production facilities to do this, and then they will provide only the service of getting the food to the consumer.

Prior to World War II there were few mobile caterers. Those that existed were like the Good Humor man, selling ice cream on a route in the summer. During World War II, trucks, vans and other mobile units, with hot or cold foods, began to visit factories, construction sites, etc., and sell food. Some cooked foods to order.

Today the mobile catering business is a significant factor in foodservice. More than 6,000 are licensed in California alone. Sales in this country in 1972 increased 15 per cent, topping $1 billion for the first time. Sales percentages were divided between industrial plants (60.8), construction sites (24.4), office buildings and complexes (12.6) and the remainder (2.2) at parks, recreational areas, special events, etc. More than 1,150,000 locations were served.

The mobile company may be a corporation or privately owned. *Vend* magazine in 1972 found 67 per cent were corporations, 21 per cent proprietorships and 12 per cent partnerships. There has been a significantly steady growth in both numbers and dollar sales since World War II, 22 per cent of the caterers starting between 1970 and 1973, 35 per cent in the 60s, 26 per cent in the 50s, with some in operation as far back as 1925.

A corporation usually hires its own salesmen to operate its trucks but it may lease them to individuals taking a percentage of sales. Some sell the foods to an individual, rent the truck to him and have him pay a commission for the route.

Proprietorships vary. Some purchase their own trucks and develop their own routes. The typical mobile catering firm has 17 trucks, each truck stopping at an average of 21 locations a day. *Vend's* 1972 study showed that 55 per cent of the truck drivers were directly employed, 27 per cent used a route lease system and the others used both procedures. Nearly 80 per cent were found to own their own commissaries.

Truck rental, including fuel, insurance and maintenance, is usually $20 to $50 a day. A route is considered worth about $40 to $50 per day for every dollar in sales it generates. Thus, a route having $200 per day in sales is worth from $8,000 to $10,000. Route leases usually run from five to 10 per cent of gross sales.

Routes are subject to pirating. To hold a business, the route operator must be regular and provide good service. The food must be of acceptable quality, attractive and moderately priced. Some routes can have up to 40 or 50 stops on a 15 to 20 mile run, but many operate shorter routes. The fewer stops the better. Some routes may have only a few stops, since enough business may be generated to give a satisfactory return. Most routes are not over 20 to 30 miles away from the pick-up spot. A good stop should generate at least $200 to $250 in an eight-hour run. Such a route may require that the work day be 10 to 12 hours, since the truck must be cleaned, serviced and loaded in addition to being operated over the route. Some routes may operate every day, but many operate only five days a week serving workers who are at the stops only during the week days.

The foods should be those that are satisfactory for such service. Usually the same foods that are easily vended are easily sold in a mobile unit, although the mobile unit may be more flexible and be able to sell a wider variety of foods. Box lunches, soft and hot drinks, sandwiches, hot lunches, coffee, desserts, bagged goods, candy, salads, crackers and cookies, etc., are all sold. The food must be filling.

Sanitation is important and many foods will have to be kept under refrigeration or frozen. Hot foods must be kept above 140°F during the time they are held.

Health Care Foodservices

There are two kinds of health care institutions, providing short- and long-term care. Short-term care facilities give intensive care and rather complex medical treatment. The patient time in the institution is usually short. In long-term care operations, people stay for long periods of time in a convalescent home, nursing home, state hospital or sani-

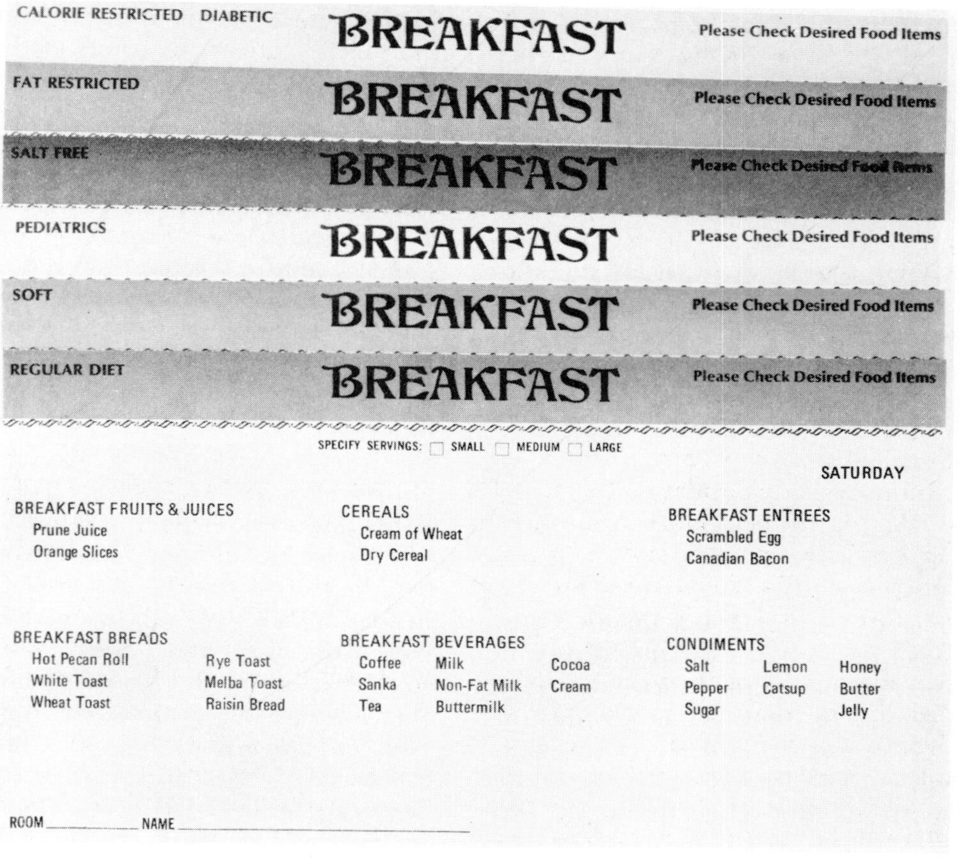

CALORIE RESTRICTED DIABETIC	**BREAKFAST**	Please Check Desired Food Items
FAT RESTRICTED	**BREAKFAST**	Please Check Desired Food Items
SALT FREE	**BREAKFAST**	Please Check Desired Food Items
PEDIATRICS	**BREAKFAST**	Please Check Desired Food Items
SOFT	**BREAKFAST**	Please Check Desired Food Items
REGULAR DIET	**BREAKFAST**	Please Check Desired Food Items

SPECIFY SERVINGS: ☐ SMALL ☐ MEDIUM ☐ LARGE

SATURDAY

BREAKFAST FRUITS & JUICES
Prune Juice
Orange Slices

CEREALS
Cream of Wheat
Dry Cereal

BREAKFAST ENTREES
Scrambled Egg
Canadian Bacon

BREAKFAST BREADS
Hot Pecan Roll   Rye Toast
White Toast   Melba Toast
Wheat Toast   Raisin Bread

BREAKFAST BEVERAGES
Coffee   Milk   Cocoa
Sanka   Non-Fat Milk   Cream
Tea   Buttermilk

CONDIMENTS
Salt   Lemon   Honey
Pepper   Catsup   Butter
Sugar   Jelly

ROOM _____ NAME _____

FIG. 2-4   Hospitals must present a well organized set of menus to meet the needs of patients. A patient on a fat-restricted diet will not get a general menu but one covering his diet. This menu will have the bacon and other foods removed that are not permitted, and other items substituted. As with other modified diets, the menu will contain as many items on the general diet as possible. (Courtesy Sunrise Hospital, Las Vegas, Nevada)

torium; little intensive care is given, but many of these units give skilled nursing care. A few give only personal care and assistance, or just residential care. We have about 1.9 million beds in both types. In 1971 health facilities spent nearly $2 billion for food for patients, staff and visitors. Some hospitals are quite large but the average number of beds is under 100.

A hospital's foodservice is usually directed by a professional food person, such as an administrative dietitian with a college degree in dietetics and an internship after that. A dietitian must be a member in good standing in the American Dietetic Association. Some hospitals use a professional foodservice manager to administrate the foodservices and use dietitians to handle only dietary problems. A chef or food production manager will work under the head of the foodservices. The food is plain, but usually of good quality. The nutritional value of the food and its sanitation are important considerations in food production.

Most hospitals operate on a general menu from which patients select foods they desire. From the general menu, modified diets are prescribed by the doctor and dietitians plan them. Thus, a low-calorie or diabetic diet will usually have many foods on the general diet with certain modifications either in kind of food or amount. Similarly, a low-sodium, low-fat, or other special diet will be drawn from the general menu but changed as required. For this reason, a general diet must be planned with a view toward its being used also for modified diets. However, it should not be dictated by this consideration.

Most hospitals use a cycle menu, which is a menu repeated several times in sequence. Since the patient's stay is usually short, most hospitals find they can often operate with a rather short cycle. The food must be nourishing, plain and not too highly seasoned. A hospital foodservice is very much a necessity rather than luxury type.

The service of the food may vary. Some hospitals have what is called centralized services where foods are dished in the central production area and then sent to the patients. Various methods of keeping the food hot or cold are used. Some have trayveyor systems that deliver food to the various floors in a short time. Others use carts into which hot or cold food is loaded and sent to floors. Or, a hot metal pellet may be put under dished food to keep it at a desirable temperature. A new insulated server is also available into which hot or cold foods can be dished with little or no loss of desirable temperature for several hours.

However, with the increasing availability of foods which are already prepared and can be quickly reconditioned for service, many new hospitals are developing decentralized systems. Only a limited amount of bulk preparation occurs in a central area. This is then sent to the various pantries on the individual floors where these foods are combined with others to make a proper meal for a patient. Thus, a foodservice may purchase all of its salad greens and other salads ready to use. Frozen or chilled entrees may also be purchased in the same condition. These foods will then be sent in the proper amount to the smaller pantries where the final preparation and dishup will occur. Some pantries wash the dishes and do a great deal of the cleanup. Heating of the food in these pantries may be by microwave ovens, quartz ovens (infra-red), convection ovens, or regular conventional ovens.

Hospitals serve patients who are ill and under considerable emotional stress because of health problems. While the food may be of good quality, patients may not think so because of their own physical or emotional condition. The food becomes a "whipping boy" on which the patient takes out his fears and frustrations. Because of this, hospitals need to "sell" patients on the food, just as commercial units must do. Foods should be attractive, properly garnished, served at the right temperature, and have good form, color, texture and flavor. While the patient may be a "captive" and have to accept the food, every attempt should be made to cater to personal tastes and whims, the same as a commercial operation must. For this reason many hospitals today, run special menus and do extra promotion to see if they can improve the patients' impressions of the food.

Long-term care facility foodservices are much like those of hospitals, but may not have the wide number of modified diets, although many patients will be on some special type of diet. The food must be nutritious and fairly plain. Many of the elderly and others may have problems in eating, so much of the food must be soft, easily chewed and easily swallowed. However, special soft and bland diets should be prepared for those who must have them so that the others can have a more normal, textured food.

Most long-term facilities operate on low budgets. The foodservice department must therefore watch its costs. The foodservice workers are not especially skilled. A foodservice manager or supervisor will have the responsibility for direct management. Most dietitians act as consultants who call once a week or sometimes as seldom as once a month. Thus, responsibility for management may rest with an individual who has had little management or dietary training.

The equipment and the layout of the foodservices will usually be fair to poor and, because of this, menus and the foods that can be produced must necessarily be restricted. While the food should be plain and home-like, it should not be monotonous and lack variety. Because the foods have to be low in cost should not mean they will all be casserole or extender dishes, with little or no relief in the way vegetables, desserts or other menu items are presented. With "a little love," even low-cost foods can be highly varied, interesting, desirable and nourishing.

Hotel Foodservices

The food and beverage department of a hotel frequently represents a fairly complex system in which a number of different types of foodservices are operated. This could include a coffee shop, banquet facilities, snack bars, foods served in bars, a night club, fine dining room, specialty restaurants, roomservice, cafeteria, employee dining room, etc.

A hotel foodservice department will usually be managed by a food and beverage manager largely responsible for seeing that the operation keeps adequate records and makes a profit. A chef may

LUNCHEON

Appetizers

Fresh Fruit Cocktail Supreme . . . 1.25
Marinated Herring in Sour Cream . . . 1.75
Fresh Chopped Chicken Livers . . . 1.50
Melon in Season . . . 1.25
Chopped Eggs with Onions and Schmaltz . . . 1.50

Shrimp or Crab Meat Cocktail . . . 2.50
Gefilte Fish with
Red Beet Horseradish . . . 1.50
Half Grapefruit Maraschino 95
Assorted Juices Small .60; Large .95

Soups

Cup .65 Bowl 1.00
French Onion au Crouton
Cold Jellied Madeline   Chicken Broth with Mazzo Balls or Kreplach
Coney Island Clam Chowder   Vichyssoise   Beet Borscht Topped with Sour Cream

Entrees

(Price of Entree Includes Potato, Vegetable, Salad, Rolls, Butter)

Caesar's Daily Special

NEW ORLEANS JUMBALAYA
On a Bed of White Rice en Casserole   3.75

FRESH CHICKEN LIVER OMELETTE with French Fried Potatoes, Garni . . . 3.25
DEEP FRIED COMBINATION SEAFOOD PLATTER, Garni . . . 3.25
PAN BROWNED CORNED BEEF HASH, Topped with Poached Egg . . . 3.00
BAKED TUNA AND NOODLE CASSEROLE . . . 3.00
LONDON BROIL, Prime Top Sirloin Sliced into Strips, Mushroom Sauce . . . 4.00
SPAGHETTI ITALIANO, Sauce Bolognese, with Meat Balls or Sausage . . . 3.25
ROAST STUFFED SPRING CHICKEN, Demi-Glaze . . . 3.50
ROAST TOP SIRLOIN OF BEEF, AU JUS . . . 4.00
French Fried or Whipped Potatoes   Carrots Vichy

From the Sandwich Board

Choice of Soup or Salad
HOT SMOKED BEEF TONGUE, Sauce
Madiera, on Rye, with Whipped Potatoes . . . 3.00

Cold Counter

COLD SLICED BREAST OF TURKEY AND SUGAR-CURED HAM, Waldorf Salad . . . 3.25
CAESARS OWN FISHERMAN'S SMORGASBORD,
Crabmeat, Lobster and Shrimp on a Bed of Crisp Lettuce, Garniture Julius . . . 4.50
SMOKED WHITEFISH PLATTER, Garnished with
Bermuda Onion, Sliced Tomatoes, Creamy Cole Slaw . . . 3.75

Desserts

Assorted Fruit Pies .75   Cheese Cake .95   French Ice Cream .65
Chocolate Cream Pie .75   Assorted French Pastries .85   Strawberry Short Cake .75
Chocolate Pudding .65   Rice Pudding with Whipped Cream .75   Strawberry Cheese Cake 1.10

Beverages

Coffee .30   Pot of Tea .35   Milk .35   Sanka .35   Postum .30
L.I.—Fre.—3/74

DINNER

Appetizers

Fresh California Fruit Supreme . . . 1.50
Marinated Herring in Sour Cream . . . 1.75
Jumbo Shrimp or Crabmeat Cocktail . . . 2.50
Half Grapefruit Maraschino . . . 1.50
Chopped Eggs with Onions and Schmaltz . . . 1.50

Fresh Chopped Chicken Livers . . . 1.50
Homemade Gefilte Fish, 1.50
Red Beet Horseradish . . . 1.25
Fresh Melon in Season 95
Assorted Juices Supreme Small .60; Large .95

Soups

Cup .65 Bowl 1.00
French Onion Soup au Crouton   Jellied Madrilene   Chicken Broth with Mazzo Balls or Kreplach
Old Fashioned Lentil Soup with Sliced Frankfurters   Vichyssoise   Beet Borscht Topped with Sour Cream

Caesar's Daily Special

ROAST PRIME TOP SIRLOIN OF BEEF, Garni   5.75

(Price of Entree Includes Potato, Vegetable, Salad, Rolls, Butter)

BROILED TURBOT with Lemon Butter . . . 4.50
VEAL SAUTE PROVENCALE, Green Peppers, Tomatoes, Pearl Onions, Sliced Mushroom Caps . . . 4.95
BAKED STUFFED BELL PEPPERS, Espagnole Sauce . . . 4.25
GRILLED GENUINE CALF'S LIVER with Canadian Bacon . . . 5.25
SHISH KEBAB, Tangiers, Noisette of Lamb, Green Peppers, Tomato, Onion, on a Bed of Rice . . . 5.50
YOUNG SPRING CHICKEN IN THE POT, Julienne of Garden Fresh Vegetables with Mazzo Balls . . . 7.50
ROAST PRIME RIBS OF BEEF AU JUS . . . 4.25
FRESHLY GROUND SIRLOIN STEAK, Mushroom Sauce, Tomato Provencale . . . 4.25
BROILED BEEFEATER LOBSTER TAILS, Drawn Butter . . . 9.50
BROILED DOUBLE RIB SPRING LAMB CHOPS, Mint Jelly . . . 6.50
BROILED PRIME T-BONE STEAK, Mushroom Caps . . . 8.50
BROILED NEW YORK CUT SIRLOIN STEAK . . . 9.50
BROILED MINUTE SIRLOIN STEAK . . . 7.50
BROILED PRIME FILET MIGNON with Mushroom Caps . . . 9.50
MARINATED RIB EYE STEAK Saute with Smothered Onions . . . 7.50
Baked Idaho   O'Brien Potatoes   French Cut String Beans   Provencale Tomatoes

From the Cold Counter

JUMBO GULF SHRIMP or ALASKAN KING CRAB LEGS LOUIE
White Asparagus Tips, Sliced Tomatoes, Hearts of Celery, Choice of Dressing . . . 4.25
CANNED GILL NETERS SALMON STEAK
Garnished with Sliced Tomatoes, Bermuda Onion, Hard Boiled Egg, Cole Slaw . . . 4.25

Desserts

Assorted Fruit Pies .75   Jell-O with Whipped Cream .65   Marble Cake .75
French Ice Cream .65   Rice Pudding with Whipped Cream .75   Sherbet .65
Assorted French Pastries .85   Strawberry Cheese Cake 1.10   Marzipan Cream Roll .75
Cheese Cake .95   Chocolate Pudding .65

Beverages

Coffee .30   Pot of Tea .30   Milk .35   Sanka .35   Postum .30
D-1 — Fre.—3/74

FIG. 2-5 A dinner and luncheon menu for a hotel dining room. These two menus are on one card, the back used for luncheon, the front for dinner. While it is crowded, close inspection will show that a rather extensive list of foods is presented in the space available. (Courtesy Caesar's Palace, Las Vegas, Nevada)

be responsible to the food and beverage manager but sometimes he may be responsible only to the manager of the hotel or his assistant. A maitre d'hotel will be in charge of the better dining areas, but a hostess might be responsible for service in a coffee shop. A banquet or catering manager will handle the catering of banquets and special parties. A steward may work with the chef in preparing menus, setting up order requirements and seeing that the linens and silver, etc. are properly handled, stored and accounted for. He may also be in charge of storage spaces for food, equipment and other supplies. A sales department of the hotel should work in close liaison with the food and beverage department since it is usually responsible for making arrangements for special catering and other functions to be handled by the food and beverage department.

Many hotels operate on the continental system in which an executive chef manages food production with his sous chef and chefs du partie working under him doing the actual food production. The operation is somewhat complex because of the variety of food that must be prepared and the number of different dining areas and special catering facilities that must be served. Much central food preparation will occur and this will be distributed to the various serving units. Thus, a grill might get many of its sauces, soups, salads and other foods from the central kitchen, preparing only sandwiches, grilled items, etc. in the grill area.

Many hotel dining rooms stress luxury-type foods and serve alcoholic beverages and wines. A table d'hôte and à la carte menu are usually combined. The menu usually features steaks, chops, roasts, poultry, seafoods and fish. Service should be in keeping with the menu.

Even a hotel's coffee shop can be fairly luxurious, although it may have a slightly different service and offer more plain foods than the main dining room. In a moderate-class hotel, the coffee shop may be quite ordinary, but in a luxury type hotel the coffee shop will very likely reflect this quality.

Banquets must be handled with high efficiency and speed. A special banquet kitchen may prepare a large part of the banquet, but the central kitchen again can be called upon to supplement many items. Since banquet service may be spasmodic, a list of individuals who can be called upon to work as waiters or waitresses, bus boys and even cooks must be maintained, or the hotel must have a contact with a union or other labor source for its needs. There are many individuals in the foodservice industry who work only for banquets and thus are available on call.

NEW TRENDS
IN HOTEL DINING

Hotels frequently have a problem in that many of the guests who have rooms will not eat at the hotel, especially lunches and dinners. The reason given for this is that customers prefer to eat elsewhere to get a change, or because the food at restaurants is better or costs less. Thus, many hotels are challenged to hold their own internal customer business. One way that has been used to do this, and also bring in outside trade, is to operate specialty restaurants such as a Trader Vics or a Benihana (Japanese).

New hotels and motels frequently do more to emphasize the food and beverage business than was true in the past. The reason is that the food and beverage business is now more looked upon as a potential source of revenue and profits. In some hotels and motels, the food and beverage income can be almost equal to that from rooms. Thus, we see many hotels and motels with rather elaborate facilities for conventions, meetings and special events. These can bring in considerable revenue in food and beverage sales as well as help fill the rooms.

Hotel foodservices have not led the market in acceptance of new types of foods. Many today cut their meats from carcass or wholesale cuts. However, there is a growing interest in these new foods as labor becomes more expensive and less skilled. Younger chefs with a broader and more management-oriented viewpoint are also beginning to take charge and bring more of these foods into the operation. In addition, young and progressive men who have had advanced training are beginning to move into management positions. They are also beginning to bring about a change in attitudes.

The following is a summary of percentages of income and expenditures that might be considered typical for a hotel:

Income

Rooms	53.2%
Food	29.3
Beverages	11.6
Rentals from stores, etc.	1.4
Telephone	2.5
Other	2.0

Expenditures

Wages and fringe benefits	36.4%
Supplies and expenses	24.8
Cost of beverages sold	3.0
Cost of food sold	9.4
Real estate taxes	4.2
Other taxes and licenses	.5
Interest	4.7
Depreciation	5.4
Profit before income taxes	11.6

Elementary and Secondary Schools

One of the largest foodservices in the world is the National School Lunch Program established by our Federal government in 1946.* The program is administered by the Department of Agriculture which distributes funds and surplus foods on the basis of the participating children in a state. In addition, it administers the Special Milk Program where a school gets a cash refund from the government for each half pint of milk it purchases for a child. To obtain cash and surplus foods, a school system must provide each student with a Class A meal. This meal must contain a specific amount of food to qualify for subsidy from the Federal government— about a third of a child's food requirements must be provided. In addition, the program should develop a knowledge of nutrition and what an adequate diet is. Elementary schools operate almost entirely on the Type A lunch program, but secondary schools may provide some

*Locally operated programs existed before this. In 1884. Mrs. Ellen H. Richards, a home economist, started probably the first program in Boston, but it was not until after World War II that the need for such a program was shown when figures for malnutrition and physical defects and some data obtained on the nutritional status of school children were analyzed.

à la carte items that do not qualify for government support, in addition to those that do. Federal regulations do not allow the sale of carbonated beverages if the program receives Federal support, but fruit punches and other non-milk beverages can be provided.

Many of the older schools in the country do not have food production facilities and consequently cannot participate in this Federal program. They can, however, participate in the milk program. New ways to provide meals to such schools are being used, however. Many school systems now prepare food in central commissaries or other units and then ship the food to the schools that lack production facilities. Because of the economies possible from such mass production, many school districts are beginning to operate largely from central commissaries. New schools are not being

		Menu for Elementary Satellite Schools		
CLARK COUNTY SCHOOL DISTRICT				APRIL 1974
MONDAY	TUESDAY	WEDNESDAY	THURSDAY	FRIDAY
Chili Dog on a Bun Potato Salad Orange Sections Homemade Cookie White or Chocolate Milk 1	Pork Chopettes Whipped Potatoes Bread and Peanut Butter Sliced Peaches Cookie – Treat 2 White or Chocolate Milk	Baked Macaroni & Cheese Buttered Green Beans Turkey Salad Sandwich Apple Crisp White or Chocolate Milk 3	Sloppy Joe Burger Tater Gems Fruit Cup Homemade Cookie Treat 4 White or Chocolate Milk	Beef & Bean Burrito Chili Beans Applesauce Homemade Cake White or Chocolate Milk 5
Cheese Dog on a Bun Potato Salad Orange Sections Homemade Cookie White or Chocolate Milk 8	Breaded Fish Sticks French Fries Peanut Butter Sandwich Fruit Cup Homemade Cookie 9 White or Chocolate Milk	Barbequed Turkey on Bun Tater Gems Orange Sections Easter Cake Treat 10 White or Chocolate Milk	SPRING VACATION 11	GOOD FRIDAY 12
SPRING VACATION 15	Cheese Dog on a Bun Potato Salad Orange Sections Homemade Cookie Treat 16 White or Chocolate Milk	Chicken Fried Steak Whipped Potatoes Bread & Butter Peach Crisp White or Chocolate Milk 17	Sloppy Joe on a Bun Tater Gems Fruit Cup Homemade Cookie White or Chocolate Milk 18	Beef & Bean Burrito with Chili Beans Applesauce Homemade Cake White or Chocolate Milk 19
Cheese Dog on a Bun Potato Salad Orange Sections Homemade Cookie White or Chocolate Milk 22	Breaded Fish Sticks French Fries Peanut Butter Sandwich Tinted Applesauce Homemade Cookie 23 White or Chocolate Milk	Spaghetti w/Meat Sauce Buttered Green Beans Cheese Sandwich Pudding White or Chocolate Milk 24	Barbequed Turkey on Bun French Fries Orange Sections Homemade Cookie Treat 25 White or Chocolate Milk	Beef & Bean Burrito Chili Beans Peaches Homemade Cake White or Chocolate Milk 26
Cheese Dog on a Bun Potato Salad Orange Sections Homemade Cookie White or Chocolate Milk 29	Chicken Fried Steak Whipped Potatoes Bread and Butter Peach Crisp White or Chocolate Milk 30			

Menu subject to change.

Emma Higby, Coordinator

FIG. 2-6 School foodservice menus under the Class A lunch program must meet certain nutritional requirements. Planning a menu which will do this, and yet satisfy the tastes of young children, can be quite a challenge. The example shown here has been designed to suit the needs of elementary school children many of whom are of Mexican descent. Note the high degree of repetition. This can be done because children would rather see foods repeated that they like, than have new, unfamiliar foods thrust upon them. (Courtesy Clark County School District, Nevada)

built with food production facilities that prepare meals but only with service units where foods that are centrally prepared and shipped in can be served to students.

A number of different methods are being used to recondition such food for service. Most frequently, convection ovens or microwave units are used for heating foods that must be served hot. The insulated server, mentioned previously for hospital foodservices, is also being used in some schools.

In general, it has been found that an hour of labor in a central commissary is as productive as 10 hours in an individual, small school kitchen. When the hours of transportation labor, clean up, serving, etc. are added in, the central commissary operation then has a saving ratio of only 1:3. Thus, while individual school kitchens produce and serve around 12 meals for every labor hour used, central commissaries produce and serve 36.

Some schools may also serve some children breakfasts because they frequently do not eat at home. Children from low income families may also get free tickets for meals. Head Start programs may also be provided food from the school foodservices. Continued extension of the services can be expected.

Much less surplus food is available today from the Federal government. The loss of this subsidy has forced schools either to raise prices or to depend more upon support from local school districts. Most school foodservices are heavily subsidized with respect to space, utilities, heat, light and power, insurance, janitorial care and even maintenance. It is now possible for a public school foodservice to be operated by a contract company. This was not true several years ago but recently the USDA changed a ruling that prohibited a profit-making company from operating in the school foodservice area.

The foods prepared for the Federal program must be simple and plain. They should have high popularity with children who have extremely sensitive food tastes and habits. Many children reflect food patterns learned at home where the food may be highly individualized and quite different from that served at school. One of the problems is to educate these children to eat different foods that provide adequate nutrition, which is no small problem. Children will also lack the food experience to be willing to try new foods and so will tend to stay with well known foods they have learned to eat. It is therefore extremely difficult to introduce other foods. Nevertheless, those administering the program over the years have done remarkable things. Today, the school foodservice system is deeply engrained into our educational system and is a tremendous force in providing adequate nutrition to many children in this country, many of whom would not be able to have this food to build strong, healthy bodies.

Colleges and Universities

School dormitories, student unions and other foodservices of colleges and universities can be huge operations doing millions of dollars of business in a year. Dormitories may be operated on a closed board plan that provides three meals a day to a student at an established rate. Regardless of whether he eats these or not, he is charged for them. Many schools have modified this program and provide fewer meals at a standard board rate and allow students to select the meals they wish and pay individually for these. Some others have worked out plans where only a specific number of meals for a week can be purchased and consumed at any time during the week.

The price of food must be modest and many schools help support the foodservices by providing free light, heat or power, space and other items. The foods must be popular with the students. Some foodservices find they have to offer organic foods on the menu along with others to satisfy all student tastes. The food must be nutritious and provide adequately for dietary needs.

Most school foodservices are cafeterias with the students serving themselves beverages, bread, butter, desserts, salads, dressings, condiments, silver, napkins, etc. For this reason many foods may have to be preportioned and dished. Students may also bus their own trays from their tables to central areas.

In addition to the main commons, a school may operate snack bars, coffee shops, faculty club and dining rooms. These will usually be typical of commercial counterparts, but slanted in price and otherwise to the campus needs. Faculty clubs must provide a somewhat luxury type food for parties, meetings, receptions, etc. They also must be able to provide food which meets faculty family needs. Alcoholic beverages may be sold in some while in others this may not be permitted. Faculty clubs frequently resemble regular social clubs. They may have recreation facilities such as swimming pools, tennis courts and even golf courses.

Usually a central department operates all foodservices on the campus. Management is usually professional. Registered dietitians may be on the staff to see that menus are balanced and adequate nutritionally. A regular staff of cooks and other personnel is maintained, along with a lot of part time student help. Many full time people will be women.

Clubs

Foodservices in clubs usually emphasize luxury or entertainment type food. They serve members who use the club for enjoyment, relaxation or the entertainment of guests. The market is usually restricted to members and guests. Social clubs have only social programs and in addition to parties may serve breakfasts, lunches and dinners. They may provide rooms for resident members. Many such clubs exist in downtown areas. Catering is usually a big source of revenue. Many clubs sell alcoholic beverages. Country clubs are social clubs, but usually have different recreational and sport facilities in addition to the foodservices. Clubs may vary from facilities for serving luxury foods to snack bars, coffee shops, grills, etc.

Most clubs have a wide fluctuation in the amount of business done. At times they will be extremely busy with every foodservice operating at full or even greater capacity, while at other times little or no business will be in operation. This makes it difficult to schedule production and labor. The menu must include food items which can be used to meet a sudden surge in business. These can be items such as steaks, chops, poultry, etc. Some convenience items may also be carried frozen or otherwise preserved so they can be quickly used if the demand arises.

Club foodservices must endeavor to attract members. Special events may be used as a drawing card. Thus, a dinner or meal featuring foreign foods may be offered, or a stag dinner may be given with some type of entertainment. Wom-

FIG. 2-7
One page of the menu of a small, club dining room where members can get food after golf, tennis or swimming. Offerings cater mainly to a need for snacks. Note provision at top for a clip-on displaying the daily special. (Courtesy Desert Inn and Country Club, Las Vegas)

en's fashion shows with a luncheon or a dessert bridge may be offered. Bingo parties, dances and other activities may be put on the social calendar to draw members.

The foods must be largely of the luxury type and more unusual than those served in ordinary foodservices. Quality must be high. The food and service must give pride to members and impress guests who eat there.

Central Commissaries

Many chain or other foodservice operations use central commissaries to produce much of the food they sell. School systems are presently using them extensively. Some large foodservices such as Horn and Hardart, Marriott's, Howard Johnson's, Horn's, Bigford's, etc. have a substantial quantity of their foods produced in them. These foods are shipped to satellite units where they are then reconditioned and served.

Some central commissaries may only receive large shipments and then reship the food items in smaller lots. Michigan State University's unit acts as a warehouse and breakdown center where fresh vegetables, groceries, meats and supplies are received and reshipped to campus units. Another central commissary in the City of Los Angeles school district does this, but prepares basic dry bakery mixes, pudding mixes, sauce mixes and other items in addition to reshipping other items after breaking them down into smaller units. The advantage in such a system is that lower prices can be obtained since now the central commissary acts as a broker in warehousing and breaking down units into smaller shipments, and the central commissary can legally qualify for brokerage rather than wholesale prices.

Other central commissaries may prepare entrees, meats, salads, vegetables, desserts, bakery items, soups, etc., ready for use. These may be shipped portioned or in bulk lots where they are conditioned for use in the satellite. Shipment may be as frozen, chilled or hot foods.

Unique distribution programs have been developed. The huge Fairfield Kitchens, operated by Marriott in Washington, D. C., ships prepared foods as far as Minnesota or Florida and has its own transportation in huge vans, each van carrying a forklift truck to handle the huge shipping containers. These containers are locked to enable the van to leave them on the loading dock at night, to be opened in the morning so that foods can then be withdrawn for use.

A central commissary is not a kitchen but a factory in which foods are mass-produced on assembly lines moving as in automotive and other factories. Special equipment must be used. Some foods are cooked in huge steam-jacketed kettles holding 2,000 gallons or more of food. The food is also cooled down in these kettles by shutting off the steam and running refrigerated glycol or water into the jacket. Huge electric stirrers must be used to move the food while cooking and cooling. Special pumps and other units must be used to put the food into the kettles and remove it. Highly sophisticated packaging machines must also be used. Such a kitchen is a far departure from the ordinary institutional kitchen.

Most foods produced in central production centers will be frozen in liquid nitrogen, contact or blast freezers. Some may be pasteurized in their wraps and then rapidly chilled and held under refrigeration until needed without freezing. Heating may occur in the plastic or other wrap of the food. Some operations using portioned packs find that heating in a microwave oven is satisfactory, provided the packaging is not metal which cannot be used in such units. Others find that heating in a water bath is satisfactory. Some use sophisticated resistance-heating units while others use quartz (infra-red) ovens, convection ovens, etc. Bulk packs under tight seal can be efficiently thawed in steam chambers and then finally heated uncovered in regular resistance ovens or in convection ovens or other dry heat units.

Before a central commissary is planned and built, a study should be undertaken to determine whether a huge investment is in order, or whether the requirement can be met with products available on the open market at a lesser cost. The production of a wider variety of foods of improved quality makes this a strong possibiltiy. One of our largest commissaries found it could purchase uncooked breaded onion rings at less cost and better quality than it could produce. It therefore converted the space for the production of this item to another purpose and purchased its needs on the open market. It also found later that it could purchase a higher quality food and soup base on the open market at a lower cost so discontinued making this product. As long as a central commis-

sary remains flexible and can move in and out of the market there is perhaps less danger of its moving into an unprofitable production position.

There are advantages to central commissary operation. The commissary can produce items it wants to have exclusively, and it can also control its own supply as to quality and cost. Portion control can also be improved by its own portion standards and production.

Many central commissaries are finding they cannot use typical professional foodservice people. These individuals are accustomed to working in large kitchens and not large factories. In the latter, items move on belt, and much of the work done by hand in a kitchen is here done by machines. Instead, food technologists and industrial engineers usually take over and interpret into mass action the standards and techniques of the chef and cook in the kitchen.

Gauging the size of the commissary has also been difficult. There is a tremendous investment in one and unless adequate production can be obtained, the operation costs can be very high. Some of our largest commissaries recently constructed have had excess capacity for present demands and have operated at heavy losses. Management has looked ahead to future demands and built to meet them, failing to realize that interim operation might be quite unprofitable. Some have been able to solve the problem by seeking other markets outside of their own units. Even the retail market has been exploited to find adequate market demands to keep the central commissary in the black.

Airline Feeding

In many respects a large kitchen producing airline meals is a central commissary but there are some very significant differences. Timing demands are tremendous. Foods must be ready at a time needed and be moved quickly. The delay of a plane because food is late would be a serious problem. But foods cannot be produced too far in advance. Much individual dishup must occur and there is a need to develop maximum efficiency in work methods. The food must be of the luxury type. A production center may produce foods for one or several airlines. A catering company may set up a central production unit and sell meals to the airlines and also operate the airport foodservices.

As an alternative, an airline may operate its own production center and provide foods to other airlines.

Each airline will have its own menus and its own standards. Food standards and purchase specifications will be precisely stated. Several menus may be required for the same plane, such as a choice for first class passengers and a choice for coach class. Thus, a center may have a very wide assortment of foods to produce at one time for different planes. Each plane may require its own type of dishes and accompanying equipment. A storage area must be provided for each. It is not unusual for a large center to produce 6,000 to 8,000 meals a day with only a limited number of common items. In addition, al-

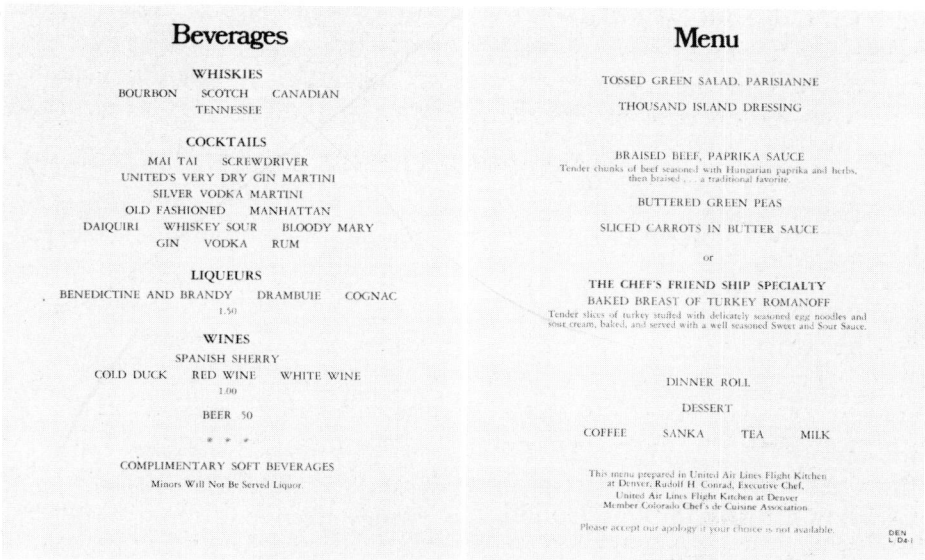

Beverages

WHISKIES
BOURBON   SCOTCH   CANADIAN
TENNESSEE

COCKTAILS
MAI TAI   SCREWDRIVER
UNITED'S VERY DRY GIN MARTINI
SILVER VODKA MARTINI
OLD FASHIONED   MANHATTAN
DAIQUIRI   WHISKEY SOUR   BLOODY MARY
GIN   VODKA   RUM

LIQUEURS
BENEDICTINE AND BRANDY   DRAMBUIE   COGNAC
1.50

WINES
SPANISH SHERRY
COLD DUCK   RED WINE   WHITE WINE
1.00

BEER .50

COMPLIMENTARY SOFT BEVERAGES
Minors Will Not Be Served Liquor

Menu

TOSSED GREEN SALAD, PARISIANNE

THOUSAND ISLAND DRESSING

BRAISED BEEF, PAPRIKA SAUCE
Tender chunks of beef seasoned with Hungarian paprika and herbs,
then braised . . . a traditional favorite.

BUTTERED GREEN PEAS

SLICED CARROTS IN BUTTER SAUCE

or

THE CHEF'S FRIEND SHIP SPECIALTY
BAKED BREAST OF TURKEY ROMANOFF
Tender slices of turkey stuffed with delicately seasoned egg noodles and
sour cream, baked, and served with a well seasoned Sweet and Sour Sauce.

DINNER ROLL

DESSERT

COFFEE   SANKA   TEA   MILK

This menu prepared in United Air Lines Flight Kitchen
at Denver, Rudolf H. Conrad, Executive Chef,
United Air Lines Flight Kitchen at Denver
Member Colorado Chef's de Cuisine Association.

Please accept our apology if your choice is not available.   DEN
L D4-1

FIG. 2-8   The menu of an airline must be suited to its needs. This menu is simple, small and yet serves the purpose for passengers and the airline. (Courtesy United Air Lines)

coholic and non-alcoholic beverages, ice, water, tea or coffee, milk, napkins, nuts and other items must be provided. This demand, plus providing the variety of services required at an airport, can require quite a complex system.

Usually an airline uses a cycle menu for six days and may change the cycle six to eight times a year. A center may be advised 14 to 30 days in advance that a plane must be loaded, but the actual count is not given until several hours before flight time although a preliminary count may have been given 24 hours before. Special meals for diabetics, Kosher meals and others must be ordered at least 24 hours in advance, but sometimes this does not occur.

Good flexibility must be established. Changes can occur rapidly and the center must be prepared to meet them. For instance, a plane may be diverted from one airport to another and have to be loaded there. The foods required have usually been well tested for their ability to hold, but holding can only be for specific time periods. Nevertheless the airlines are serving a constantly increasing number of rather perishable products, such as steaks or roasts, done to the passenger's order, omelets, scrambled eggs, hot cakes and other items normally thought to be possible only with immediate service.

An airline likes to have the equipment it brings in on a flight ready for takeoff about four hours later. This means the center must work out a rapid system for unloading a plane and getting the equipment washed and ready for turnaround.

No food or beverages returned on one plane can be used on another unless it is in the form of packaged units such as canned pop, bagged nuts, etc. The U. S. Public Health Service has jurisdiction over sanitation on all public carriers moving across interstate lines and the rules are quite stringent. Because of the large inventory of different kinds of dishes, tableware, equipment and other items that must be held, the center must have considerable storage space for each airline. If good organization of storage is not established, chaos can result. Transportation to and from the center to the planes must also be well organized. Work methods in production should be well developed because of the large number of motions workers have to make in preparing and assembling foods.

One of the great benefits of the technical knowledge gained by airline feeders is that they have been willing to experiment, attack and solve problems and come up with new and novel methods for preparing and serving meals. This knowledge is spilling over into other foodservice operations and causing marked change in some procedures.

TRENDS IN THE INDUSTRY

The foodservice industry is not a static one. It is a dynamic, changing entity and, while the changes that are occurring may not seem to be revolutionary, their steady pace is creating a very different industry. If one looks back 50 years and compares production and service then and now, he will recognize that vast changes have occurred. Our foods 50 years ago were not as fresh nor sanitary as they are today. Our grading standards and our ability to hold quality in foods were not as good. Many foods now come to us processed to such a degree that we do not have to use as much labor to get them ready for service. For instance, the tedious and painstaking chore of making almond paste has gone because prepared paste of high quality is available. Many different kinds of cooked foods, ready for service, are on the market. Frozen foods, as we use them today, are less than 50 years old.

It is not much more than 50 years ago that foodservices began to use mechanical dishwashers and mixers. Coal, wood or fuel oil ranges and ovens were quite common in comparison with a thermostatically controlled unit such as we use today. There were no electrical meat saws, cubers or grinders. Steam-jacketed kettles and pressure cookers were just appearing. The modern deep-fat fryer was unknown. Potatoes and other vegetables and fruits were pared by hand. No bleaches or anti-oxidants had been developed to prevent fruits and vegetables from tarnishing and so they were soaked in water with a heavy nutrient loss. Canned products had just begun to be widely used and had lost their stigma. They were the "convenience foods" of the time, just as in our day portion-cut meats, preblanched frozen potato strips and other products are commonly accepted. We can look forward in the next 50 years to even greater progress because we have available far, far more technology and resources than we had 50 years ago and the pace of change is even faster.

Types of foodservices and modes of operation have also changed and the industry is serving a much larger and more diverse market. Chains or multiple operations and franchises are a very important part of the industry today and the volume of business they do is impressive. These will continue to grow and the trend for independently owned units to decline will go on. Volume will continue to increase per unit and ways will have to be found to produce food in greater amounts and serve it to larger numbers of people. Central commissaries will continue to take over more and more production tasks. Foodservice outlets will become more and more distribution, service and merchandising facilities. In a way, the Industrial Revolution will begin to take place as more and more products are manufactured this way and distributed and served in retail and service outlets.

Man's biological need for food and his appreciation of it will not change, nor will our foods. A pill will not be satisfactory. But our methods of producing, distributing and reconditioning foods will change. Modes of service will not change as much. It will be the alert individual who looks ahead and anticipates change who will be most successful. Those who stay with things as they are and refuse to accept change will find they are losing ground and customer favor and, finally, will pass on just as did the dodo and dinosaur.

The ability to meet change successfully requires that one not only be able to adapt to it; he must also be able to evaluate it and resist it when it leads to undesirable conditions. Too rapid an adaptation can be as harmful as a failure to adapt. The bankruptcy courts are filled with cases of enterprises which pushed an idea before its time had come.

Part I Bibliography

Brodner, J., Carlson, H. M., Maschal, H. T., *Profitable Food and Beverage Operation,* 4th edition, Ahrens Publishing Co., New York City, 1962.

Fay, G. T., Rhoads, R. C. and Rosenblatt, R. L., *Managerial Accounting,* Wm. C. Brown Co., Dubuque, Iowa, 1971.

Fitzgerald, Jean, *The Foodservice Business,* Bank of America, Small Business Advisory Service, San Francisco, 1968.

National Restaurant Association, Facts About the Foodservice Industry, Chicago, 1970.

National Restaurant Association, *Washington Report,* Vols. 16 through 22 (January 28, 1974), Chicago, Ill.

Watson, Betty, "Cooks, Gluttons and Gourmets," Doubleday and Company, Garden City, N. Y., 1962.

U. S. Department of Labor, "Eating and Drinking Places Industry," *Industry Manpower Surveys,* No. 115, Washington, D. C., 1969.

PART TWO

THE MENU: BLUEPRINT AND SHOWCARD

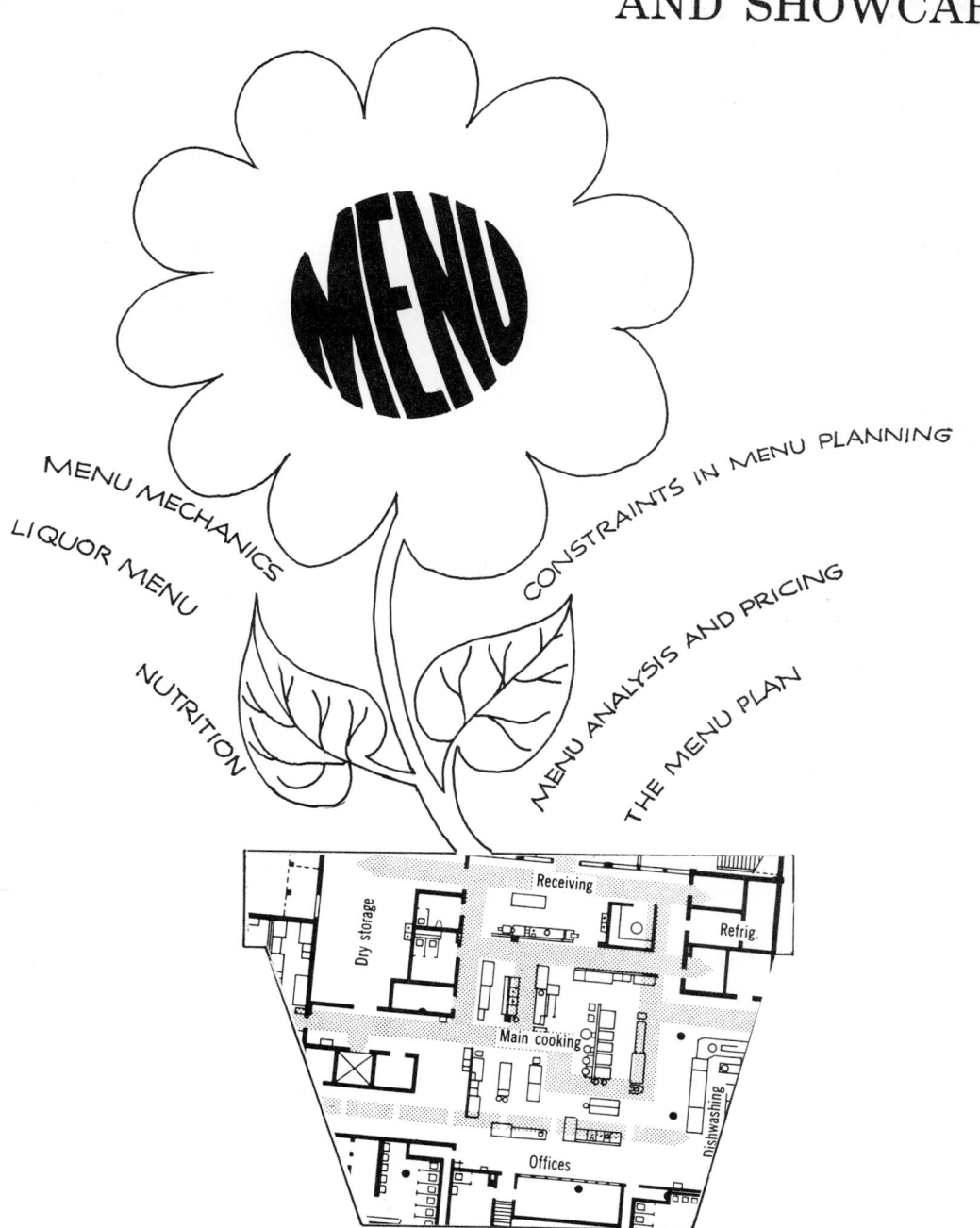

MENU

MENU MECHANICS

LIQUOR MENU

NUTRITION

CONSTRAINTS IN MENU PLANNING

MENU ANALYSIS AND PRICING

THE MENU PLAN

Receiving

Dry storage

Refrig.

Main cooking

Dishwashing

Offices

FOR most of us the term menu conjures up an image of the bill of fare, a list, often presented as an elegant folio, showing the food and drink offered by a restaurant. For the operating personnel of a food-service establishment it signifies something more: It is the production plan governing almost every phase of the work.

The menu has few names but many uses. Simply to recite these uses is to demonstrate how integral the menu is to the functions of a foodservice. That indeed is the recurring theme of this management study and the dominant note in our present discussions.

In considering the menu as a written, graphic instrument, we can think of it generally in two ways: as a working document for the back-of-the-house, and as a published announcement to the patron out front. In the first model it serves a variety of functions. It is a purchasing guide, a work order to the kitchen or pantry, a service schedule — the basis for charting staff assignments in all departments. In the second model it is the product list and price schedule, and the primary means of advertising the food, beverages and service available. A good menu should lead a patron to food selections which satisfy both his dining preferences and the merchandising priorities of the proprietor. It can also inform patrons of the hours of operation, of special services available, and may include narrative material on the history of the establishment and its locale.

The design of the menu card is itself a specialized project involving judicious use of the graphic arts coupled with a keen understanding of the foodservice profession.

In a larger sense the menu can be seen as a powerful factor in establishing a foodservice enterprise, large or small. At the initial stage of planning it describes the very nature of the undertaking and the scope of the investment. It determines the design and construction features of buildings and facilities, the mode of operation, cuisine and style of service. From the investor's standpoint it names the product, selects the market and calls the tune in merchandising and sales promotion. For the multi-unit operation with a highly distinct product it may even be the trademark of the business.

"Start with the menu." This familiar byword of the restaurant trade is laden with meaning for the operator, suggesting not only the procedure in conducting a successful business, but the careful and orderly approach required of the professional who takes his public service commitment seriously. In an industry facing the prospect of serving half the meals consumed by a nation of 220 million, a significant degree of "scientification" seems inevitable. This means increased attention to nutrition and health, as well as to culinary excellence.

From start to finish, and from back to front, the menu is clearly the blueprint and showcard of a foodservice. And, as we shall see in more detail, menu writing is a very important craft. The following chapters incorporate numerous observations about menus and menu planning. All are not applicable to every menu. What is intended is a broad discussion of the many factors affecting menus and their planning. The planner will need to select those which best fit a specific situation. Ingenuity and imagination are a prime requisite. If science is an organized body of knowledge, and art the application of it, the material that follows is the science; the menu maker must supply the art.

CHAPTER 3

Menu Planning

As far as we know, the first coffee houses and restaurants did not use written menus. Instead, waiters or waitresses recited available items from memory. Later, some restaurants in Paris originated the custom of writing on a small board a list of foods offered. The waiter hung this from his belt to use to refresh his memory. Other early foodservices set up a large board which listed menu items. No doubt the need to have some record, not only for customers but for cooks and others, led to the written menu. These finally evolved into some of the elaborate merchandising mediums we see today.

The word "menu" comes from the French and means "a detailed list." The term is derived from the Latin *minutus* meaning "diminished" from which we get our word "minute." Based on this, perhaps, we can say that a menu is "a small detailed list."

Instead of "menu" some may use the term "bill of fare." A "bill" is an itemized list and "fare" means food, so we can say the term means "an itemized list of foods." This works out to be pretty much the same thing as "menu."

As we have noted, the menu is an extremely important working document influencing almost every facet of the operation. It is the central document out of which almost all operations proceed. No good planner of the layout and equipment for a foodservice would start his plan until a copy of the menu was available. No program for sales promotion and merchandising should be started without a menu as the basis of planning. No food can be ordered, cooked or served until there is a menu to tell what is needed.

The job of a menu is basically to inform. It must inform patrons of what is available to be served and, frequently, the cost. A menu also informs workers of what is to be produced and what may be ordered. Thus, the problem of a good menu construction is basically one of achieving good communications. The terms used must mean the same thing to the menu planner and the reader. They should be simple, clear, graphic words that present an exact description of what the patron is to get. They should not be confusing, nor should they over-promise. The list should avoid foreign words readers will not understand. If such words are used, an English explanation of the meaning is usually desirable. Too often foreign menu terms are used more for ostentation than to inform. The planner must be sure of the background of the patron before presenting him with highly sophisticated terminology. Keeping the language simple is a good general rule.

A menu should be constructed so that it is quickly interpreted by the reader. Items should stand out, especially those management wishes to sell. The menu should not be cluttered. Just as there is a correct and proper way to write a business letter, so there is a correct and proper way to write a menu. There is a given order for presenting foods and this is usually in the order in which they will be eaten. Many menus must sell—even institutional menus should sell, if seen by patrons—and the art of presenting menu items, selecting words to describe them to encourage a sale, should be particularly studied.

PLANNING A MENU, GENERAL

Because of its importance, a menu should be planned by one who knows how. It is a time-consuming and detailed job, and should not be attempted by a person who is fatigued or rushed, who is apt to be distracted or who is not in a proper frame of mind. The work place should be quiet. Enough equipment, information and aids should be available to do the job.

Planning must occur sufficiently in advance of actual production to allow for the delivery of items, the required labor to be scheduled and the menu to be prepared for use. Some menus, once

they are planned, never change. Some that do change, must be planned at least three days, a week, a month or even several months ahead.

Menu reminder lists of items should be kept up by the menu planner. These should be in food groups, usually in the order in which they appear on the menu. This list may also indicate seasonality, the item popularity, portion costs, good food combinations or accompaniments, special occasion foods, etc. A menu diary is helpful to indicate past acceptance of items, amounts prepared versus amounts sold, weather, day of the week, season or any other information that might be helpful.

It is advisable before planning a menu to check first-hand the inventory and condition of perishable foods in storage. It is also customary for responsible personnel to send to the planner reminder lists of menu needs and suggestions, foods that must be used, parties or special events, etc. In fact, before starting to plan a menu, a check should be made to see if all the required information for planning is on hand. A check list of what should be there can be used until the planner knows it well.

THE MEAL PLAN. An à la carte menu offers food separately. Each food is independently priced. A table d'hôte menu combines foods in groups and offers these together at a set price. A meal plan is the manner in which foods are grouped for particular meals in a day. Thus, a breakfast may have a fruit, cereal, main dish, bread and beverage. For a table d'hôte menu, some knowledge of the meal plan to follow is required even for partial meals. On an à la carte menu, a meal plan is not needed since the individual establishes his own meal plan in selecting his items.

The normal meal plan is three meals a day with about a fourth of the day's calories eaten at breakfast, a third at lunch and slightly over 40 per cent at dinner although some may reverse the lunch and dinner percentages.

In this country, food patterns have been changing and some menus may be written for a four-meal or five-meal-a-day plan. This gives a greater division of calories but the same total amount in a day. Most meal plans call for all the food to be consumed within a 10-hour period, but if a snack is served at night the fasting period may be less than 14 hours.

Staying too strictly with a meal plan can lead to menu monotony, so it is recommended that a plan be broken and a different one introduced occasionally. Thus, a supper of hot cakes rolled around hot, spicy applesauce and served with pork sausage links may be a relief from the usual meat, potatoes and gravy dinner. On a commercial menu, such a supper could be introduced by a clip-on.

PLANNING A MENU, COMMERCIAL

The job of planning a commercial menu differs from that of planning an institutional menu. A commercial menu usually emphasizes merchandising. More à la carte and specialty items are usually offered. Many more commercial operations will emphasize the "occasion" nature of food rather than convenience. Service also is usually different. Customers in the commercial unit usually have free food selection and they pay for what they select. In an institution, no payment occurs for a specific meal. Also, no selection may be possible. To satisfy patrons' needs, a foodservice operated for profit must have a quite different group of menus from those used by non-profit operations.

Many commercial foodservices have a permanent menu printed on rather heavy, stiff, glossy paper. Frequently a large part lists à la carte items, although some may list food combinations sold together as a group. This permanent menu is printed in large quantity and is not changed until management wants to revise it or the printed lot runs out. Many foodservices have more than one menu for use during a day: perhaps one for breakfast, one for snack foods, another for lunch, another for dinner, and even a special "after hours" or evening menu. Each one may be a permanent menu. Frequently, along with the permanent menu, a menu that changes either by meal or by day is used. This is usually on lighter paper and attached to the stiffer, permanent one. The offerings on this lighter paper will often be table d'hôte or specials for the day. Clip-ons may also be used with the permanent menu card.

A table d'hôte menu is usually planned by selecting the entrée or main dish items first and then the accompanying vegetables, potatoes and the salads. Appetizers, soups and desserts may then follow. Breads and beverages may or may not be named. It is not necessary to list all the menu items that are customarily served with a given dish. Thus, crackers served with soup or butter with bread need not be named.

$\mathcal{T}$ABLE D'HOTE

Our Complete Dinners

Choice of Soup or Salad with your favorite dressing

The Outrigger
Tender morsels of creamed chicken served with
rice in half a fresh Hawaiian pineapple 7.50

Breaded Center Cut Pork Chops
Served with nutted applesauce 8.00

Chopped Sirloin Steak
Aged ground sirloin broiled to your preference, with
french fried onion rings and baked potato 6.75

Filet of Chinook Salmon
Grilled or poached, with Sauce Bernaise 8.25

London Broil
Rare, juicy slices of marinated beef flanks
served with a burgundy mushroom sauce 7.75

Sirloin Steak
Broiled to perfection served with mushrooms and
baked potato 9.75

*Your choice of assorted ice creams and sherbets, coffee, decaf or tea included
in the complete dinner.*

FIG. 3-1
A group of table d'hôte
dinners found on menu
of the Hilton Inn of
Seattle. This menu
indicates that a fairly
complete meal, with
soup or salad, dessert
and beverage, will be
obtained by ordering
the entrée. (Courtesy
Hilton Inn)

TRY A Glorified Steakburger

Not the garden variety Hamburger, but a Super-Special, open-face sandwich that packs 5 full ounces of freshly ground choice Steer Beef partly grilled to your individual preference and served on a well buttered toasted bun, with a full portion of French Fried Potatoes, Cole Slaw, and garnished with French Fried Onion Rings.

1.95

Appetizers—Soups

SEAFOOD APPETIZERS—One Dozen
French Fried Scallops	1.75
Chilled or French Fried Shrimp	2.75
Mixed—French Fried Shrimp and Scallops	2.25
SHRIMP COCKTAIL	1.25
Fresh Chilled Gulf Shrimp	

HOMEMADE SOUPS
Savory and tempting, served in a cup .35
Or a larger portion served in a bowl .40

TOMATO JUICE
Large glass 35   Small glass 20

ORANGE JUICE Large .35 Small .20

Desserts
Pie ....40 Ice Cream or Sherbet	.40
Pie a la mode	.55
with Cheddar Cheese	.45
Sundaes — Chocolate	.45
Large	.60

SOUP'S ON!

this is the season when soup tastes so good—BILL KNAPP'S are making a special effort with their FAMOUS HOME MADE SOUP. Check the list — it's a happy habit.

MONDAY	Vegetable—Bean—Mushroom
TUESDAY	Vegetable—Bean—Chicken Noodle
WEDNESDAY	Vegetable—Bean—Mushroom
THURSDAY	Vegetable—Bean—Chicken Noodle
FRIDAY	Vegetable—Bean—Cream of Tomato
SATURDAY	Vegetable—Bean—Chicken Noodle
SUNDAY	Vegetable—Bean—Chicken Noodle

BOWL 40c   CUP 35c

SOUP TO GO - HOT OR COLD - PT. 45 QT. .90

Chicken 'n Biscuits

Our own oven fresh Buttered Biscuits smothered with tender bits of Chicken in rich, yellow Gravy. Tossed Salad, or Cole Slaw.

1.75

Bill Knapp's Sandwiches

TOASTED IF YOU WISH!
OUR HOMEMADE WHITE OR WHOLE WHEAT

1. STEAKBURGER
Our own freshly ground Round Steak tucked in one of Bill Knapp's Homemade Buns 65
Jumbo Size ($.13) .95

2. CHEESEBURGER .75
Jumbo Size ($.12) .95

3. STEAKBURGER DELUXE
Our Steakburger with Lettuce, Tomato, and Mayonnaise 75

4. GRILLED HAM
Mustard or Lettuce and Mayonnaise 75

5. CHICKEN—SLICED
With Lettuce and Mayonnaise 95

6. BACON, LETTUCE, TOMATO 75

7. GRILLED CHEESE .55
With Bacon or Ham 85

8. HAM SALAD .65

9. TUNA FISH SALAD .65

10. CHICKEN SALAD .85

11. CLUB SANDWICH 1.55

14. FISH SANDWICH .75

15. TENDERLOIN STEAK SANDWICH 2.25

Try a Sandwich SPECIAL
With French Fried Potatoes and Cole Slaw. 50c extra

"Good Things To Eat"

Dinner Plates

1. CHOPPED STEAK—One-half pound of freshly ground choice Steer Beef, assuring a rich full bodied flavor, garnished with French Fried Onion Rings. **2.35**

2. SOUTHERN FRIED CHICKEN— A real "he-man" portion of tender spring Chicken, skillfully fried to a luscious Golden Brown. Gravy on request. **2.65**

3. TENDERLOIN STEAK— A choice Tenderloin of properly aged Steer Beef, cooked as you like it, garnished with French Fried Onion Rings. **2.95**

4. HAM STEAK— A generous slice of savory Hickory Smoked Ham, cooked on the grill and served piping hot. **2.35**

5. PORK CHOPS— Two grilled center cut Chops, 4 oz each chosen from tender young stock. Apple Sauce on request. **2.35**

6. OCEAN PERCH FILLETS— Delightfully tender Boneless Fillets coated with our own Biscuit Crumbs. **2.35**

7. FRENCH FRIED SHRIMP— Jumbo Shrimp from the Gulf Coast. Served with our special Tartar Sauce. Cocktail Sauce on request. **3.45**

17. FRENCH FRIED SCALLOPS—Direct from New England. The tender, sweet, deep sea morsels are cooked with our own special breading. **2.65**

8. SEA FOOD PLATTER—Boneless Fillet of Ocean Perch, French Fried Shrimp, Scallops, and Genuine African Rock Lobster Tail. Drawn Butter ... **4.95**

9. AFRICAN ROCK LOBSTER TAIL—One-half pound genuine African Rock Lobster Tail - tops in excellence and flavor - firm - white and moist.

For the hearty eater .... Three quarter pound of lobster. **4.95**

10. SIRLOIN STEAK— The king of all Steaks. A really tender cut of U.S. Prime Strip Sirloin, cooked as you like it and garnished with French Fried Onion Rings. **4.95**

Choice of Bill Knapp's Cole Slaw or Tossed Salad Bowl
Choice of Our Famous Au Gratin or French Fried Potatoes
Dinners Served with Homemade Buttered Biscuits

Meal in a Basket

1. STEAKBURGER-IN-A-BASKET
A Bill Knapp Steakburger, our own Toasted Bun and ground Steak nesting in a basket of French Fried Potatoes. **1.05**

2. CHICKEN-IN-A-BASKET
A generous portion of tender Fried Chicken, French Fried Potatoes, Home-made Buttered Biscuits. Gravy on request. **1.95**

3. CHEESEBURGER-IN-A-BASKET
Steakburger and Melted Cheese plus a large portion of French Fried Potatoes. **1.15**

4. FISH-IN-A-BASKET
Golden Brown Fillets of Ocean Perch, French Fried Potatoes. Homemade Buttered Biscuits, and Tartar Sauce. **1.75**

5. DELUXE STEAKBURGER-IN-A-BASKET
Choice Ground Beef, sliced Tomato, Lettuce and Mayonnaise on Toasted Bun, French Fried Potatoes. **1.15**

17. SCALLOPS-IN-A-BASKET
Golden Breaded Scallops, French Fried Potatoes, Homemade Buttered Biscuits, and Tartar Sauce. **1.95**

Pancakes

Our Famous/Malted Pancakes/served with melted butter and a jug of warm syrup 85
With Bacon, Ham or Sausage. 1.35

Waffle

Our Famous Crisp Malted Waffle served with melted butter and a jug of warm syrup. 85
With Bacon, Ham or Sausage. 1.35

Luncheon or Supper Plates

CHOPPED STEAK	1.85
HAM STEAK	1.85
PORK CHOP	2.05
SOUTHERN FRIED CHICKEN	1.85
FRENCH FRIED SCALLOPS	1.85
FRENCH FRIED SHRIMP	2.25
OCEAN PERCH	1.85

These are luncheon portions of our Dinner Plates and include Homemade Buttered Biscuit, Crisp Tossed Salad or Cole Slaw and French Fried Potatoes (Au Gratin Potatoes 10c extra)

Two golden brown Ham Croquettes served with Chicken Gravy, Homemade Buttered Biscuit, Crisp Tossed Salad or Cole Slaw and French Fried Potatoes (Au Gratin 10c extra.)   **1.75**

Salads

COLE SLAW	.35
TOSSED SALAD	.45
COTTAGE CHEESE AND PEAR	.75
CHICKEN SALAD	1.35
TUNA FISH SALAD	1.35

Diet Plates

CHOICE OF
SLICED CHICKEN
FRIED SCALLOPS
OCEAN PERCH
CHOPPED STEAK
HAM STEAK
1.85
CHILLED SHRIMP
2.25
Served with Sliced Tomatoes
Cottage Cheese Melba Toast
Skimmed Milk Available .20

Eggs

With Buttered Toast and Jelly	
One Egg	.45
With Ham, Bacon or Sausage	.95
Two Eggs	.75
With Bacon, Ham or Sausage	1.25

Donut—Sweet Rolls
Donut	.10
Sweet Roll	.20

French Toast

Our homemade Butter and Egg Bread dipped in Country Fresh Eggs and grilled until golden brown. Warm syrup and hot melted butter. 85
With Bacon, Ham or Sausage. 1.35

FIG. 3-2 A good example of a California style menu which offers anything from a snack to a full meal at almost any time of day. This is a family-type, seated-service restaurant with some of the features of a fast-food operation. (Courtesy Bill Knapp's Grand Rapids, Michigan)

The California Menu

Some operations may use a menu called the "California" because it originated there. This is a menu that does not change. It is usually printed on stiff, durable paper. It differs from an ordinary menu in that it lists a wide variety of foods so that at any time of the day or night a customer can get a breakfast, a meal, a fountain item or a snack or a partial meal. This menu is used during the entire period the place is open. It can also act as a cover for items printed on lighter paper and changed frequently, such as chef's specials, table d'hôte meals, etc. Clip-ons may also be used with it but essentially it stands on its own with wide flexibility of different foods offered.

The Breakfast Menu

Some breakfast menus are printed on the regular menu cover while others are separate menus. A California or similar menu that offers breakfast during all hours of operation may list the breakfast on a side panel or in a special space. Some have the breakfasts on the back. A placemat may carry them. If desired, a children's breakfast menu may be available.

Both à la carte items and table d'hôte breakfasts should be on a breakfast menu normally. Table d'hôte offerings should list a continental breakfast which includes a juice (usually orange), a break item (usually a sweet roll, but a croissant is more typical) and a beverage (usually coffee). It should also list heavier breakfasts. A juice or fruit may or may not be included with these. Meat, eggs or other main dishes will be accompanied by toast, hot breads or rolls and perhaps hashbrown potatoes—grits in the South—which are not served with hotcakes and waffles. A beverage is usually included with these breakfasts.

The offerings of table d'hôte breakfasts should be balanced. A familiar one is simply eggs fixed any style and priced for one or two eggs. Omelettes or eggs with bacon, ham or sausage are other offerings. Meats alone may also be offered. A pancake and a waffle breakfast is usual. Sometimes a cornbeef hash, main dish with or without poached eggs, steak plain or with eggs, creamed chipped beef, finnan haddie or other main dish may be on table d'hôte listings. Items such as eggs Benedict, eggs Florentine or other more "occasion" foods will be included depending upon the type of operation. Specials such as a low-calorie breakfast, a steak and egg breakfast, a high-protein breakfast, or a child's breakfast may be offered.

There is a tendency for Americans to eat a lighter breakfast or a snack, such as doughnuts or toast and coffee. Therefore, breakfasts such as table d'hôte, that bring in a higher check average, should be in the most prominent place. These higher income items should also be given as effective presentation as possible with large type, bracketing, effective description, etc. Numbering breakfasts makes them easier to order, both for the patron and waitress. Specialties such as a variety of syrups with waffles or hotcakes, or a group of desirable jellies and jams may serve to draw choices.

The number of items on a breakfast menu should receive consideration. One factor to consider is how important breakfast is as a meal to the operation. If it is important, probably more items are warranted than if it is just a casual meal with low volume. A limited menu is desirable but not so limited as to shut off profitable selections. Thus, perhaps 10 juice and fruits might be too much, while five might be adequate. Some menus may list only three or four juices, prunes or fruits. Many find they must have at least one hot cereal, and perhaps two, plus a wide offering of dry cereals. With eggs, meat dishes and other breakfast items plus waffles, pancakes, breads and beverages, the number of items can quickly mount. Perhaps 60 items should be considered a maximum on a breakfast menu, with the normal operation offering from 35 to 45 items to meet demand.

The menu order is usually (1) fruits and juices, (2) cereals, (3) eggs alone or combined, (4) omelettes, (5) meat and other main dishes, (6) pancakes, waffles and French toast, (7) toast, rolls and hot breads and (8) beverages. Side orders must be placed in available space. On the à la carte menu, items should be grouped together and set apart from each other in about this same order.

Breakfast menus should cover less space than many others and usually should have larger type. Do not list items only as "juices" or "cereals" but list each separately. Also list essential information such as how long breakfasts are served, special breakfast facilities, etc.

Special breakfasts may have to be catered. A wedding breakfast may start with champagne, silver gin fizzes, fruit punch or juices, etc. A fresh fruit cup is often served as the first course. If

not, then a fruit salad or molded fruit salad is appropriate. A typical main dish is served with a high quality sweet roll. Eggs Benedict would be suitable for the early breakfast, or eggs with sausages, ham, bacon, etc. An omelette of some type would be suitable. If the affair is late, the main dish can be creamed chicken, creamed ham and mushrooms, or creamed sweetbreads and ham in a patty shell with perhaps a few green peas. A beverage choice is offered. If wine is served at the table, it is usually a chilled white wine or an off-dry rosé.

Buffet breakfasts are popular. Some may be offered to allow guests to quickly obtain what they want and leave. Many people at conventions or meetings in the morning are in a hurry and may patronize the foodservice if they feel they can get what they want quickly. Some who usually skip breakfast may be enticed to come in and get a quickly served buffet continental breakfast.

A buffet breakfast for more leisurely dining may be much more elaborate and feature a wide choice of juices and fruits, cold items such as cheese, sliced baked ham, lox and bagels, chopped chicken livers or even salads with hot dishes such as scrambled eggs, assorted breakfast meats, chicken livers and mushrooms, pepper steaks, cornbeef hash, creamed chipped beef, eggs Benedict, etc. Side dishes such as hash brown potatoes or grits are often available. Assorted hot breads and sweet rolls are offered along with a beverage choice. The drink is often poured at the table by service personnel, the guests selecting the other foods they wish at the buffet. On the most elaborate buffets, a dessert may be offered. Depending upon the occasion, champagne or alcoholic beverages may be provided. Wine service may be offered with a white wine (not completely dry) or a rosé.

A hunt breakfast is an elaborate buffet which may include broiled lamb chops, steaks, roast beef, grilled pork chops, pheasant, hare, venison or other items. A hunt breakfast originated as a meal before or after the hunt and was intended for hearty eaters leading a vigorous life. They had to eat that way!

A chuck wagon should feature sourdough hotcakes, steaks, eggs, hash brown potatoes, and perhaps freshly cooked doughnuts. Grits or biscuits can be substituted for the breads. A family-style breakfast would be one in which the

breakfast

DOUBLETREE EYEOPENER
2 eggs (any style), toast, hashbrowns, bacon or sausage, and a hottle of coffee or tea. 3.30

DOUBLETREE CONTINENTAL
Chilled orange juice, fresh hot cinnamon roll, and a hottle of coffee or tea 1.50

GOOD MORNING OMELETTE
Stuffed full of mushrooms, ham or cheese, served with toast, hashbrowns and coffee or tea . . 3.00

DOUBLETREE INN
Room Service Hours — 6:30 a.m. - Midnight
Minimum Room Service Charge — $1.00
DIAL 160 — ROOM SERVICE

beverages

COFFEE or TEA . . . . . . by the hottle .60
by the pot 2.00

SOFT DRINKS 50

MILK or FRUIT JUICES . . . regular .50
large .75

snacks

SEAFOOD APPETIZER
A combination of fresh seafoods, deep fried to perfection. 4.25

MIXED NUTS 1.50

FRUIT BASKET
Fruits in Season 2.00

CHEESE & CRACKERS — per person .75

ICED PRAWNS
Perfect for get togethers, served fresh with zesty cocktail sauce and tarter —
. . . by the dozen 5.00

anytime

DOUBLETREE FRIED CHICKEN
Served with French fries, roll and butter . 3.95

DELICIOUS DOUBLETREE BURGER
Served with French fries 2.25

DOUBLETREE CLUB BURGER
Topped with hickory bacon, sliced tomato and American cheese 2.95

FRENCH DIP
Steaming au jus and French fries 2.65

BACON, LETTUCE & TOMATO SANDWICH
Served with potato salad . . . it's a favorite . . . 1.95

LO-CAL CHOPPED SIRLOIN
Served with sliced tomatoes and cottage cheese . . 2.85

FILET OF SALMON
From Pacific waters, served with French fries and cole slaw 4.25

CHEF'S SALAD
Fresh vegetables, meats and cheeses . . . with your favorite dressing 4.10

OLYMPIC STEAK SANDWICH
Char-broiled and served with a French roll and fries 4.45

FIG. 3-3
A room service menu that offers a wide choice of items from breakfast through the evening TV snack. (Courtesy Double Tree Inn)

Fruits & Juices

Grapefruit Sections .40
Grapefruit Half (in season) .45
Stewed Prunes .40
Juices: Orange, Tomato or Grapefruit .35
  Large .50

Toast & Pastries

Toasted and Buttered
Blueberry 'Toastees' or Corn 'Toastees' .35
Buttered Toast .30
Toasted English Muffin .30
Marmalade and Jelly with Above
(Orange Marmalade, Apple or Grape Jelly)
Danish Pastry .35

Cereals

Your Choice of
Crisp Cereal or Hot Oatmeal
Served with Milk .45
Cereal topped with Sliced Banana .60

From the Grill

French Toast (Three Slices)
Whipped Butter and Warm Syrup .95
Breakfast Ham .85
Grilled Link Sausages (Three Links) .80
Crisp Sliced Bacon (Three Strips) .80
Hashed Brown Potatoes .40

Eggs

Two Eggs
Large Grade A, Any Style
Toast, Marmalade and Jelly .95
Single Egg
Large Grade A, Any Style
Toast, Marmalade and Jelly .70

Combination Breakfast

Tomato or Orange Juice
Two Eggs
Scrambled in Butter
Buttered Toast with Marmalade and Jelly
Beverage **1.45**

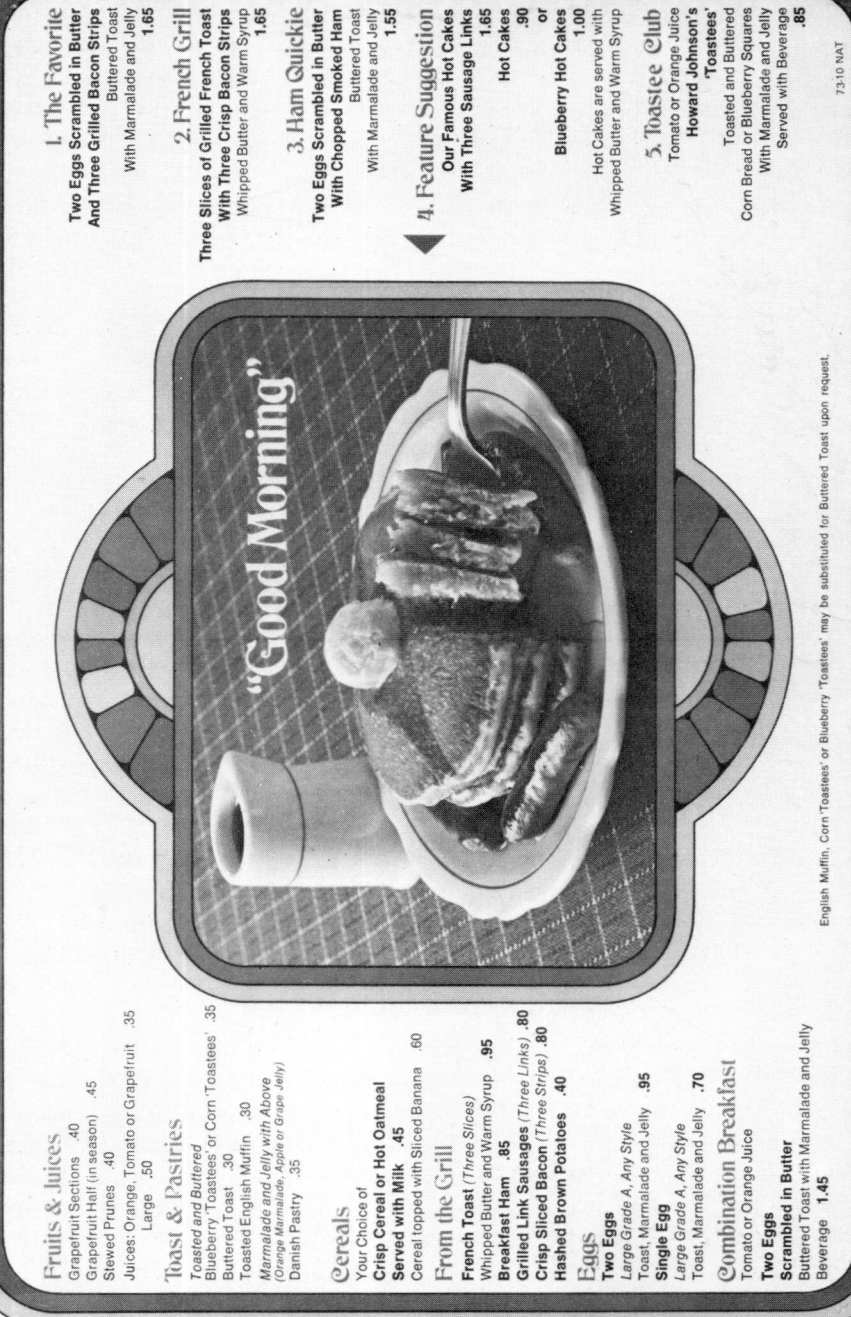

"Good Morning"

1. The Favorite

Two Eggs Scrambled in Butter
And Three Grilled Bacon Strips
Buttered Toast
With Marmalade and Jelly 1.65

2. French Grill

Three Slices of Grilled French Toast
With Three Crisp Bacon Strips
Whipped Butter and Warm Syrup 1.65

3. Ham Quickie

Two Eggs Scrambled in Butter
With Chopped Smoked Ham
Buttered Toast
With Marmalade and Jelly 1.55

4. Feature Suggestion

Our Famous Hot Cakes
With Three Sausage Links 1.65
Hot Cakes .90
or
Blueberry Hot Cakes 1.00
Hot Cakes are served with
Whipped Butter and Warm Syrup

5. Toastee Club

Tomato or Orange Juice
Howard Johnson's
'Toastees'
Toasted and Buttered
Corn Bread or Blueberry Squares
With Marmalade and Jelly
Served with Beverage .85

English Muffin, Corn 'Toastees' or Blueberry 'Toastees' may be substituted for Buttered Toast upon request.

73-10 NAT

FIG. 3-4   A breakfast menu takes on good meaning when it is presented to the patron as a place mat.

food is brought to the table and individuals serve themselves.

Group breakfasts should be planned carefully. Eggs and some other items cool rapidly. Do not attempt difficult egg preparations such as omelettes or eggs Benedict unless the kitchen can prepare them. Toast is difficult to serve because it gets cold and clammy quickly. Hot breads are easier to handle such as biscuits, muffins or cinnamon rolls. American service is usually used, but Russian service *could* be used.

A brunch menu should combine items usually found on breakfast and lunch menus, and be a rather substantial meal. A fruit juice or fruit should be offered. The main dish should be substantial— omelettes with creamed ham or chicken or mushrooms, creamed chicken on toast points, a soufflé, a small steak with hash browns, chicken livers and bacon, a mixed grill which includes a lamb chop, grilled liver, small sausage and sliced bacon with a grilled tomato slice, finnan haddie with boiled potato and melted butter, etc. Hot breads and a beverage choice should be offered and vegetables can be served. A salad is not too appropriate but it could be a fruit salad or a molded fruit salad *filled* with fruit.

The Lunch Menu

Luncheon menus may contain a wide assortment of foods from complete table d'hôte meals to snacks. Offer a wide number of à la carte items with combinations such as sandwich and milk shake; cup of soup, salad and dessert with beverage; a blue-plate special; along with perhaps several full lunch table d'hôte lunches. A few casserole or "made" dishes can be offered. They need not be as typical as breakfast or dinner items. Items such as sandwiches, salads, soups and fountain products can be stressed. A luncheon menu can more easily feature economical purchases than the breakfast or dinner menu.

Many units have moderately priced items and attempt to cover costs with volume and fast turnover. Office, factory, laboratory or mid-management workers and others with moderate incomes are customers as are women shoppers. "Occasion" foods may be profitable, if especially slanted to the trade. Executives and expense account patrons wish more elaborate menus. Thus, a club, better hotel or fine restaurant which they patronize may feature a higher priced list. Alcoholic beverages should be offered.

Lunch menus have permanent à la carte offerings on the firm cover but will also present daily offerings. The permanent menu offers sandwiches, salads, fountain items, desserts, etc. Flexible menus are more typical of lunch than any other meal. Inserts or other means may be used to introduce such flexibility.

Lunches for groups usually are complete meals. Clubs or organizations may meet at lunch time and a main dish with vegetables, a salad, dessert and beverage will be eaten. A first course will be included on a more elaborate luncheon. If men form the group, a heavier entrée may be offered than for a women's group. Party or "occasion" foods may be offered, but since most diners have little time, the menu must allow them to eat quickly, have time for the speaker and get back to work. However, if the luncheon is to last for a longer period and is an

DESSERTS

Orange angelfood cake ..... .55
fresh orange icing

Field's cheese cake ..... .65
Our treasured recipe from decades ago

Pineapple chiffon pie ..... .60
A zephyr-light filling with a luscious pineapple taste, topped with whipped cream

Strawberry-rhubarb pie ..... .60
A fruitful delight—rhubarb and strawberries in a flaky double crust

Field's fresh apple pie ..... .55
One of the tastiest apple pies that ever came brown and fragrant from the oven
... for a special treat—a time honored combination

... with New York cheddar cheese ..... .65
or
... with Field's vanilla ice cream ..... .70

Select a decorated European torte slice ..... .90
fillings of fruits, creams, brittles and liqueurs in traditional old world fashion

Cherry crunch pudding served a la mode ..... .55
Semolina, spiced, sweet red cherries baked in a crumbly butter crust, with Field's vanilla ice cream

A mound of chilled watermelon ..... .40

Specialties

TROPICAL PARFAIT ..... .75
Our own rich vanilla and cranberry ice creams, with strawberries, pineapple and shredded coconut

Field's chocolate Frango®-mint ice cream pie ..... .60
A delicious ice cream pie filled with chocolate Frango-mint ice cream, then topped with French mint nougat, all in a graham cracker crust

Field's English Toffee Ice Cream Pie ..... .55
English toffee ice cream with its rich butterscotch almond crunch fills its graham cracker shell. Field's candy-makers add their special touch to the toffee topping

Ice Creams

Field's Ice Cream ..... .45
Lemon chiffon (root tartness of lemon—creamy and satisfying)
Strawberry, coffee, vanilla or chocolate

Special flavor of ice milk ..... .40

Red raspberry or apricot sherbet ..... .40

Thick and creamy malts or a delicious ice cream soda ..... .40
(chocolate, vanilla or strawberry)

Sm...
Field's chocolate, butter...
Hot fudge

Bev...
Coffee 30
Pasteurized grade "A" m...
De-Caffeinated

Coca-Cola 25-30

THE WALNUT ROOM

Appetizers

Cream of spinach soup, by the cup 40; or tureen 80

Chicken noodle soup, by the cup 35; or tureen 70 ..... .75

Chicken liver pate', watercress garnish 45

Chilled fresh fruit cup 40

Luncheons

3—An Individual Chicken Pie 2.70
Served in our tea rooms since Grandma was a belle. Under the flaky puff pastry topping are generous strips of white and dark meat chicken in a rich fricassee gravy. A touch of tartness: sweet mixed pickles.

Baked Loin Pork Chop 2.80
...tier flavorful center cut pork chop, gravy, cut green ...u and Bavarian red cabbage

...of Haddock, Epicurean Style 2.85
...herbed crumbs, then deep fried to a crisp brownness, ...h Epicurean sauce, whipped potatoes, and a mixed ... Field's French dressing

...Brisket 2.80
...ained steady until fork tender; served with ...pan gravy, cut green beans and whole

...Soup and Sandwich 2.65

Cocktails

From Our Cocktail Menu . . . .
May we suggest . . . .

Jamaican Elegance—a tall, chilled cocktail blended with rum, brandy and pineapple juice 1.25

Fresh Strawberry Daiquiri 1.25

Sangria—A Spanish custom. Chilled red wine, orange, lemon and other fruits combine to give this punch its refreshing, cool taste 1.00

Rum Verdi—your favorite Daiquiri with a new and exciting dimension—our secret 1.25

Sandwiches

4—Our Special Sandwich 2.45
Special indeed! Rye bread laden with turkey, lettuce and Mountain Swiss cheese, topped with our own Thousand Island dressing and garnished with tomato and egg slices. ...crisp bacon strips and a ripe olive

The Pilgrim $2.10
Thinly sliced turkey with lettuce, mounded on a sesame seed bun, ham, peach half filled with cranberry-orange relish, garnished with celery and carrot sticks

23—Taurus Burger 2.20
A larger-size grilled hamburger patty, tomato, crisp bacon strip, and lettuce on a toasted bun. Thousand Island dressing, French fried potatoes

31—Ham Salad 1.40
served on black rye bread, sweet mixed pickles

32—Whitemeat Tunafish Salad 1.55
on homemade bread, with assorted olives

33—Soup and Sandwich 2.05
Choice slices of roast round of beef on whole wheat bread, served with a cup of cream of spinach soup

Salads

10—Oriental Turkey Salad 2.10
Cubes of whitemeat turkey, rice and water chestnuts tossed with special dressing, served in a crisp lettuce cup, garnished with candied ginger

11—Fruit and Cheese Festival 2.05
A bowl of mixed fresh fruits and creamy cottage cheese served on crisp salad greens, Field's French dressing

An amount will be added to quoted prices to cover Use and Occupation Taxes

4-12

Mixed green salad with Field's French dressing ..... .30

FIG. 3-5 This luncheon menu is designed to suit the needs of the busy shopper who wants a rather nice meal but will want to eat it and leave quickly. (Courtesy Marshall Field of Chicago)

"occasion" meeting with an important speaker, the group may want to feature a little more luxury-type food. The foods should fit the occasion.

Afternoon Menus

Many operations "die" in the afternoon following lunch. To bring in trade a different menu can be designed to catch the afternoon and shopper trade with specials. Alcoholic beverages may also be priced to attract patrons. These menus should be the conversational type that might appeal to women and other afternoon-free individuals with time on their hands. The foods should be snack-type with considerable "occasion" appeal, different from the usual menu. Thus, after the lunch hour rush, an operation might put on a special menu with tiny fancy sandwiches, desserts, fountain items, snack fruit plates, fancy cookies, pastries, etc. withdrawing it just before the dinner hour.

The Dinner Menu

The dinner menu usually has more specialty items than others and attempts to feature more "occasion" foods. The menu must be carefully directed to the patron.

The normal meal plan in the American home is a main dish, potato, vegetable, salad, dessert and beverage. For a foodservice seeking to gain family trade, this plan should be followed but not in a stereotyped form. Interesting differences can be introduced. A soup, fruit cocktail, juice or other appetizer may be served as a first course. Regular steaks, but also hamburger, Swiss, cubed and other steaks can be on the menu.

Chicken and other poultry, fish and seafood should also appear but interesting casserole dishes, Italian pastas and some specialty foods may also be offered. A family dines out usually for an "occasion" but wants food it knows and which will be liked and consumed. Not too many of the group will want to experiment in a major way but will appreciate some favorite dressed up in a slightly different form. Thus, a delightful chicken pie, topped with biscuits, and served in a very interesting small chicken-shaped dish can win approval. A family meal with the food brought to the table in big platters, so that individuals can help themselves, may also be liked. Interesting desserts also can help to create the feeling of difference. A hot, spicy Apple Betty, served with a rum sauce, is low in cost but can win friends.

Menus are also needed which feature moderate cost items for those who want convenience foods rather than the luxury type. Some individuals in modest housing and eating in a downtown cafeteria will not have much to spend but will want enough to eat. Some operations may also find this type of trade a satisfactory source of revenue.

In attempting to develop dinner menus of the "occasion" type, it is important to remember that service and décor are as essential as the food. Complete follow-through on *all* details of an idea is a requirement. Too many menus attempt to create a food "atmosphere" on the menu only to have the rest of the performance a dismal failure, or vice versa. The operation must be constantly watching to see that there is complete follow-through. If a menu features

the Copa Room

Copa Room

Sands

DINNER

- Appetizers -
(Choice of Soup or Salad)

Supreme of Fruit 1.00   Chopped Chicken Livers 1.00   Marinated Herring in Sour Cream 1.00

Gefuelte Fish, Beet Horseradish 1.00   Chilled Tomato or Fruit Juice .75

Fresh Jumbo Shrimp, Lobster, Dungeness Crabmeat Cocktail, $2.00 *extra*

Consomme Maison   Chicken Broth with Matzo Ball

Jellied Madrilene   Soup du Jour   Creme Vichyssoise

— *or* —

Tossed Green Salad — French, Thousand Island, Roquefort or Continental Roquefort Dressing

- Entrees -

OUR *CHINESE* CHEF
Recommends . . .

PEPPER STEAK (Sliced Tenderloin of Beef,
Bamboo Shoots, Water Chestnuts,
Green Pepper, Mushrooms, Fresh Tomatoes) 12.50

Boneless Colorado Rainbow Trout Saute with Shrimps and
Capers, Havraise 12.50

Broiled Salmon Steak, Anchovy Butter 12.00

Chopped Prime Sirloin Steak Saute, Sauce Chasseur 13.00

Roast Tom Turkey, Chef's Dressing, Giblet Gravy, Cranberry Sauce 12.00

Baked Rock Cornish Game Hen, with Wild Rice Stuffing,
Diced Mushrooms, Olives, Ham, Financiere 13.00

Roast Prime Ribs of Beef au jus 14.00

Charcoal Broiled Prime New York Cut Sirloin Steak Maitre d'Hotel 15.00

ONE DRINK INCLUDED IN PRICE OF ENTREE

Fresh Vegetable   Potato

Coffee   Tea   Postum   Milk

- Desserts -

Layer Cake 1.00   Sands Special Pie 1.10   Ice Cream Roll with Brandied Cherries 1.10

Apple Pie 1.00   Strawberry Cheese Cake 1.10   Rainbow Sherbet .90   Parfait and Sundaes 1.10

Fresh Cheese Cake 1.00   Assorted Ice Cream and Sherbet .90

FIG. 3-6   A simple dinner menu of the Sands Hotel, Las Vegas. Although there are only a few entrées, the choice is broad enough to cover almost any patron's wants. (Courtesy Copa Room, Sands Hotel)

Mexican, French or another culture's foods, the performance should be absolutely authentic. Research is necessary to verify authenticity, yet modification is also needed to suit the non-authentic palate. A very hot Indian curry served with Bombay duck and all the side dishes may be delicious to one who knows this food but could be a disappointment to one who isn't familiar with it. A very important consideration in featuring many foreign foods is that they usually do not require the most expensive ingredients, but use the less expensive ones. Thus, they may be more profitable to serve than some American foods. Also, the fact that these foods are not normally a part of our diet gives them a true "occasion" flavor. Novelty can also be achieved by good and different service.

Some occasion-service operations may have nothing but an à la carte menu from which to make dinner selections. These are usually the luxury type units and not too many find this type of trade enough to make the practice successful. Most operations offer an à la carte menu but find that more than 90% of the trade comes in selections from the table d'hôte offerings.

It is becoming more and more common on table d'hôte meals to omit the first course and desserts seeking to have these selected from à la carte items. Furthermore, many operations today serve the salad as a first course, making it fairly substantial, and then omit the salad with the main course, also omitting the vegetable.

The number of items on a table d'hôte dinner or as dinner entrées can be as few as five and for some operations can be fewer. More and more specialty units are successful where only one main dish is served, such as roast ribs of beef, a bouillabaise, etc. The fewer items there are, the better control one has of costs, quality and production. One of the essentials in having a limited menu is to have superb quality in all items offered. It is important to have customers know that no matter what they take, the quality will be so high that they will be pleased with the item. Such pleasure can do much to reduce the feeling of customers that they cannot find something they like on a restricted menu.

Evening Menus

Some places operate after dinner hours. This may be to catch those who are out at the theater, some athletic event or other attraction, or it may be that there is a good trade potential for night workers. Some operations may attempt to attract business with entertainment that may be quite elaborate, such as a night club revue. Others may be simple places that act more as social gathering houses than as true eating places. It is possible to combine night customers—with separate areas for those who want entertainment and those who want quick service.

Many operations open for night business remove the specials and table d'hôte dinners from the à la carte covers and only offer customers a selection of à la carte items. Some may "pull" the whole dinner menu and have another completely different one emphasizing snack foods such as hamburgers, milk shakes, pies, cakes, fountain goods, etc. Such a menu may be desirable to reduce the need for a large kitchen staff after dinner hours. In this case, most menu items are available up front where service personnel can get them. If an operation is near an after-theater or similar trade, the menu should emphasize good desserts and perhaps light supper items.

A good analysis of the desires of the market and its potential should be made if one hopes to draw a trade that seeks entertainment. The menu should then be designed to meet the demand for the right kind of entertainment rather than attempt to create a demand. The menu should be supported by proper emphasis on props such as the dress of service personnel, dishes and glassware, table appointments, lighting, entertainment, etc.

Special Occasion Menus

Quite a few hotels, clubs and restaurants are able to develop a substantial party or catering business. This can be profitable and considerably supplement the overall income. The proper handling of the details for such events is not easy, and experience is of great assistance.

The special-occasion menu must be planned in detail to suit the occasion. While there is a general pattern to events such as wedding receptions, buffet dinners, cocktail parties, etc., each should be differentiated by its own special arrangements. Thus, many menus may have to be planned for a special occasion and not used again. Some events will be quite formal while others will be very informal. The menu should carry out the spirit of the theme. Creativity and ingenuity are required. Color, décor, props, foods and service should be cleverly combined to give correctness and novelty to the occasion.

A menu for a party should be carefully analyzed to see that it does not make excessive requirements for service, dishware or other factors. The foods selected should be easy and fast to serve and be kinds that can stand delays in service. They should be suitable for the occasion. A football buffet after a game may suitably feature hot chili which hardly would go at a wedding reception.

Formal Dinners

Very few formal dinners are served today that follow the traditional French style of three settings with a progression of courses within each setting. People find it difficult to eat this much food today. Even a more simple formal meal can be exhausting and overpowering unless properly planned. Portions for a formal dinner should be adequate but restrained. The food should be selected to give a progression of flavor sensations, avoiding any heavy sweetness until the very end of the meal when sweetness is desired to "silence the appetite."

Wines and alcoholic beverages for this meal should be selected carefully. Cocktails made from spirits such as martinis, manhattans, or scotch and soda, blunt the taste buds. Apéritif wines such as dubonnet, cocktail sherry, etc. are more suitable to promote the appetite. Nevertheless, Americans prefer the former. Sweet wines and sweet drinks should be avoided except at the end of the meal, where a sweet dessert wine may be served with the dessert, sweet liqueurs afterwards. A formal meal should give time for the guests to appreciate the food and service, to converse and to allow the body time to assimilate the food of one course before another follows.

The most formal meal today usually does not have more than eight courses. At one time, this was a standard formal meal for diplomatic occasions, but inspection of menus today shows that this is no longer true.

The first course of a formal meal can be oysters or clams on the half shell, a seafood cocktail of some type, a canapé, or fruit such as melon or mango. Some may omit this course if cocktails and good appetizer hors d'oeuvres are served before. Soup is the next course and this should be quite light, such as a turtle broth, consommé, bouillon or a light cream soup, purée or bisque. Cheese straws may be the accompaniment. On all courses, garniture is important and may be the only item accompanying the food.

The fish course comes after the soup, followed by the poultry course. If more than eight courses are served, an entrée such as a light timbale or creamed dish might be served next.

The roast or joint, with perhaps potato and vegetable, is the next course. The salad course is next, followed in turn by cheese and then the dessert course. In some formal meals an ice or sherbet may come right after the roast course. The meal may end with demi-tasse coffee, nuts, mints and bon bons.

A wine such as sherry may be served with the first course and soup. A light, white dinner wine should follow with the fish and poultry. A rather full-bodied dry red wine should be served with the main course. Usually no wine is served with the salad. A very good dry red wine may be served with the cheese followed by a light-bodied but refreshing sweet dessert wine. Port, Madeira or similar wine can be served after the dessert. As with foods, the tendency in formal meals is to limit the number of wines and as few as one or two wines may suffice for such a dinner today.

A properly planned formal dinner should compare to a symphony or concerto. It should have different movements and themes in the foods and wines. The progression of themes should lead to a taste climax and then gradually recede in intensity as other foods follow. There are places in the meal where the foods should be modest, quiet and subtle in flavor, and in others where the food and flavor should stand out in a loud crescendo.

Lightness and delicacy should be the motif of the appetizer and soup. Both should be refreshing and somewhat zestful to whet the appetite. They should be a good introduction in flavor and other factors for the foods to follow. The fish course should be bland but sufficiently poignant to give a contrast to the courses that have preceded it and to the more pronounced flavors in the poultry course that follows. The poultry course should be light and delicate and not rich. Each course should lead into the next and the meal should be a continuity of related taste themes just as in a good symphony. The roast can be a red meat such as venison, beef or lamb, and should be the peak, or center, of the meal. At this point, flavor values are more pronounced, but excessive richness, sweetness or sharpness in flavor should be avoided. Piquant, brilliant flavors with some subtlety, can reduce richness but they, in turn, should not be

```
THE WHITE HOUSE
WASHINGTON




MENU FOR BREAKFAST CONFERENCE GROUP



Fresh Orange Juice

Scrambled eggs and bacon

Poached eggs on toast


Toast points

Danish Pastry


Coffee
```

FIG. 3-7   A "working" breakfast at the White House. the menu is special-purpose; the meal itself is about as conventional as an American breakfast could be.

(Illustrations on these pages courtesy Chefs Haller and Bender of the White House)

```
THE WHITE HOUSE
WASHINGTON


A SIMPLE LUNCHEON MENU

Fresh Fruit Cup

French pancakes à la Reine
(filled w/ diced capon & mushrooms)
Early June peas in butter

Bibb Lettuce salad

Lemon Sherbet
Petits fours
_____

ELABORATE LUNCHEON MENU

Coquille of Seafood Neptune
Cheese Straws

Piccata of Veal Luganese
Saffron rice
Asparagus tips

Champagne Mousse

Bernkasteler Doktor 1969
```

```
THE WHITE HOUSE
WASHINGTON

SIMPLE AFTERNOON TEA MENU

Assorted Petits fours
Raisin Pound Cake

Coffee

Tea

_____


MORE ELABORATE TEA MENU

Assorted Tea Sandwiches

Selection of miniature French Pastry

Fruit Cake


Coffee

Tea
```

FIG. 3-8   Typical luncheons and teas served at the White House in 1974. Note that the lunch menus offer relatively few, but well balanced, selections. The tea menus are both quite simple, including the "more elaborate" one.

Dinner

Johannisberger
Klaus
1970

Timbale of Seafood White House
Fleurons Dorées

Louis Martini
Cabernet Sauvignon
1968

Châteaubriand Béarnaise
Pommes Soufflées
Artichokes Andalouse

Bibb Lettuce Salad
Brie Cheese

Dom Pérignon
1964

Fresh Peaches Glacées Monticello
Sauce Framboise

THE WHITE HOUSE
Tuesday, July 24, 1973

FIG. 3-9 A diplomatic formal dinner served at the White House. Note the simplicity of the menu. This is perhaps indicative of the trend nowadays toward fewer courses and less elaborate service, even on formal occasions.

too overpowering. The most formal meals are served without bread or butter. Salts and peppers are not on the table. In fine commercial dining rooms, bread and butter, salts and peppers and even ash trays will be found on the table even for very formal dinners.

The salad should be a relieving course, its cool crispness and slightly tart flavor should be delicate and possess a distinctive quality, giving a respite from the heavier foods that have come before. The Italians say the salad should "clean the palate and the teeth." Any oiliness or sharpness in flavor should be avoided.

The tangy cheese course which may follow should renew the jaded palate and set it properly for the concluding course—a sweet dessert. This should be light and delicate, not cloyingly sweet. It should end the meal with some finality but not on a heavy note.

A less formal dinner may have only three to five courses. The first course can be a fruit cup, juice or seafood cocktail, melon, canapé, oysters or clams, followed by a soup and then a fish course. Or there can be either an appetizer or soup and no fish course. The main course is next, accompanied by a potato and vegetable. A salad is served usually with the main dish. A dessert follows. Rolls and butter are usually served.

Parties

A wide variety of parties may be served by a catering department. These may be as simple as punch at a dance or coffee at a meeting. Others may be a simple dessert served before bridge or a style show. The complexity of the foods can increase until it becomes a formal luncheon or dinner.

There are high and low teas. A low tea might be simply tea, served perhaps with lemon, milk and sugar as desired. A more elaborate tea would add a simple dessert item or cookie, mints, bon bons, nuts, and a still more elaborate one might add a frozen dessert and fancy sandwiches. Often a tea is served from a table with the beverage served by an honored hostess at one end of the table and coffee served at the opposite end by another honored hostess. These hostesses are usually changed at set times.

The placement of the tea table should be considered carefully because traffic can be a problem. A high tea is somewhat like a meal. It is served late in the afternoon and is more substantial than a low tea. It is often used as a light meal between lunch and a late evening dinner. It is most frequently served in homes and not in commercial operations.

A tea may be used as a reception event for a speaker, followed by a talk in some room close by. It can also be used to honor some individual, individuals or event.

Receptions resemble teas and may be almost the same thing. Receptions may feature alcoholic beverages. A wedding reception usually has a punch made of fruit juice, brandy and champagne although almost any other drink combination would be satisfactory. At some receptions, cocktails with canapés, hors d'oeuvres and other tangy foods may be served. These may be picked up by guests at a buffet or they may be passed. When passed, the service is called "flying service," from the Russians who originated the service and called the trays of foods carried around "flying platters." It is usual to estimate that guests will consume two to eight small pieces of food at such gatherings. The variety served may affect the quantities required. The type of function, its length of time and other factors will have much to do with the amount of food required. Bowls of dips and platters of crisp foods, pickles, olives, etc., which are easy to replenish, may assist in giving flexibility. Some operations plan a run-out time and toward the end of service leave only a few foods remaining. The number of drinks served may also vary. Men usually consume, on the average, two to four alcoholic drinks per hour of service and women one to three.

Since the preparation of a large quantity of fancy canapés, sandwiches and hors d'oeuvres can require much labor, ways should be found to reduce preparation time by purchasing items such as tiny baked puff shells or other items that can be filled and made to look as if they were prepared on the premises. A tray of canapés or fancy sandwiches need not have every item on it highly decorated. If a few fancy ones are properly spaced among plain ones that take little labor to produce, the effect is still good and labor requirements are considerably reduced.

Party menus will vary according to the event and thus there may be constant change. However, some operations preplan menus and have these available for clients when they call to discuss an event. This helps to standardize production and allows an accurate calculation of cost. If a special menu has to be planned, the individual planning the menu and establishing the price should know the costs so that an adequate price can be charged.

Most operations doing party business have standard printed forms on which to put information about events. Some of these are shown here. The number of copies distributed may vary and each operation will have its own specific procedure. It is important that all departments affected have a coordinated plan and that the system work smoothly. There are many details. Party business can be profitable but is very demanding

upon many of those working in it. Good forms and a smooth, efficient system can do much to add to profits and make its functioning less demanding upon personnel. Figures 3-10, 3-11, and 3-12 show some of the records and forms used to record catering information.

Buffets

The use of buffets for breakfast has been mentioned, and additional material will be found in a discussion on service. Originality in buffet menu items should be sought. Too many foodservices today use kidney bean and onion salad, pickled corn, pickled or sliced pickled beets, fruit gelatin salads made with canned fruit cocktail, etc. If taken from the can, they should be given some differentiation and personality of their own with garniture or in combination with other foods. The effectiveness of a buffet depends much upon the originality and presentation of the food. If these are not emphasized, the purpose is lost. Foods that look tired, excessively garnished, off-color or messy will not satisfy. Unless correctly done, a buffet can lose patrons.

The number of foods to put on a buffet can differ with the occasion. For a simple meal, only a few may be used along with rolls and butter, beverage and dessert. A dessert buffet luncheon may be only a dessert and beverage. A slightly more elaborate buffet may have four to six cold foods including appetizers and salads, several hot entrées with vegetables and perhaps a potato dish, a selection of bread or rolls and butter, and perhaps several desserts. There may be a score or more of cold foods on an

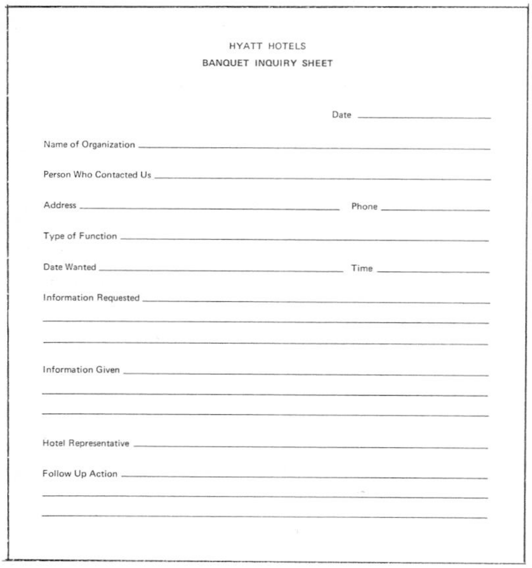

```
                    HYATT HOTELS
                 BANQUET INQUIRY SHEET


                                    Date _____

Name of Organization _____

Person Who Contacted Us _____

Address _____  Phone _____

Type of Function _____

Date Wanted _____  Time _____

Information Requested _____
_____
_____

Information Given _____
_____
_____

Hotel Representative _____

Follow Up Action _____
_____
_____
```

FIG. 3-10   A record of party or banquet data which could be maintained by the sales or catering department. Frequently it is important to have such information available to know who originally arranged a function and how the inquiry came about. (Courtesy Hyatt Corporation)

elaborate buffet, eight or more hot entrées with a number of different hot vegetable dishes, potatoes, a variety of hot breads and rolls, cakes, puddings, pies and other desserts.

The number of items and their presentation will decide the degree of elaborateness. Certainly an over-offering is a mistake and can lead to waste. The purpose of a buffet is to give guests the feeling that they can help themselves as much as they desire but it should not lead to waste.

Some buffets require particular foods. A Smorgäasbord, the Scandinavian buffet, must have pickled herring or herring of some kind, rye bread and myost or gjetost cheese in addition to many cold foods, hot foods such as liefse, Swedish meat balls, and a dessert such as a pancake in which ligonberries are rolled. The cold foods are eaten first and then the hot ones. Dessert is last with coffee. A Russian buffet should have caviar served from the table center, either from a beautiful glass bowl or from a bowl made of ice. Dark rye bread and butter must accompany it. The other foods should be typical of a buffet. A true Smorgäasbord usually has acquavit or schnapps served with it in tiny glasses. The Russian buffet has small glasses of vodka served, at least with the first foods.

How Many Menu Items?

The number of items to place in the various food groups on a menu card may vary depending upon the type of operation. In most instances, the least number possible is the desirable one. This will depend upon what is required to suit patrons' desires.

It is also necessary to balance selections within groups. Thus, for appetizers probably there should be several juices, a fruit and a fish cocktail. This perhaps is a minimum, but still gives some balance for different tastes. If only two juices are on the menu card for appetizers, one

FIG. 3-11   An example of a record that is completed at the time a reservation is made for a catering event. A considerable amount of detail is required to see that events are properly booked and that all arrangements and requirements are known. (Courtesy Hyatt Corporation)

CONTINENTAL HYATT HOUSE
BANQUET PROSPECTUS

Name of Organization

Address _____ Phone

Nature of Function

Day _____ Date _____ Time

Room _____ Rent

Name of Engagor

Address _____ Phone

Responsibility of Party

Price per Person $ _____ Gratuity: _____ Minimum Number Guaranteed: _____ Maximum Attendance:

FOOD MENU

BEVERAGE MENU

Cash: _____ Charge:

Corkage:

Room for Bar:

Open: _____ Close:

Bartender Charge:

Minimum Charges (4Hrs)

Types of Beverages

Staff:

Table Arrangements:	Set Up By:		Head:
Flowers:	Centerpieces:		Checking:
Ticket Table:	Blackboard:	P.A.:	Stage:
Lectern:	Screen:	Piano:	Music:
Cigars:	Cigarettes:	Platform:	Dance Floor:

REMARKS:

COMMENTS BY PARTY:

Copies to:

☐ Customer ☐ Chef:
☐ Catering Office ☐ Houseman·
☐ Maitre D' ☐ Bar:
 ☐ Accounting

Date Booked:

BY_____

should be a fruit and the other a vegetable juice.

The number and kind of soups to put on a menu card depends upon the meal. For lunch, some customers may only want a bowl of soup. This usually is a substantial one such as vegetable, chowder, chicken or beef and rice. A consommé or bouillon is too light to satisfy a good appetite but proper for one who wants only a few calories. Soups could also start a fairly substantial meal. Some dinner menus may have only one or two soups. Many usually have as many as four. If a dinner menu is to offer wide selection, it can list a consommé or bouillon or both, a light cream soup or bisque, a purée and a mixed soup such as vegetable, chowder or beef rice. Six soups might be the most that any menu needs. Balance should be obtained between light clear soups, purées, creams and bisques, and heavier soups such as vegetable, minestrone, chowder, or Philadelphia pepper pot.

The ordinary menu probably needs at least five or six main dish offerings, but some can have only one or two and be successful in a specialty restaurant. If a balance is required, the entrée should be divided between beef—more than 60 per cent of the meat consumed in this country is beef—pork or cured pork, poultry, lamb or veal, shellfish, fish, egg dishes, cheese dishes and perhaps a non-meat item. If two meats appear, they can both be beef with one a steak and the other a roast or other beef dish, or as an alternate, one beef and another meat such as ham, pork, veal or lamb. If two fish or shellfish appear, they should be quite different, such as a lean white-fleshed fish and a fatter one such as salmon, or one fish and one shellfish. Shrimp and lobster are two crustaceans too much alike to appear together unless there is a long list of shellfish.

The menu should also provide for a balance and variety in vegetables, sauces and potatoes. These must be selected to complement the entrées. Thus, on a menu in which there is ham or chicken, the offering of sweet potatoes or yellow winter squash is good. Roast beef, veal loaf, pot roast of beef, etc., go well with mashed potatoes. Vegetables should be selected for their flavor, color and texture contrasts. A popular vegetable such as peas, string beans, carrots or asparagus should be one of the vegetables offered. Other vegetables can be less popular but should go well with some of the entrées. Different treatment in cooking also can help to give variety, such as serving a vegetable creamed, deep-fried, au gratin, baked, mashed, diced, julienne or as fritters, or with a sauce such as hollandaise, tomato or cheese.

Two potatoes are usually sufficient but more can be offered if the menu selections in other food categories are somewhat elaborate. Similarly, several vegetables may be offered but probably four to six vegetables, including potatoes, will meet most needs.

The number of salads offered has decreased. For many years table d'hôte meals included a choice of salads. Today, usually only one is served such as a tossed green salad with a choice of dressings. This is served at the beginning of the meal and no vegetable except a potato is served with the main dish. If salad bowls or à la carte salads are of-

Regal des Gourmets

MEDALLIONS OF CALF'S SWEETBREAD, FORESTIERE 6.75
SUPREME OF CAPON SAUTE, BASQUAISE 6.75
BRAISED QUAIL AND TOURNEDOS, ROSSINI 8.75
SLICED TENDERLOIN of BEEF "STROGANOFF" with WILD RICE 7.95
(Entrees are presented with Fresh Vegetable, Potato and Salad)

ROAST LEG OF VENISON GRAND VENEUR 8.25

FILET OF ROCKFISH SAUTE MURAT 7.25

Entrees are presented with Fresh Vegetables, Potato, and Salad

A la Carte Vegetables

Peas and Mushrooms, Farmer Style 1.15   Artichoke Hearts Niçoise 1.35
French Fried Mushrooms 1.30   Braised Hearts of Celery 1.65

Appetizers

Bouquet of Shrimps Supreme 2.75   Fresh Lump Crabmeat, Louis 2.75
Smoked Filet of Trout, Raifort 1.95   Macedoine of Fresh Fruit Ambrosia 1.10
Iced Melon 1.50   Iced Melon with Virginia Ham 2.50
Cherry Stone Clams on Ice 1.95   Coquille Gastronome 2.65
Chesapeake Oysters on Half Shell 2.45   Nova Scotia Smoked Salmon 3.25

Soups

Consomme Double with Dry Sack .75   Cream of Watercress .75
Lobster Bisque Chantilly 1.10   Gazpacho San Sebastian .95
Vichyssoise Supreme .75   Chilled Crab Gumbo .95

Seafood

BOUILLABAISSE MARSEILLAISE 7.25
FROG LEGS SAUTE PROVENÇALE 7.75
VIRGINIA CRABMEAT SAUTE "RANDOLPH" 7.25
SPANISH SCAMPI MONTE CARLO 7.50
(Entrees are presented with Fresh Vegetable, Potato and Salad)

Grill

FRENCH LAMB CHOPS WITH MINTED PEARS 8.25
BROILED FILET MIGNON WITH CHAMPIGNON 9.50
PRIME SIRLOIN STEAK MAITRE D'HOTEL 9.75
ROAST PRIME RIB OF BEEF AU JUS, YORKSHIRE PUDDING 8.50
(Entrees are presented with Fresh Vegetable, Potato and Salad)

Salads

Boston Lettuce   Chilled Fruit Salad   Hearts of Romaine
Sliced Tomato with Watercress 1.25   Caesar Imperator 1.50
Hearts of Artichokes, Quartered Mushrooms, Tomato Wedges Vinaigrette 1.65

10/73

FIG. 3-13   An elegant menu but with very few items listed. Menus need not show a large number of offerings to satisfy guests. It is much more important for the items offered to be of excellent quality and well served. (Courtesy Williamsburg Inn, Williamsburg, Virginia)

fered, a balanced choice of four—perhaps an egg, a shellfish, a fish or meat and a fruit salad—may be offered. Specialty salads such as a fruit with sherbet, a stuffed tomato or stuffed avocado salad may additionally appear. Variety should be gained by offering different salad dressings.

Desserts have been falling in menu and patron popularity and menus today offer fewer. Some operations find that ice cream or sherbet may be all that is required. Others combine these with a limited number of pies or cakes. Some puddings may appear if the dessert list is extended. If further extension is desired, fresh, canned or dried fruits may be offered. The number of desserts should be guided by the number and type usually sold.

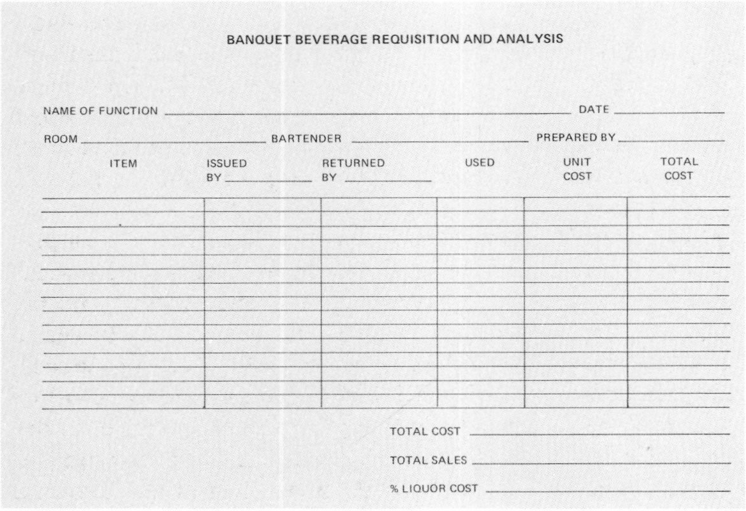

BANQUET BEVERAGE REQUISITION AND ANALYSIS

NAME OF FUNCTION _____ DATE _____

ROOM _____ BARTENDER _____ PREPARED BY _____

ITEM	ISSUED BY _____	RETURNED BY _____	USED	UNIT COST	TOTAL COST

TOTAL COST _____

TOTAL SALES _____

% LIQUOR COST _____

FIG. 3-12
An accurate record is needed of liquor ordered and used for banquets and special parties. Here is a typical form showing returns as well as charge-outs. (Courtesy Hyatt Corporation)

THE INSTITUTIONAL FOODSERVICE MENU

Non-commercial institutions have needs different from commercial operations and therefore different menu requirements. Many individuals in them will obtain all or most of their meals there. This makes it necessary to see that the foods served are nutritionally adequate. Because many individuals stay at the institution for long periods of time, it is also necessary to see that there is good variety and not too much repetition.

Most institutional menus are built around the three-meal-a-day plan. Breakfast is a fruit or juice, cereal and milk, a main dish such as eggs, and/or meat, hotcakes, Danish pastry, toast or bread with margarine or butter, jelly or jam, and beverage. Lunch may include as much as an entrée, vegetable, salad, bread and butter, beverage and dessert, or as little as a soup, beverage and dessert. The institutional dinner may have a first course, such as an appetizer or soup, followed by a main dish with vegetable and potato or starch food, a salad, bread and butter or margarine, a dessert and beverage. There is usually a 10-hour span between breakfast and dinner and a 14-hour fast between dinner and breakfast unless a snack is served in the evening.

Some institutions find that a four-meal or five-meal plan is more suitable for their needs. In the four-meal plan, a light continental breakfast is served at 7:00 a.m. A substantial brunch follows it at 10:30 a.m. At 3:30 p.m., the main meal is served followed by a light supper in the evening.

The five-meal plan is similar, with a continental breakfast at 7:00 a.m., a brunch at 10:00 a.m., a light snack about 12:30 or 1:00 p.m. with the main meal following between 3:00 and 4:00 p.m. A light snack is served between 6:30 and 8:00 p.m.

The four-meal or five-meal plans may reduce the labor required in the kitchen since the two big meals of the day are close enough together for one shift to prepare them. The other meals are light enough to be prepared by skeleton crews.

Some hospitals also find that the four-meal or five-meal plans permit patients to be gone for early morning examinations without losing out on a full meal. Even though the patient has had to forego a breakfast, just about the time he is released from examination and is returning, one of the heavier meals of the day is being served.

Not all attempts to change to a four-meal or five-meal plan have been successful. The failure has usually been one of planning. It is essential that the plan be thoroughly discussed with the staff members who may be affected. The plan must have the complete support of the staff and solid backing from the administration. Communication of the plan, and a complete discussion of the benefits and disadvantages, should occur a long time in advance of implementation. If, after complete discussion and communication, there remains a degree of opposition, it is best not to start the plan. Experience has shown it will not succeed.

The change must consider every factor. For instance, a large state mental hospital changed to a five-meal plan and found that the patients felt they were not getting a breakfast because cereal was not a part of the first meal served. Adding either cold or hot cereals to the continental breakfast resulted in eliminating most complaints. In implementing these four-meal or five-meal plans, the amount of sugar, flour and fat should be watched. Sweet rolls or other breakfast pastries and evening snacks (which might be cookies, cakes or other sweet and rich products) cause undesirable weight gain with a failure on the part of patients to consume adequate amounts of other essential nutrients.

Different institutions need different menus. A school program on the Class A lunch must serve at least two ounces of high protein food, three-fourths cup of vegetables or the equivalent in salad, bread or roll with butter or margarine, and a half pint of milk, to meet federal requirements. Many hospitals and nursing homes must plan a general menu and from this develop the required modified diets. In college foodservices, young growing people will want different foods that have a higher caloric value than diets served to older people. Some individuals will want "soul" foods.

Sunday	Monday	Tuesday	Wednesday
Unsweetened Orange Juice - ½ c. FF Scrambled Egg - 1 Malt-o-meal - ½ cup Toast - 1 slice Crisp Bacon - 1 strip Margarine - 1 pat Milk (for cereal) - ¼ cup as desired	Diet Stewed Prunes - 2 Poached Eggs - 1 Cream of Rice - ½ cup Toast - 1 slice Biscuit - 2" diameter - 1 Margarine - 1 pat a.d.	Unsweetened Grapefruit Juice - ½ c. Soft-cooked egg - 1 Cream of wheat - ½ c Toast - 2" diameter - 1 sl. a.d.	Unsweetened Pineapple Juice - 1/3 cup FF Scrambled Egg - 1 Oatmeal - ½ cup Toast slice - 1 a.d.
Meat loaf - 2 oz. FF Mashed Potatoes - #8 scoop Bread - 1 slice FF Green Beans Stewed Tomato Cubes Diet pear halves (2) Milk - 3/4 cup Margarine - 1 pat	Lean Roast Beef - 2 oz. Cream of Chicken Soup made with water - 3/4 cup Saltines - 5 squares FF Leaf Spinach w/vinegar Diet Pineapple - 2 slices	Broiled Beef Pattie (2 oz.) w/ tomato sauce - free w.k. corn - 1/3 cup Bread - 1 slice FF Asparagus Diet Peach halves - 2	stew { Tender Beef Cubes - 2 oz. Potato cubes - ¼ cup Mixed vegetables - ¼ cup (+ 1 bread) + Broth, tomatoes, Celery to make stew. Biscuit - (2" diameter) - 1 Fine chopped cabbage w/ zero Drsg. Diet Hot Cinnamon Apples - ½ cup Margarine - 1 pat Milk - 3/4 cup
Stewed Chicken - 3 oz. FF Savory Noodles - ½ c. (cooked in FF Broth) Plain Angel Food Cake (1/20 of 9"cake) Finely shredded lettuce, FF Peas with a hint of mint Diet Baked Apple (2") Margarine - 1 pat French Drsg. - 1 Tbsp. Milk - 1 cup Saltines - 5 squares Vegetable Soup-diluted-1 cup Cheese - 1 oz. slice	FF Parslied Catfish Fillet - 3 oz. Baked Potato (2"diameter) - 1 Hot Roll (2"diameter) - 1 Mixed Green Salad (finely chopped) FF Beet Cubes w/grated lemon rind Sliced Orange - 1 small Margarine - 1 pat Mayonnaise - 1 tsp. Buttermilk (3.5% butterfat) 1 cup Sandwich: 2 slices w.w.bread lean roast beef - 1 oz. (Held over from noon) Lettuce as desired	Roast turkey - 3 oz. Sage Bread Dressing - #8 scoop (omit 1 Fat) Hot roll (2"diameter) - 1 Diet cranberry sauce FF Green Peas & Carrots - ½ c. Diet fruit cocktail - ½ c Margarine - 1 pat (other fat is in Drsg.) Milk, skimmed - 1 cup (2 Fat Exchange go for Ice Cream) Vanilla Ice Cream - #8 Scoop (= 1 Bread + 2 Fat (from milk) Gingersnaps, small - 6 Peanut Butter - 2 Tbsd.	Baked pork cutlet - 3 oz. Parslied Savory Rice - ½ cup FF Green Beans Acorn squash - ½ c. of small + 1 pat margarine Diet plums - 2 Margarine - 1 pat (other is on squash) Milk - ½ cup Cream of Tomato Soup (6 T undiluted Tom. Soup ½ cup milk) Saltines - 5 squares Wiener - 1 - hot + cut up in tomato soup

FIG. 3-14   A planning form for an institutional general menu which allows for modified diets.

Basics in Planning
The Institutional Menu

It is best in planning the institutional menu to work with a sheet large enough to hold the menu for an entire period. Obviously, if the menu is to run for a long period, such as a quarter or more, this cannot be done. The proper headings should be set up with days, date, meals, etc., designated for columns and rows.

Most planners start with the main dishes for a meal, beginning first with dinners, then with lunches and then breakfasts. Balance and variety must be sought between days and also between the meals of a day. The frequency of the types of meats to use should be established and a table can be set up for this. For instance, in a week beef may be served twice, pork or cured pork once, poultry once, fish or shellfish once, a casserole dish once along with an occasional selection of variety meat, veal, lamb, sausage, eggs, cheese or other non-meat dish. Similarly, a table may be set up to indicate the frequency desired for various vegetables and other foods. A desired frequency table can be set up for breakfast and lunch items also.

After the main dishes are selected, the vegetables and potato, or other starch items, are added, followed by salads and dressings. Again, these must be balanced against the various foods used in a day and from day to day. After adding these major items, the planner may select the breakfast fruits and cereals. Breads for each meal, desserts and beverages can follow in that order.

After this, the menu is checked to see that balance has been maintained, nutritional needs met, cost restraints not exceeded and other factors such as equipment balance, skill of labor, etc., considered. Modified diets based on this general menu, should be planned by an individual trained in nutrition.

It is important in most institutional foodservices to check the menu carefully to see that the meals are adequately balanced nutritionally. This should be a detailed check such as checking to see each day if a good source of ascorbic acid has been provided, etc. (Also see the chapter on nutrition.)

CHAPTER 4

Constraints in Menu Planning

Few individuals have a free hand in menu planning. A number of restrictions must be considered such as cost, the patron, the meal, the season, the occasion, the layout or equipment, personnel, the service, the availability of foods, quality and the practicality of producing a given menu item. All factors must be considered and the menu constructed around them or it most likely will be a failure. It is not enough to consider some and fail to consider others. All must be considered for a successful menu.

Physical Constraints

The menu must be written so that the physical facilities of the operation are capable of producing the right quality and quantity of items. These facilities must also be such that the proper service can follow. A menu requiring a dinner of escalloped potatoes and ham, candied squash, baked tomatoes, cornbread and chocolate cake makes too much demand on the ovens and not enough on other equipment. Planning a buffet dinner for a dining room where there are not units to keep food warm is another example of a failure to consider limitations. To ask a baker to make hard rolls is a mistake if the ovens do not have steam connected to them because it takes steam to produce the hard, crisp crusts.

Menus must be planned to suit equipment capacity. A 20-gallon steam-kettle is capable of producing only 16 gallons of soup. To plan for more can create problems. Also, a griddle 24 by 36 inches in size can produce 80 orders of hot cakes, three cakes per order, in an hour. To plan for a production of 100 such orders, plus bacon, ham, hashbrowns, eggs, etc., would be another example of failing to consider equipment limitations.

The time required to process foods through the equipment must also be known. Work benches, mixers, ovens, sinks, top-of-the-range space and other units all can handle just so much work in a given time. If a planner asks for more than the kitchen is capable of producing, the whole system may collapse because workers cannot meet the quota.

Many planners of menus observe limitations in the areas where the last stages of production occur, but frequently fail to consider requirements previous to that, such as limitations in storage areas, pre-preparation units and other support areas. Often the fault may not be in the original planning. Sometimes a facility may outgrow these units, creating problems. Or it may be that faulty use of these facilities is occuring. A walk-in refrigerator may be adequate to handle the loads but, because of misplanning, too heavy a load of carryovers, or poor use of space makes the refrigerator appear inadequate. With better planning of its use, reducing the amount of carry-over food or by reorganizing the space, the problem may be corrected. Whatever the cause, the menu planner must consider such limitations and work around them in designing a menu.

The menu planner can often be helpful in indicating to those in production and service how to avoid an equipment overload. An employee may feel there is a lack of equipment but if he is shown that limitations can be overcome with planning or a procedural change, the problem may not appear. For instance, a seeming lack of griddle space can be corrected by first browning off hash brown potatoes in an oven and then finishing them on the griddle for service. A stew can be cooked in a roasting plan in the oven as well as on top of the stove. Vegetables can be steamed, baked or sautéed as well as they can be boiled. A change in the menu to one of these other methods of cooking can avoid overloading the range or steam-jacketed kettle units.

The purchase of already prepared foods may help solve equipment limitations. Many planners today find that they can considerably extend the production capacity of a kitchen by purchasing prepared banquet items. This allows the addition of items without additional equipment or facilities. Salad greens can be obtained washed and ready to serve, as can many vegetables. Stuffed baked potatoes can also be purchased, thereby saving space in the vegetable preparation area as well as saving on personnel.

The menu planner must also see that the ability of the operation to serve the food is not exceeded. A dining area can serve only a given number and after that the quality of service drops and heavy customer disapproval results. Also, a foodservice will have just so many dishware items for service. If the menu requires more of a specific type of dish than it has, the quality of service sags. The planner should also know that some foods take longer to prepare and serve than others. Too many such offerings on a menu may slow down service to a point where desirable turnover is not achieved, customers are not served promptly and customer dissatisfaction occurs.

Personnel Constraints

The menu must be planned to suit the ability of the cooks to prepare the items, the service personnel to serve it and management to control it properly. In addition to having the ability to do what is required, the amount of work assigned should be within the limits that an individual is capable of doing.

Workers should be given enough to do to keep them busy but not so much that the work is not done or is done poorly.

Observation of the kitchen and dining areas may indicate how labor can be stored, how jobs can be combined and if there is a deficiency in planning the menu for best labor utilization. Workers are adept at practicing Parkinson's law which says, "Work expands to fill the time available." Being able to fill out the peaks and valleys in work takes experience on the part of the planner but, once learned, can be a valuable tool to reduce labor cost, avoid times when the work load is excessive and keep a happier crew.

Labor may be stored by seeing to it that jobs are done ahead. It is wise to set up pre-preparation tasks that can be done when workers have time. Some operations prepare certain dishes when there is slack time and then freeze them for later use. A menu should avoid having everything prepared at the last minute, for this may mean that employees stand around for a good share of the time and then are overloaded during the service period. Planning ahead to store labor can also be achieved by having an item such as roast turkey on one day and then several days later using the carry-over for turkey à la king. Or the menu can have pot roast of beef for dinner and hot roast beef sandwiches for lunch the next day. If meat balls and spaghetti are on the menu and meatloaf is to follow a week later, both can be mixed at the same time, the meat loaves formed and frozen and then used at the required time.

Every job has a "get ready", a "do" and a "clean up and put away." Planning work to get more "do" for the "get ready" and "clean up and put away" time can considerably increase the amount done. About the same time is required in doing a small or large lot in "get ready" and "clean up and put away." Thus, doing bigger batches or combining jobs can do much to increase the productivity of workers in an operation.

The fact that workers may lack skills to produce menu items may be a limitation at the time of writing, but it need not be a permanent one. Every operation should have a training program designed to improve workers' skills and job competency. An operation also can send employees to classes where they can learn to do jobs they were not able to do previously.

Flexibility should be built into staffs so that labor can be shifted around to meet variable work demands. Busboys should be utilized in slack times in back-of-the-house jobs such as in vegetable preparation, dishwashing, cleaning or other tasks. Kitchen helpers should be flexible enough to be able to work in other sections as well as their assigned one. Sometimes labor unions restrict too variable a use of labor. Thus, job descriptions and titles should be carefully assigned so that better flexibility can be obtained when such restrictions exist.

Food Availability

Before an item is put on the menu, the availability of its ingredients on the market should be known. Menus planned for use over a long period, such as a permanent à la carte menu, should not list too many seasonal items. If they are on the menu card, a notation should indicate that they are available only in season. For instance, a breakfast menu might list "melon, in season." If a menu card changes frequently, items having seasonality can be featured when they are on the market, but the planner should know beforehand whether the season is running normally or not. At times there can be a wide variability on the arrival or the disappearance of items on the market and the menu planner should not get caught having something on the menu that has not yet reached the market or has left it. Price stability should also be investigated. An item might appear on the market at the time planned but be so high in price that it cannot be used.

Some menu planners keep lists noting when items are in season and at their best quality. They also keep track of prices. Usually an item is at its highest quality and lowest in price when it is at its seasonal peak. Featuring foods at this time may be good merchandising. Grapefruit is at its peak supply and quality in December through February and this is the time to feature it.

Plans should be made considerably ahead for the offering on menu cards of specials on seasonal items. It is often desirable to have cards printed that show an attractive serving of a fresh strawberry shortcake, or a baked Rome Beauty apple stuffed with mincemeat and served with a hot butter rum sauce. In the spring, fresh water smelt leave Lake Michigan and go up the streams to spawn. At this time they are caught in large numbers. These smelt are high in quality and low in price. Some operations purchase them at this time and offer them crisply fried with French fried potatoes and a succulent cole slaw.

Free marketing information on when foods are plentiful and low in price is available from government agencies. They will mail daily market reports on many commodities to those who request them. Newspapers and other information media also publish lists of foods plentiful on the market. Salesmen can often be helpful in indicating whether foods are in good supply or scarce.

Patron Constraints

Food must serve physiological, social and psychological needs of people. To plan a menu which adequately does all three requires a considerable amount of knowledge and ability.

Planning to meet physiological needs requires a good background in nutrition and the part foods play in maintaining health and well-being. While commercial foodservices may not have the responsibility for providing those they serve with an adequate diet, they should see that the foods served are high in essential nutrients. While they cannot force people to select a balanced diet, the selection of such a diet should be possible from the menu card if it offers complete meals. If snack type foods are served, they should be as nutritious as possible—in fact, all food served should contain as many nutrients as possible.

Food can also play a tremendously important part in our social lives because it is frequently the vehicle on which many social activities ride. Many business functions revolve around food and often some of the most important events in the life of an individual will be built around food.

The psychological considerations involving food are deep, complex and varied. Food can be comforting and give deep animal satisfaction. Food can be the method by which we display pride and show off to our friends, acquaintances and relatives. Patterns of eating arise from deeply ingrained habits, ethnic backgrounds and personal characteristics. Our feelings of security and safety can be closely tied to food and when we are disturbed and insecure we may overeat.

Whether physiological or psychological needs are greatest in importance may be argued. If physiological needs are not met, an individual may lack health and well-being and may even die. However, if psychological needs in food are not met, an individual can refuse to eat and the result can be the same. Both are powerful drives. Not far behind these two as drives in creating human action are the social ones that revolve around food. There are times when even social considerations involving food may take precedence over others. We may eat something we know is not good for us, or that we do not like, just because of social pressures.

PHYSIOLOGICAL NEEDS

Food is essential to produce and maintain life. People are what they eat, and what is eaten has much to do with their health, how active they are, their vitality and how long and how well they live. An inadequate food intake during the later stages of a pregnancy can cause a woman to give birth to a mentally retarded child. Infants and young children who fail to get adequate food may fail to develop mentally as well as physically. Hungry children cannot learn. An improper food intake may contribute to an adolescent's poor posture and skeletal structure, inadequate growth and a failure to build a strong body.

Our need for food to support life has been a tremendous motivator in spurring human action in man's history. Stalin said, "You can't argue with a hungry man," indicating that until man's basic need for food is met, there is little use in trying to interest him in anything else.

The physiological needs for food vary according to age, sex, activity, environmental factors and physiological make-up. Babies must have large amounts of food because of their rapid growth; in a very short time they double their birth weight.

Individuals vary in the speed at which their bodies function. The body cells of some people metabolize food more slowly and react more slowly. This makes a difference in the amount of food they need. An individual with active cells will require more food than one whose cells function more slowly.

The hormone and endocrine secretions of the body also affect food needs. Young people need more food not only because they are growing and are more active but because their body cells function more rapidly and have a different hormone makeup from that of elderly people. After 55, human beings begin to slow down and many of the body's functions change.

Small people require less food than larger ones but the shape of the body, or the amount of fat covering it, can also be factors in deciding how much food one needs. A tall, thin person with a lot of body surface and little fat covering will need more calories than a more compact person who has a good fat layer over the body. The compact person loses less heat than the tall thin one and the layer of fat also helps to reduce the heat loss. If less heat is required, we need less food to keep our bodies warm.

Activity is also a factor in deciding how much food we need. It takes a lot of calories to play football or tennis. If we do not move about much we need fewer calories than if we are quite active.

It is interesting that while our need for calories can drop as we get older our need for other nutrients, such as vitamins or minerals, does not. A frail bedridden woman of 80 may need only around 1,200 calories a day but will need the same amount of most vitamins and minerals as an active girl of 18. When an individual consumes less than 1,200 calories of food per day, it is difficult to get all the vitamins, protein and minerals needed in the diet to maintain good health.

We also need more calories in the winter than in the summer because we have to burn more food to keep our bodies warm. In our society today, people are less active and live in warmer houses, use electric blankets to keep warm in bed, and so use fewer calories than they needed in the past.

SOCIAL NEEDS

Food may be more a part of our social lives than we realize. Family gatherings around the table are social events and eating is only a vehicle for a "family get-together." When individuals go out for a coffee break at the office, the purpose may be more for getting together than simply to get food. Food serves as an excuse for the conversation and social interaction. The coffee house became popular because people could sit and talk. The English pub today gains its popularity much for the same reason. Food or drink is often incidental at a cocktail party or reception.

The use of food as a social vehicle can vary. A hungry person has far less social need than one who is not hungry. A truck driver who stops to have food is not as interested in the social contacts he may gain (although he may appreciate visiting with others after being so long alone in the cab) as he is in obtaining satisfying food and being on his way again. Social togetherness, on the other hand, may be the purpose of a stop by two young people at a drive-in, or for two women who have just come from an afternoon theater and enter a lounge for an afternoon cocktail. The menu designed to cater to such occasions must reflect social needs and, as much as possible, establish the proper vehicle for satisfying them.

Other menus must also be purposely planned for the social event. A Fourth of July picnic, at which the bigwigs of the local Democratic party bring in a prominent politician to make a speech, will require very different foods and drink from those served at a style show for women. Fitting the foods to the theme and carrying it out with originality and creativity can do much to enhance the success of a social function.

PSYCHOLOGICAL NEEDS

There are many ways in which food can meet psychological needs of individuals. Hunger creates anxiety and a restlessness which eating quiets. This property of food is often called its "satiety value." Some individuals overeat when they are frustrated or disturbed. The satiety or peaceful feeling they get from food tends to quiet them and soothe their emotional disturbances. This overeating can be done to the extent than an individual becomes overweight.

The part food plays in satisfying emotional needs has been the subject of a number of studies. Some investigators believe than in infancy one's world is largely interpreted through food and thus many of our basic emotions are tied to food very early. When the baby is hungry, it cries and thrashes about. Food satisfies it and it goes to sleep. When it gets hungry again, it wakes and cries. Some have postulated that mother love is based on the fact that the mother feeds the child and the child, associating the mother with the satisfaction of a basic need, develops a

strong attachment for her. As an individual gets older, he learns to submerge emotions attached to food. He no longer cries when hungry, but he can be disturbed when he lacks food and can be more satisfied after he has eaten. When he is upset, food still can give comfort. Emotions are quieted by food. College students often show distinct tieups between frustrations and food. Arriving at school in the fall, their spirits are high and they enjoy their new experiences. At this time, the food is considered good. (This is the time for the foodservice department to save money on its budget.) However, as the newness wears off, students miss home and loved ones. The rigors of classes, assignments, term papers and examinations begin to create problems and frustrations and the students begin to take out their frustrations on the food they are getting. Even food riots can be a result. It is no coincidence that troubles on campus rise with such pressures. Students don't realize that the food they once liked now is cause for great dissatisfaction. (This is now the time to put the money previously saved on the budget into better food.)

Adults can show the same reactions and use food as a "whipping boy" for emotional disturbances. A business executive at his club may find the food totally unacceptable while others at the table enjoy it. The problem may be that frustrations at the office did more to ruin the man's appreciation of his food than the chef, the waiter or anything else at the club.

Many times institutional food of much higher quality than individuals get at home is criticized for its quality because diners miss the home atmosphere, friends, etc. People learn to eat amid familiar surroundings. There is comfort and security in being at home eating with those one loves. The security and comfort is deeply set and tied to food. It has been built up over a long period of time. Then suddenly, when an individual must eat elsewhere away from his loved ones, there is an insecurity, lonesomeness and a desire for familiar things associated with food. So, it is not the food that is lacking quality but environmental factors associated with it. An individual who is hospitalized and ill has little appetite anyway and under the stress of illness and the loss of familiar surroundings it is not surprising that the hospital's food is not liked. The wonder is that hospital food is liked as well as it is.

Food patterns learned early in life are apt to stay with one all through life. In fact, we have medical evidence to show that overfeeding a child can develop body cells that will want to build fat all during the lifetime of this individual.

Some people learn to eat certain kinds of food and if they cannot have this assortment they become upset and even develop fantasies of persecution and illness. Many individuals of specific ethnic backgrounds, having different food habits, find they must have this food or they cannot function well. The cafeteria at the East-West Center of the University of Hawaii, where many Orientals live, must serve large quantities of rice at every meal to keep these students satisfied. If they do not get it, they say they cannot study. Some students have left and gone back to their own countries, forsaking their educations, because they have missed the foods they were accustomed to.

"Soul" foods today must be served in many college dormitories and institutions and even in commercial operations to satisfy deep-set feelings of individuals about food. Individuals may also believe that foods can have medicinal or other harmful or beneficial effects on the body. Some believe that raw oysters stimulate the sex drive. Others believe that saltpeter (potassium nitrate) used to pickle meat is a sexual depressant.

Fact and fancy are frequently interwoven in our notions about food. Thus, some individuals eat certain foods because they feel they are beneficial. Some of these beliefs are right and others are wrong. It is doubtful if carrots grown in organic soil are more nutritious than those grown in a soil artificially fertilized, but because of a belief that they are, some people will eat only these "organic" carrots. Some people believe that "an apple a day keeps the doctor away," and there is a reason for this. Apples contain a small quantity of magnesium, which is a mild laxative and helps in promoting good body elimination. Once such beliefs are ingrained in an individual, it is extremely difficult to eradicate them. Some authorities have stated that it is easier to change religious beliefs than it is to change beliefs about food or to change deeply ingrained food habits.

Food can have religious significance. The unleavened Passover bread has deep religious meaning for the Jew. His acceptance or rejection of food may be so deeply tied to some of his religious concepts that he would die before he would eat food violating these beliefs. To the Seventh Day Adventist who will not eat meat, the sight of meat can cause repugnance and nausea. The Roman Catholic believes that the bread and wine he receives at the altar rail has been changed into the body of Christ, even though he sees no physical change as he receives them. At one time he was taught it was a sin to eat meat on Friday. Now he knows it was just a belief.

In many religions food is a symbol, and this is linked to some of the basic philosophies and beliefs of man. The fact our bodies can take inanimate things, such as food and drink, and convert them into living cells is in truth a miracle. Thus, the fact that food or drink may have deep religious significance for some people should be respected.

What Makes Foods Good?

Eating can give mental pleasure as well as "gut" satisfaction, as has been noted. Many people enjoy seeing good food and take pleasure in tasting it. A discriminating taster who enjoys food can become somewhat like a discriminating listener to music, taking pleasure in noting the subtle sense differences which foods can give. That people "eat with their eyes" has been substantiated and many will accept food that appears good to them while they reject food that does not look good. Color, form or shape, temperature, texture and consistency can affect one's feeling about food. Of course, taste is also tremendously important.

Red, red-orange, butter-yellow, pink, tan, light or clear green, white or light brown colors enhance the appeal of food, while purple, violet, yellow-green, mustard yellow, gray, olive and orange-yellow do not. Contrasts in acceptable colors should be sought. A myriad of bright colors in a fruit cup or salad can heighten interest. Freshness in color is important. Too vivid colors, especially if they are combined or massed together, can be disagreeable. Natural colors are desirable.

Differences should also appear in the form or shape of foods. Variations on a plate, such as a slice of baked ham dressed with a small quantity of light brown raisin and shredded pineapple sauce, diced beets with a light gloss or sheen of butter, mashed sweet potatoes graced with a small spray of parsley, will achieve a difference in form (plus color) that is agreeable. Too many mounds, cubes, balls or similar shapes cause a loss of interest.

It is also important to have foods of a different height. While this may not be possible on one plate, it can be done by using different heights in different foods. Thus, salads or desserts can be planned which have height and contrast with foods that are flat. Tall glasses or other dishes can be used to give a variation in height.

It is also important that the form of foods be kept natural. Foods that are chopped, puréed or otherwise changed in shape too much from what one expects, can bring rejection just because they do not have the shape expected. This does not mean that a difference in form or shape of a food cannot be used to give variety but that dramatic or garish change should be avoided.

The rule of having "hot foods hot and cold foods cold" is probably well known to many in foodservice work. It is therefore amazing that the rule is so frequently transgressed. One can step up to a buffet lined with a tempting array of cold foods sitting in a bed of ice and experience the deepest disappointment when, grasping the plate on which he is to serve himself, he feels the plate is very warm. Or, he can have the same sensation when he touches a plate on which he is to put hot foods and finds the plate is very cold. Having "hot foods hot and cold foods cold" requires planning and care—production and services personnel *should care* because unless they do, the rule will be breached.

In the planning of foods, contrasts in temperature should be sought. A small cup of cranberry ice is a delightful contrast to a hot plate of food at a Thanksgiving dinner. A cold, crisp salad of greens can be a refreshing item with a piping hot steak and mushrooms, accompanied by a hot, baked potato. A cool, crisp dill pickle can be not only a good flavor and texture contrast to a New England boiled dinner but also a pleasing temperature contrast.

The cooking of food frequently softens its texture and, unless such softening is watched, can result in a meal which is very little other than a soft, mushy mass. Texture contrasts should be planned: a crisp cracker with a soft salad, or a crisp piece of stuffed celery with a seafood cocktail. Crisp or crunchy foods can be blended with soft ones to give a desirable difference in texture. Thus, toasted almonds in an almandine sauce can enliven the soft texture of sole with which it is served. Some crispness left in vegetables as they come to the steam table is also desirable, not only from the standpoint of freshness, but also because this gives them a textural contrast. Having a difference between the texture of foods on a plate or between courses can help to give desirable contrasts. An excess of one texture or too much crispness without some softness can be objectionable.

Consistency is important not only to the sight but also to give a proper feel in the mouth. Some children will reject food saying they do not like its taste when actually they are rejecting it because of its consistency. Foods that appear runny on a dish will fail to receive approbation. So do foods that are pasty, sticky or that have too much of a contrasting consistency. A slickness can be objectionable. Soda added to the cooking water to keep vegetables green can also soften the cellulose to a point where the vegetable becomes slick and slimy.

Flavor in food is made up of taste and odor. We have four tastes: sweet, sour, bitter and salt. Our sweet and sour taste buds are in the center and near the front of the tongue while the salt buds are in the middle and slightly farther back. Bitter taste buds are farthest back. Flavor is the joining of these four tastes, or some of them, with an odor or odors. If the nose is held, many individuals cannot tell what some foods are. They can identify them as bitter, salt, sweet or sour but, because the odor is missing, they miss *what* they are.

Flavor differs as the intensities of the tastes and the differences in the odors differ. What is pleasant or disagreeable in flavor differs with individuals. Most object to too sharp a flavor but once one learns to like such a flavor, as in a sharp cheese, he will look for it in the product and like it.

Our senses are sharpest around the age of 20 to 25 and after this slowly decline. However, young people may not be as good tasters as older ones, not because of flavor acuity, but because flavor identification requires experience to be able to tell which flavors are which. Older people have tested more things and so know more flavors, and this helps them even though they do not have as good taste acuity as young persons. Young people do not like to experiment with foods they do not know and thus may build restricted food patterns. Older people, being more adventurous, eat a wider range of foods and know a wider range of flavors.

However, as people age, they lose their ability to taste. Many old people cannot identify flavors unless they see the food. Because the sweet and salt taste buds are first to atrophy, older people usually lose their ability to taste salt or sweet first.

If a man is hungry, the sight of food can increase his desire to eat. Thus, food displayed where hungry people can see it may help increase sales.

Investigators have also found that visually sighting food is needed for some individuals to recognize food flavors. When these people are blindfolded, food prepared so that it texture does not identify it cannot be detected by flavor alone—even if the flavors are as pronounced as in a banana, or lemon or coffee-flavored pudding.

Food can be used as a means of display or ostentation. A business executive wishing to impress a client is willing to pay for an elaborate meal he normally would not select. Lavish display may satisfy the ego of individuals or a group. Some wedding and party gatherings may have an extravagant display of food in an attempt to make it noteworthy. There is snob appeal in eating some foods. Thus, one who eats chocolate-coated ants may detest them but, because they set him apart as a connoisseur of food delicacies, he eats them.

Rating Food

Food preferences must be considered in writing menus. People are influenced by food habits acquired over a long period. As previously noted, many individuals do not like foods which they do not know. They may even be unwilling to try them. Some menu planners may use the results of food preference tests to ascertain what should be put on the menu. However, food preferences do not necessarily mean that foods preferred are the most frequently selected. Thus, it is also necessary to pay attention to what people select as well as what they say they prefer.

Preference ratings are frequently indicated as a percentage. Thus, we may say that 78 per cent prefer coffee black to coffee with cream. However, it is becoming more and more common to indicate a relative degree of preference based on a hedonic scale from 9 to 1. To do this, individuals are asked if they like a food extremely (9), like it very much (8), like it moderately (7), like

Food Preference Questionnaire

Now I am going to ask you to rate the food you just ate. For each food, will you tell me if you liked it extremely, liked it very much, liked it moderately, liked it slightly, neither liked nor disliked it, disliked it slightly, disliked it moderately, disliked it very much, or disliked it extremely. This card has a list of these ratings. (Interviewer circle number.)

a. What main dish?

_____ 1 2 3 4 5 6 7 8 9

b. Any other main dish?

_____ 1 2 3 4 5 6 7 8 9

c. Vegetable(s)?

_____ 1 2 3 4 5 6 7 8 9
_____ 1 2 3 4 5 6 7 8 9

d. Drink(s)?

_____ 1 2 3 4 5 6 7 8 9
_____ 1 2 3 4 5 6 7 8 9

e. Breads or cereals?

_____ 1 2 3 4 5 6 7 8 9
_____ 1 2 3 4 5 6 7 8 9

f. Potatoes or starches?

_____ 1 2 3 4 5 6 7 8 9

g. Salads?

_____ 1 2 3 4 5 6 7 8 9
_____ 1 2 3 4 5 6 7 8 9

h. Soup?

_____ 1 2 3 4 5 6 7 8 9

i. Desserts?

_____ 1 2 3 4 5 6 7 8 9
_____ 1 2 3 4 5 6 7 8 9

(For breakfast, ask only for main dishes, beverages, breads and cereals, and fruits.)

Overall, how would you rate the meal you just ate, using the same scale? (Circle)

1   2   3   4   5   6   7   8   9

How did this meal compare with other Army meals you have had?

_____ Much better?   _____ About the same?   _____ A little worse?

_____ A little better?   _____ Much worse?

Respondent's name _____ Number _____

Interviewer _____

FIG. 4-1   A form used by an interviewer obtaining data on food acceptability. Depending on the answer of the respondent, the interviewer would circle the proper number. These then were totaled for each food and divided by the number of respondents, to give a hedonic rating for the various foods.

it slightly (6), neither like nor dislike it (5), dislike it slightly (4), dislike it moderately (3), dislike it very much (2) and dislike it extremely (1). The value in parentheses is the score given this answer.

These scores are then added together and divided by the number of individuals making up the total score. Thus, if 10 people's scores added up to 64, the average rating of 6.4 for the food

item means it was between "liked slightly" and "liked moderately", while a value of 3.0 would indicate it was "disliked moderately." Figure 4-1 is taken from a page of a questionnaire used in 1971-72 by the U. S. Army Natick Laboratories at Fort Lewis, Wash., to obtain hedonic rating of foods. Table 4-1 shows the hedonic ratings for 25 of the most-liked and 25 of the least-liked foods obtained in the Fort Lewis study.

Table 4-1

Foods Best & Least Liked on Hedonic Scale

a. 25 MOST PREFERRED FOODS

b. 25 LEAST PREFERRED FOODS

Food Name	Hedonic Preference	Food Name	Hedonic Preference
Milk	8.03	Pickled beat/onion salad	3.01
Orange juice	7.65	Parsnips	3.10
Grilled steak	7.61	Zucchini squash	3.21
Hot rolls & buns	7.46	Iced coffee	3.31
Fried chicken	7.43	Eggplant	3.43
Chocolate milk	7.42	Rutabagas	3.48
Oranges*	7.33	Carrot, raisin & celery salad	3.56
Ice cream	7.32	Raisin pie	3.67
Corn-on-the-cob	7.29	Manhattan clam chowder	3.73
French fried potatoes	7.28	Butterscotch sauce	3.77
Eggs to order	7.27	Cucumber/onion salad	3.80
Chicken	7.26	Canned figs	3.86
Bacon, lettuce & tomato sandwich	7.23	Succotash	3.88
Fresh apples	7.20	Cabbage & sweet peppers	3.88
White bread	7.18	Yellow squash	3.88
Oranges*	7.16	Cheese soup	3.88
Milk shake	7.15	Stuffed celery/peanut butter	3.88
Toast	7.14	Cooked onions	3.88
Cola	7.14	Mustard greens	3.89
Strawberry shortcake	7.14	Turnip greens	3.89
Bacon	7.12	Pepper pot soup	3.89
Fried eggs	7.05	Onion soup	3.89
Banana split	7.05	Kidney bean salad	3.91
Ice cream sundae	7.05	Mincemeat pie	3.93
Fresh peaches	7.04	Sukiyaki	3.94

*For control purposes a food may in some cases have been listed more than once.

This study showed, among other things on food preferences, that subjects might indicate they preferred certain foods, but did not always select them, and would frequently select foods which they said they least preferred. Table 4-2 gives in Column 1 the 24 most preferred foods, 14 of which were most frequently selected but 10 of which were not. Column 2 indicates 11 foods which were not the most preferred foods but were frequently selected.

Table 4-2

Preferences and Selections of Foods

COLUMN 1

Most Hedonically Preferred and Most Frequently Selected

1. Milk
2. Regular orange juice
3. Toast
4. Cola
5. Oranges
6. Chocolate milk
7. Strawberry shortcake
8. Eggs to order
9. Hot rolls and buns
10. Fresh apples
11. Bacon
12. White bread
13. Milk shake
14. Ice cream

Most Hedonically Preferred but NOT Most Frequently Selected

1. Grilled steak
2. Fried chicken
3. Corn-on-the-cob
4. French fries
5. Chicken
6. Bacon, lettuce, tomato sandwich
7. Fried eggs
8. Banana split
9. Fresh peaches
10. Ice cream sundae

COLUMN 2

Least Hedonically Preferred but Frequently Selected

1. Fresh coffee
2. Beer
3. Tea
4. Instant orange juice
5. Lettuce & tomato sandwich
6. Iced tea
7. Tossed green salad
8. Thousand Island dressing
9. French dressing
10. Biscuits
11. Hot Cross buns

Thus, in menu planning it is wise not to put items on the menu based on what people say but what the menu planner learns that people take.

Many foodservices have their own rating systems, using cooks, waiters, waitresses, clerks and other personnel to taste foods and indicate how well they are liked. A rating such as "very acceptable," "acceptable," "probably acceptable" and "unacceptable" may be used. Informal checks of acceptability can be made by noting how food is consumed when plates come back to the dishwashing unit.

Food preferences will usually be less varied for breakfast and about evenly divided in variability between lunch and dinner. Young people usually have more violent dislikes and likes than mature adults. They will also accept more food repetition of food they like. Older people also have greater dislikes and likes than middle-aged people. Meal plans therefore can be varied less for breakfast than for other meals and can be varied less for young and old people than for middle-aged ones.

COST CONSTRAINTS

Perhaps no other constraint occupies more time in menu planning than trying to keep costs within prescribed bounds. So much emphasis, however, can be given cost control from the standpoint of menu planning that other constraints are neglected. This neglect can further magnify the cost control problem. Attention to other constraints might significantly reduce the cost problem.

To control costs, one must be able to isolate and identify them and know their cause which must then be attacked. Too many people feel that if they know their costs, they have the proper tool to control them. This is not true. They only know a symptom and not the cure. It is the same as if a medical doctor took a patient's temperature and found it far above normal and then depended upon this information alone as to how to cure the patient. The doctor immediately sets about finding ways of curing the problem once he sees the danger signal of the temperature reading. This is what should be done by management in cost control.

Any foodservice seeking to control food costs must have reliable, accurate information on costs *in time* to do something about them. Often vital control information comes too late to do anything about the problem.

Pre-costing is one way in which information can be available in sufficient time to control costs. This is the estimation of costs before events take place. It can be done by a number of methods. The total costs of a recipe can be calculated and then the number of portions divided into this cost to ascertain the portion cost. If this is too high, some other food can be offered.

CAMP and Transtech are two computer systems that pre-cost. This is done in the same way it is done manually. The recipe cost is obtained and then the number of portions the recipe produces is divided into the total cost to obtain the cost per portion.

The pre-costing of menu items—e.g. steaks—which are purchased as units is calculated differently, but pre-costing for these is similarly possible. (See in later passages the discussion on food costing and the calculation of portion costs and selling prices.)

Commercial operations may have some difficulty in calculating costs when only part of a recipe is sold. If the carry-over food has a value, this can be deducted from the recipe's total cost, the number of portions served divided into the remainder and a cost per portion sold obtained.

Controlling food costs *after* events have occurred is manifestly not possible.

However, getting accurate information on what has happened can frequently be helpful in indicating to management what should be done to control future costs. Thus, on a manager's desk in the morning a food cost summary such as follows may appear:

Table 4-3
Food Cost Summary

	Sales $	Food Cost $	%	Labor Cost $	%	Other Costs $	%
1/14/75 (yesterday)	1,050	395	37.6	310	29.5	295	28.1
Cumulative through 1/14/75	18,000	6,480	36.0	6,000	30.0	5,000	27.7
Last year this date	1,200	432	36.0	348	29.0	295	24.6
Cumulative last year	24,000	9,200	38.3	7,200	30.0	6,000	25.0

In some of these summaries the increase or decrease in dollars and the percentages may be shown. It is important that the information be used. It should also not cost much. The cost of obtaining such information and the need for it should be evaluated by management from time to time.

Every operation should establish cost standards which are meaningful and are realistic. Costs may vary considerably among different types of foodservices and also between any two of the same type. Some foodservices may be subsidized, and costs which others have may not be paid by them. Thus, heat, light and power may be furnished at no cost to an elementary school foodservice. A hospital's administrative department could conceivably pick up some of the dietary department's costs. A hotel foodservice may obtain security at no cost, these costs being borne by another operating division. An in-plant operation for an office building may operate at a cost greater than income but the parent company may pick up the loss each month, considering this a fringe benefit to its employees.

In the past, a broad rule for profitability in commercial operations was that combined food and labor costs should not be over 75 per cent. Today, this standard is 65 per cent and there are indications that this may be too high. Institutions that do not use percentage of food and labor costs as a standard may establish a standard such as so many dollars per patient day or so much per meal, etc. Thus, a hospital might allow its foodservice department to have six dollars per patient day to cover costs.

Other costs in many foodservices may average somewhere within these ranges:

Supplies (cleaning, office, etc.)	2 to 4%
Repair and maintenance	1 to 2%
Laundry and uniforms	2 to 3%
Employee meals	2 to 4%
Advertising	0 to 1%
Rent or space costs	5 to 15%
Dishes, glasses, silverware, etc.	1½ to 2%
Heat, light, power, water, etc.	2 to 4%
Capital expenditures	2 to 4%
Office costs (telephone, etc.)	1½ to 2%
Insurance	½ to 1%
Miscellaneous	1 to 2%

The following are some of the costs a commercial foodservice might have:

CONTROLLABLE EXPENSES
Payroll
Payroll taxes and insurance
Employee benefits
Employee meals
Reserve for bonuses, vacations, etc.
Service charge distribution

DIRECT OPERATING EXPENSES
Uniforms and laundry or linen
Music and entertainment
Heat, light, water, power, fuel
China, glassware, silver, utensils
Cleaning supplies
Cleaning
Menus and beverage lists
Printing and stationery
Decorations
Banquet expense
Accounting
Licenses
Bar expenses
Wine cellar expenses
Trash removal
Ice
Advertising and sales promotion
Miscellaneous
Administrative and general expenses
Capital costs
Rent or occupation costs

Budgeting to Control Costs

Many foodservices prepare a budget which is to act as a guide for directing operations and controlling costs. The budget should indicate what the expected income and costs will be for the period it covers. It should be based on realistic projections and not hopes. If conditions change, a budget may have to be changed but, usually, management tries to hold to a budget once it is established. If it is changed too often, it becomes then a document that is subject to the operating conditions rather than controlling them.

Budgets are fixed or flexible. A flexible budget is used where sales vary and where costs vary as a percentage of sales. Fixed costs do not vary and therefore a fixed budget will have costs which are not changed. Usually the expected income is also stable and does not change. Thus, a rental item of a specified amount per month would be in a fixed budget, but if the rental is based on a percentage of sales, then the budget would be considered a flexible one.

A budget should not be looked upon as a record of how much *is* to be spent but as a planning instrument for operations and also as a guide to actual expenditures. Experience can be helpful in establishing what a budget should be but the budget should not be based on past performance alone. Using figures of the past may repeat mistakes and faulty calculations. They should only be guides and used to indicate what costs *were* under the conditions of the past. If a budget is based on the past, it is a good budget for conditions as they existed in the past, but not necessarily on conditions as they might occur in the future. Thus, today some operations wipe out all past budget figures and start anew. They first study expected conditions and then make up estimates of costs based on them—not past conditions. More and more operations are also setting up variable budgets and variable costs to enable management to make decisions as to what and how much to spend. Trade-offs may occur. Management may decide that it is unwise to spend 25 per cent of a budget for an expected 10 per cent increase in achievement in one area but rather to take limited resources and put them in another area where the pay-off is greater. Alternative actions are defined and evaluated. Such budget planning is called zero-base budgeting. If such a budget is well researched and all data presented with alternatives for action, management has a better chance of evaluating factors requiring management decision. For instance, management may wish to know if it is better to purchase ready-to-serve bakery goods rather than to remodel the bakeshop. If budgetary projections are made properly, management can evaluate the costs and then make a decision.

INCOME FACTOR

While budgets deal largely with expenditures and their control, it is also necessary that they consider income. This is especially true when a budget is established as a percentage of sales, because income is directly associated with it and decides many expenditures.

Food Costs

Some food costs are not difficult to identify and calculate. It is often a simple process of assembling costs and adding them up. Normally, the cost of food used or sold is calculated as follows:

Beginning inventory	xxx
+ Purchases, including transportation, delivery and other charges	xxx
Total food available for the period	xxx
— Ending inventory	xxx
Cost of food	xxx

Many costs in a budget or in cost control are calculated as a percentage of sales as mentioned previously. This calculation is not difficult if one knows what the sales are and the cost of the food sold. The percentage is then obtained by dividing sales into the cost of the food sold. For instance, if the cost of food is $400 and sales are $1,500, the calculation is $400/$1,500 = .33-1/3 or 33-1/3%.

It is relatively easy to calculate a food cost percentage for a single item or even a meal. It is much more difficult to estimate food cost for a large group of diverse items having differing cost percentages that may have a variable sales mix. Some operations find it necessary, after calculating the basic cost of a menu item or group, to add on from 5 to 10 per cent for the cost of frying fats, parsley garnish, dusting flour, etc. Thus, if an item is found to have a basic cost of 60¢ and a policy of adding 10 per cent is followed for these items, the cost would be placed at 66¢.

Many commercial operations with 60 or more items on the menu may have a very difficult time predicting what food cost will result from the sale of these items. Since customers have free selection, with no established pattern of sales possible, predictions can be considerably thrown off because selections may, for some reason or other, concentrate on high food cost items or low food cost items.

An experienced menu planner can do much to select items and present them so that a desirable food cost results. There are ways of using menu arrangement, the listing of items, sales promotion, item descriptions and other means to direct sales to certain types of items. Service personnel can be instructed to "push" certain items helping bring about a desirable sales mix. Clip-ons can be used to push specials.

If the food cost percentage for each of a large group of items is known, and if management can estimate the sales mix accurately, a good estimate of food cost can be made. For instance, if a drive-in predicts sales for a day of $2,121 (100 per cent), made up as follows: hamburgers $875 or 41.2 per cent of sales, milk shakes $410 or 19.3 per cent of sales, french fries $550 or 26 per cent of sales and carbonated beverages $312 or 13.5 per cent of sales (with respective food cost percentages of 39 per cent, 32 per cent, 27 per cent and 30 per cent) the food cost percentage prediction would be:

Hamburgers	41.2% × 39%	= 16.1%
Milk shakes	19.3% × 32%	= 6.2%
French fries	26.0% × 27%	= 7.0%
Carbonated beverages	10.5% × 30%	= 6.2%
	100.0%	35.5%
	(Total)	(Average)

The steps in making the calculation are:

1. Predict total sales and per cent contribution each item or group makes of these.
2. Calculate the food cost per cent for each item or group.
3. Multiply each item's or group's per cent food cost times its per cent of sales.
4. Total these results for an average food cost percentage.

The food cost of individual items may be simple or difficult to calculate. If an operation purchases 10-ounce top butt sirloin steaks at so much each, the cost is not difficult to calculate. Similarly, if frozen peas cost $13.60 per case of 12 five-pound packages, the cost is 22.7¢ per pound (12 × 5 lb = 60 lbs divided into $13.60 = 22.7¢) and, since a three-ounce portion is served or five portions per pound, the cost per portion is 4.54¢.

It is obvious that to do good food costing, accurate yields from food and portion sizes must be known. To calculate the cost of a serving of butter, for instance, one should know how many pats are in a pound and how many an average customer gets.

Calculating the food cost of some other items may be more difficult. For instance, if pre-blanched frozen potato strips are purchased and fried, what is the cost of a two-ounce portion? If the strips cost 21¢ a pound and they lose a third of their weight in frying, the cost per pound of finished potatoes is .21 ÷ .67 (if a third is lost, 2/3 or .67 remains) = 31.34¢ per pound of finished product. There is also the cost of frying oil. These potatoes absorb 6 per cent of their weight in oil. Thus, a pound of finished potatoes has about an ounce of new frying oil in it (16 oz $\times$ 6 per cent = .96 oz) [1] If the cost of the frying fat is 50¢ per pound the cost of oil in the finished product is 3.13¢ ($.50 ÷ 16 oz = 3.13¢). Thus, for 17 ounces of finished product (16 ounces of potatoes plus an ounce of fat) we have a cost of 31.34¢ + 3.13¢ = 34.47¢, and therefore an ounce costs 34.47¢ ÷ 17 = 2.022¢ and a two-ounce portion costs 4.044¢. It is clear that before one can calculate some food costs a considerable amount of accurate operating information is required.

Calculating the cost of some meats may also be complicated. In preparing meat on the block there is frequently a loss in bones and fat. There is also trim which does not have the same value as the main meat product. In addition, there is always a shrink which may be about 1 per cent of the original weight. (Meat also shrinks about 1 per cent per day when it hangs in a refrigerator.) Thus, if a boned strip loin is purchased for New York steaks, the cost calculation may be made as shown in the ruled panel below, based on a cutting test.

The $1.575 value of the trimmed meat (used for kabobs or ground meat) has to be known to arrive at the cost per steak.

A more difficult calculation will be required to arrive at the cost of different meats obtained from large wholesale, side, quarter or carcass cuts. For instance, a top choice full loin weighing 54½ pounds and costing $1.09 per pound yields cuts totaling $59.41 in value. (See ruled panel on following page.)

Continuous cutting and yield tests should be made by operations that cut out their own meats to see if the costs are those predicted. There is a great variabiltiy in yields and so the results of tests can only be indicative of an approximate cost. This may be the reason why so many operators have gone to portion cuts. When they buy portion cuts, they know more exactly the cost of the item they serve.

Calculating the food cost of cooked meats requires that some record be kept of the number of portions obtained. For instance, a cook records 32 orders ob-

---

COST OF STEAK

Boneless strip, No. 180, 12 lb @ 1.89/lb*   = $22.680

YIELD:

Steaks (16 @ 10 oz each) 10 lb
Trimmed meat 10 oz @ $1.40/lb   =   1.575
Suet 12 oz (no value)

Cost of meat used for steaks $21.105
Cost per steak ($21.105 ÷ 16)   = $ 1.318
(Weight verification: 10 lb steak + 18 oz trimmed meat + 12 oz trim = 11 lb 14 oz; loss by shrink 2 oz)

*The prices quoted in this text usually represent early 1973 prices.

---

[1] The frozen pre-blanched strips usually contain around 11% fat when purchased. Thus, the finished potatoes will contain around 17% fat when sold. Investigations have shown that about a 17% fat content results in potatoes having the highest acceptability with customers.

YIELD FROM BEEF LOIN

Total cost	54½ × $1.09		=	$59.41
CUTTING YIELD:	VALUE/LB	COST/STEAK		TOTAL VALUE
Strip steaks 20 lb (32 10-oz steaks)	$1.65	$1.03		$33.00
Top sirloin steaks 4 lb (8 8-oz steaks)	1.25	.63		5.00
Butt sirloin steak 4 lb (8 8-oz steaks)	1.20	.60		4.80
Tenderloin steak 6 lb (12 8-oz steaks)	1.85	.93		11.10
Kabob cubes 3 lb (8 6-oz orders)	.95	.36		2.85
Trim meat 3 lb (12 4-oz ground patties)	.70	.18		2.10
Bone 8¾ lb @ 5¢/lb				.44
Suet 5¾ lb @ 2¢/lb				.12
				$59.41

tained from a 25-pound No. 109 rib roast. In addition 1¾ lb of cooked meat is left for use as hash or other meat dishes. The cost of the roast was $18.75. The value of the cooked meat was considered 70¢ per pound or $1.13 for the 1¾ pounds. The cost per portion was then

25 lb × $.75	= $18.75
Value of trimmed meat	— 1.13
Cost of 32 portions	$17.62
Cost per portion	.55

The Winn Schuler Restaurants in Michigan keep a record of the number of portions obtained from every roast they cook. This gives them an excellent basis for judging the portion cost.

Prepared items such as soup, salads, entrée dishes, etc., are difficult to cost out. Usually the cost of a portion is calculated by figuring the cost of a recipe and then dividing this total cost by the number of portions obtained. For instance, if a vegetable soup recipe makes 50 eight-ounce portions (3⅛ gallons) of soup, the calculation is as shown below.

BEEF VEGETABLE SOUP

Yield: 50 8-oz portions (3⅛ gal)   Portion: 1 cup or 8 oz

	Amount	Cost per unit	Total cost
Bones, beef	15 lb	$.05	$ .75
Celery, diced	3½ lb	.20	.40
Carrots, diced	4 lb	.12	.48
Onions, diced	2 lb	.06	.12
Tomatoes, chopped	2 No. 10's	.83	1.66
Rice	2 lb	.12	.24
Diced beef	3 lb	.70	2.10
Total cost			$6.75
Cost per portion ($6.75 ÷ 50)			.13½

It is usually desirable to check recipe costs every six months to see if they reflect current prices. Some operations do this less often but move the total cost of the recipe up or down as the price index of food moves and then, once a year or so, recalculate recipe prices. Prices in recipe costing are usually rounded off to an even cent, with portion costs carried to a tenth of a cent. Some ignore a calculation for seasonings, while others take the total spent for seasonings, flavorings, etc., in a year and get a percentage of this against all food purchases for the year. The recipe cost without seasonings is then multiplied by this percentage and the result added to the recipe cost as a seasoning cost. Thus, if an operation spent $35,000 for food for a year, $700 of which is for seasonings, flavorings, etc., the percentage factor for seasonings is 2 per cent. If a recipe costs $6.25 without seasonings, $6.25 × 2 per cent = $12\frac{1}{2}¢$, giving the estimated seasoning cost. Adding this to $6.25 gives a total cost of $6.37\frac{1}{2}$. Some accept a 2 per cent estimate because this is about what the average institution spends for seasonings.

Is a High Food Cost Bad?

Many operations emphasize food cost more than they should with reference to the part it plays in making a profit. A high food cost does not necessarily mean an unprofitable unit. It might be a good omen indicating that patrons are getting a lot for their dollar. Recognizing this, patrons might be drawn to the unit.

Some low-cost steak and pancake houses operate at rather high food cost—a low-cost steak house may have a food cost of 60 per cent but other costs are so low that it makes a good profit. A high food cost coupled with a low profit might be undesirable but, if the volume is good, the high food profit is no problem. It is better to sell 10 items at a 10¢ profit each than one item at a 50¢ profit.

Some operators spend so much time trying to control food cost that they fail to control other costs. They may serve what they think are low-cost items when actually the items are high in cost. A cole slaw salad or sliced orange salad may be low in food cost but when the labor used in making them is added in, they become rather expensive salads. A beef stew may also have a much lower food cost than a steak but when the labor cost of preparing either is considered, the stew becomes the more expensive item.

As labor cost takes a greater share of the patron's dollar, it has become more necessary to consider this element and try to bring the combined food and labor cost within a desired limit. Also, as costs other than food and labor have risen in ratio to labor and food cost, it has become more important to consider these in controlling costs. Thus today, management needs to put more emphasis into controlling *all* costs and not food cost alone.

FAIR INCOME A MUST

A high food cost may arise because the sale price is not high enough. An item with a food cost of 25¢ selling for $1.00 has a food cost of 25 per cent, but if it sells for 60¢ the food cost will be nearly 42 per cent. Similarly, if an institution budgets 90¢ a day per individual for food and prices rise, as they did in 1973 and 1974, this allowance is not sufficient and more money must be allotted. In this case, the cost of food is not too high based on food prices but the amount of income is not enough for the price of food. Any foodservice, whether operated for profit or non-profit, that established a price or an allowance for food based on certain costs must expect to increase menu prices or the allowance to meet the change in conditions if these costs rise.

Food Cost Control

Different foodservices must operate under different food and other costs. A restaurant having to make a profit must meet many costs that a school lunch operation would not have to. The restaurant's prices must therefore be higher to cover these additional costs. A hotel may find it has to operate at a 27 per cent food cost, a restaurant at 30 per cent, a club at 45 per cent, while a hospital can spend 55 per cent of its budget for food and a highly subsidized school foodservice may spend 85 per cent of its cash income for food.

Experience has shown that it is seldom possible to reduce quality or quantity to achieve a lower food cost. There is a certain minimum below which a foodservice can go not only in quality but in food cost, labor and other costs. Attempts to go below these minimums usually bring about failure. The day when a cook could walk into a kitchen "with a knife under one arm and a ham bone under the other and come up with a meal" is gone, if it ever existed. The saying "you can't make a silk purse out of a sow's ear" is as true today as it was in Shakespeare's time. A patron must get enough food of the proper quality to satisfy him for what he has paid. When an operation fails to create such patron satisfaction, it has failed in one of its major goals.

Food cost can also be increased by a failure to portion properly, by pilferage or by waste. Management should establish procedures for the control of each of these.

Steaks costing $1.76 per pound to be portioned at 10 ounces each but actually portioned instead at $10\frac{1}{2}$ ounces each are costing $1.15\frac{1}{2}$ instead of $1.10. If management sells these steaks for $3.50, thinking they have a food cost of 31.4 per cent ($1.10 \div 3.50 = .314$), it is mistaken. The actual food cost is 33 per cent ($1.155 \div \$3.50 = .33$). If 600 steaks are sold, the loss in profit is $33. If the expected profit should be 5 per cent, it is now actually only 3.4 per cent or 32 per cent less than planned.

If a six ounce portion of food is planned but a seven ounce one is consistently dished, only 86 per cent of the planned portions will be obtained. Because of the need to see that portions are what management determines, portioning information should be posted where employees can see it. Recipes should list the portions and checks should be made frequently to see that proper portions are given. Every operation should use portioning scales and other portioning equipment. Frequently a 1 or 3 per cent difference is found between predicted and actual food cost because of a failure to properly portion, because of overproduction or because of waste. Good control can eliminate such an overage.

A failure to give adequate security to food can also raise food cost. If an operation has $1200 in sales and uses $400 worth of food, the food cost is 33-1/3 per cent, but if there is a theft of $35 worth of this food, the food cost becomes 36¼ per cent. A failure to protect cash can raise food cost. If $50 of the $1200 income is taken from the cash register by a dishonest employee, the $400 food cost then becomes not 33-1/3 per cent but 34.8 per cent.

Waste also takes a heavy toll of food cost. If an operation prepares 50 orders at a cost of $15, planning to sell them for $1.00 each, but then throws out 20 orders, the food cost is not 33-1/3 per cent as planned but 50 per cent.

In the previous illustration on roast beef, $1.13 worth of meat trim was taken from the bones. If this had been thrown out instead of saved for hash, diced beef and mushrooms, chili or diced for soup, the food cost would be 35% instead of the expected 33.6 per cent.

It is extremely important to see that all the food produced is sold and, if not sold, utilized in some way to bring in the expected revenue. Feeding carryover food to employees is not the answer. Better control of amounts produced and improved forecasting should take place when there is too much overproduction or underproduction.

Reworking food into saleable items is not the best mode of operation. Additional labor must be spent in the new preparation of the item. Frequently, there is also a quality loss in reworking food.

A menu card that features items that are prepared only after they are ordered can reduce the loss that comes from overproduction. However, this may increase customer waiting time and delay turnover. The use of foods which can be reheated quickly, such as frozen entrées and others, helps to eliminate the overproduction problem and, in part to solve the waiting time factor.

Food cost is affected also by the manner in which the purchasing task is accomplished. The best cost results when the market is searched and the best product for the production need is purchased at the lowest possible cost. Knowing where to buy and when to buy is important. Knowing when foods are best in quality and at a favorable price can also reduce food cost. Buying in amounts which save (but not in such amounts that may cause waste) is important. Buying should be planned with the portion in mind; if a peach and cottage cheese salad is on the menu and a 35-45 count peach half is to be used, the buyer should not purchase a 22 count per No. 10 can, because the food cost will be materially increased.

Constant search of the market should be made to see if better products cannot be obtained which lowers food costs. Also, if other costs are reduced more than food cost raised, it might still be advisable to allow food cost to rise and thereby gain a lower overall cost. In a recent study, a foodservice changed much of its production to ready-prepared foods so that the food cost rose 5 per cent but labor cost dropped 11 per cent. The overall reduction in costs of 6 per cent was significant.

A later section of this book is devoted to showing how the purchasing task can be performed more adequately for menu planning.

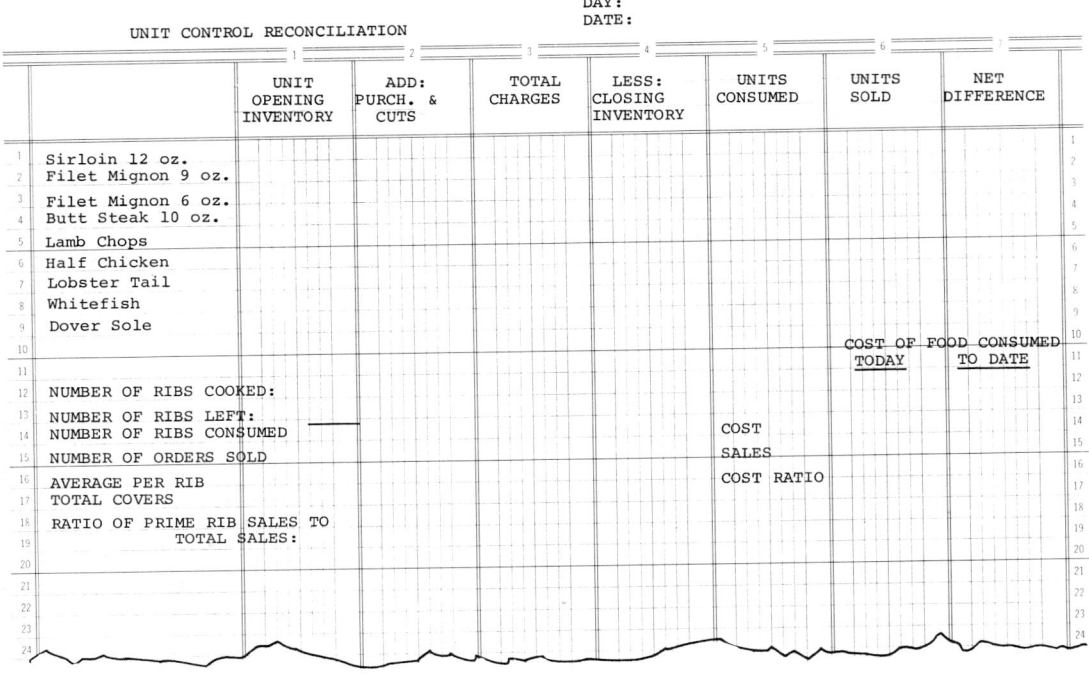

UNIT CONTROL RECONCILIATION							DAY: DATE:

	UNIT OPENING INVENTORY	ADD: PURCH. & CUTS	TOTAL CHARGES	LESS: CLOSING INVENTORY	UNITS CONSUMED	UNITS SOLD	NET DIFFERENCE
Sirloin 12 oz.							
Filet Mignon 9 oz.							
Filet Mignon 6 oz.							
Butt Steak 10 oz.							
Lamb Chops							
Half Chicken							
Lobster Tail							
Whitefish							
Dover Sole							
						COST OF FOOD CONSUMED	
						TODAY	TO DATE
NUMBER OF RIBS COOKED:							
NUMBER OF RIBS LEFT:							
NUMBER OF RIBS CONSUMED				COST			
NUMBER OF ORDERS SOLD				SALES			
AVERAGE PER RIB				COST RATIO			
TOTAL COVERS							
RATIO OF PRIME RIB SALES TO							
TOTAL SALES:							

FIG. 4-2   High-cost items require special control. This can be provided by a chart such as the one shown here. In addition, it can give good information about the popularity of menu items. (Courtesy Don Roth, Black Hawk Restaurants, Chicago)

Non-profit institutions do not use a percent food cost for information and control as much as commercial ones do. When they do calculate a percentage of raw food expenditures against income or budgeted allowance, the food cost frequently runs 50 per cent or more of total costs. This can happen even when some institutions are subsidized and costs other than for food and labor may be minimized.

Normally, institutional foodservices operate on budgeted allowances per person for a day, or meal, or for an established period. Some state institutions may, for instance, operate on an allowance per person per quarter. Budget planning for such institutions usually makes an allowance per day for a year with a review each quarter. Thus, a budget may allow $2.80 per day per person, to be divided $1.30 for food, $1.00 for labor and $.50 for other costs.

The institution plans to divide this among meals as following panel shows. Another institution might divide the $2.80 equally between three meals for an allowance of $.93-1/3 per meal, breaking the allowance down into 43-1/3¢ food, 33-1/3¢ labor and 16-2/3¢ for other costs. The annual total allowance would be $1022 with $474.50 for food, $365 for labor and $182.50 for other costs per person.

	Breakfast	Lunch	Dinner	Total
Food (46.4%)	$ .39	$ .39	$ .52	$1.30
Labor (35.7%)	.30	.30	.40	1.00
Other (17.9%)	.15	.15	.20	.50
Total (100.0%)	$ .84	$ .84	$1.12	$2.80

Some institutions not only get a dollar allowance but also a food ration allowance. This allows various quantities of different kinds of food per person per specified period. Thus, in a month the allowance may be 15 lb of meat, 4 lb of orange or yellow or leafy green vegetables, 9 lb of potatoes, etc.

Institutions on such a ration allowance are assured to a degree that the meals will also be nutritionally balanced if the ration allowance is used as permitted. Some ration allowances are based on recommended weekly allowances developed each year by the USDA based on current prices. There are three of these allowances, low, moderate and liberal. Most state institutions use the low cost plan but some, such as the State of California, add a bit more meat to give better palatability and acceptability.

After the type of ration allowance is decided, a cost for it is calculated. Thus, the average price of meat may be calculated for the geographic area and multiplied by the pounds allowed in the ration for the period. These costs are calculated for all food groups in the amounts allowed and, when totaled, give a dollar allowance that must not be exceeded. An institution on such a ration system has two restraints: 1) cost and 2) a specified quantity of food based on the ration allowance.

Jane Hartman* has recommended a ration allowance for institutions based on the 17 food groups in the low-cost plan of the USDA. Instead of weekly amounts, she translates these into monthly allowances. Table 4-4 indicates that such a breakdown would establish about a $1.30 per day allowance for 1973.

The USDA operates the school food-service program and requires that a Class A meal have two ounces or more of a good protein food such as eggs, cheese, fish, poultry or meat, a half pint of milk, along with a good portion of vegetables or equivalent in salad, a slice of bread with butter or margarine and perhaps a dessert. It should give approximately a third of the child's food needs for a day.

Institutions usually calculate the total cost of food as commercial units do. For instance, such a calculation might be:

Beginning inventory	$ 2,378.90
Purchases and other logical costs	10,333.45
Total food available	$12,712.35
Less ending inventory	2,111.45
Cost of food used	$10,600.90

Employee meals are considered a fringe benefit and a part of operating expenses. Therefore, when the cost of food for employee meals is included in

*"Proper Budgeting Aids Food Service Planning," *Modern Hospitals,* June, 1969.

the cost of food used, it must be deducted. The value for deducting an employee meal can be based on either 1) the actual cost of the meal, 2) on experience, 3) a standard charge made in the area for meals, or 4) an arbitrary amount. Actual cost may be menu prices with a discount given to the employee. In some areas it may be a practice to deduct a predetermined amount for employee meals, a plan followed by a number of foodservices. The arbitrary amount may be only a nominal charge but one which the foodservice thinks is adequate to cover its costs, or at least a major portion of them.

After a value for an employee meal is set, the number of meals consumed times this value gives a value for all meals consumed by employees. If this total includes more than food, an estimate has to be made on the value of the food in these meals. Most operations take their average food cost percentage and use

Table 4-4

Food and Dollar Ration Allowance

Food group	AP[1] allowance/ day	AP[1] lb/person/ mo.		Average unit price/lb[2]	Cost/ individual/ mo.
Meat, fish and poultry	6½ oz raw	12.30		$ 1.05	$12.92
Eggs	¾ egg	3.15	(20 eggs)	0.35	1.10
Milk, liquid	½ pt (lc)	15.00	(7½ qt)	0.38	5.70
Milk, non-fat, dry[3]	1/3 c instant	1.80		0.70	1.26
Margarine	½ oz (1 T)	.60		.0.32	.19
Other fats	2/3 oz (1½ T)	1.50		0.38	.57
Sugar, jam, sirup, etc.	1 oz (1½ T)	2.20		0.17	.37
Grains or cereals[4]	5 oz	9.00		0.24	2.16
Dry legumes, nuts, etc.	½ oz	1.00		0.30	.30
Vegetables, yellow or green leafy	2 oz	4.00		0.36	1.44
Tomatoes[5]	1 oz	2.00		0.38	.76
Fruit, citrus group	2 oz	4.00		0.36	1.44
Fruit, non-citrus	4 oz	8.00		0.35	2.80
Fruit, dried	2/3 oz	1.25		0.75	.94
Potatoes	5 oz	9.00		0.08	.72
Other vegetables	4 oz	8.00		0.30	2.40
Coffee	½ oz (2 T)	1.00		1.00	1.00
Tea	.05 oz (2 t)	.15		1.86	.28
Miscellaneous					.15
					$36.60

[1] AP = As Purchased. [2] These prices are hypothetical; use those in effect in your local area. [3] Can be used in cooking. [4] Price is based on the purchase in part of bakery bread. [5] This can be adjusted to serve, for instance, a three-ounce serving as a vegetable every third day, or in salads, etc. If a citrus juice of four ounces is served on a day, the tomatoes can be omitted. If a fruit or vegetables of good ascorbic acid yield is served on a day, both the tomatoes and citrus can be omitted.

this to arrive at a value for the food used for employees' meals. Thus, if the food cost is 35 per cent and a total value of $800.19 is assigned to the employees' meals for a period, the value of the food in these meals may be .35 × $800.19 or $280.17. If the cost of food used is calculated as previously done:

Beginning inventory	$ 2,378.90
Purchases and other chargeable costs	10,333.45
Total food available	$12,712.35
Less ending inventory	2,111.45
Cost of food used	$10,600.90,
The cost of food used in employee meals is deducted to give as the cost of food sold	280.17
	$10,320.73.

If sales for this period were $30,000, then the food cost percentage is 34 per cent ($10,320.73 ÷ $30,000).

Where employees consume the same meals as patrons do in some institutions, the cost of an employee's meals may be calculated differently. The panel below illustrates an operation having total costs of $11,400 for 15,571 meals served during the period, 1,240 of these meals being consumed by employees.

In this example, the cost of food sold is calculated as follows:

Beginning inventory	$ 890.14
Purchases	5,300.28
Total food available	$6,190.42
Less ending inventory	793.21
Cost of food used	$5,397.21
Less cost of food used for employee meals	414.16
Cost of food sold	$4,983.05

Since the total number of meals served in the period was 15,571 and the number of employees' meals 1240, the number of patron meals was 15,571 − 1,240 = 14,331 and the cost of food per patron was $4,983.05 ÷ 14,331 = 34.8¢.

The cost of food sold is needed if a per cent food cost is to be obtained and the above procedures are the most standard used to obtain it. The per cent food cost for a period is calculated by dividing total sales into the cost of food sold. For instance, where the cost of food sold above was $10,320.73 and sales were $30,000, the food cost percentage was 34 per cent ($\frac{\$10,320}{\$30,000} = 34.4$ per cent).

Management should analyze its food cost control system and make it as sim-

---

Steps	Example
1. Ascertain the number of employee meals.[1]	Number of meals consumed as indicated by a meal sign-in sheet was 1,240.
2. Calculate the individual meal cost.	$11,400 ÷ 15,571 = 66.8¢ per meal.
3. Consider food for employees' meals as 50% of the cost of a meal.[2]	66.8¢ × .50 = 33.4¢ food cost per employee meal.
4. Multiply the number of employee's meals × food cost per employee meal.	1,240 × $.334 = $414.16 cost of food for employee meals.

[1] This can be obtained from payroll records, a sign-in sheet, estimate or other method.
[2] Calculating that the cost of a meal is 50% food is a standard procedure among institutions operating on a non-profit basis.

ple and efficient as possible. In making the analysis, questions like these could be asked:

Are menu item abstracts being made? Are portions standardized?

Are recipe costs being made and kept uptodate? Is storeroom security adequate?

Are purchasing specifications set up and being used? Is buying competitive?

Are requisitions used? Is receiving adequate and receiving sheets used? Are scales used?

Are inventories taken and reconciled? Are par stocks in effect?

Is ordering systematized from departments and are quantities ordered correct?

Are employee meals recorded and properly administered?

Are high cost foods inventoried and checked properly? Do they have good security?

Who signs requisitions and purchase orders? Who issues from the storeroom?

Who is authorized to order? Are invoices checked for prices and accuracy?

Are procedures simple and carried out in scheduling special parties?

Is forecasting accurate? Is there food waste? Over production? Under production?

Is value analysis on purchases being carried out such as meat tests, etc?

Labor Cost

Labor cost is made up of wages, salaries, payroll taxes, employee meals and other costs associated with labor and its benefits. The cost of labor may vary considerably in various operations. In some, labor cost may be higher than food cost. Some clubs may have a labor cost over 50 per cent of sales because they must have considerable labor on hand regardless of whether members are there or not. A take-out unit, however, may have a labor cost of around 15 per cent. Deciding what is proper must therefore be left to the individual unit.

Most commercial operations seek to keep labor cost within a certain percentage of sales. For instance, if an operation has $895.35 in sales and wishes to have a 30 per cent labor cost, it might allocate $268.50 for labor. Another might attempt to allocate labor according to the dollar sales labor produces; for instance, for each $6.00 in sales, an hour of labor might be allocated or one employee might be allowed on the payroll for every $15,000 of sales per year.

Some units allow one worker per a specific number of covers or other units produced. For instance, it is said that there should be a waiter for every 20 to 25 breakfasts or lunches served and one for 15 to 20 covers at dinner. Some foodservice authorities say that a hostess should be able to take care of 200 people at a meal, and a cook should be able to prepare 100 meals during an eight-hour shift.

Agencies can develop staffing recommendations for the allocation of labor, such as the USDA's school for foodservices. (See Table 4-5). Formulas have been developed by which staffing requirements can be established. One of the most common standards used today for non-commercial operations is the number of meals produced per labor hour used. (See Table 4-6). Thus, if an operation produces 15,000 meals in a month and wanted to produce four meals for every hour of labor used on the payroll, 3,750 hours of labor is allocated.

Table 4-5

The USDA's Recommended Allowances for Workers in School Lunch

No. Meals/Day	Worker Type	No. Workers	Shift Time	Total Hrs/Day
350 to 500	Head cook	1	7:30 a to 2:00 p	6
	Assistant cooks	3 to 4	7:30 a to 2:00 p	18 to 24
	Kitchen and lunch-room helpers	2 to 4	10:30 a to 2:00 p	6 to 12
	Janitorial	1	Intermittent	2
Total		7 to 10		32 to 44
700 to 1000	Lunchroom supervisor	1	Intermittent	
	Head cook	1	7:00 a to 2:30 p	3 to 4
	Assistant cooks	6 to 9	7:30 a to 2:00 p	36 to 54
	Kitchen and lunch-room helpers	1 to 2	10:30 a to 2:00 p	3 to 6
	Dishwashers	3 to 4	10:30 a to 2:00 p	9 to 12
	Janitorial	1	Intermittent	3 to 4
Total		13 to 18		61 to 87
1400 to 2000	Lunchroom supervisor	1	Intermittent	4 to 5
	Head cook	1	7:00 a to 3:30 p	7 to 8
	Assistant cooks	10 to 15	7:30 a to 3:00 p	70 to 105
	Kitchen and lunch-room helpers	3 to 4	9:30 a to 2:00 p	12 to 16
	Dishwashers	4 to 5	10:30 a to 3:00 p	16 to 20
	Janitorial and maintenance	1	Intermittent	3 to 6
Total		20 to 27		112 to 160

Table 4-6

Average Number of Meals per Labor Hour

Type Operation	Meals Produced/Hour
Hotels and clubs	1.25 to 1.75
Restaurants	1.50 to 3.00
Cafeterias	3.50 to 8.50
School lunches	11 to 13
College dormitories	$11\frac{1}{2}$
Hospitals	3 to 6
Nursing homes	5
Large state hospitals	11.6

The quantity of labor used between service and back-of-the-house areas varies for different foodservices. A cafeteria or a buffet operation may use less labor for service than a seated-service restaurant or club. Some seated-service restaurants have found that an allocation of seven hours for back-of-the-house compared to 10 hours for service is adequate but no standard can be properly set; every operation should work out its own. Some operations work out labor budgets that allocate a given number of hours for various departments in a period. Thus, a small foodservice could allow 1,776 hours for a month as follows: cook-manager 162, first and second cooks 244, assistant cooks or helpers 275, consulting dietitian 16, kitchen or lunchroom workers including dishwashers, storeroom, porter, clerical, etc., 26, and accounting 16. Some may allocate labor on the basis of a percentage for various types of workers such as in an institutional cafeteria where management may get 10 per cent of the total hours, service and cashiers 20 per cent, clerical and accounting 3 per cent, food production 44 per cent, janitorial and cleanup 12 per cent,

maintenance three per cent and miscellaneous 6 per cent. If a labor budget is set up, it should be extremely flexible and allow for the shifting of labor between departments.

Formulas used to allocate labor can give broad estimates of requirements. In 1950, John F. Johnson[1] developed a formula for staffing cafeterias which indicated that the number of employees on the staff (Y) equaled 2.99 plus 0.82 times the number of thousands of meals served per month (X). This formula was $Y = 2.99 + 0.82X$. Thus, a cafeteria serving 90,000 meals in a month would be allocated $2.99 + 0.82 \times 90 = 100.37$ employees. Some hospitals find that a better formula for them is $Y = 2.99 + .9X$. This allows for the additional labor used to handle special diets, meal delivery, etc. Professor Broten[2] of Cornell, using Johnson's technique, also devel-

---

[1] "A Statistical Analysis of the Relationship between the Number of Meals Served and Number of Employees in 171 Cafeterias," M. A. thesis, University of Chicago, School of Business, 1950.
[2] "Controlling Restaurant Costs." M.A. thesis, College of Hotel Administration, Cornell University, 1953.

oped formulas for hotels, clubs, schools and hospitals as follows:

Hotels	$Y = 2.34 + 2.2X$
Clubs	$Y = 2.34 + 2.2X$
Schools	$Y = 6.44 + .92X$
Hospitals	$Y = 4.01 + 1.08X$

indicating his formulas were for the full time employees needed who worked an average of 206 hours per month. This would mean that a worker would average around 310 days a year.

In allocating labor it is necessary to differentiate between the number of employees on the payroll and the number of positions allowed. More employees will be on the payroll than allowed positions because a single position frequently must be filled by more than one person in seven days of the week. In seven days a shift position requires 56 hours to cover it. This means that 1.4 workers must be on the payroll to cover it ($56 \div 40$ hours/week $= 1.4$). However, this does not provide for days off, holidays, vacations, etc., and so it is usual to have 1.5 to 1.6 workers on the payroll to cover a seven-day position. Many workers work about 232 days a year, or about 67 per cent of 365 days. Some operations allow 1.1 workers on the payroll for a five-day week (40 hours a week) position to take care of sick leave, absenteeism, vacations, etc.

Controlling Labor Cost

Authorities agree that a high labor waste occurs in foodservices and that more emphasis should be given to improving the use of labor. At the present time programs for doing this are directed toward four areas: hiring and training, labor-saving devices and foods, improving layouts, and improving forecasting and scheduling of labor.

Many operations use poor methods in selecting employees with the result that they get employees who do not have the requisite skills, knowledge or motivation to do an adequate job. Furthermore, after hiring them, these operations do little to see that they become more effective employees.

More attention should be given to hiring techniques to eliminate the undesirable employee and hire those who will do the job. A "job specification" is frequently written to indicate what type of employee should be hired for a specific position and this is used in interviews and in seeking potential employees to improve the selection process. The specification usually covers the job and some of its work requirements, the age of employee needed, sex (consistent with federal regulations requiring equal job opportunities), skills, knowledge required, etc.

After an employee is hired, many operations do little to see that he quickly becomes oriented to the company, the position and to those he is responsible to and with whom he works. A "job description" frequently is written to indicate what an employee is to do on the job. Such a document can be of considerable assistance to an employee in orienting himself and in getting started correctly and quickly.

Training can also do much to improve job performance. Employees should be given the opportunity to learn on the job or to take formal or correspondence courses to become better employees and of more value to the company. Some foodservices use "job evaluations" to assist management and employees in knowing how new personnel are doing on the job and what could be needed for improvement.

Most printed materials on personnel management cover these techniques of improving work performance through the use of job specifications, job descriptions and job evaluations.

Most workers have never been taught how to make their jobs easier and still more productive. Efficient workers usually become so because they are basically efficient by nature and learn the short-cuts quickly. However, workers can be taught these and how to work more efficiently. By planning work, arranging work places to be more convenient and reducing motions and energy in doing work, most jobs can be simplified and made more efficient.

This field of knowledge on how to improve jobs is called work simplification, human engineering or work methods improvement. Foodservices that have taught workers to improve jobs frequently find that productivity is not only increased but worker morale is also. Workers then no longer get as tired working. Considerable material on this subject is available for use in foodservices.*

Studies of the kind of work indicate that skilled workers frequently do too many unskilled jobs and not enough skilled ones. While it is not possible to eliminate this situation completely, it has been found that perhaps an upper limit of spending 25 per cent of a skilled worker's time doing unskilled jobs is sufficient in most cases. If it is more, investigation should be made to see if some of the unskilled work cannot be shifted to less skilled workers.

*A recently published text entitled *Increasing Productivity in Foodservice*, Cahners Press, Boston, Mass., 1973, is a most worthwhile contribution to knowledge in this area.

Investigations have also shown that many employees travel too much in doing work. The use of an ingredient room (a center in which all materials for foods to be produced are assembled and then brought to the worker's area) eliminates travel and increases worker productivity. Better arrangement of equipment, the use of mobile equipment and changes in work procedures can also assist in reducing travel.

The foodservice industry remains a handicraft industry and is not particularly oriented toward the use of labor-saving equipment. However, with labor costs increasing rapidly, many foodservices find the use of pie dough rollers, cookie droppers, automatic fryers, trayveyors and other automated equipment to be less expensive than hiring additional labor to do the work. They are also finding that as labor costs increase, skills decline and good labor becomes more difficult to find, and that new foods that eliminate labor help reduce problems.

The increasing use of central commissaries is also reducing labor requirements. On a production basis, one hour of labor in a central commissary is equivalent to about 10 on the job in the small unit kitchen. However, when transportation of food and other labor requirements are considered, along with serving the food, the saving falls to about 1 to 3. Also it is not necessary to have the same amount of skilled labor in mass producing units; work can be more specialized and more automated equipment can be used.

As a result of central commissaries, simplified menus and the use of labor-saving equipment and new labor-saving

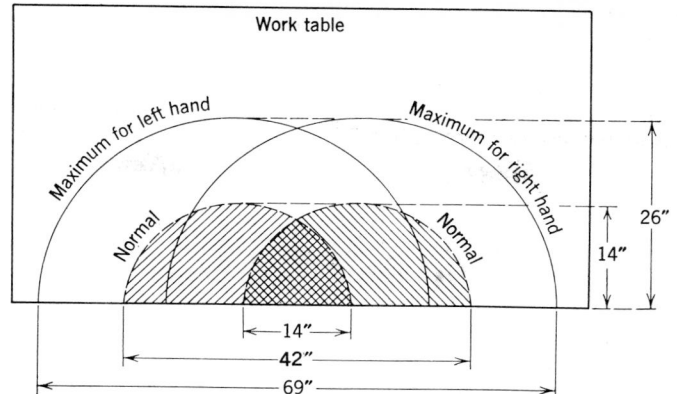

Sitting

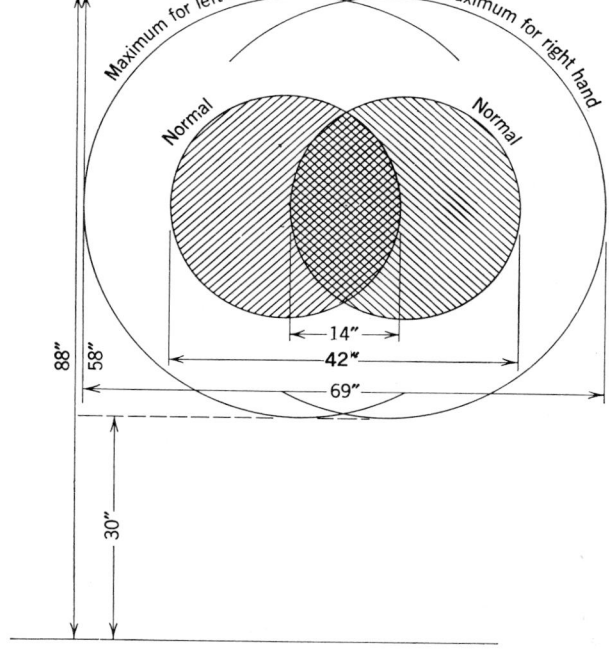

Standing

FIG. 4-3   A chart of maximum and normal work center areas for a sitting and standing man (10% less for a woman). In work center planning, industrial engineers try to confine work to within the normal reach whenever possible, and never have a work motion go farther than the maximum reach. If this is done properly, a worker does all of his work in this area and does not have to move out of it.

foods, layouts of foodservices are changing. Less space is needed in the average kitchen than was required in the past. The use of service islands, conveyor units and other factors is also reducing the travel of service personnel and making it possible to increase productivity. Mobile equipment is now used to assist in achieving this end.

As a result of better knowledge in designing work areas, organizing the flow of work and adding labor-saving equipment, layouts are changing. The flow of materials through units is also changing. Storage areas are being brought closer to work areas and equipment arrangement is conforming more to desirable work center design. This is not only acting to reduce labor but also is improving the quality of the items produced. The increasing cost of equipment has made planners challenge its use more and eliminate it if it does not get enough use to warrant its cost.

As a result of these factors foodservice production and, to a lesser extent, service areas are becoming more streamlined and efficient. We can expect continued movement in this direction because the conditions existing in the past that generated these changes are not expected to reverse themselves.

In many foodservices, the scheduling of labor and forecasting of the amount of labor required is poorly done. Few make attempts to ascertain whether the labor scheduled is needed or if more or less might be required. Fewer make evaluations on whether it is efficiently used. Many managers are not willing to

take the time to utilize information, easily available to them, which can make the forecasting of how much labor is required and how to schedule it more properly. An over or under use of food is frequently noted and corrected but this is not done nearly as much with labor. Of course, labor is less flexible than food in the management of quantity and it is not possible to increase or decrease it as easily as can be done with food. However, observation shows that many operations are extremely wasteful of labor and that it is often scheduled when management knows it will not be needed and not scheduled when management knows that it will be needed.

Counts of customers in an operation and the amount of labor on hand can do much to indicate when service personnel should be available. A knowledge of the time and the amount of labor required to produce items can also assist in indicating the amount of production labor needed.

Scheduling

Schedules for workers will be used for different purposes. One kind shows when workers are to be on the job and is usually called a work schedule. A second kind shows days off or when vacations are to be taken, and a third shows the production tasks for workers on the job. It is possible to combine the first and last kinds.

A work schedule should indicate the worker and time at work for a specific period. This is done differently, depending upon the type of schedule, and the

PRODUCTION SCHEDULE   Date _____

Meal and Item	Worker	Amount	No. Portions	Portion Size	Comment
Breakfast					
Tomato juice	F	12 46 oz	87	6 oz	Do Tues pm
Pineapple juice	F	1 No. 10	12	6 oz	Do Tues pm
Prunes	F	2 No. 2½	16	3 prunes	Do Tues pm
Oatmeal (R-1)	B	4 gal	60	1 c cooked	
Dry cereals	F	(Assorted)		1 pkg	Send to floors
French toast (B-8)	B		84	3 half slices	
Sirup	G		84	1 packet	
Butter	G		84	1 pat	
Coffee (G-2)	B	4 gal	60	1½ c	Send in pitchers
Milk	G	138-½ pts		1	

Other Assignments

Morning

Clean refrigerators 1 and 3 and storeroom.

Preprep: Wash lettuce and separate leaves for dinner salads.
Peel 40 lb AP potatoes for dinner
Make cream sauce for croquettes for Thursday (2 gal)
(C-11 recipe).
Pick over split peas for Thursday lunch soup.
Take turkey meat from bones stored in refrigerator 2.
Check salad dressings and make up those necessary.

Lunch

	Worker	Amount	No. Portions	Portion Size	Comment
Turkey shortcake (A-7 recipe)	B	7 gal	147	6 oz (2/3 c)	
Cornbread for shortcake (S-10)	A	3 12 x 20 pans	147	2 in. sq	Turkey over cornbread

FIG. 4-4   Above is a typical production schedule indicating the work to be done, the worker assigned to do it, and operating procedures to ensure that management's instructions are carried out. (R-1, B-8, etc., are recipe numbers.)

particular operation. A production work schedule frequently shows:

1. Period covered
2. Work to be done
3. Who does the work
4. Amount to produce
5. Recipe to use
6. Portion size
7. Meal or completion time required
8. Run-out time
9. Comments
10. Slack time assignments

Figures 4-4 through 4-11 are various kinds of schedules used to control and utilize labor. Figure 4-7 shows a labor bar graph. This is a helpful visual chart to indicate when labor is scheduled. Management can note quickly if there is a sufficient density of bars at particular times when most work must be done.

It is extremely important that employees be properly informed of days off and when they can expect to take vacations. A worker has a right to know at least a week ahead on which day he can be off so that he can arrange his own personal time. Nevertheless, days off should be somewhat guided by business activity and operational needs. Workers must be there when the work is there. However, management should attempt to keep scheduling as flexible as possible so that workers can, in times of personal need, be off from their duties.

There are state and federal regulations which control the number of hours that children, women and general labor can work. There also may be times when a specific kind of person, such as a child or young person, can be on the job. The number of hours will be controlled and all hours worked over a certain time must be paid in overtime. There are different overtime rates and, in scheduling employees, it is important to avoid overtime payment, especially at high penalty rates. Workers should not be allowed to be absent from the job and then, later, attempt to qualify for overtime because they work special days. Good control of scheduling can do much to reduce loss from time manipulations by employees.

The planning of vacations also should be done with care. There are certain times when labor requirements may be less and this is the time to schedule vacations. It may be possible, with proper planning, to take care of much vacation time without having to hire additional labor to take its place. Planning ahead can do much to please workers.

FORECASTING LABOR

Projecting labor requirements can be very valuable. Management can usually work with department heads to establish accurate forecasts of needs. Often department heads are required to submit forecasts on labor requirements and to have this approved by the accounting division.

After actual events have occurred, it is always necessary to compare the forecast with what happened, to see if the forecast could have been improved. Too much labor may have been scheduled, or not enough, or perhaps it was not timed to the best advantage. There will always be a range of error but, if there is accurate historical data, business trends, advance reservations, house occupancy, bookings, local or regional events and other factors, such as the season, internal factors, etc., the range of error can be reduced, especially if the forecast is critiqued afterward.

Systems should be established whereby information is funneled to those making the forecast. For instance, at a university the dormitory proctors or others may be instructed to call in to the foodservices on late Thursday afternoon, giving the expected dormitory occupancy for the weekend. Nursing staffs can alert the foodservices on probable checkouts. Airlines have worked out excellent systems whereby the count is usually down to only a small margin of error. In a heavy sea, the chef should know that a lot of passengers who have not yet acquired their "sea legs" will not show up for meals. Room occupancy predictions in a hotel can be very helpful in indicating the amount of business that will be done.

WORK SCHEDULE BY ASSIGNMENT

Date _____

Assistant Cook	Cook's Helper	Pantry and Baker
Make coffee and hot cereal	Pick turkey meat from bones	Put ice into bins
Prepare French toast (B-8)	Pare potatoes	Cut butter and margarine
Prepare cream sauce	Wash lettuce and fix leaves	Help dish breakfast
Mash potatoes	Help dish breakfast	Make and dish up lunch salads
Cook string beans	See cafeteria counter is properly filled	Make 3 pans cornbread (S-10)
Help dish lunch	Prepare 1½ qts diced pepper	Make 2½ gal hotcake batter for Thurs. breakfast (S-8)
Help clean refrigerators	Chop 1 c pimiento	Make lemon pudding (R-15)
Help clean storeroom	Clean up cafeteria counter	Dish pudding
Do preprep as instructed for next day	Make gelatin salads for night	Set up gelatin salads
Bread mock chicken legs	Help clean refrigerators and storeroom	Help dish lunch and supervise lunch counter
Get vegetables ready for dinner	Help set up lunch counter	Do preparation for apple pie on Thurs.
Pan baked potatoes and get ready for baking	Do preparation as instructed	Clean own unit and do own pots and pans
	Help dish up lunch	Make 10 doz muffins for dinner (S-17)
	Clean lunch counter	
	Do pots and pans as required	
	Clean cook's shelves	

FIG. 4-5   An assignment sheet may be made out to indicate what a worker should do on a shift. Here is one illustrating how such instructions might be prepared for a small operation.

GOLD ROOM SCHEDULE

Morning Shift 7 to 3:30	Station	Afternoon Shift 3:00 to 11:30
Alice Tilton	1	G. Smith
Bert Sivay	2	Gloria Rutter
Sylvia Tubbs	3	Cora Spotler
Rosy Stephan	4	Julia Oilan
Grace Abrams	5	Mabel Morris
Mary Crowder	6	Silvia Field
E. Turner	7	Helen Peller
Bess Manor	8	Mary Sage
Marie Scott	9	closed
Clara Tourney	10	closed
Sam Baker	1,2+3	Teddy Holt
Mike Benner	4,5+6	Arais Vicune
Gary Dentor	7,8+9	Stan Starford (7+8 only)
Sandra Holman 11-3:30	11	closed
Phyllis Loch 11-3:30	12	closed
T. Crane 11-3:30	14	closed
Barry Tucker 11-3:30	11,12+14	closed

Date Feb. 20, 1974   Signed George Bell

FIG. 4-6   Such a work schedule as this could appear on the employee bulletin board, indicating which station various waitresses would take and which bus boys would be assigned, each bus boy having three stations. Several part-time waitresses are also indicated, working shorter hours than a full shift.

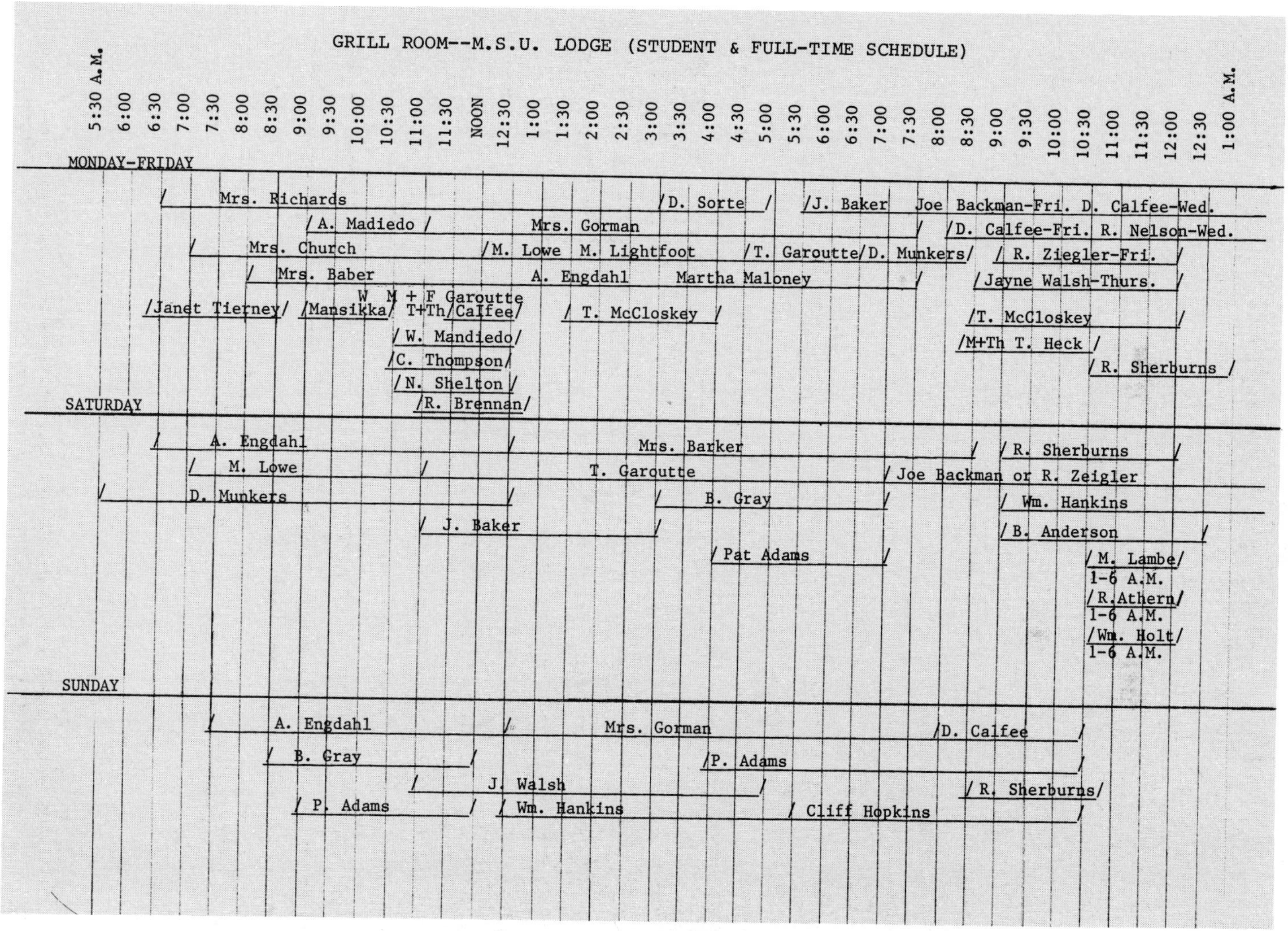

FIG. 4-7 A time-line schedule showing at a glance the hours of coverage assigned to individuals on a foodservice staff.

NEIMAN MARCUS

Food Production Schedule

DEPT. _____

	MONDAY	TUESDAY	WEDNESDAY	THURSDAY	FRIDAY	SATURDAY
ZODIAC						
LITTLE DIPPER						
PRESTON CENTER AND HASKELL						
SPECIAL ORDERS						

FIG. 4-8 Adapted from menu planning form used by Helen Corbitt at Neiman Marcus. Note that every day of operation and various dining areas are covered.

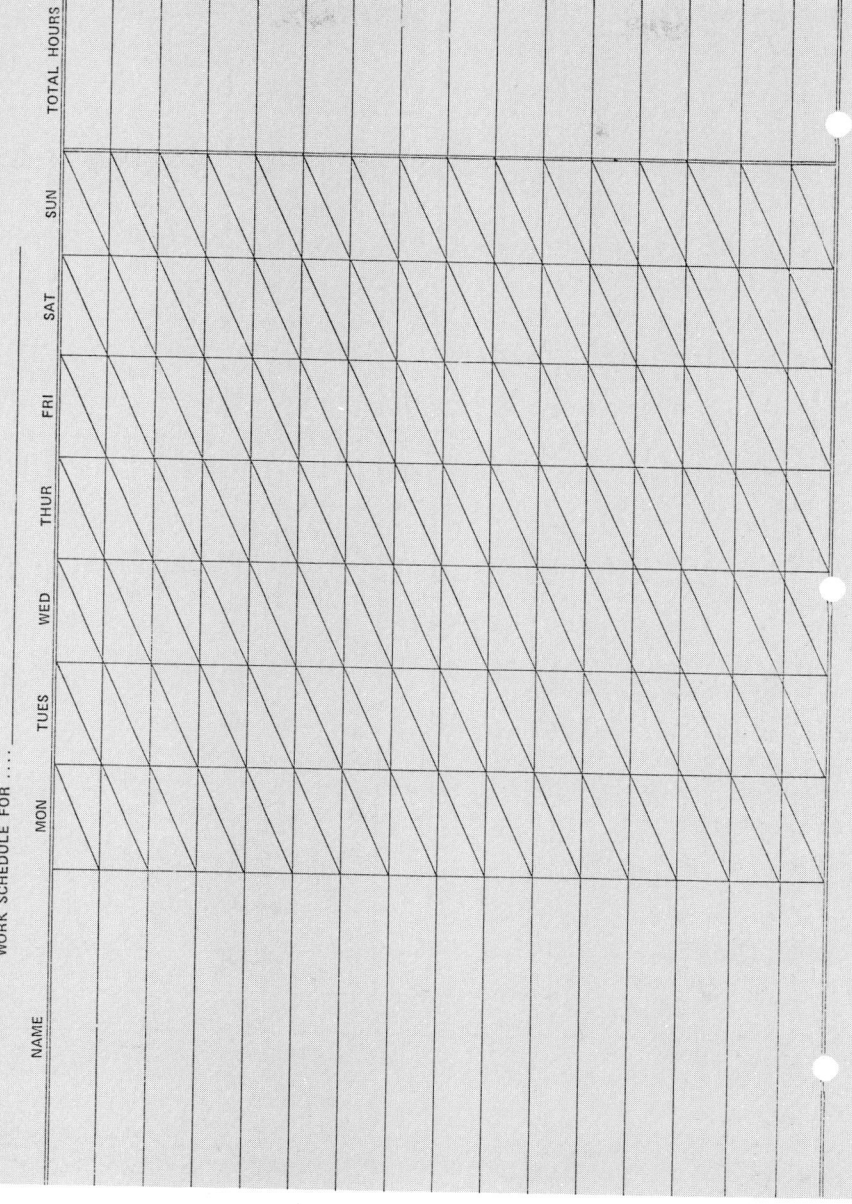

FIG. 4-9 A work schedule used to indicate hours of work for different employees. If a split shift is worked, the top and bottom parts of the square indicate the hours. (Courtesy Hyatt Corporation)

HYATT HOTELS DAILY TIME SHEET

Department_____

No.	Name	TIME		HOURS		WAGES		Rate	Other
		In	Out	Reg.	O.T.	Reg.	O.T.		
2									
3									
4									
5									
6									
7									
8									
9									
10									
11									
12									
13									
14									
15									
16									
17									
18									
19									
20									
21									
22									
23									
24									
	STAFF ALLOWANCE								
	TOTALS								

Total Wages $_____   Dept. Head_____   Day_____   Date_____19____

F & B NO. 7 H-2317 6-72

FIG. 4-10 A daily time sheet used by Hyatt Hotels. Note that a staff allowance figure is used to compare the actual use of labor with that projected. If time cards and a time clock are not available, this can be a sign-in and sign-out record filled in by employees and then checked, completed and signed by the department head. (Courtesy Hyatt Corporation)

Management can also set up systems whereby historical information is compiled. For instance, a diary may be kept that gives the amount of business for a specific day as compared with the prevailing weather, events occurring nearby, holidays, general business conditions, etc. This can be referred to in setting up schedules to give an idea of what might be expected to happen at another time. On days when it rains a foodservice near office buildings will find it has more business than it has on nice days when office workers might wish to walk farther to obtain food.

Some forecasts are based on dollar sales. Others are made on the number

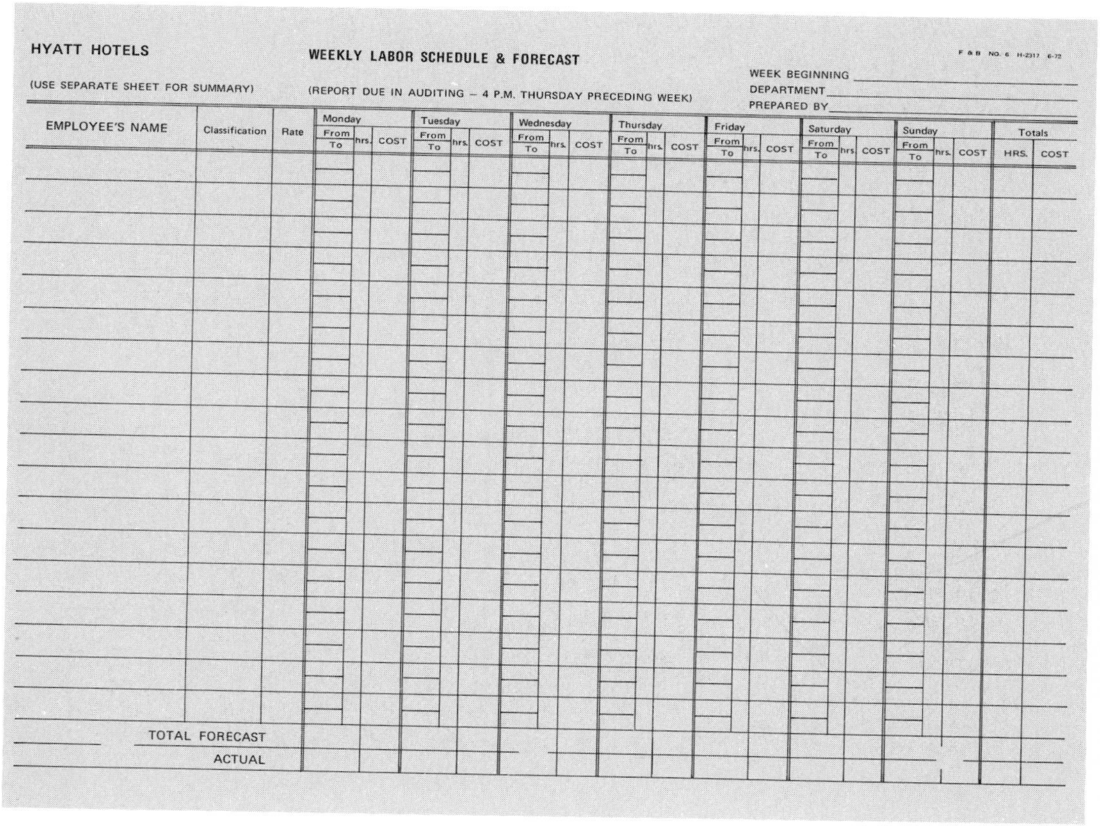

EMPLOYEE'S NAME	Classification	Rate	Monday From To	hrs.	COST	Tuesday From To	hrs.	COST	Wednesday From To	hrs.	COST	Thursday From To	hrs.	COST	Friday From To	hrs.	COST	Saturday From To	hrs.	COST	Sunday From To	hrs.	COST	Totals HRS.	COST

HYATT HOTELS (USE SEPARATE SHEET FOR SUMMARY)

WEEKLY LABOR SCHEDULE & FORECAST (REPORT DUE IN AUDITING — 4 P.M. THURSDAY PRECEDING WEEK)

F & B NO. 6 H-2317 6-72

WEEK BEGINNING _____
DEPARTMENT _____
PREPARED BY _____

TOTAL FORECAST
ACTUAL

FIG. 4-11   A labor forecast and schedule sheet that makes possible the comparison of actual and projected labor use. (Courtesy Hyatt Corporation)

of meals to be served, number of guests or other factors. The assignment of labor should be made on the basis of one of these factors. For instance, it is usual for a foodservice to assign waiters or waitresses on the basis of a specific number each will handle in a meal. If the forecast is based on dollar sales, a standard should be worked out allowing for a specified amount of labor for a partic-

ular work assignment according to dollars in sales. Some allow an hour on the payroll for every $6.00 in sales, for instance. If properly done, there should be little difference in the amount of labor allocated by any standard selected. Figure 4-12 shows how a forecast for a dining room, catering rooms and bar might work out based on dollar sales.

DOLLAR VOLUME FORECAST FOR 9/10 WEEK

Unit and Meal	Sun 9/10	Mon 9/11	Tues 9/12	Wed 9/13	Thurs 9/14	Fri 9/15	Sat 9/16	Weekly Total
Dining Room								
Breakfast	$150	$185	$190	$195	$195	$215	$280	$1,410
Lunch	120	160	175	210	210	225	235	1,335
Dinner	220	300	335	365	365	385	400	2,370
Total	$490	$645	$700	$770	$770	$825	$915	$5,115
Catering								
Breakfast	$160	$	$20	$40	$40	$	$ 30	$290
Lunch		130	40	40	60	40	100	330
Dinner	20	50	25	40	120	410	260	665
Total	$180	$180	$85	$120	$220	$450	$390	$1,285
Bar	$120	$250	$325	$270	$300	$375	$400	$2,040
Total for all	$790	$1,075	$1,110	$1,160	$1,290	$1,650	$1,705	$8,440

FIG. 4-12   Based on the amounts shown in this sales forecast, a manager would then make up a projected labor schedule. If he wished to achieve a 20 per cent labor cost, the total labor cost for these units for this week should not exceed $1,688.

CHAPTER 5

Menu Analysis and Pricing

Before planning and writing a menu, it is necessary to know how much revenue it will produce. It is also necessary to know whether menu items will meet with good patron acceptance and satisfy customers' needs as well as the needs of the operation. Menu pricing should include tests to see if they meet with patron approval, yield the desired revenue and adequately cover costs, etc. Selections on the menu should be balanced so that costs are properly balanced between high-revenue producing and lower-revenue producing items. Menu space is extremely valuable and each item on the menu card should carry its own weight in providing revenue and customer satisfaction.

SALES ANALYSIS

A good sales analysis should be made prior to writing a menu to indicate its overall profitability and patron acceptability. The number of items that must be sold to produce the necessary revenue should be accurately estimated. A good projection of the sale-mix is necessary. A menu that is written to produce one sales-mix but actually makes a quite different one can cause real problems. The point at which the projected menu makes a satisfactory profit, where it breaks even and where it is producing a loss, should be known. If catering is a part of the action, the analysis should include this. If the analysis is properly done, it can indicate to management where further investigation might be needed and where further study of the results may indicate better courses for management action and decisions.

The analysis should include not only investigation from the front of the house, but also factors in the back of the house which might influence costs, ability to produce the menu items, quality control, etc. In fact, the analysis may be a far bigger job than the actual planning and writing of the menu.

The Popularity Index

Menu items within a specific food group can compete against each other for patron selection. One or more items in a group can completely kill the sale of others because of their high popularity. Groups of foods such as soups and sandwiches can also compete against each other. The relative popularity of separate items among each other and the relative popularity of different food groups should be known so their contribution to the sales-mix can be estimated and the potential of the menu as a revenue producing item or as a means of satisfying customers' needs can be estmated. Even a non-profit foodservice needs to study carefully the relative popularity of its menu items and groups. Both profit and non-profit foodservices should also study trends in patron selections and for this a continuing record of selections is needed over a period of time. Not all menu items should be expected to have a high popularity. Some may be on the menu because management feels they must be, even though only a few patrons select them.

Some operations compile a sales ratio or popularity index for menu items as follows:

1. A count of the separate item selections is made within a group to be studied,

2. The total selections within the group are summed, and

3. The percentage each separate item is of the total is calculated. The percentage obtained for each item indicates its popularity when competing with the other items of its group. This may be called the sales ratio or popularity index.

For instance, the following might be obtained from five menu items:

Item	No. Sold	Popularity %
New York Steak with Béarnaise Sauce	44	24
Breast of Chicken Nanking	38	21
Broiled Lobster Tails Meunière	14	8
Roast Pork Loin with Chestnut Dressing	54	30
Lamb Shish Kebab Iranian	32	18
	182	101%

A similar ratio can be calculated for groups of foods. Such information can be revealing. For instance, such a calculation may show that the sandwich group is far more popular than luncheon items, or that fountain items are destroying the sale of desserts.

A popularity index for a single day is not too informative. It becomes so when calculations cover a 30-day period or more. Items vary in popularity according to how they are combined with others. The results of such studies should be analyzed carefully. A continued low ratio should be checked. In some cases, as noted, this can be expected. Items are purposely put on the menu even though they may be known to have a low or moderate popularity. Thus, diced rutabagas might have a relatively low index but if they are selected enough times, it might be well to leave them on the menu for the few who appreciate them. It is also advisable to check the popularity index with the menu price. If low priced items are

SALES RATIO FORM

Date 1-25-74 Day Friday Dining Area Cobra CoffeeShop Weather Rain/sleet Special Events Women's bridge & Dental Convention

Meal Lunch Total Covers 443 Items covered Entrées

(1) ITEM	(2) FORE-CAST	(3) TABLE D'HOTE Price $	FC* $	% FC*	(4) À LA CARTE Price $	FC* $	% FC*	(5) PORTIONS SERVED	(6) % TO TOTAL FC*	Sales	Gross Profit	(7) SALES RATIO	(8) RATIO TO DATE	(9) QUALITY OF ITEM	(10) COMMENTS
grilled cube steak	60	2.25	.67	29.8	1.65	.55	33.3	21/48	24.1	23.4	23.1	17.5	16.0	Fair-sometimes overdone	-
Chili-burger	80	1.50	.40	26.6	1.00	.25	25.0	38/62	18.9	21.5	22.6	25.3	22.6	Fair-little runny	Sold out-12:42.
Baked Salmon	45	1.70	.48	28.2	1.20	.30	25.0	9/21	7.2	7.0	7.3	7.6	12.4	Poor-too dry.	Usually better quality.
Corned beef	80	1.85	.54	29.2	1.25	.40	32.0	28/49	20.7	20.6	20.6	19.5	16.0	Good	Sold out-1:50.
Hot turkey Sandwich	100	1.60	.48	30.0	1.10	.40	36.4	48/71	29.3	27.3	27.3	30.1	27.9	Good	Price helps sales.
TOTALS	365	-	-	-	-	-	-	144/251	100	100	100	100	94.9	-	-

*Food Cost

Contributions of Items to:

(11) ITEM	(12) SALES À la carte $	Table d'hote $	Total $	(13) FOOD COST À la carte $	Table d'hote $	Total $	(14) GROSS PROFIT À la carte $	Table d'hote $	Total $
Steak	34.65	108.00	142.65	11.55	32.16	43.71	23.10	75.84	98.94
Burger	38.00	93.99	131.99	9.50	24.80	34.30	28.50	68.20	46.70
Salmon	8.40	35.70	44.10	2.70	10.08	12.78	5.70	25.62	31.32
Corned beef	35.00	90.65	125.65	11.20	26.46	37.66	23.80	64.19	87.99
Turkey	52.80	113.60	166.40	19.20	34.08	53.28	51.60	79.52	131.12
TOTALS	168.88	440.95	609.80	54.13	127.58	181.73	132.70	313.37	446.07

General Comments:

After four complaints on the salmon, it was taken off the menu.

Compiled by: _____

FIG. 5-1 The above sales ratio tabulation gives considerable information which can lead to valuable data on how menu items perform. The "% to Total" column (6), covers the percentage each item contributes to the total food cost, total sales and total gross profit. Details for making these calculations appear in the data following on "Contributions of Items" to sales, food cost and gross profit. "Ratio to Date" figures do not add up to 100 per cent because these items do not always appear together.

much higher in popularity than the higher priced ones, patrons may be showing price consciousness. A review of pricing and the type of items offered may thus be advisable.

Popularity figures can be misleading; any analysis should look behind the ratio to see if some hidden factors are at work to affect them. Most forms used by foodservices for calculating the sales ratio leave a space for comments so that such factors may be weighed in evaluating the popularity of items. For instance, selections can differ depending upon the day of the week they are offered. Sundays are quite different from other days. Mondays may also be. Special events near the foodservice or in the same building can influence selections. A rock concert in a convention center nearby may affect the selection of items which young people might like, while a convention of car salesmen in the same center would create an entirely different popularity index. Running out of some popular items may force patrons to take different selections than they would have if the run-out had not occurred. Therefore, some record of run-outs and the time might be maintained. Weather can affect selections. On a cold day, soup may have a higher selection compared to cold appetizers. Seasons can be influential. Fresh strawberry shortcake may have a higher popularity when fresh strawberries are first on the market. A sudden shift in popularity might also mean that the item suffered a variation in quality that day and complaints from customers made it necessary to remove it from the menu. Menu placement, presentation on the menu, descriptions, and many other factors must be weighed.

Some differentiation in counts may be desirable for à la carte and table d'hôte items. This may be done by writing 22/34 in a count for an item indicating that 22 à la carte and 34 table d'hôte items were sold for a single item. It is also common to calculate the contribution an item or a group makes to total sales, gross profit and net profit plus other factors.

Figure 5-1 shows how a sales ratio plus other desirable information might be compiled on a form. Figure 5-2 shows how it might be done for only one item on a record card. Any form used should quickly reveal data for specific items.

The magnitude of a sales ratio depends upon the number of items against which an item competes. If an item is one of four in a group, one would expect it to have a ratio of .25. If it is one of five, it would hold its own against the others with a popularity rating of .20. However, if one in four and it has a rating of .42, it is more than holding its own and, if it is one in five, with a rating of .12, it is not holding its own.

It is difficult to compare the rating of items when they come from groups not having the same number of items in competition with each other. For instance, if an item which is one of four and has a popularity index of .25 is compared with one which is one in five and has a popularity index of .20, one might conclude that the first is more popular than the second because one has a higher popularity index than the other. This might not be true. To remove this difficulty, some calculate a popularity factor. This is done by dividing the popularity index an item would have if it competed as expected in its group into its actual popularity index. Thus, an item which is one of five, would be expected to have a popularity index of .20. If it actually had a popularity index of .20 then the popularity factor would be 1.00 (.20 ÷ .20 = 1.00). However, if it had a popularity index of .25, the popularity factor would be 1.25 (.25 ÷ .20 = 1.25). Using the popularity factor makes it possible now to compare a wide number of popularity indexes of items not in the same group. For instance, suppose it is desired to compare the popularity of an item which is one of a group of eight (expected popularity .125) having a popularity index of .15 with one of a group of five (expected popularity .20) having a popularity index of .15 also. The popularity factor of the first is 1.20 (.15 ÷ .125 = 1.20) and that of

the second is .75 (.15 ÷ .20 = .75) showing that in spite of the fact both have the same popularity index or sales ratio, a popularity factor shows they differ in popularity. Calculating the popularity factor puts them on the same basis for comparison. A popularity factor of more than one indicates the item more than holds its own, while a popularity factor of less than one indicates it does not. If an item has a popularity factor of .68 while another has one of 1.30, we know that the latter is about twice as popular in its group as the first is in its group. Figure 5-3 indicates how three menu items could be tabulated to show a popularity factor, plus other desirable information. The popularity factor in this figure was derived by dividing the expected popularity index into the actual (.13 ÷ .333 =

Baked Salmon and Dressing							
					(Item)		
Date Served	Fore-cast	Amount Sold	Sales Ratio	Accumulated Ratio to Date	Contribution to:		
					Sales %	Food Cost %	Gross Profit %
1/25/74	45	30	⑤ 7.6%	7.6%	7.0	7.2	7.6
2/12/74	40	38	⑤ 12.4%	10.0%	8.1	7.8	7.9
4/1/74	40	34	⑤ 10.4%	10.1%	8.1	7.8	7.8
5/20/74	40	40	⑤ 14.2%	11.4%	8.2	7.9	8.0

FIG. 5-2   An example of a card used to record the relative popularity of a menu item. The circled figure in the sales ratio column indicates the number of items in the group in which it competed. Contribution of the item is calculated against the toal sales, total food cost and total gross profit for the five items.

RAW SALES DATA

Item	No. Sold	Selling Price	Revenue	Food Cost	Total Food Cost	Gross Profit	Total Gross Profit
Sole	26	$3.25	$ 84.50	$ .41	$ 10.66	$2.84	$ 73.84
Chicken	76	3.60	273.60	1.09	82.84	2.51	190.76
Beef	98	4.50	441.00	2.57	251.86	1.93	189.14
	200		$799.10		$345.36 (43.2%)		$453.74 (56.8%)

COMPARATIVE POPULARITY AND PROFIT VALUES

| | | | CONTRIBUTION OF ITEM TO: | | | | | |
| | | | FOOD SALES | | TOTAL FOOD COST | | GROSS PROFIT | |
Item	Sales Ratio	Popularity Factor	%	Factor	%	Factor	%	Factor
Sole	.13	.39	.106	.32	.031	.09	.163	.49
Chicken	.38	1.14	.342	1.03	.240	.72	.420	1.26
Beef	.49	1.47	.552	1.66	.729	2.19	.417	1.25

FIG. 5-3   The information on sole, chicken and beef in the tabulation at top is standard information frequently compiled on menu items. The data in the bottom tabulation on these items are derived from the data above. Sole has a sales ratio of .13 compared to the other two. Its popularity is correspondingly low. Its contribution to sales and gross profit is also low but it has a very low food cost. And this may be the reason management lets it remain on the menu — to offset the much higher food cost of the beef.

.39, .38 ÷ .333 = 1.14, and .49 ÷ .333 = 1.47). Similarly, the factors for the contribution to sales, total food cost and gross profit were similarly calculated by dividing .333, the expected factor, into the actual one such as .106 ÷ .333 = .32 for the factor for contribution to sales. A factor over 1.00 indicates that the item in this category is more than holding its own. A factor under 1.00 indicates that it is not.* For instance, the factor of 1.66 for beef in sales indicates it is contributing more than its share here while the factor of .49 for the sole for its contribution to gross profit indicates it is doing poorly in this category.

A management individual looking at the data found in Figure 5-3 would clearly see that the sole does not sell well compared with baked chicken and roast beef. It also does not contribute its share of dollars in sales and gross profit but it does have a very good food cost. In studying these figures management may decide to keep it on the menu because of its food cost and because it may sell as well as any other fish item. The baked chicken more than holds it own in popularity and contributes about its fair share of revenue and gross profit. Its food cost is adequate and therefore it is perhaps a fairly satisfactory menu item. The roast beef may appear from this analysis underpriced to management. Its food cost is high compared with the other items. However, it is contributing more than its fair share of revenue dollars as compared with the other items, and it is doing all right in its contribution to gross profit. After

*Except for the food cost factor.

reviewing these data, management may decide it should raise the price of roast beef slightly and, perhaps, let the others remain priced as they are. A later analysis might show some shift in these data and then management again could take action if it felt it should. The compilation of such data gives good information to management for making decisions. The consistent recording of such information will make possible cautious adjustments in various menu factors until a desirable situation is achieved.

The important thing in making such an analysis is that management is able to see more clearly how menu items perform in making their contribution to sales and gross profit, and how they stand in food cost compared to others. Knowing this, management can make

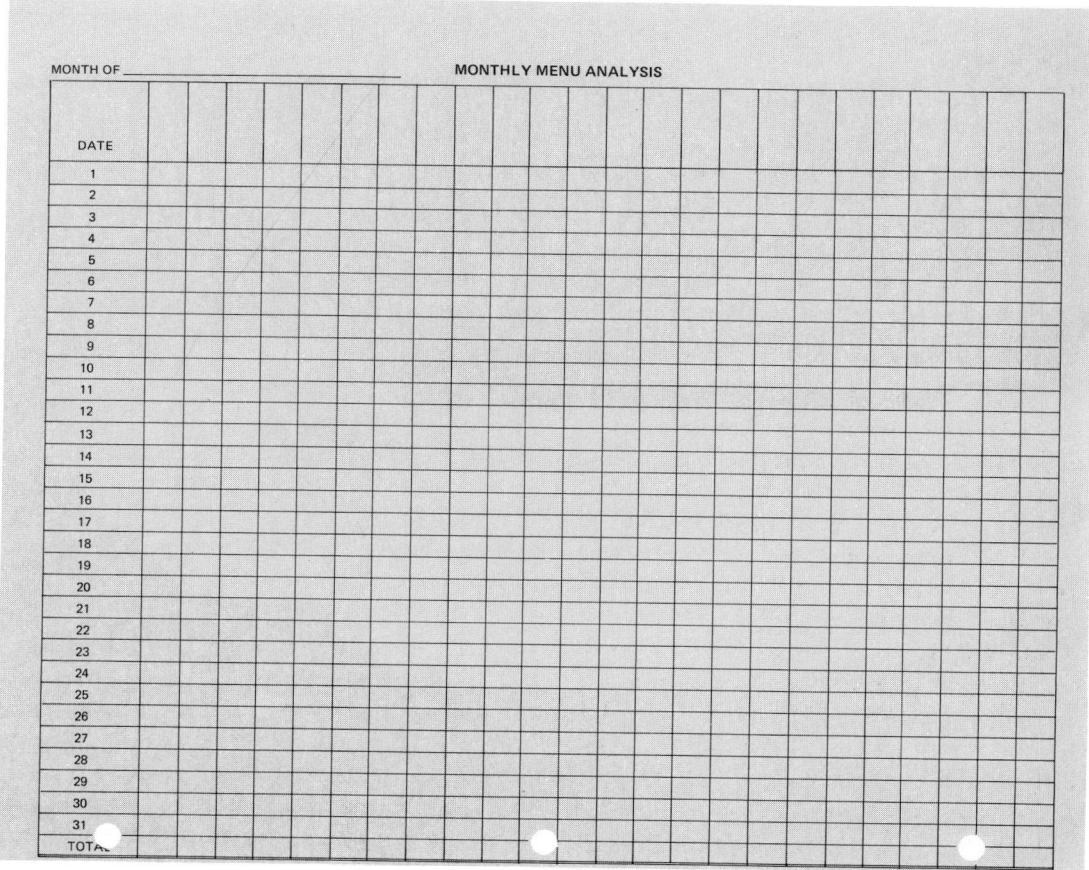

MONTH OF _____   MONTHLY MENU ANALYSIS

DATE

1
2
3
4
5
6
7
8
9
10
11
12
13
14
15
16
17
18
19
20
21
22
23
24
25
26
27
28
29
30
31
TOTAL

FIG. 5-4   This monthly menu analysis sheet lists menu items with the number of sales made of each per day. Note there are rows for a month of 31 days. Menu items are written in at the top of the column. The last column may be used for the total number of covers served that day. A percentage can be calculated for the relative popularity of a menu item based on the number of times it was selected compared with the total.

BLACKHAWK RESTAURANT

DAILY LUNCHEON AND DINNER FOOD SERVICE AND ENTRÉE COUNT

Date_____   Weather_____

Pre-Set Entrée Key	ENTRÉE	ENTRÉE PORTION COUNT	VOID PORTION COUNT	NET PORTION COUNT	ENTRÉE PRICE	DOLLAR EXTENSION
1						
2						
3						
4						
5						
6						
7						
8						
9						
TOTALS				(3)		
GROUP TOTAL REGISTER READING						
LESS PRE-SET MONEY VOIDS						
NET GROUP PRE-SET MONEY VOIDS						
NET GROUP PRE-SET ENTRÉE TOTAL						(1)
OPEN #1 Coffee Tea Milk						
OPEN #2 Desserts						
OPEN #3 Appetizers (Misc.)						
OPEN #4 All Other				(4)		
TOTAL OPEN FOOD SERVICE						
LESS OPEN FOOD VOIDS						
NET OPEN FOOD SERVICE						(2)
TOTAL NET FOOD SERVICE	ADD (1) plus (2)					
TOTAL COVER COUNT	ADD (3) plus (4)					

FIG. 5-5 A sheet used to record and analyze sales of entrées and other menu items. (Courtesy Don Roth, Blackhawk Restaurants, Chicago)

MAIN DINING ROOM LUNCHEON   Day:_____ Date:_____

Total Covers:_____

A - Prime Rib

B - Filet

B - Butt Steak

C - Blackhawk

D - Corned Beef

E - Hollander

F - Chopped Steak

G - Baked Ham

H - Calves Liver

1 - New Orleans

2 - Don Roth's

3 - Palm Beach

4 - Hollywood

13 - Pirate

25 - Cold Cuts

43 - Manhattan

5 - Chicken Sandwich

7 - Club Sandwich

Giraffe   Bear   Elephant   Seal

#19

9

Flyer: Dinner Items:

Miscellaneous:

FIG. 5-6   Another sheet used to record menu item sales in a simple manner. (Courtesy Don Roth, Blackhawk Restaurants, Chicago)

evaluations and decisions more satisfactorily.

Some operations keep a history of their pricing on various items. This record indicates by date the food cost, the selling price and the basis for each, and could be tied in with a popularity index. Changes in any of these factors are recorded. It allows an evaluation of costs and the selling price. It also can show if prices are properly charged in the various dining areas. It has been observed in some large operations where the same item is sold in different dining areas that prices may differ, with a supposedly higher priced dining area selling an identical product for less. Figure 5-7 indicates how such a record might be maintained on the back of the same card on which a sales record is maintained for an item.

Break-Even Point

If one covers all costs in doing business, he breaks even. If he does not, there is a loss. If costs are exceeded by income, a profit is made. To know where a menu breaks even can be calculated by totaling all costs. Thus, if *all* costs for serving 100 people are $400 and there is a $400 income, the operation breaks even.

At times it may be desirable to obtain a break-even point based on an estimate made prior to doing business. For instance, a menu planner may wish to know how many dollars in sales a menu must generate before it breaks even. To calculate this, fixed costs must be known. Fixed costs are those incurred, regardless of whether or not a sale is made, such as rent, light, admin-

Price Comparison Card				
Item Veal Parmigiana		Portion Size 6oz A la carte; 4oz Table d'hôte		
Where Served	Date	Selling Price À la T d'hôte	Food Cost À la T d'hôte	Accompaniments
Leaf Rm.	1/8/74	$3.40 $5.10	1.12 % 30. 1.43 28%	A la - Rice, bread & butter. (b+b) t d'h - Minnestrone, pasta, salad."
Coffee Shop	1/12/74	1.80 4.00	1.12 40 1.43 36.	A la - Rice, b+b. t d'h - minnestrone, pasta, salad, b+b
Coffee Shop	1/20/74	3.00 4.40	1.12 37. 1.43 32.5	A la - Rice, b+b. t d'h - minnestrone, pasta, salad, b+b
Gold Rm.	1/24/74	- 5.50	- - 1.73 32.5	Minnestrone, salad, pasta, coffee, tortoni
party Leaf Rm.	2/20/74	3.80 5.50	1.20 31.5 1.52 27.5	Rice, b+b. Minnestroni, salad, pasta, b+b.
Coffee Shop	2/24/74	3.40 4.60	1.20 35. 1.52 33	Rice, b+b. Minnestroni, salad, pasta, b+b.

FIG. 5-7   The same item may be on the menu in different dining areas, selling at different prices. Management will often want to maintain some record of sales and performance, as is done here for Veal Parmigiana.

istrative salaries and licenses. These are sometimes called "turn-key expenses" because as soon as the key is turned in the door in the morning, before any business is done, they are incurred.

To calculate break-even point, one should know what the percent of all costs these fixed costs are, plus what the average check is. Knowing these, the calculation is not difficult.

If we assign symbols to the various factors as follows,

$$BE = \text{break even}$$
$$FC\% = \text{per cent fixed cost}$$
$$FC = \text{fixed cost}$$
$$AC = \text{average check}$$

the formula for the break-even point is:

$$BE = \frac{FC}{AC \times FC\%} \times AC$$

Thus, if an operation has fixed costs that are 43.3 per cent of all costs, fixed costs are $200 and average check is $1.50, the calculation will be:

$$BE = \frac{\$200}{\$1.50 \times .433} \times \$1.50 = \$461.54$$

Thus, the operation needs $461.54 to break even.

If management wanted to know how many customers the menu would have to generate to break even, the formula would be

$$BE = \frac{FC}{AC \times FC\%} = \frac{\$200}{\$1.50 \times .433}$$

= 308 customers which, at an average income of $1.50 (average check), would equal $462.

If this same operation wanted to make a profit of $100 a day, a slightly differ-

ent calculation would be made which could be represented by:

$$BE + \text{Profit} = \frac{FC + P \ (\text{Profit})}{AC \times FC\%}$$

$\times$ AC. Translated numerically, using the figures in our above example, this would be:

$$BE + P = \frac{\$200 + \$100}{\$1.50 \times .433} \times \$1.50$$

$$= \frac{\$300}{\$ .65} \times \$1.50 = \$692.31 \text{ in sales to}$$

cover all costs and make this profit. Figure 5-8 shows how one might arrive at this same information by using a graph.

Break-even point can also be used to ascertain the number of items that must be sold to cover departmental fixed costs. The basic formula is:

$$BE = \frac{FC}{\dfrac{SP - VC \ (\text{variable cost})}{SP \ (\text{selling price})}}$$

As an example, suppose a central commissary manufactures pies and the average selling price is $1.20 each. Variable costs are $.80 per pie. How many pies would have to be sold to pay off $30,000 a year in fixed departmental costs? How many would have to be sold to make a $10,000 profit for the year? The first calculation is

$$\frac{\$30,000}{(\$1.20 - \$.80)/\$1.20} = 90,000 \text{ pies}$$

must be sold to recover fixed costs. The second calculation is

$$\frac{\$30,000 + \$10,000}{(\$1.20 - \$.80)/\$1.20} = 120,000 \text{ pies}$$

to make $10,000 profit in a year.

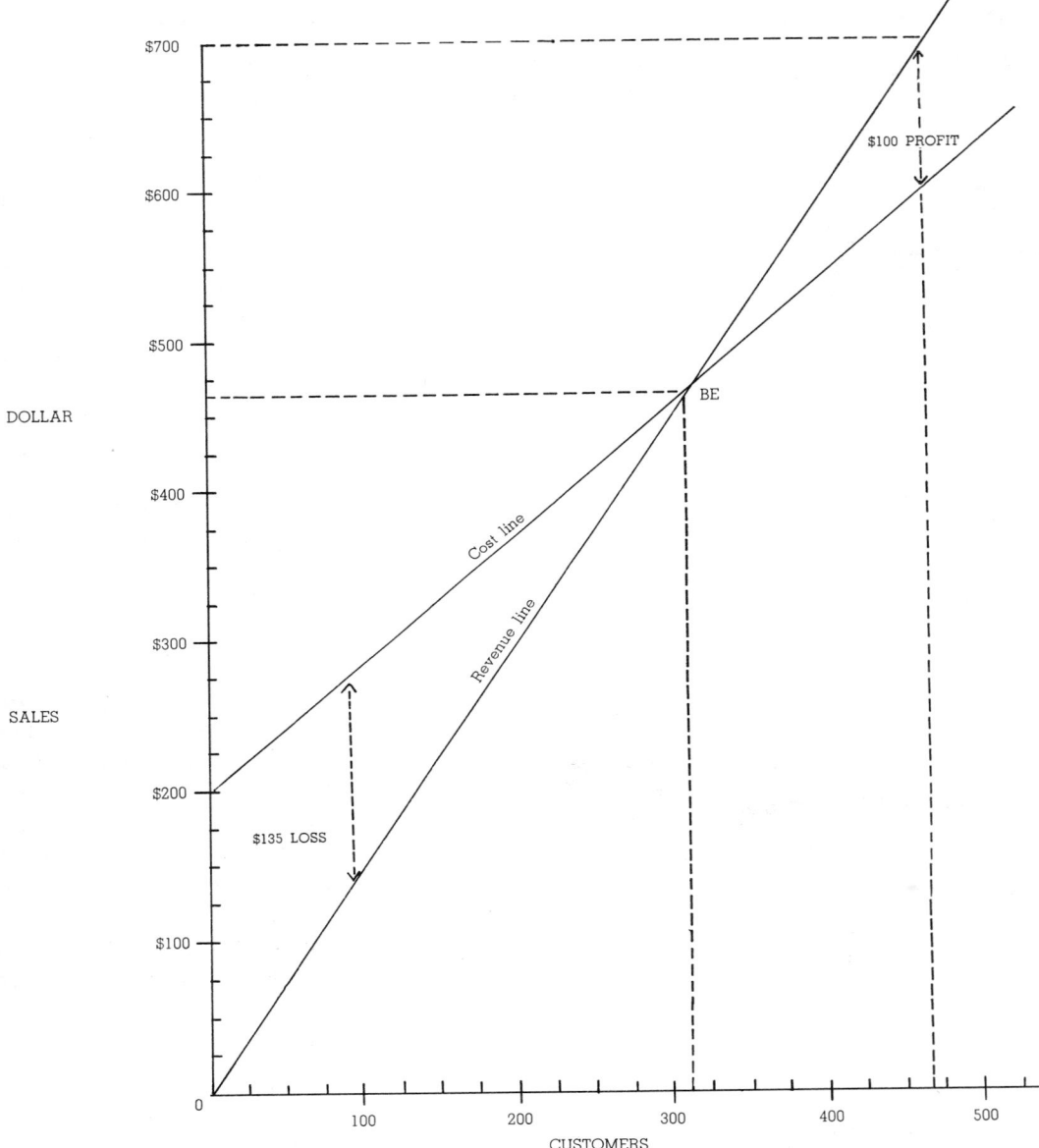

FIG. 5-8   This break-even chart shows that at zero sales (no customers) the loss is $200, equal to minimum cost. But as revenue increases it overtakes costs until, at 308 customers and a revenue point of approximately $462, revenue and costs meet, the juncture of the two dotted lines at BE, the break-even point. With a sale of 100 units (100 customers) the **loss** is $135 — $275 costs minus $140 revenue. With a sale of 462 units the **profit** is $100 — $700 revenue minus $600 costs.

Many operators feel that if they stay open longer hours they can get enough sales that will help to defray fixed costs. This is true since the fixed costs are there, regardless of whether the place is open or not. Even though some business may not look profitable, it might be most worthwhile because even a small contribution to fixed costs helps increase the profit picture.

Suppose an operation open 10 hours a day has an income of $300 per day divided as follows:

30% food cost	$ 90.00	
20% labor cost	60.00	
20% other variables	60.00	
Fixed costs	60.00	
Total costs	$270.00	
Profit	30.00	(10%)
Total	$300.00	

It decides to stay open three more hours and bring in $20.00 more. The operator's analysis shows that an average of $6.70 an hour income, versus $30.00 per hour in regular hours of operation, is worth while. His analysis now on a $320 income is as follows:

30% food cost	$ 96.00	
20% labor cost	64.00	
20% other costs	64.00	
Fixed costs	60.00	
Total costs	$284.00	
Profit	36.00	(11¼%)
Total	$320.00	

Thus, profit rises 1¼ per cent which over a year of 365 days of operation will result in a change of $10,950 profit to $13,140 profit or $2,190 more, a sum that might be worth while to a small business.

THE EFFECT OF VOLUME

Some individuals may think that if a selling price is established including an allowance for profit, the first item sold makes a profit. This is not true. If there are fixed expenses, these must be paid first before a profit is made. For instance, if a company operating mobile truck food routes finds its average sale per customer is 60¢ and its fixed costs per day for operating a truck, etc. are $25 with the driver's commission being 25 per cent, food cost 35 per cent and other variable costs 5 per cent, it would have to have 119 sales before a profit is made. Thus, no profit would be made until the 120th sale. The calculation for this is the same as used before:

$$BE = \frac{FC}{AC \times FC\%}$$

We know the fixed costs are $25 and the average check (average sale) is 60¢. To get the fixed cost per cent (FC%) we total the variable costs of 25 per cent commission, food cost 35 per cent and other variable costs 5 per cent to get 65 per cent and, if we deduct 65 per cent from 100 per cent (all costs including fixed), we find that the fixed costs are 35 per cent of the average sale. Numerically, we can make the calculation as

$$BE = \frac{\$25}{\$.60 \times .35} = \frac{\$25}{\$.21} = 119.05.$$

The company may wish to know, for instance, what happens if the driver sells to 400 customers on the route in one day. How much profit is made? There are 21¢ of each 60¢ average sale available for profit after the 119th sale. Thus, if there are 400 sales and 119 are required to take care of expenses, the profit made from 400 sales is 400 less 119 or 281 sales on which a 21¢ profit is made and .21 × 281 = $59.01 profit. This proves out as follows: If we have 400 sales at 60¢ each, total sales are $240. If food cost is 35 per cent, commission 25 per cent and other variable costs 5 per cent with fixed costs $25, total costs are respectively $84, $60, $12 and $25 or $181. If we deduct these costs from $240 ($240 − $181) we get $59 for profit. Thus, after taking care of fixed costs, profits can mount up considerably. This is why operations may strive for volume which pushes sales far over the level of the break-even point. The following indicates what happens if there are 480 sales in a day:

35%	Food cost	$100.80
25%	Sales commission	72.00
5%	Other variable costs	14.40
	Fixed costs	25.00
	Total costs	$212.20
	Profit	75.80
	Total sales	$288.00

(480 sales × 60¢ per sale = $288.00).

Figure 5-9 gives another illustration of the effect of volume on profit for an operation having a food cost of 30 per cent, variable labor cost of 26 per cent, other variable costs of 19 per cent, fixed costs of $200 per day and a profit of 5 per cent on the first $1,000 in sales done per day. The effect of volume on profit in doing $1,000, $1,200 and $1,400 in sales a day is substantial.

Management would do well to examine the nature of its fixed costs. Some thought to be fixed may be what are called "programmed" costs, that is, they are programmed into operation, and these sometimes can be controlled or changed. For instance, the cost of electricity for lights, water, heat for cooking or the making of steam, or the cost of cleaning supplies may be programmed into operation as fixed costs, but if lights are turned off more frequently, supplies are used properly, leaking faucets are fixed to reduce the use of hot water, and broilers, griddles and steam equipment are turned off when not in use, some of these costs may be reduced. A small change may make a considerable difference in the amount of sales required to pay for these fixed costs.

Management should also consider the effect of capital investment on fixed costs. If a $20,000 investment saves

The Effect of Volume on Profit

		$1000 Sales/Day	$1200 Sales/Day	$1400 Sales/Day
30%	Food cost	$ 300	$ 360	$ 420
26%	Labor cost	260	312	364
19%	Other variable costs	190	228	266
	Fixed costs	200	200	200
	Total costs	$ 950	$1100	$1250
	Profit	50 (5%)	100 (8⅓%)	150 (12%)
100%	Total sales	$1000	$1200	$1400

FIG. 5-9   The effect on profit of three levels of volume is demonstrated in this table.

$5,000 a year in costs, four years recovers the investment. Some of this saving could be considered to be profit and add that much more to the bottom line. For instance, if an operation has a profit of 10 per cent on a $100,000 yearly income with fixed costs of $15,000 and with an investment of $20,000 and it can save $5,000 a year, the following is true:

At 8% interest, the $20,000 investment costs $1,600 a year,

And, the $5,000 saved less interest cost is $3,400 a year saved in 10 years.

Now, if the investment is written off in 10 years, $34,000-$20,000/10 = $1,400 per year and, if this $1,400 is applied to fixed costs, they are now $13,600 ($15,000 — $1,400 = $13,600.)

Now, instead of $100,000 in sales to make a $10,000 profit, sales need only be $94,400 to produce it.*

This is evident from the following:

Total sales: $94,400
(100% — 10% profit — 15% fixed costs = 75% variable costs)
.75 × $94,400 = $70,800 variable costs
$70,800 variable costs + $13,600 fixed costs + $10,000 profit = $94,400.

*The calculation is $BE = \dfrac{FC+P}{FC\% + P\%} = \dfrac{\$13,600 + \$10,000}{.15 + .10} = \$94,400.$

THE HURST METHOD OF MENU SCORING[1]

In 1960 Professor Michael Hurst of Michigan State University published a unique method of evaluating a menu including pricing, item popularity, gross profit contribution, etc. It was intended to be a tool to assist management in evaluating menu changes by comparing the various scores menus made, based on management decisions affecting prices, items to offer, their food cost and their popularity. The method was not complex and could be quickly calculated from only a few statistics easily obtainable from accounting data.

To use the Hurst method, management had to decide on a period for which the scoring was to be made. It could be a single meal or a series of meals in which the same menu was used. The period should be typical and not one in which unusual events, such as bad weather or Christmas, would keep patrons away.

The steps in scoring the menu or menus were as follows:

A. Determine the items that contribute a major portion of sales income and select those to be evaluated. Unless the income from sandwiches, salads, beverages or others is significant, do not include these.

B. Calculate the food cost for each item to be evaluated.

C. Prepare a menu count of sales for the period of the items to be evaluated.

D. Prepare a count for the period, customers selecting each of the items to be evaluated.

E. Calculate the menu score as follows by obtaining:

1. Total item sales dollars (number of items sold × their selling price).

2. Total item food cost dollars (sales dollars obtained in (1) × the item's food cost percentage or number of items sold × item food cost).

[1] Permission to summarize this method of evaluating a menu has been granted by its originator, Professor Michael Hurst, Florida International University, Miami, Florida.

3. (a) Total sales dollars for all items to be evaluated, (b) total food cost dollars for all items to be evaluated and (c) the total number of items sold of those to be evaluated in the period.

4. Dollar meal average—total sales dollars obtained in (3a) divided by total number of items sold in (3c).

5. Gross profit percentage of items evaluated during the period (dollar sales—(3a) less dollar food cost (3b), equals gross profit for items evaluated during the period. This divided by dollar sales (3a)

gives the gross profit percentage.

6. Average gross profit per meal—dollar meal average (4) times gross profit percentage (5).

7. Percentage of customers eating items evaluated—divide total number of items sold (3c) by total number of customers served by the operation during this period.

8. Menu score—gross profit average (6) times percentage of customers eating items evaluated (7).

The example given by Mr. Hurst in 1960 to illustrate his menu scoring and pricing method was as shown in the ruled panel below.

EXAMPLE OF HURST METHOD

Given:[1]

Items to be evaluated and other data —

ITEM	NO. SOLD	SELLING PRICE	FOOD COST %
Shrimp	100	$3.00	$33\frac{1}{3}$
Prime Ribs	500	$4.00	41
Turkey	400	$3.00	40

Total customer count: 1500

Solution:

Shrimp	100	$3.00	$ 300 (E1)[2]	$ 100 (E2)[2]
Prime Ribs	500	$4.00	$2000 (E1)	$ 820 (E2)
Turkey	400	$3.00	$1200 (E1)	$ 480 (E2)
	1000 (E3c)[2]		$3500 (E3a)[2]	$1400 (E3b)[2]

Meal Average $3500/1000 = $3.50 (E4)[2]

Gross Profit Percentage $3500 — $1400/$3500 = 60% (E5)[2]

Gross Profit Average $3.50 × 60% = $2.10 (E6)[2]

Percentage of Meals Evaluated to Total Meals 1,000/1,500 = $66\frac{2}{3}$% (E7)[2]

Menu Score $2.10 × $66\frac{2}{3}$% = 1.40 (E8)[2]

---

[1] Mr. Hurst in 1960 was executive vice president of the Win Schuler Restaurants in Michigan while, at the same time, on the staff of the HRI School at Michigan State University, and used figures typical of restaurants of that date.

[2] These figures in parentheses indicate which step is being used of those enumerated previously in the explanation of Mr. Hurst's method.

DAILY DINNER MENU SCORE

WIN SCHULER'S OF_____

Labor etc.

DATE_____

DAY_____

Unit Sold	Item	Selling Price	Food Cost	Dollar Sale	Dollar Cost	Profit	%
	ANGELS ON HORSEBACK	$1.25					
	SHRIMP SUPREME	1.00					
	MAIDS OF HONOR	.95					
	COLCHESTER FEAST	1.25					
	CANTERBURY BEEF	3.45					
	BRAISED SHORT RIBS	3.65					
	GROUND STEAK	3.25					
	PRIME RIB	4.25					
	FILET	5.35					
	STRIP	4.95					
	CRABLEGS & CLAWS	3.95					
	MARINER SOLE	3.75					
	LOBSTER TAILS	4.25					
	TURKEY	3.50					
	BEEF & BIRD	3.95					
	HOT-POT	3.85					
	LAMB CHOPS	4.50					
	HAM STEAK	3.75					
	HARVEST OF THE SEA	4.25					
	SCALLOPS	3.35					

Average Check_____

% Customers_____

Gross Profit Average_____

Menu Score_____

FIG. 5-10   The above form was used by the Win Schuler restaurants in Michigan to record data for use in menu scoring. (Courtesy Professor Mike Hurst)

MENU SCORING WORKSHEET

Restaurant __Neverfail__   Date __24-March 1974__

Person Scoring __OBA__   Period __Dinner – 23 March__

Steps:

A. Decide on the period to be covered.
B. Decide on which menu items or meals are to be evaluated. Enter in Column 1 below.
C. Get the number of orders for each item evaluated and enter in Column 2.
D. Put the sales price of the item in Column 3.
E. Put the food cost per cent to selling price of each item in Column 4.
F. Enter the *total* number of meals served during the period in Space 11.
G. Fill in the other columns or spaces.

(1) Menu Item	(2) Number Sold	(3) Selling Price	(4) Food Cost %	(5) Total Sales (2) × (3)	(6) Total Food Cost (4) × (5)
Sole Mariner	200	$ 4.75	30.0	$ 950.00	$ 285.00
Steak	150	7.50	40.0	1,125.00	450.00
Ribs	300	6.75	35.0	2,025.00	708.50
Chicken	300	5.50	30.0	1,650.00	495.00
Ham	200	5.75	30.0	1,150.00	345.00
	1150 Total (2)			$ 6,900.00 Total (6)	$ 2,283.50 Total (5)

(7) Meal Average Total (5) ÷ Total (2)	(8) Gross Profit Total (5) minus Total (6)	(9) Gross Profit Percentage (8) ÷ Total (5)
$ 6.00	$ 4616.50	66.9 %

(10) Gross Profit Average (7) × (9)	(11) Total Meals Served	(12) Percent of Customers Total (2) ÷ (11)
$ 4.014	1643	70.0 %

(13) Menu Score (10) × (12)	(14) Comments: Slow night on steaks and ribs; lots of family business and little expense account business.
$4.014 × 70.% = $2.81	

FIG. 5-11   An example of the kind of worksheet used by Professor Hurst.

A menu score by itself means little. It is an indicator of how prices, sales mix, gross profit and other factors affect it. It must be compared and analyzed with other possible situations. The higher the score, the more profitable the menu. Mr. Hurst has indicated that a difference as small as several tenths of a point is significant.

A low score could be the result of too low a meal (check) average. If so, management should take steps to correct the situation. The effect of increasing prices or offering other items can be quickly evaluated by running another score after the change is made. A food cost that is too high, giving a low gross profit, can also lower the menu score. Management can take steps to correct this by offering

other items, with a better gross profit, or pushing sales on items which have a higher gross profit. Increasing menu prices can also increase the gross profit. A poor sales mix, because of item popularity, can also lower the score and steps may have to be taken to improve the merchandising on some items, or change them to items which will be more popular. Perhaps pricing is wrong. There are many possibilities and management should carefully investigate all to understand how to improve the menu score. The following indicates how the sales of 700 rib of beef dinners, 100 shrimp dinners and 200 turkey dinners against 1,500 total customers would affect the menu score based on Mr. Hurst's example.

100 shrimp	$3.00	$ 300	$ 100
700 ribs of beef	$4.00	$2800	$1148
200 turkey	$3.00	$ 600	$ 240
1000 (E3c)		$3700 (E3a)	$1488 (E3b)

Meal Averages ($3,700/1,000) = $3.70 (E4)
Gross profit percentage ($3,700 — $1,488/$3,700) = 59.8% (E5)
Gross profit average ($3.70 × 59.8%) = $2.21 (E6)
Percentage of meals to total meals (1,000/1500) = 66 2/3% (E7)
Menu score ($2.21 × 66 2/3%) = 1.474

Thus, the change to a higher food cost item, with a lower gross profit, still can result in an improved score because of the higher price which gives a greater dollar gross profit contribution.

Menu scoring is an effective tool when management wishes to compare the performance of different units in a multiple operation. It must use the same menu and have other similar factors such as food cost, prices, etc. Figure 5-10 shows the Daily Dinner Menu Score Sheet used by the Schuler Restaurants. Figure 5-11 shows a worksheet that could be used for menu scoring.

The effect of higher selling prices and higher gross profit can be seen in the example shown in Figure 5-11. Thus, today instead of a good menu score being 1.40 as it might have been in 1960, one around 2.80 or so may be required to indicate a satisfactory relationship between customer selections, price and gross profit.* It should also be noted that the effect of a higher percentage of customer selections can alter the size of the menu score and, as one selects more items which give a greater percentage of the total number of customers served, the menu score will be higher. It is therefore important when comparing and evaluating menu scores that very parallel conditions exist between menus since the variation of the number of items selected, kinds of items, etc., can produce considerably different menu scoring results.

Menu Evaluation

Menus should be analyzed not only for their profitability and ability to generate revenue but also on how well they do their job in other ways, such as pleasing customers and helping to establish a background for the décor and atmosphere.

One of the problems with menu evaluation is that menus differ so greatly that what may be established as evaluation criteria for one does not necessarily work well for others. Thus, each operation should establish its own evaluation procedure. One can set up a large number of factors which a menu should include and then give each a value. The total score can indicate how well the menu meets the standards. Some operations use a total score of 85 to 100 as excellent, 84 to 70 good, 69 to 55 fair and below 55 poor. But a different scoring method can be used. If there are a large number of factors to be evaluated, perhaps a total score of 1000 should be established.

Some of the criteria established as factors for evaluating a menu might come from questions such as the following:

Do guests find on the menu items they want and like? Does it sell the patron? Does it have good color and design? Does it present items in the proper order? Can one find items easily? Does it have good variety? Does it have enough variety? Does it need other items? Are the listings and descriptions easily understood? Are the descriptions adequate and do they sell? Does the menu meet the needs of the market? Does it fit into the décor and atmosphere of the operation? Is the paper adequate? Does it list prices properly? Are the prices right for the market and items offered? Does it provide proper space for clip-ons and specials? Is the menu large enough to carry all the items but not too large for good handling? Does it attempt to call attention to the more profitable items by placement, type size, description? Does it list items in a form that makes for good, legible copy? Is it sufficiently simple to be understood? Do customers know what they are going to get when they order? Are groups of foods sold for one price prop-

---

*For instance, if out of 1,500 customers, 200 orders of lobster tails at $9 (food cost 40%), 600 orders of prime ribs of beef at $7.50 (food cost 35%) and 200 orders of turkey at $6 (food cost 30%) were sold, total sales would be $7500 and food cost $2655. The percent of customers eating the meals evaluated to total customers would be 66-2/3% and the gross profit per meal average would be $4.845 giving a menu score of 3.23.

erly and clearly presented? Does it adequately meet the needs of the operation? Is it sufficiently unusual? Does it list the telephone number of the operation, the hours and days of operation, the address, credit card policy and other desirable and necessary information?

Such criteria can be grouped into classifications such as format, pricing, merchandising, artwork and color, etc. Each group can then be given an overall score value and the items included in the group weighted so as to produce this total score for the classification. Some factors which are more important in making a good menu should be more heavily weighted than others. The important thing is to have the evaluation be meaningful to the operation, give information which will improve the next menu that is produced and indicate strengths and weaknesses in the operation.

PRICING

A PRICING CRITIQUE. Some authorities have criticized the foodservice industry's pricing methods, stating that they are archaic, fail to achieve desired goals and are frequently based on false premises and information. They state that pricing theory has moved a long way in the last few years but that foodservices do not seem to know it. Many foodservices, they point out, establish prices on food cost. They agree that cost should be considered in price establishment but that price should be based on *all* costs and not just food cost. Food cost may not reflect the cost of labor and other costs incurred. These authorities say, furthermore, that most foodservices don't know their food costs and hence prices based on what they use are not reliable. They point out that better cost information should be available so that prices can be more reliably established.

These authorities state further that foodservices should base their prices more on market demand and economic laws, and that often menu prices are established with only the slightest consideration for the type patron they serve, how much the patron has to spend for items and how much he wants to spend for them. Prices, they say, should be established only after an in-depth study is made of the market and the customer.

There are psychological values to consider in pricing. A high price may be desirable where expense account spending is prevalent because there can be prestige in bringing a client into an operation and "laying it on." A low price is frequently associated with low quality while a higher price indicates something better. Some customers are driven away by "cheap" prices.

Pricing experts agree that price should be equated to value and that the value should be largely the patron's and not what the menu planner, or someone else in the business, thinks it is. Value may be something quite different in a patron's mind from what the menu planner thinks it is. A moderately priced meal which supplies all the necessary nutrients may represent a terrific value to a dietitian but may represent just junk to a patron interest in satisfying egocentric needs and not nutritional ones.

Pricing, experts say, should be based on economic considerations and few individuals who price menus are aware of them, let alone know how to use them. Any price should cover costs but how much a price should be above cost depends upon a number of factors.

Under highly competitive conditions, prices to vie with competition may have to be too close to costs to keep a business healthy. Experts say the product, in such a case, should be improved to a point where it rises above that of competition. Then, a higher price can be charged. Such a product becomes, in the patron's mind, a *differentiated* product unlike the others offered by competition. It is now much more desirable because it is of better quality even though higher in price. The customer is willing to pay more for it because he thinks it is a better value and he cannot get a similar item from competition.

If an enterprise makes a better product which finds a market, it has better control over pricing and reduces the pressure of competition. Thus, in trying to meet competition in a drive-in hamburger market, it may be wiser to produce a *better* hamburger and charge more for it than to stay with competition and fight it out meeting competition's prices and quality. Not only has the operation risen above its competition but it also has saved itself from a very small margin in the selling price over cost because now it can increase this margin without as much restriction.

Most operators, experts say, like to have a big market—as big as possible. Under certain economic conditions this may not be desirable. It may be more profitable, if one has a differentiated product from others, to restrict the supply and charge more because there is more demand for it. Some economic laws support this.

Some operators may feel that lowering prices will develop a larger market giving them more profit. This may not be true. Demand may be what is called inelastic—it does not increase when prices are lowered and it does not become less when prices are raised. Thus, reducing prices reduces profit and does not stimulate a larger demand. Also, if demand is increased by lowering price, competition may come in and supply a part of this demand. Then, everybody shares in smaller prices because prices are lower but demand is no greater.

If an operation has a market which is not price conscious, it may find that lowering prices does not increase the number of patrons and that raising prices also does not stop them from coming. It may be better, under such conditions, to restrict the number of patrons and charge a fairly high price. Thus, an operation that limits reservations and can consistently fill this number of reservations can exploit an inelastic market to best advantage. It is desirable to put an enterprise in such a position but extremely difficult.

The relationship between cost and price must also be considered. If the profit margin is small, a reduction in price narrows this even more. It could be that, even though a much larger market is developed, less profit is made. Thus, if hamburgers are sold at 25¢ each with a 2½¢ profit, and the price is dropped to two for 45¢, the profit is not 1¼¢ per hamburger. To make the same profit twice as many hamburgers have to be sold. This may not be possible. The facility may not have the productive capacity to do it. It could also be there are not that many customers wanting that many hamburgers.

Dropping a price temporarily may be a good ploy to attract customers but continuing it may be disastrous. In establishing prices, it is important that their effect be evaluated before deciding to act. Indiscriminate cutting of price in the hope of increasing profits may end in heavy disappointment.

The effect of pricing on the sales-mix should also be examined. It is better to sell a steak dinner for $7 with a food cost of 40 per cent than a chicken dinner for $5 with a food cost of 30 per cent. The following illustrates why:

	Steak	Chicken
Selling price	$7.00	$5.00
Food cost	2.80 (40%)	1.50 (30%)
Gross profit	$4.20	$3.50

In the above case, $4.20 is available to pay for labor, fixed expenses, other variable expenses and profit as against $3.50. Usually these costs are the same for any menu item. Thus, the steak dinner leaves more to pay for these expenses and profit than the chicken dinner does. Even though the food cost of the chicken is lower, it does not end up doing the operation the most good. We can look at this in a different way. If $1,000 in sales at 30 per cent food cost are gen-

erated by a menu, $700 remains for other costs and profit. If $1,500 in sales at 40 per cent food cost are generated, $900 remains for the same thing. Which is better?

Good pricing should influence patron selections. Pricing should be accompanied by attempts to let patrons see value in menu card items. If this can be done, patrons may be better satisfied and the aims of management can also be promoted.

The effect of price manipulation on menu items must be discovered. Dropping a price on a low food cost item may do more harm than good because it draws customers away from items with a higher gross profit. For instance, if between two periods, Period I and Period II, the same number of customers patronized the place and the same food costs were in effect, the results, seen below could occur with a distinct loss in profit to the operation.

In both Periods I and II, the number of selections were the same but there was a shift of 2,000 selections from higher priced items in Period I to lower priced items in Period II because management dropped price. The food cost for both periods is about the same, being respec-

Menu Item	PERIOD I Menu Price	Selections	Food Cost	Total Gross Profit	Total Revenue	PERIOD II Menu Price	Selections	Food Cost	Total Gross Profit	Total Revenue
Roast Ribs of Beef	$8.50	8000	$4.00	$ 36,000	$ 68,000	$8.50	7000	$4.00	$ 30,000	$ 59,500
Duck à l'Orange	7.50	6000	3.50	24,000	45,000	7.50	5500	3.50	22,000	41,250
Broiled Lamb Chops	8.00	7000	4.00	28,000	56,000	8.00	6500	4.00	26,000	52,000
Crab Newburg	6.50	4000	2.50	16,000	26,000	6.00	5000	2.50	17,500	30,000
New Orleans Omelette	6.50	3000	2.00	13,500	19,500	6.00	4000	2.00	16,000	24,000
Total		28000		$117,500	$214,500		28000		$111,500	$206,750
Difference									—$6,000	—$7,750

tively 45.2 per cent and 45.3 per cent. This is not enough to cause the $6,000 difference in gross profit. The undesirable difference in both gross profit ($6,000) and in total revenue ($7,750) in Period II is caused by a shift to lower priced items that do not have as good a gross profit as the higher priced items.

It is important to remember in pricing that on the average every patron who passes through the doors represents a check, that it is necessary to get a maximum return on this check, and that the total must cover the cost of serving the patron plus a profit if the operation is profit oriented. This is not necessarily meant to get the largest dollar sale, but to get the largest gross profit from the check.

Those who price menus should study the techniques of others who price other merchandise in retail establishments. There may be little difference between a price of $3.00 and $2.95 but, psychologically, it may bulk large in the patron's mind. The supermarkets have learned a lot about pricing. They utilize psychological factors relating to prices. "Loss leaders" that draw patrons in and, in addition to the leaders, pick up other products that make a profit are often used. In the end the leaders plus the others give a satisfactory margin over costs. This must be done carefully but can be a tremendous motivating factor in creating sales. Thus, the price on the menu may not only represent profit and cost but a basic factor that draws sales and compels selections. It is very important that menu planners look behind the obvious factors and understand also hidden ones that may be the true, effective ones in bringing about

a price that satisfies the patron and makes a satisfactory contribution to the enterprise.

Price and Economic Theory

Supply and demand both influence price. If a large supply exists to meet demand, prices are lower. If supply is restricted, as could occur in a limited supply of beef, prices rise. Market prices move frequently with supply and demand.

When demand is large, prices rise because buyers compete for the supply. Conversely, if demand is light and there are few buyers, prices drop.

If both supply and demand move together in the same way, the counter-effect of each balances and prices do not change much. Thus, if there is a large demand for turkeys but the supply also increases, prices tend to stay steady. If demand drops but supply does also, fewer buyers compete for a decreasing supply and prices again tend to remain steady.

Figures 5-12 and 5-13 indicate how these economic laws work. Figure 5-12a indicates that as supply increases prices tend to drop; Figure 5-12b shows that as demand increases prices tend to rise. And thus, in 12a as supply decreases the line moves from right to left and prices rise; in 12b as demand moves in a similar direction prices drop. Figure 5-13 shows three differing conditions, an inelastic condition, I, an elastic condition, E, and a condition where both inelasticity and elasticity exist, F. In an inelastic situation it is difficult to make a change. A change in price, supply or demand would not tend to make much change. In an elastic situation, the oppo-

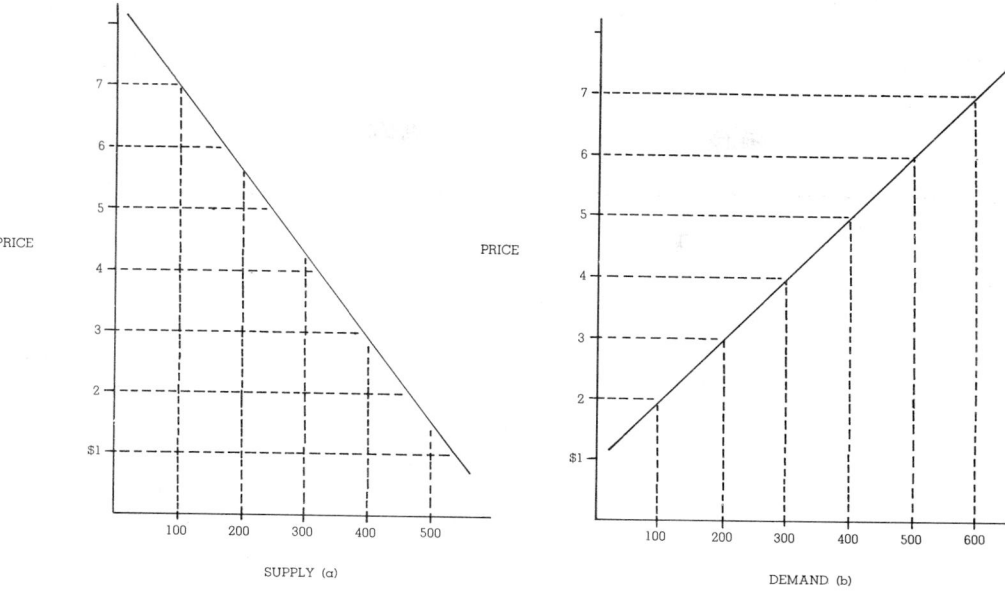

FIG. 5-12   The basic laws of supply and demand are shown at work here. In the **SUPPLY** case, (a), when only 100 units are available a price of $7 occurs; when 200 are on the market, the price drops to around $6. Thus, as supply increases price drops. Demand may also. In the **DEMAND** case, (b), when demand is for 100 units a price of $2 exists, but when demand rises the price also rises. [Note: In (a) demand is considered fixed while supply varies; in (b) supply is considered fixed as demand varies.]

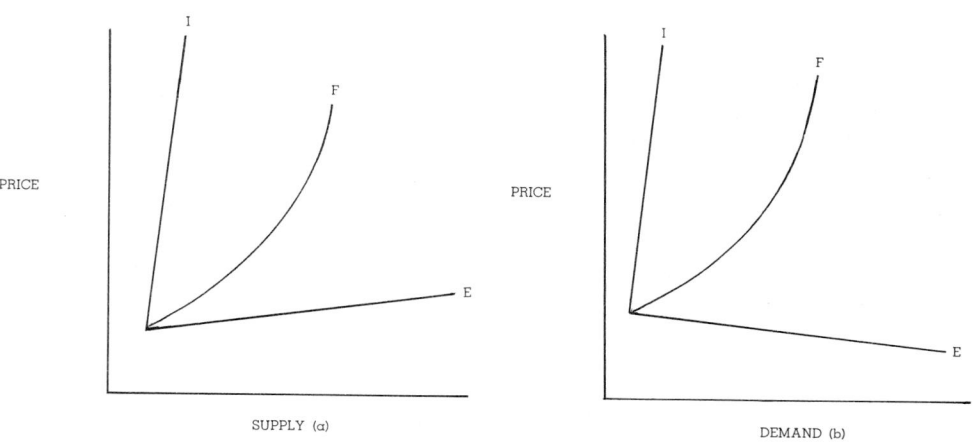

FIG. 5-13   The effects of an elastic or inelastic supply or demand are shown. In (a), line I shows an inelastic supply where a rise in price does little to increase supply, and a drop in price does little to reduce it. Line E shows considerable elasticity, a small change in price causing a significant change in supply. In (b), Line I shows an inelastic demand with neither a high nor a low price causing much change. Line E reflects an opposite condition with a small change in price causing a considerable elasticity in demand. Line F in either (a) or (b) shows some elasticity but after a certain point is reached, inelasticity sets in.

site is true. In lines F an elastic situation exists and then suddenly an inelastic situation sets in. This means that customers might respond to price changes up to a point and then cease reacting this way as prices increased above a certain point.

For economic laws to work freely, no restriction in either supply or demand can occur. Competition must be able to function freely and supply a greater demand if one occurs. In a monopoly, supply can be restricted and prices will probably rise without fear that competition will move in and drop them. In a monopoly, only that part of the market that wishes to pay the higher prices need be supplied.

A differentiated product mentioned previously—a product that no one else produces—creates somewhat of a monopolistic condition and the producer has more control of his market. Therefore, he can raise the price and restrict the supply to support it.

The amount of influence price has on supply or demand or the amount of influence supply or demand has on price is important in pricing. If price has a considerable effect on supply, a small raise in price increases supply considerably, while a small drop may cause a big drop in supply. This is shown in line E in Figure 5-13. If price has little effect on supply, the price can be increased or decreased without making a material change in supply, as shown by line I in Figure 5-13.

If price has a considerable effect on demand, demand can drop off sharply when the price is increased. It will drop off quickly when the price is raised as seen in line E in Figure 5-13. How-ever, if price has a small effect on demand, a rise in price may not cause much of a drop in demand. (See line I in Figure 5-13).

When price has a considerable effect on either demand or supply, or when demand or supply have a considerable effect on price, we say that the situation is elastic. [See lines E in Figures 5-13 (a and b).] In elastic situations, price manipulations can have a considerable effect on either supply or demand, and supply or demand may also considerably influence price.

When there is little effect on price in increasing or reducing either supply or demand, or by manipulating price on supply or demand, we say the situation is inelastic. [See lines I in Figures 5-13 (a and b).] Inelastic situations allow an opportunity to see if pricing cannot be manipulated to create a more favorable pricing structure.*

Anyone who seeks to manipulate prices or supply or demand should carefully check all possibilities that could arise in such manipulations and also understand what is being done and the results to be expected. Where there is an elastic demand, putting a price a bit higher can only drive off considerable business, while putting price only slightly lower can considerably increase the demand. If price has little effect on demand, we can put prices up without disturbing demand much. Almost the same amount of demand is present as will be seen in

---

*This discussion on economic laws is extremely simplified and very basic. One seeking to understand the ramifications and further complexities in economic theory should consult some of the references listed in the bibliography.

line I of Figure 5-13. Such an inelastic demand might be represented by a customer who, regardless of price, will patronize a particular place. However, if demand is highly sensitive to price, then prices must be kept low if demand is to be stimulated and held.

Competition must be considered in pricing. Raising prices may invite competition in. If demand is elastic, an operator knows he can get a bigger market by dropping prices. He may do this only to find that competition enters the market to satisfy the extra demand created by the lowered price. He is now at a disadvantage because he is now operating with about the same demand as before but at a lower price. Such a situation has previously been demonstrated. If there is no competition, one might be able to restrict supply and force a price increase without fear that competition will enter the market and bring prices down.

Traditional Menu Price Testing

Experience is one of the best testers of menu prices. Most menus are priced out and then tried out to see if they meet customer approval and also make a profit. While this is a rather accurate way of testing, it is dangerous and, perhaps, this is one of the reasons why so many food-services start up and fail soon after.

PRICING METHODS

A variety of pricing methods is used in the industry. Some of the most common are:

1. Direct food cost and/or direct labor cost
2. What the market will bear
3. Competition
4. One average selling price plus a desired profit
5. All costs plus profit
6. Minimum sale per patron to give adequate profit and cover costs
7. Tradition

Direct Cost Pricing

One of the most common methods of pricing is to base selling price on food cost. This is the usual formula: Selling

$$\text{Price (SP)} = \frac{\text{Cost of Food}}{\% \text{ Food Cost Desired}}. \text{ For}$$

instance, if management wants a 30 per

cent food cost and an item has a food cost of 70¢, the selling price will be $2.35

$$\left(\text{SP} = \frac{70¢}{.30} = \$2.33\right). \text{ Or if it wants a}$$

25 per cent food cost, the selling price is $2.80

$$\left(\text{SP} = \frac{70¢}{.25} = \$2.80\right).$$

Some operations may wish to use a factor to get the selling price in dollars rather than a per cent. Such a factor is derived from the per cent food cost desired. For instance, if an operation wants a 25 per cent food cost, it can divide 25 per cent into 100 per cent to obtain a factor of four and use this to multiply the cost of the food to arrive at a selling price. Thus, 100 per cent/25 per cent = 4 and 4 × 70¢ food cost = $2.80. Or, if it wants a 33-1/3 per cent food cost, it divides 100 per cent by 33-1/3 per cent to get a factor of 3 and multiplies the cost of the food by this ($3 \times 70\textcent =$ $2.10). A 2.7 factor indicates a desired food cost of 37 per cent (100 per cent/ 2.7 = 37 per cent).

Few operations base selling prices on labor cost but some do combine food and labor. The method is the same as used to calculate selling price from food cost. Food and labor cost are totalled and a desired combined food and labor cost percentage is established and the selling price calculated. For instance, if the combined food and labor cost is $1.20 and management wants a combined food and labor cost percentage of 60 per cent, the selling price is $2.00 (SP $= \dfrac{\$1.20}{.60} = \$2.00$). A factor can also be established for doing this the same way as was done for calculating selling prices on food cost. For instance, if management wants a 60 per cent combined food and labor cost, 60 per cent is divided into 100 per cent to get a factor of 1.67. Now, with a combined food and labor cost of $1.20, the factor is used as follows: $1.67 \times \$1.20 = \$2.00$.

One of the problems in using labor cost is that few operations know what it is. They know they have an average labor cost based on sales and this could be used. However, this is only an estimate and does not necessarily reflect the true amount of labor used on a specific menu item. Usually, the task of making a time study to find out how much labor is used to produce a specific product is time consuming and costly. If the total time used to produce a number of items is recorded by workers as they work, the number of items divided into the total time will give the time required per unit. This figure based on

the wage cost, can then be added to the food cost to get a combined food and labor cost. For instance, if a cook in two hours makes 25 chicken pot pies and is paid $4.00 an hour, the labor cost is $8.00 for all of the pies, and the cost per pie is 32\textcent. If each pie has a food cost of 40\textcent, the combined food and labor cost would be 72\textcent. If the desired combined food and labor cost is 60 per cent, then the selling price for a chicken pie on the à la carte menu would be $1.20 (SP $= \dfrac{72\textcent}{.60} = \$1.20$).

Experience has shown that the actual food and labor costs are usually above those calculated, and it is wise to add a safety factor to compensate for this. Many use a factor of 10 per cent to cover missed labor costs, frying fat, dredging flour, seasonings, etc.

Basing a selling price on food or labor cost is not considered good practice. This is because the food and/or labor cost is thought to reflect other costs. They may not. If an item has a food cost of 30\textcent and if management wishes a 30 per cent food cost, the selling price is a dollar. This assumes that the other costs are less than 70\textcent so that a profit is made. However, the assumption may not be true. Labor could be 40\textcent and other costs 35\textcent so that the item is being sold for less than cost.

What the Market Will Bear

A method of pricing used by some companies is to design a product and then test market it at a given selling price. The product may be put on several markets at different prices and the reaction of customers studied to ascertain what is the best price.

Marketing specialists state that one of the best routes to success is to develop a product the market wants and then to price it so that a profit is made. With proper pricing and a good demand, these specialists say there is a high chance of developing a successful market. They recommend that a study be made to ascertain what the value of the product is in the minds of patrons and to charge accordingly. Some items may have to bear only a small markup above cost to be accepted by the market while others can have a much higher margin.

Establishing a selling price based on what the market will bear is not just a trial and error method, but should be based on some rather good information. To some extent, prices can be tested to see how well patrons accept them but not too much experimentation can be done. Perhaps several prices can be tested on an item and then the testing must be stopped, for otherwise, patrons might reject the item because of the instability of the price.

Pricing according to what the market will bear is much more commonly done today than in the past and has become a commonly followed method by a number of industries. It is a perfectly legitimate system. If a customer attaches a certain value to a product and is willing to pay that much for it, there is no reason why it should not be marketed at that price. Patrons are not interested in what it costs to produce and market an item. They are much more interested in getting something which represents a good value for their money. If the price is within the value, the patron is happy. If he feels that a meal priced at $4 is worth this even though its cost is only $2.50, there is nothing wrong in charging $4 for it. However, if a meal costs $4 to produce, and the patron considers it worth only $2.50, he will not buy it even if it represents a bargain from the standpoint of cost.

Success in pricing according to what the market will bear is enhanced if some attempt is made to show customers the "value" of the menu item. It is often difficult for patrons to see the value in atmosphere, service, fine tableware and linens, and in foods that are somewhat out of season or brought in at additional cost. If a way is found to get patrons to understand that these increase costs and have value, they may be willing to pay the price.

A differentiated product is something that stands out above others on the market. When a customer thinks of purchasing a specific item, his mind immediately thinks of the specialized item rather than competitive ones. Foodservice should attempt to achieve such differentiation in the customers' minds. This can be done by featuring specialty products on the menu. Some find that if a menu card has from one to a dozen distinct and different items, customers associate the menu and the enterprise as one that is differentiated. It is entirely possible to establish in the patron's mind the same kind of feeling with just one product. An establishment may serve a martini cocktail in a glass that it keeps in dry ice. The glass is so cold that when the drink is served in it, it clouds and frosts. There is an operation called Delmonicos in Mexico City that does just exactly this and has an international reputation for serving "the finest dry martini in the world."

Food is also not the only thing that can differentiate an operation. A location, a smiling host at the door greeting people by name, bunny girls, excellent service, etc., all can. Grandma Young, the mother of Paul Young who operates a famous restaurant in Washington, D. C., gave that establishment differentiation. One was the cheesecake which she baked herself for the guests. The other was herself as she circulated among the famous guests while they ate, checking to see that they were happy with the food and service. Today a picture of Grandma Young hangs in a prominent place in the restaurant to remind patrons that, even though she is gone, her quality standards still remain.

Competition Pricing

One of the most common pricing methods is to base the price on what competition charges. While it is wise to pay attention to competition's pricing, it is unwise to base prices completely on it. What the competition charges may bear no relation to *your* costs. Pricing in this manner assumes that the competition's prices are also satisfactory for your customers. Copying competition's prices does little to differentiate an operation.

If competitive pricing is indicated, a unit should study its own costs to analyze how it can shade prices to produce a more favorable response than the prices charged by competition. A competitor's price may be studied to reveal information about his food, labor and other costs. Food and labor are standard commodities which have a known price. A close scrutiny of these may indicate what competition might be doing to achieve a favorable price structure. While the thesis that the selling price should be based on costs or what the market will bear is a tenable one, a study of competitive pricing and its effect against what it might be doing to one's own business is also warranted and prices may have to reflect the influence of competition.

Average Cost Plus Profit

If a menu has a relatively homogeneous group of items which have production costs that are much alike, such as one might find in a doughnut shop, an individual doughnut is not priced but one price is charged for any dozen of doughnuts. In doing this, management has an overall cost which it wishes to cover and hopes for a sales mix of the various products under this one price to cover these plus produce a profit. Since the ingredients for each type food sold are rather alike as is the labor, using such a pricing method is warranted. If these were quite different, one price might not be possible.

This method of pricing can also be used where the food is only a part of the service rendered. Thus, a night club or night show which offers entertainment and other things in addition to food and drink may have just one price which will cover costs and yield a profit. Also, some table d'hôte operations may find that just one price for a dinner regardless of what is selected is satisfactory.

All Costs Plus Profit

The most approved method of pricing is to calculate all costs and then add the desired profit. Recently many operations have been trying to ascertain their total costs and then price on this basis. This is time consuming and difficult. It may also take detailed studies on the amount of labor consumed in producing individual items plus other costs. The difficulty in obtaining accurate labor costs has been previously mentioned. The more labor and other costs are averaged or estimated in calculating total costs, the less accurate the calculation may be. Basing a pricing structure on an inaccurate estimate can be dangerous.

As we move more toward prepared foods which eliminate labor and as we move into central food production, we may be able to obtain more accurate costs upon which to base prices. The adoption of better cost accounting procedures can also assist in giving more accurate cost information.

The calculation of selling price based on cost plus profit is not difficult. If an operation wishes a 10 per cent profit, the costs are totaled and this is considered 90 per cent of the selling price. Thus, by dividing .9 into these costs, a selling price is obtained. For instance, if an item costs $2.70, the selling price would be $2.70 ÷ .9 = $3.00. This leaves 30¢ or 10 per cent of the selling price for profit.

An operation may also decide that it needs a standard profit from every patron who enters. The rationale behind this is that every customer who comes through the door costs so much to serve and it does not matter what is ordered, for the cost is still there. Also, the operation may reason that it wants a set amount of profit from every patron. Therefore, total costs may be calculated and then a set amount added to this. For instance, an operation may find it

has an average of 400 patrons a day and it wants to make $100 profit a day. If it adds 25¢ to the cost of every item sold, this can be achieved. It should be recognized that this can be done only when a rather standard type item is sold and the basic cost is sufficient to bear a 25¢ charge. To have a cost of 18¢ for coffee and doughnuts and then add on 25¢ for profit might discourage customers.

Minimum Sale Pricing

Pricing on the basis of a minimum price to cover costs and give a desired profit in a commercial operation is much the same as calculating the price based on costs plus profit previously discussed. The rationale for this method is also much the same. Every customer costs a certain amount to serve and by having a minimum charge these costs will be covered. A hospital or convalescent home may use such a method as well as night clubs, Las Vegas shows and others. A club may have a minimum for certain rooms where food and beverage service is provided. Such a policy is also not uncommon in some commercial dining rooms. Pricing may be "arranged" on a menu card also to make it impossible to obtain service below a certain price. For instance, the Four Seasons Restaurant in New York City may not want to see a price of less than $8.50 for lunch. They will test out various luncheon combinations such as a soup or small salad, omelette, beverage and dessert. If this produces the desired result it will be priced accordingly.

Some operations may state on the menu card that there is a check minimum. If a customer does not order enough food to meet this minimum, the least that can be paid is the minimum. As noted previously, clubs may require that members spend a specific amount during a period on food and beverage so that the foodservice department receives enough income to operate. If the member does not spend this amount during the period, the balance is added to his bill.

Traditional Pricing

Some prices are considered traditional and almost have to be used on the menu card for an item. One has little freedom under such circumstances. For years, foodservices charged 5¢ for a cup of coffee and, even when it was obvious that the operation was losing money at this price, the price was continued. Finally, the dam broke and the industry quickly converted to the 10¢ cup of coffee which is now begining to be difficult to find. If an operation has a tight control on its market and pricing structure, it is possible to vary a traditional price and not meet customer criticism. In fact, such a variation may be desirable to differentiate the operation from others. It may give the operation some distinction in flaunting tradition and varying the price.

Many operations look upon a traditional price as perhaps a leader and something that brings in other business that is more profitable.

Tradition in pricing may relate not only to a specific price but also to the pricing structure. Many operations find that they cannot get as high a markup for California wines as they can for European ones although the California product may be of equal or better quality. Tradition has it that the domestic product is usually lower in price and therefore the pricing structure must be varied to suit this tradition. Different types of operations will also find that the pricing structure they must follow is one in which a lower markup must be taken than another type of foodservice. Thus, while two operations may sell exactly the same thing—a glass of milk, for instance—one will be able to price on a different basis from the other.

Some operations may find that they have prices established for such a long time that they become traditional with their customers and when they attempt to change prices meet with very strong sales resistance and customer dissatisfaction. Thus, they may decide not to change the price on a particular item but get a higher markup on other items which are not so restricted.

It is possible for a price to become traditional because a leader in the market charges this price. Thus, McDonalds' prices often become a traditional price among drive-ins because of competition and because McDonalds, as the leader, can establish a price which may become traditional.

PRICING METHODS SUMMARY

Few operations use one method of pricing. Most use a combination to best meet their needs and the needs of the patron. Certainly pricing against competition only is not a good method, but considering the prices of competition, when establishing one's own, is advisable. Using a standard markup over an accurate cost determination gives a fairly good and precise price basis and one that usually assures an adequate profit or budget performance, but vary-

Table 5-1

Markup Factors for Pricing

Food Cost %	Factor	Food Cost %	Factor	Food Cost %	Factor
20	5.00	30	3.33	40	2.50
21	4.76	31	3.23	41	2.43
22	4.55	32	3.13	42	2.38
23	4.35	33	3.00	43	2.32
24	4.17	34	2.94	44	2.27
25	4.00	35	2.85	45	2.22
26	3.85	36	2.78	46	2.17
27	3.70	37	2.70	47	2.12
28	3.57	38	2.63	48	2.08
29	3.45	39	2.56	49	2.04
				50	2.00

NOTE: Decide what percentage food cost you wish and them multiply actual food cost by the desired percentage factor to arrive at desired selling cost. Example: If an item has a food cost of 25¢ and you want a food cost of 28%, look up the factor opposite 28 (3.57) and multiply this times 25¢ (25¢ × 3.57 = 89.3¢). The selling price would probably be 90¢.

ing margins over cost based on what the market will bear should also be considered as should volume and pricing based on it. Markups perhaps should be varied to promote merchandising and leaders certainly which have a low markup but bring in business may be advisable. Thus, a drive-in may not make as much on its hamburgers and hot dogs as it does on milk shakes, carbonated beverages and fries, but in the end the sales mix achieved gives a very desirable markup level.

And, finally, pricing is not something which is done and then is over. There is a need to evaluate prices constantly, to study how customers react to prices and to gather data on costs, etc. Just because a price has been established is no reason why it cannot be refined and improved. Too many times no followup or continuing study occurs and, when a revision of menus and prices is neces-

sary for a new menu, there is a lack of adequate information for an improved job. The gathering, compiling, collating and filling of data to be used in pricing are as much a part of the pricing function as the establishment of the final price itself.

Pricing in Non-Profit Institutions

While the previous discussions on pricing may have been oriented more to pricing of menus for commercial operations, from time to time the application of particular methods discussed has indicated that non-profit institutions can price their menus in the same way.

Many non-profit institutions do not need to include in a price an allowance for profit. They are required to meet costs and perhaps make a slight margin above this as a safety factor which can be accumulated to bridge times when costs are not covered.

Where an institution must price to cover costs alone, accurate cost information must be available from operating records. The information must be timely so that action can be taken promptly to bring costs into line when they vary from desired levels. Many institutions estimate costs for a period and are given an allowance to cover this estimate. Usually the amount to be expended and the amount of income to be used can be shown in a budget. When costs for a future period must be estimated, information from federal agencies, economic indexes, price predictions, etc. can be used. While many operations are non-union, what is done in union operations on wages and salaries may affect the pay scales of the non-union unit. If it is known that negotiations for a pay raise and benefits are to be entered into by the unions and foodservices in the area, some estimate of the probable increase in labor cost should be worked into the budget. In many instances, pricing in a non-profit institution may be as difficult or even more so than pricing for a profit-motivated operation.

Changing Menu Prices

At times a change in a menu card price is necessary. If it is an item appearing frequently on the menu and has good acceptance, this may present difficulties. Customers may resent the change and may no longer order the item to show their displeasure. Sometimes this does not last too long and the item gradually assumes its former importance as a seller.

In periods in which prices increase rapidly, most customers recognize the need to increase prices and will accept them. In periods when prices are stable but some other factor makes a change necessary, customers may not be so willing to accept a change.

Some operators attempt to change a price by removing an item from the menu for a time and then bringing it back at a new price. If it also comes back in a somewhat new form, or in a new manner of serving and a slightly different menu name, the price change is noticed less.

Prices are frequently changed when a new menu card is printed. In fact, the need to change menu card prices may sometimes stimulate a menu change more than the need to change items. Clip-ons for menu prices, to be put into blank spaces where prices normally appear, are becoming more and more popular. This obviates the need to have a number of new menu cards printed just to incorporate new prices, and avoids having to cross out old prices and put in new ones.

In some instances, if a general rise in menu prices must occur, an operation may change several items five or 10 cents each and then let these remain at this price while changing few others. In this manner prices are gradually worked up to the desired level. This has its disadvantages, however, since customers get the feeling of instability in the menu and its prices.

Some announcement, by using a clip-on or table tent, can be helpful in indicating to patrons why a change in menu prices is necessary. This can also have the undesirable effect of calling to the attention of patrons that a price change has occurred which some customers may never notice otherwise.

Portion Pricing

To be able to price portions adequately, it is first necessary to calculate their cost. This may be simple or difficult to do. If a product is purchased which can be portioned without any loss, such as cake, calculating the cost is not difficult. One calculates the number of portions obtained and divides this into the total cost. For instance, if a cake costs $1.76 and cuts into 16 portions, the cost is 11¢ per portion ($1.76 ÷ 16 = 11¢). Sometimes, if the item is purchased by the pound and is portioned we may have to ascertain the cost per ounce and then multiply this times the ounce size of the portion. Thus, if cottage cheese is purchased at 40¢ a pound and a portion is three ounces, the cost per ounce is 40¢ divided by 16 ounces or 2½¢ per ounce, and this times three ounces equals 7½¢ per portion.

Similarly, volume portion costs are not difficult to calculate. If tomato juice is purchased in 46 oz cans for 50¢ a can and the portion is four ounces, the cost per ounce is 1.087¢ (50¢ ÷ 46 oz = 1.087¢), which gives a portion cost of 4.35¢ (4 × 1.087¢). Portioning on the basis of count is also simple. If there are three apples per pound and the cost is 21¢ per pound, an apple is 7¢.

Portion costs from recipes are not too difficult to calculate. The total cost of the recipe's ingredients must be calculated and this is divided by the total number of portions obtained. Thus, if a cheese dish with crab sauce costs a total of $12, and 40 portions are obtained, the cost is 30¢ per portion ($12 ÷ 40 = 30¢).

When it is necessary to calculate portion costs of items which lose weight in preparation and/or cooking, the calculation is more difficult. Frequently, in food work we use the symbols AP to indicate "as purchased", EP to indicate "edible portion" and AS to indicate "as served". Sometimes an item can be served AP with no loss, such as prepared grapefruit sections. At other times items must be prepared to an EP state and then portioned, such as grapefruit sections from fresh grapefruit. Or the item purchased AP must be prepared and then cooked to an AS state which gives two losses, one in getting it to the EP state and the second in getting it from an EP to an AS state.

FORMULAS

There are some formulas which are helpful in calculating portion costs in these circumstances. These are:

AP to EP portion cost:

Step 1

$$\text{Cost AP per lb} \times \frac{\text{Wt AP}}{\text{Wt EP}} = \text{Cost EP per lb.}$$

Step 2

Cost EP per lb ÷ 16 oz = Cost EP per oz.

Step 3

Cost EP per oz × Portion size in oz = Cost per EP.

AP to AS portion cost:

Step 1

$$\text{Cost AP per lb} \times \frac{\text{Wt AP}}{\text{Wt AS}} = \text{Cost AS per lb.}$$

Step 2

Cost AS per lb ÷ 16 oz = Cost AS per oz.

Step 3

Cost AS per oz × Portion in oz = Cost per portion AS.

AP to EP to AS portion cost:

Step 1

$$\text{Cost AP per lb} \times \frac{\text{Wt AP}}{\text{Wt EP}} = \text{Cost EP per lb.}$$

Step 2

Cost EP per lb $\times \dfrac{\text{Wt EP}}{\text{Wt AS}} =$ Cost AS per lb.

Step 3
Cost AS per lb $\div$ 16 oz $=$ Cost AS per oz.

Step 4
Cost AS per oz $\times$ Portion in oz $=$ Cost per portion AS.

EXAMPLES

An example of each could be:

AP to EP portion cost:

Fresh tomatoes are purchased at 40¢ per lb. They lose 2 oz in preparing for sliced tomatoes*. Two ounces is the portion. The weight EP from a pound AP is 14 oz.

STEP 1

$40¢ \times \dfrac{16 \text{ oz}}{14 \text{ oz}} = 40¢ \times 1.143 = 45.72¢$ per lb EP.
(16/14 $=$ 1.143).

STEP 2
45.72¢ $\div$ 16 oz $=$ 2.8575¢ per oz EP.

STEP 3
2.9575¢ $\times$ 2 oz portion $=$ 5.715¢ portion cost of tomatoes; in addition, the cost of the lettuce leaf, shredded lettuce and dressing would have to be added if served as a salad.

AP to AS portion cost:

Sole is purchased at 80¢ per pound; 36 lb AP end up as 20 lb AS poached. The portion is four ounces.

STEP 1

$80¢ \times \dfrac{36 \text{ lb}}{20 \text{ lb}} = 80¢ \times 1.8 = \$1.44$ per lb AS.
(36/20 $=$ 1.8)

STEP 2
$1.44 $\div$ 16 oz $=$ 9¢ per oz AS.

STEP 3
9¢ $\times$ 4 oz portion $=$ 36¢ per portion AS.

*Standard preparation losses have been detailed in publications of the USDA, Washington, D. C. *Quantity Food Purchasing* (Kotschevar) published by John Wiley & Sons, New York, 2nd edition, 1975, also indicates what a number of these losses are.

AP to EP to AS portion cost:

A 12 lb trimmed pork loin is purchased at 88¢ a lb. After removing the chine bone, shoulder blade and excess fat, 9 lb is left for roasting—the bone and fat are not considered to have a value. After roasting and slicing only 7 lb are left. The portion is 3 oz.

STEP 1

$88¢ \times \dfrac{12 \text{ lb}}{9 \text{ lb}} = 88¢ \times 1.333 = \$1.173$ per lb EP
(ready for roasting). (12/9 $=$ 1.333).

STEP 2
$\$1.173 \times \dfrac{9 \text{ lb}}{7 \text{ lb}} = \$1.173 \times 1.2857 = \$1.5081$ per lb AS. (9/7 $=$ 1.2857).

STEP 3
$1.5081 $\div$ 16 oz $=$ 9.42¢ per oz AS.

STEP 4
9.42¢ $\times$ 3 oz portion $=$ 28.3¢ per portion AS.

OTHER FORMULAS

At times it may be desirable to calculate a portion cost of AP, EP or AS items based not on the actual weight loss but on the percentage of loss. Thus, if an item costs 80¢ a pound, what is the serving cost per pound, if in preparation it loses 25 per cent of its weight? The formula for making the calculation is:

Cost per lb AP $\times \dfrac{100\%}{\% \text{ of AP wt remaining}} =$ Cost per lb AS which in this example would be $80¢ \times \dfrac{100\%}{75\%} = \$1.067$ serving cost per pound.

The formulas used to calculate AP costs to other EP or AS costs are slightly different when percentage losses are used from those previously used to calculate the cost when employing actual weights. These are formulas based on percentage losses using the same examples as previously:

AP to EP portion cost:

Step 1

$$\text{Cost AP per lb} \times \frac{100\%}{\% \text{ EP wt is of AP wt}} = \text{Cost per lb EP.}$$

Step 2

$$\text{Cost per lb EP} \div 16 \text{ oz} = \text{Cost per oz EP.}$$

Step 3

$$\text{Cost per oz EP} \times \text{oz portion size} = \text{Cost per portion EP.}$$

AP to AS portion cost:

Step 1

$$\text{Cost AP per lb} \times \frac{100\%}{\% \text{ AS wt is of AP wt}} = \text{Cost per lb AS.}$$

Step 2

$$\text{Cost AS per lb} \div 16 \text{ oz} = \text{Cost per AS oz.}$$

Step 3

$$\text{Cost per AS oz} \times \text{oz portion size} = \text{Cost per portion AS.}$$

AP to EP to AS portion cost:

Step 1

$$\text{Cost AP per lb} \times \frac{100\%}{\% \text{ EP wt is of AP wt}} = \text{Cost per lb EP.}$$

Step 2

$$\text{Cost EP per lb} \times \frac{100\%}{\% \text{ AS wt is of EP wt}} = \text{Cost per lb AS.}$$

Step 3

$$\text{Cost per lb AS} \div 16 \text{ oz} = \text{Cost per oz AS.}$$

Step 4

$$\text{Cost per oz AS} \times \text{portion size in oz} = \text{Cost per portion AS.}$$

If we use the examples previously used of tomatoes, sole and pork, examples of this translation using percentages would be:

Tomatoes:

$$40\cancel{c} \times \frac{100\%}{87\frac{1}{2}\%} = 40\cancel{c} \times 1.143 = 45.726\cancel{c}$$

per lb EP. $(100/87\frac{1}{2} = 1.143)$.

$45.726\cancel{c} \div 16 \text{ oz} = 2.856\cancel{c}$ per oz EP.

$2.856\cancel{c} \times 2 \text{ oz} = 5.712\cancel{c}$ per portion EP.

Sole:

$$80\cancel{c} \times \frac{100\%}{55\frac{1}{2}\%} = 80\cancel{c} \times 1.8 = \$1.44 \text{ per}$$

lb AS. $(100/55\frac{1}{2} = 1.8)$.

$\$1.44 \div 16 \text{ oz} = 9\cancel{c}$ per oz AS.

$9\cancel{c} \times 4 \text{ oz portion} = 36\cancel{c}$ per portion AS.

Pork:

$$88\cancel{c} \times \frac{100\%}{75\%} = 88\cancel{c} \times 1.333 = \$1.173$$

per lb EP. $(100/75 = 1.333)$.

$$\$1.173 \times \frac{100\%}{77.7\%} = \$1.173 \times 1.286 =$$

$\$1.51$ per lb AS. $(100/77.7 = 1.286)$.

$\$1.51 \div 16 \text{ oz} = 9.43\cancel{c}$ per oz AS.

$9.43\cancel{c} \times 3 \text{ oz} = 28.29\cancel{c}$ per portion AS.

The NCR System

The National Cash Register Company* has devised a system that quickly indicates the allowed food cost over and above the cost of an entrée to give a desired selling price at a desired food cost percentage. The entrée cost should be accurately determined and the cost of other items to be served with the entrée, such as the vegetable, salad, roll and butter, beverage and miscellaneous things such as condiments, etc. This NCR system uses charts from which the desired information can be obtained.

(Table 5-5 at the end of this chapter presents extracts from these NCR charts, for food costs of 35%, 40% and 45%.)

---

*The National Cash Register Company, Marketing Services Department, Dayton, Ohio, 45409, "Restaurant Menu Pricing Charts."

To obtain the permitted cost of additional items (NCR calls these "trimmings"), the cost of the entrée is located on the chart of the desired food cost percentage. The row to the right of this entrée cost is then followed until the desired selling price is obtained. Reading up the column from this desired selling price one finds the maximum amount to spend for the additional food items. Thus, if an entrée costs 36¢, and a 40 per cent food cost and a $1.75 selling price are desired, we will find referring to Table 5-5, the 40 per cent food cost chart, the cost of the entrée on the far left column at .36. We next follow to the right on this row to $1.75 and then up this column to the top where .34 is indicated as the maximum amount that can be spent for trimmings.

These NCR charts also can be used to determine a selling price based on a desired food cost percentage. The entrée price must be known as must the cost of the additional items. The selling price is determined by finding the entrée cost in the proper cost column and the cost of the additional items in the cost of trimmings row. At the juncture of the entrée cost column and the trimmings row the selling price is found. For instance, if an operation wished to maintain a 35 per cent food cost and the cost of the entrée was $1.50 and the cost of trimmings 60¢, the juncture of the column and row on the 35 per cent food cost chart, Table 5-5, indicates the selling price is $6.00.

If one knows the cost of the additional items served with the entrée but not the cost of the entrée itself, and wants a desired selling price at a desired food cost, he can also quickly determine the maximum cost of the entrée. For instance, if the cost of trimmings is 36¢ the food cost is 45 per cent and a selling price of $3.75 is desired, the entrée cost can be obtained by consulting the 45% table (See Table 5-5). One finds the 36¢ trimming cost and reads down the column until $3.75 is reached. He then moves left along this row to the entrée cost column. Here he sees that the entrée should not cost more than $1.32 to give the desired results.

If a chart is desired based on a different food cost other than those prepared by NCR, it can be easily made up. For instance, if a 30% chart is desired starting with an entrée cost of 40¢ and going up in 5¢ steps and starting with a trimming cost of 6¢ and going up in steps of 2¢, the following would be some of the calculations made:

Entrée Cost	+	Trimming Cost	=	Total Food Cost	÷ .30 =	Desired Selling Price
.40		.06		.46		1.53
.40		.08		.48		1.60
.40		.10		.50		1.67
.40		.12		.52		1.73
				etc.		
.45		.06		.51		1.70
.45		.08		.53		1.77
.45		.10		.55		1.83
.45		.12		.57		1.90
				etc.		

The calculations would be continued until all desired possibilities had been explored. They could then be set into a table as follows:

30% FOOD COST CHART

| Cost of Entrée | Cost of Trimmings | | | | |
	.06	.08	.10	.12	etc.
.40	1.53	1.60	1.67	1.73	etc.
.45	1.70	1.77	1.83	1.90	etc.
etc.					

Once a portion cost is ascertained, management has a basis for pricing the item. The pricing methods discussed in this chapter can be used. It might be that after knowing cost, management decides to price the item more on what the market will bear and either puts a lower or higher price than if cost, plus a standard markup, were used. It might also consider competition, tradition, etc. rather than cost in setting the price.

PORTION CONTROL

Management is responsible for establishing the size portion for the menu item and seeing that this portion is served. There are many standard sizes for different foods. For instance, a standard portion of vegetables is usually three ounces or about a half cup. An oven baked potato, or a portion of mashed potatoes, is usually considered to be five ounces. A standard portion of gravy is considered to be two ounces. Meat portions may vary according to the type operation and the meat. Normally, menu planners calculate three portions to the pound AP of a roast that has some bone in it. This gives about three 3-oz portions. If dressing is served with the meat, the meat portion may be only two ounces with two or three ounces of dressing. Ground meat items usually give four portions to the pound AP and an AS weight usually of about three ounces per portion.

A table of standard size portions is usually found in many of the standard recipe books used by foodservices*.

*Quantity Food Production, 3d edition, by Kotschevar, published by Cahners Books. 89 Franklin Street, Boston, Mass., 02110, has a large number of tables indicating portions and yields.

Foodservices should also compile their own lists and see that employees follow them. Portion sizes can be indicated on the production schedules, recipe or service charts.

There are many ways to achieve the right size portion. Items can be dished into small paper cups or dishes. A portion scale can be used. This is set at the portion weight desired and food is added until the scale pointer indicates the correct amount is obtained. Such a scale is often used in portioning meats, cheese and other items for sandwiches, cold plates, etc. It can also be used for hot sliced meat, etc. A portion scale should be in the meat preparation area so that items cut there can be weighed to see if the portions are correct.

Portioning tools such as scoops or ladles can also be used to control portion size. The size of the scoop indicates how many portions the scoop gives per quart when it is level full. Thus, a No. 12 scoop (2 2/3 oz) will give 12 scoops from a quart, if level full, but in fast work in dishing, employees seldom take the time to see that the scoop is level full. For this reason, it is better to use a smaller scoop, let it be rounded and obtain a faster dishup. Actually, if rounded just slightly the portion in a No. 12 scoop is about three ounces. A lightly rounded dishup spoon (basting spoon) gives also about a three ounce portion. It is good to use for dishing vegetables. Ladle sizes are usually numbered by the ounces they contain when level full. There are also standard measures which can be used. Normally, we work with volume, not weight measure, in portioning. Table 5-4 indicates the quantities that some common measures hold.

Table 5-2: Costs per Portion

Cost/lb	Cost per Portion					Cost/lb	Cost per Portion				
	1 oz.	1.5 oz.	2 oz.	2.5 oz.	3 oz.		1 oz.	1.5 oz.	2 oz.	2.5 oz.	3 oz.
.20	$.0125	$.0187	$.0250	$.0312	$.0375	.85	.0531	.0796	.1062	.1327	.1593
.21	.0131	.0196	.0262	.0328	.0394	.86	.0538	.0806	.1076	.1344	.1614
.22	.0137	.0205	.0275	.0344	.0413	.87	.0544	.0816	.1088	.1359	.1632
.23	.0143	.0214	.0287	.0359	.0431	.88	.055	.0826	.110	.1374	.1650
.24	.0150	.0225	.0300	.0375	.0450	.89	.0556	.0834	.1113	.1389	.1668
.25	.0156	.0234	.0313	.0390	.0469	.90	.0562	.0842	.1124	.1404	.1686
.26	.0162	.0243	.0325	.0406	.0483	.91	.0571	.0856	.1142	.1427	.1713
.27	.0168	.0252	.0337	.0422	.0506	.92	.058	.087	.116	.145	.174
.28	.0175	.0262	.0350	.0437	.0525	.93	.0583	.0874	.1166	.1457	.1749
.29	.0181	.0271	.0362	.0453	.0548	.94	.0586	.0878	.1172	.1464	.1758
.30	.0187	.0280	.0375	.0469	.0563	.95	.0593	.0889	.1186	.1482	.1779
.31	.0193	.0289	.0387	.0484	.0581	.96	.06	.09	.12	.15	.18
.32	.0200	.0300	.0400	.0500	.0600	.97	.061	.0915	.122	.1525	.183
.33	.0206	.0309	.0412	.0515	.0619	.98	.062	.093	.124	.155	.186
.34	.0212	.0318	.0425	.0531	.0638	.99	.0622	.0933	.1244	.1555	.1866
.35	.0218	.0327	.0437	.0547	.0656	1.00	.0624	.0936	.1248	.156	.1872
.36	.0225	.0337	.0450	.0562	.0675	1.01	.0631	.0946	.1262	.1577	.1893
.37	.0231	.0346	.0462	.0577	.0694	1.02	.0638	.0956	.1276	.1594	.1914
.38	.0237	.0355	.0475	.0594	.0713	1.03	.0644	.0965	.1288	.1609	.1932
.39	.0243	.0364	.0487	.0609	.0731	1.04	.0650	.0974	.130	.1624	.1950
.40	.0250	.0375	.0500	.0625	.0750	1.05	.0656	.0983	.1312	.1639	.1968
.41	.0255	.0382	.0512	.0640	.0769	1.06	.0662	.0992	.1324	.1654	.1986
.42	.0262	.0393	.0525	.0656	.0788	1.07	.0668	.1001	.1336	.1669	.2004
.43	.0268	.0402	.0537	.0672	.0806	1.08	.0674	.1010	.1348	.1684	.2022
.44	.0275	.0412	.0550	.0687	.0825	1.09	.0681	.1021	.1362	.1702	.2043
.45	.0281	.0421	.0562	.0703	.0844	1.10	.0688	.1032	.1376	.172	.2064
.46	.0287	.0430	.0575	.0718	.0863	1.11	.0694	.1041	.1388	.1735	.2082
.47	.0293	.0439	.0587	.0734	.0881	1.12	07	.1050	.14	.1750	.210
.48	.0300	.0450	.0600	.0750	.0900	1.13	.0706	.1059	.1412	.1765	.2118
.49	.0306	.0459	.0612	.0765	.0919	1.14	.0712	.1068	.1424	.178	.2136
.50	.0312	.0468	.0625	.0781	.0938	1.15	.0718	.1077	.1436	.1795	.2154
.51	.0318	.0477	.0637	.0797	.0956	1.16	.0724	.1086	.1448	.1810	.2172
.52	.0325	.0487	.0650	.0812	.0975	1.17	.0729	.1096	.1462	.1827	.2193
.53	.0331	.0495	.0662	.0828	.0994	1.18	.0738	.1106	.1476	.1844	.2214
.54	.0337	.0505	.0675	.0844	.1013	1.19	.0744	.1115	.1488	.1859	.2232
.55	.0343	.0514	.0687	.0859	.1031	1.20	0750	.1124	.15	.1874	.2250
.56	.0350	.0525	.0700	.0875	.1050	1.21	.0756	.1133	.1512	.1889	.2268
.57	.0355	.0532	.0712	.0890	.1069	1.22	.0762	.1142	.1524	.1904	.2286
.58	.0362	.0543	.0725	.0906	.1088	1.23	.0768	.1151	.1536	.1919	.2304
.59	.0368	.0552	.0737	.0922	.1106	1.24	.0774	.116	.1548	.1934	.2322
.60	.0375	.0562	.0750	.0937	.1125	1.25	.0781	.1171	.1562	.1952	.2343
.61	.0381	.0571	.0762	.0953	.1144	1.26	.0788	.1182	.1576	.1970	.2364
.62	.0387	.0580	.0775	.0968	.1163	1.27	.0794	.1191	.1588	.1985	.2382
.63	.0393	.0589	.0787	.0984	.1181	1.28	.08	.12	.16	.20	.24
.64	.0400	.0600	.0800	.1000	.1200	1.29	.081	.1215	.162	.2125	.243
.65	.0405	.0608	.0812	.1015	.1219	1.30	.082	.1230	.164	.2050	.246
.66	.0412	.0618	.0825	.1031	.1238	1.31	.0822	.1233	.1644	.2055	.2466
.67	.0418	.0627	.0837	.1046	.1256	1.32	.0824	.1236	.1648	.206	.2472
.68	.0425	.0637	.0850	.1062	.1275	1.33	.0831	.1246	.1662	.2077	.2493
.69	.0431	.0646	.0862	.1078	.1294	1.34	.0838	.1256	.1676	.2094	.2514
.70	.0437	.0655	.0874	.1092	.1311	1.35	.0844	.1265	.1688	.2109	.2532
.71	.0444	.0666	.0888	.1109	.1335	1.36	.085	.1274	.170	.2124	.2550
.72	.0450	.0674	.09	.1124	.1350	1.37	.0856	.1283	.1712	.2139	.2568
.73	.0456	.0683	.0912	.1139	.1368	1.38	.0862	.1292	.1724	.2154	.2586
.74	.0462	.0692	.0924	.1154	.1386	1.39	.0868	.1301	.1736	.2169	.2604
.75	.0468	.0701	.0936	.1169	.1404	1.40	.0874	.1310	.1748	.2184	.2622
.76	.0474	.0710	.0948	.1184	.1422	1.41	.0881	.1321	.1762	.2202	.2643
.77	.0481	.0721	.0962	.1202	.1443	1.42	.0887	.133	.1774	.2217	.2661
.78	.0488	.0732	.0976	.122	.1464	1.43	.893	.1339	.1786	.2232	.2679
.79	.0494	.0741	.0988	.1235	.1482	1.44	.09	.135	.18	.225	.27
.80	.05	.075	.10	.125	.15	1.45	.0906	.1359	.1812	.2265	.2718
.81	.051	.0765	.102	.1275	.153	1.46	.0912	.1368	.1824	.2280	.2736
.82	.052	.078	.104	.13	.156	1.47	.0919	.1378	.1838	.2297	.2757
.83	.0522	.0783	.1044	.1305	.1566	1.48	.0925	.1387	.1850	.2312	.2775
.84	.0524	.0786	.1048	.1310	.1572	1.49	.0931	.1396	.1862	.2327	.2793
						1.50	.0937	.1405	.1874	.2342	.2811

Table 5-3

Number of Portions Available from Standard Containers

HOT AND COLD FOOD VESSELS

Portion size →	2½ oz.	3 oz.	3½ oz.	4 oz.	5 oz.	6 oz.	7 oz.	8 oz.	10 oz.	12 oz.
			NUMBER	OF	PORTIONS					
No. 2 Can	7	6	5	5	4	3	2	2	2	1
No. 2½ Can	10	9	8	6	5	4	4	3	3	2
One Quart	13	11	9	8	6	5	5	4	3	3
5 Lb. Tin (80 ounces)	32	27	23	20	16	13	11	10	8	7
7 Lb. Tin (No. 10 Can)	45	37	32	28	22	19	16	14	11	9
1 Gallon	51	43	37	32	26	21	18	16	13	11
10 Lb. Can	64	53	46	40	32	27	23	20	16	13

SOUFFLE CUPS, CREAMERS, ETC.

Portion size →	¾ oz.	1 oz.	1½ oz.	2 oz.	3 oz.	3¾ oz.	5 oz.	5½ oz.
		NUMBER	OF	PORTIONS				
No. 2 Can	24	18	12	9	6	5	4	3
No. 2½ Can	34	26	17	13	9	7	5	5
One Quart	43	32	21	16	11	9	6	5
5 Lb. Tin (80 ounces)	106	80	53	40	27	21	16	15
7 Lb. Tin (No. 10 Can)	148	112	75	56	37	30	22	20
1 Gallon	171	128	85	64	43	34	26	22
10 Lb. Can	212	160	107	80	53	43	32	29

PORTION CUPS

Cup number	050	075	100	125	200	250	325	400	550
Cup size →	½ oz.	¾ oz.	1 oz.	1¼ oz.	2 oz.	2½ oz.	3¼ oz.	4 oz.	5½ oz.
			NUMBER	OF	PORTIONS				
No. 2 Can	36	24	18	14	9	7	5	5	3
No. 2½ Can	52	34	26	20	13	10	8	6	5
One Quart	64	43	32	26	16	13	10	8	6
5 Lb. Tin (80 ounces)	160	106	80	64	40	32	24	20	15 L
7 Lb. Tin (No. 10 Can)	224	148	112	90	56	45	34	28	20
1 Gallon	256	171	128	102	64	51	39	32	22
10 Lb. Can	320	212	160	128	80	64	50	40	29

(Adapted from NRA data)

Table 5-4
Capacity of Measures

Measure	Abbre-viation	Quantity in Liquid Volume
Teaspoon	t	1/6 oz or 1/3 T
Tablespoon	T	1/2 oz; 16 T = c
Cup	c	8 oz; 2 c = pt
Pint	pt	1 lb; 2 pt = qt
Quart	qt	2 lb, 4 c, 2 pt
Ounce	oz	2 T
Gallon	gal	8 lb, 128 oz, 4 qt, 8 pt, 16 c

NOTE: 5-1/3 T = 1/3 c; 4 T = 1/4 c; a pinch equals about 1/16 t and a dash less than 1/8 t.

Individuals who work in food production should be trained to watch portioning and see that the right number of portions are prepared. Some operations have stainless steel measuring rods which, when inserted into a steam-jacketed kettle, indicate the number of gallons in the kettle. Thus, if an operation plans to have 400 portions of soup, each portion to be eight ounces, the rod should show at a certain mark that there are 25 gallons of soup in the kettle. Since evaporation can occur in cooking, this measure should be made just before service. Some operations install mechanical measuring devices which measure and shut off automatically.

Pan weights should also be carefully worked out for proper portions of specific items. Suppose chicken meat pie is to be dished into 12 × 20 inch steam table pans, topped with biscuits and baked. Each portion is to be six ounces, topped with a small biscuit; 32 portions are to come from each pan. Then, the panning instructions should indicate that 1½ gallons of pie mixture (six quart ladles full) are to be put into the pan, topped with 32 biscuits in four columns and eight rows.

Some pannings instructions in recipes may be stated in weights. If this is so, then it is wise to stamp metal pans with their weight so that one knows the net weight of the pan when filled. Sometimes an average weight is taken for a type of pan and used as a tare weight. Thus, a 17 × 25 inch roasting pan may be stamped "4½" indicating it weighs 4½ lb. If 20 pounds of hash are to be baked in such a pan giving 40 8-oz portions, the pan after filling should weigh 24½ pounds.

Insofar as possible, foods should be marked to indicate portions. Thus, if food in a 12 × 20 inch pan is to be cut into four column, six row portions, markings should be put on the food before or after baking. For instance, a meat pie crust could be marked lightly before baking to indicate cutting into 4 × 6. There are many markers available for use in cutting pies and cakes.

Hidden factors can disrupt portioning. Thus, while a No. 12 scoop gives 12 scoops per quart of solid material such as pudding, it will not give this in ice cream or sherbet because these pack in the scooping. Instead of 12 scoops per quart one is more apt to get seven.

Items can lose weight and volume in cooking or baking. One may think there are three gallons of sauce in a kettle, because that was the original volume, but it might be only 2½ gallons because of the evaporation loss. There is usually a 4 to 16% baking loss in baking bread, cakes, etc. Thus, if a baker expects to have a loaf of bread weighing 16 ounces, he must pan one weighing 18 ounces.

Meat can shrink considerably in cooking. Normally a 25 per cent shrink is moderate but many meats shrink 35 per cent or more in cooking.

Even after an item is cooked, there is no assurance that the entire cooked weight will end up as portions. Meat, in being sliced, frequently loses as much as 5 per cent of its weight in shreds and non-usable pieces, juice, etc. Other items can lose weight similarly or lose volume in being portioned. Experience can be helpful in indicating some hidden factors occurring in portioning.

**Table 5-5
NCR Food Cost Charts
(next 12 pages)**

35% FOOD COST CHART

COST OF TRIMMINGS

COST OF ENTREE	.06	.08	.10	.12	.14	.16	.18	.20	.22	.24	.26	.28	.30	.32	.34	.36	.38	.40	.42	.44	.46	.48	.50	.52	.54	.56	.58	.60	.62
.10	.46	.51	.57	.63	.69	.74	.80	.86	.91	.97	1.03	1.09	1.14	1.20	1.26	1.31	1.37	1.43	1.49	1.54	1.60	1.66	1.71	1.77	1.83	1.89	1.94	2.00	2.06
.12	.51	.57	.63	.69	.74	.80	.86	.91	.97	1.03	1.09	1.14	1.20	1.26	1.31	1.37	1.43	1.49	1.54	1.60	1.66	1.71	1.77	1.83	1.89	1.94	2.00	2.06	2.11
.14	.57	.63	.69	.74	.80	.86	.91	.97	1.03	1.09	1.14	1.20	1.26	1.31	1.37	1.43	1.49	1.54	1.60	1.66	1.71	1.77	1.83	1.89	1.94	2.00	2.06	2.11	2.17
.16	.63	.69	.74	.80	.86	.91	.97	1.03	1.09	1.14	1.20	1.26	1.31	1.37	1.43	1.49	1.54	1.60	1.66	1.71	1.77	1.83	1.89	1.94	2.00	2.06	2.11	2.17	2.23
.18	.69	.74	.80	.86	.91	.97	1.03	1.09	1.14	1.20	1.26	1.31	1.37	1.43	1.49	1.54	1.60	1.66	1.71	1.77	1.83	1.89	1.94	2.00	2.06	2.11	2.17	2.23	2.29
.20	.74	.80	.86	.91	.97	1.03	1.09	1.14	1.20	1.26	1.31	1.37	1.43	1.49	1.54	1.60	1.66	1.71	1.77	1.83	1.89	1.94	2.00	2.06	2.11	2.17	2.23	2.29	2.34
.22	.80	.86	.91	.97	1.03	1.09	1.14	1.20	1.26	1.31	1.37	1.43	1.49	1.54	1.60	1.66	1.71	1.77	1.83	1.89	1.94	2.00	2.06	2.11	2.17	2.23	2.29	2.34	2.40
.24	.86	.91	.97	1.03	1.09	1.14	1.20	1.26	1.31	1.37	1.43	1.49	1.54	1.60	1.66	1.71	1.77	1.83	1.89	1.94	2.00	2.06	2.11	2.17	2.23	2.29	2.34	2.40	2.46
.26	.91	.97	1.03	1.09	1.14	1.20	1.26	1.31	1.37	1.43	1.49	1.54	1.60	1.66	1.71	1.77	1.83	1.89	1.94	2.00	2.06	2.11	2.17	2.23	2.29	2.34	2.40	2.46	2.51
.28	.97	1.03	1.09	1.14	1.20	1.26	1.31	1.37	1.43	1.49	1.54	1.60	1.66	1.71	1.77	1.83	1.89	1.94	2.00	2.06	2.11	2.17	2.23	2.29	2.34	2.40	2.46	2.51	2.57
.30	1.03	1.09	1.14	1.20	1.26	1.31	1.37	1.43	1.49	1.54	1.60	1.66	1.71	1.77	1.83	1.89	1.94	2.00	2.06	2.11	2.17	2.23	2.29	2.34	2.40	2.46	2.51	2.57	2.63
.32	1.09	1.14	1.20	1.26	1.31	1.37	1.43	1.49	1.54	1.60	1.66	1.71	1.77	1.83	1.89	1.94	2.00	2.06	2.11	2.17	2.23	2.29	2.34	2.40	2.46	2.51	2.57	2.63	2.69
.34	1.14	1.20	1.26	1.31	1.37	1.43	1.49	1.54	1.60	1.66	1.71	1.77	1.83	1.89	1.94	2.00	2.06	2.11	2.17	2.23	2.29	2.34	2.40	2.46	2.51	2.57	2.63	2.69	2.74
.36	1.20	1.26	1.31	1.37	1.43	1.49	1.54	1.60	1.66	1.71	1.77	1.83	1.89	1.94	2.00	2.06	2.11	2.17	2.23	2.29	2.34	2.40	2.46	2.51	2.57	2.63	2.69	2.74	2.80
.38	1.26	1.31	1.37	1.43	1.49	1.54	1.60	1.66	1.71	1.77	1.83	1.89	1.94	2.00	2.06	2.11	2.17	2.23	2.29	2.34	2.40	2.46	2.51	2.57	2.63	2.69	2.74	2.80	2.86
.40	1.31	1.37	1.43	1.49	1.54	1.60	1.66	1.71	1.77	1.83	1.89	1.94	2.00	2.06	2.11	2.17	2.23	2.29	2.34	2.40	2.46	2.51	2.57	2.63	2.69	2.74	2.80	2.86	2.91
.42	1.37	1.43	1.49	1.54	1.60	1.66	1.71	1.77	1.83	1.89	1.94	2.00	2.06	2.11	2.17	2.23	2.29	2.34	2.40	2.46	2.51	2.57	2.63	2.69	2.74	2.80	2.86	2.91	2.97
.44	1.43	1.49	1.54	1.60	1.66	1.71	1.77	1.83	1.89	1.94	2.00	2.06	2.11	2.17	2.23	2.29	2.34	2.40	2.46	2.51	2.57	2.63	2.69	2.74	2.80	2.86	2.91	2.97	3.03
.46	1.49	1.54	1.60	1.66	1.71	1.77	1.83	1.89	1.94	2.00	2.06	2.11	2.17	2.23	2.29	2.34	2.40	2.46	2.51	2.57	2.63	2.69	2.74	2.80	2.86	2.91	2.97	3.03	3.09
.48	1.54	1.60	1.66	1.71	1.77	1.83	1.89	1.94	2.00	2.06	2.11	2.17	2.23	2.29	2.34	2.40	2.46	2.51	2.57	2.63	2.69	2.74	2.80	2.86	2.91	2.97	3.03	3.09	3.14
.50	1.60	1.66	1.71	1.77	1.83	1.89	1.94	2.00	2.06	2.11	2.17	2.23	2.29	2.34	2.40	2.46	2.51	2.57	2.63	2.69	2.74	2.80	2.86	2.91	2.97	3.03	3.09	3.14	3.20
.52	1.66	1.71	1.77	1.83	1.89	1.94	2.00	2.06	2.11	2.17	2.23	2.29	2.34	2.40	2.46	2.51	2.57	2.63	2.69	2.74	2.80	2.86	2.91	2.97	3.03	3.09	3.14	3.20	3.26
.54	1.71	1.77	1.83	1.89	1.94	2.00	2.06	2.11	2.17	2.23	2.29	2.34	2.40	2.46	2.51	2.57	2.63	2.69	2.74	2.80	2.86	2.91	2.97	3.03	3.09	3.14	3.20	3.26	3.31
.56	1.77	1.83	1.89	1.94	2.00	2.06	2.11	2.17	2.23	2.29	2.34	2.40	2.46	2.51	2.57	2.63	2.69	2.74	2.80	2.86	2.91	2.97	3.03	3.09	3.14	3.20	3.26	3.31	3.37
.58	1.83	1.89	1.94	2.00	2.06	2.11	2.17	2.23	2.29	2.34	2.40	2.46	2.51	2.57	2.63	2.69	2.74	2.80	2.86	2.91	2.97	3.03	3.09	3.14	3.20	3.26	3.31	3.37	3.43
.60	1.89	1.94	2.00	2.06	2.11	2.17	2.23	2.29	2.34	2.40	2.46	2.51	2.57	2.63	2.69	2.74	2.80	2.86	2.91	2.97	3.03	3.09	3.14	3.20	3.26	3.31	3.37	3.43	3.49
.62	1.94	2.00	2.06	2.11	2.17	2.23	2.29	2.34	2.40	2.46	2.51	2.57	2.63	2.69	2.74	2.80	2.86	2.91	2.97	3.03	3.09	3.14	3.20	3.26	3.31	3.37	3.43	3.49	3.54
.64	2.00	2.06	2.11	2.17	2.23	2.29	2.34	2.40	2.46	2.51	2.57	2.63	2.69	2.74	2.80	2.86	2.91	2.97	3.03	3.09	3.14	3.20	3.26	3.31	3.37	3.43	3.49	3.54	3.60
.66	2.06	2.11	2.17	2.23	2.29	2.34	2.40	2.46	2.51	2.57	2.63	2.69	2.74	2.80	2.86	2.91	2.97	3.03	3.09	3.14	3.20	3.26	3.31	3.37	3.43	3.49	3.54	3.60	3.66
.68	2.11	2.17	2.23	2.29	2.34	2.40	2.46	2.51	2.57	2.63	2.69	2.74	2.80	2.86	2.91	2.97	3.03	3.09	3.14	3.20	3.26	3.31	3.37	3.43	3.49	3.54	3.60	3.66	3.71
.70	2.17	2.23	2.29	2.34	2.40	2.46	2.51	2.57	2.63	2.69	2.74	2.80	2.86	2.91	2.97	3.03	3.09	3.14	3.20	3.26	3.31	3.37	3.43	3.49	3.54	3.60	3.66	3.71	3.77
.72	2.23	2.29	2.34	2.40	2.46	2.51	2.57	2.63	2.69	2.74	2.80	2.86	2.91	2.97	3.03	3.09	3.14	3.20	3.26	3.31	3.37	3.43	3.49	3.54	3.60	3.66	3.71	3.77	3.83
.74	2.29	2.34	2.40	2.46	2.51	2.57	2.63	2.69	2.74	2.80	2.86	2.91	2.97	3.03	3.09	3.14	3.20	3.26	3.31	3.37	3.43	3.49	3.54	3.60	3.66	3.71	3.77	3.83	3.89
.76	2.34	2.40	2.46	2.51	2.57	2.63	2.69	2.74	2.80	2.86	2.91	2.97	3.03	3.09	3.14	3.20	3.26	3.31	3.37	3.43	3.49	3.54	3.60	3.66	3.71	3.77	3.83	3.89	3.94
.78	2.40	2.46	2.51	2.57	2.63	2.69	2.74	2.80	2.86	2.91	2.97	3.03	3.09	3.14	3.20	3.26	3.31	3.37	3.43	3.49	3.54	3.60	3.66	3.71	3.77	3.83	3.89	3.94	4.00
.80	2.46	2.51	2.57	2.63	2.69	2.74	2.80	2.86	2.91	2.97	3.03	3.09	3.14	3.20	3.26	3.31	3.37	3.43	3.49	3.54	3.60	3.66	3.71	3.77	3.83	3.89	3.94	4.00	4.06
.82	2.51	2.57	2.63	2.69	2.74	2.80	2.86	2.91	2.97	3.03	3.09	3.14	3.20	3.26	3.31	3.37	3.43	3.49	3.54	3.60	3.66	3.71	3.77	3.83	3.89	3.94	4.00	4.06	4.11

35% FOOD COST CHART

COST OF TRIMMINGS

COST OF ENTREE	.06	.08	.10	.12	.14	.16	.18	.20	.22	.24	.26	.28	.30	.32	.34	.36	.38	.40	.42	.44	.46	.48	.50	.52	.54	.56	.58	.60	.62
.84	2.57	2.63	2.69	2.74	2.80	2.86	2.91	2.97	3.03	3.09	3.14	3.20	3.26	3.31	3.37	3.43	3.49	3.54	3.60	3.66	3.71	3.77	3.83	3.89	3.94	4.00	4.06	4.11	4.17
.86	2.63	2.69	2.74	2.80	2.86	2.91	2.97	3.03	3.09	3.14	3.20	3.26	3.31	3.37	3.43	3.49	3.54	3.60	3.66	3.71	3.77	3.83	3.89	3.94	4.00	4.06	4.11	4.17	4.23
.88	2.69	2.74	2.80	2.86	2.91	2.97	3.03	3.09	3.14	3.20	3.26	3.31	3.37	3.43	3.49	3.54	3.60	3.66	3.71	3.77	3.83	3.89	3.94	4.00	4.06	4.11	4.17	4.23	4.29
.90	2.74	2.80	2.86	2.91	2.97	3.03	3.09	3.14	3.20	3.26	3.31	3.37	3.43	3.49	3.54	3.60	3.66	3.71	3.77	3.83	3.89	3.94	4.00	4.06	4.11	4.17	4.23	4.29	4.34
.92	2.80	2.86	2.91	2.97	3.03	3.09	3.14	3.20	3.26	3.31	3.37	3.43	3.49	3.54	3.60	3.66	3.71	3.77	3.83	3.89	3.94	4.00	4.06	4.11	4.17	4.23	4.29	4.34	4.40
.94	2.86	2.91	2.97	3.03	3.09	3.14	3.20	3.26	3.31	3.37	3.43	3.49	3.54	3.60	3.66	3.71	3.77	3.83	3.89	3.94	4.00	4.06	4.11	4.17	4.23	4.29	4.34	4.40	4.46
.96	2.91	2.97	3.03	3.09	3.14	3.20	3.26	3.31	3.37	3.43	3.49	3.54	3.60	3.66	3.71	3.77	3.83	3.89	3.94	4.00	4.06	4.11	4.17	4.23	4.29	4.34	4.40	4.46	4.51
.98	2.97	3.03	3.09	3.14	3.20	3.26	3.31	3.37	3.43	3.49	3.54	3.60	3.66	3.71	3.77	3.83	3.89	3.94	4.00	4.06	4.11	4.17	4.23	4.29	4.34	4.40	4.46	4.51	4.57
1.00	3.03	3.09	3.14	3.20	3.26	3.31	3.37	3.43	3.49	3.54	3.60	3.66	3.71	3.77	3.83	3.89	3.94	4.00	4.06	4.11	4.17	4.23	4.29	4.34	4.40	4.46	4.51	4.57	4.63
1.02	3.09	3.14	3.20	3.26	3.31	3.37	3.43	3.49	3.54	3.60	3.66	3.71	3.77	3.83	3.89	3.94	4.00	4.06	4.11	4.17	4.23	4.29	4.34	4.40	4.46	4.51	4.57	4.63	4.69
1.04	3.14	3.20	3.26	3.31	3.37	3.43	3.49	3.54	3.60	3.66	3.71	3.77	3.83	3.89	3.94	4.00	4.06	4.11	4.17	4.23	4.29	4.34	4.40	4.46	4.51	4.57	4.63	4.69	4.74
1.06	3.20	3.26	3.31	3.37	3.43	3.49	3.54	3.60	3.66	3.71	3.77	3.83	3.89	3.94	4.00	4.06	4.11	4.17	4.23	4.29	4.34	4.40	4.46	4.51	4.57	4.63	4.69	4.74	4.80
1.08	3.26	3.31	3.37	3.43	3.49	3.54	3.60	3.66	3.71	3.77	3.83	3.89	3.94	4.00	4.06	4.11	4.17	4.23	4.29	4.34	4.40	4.46	4.51	4.57	4.63	4.69	4.74	4.80	4.86
1.10	3.31	3.37	3.43	3.49	3.54	3.60	3.66	3.71	3.77	3.83	3.89	3.94	4.00	4.06	4.11	4.17	4.23	4.29	4.34	4.40	4.46	4.51	4.57	4.63	4.69	4.74	4.80	4.86	4.91
1.12	3.37	3.43	3.49	3.54	3.60	3.66	3.71	3.77	3.83	3.89	3.94	4.00	4.06	4.11	4.17	4.23	4.29	4.34	4.40	4.46	4.51	4.57	4.63	4.69	4.74	4.80	4.86	4.91	4.97
1.14	3.43	3.49	3.54	3.60	3.66	3.71	3.77	3.83	3.89	3.94	4.00	4.06	4.11	4.17	4.23	4.29	4.34	4.40	4.46	4.51	4.57	4.63	4.69	4.74	4.80	4.86	4.91	4.97	5.03
1.16	3.49	3.54	3.60	3.66	3.71	3.77	3.83	3.89	3.94	4.00	4.06	4.11	4.17	4.23	4.29	4.34	4.40	4.46	4.51	4.57	4.63	4.69	4.74	4.80	4.86	4.91	4.97	5.03	5.09
1.18	3.54	3.60	3.66	3.71	3.77	3.83	3.89	3.94	4.00	4.06	4.11	4.17	4.23	4.29	4.34	4.40	4.46	4.51	4.57	4.63	4.69	4.74	4.80	4.86	4.91	4.97	5.03	5.09	5.14
1.20	3.60	3.66	3.71	3.77	3.83	3.89	3.94	4.00	4.06	4.11	4.17	4.23	4.29	4.34	4.40	4.46	4.51	4.57	4.63	4.69	4.74	4.80	4.86	4.91	4.97	5.03	5.09	5.14	5.20
1.22	3.66	3.71	3.77	3.83	3.89	3.94	4.00	4.06	4.11	4.17	4.23	4.29	4.34	4.40	4.46	4.51	4.57	4.63	4.69	4.74	4.80	4.86	4.91	4.97	5.03	5.09	5.14	5.20	5.26
1.24	3.71	3.77	3.83	3.89	3.94	4.00	4.06	4.11	4.17	4.23	4.29	4.34	4.40	4.46	4.51	4.57	4.63	4.69	4.74	4.80	4.86	4.91	4.97	5.03	5.09	5.14	5.20	5.26	5.31
1.26	3.77	3.83	3.89	3.94	4.00	4.06	4.11	4.17	4.23	4.29	4.34	4.40	4.46	4.51	4.57	4.63	4.69	4.74	4.80	4.86	4.91	4.97	5.03	5.09	5.14	5.20	5.26	5.31	5.37
1.28	3.83	3.89	3.94	4.00	4.06	4.11	4.17	4.23	4.29	4.34	4.40	4.46	4.51	4.57	4.63	4.69	4.74	4.80	4.86	4.91	4.97	5.03	5.09	5.14	5.20	5.26	5.31	5.37	5.43
1.30	3.89	3.94	4.00	4.06	4.11	4.17	4.23	4.29	4.34	4.40	4.46	4.51	4.57	4.63	4.69	4.74	4.80	4.86	4.91	4.97	5.03	5.09	5.14	5.20	5.26	5.31	5.37	5.43	5.49
1.32	3.94	4.00	4.06	4.11	4.17	4.23	4.29	4.34	4.40	4.46	4.51	4.57	4.63	4.69	4.74	4.80	4.86	4.91	4.97	5.03	5.09	5.14	5.20	5.26	5.31	5.37	5.43	5.49	5.54
1.34	4.00	4.06	4.11	4.17	4.23	4.29	4.34	4.40	4.46	4.51	4.57	4.63	4.69	4.74	4.80	4.86	4.91	4.97	5.03	5.09	5.14	5.20	5.26	5.31	5.37	5.43	5.49	5.54	5.60
1.36	4.06	4.11	4.17	4.23	4.29	4.34	4.40	4.46	4.51	4.57	4.63	4.69	4.74	4.80	4.86	4.91	4.97	5.03	5.09	5.14	5.20	5.26	5.31	5.37	5.43	5.49	5.54	5.60	5.66
1.38	4.11	4.17	4.23	4.29	4.34	4.40	4.46	4.51	4.57	4.63	4.69	4.74	4.80	4.86	4.91	4.97	5.03	5.09	5.14	5.20	5.26	5.31	5.37	5.43	5.49	5.54	5.60	5.66	5.71
1.40	4.17	4.23	4.29	4.34	4.40	4.46	4.51	4.57	4.63	4.69	4.74	4.80	4.86	4.91	4.97	5.03	5.09	5.14	5.20	5.26	5.31	5.37	5.43	5.49	5.54	5.60	5.66	5.71	5.77
1.42	4.23	4.29	4.34	4.40	4.46	4.51	4.57	4.63	4.69	4.74	4.80	4.86	4.91	4.97	5.03	5.09	5.14	5.20	5.26	5.31	5.37	5.43	5.49	5.54	5.60	5.66	5.71	5.77	5.83
1.44	4.29	4.34	4.40	4.46	4.51	4.57	4.63	4.69	4.74	4.80	4.86	4.91	4.97	5.03	5.09	5.14	5.20	5.26	5.31	5.37	5.43	5.49	5.54	5.60	5.66	5.71	5.77	5.83	5.89
1.46	4.34	4.40	4.46	4.51	4.57	4.63	4.69	4.74	4.80	4.86	4.91	4.97	5.03	5.09	5.14	5.20	5.26	5.31	5.37	5.43	5.49	5.54	5.60	5.66	5.71	5.77	5.83	5.89	5.94
1.48	4.40	4.46	4.51	4.57	4.63	4.69	4.74	4.80	4.86	4.91	4.97	5.03	5.09	5.14	5.20	5.26	5.31	5.37	5.43	5.49	5.54	5.60	5.66	5.71	5.77	5.83	5.89	5.94	6.00
1.50	4.46	4.51	4.57	4.63	4.69	4.74	4.80	4.86	4.91	4.97	5.03	5.09	5.14	5.20	5.26	5.31	5.37	5.43	5.49	5.54	5.60	5.66	5.71	5.77	5.83	5.89	5.94	6.00	6.06
1.52	4.51	4.57	4.63	4.69	4.74	4.80	4.86	4.91	4.97	5.03	5.09	5.14	5.20	5.26	5.31	5.37	5.43	5.49	5.54	5.60	5.66	5.71	5.77	5.83	5.89	5.94	6.00	6.06	6.11
1.54	4.57	4.63	4.69	4.74	4.80	4.86	4.91	4.97	5.03	5.09	5.14	5.20	5.26	5.31	5.37	5.43	5.49	5.54	5.60	5.66	5.71	5.77	5.83	5.89	5.94	6.00	6.06	6.11	6.17
1.56	4.63	4.69	4.74	4.80	4.86	4.91	4.97	5.03	5.09	5.14	5.20	5.26	5.31	5.37	5.43	5.49	5.54	5.60	5.66	5.71	5.77	5.83	5.89	5.94	6.00	6.06	6.11	6.17	6.23

35% FOOD COST CHART

COST OF TRIMMINGS

COST OF ENTREE	.06	.08	.10	.12	.14	.16	.18	.20	.22	.24	.26	.28	.30	.32	.34	.36	.38	.40	.42	.44	.46	.48	.50	.52	.54	.56	.58	.60	.62
1.58	4.69	4.74	4.80	4.86	4.91	4.97	5.03	5.09	5.14	5.20	5.26	5.31	5.37	5.43	5.49	5.54	5.60	5.66	5.71	5.77	5.83	5.89	5.94	6.00	6.06	6.11	6.17	6.23	6.29
1.60	4.74	4.80	4.86	4.91	4.97	5.03	5.09	5.14	5.20	5.26	5.31	5.37	5.43	5.49	5.54	5.60	5.66	5.71	5.77	5.83	5.89	5.94	6.00	6.06	6.11	6.17	6.23	6.29	6.34
1.62	4.80	4.86	4.91	4.97	5.03	5.09	5.14	5.20	5.26	5.31	5.37	5.43	5.49	5.54	5.60	5.66	5.71	5.77	5.83	5.89	5.94	6.00	6.06	6.11	6.17	6.23	6.29	6.34	6.40
1.64	4.86	4.91	4.97	5.03	5.09	5.14	5.20	5.26	5.31	5.37	5.43	5.49	5.54	5.60	5.66	5.71	5.77	5.83	5.89	5.94	6.00	6.06	6.11	6.17	6.23	6.29	6.34	6.40	6.46
1.66	4.91	4.97	5.03	5.09	5.14	5.20	5.26	5.31	5.37	5.43	5.49	5.54	5.60	5.66	5.71	5.77	5.83	5.89	5.94	6.00	6.06	6.11	6.17	6.23	6.29	6.34	6.40	6.46	6.51
1.68	4.97	5.03	5.09	5.14	5.20	5.26	5.31	5.37	5.43	5.49	5.54	5.60	5.66	5.71	5.77	5.83	5.89	5.94	6.00	6.06	6.11	6.17	6.23	6.29	6.34	6.40	6.46	6.51	6.57
1.70	5.03	5.09	5.14	5.20	5.26	5.31	5.37	5.43	5.49	5.54	5.60	5.66	5.71	5.77	5.83	5.89	5.94	6.00	6.06	6.11	6.17	6.23	6.29	6.34	6.40	6.46	6.51	6.57	6.63
1.72	5.09	5.14	5.20	5.26	5.31	5.37	5.43	5.49	5.54	5.60	5.66	5.71	5.77	5.83	5.89	5.94	6.00	6.06	6.11	6.17	6.23	6.29	6.34	6.40	6.46	6.51	6.57	6.63	6.69
1.74	5.14	5.20	5.26	5.31	5.37	5.43	5.49	5.54	5.60	5.66	5.71	5.77	5.83	5.89	5.94	6.00	6.06	6.11	6.17	6.23	6.29	6.34	6.40	6.46	6.51	6.57	6.63	6.69	6.74
1.76	5.20	5.26	5.31	5.37	5.43	5.49	5.54	5.60	5.66	5.71	5.77	5.83	5.89	5.94	6.00	6.06	6.11	6.17	6.23	6.29	6.34	6.40	6.46	6.51	6.57	6.63	6.69	6.74	6.80
1.78	5.26	5.31	5.37	5.43	5.49	5.54	5.60	5.66	5.71	5.77	5.83	5.89	5.94	6.00	6.06	6.11	6.17	6.23	6.29	6.34	6.40	6.46	6.51	6.57	6.63	6.69	6.74	6.80	6.86
1.80	5.31	5.37	5.43	5.49	5.54	5.60	5.66	5.71	5.77	5.83	5.89	5.94	6.00	6.06	6.11	6.17	6.23	6.29	6.34	6.40	6.46	6.51	6.57	6.63	6.69	6.74	6.80	6.86	6.91
1.82	5.37	5.43	5.49	5.54	5.60	5.66	5.71	5.77	5.83	5.89	5.94	6.00	6.06	6.11	6.17	6.23	6.29	6.34	6.40	6.46	6.51	6.57	6.63	6.69	6.74	6.80	6.86	6.91	6.97
1.84	5.43	5.49	5.54	5.60	5.66	5.71	5.77	5.83	5.89	5.94	6.00	6.06	6.11	6.17	6.23	6.29	6.34	6.40	6.46	6.51	6.57	6.63	6.69	6.74	6.80	6.86	6.91	6.97	7.03
1.86	5.49	5.54	5.60	5.66	5.71	5.77	5.83	5.89	5.94	6.00	6.06	6.11	6.17	6.23	6.29	6.34	6.40	6.46	6.51	6.57	6.63	6.69	6.74	6.80	6.86	6.91	6.97	7.03	7.09
1.88	5.54	5.60	5.66	5.71	5.77	5.83	5.89	5.94	6.00	6.06	6.11	6.17	6.23	6.29	6.34	6.40	6.46	6.51	6.57	6.63	6.69	6.74	6.80	6.86	6.91	6.97	7.03	7.09	7.14
1.90	5.60	5.66	5.71	5.77	5.83	5.89	5.94	6.00	6.06	6.11	6.17	6.23	6.29	6.34	6.40	6.46	6.51	6.57	6.63	6.69	6.74	6.80	6.86	6.91	6.97	7.03	7.09	7.14	7.20
1.92	5.66	5.71	5.77	5.83	5.89	5.94	6.00	6.06	6.11	6.17	6.23	6.29	6.34	6.40	6.46	6.51	6.57	6.63	6.69	6.74	6.80	6.86	6.91	6.97	7.03	7.09	7.14	7.20	7.26
1.94	5.71	5.77	5.83	5.89	5.94	6.00	6.06	6.11	6.17	6.23	6.29	6.34	6.40	6.46	6.51	6.57	6.63	6.69	6.74	6.80	6.86	6.91	6.97	7.03	7.09	7.14	7.20	7.26	7.31
1.96	5.77	5.83	5.89	5.94	6.00	6.06	6.11	6.17	6.23	6.29	6.34	6.40	6.46	6.51	6.57	6.63	6.69	6.74	6.80	6.86	6.91	6.97	7.03	7.09	7.14	7.20	7.26	7.31	7.37
1.98	5.83	5.89	5.94	6.00	6.06	6.11	6.17	6.23	6.29	6.34	6.40	6.46	6.51	6.57	6.63	6.69	6.74	6.80	6.86	6.91	6.97	7.03	7.09	7.14	7.20	7.26	7.31	7.37	7.43
2.00	5.89	5.94	6.00	6.06	6.11	6.17	6.23	6.29	6.34	6.40	6.46	6.51	6.57	6.63	6.69	6.74	6.80	6.86	6.91	6.97	7.03	7.09	7.14	7.20	7.26	7.31	7.37	7.43	7.49
2.02	5.94	6.00	6.06	6.11	6.17	6.23	6.29	6.34	6.40	6.46	6.51	6.57	6.63	6.69	6.74	6.80	6.86	6.91	6.97	7.03	7.09	7.14	7.20	7.26	7.31	7.37	7.43	7.49	7.54
2.04	6.00	6.06	6.11	6.17	6.23	6.29	6.34	6.40	6.46	6.51	6.57	6.63	6.69	6.74	6.80	6.86	6.91	6.97	7.03	7.09	7.14	7.20	7.26	7.31	7.37	7.43	7.49	7.54	7.60
2.06	6.06	6.11	6.17	6.23	6.29	6.34	6.40	6.46	6.51	6.57	6.63	6.69	6.74	6.80	6.86	6.91	6.97	7.03	7.09	7.14	7.20	7.26	7.31	7.37	7.43	7.49	7.54	7.60	7.66
2.08	6.11	6.17	6.23	6.29	6.34	6.40	6.46	6.51	6.57	6.63	6.69	6.74	6.80	6.86	6.91	6.97	7.03	7.09	7.14	7.20	7.26	7.31	7.37	7.43	7.49	7.54	7.60	7.66	7.71
2.10	6.17	6.23	6.29	6.34	6.40	6.46	6.51	6.57	6.63	6.69	6.74	6.80	6.86	6.91	6.97	7.03	7.09	7.14	7.20	7.26	7.31	7.37	7.43	7.49	7.54	7.60	7.66	7.71	7.77
2.12	6.23	6.29	6.34	6.40	6.46	6.51	6.57	6.63	6.69	6.74	6.80	6.86	6.91	6.97	7.03	7.09	7.14	7.20	7.26	7.31	7.37	7.43	7.49	7.54	7.60	7.66	7.71	7.77	7.83
2.14	6.29	6.34	6.40	6.46	6.51	6.57	6.63	6.69	6.74	6.80	6.86	6.91	6.97	7.03	7.09	7.14	7.20	7.26	7.31	7.37	7.43	7.49	7.54	7.60	7.66	7.71	7.77	7.83	7.89
2.16	6.34	6.40	6.46	6.51	6.57	6.63	6.69	6.74	6.80	6.86	6.91	6.97	7.03	7.09	7.14	7.20	7.26	7.31	7.37	7.43	7.49	7.54	7.60	7.66	7.71	7.77	7.83	7.89	7.94
2.18	6.40	6.46	6.51	6.57	6.63	6.69	6.74	6.80	6.86	6.91	6.97	7.03	7.09	7.14	7.20	7.26	7.31	7.37	7.43	7.49	7.54	7.60	7.66	7.71	7.77	7.83	7.89	7.94	8.00
2.20	6.46	6.51	6.57	6.63	6.69	6.74	6.80	6.86	6.91	6.97	7.03	7.09	7.14	7.20	7.26	7.31	7.37	7.43	7.49	7.54	7.60	7.66	7.71	7.77	7.83	7.89	7.94	8.00	8.06
2.22	6.51	6.57	6.63	6.69	6.74	6.80	6.86	6.91	6.97	7.03	7.09	7.14	7.20	7.26	7.31	7.37	7.43	7.49	7.54	7.60	7.66	7.71	7.77	7.83	7.89	7.94	8.00	8.06	8.11
2.24	6.57	6.63	6.69	6.74	6.80	6.86	6.91	6.97	7.03	7.09	7.14	7.20	7.26	7.31	7.37	7.43	7.49	7.54	7.60	7.66	7.71	7.77	7.83	7.89	7.94	8.00	8.06	8.11	8.17
2.26	6.63	6.69	6.74	6.80	6.86	6.91	6.97	7.03	7.09	7.14	7.20	7.26	7.31	7.37	7.43	7.49	7.54	7.60	7.66	7.71	7.77	7.83	7.89	7.94	8.00	8.06	8.11	8.17	8.23
2.28	6.69	6.74	6.80	6.86	6.91	6.97	7.03	7.09	7.14	7.20	7.26	7.31	7.37	7.43	7.49	7.54	7.60	7.66	7.71	7.77	7.83	7.89	7.94	8.00	8.06	8.11	8.17	8.23	8.29
2.30	6.74	6.80	6.86	6.91	6.97	7.03	7.09	7.14	7.20	7.26	7.31	7.37	7.43	7.49	7.54	7.60	7.66	7.71	7.77	7.83	7.89	7.94	8.00	8.06	8.11	8.17	8.23	8.29	8.34

35% FOOD COST CHART

COST OF TRIMMINGS

COST OF ENTREE	.06	.08	.10	.12	.14	.16	.18	.20	.22	.24	.26	.28	.30	.32	.34	.36	.38	.40	.42	.44	.46	.48	.50	.52	.54	.56	.58	.60	.62
2.32	6.80	6.86	6.91	6.97	7.03	7.09	7.14	7.20	7.26	7.31	7.37	7.43	7.49	7.54	7.60	7.66	7.71	7.77	7.83	7.89	7.94	8.00	8.06	8.11	8.17	8.23	8.29	8.34	8.40
2.34	6.86	6.91	6.97	7.03	7.09	7.14	7.20	7.26	7.31	7.37	7.43	7.49	7.54	7.60	7.66	7.71	7.77	7.83	7.89	7.94	8.00	8.06	8.11	8.17	8.23	8.29	8.34	8.40	8.46
2.36	6.91	6.97	7.03	7.09	7.14	7.20	7.26	7.31	7.37	7.43	7.49	7.54	7.60	7.66	7.71	7.77	7.83	7.89	7.94	8.00	8.06	8.11	8.17	8.23	8.29	8.34	8.40	8.46	8.51
2.38	6.97	7.03	7.09	7.14	7.20	7.26	7.31	7.37	7.43	7.49	7.54	7.60	7.66	7.71	7.77	7.83	7.89	7.94	8.00	8.06	8.11	8.17	8.23	8.29	8.34	8.40	8.46	8.51	8.57
2.40	7.03	7.09	7.14	7.20	7.26	7.31	7.37	7.43	7.49	7.54	7.60	7.66	7.71	7.77	7.83	7.89	7.94	8.00	8.06	8.11	8.17	8.23	8.29	8.34	8.40	8.46	8.51	8.57	8.63
2.42	7.09	7.14	7.20	7.26	7.31	7.37	7.43	7.49	7.54	7.60	7.66	7.71	7.77	7.83	7.89	7.94	8.00	8.06	8.11	8.17	8.23	8.29	8.34	8.40	8.46	8.51	8.57	8.63	8.69
2.44	7.14	7.20	7.26	7.31	7.37	7.43	7.49	7.54	7.60	7.66	7.71	7.77	7.83	7.89	7.94	8.00	8.06	8.11	8.17	8.23	8.29	8.34	8.40	8.46	8.51	8.57	8.63	8.69	8.74
2.46	7.20	7.26	7.31	7.37	7.43	7.49	7.54	7.60	7.66	7.71	7.77	7.83	7.89	7.94	8.00	8.06	8.11	8.17	8.23	8.29	8.34	8.40	8.46	8.51	8.57	8.63	8.69	8.74	8.80
2.48	7.26	7.31	7.37	7.43	7.49	7.54	7.60	7.66	7.71	7.77	7.83	7.89	7.94	8.00	8.06	8.11	8.17	8.23	8.29	8.34	8.40	8.46	8.51	8.57	8.63	8.69	8.74	8.80	8.86
2.50	7.31	7.37	7.43	7.49	7.54	7.60	7.66	7.71	7.77	7.83	7.89	7.94	8.00	8.06	8.11	8.17	8.23	8.29	8.34	8.40	8.46	8.51	8.57	8.63	8.69	8.74	8.80	8.86	8.91
2.52	7.37	7.43	7.49	7.54	7.60	7.66	7.71	7.77	7.83	7.89	7.94	8.00	8.06	8.11	8.17	8.23	8.29	8.34	8.40	8.46	8.51	8.57	8.63	8.69	8.74	8.80	8.86	8.91	8.97
2.54	7.43	7.49	7.54	7.60	7.66	7.71	7.77	7.83	7.89	7.94	8.00	8.06	8.11	8.17	8.23	8.29	8.34	8.40	8.46	8.51	8.57	8.63	8.69	8.74	8.80	8.86	8.91	8.97	9.03
2.56	7.49	7.54	7.60	7.66	7.71	7.77	7.83	7.89	7.94	8.00	8.06	8.11	8.17	8.23	8.29	8.34	8.40	8.46	8.51	8.57	8.63	8.69	8.74	8.80	8.86	8.91	8.97	9.03	9.09
2.58	7.54	7.60	7.66	7.71	7.77	7.83	7.89	7.94	8.00	8.06	8.11	8.17	8.23	8.29	8.34	8.40	8.46	8.51	8.57	8.63	8.69	8.74	8.80	8.86	8.91	8.97	9.03	9.09	9.14
2.60	7.60	7.66	7.71	7.77	7.83	7.89	7.94	8.00	8.06	8.11	8.17	8.23	8.29	8.34	8.40	8.46	8.51	8.57	8.63	8.69	8.74	8.80	8.86	8.91	8.97	9.03	9.09	9.14	9.20
2.62	7.66	7.71	7.77	7.83	7.89	7.94	8.00	8.06	8.11	8.17	8.23	8.29	8.34	8.40	8.46	8.51	8.57	8.63	8.69	8.74	8.80	8.86	8.91	8.97	9.03	9.09	9.14	9.20	9.26
2.64	7.71	7.77	7.83	7.89	7.94	8.00	8.06	8.11	8.17	8.23	8.29	8.34	8.40	8.46	8.51	8.57	8.63	8.69	8.74	8.80	8.86	8.91	8.97	9.03	9.09	9.14	9.20	9.26	9.31
2.66	7.77	7.83	7.89	7.94	8.00	8.06	8.11	8.17	8.23	8.29	8.34	8.40	8.46	8.51	8.57	8.63	8.69	8.74	8.80	8.86	8.91	8.97	9.03	9.09	9.14	9.20	9.26	9.31	9.37
2.68	7.83	7.89	7.94	8.00	8.06	8.11	8.17	8.23	8.29	8.34	8.40	8.46	8.51	8.57	8.63	8.69	8.74	8.80	8.86	8.91	8.97	9.03	9.09	9.14	9.20	9.26	9.31	9.37	9.43
2.70	7.89	7.94	8.00	8.06	8.11	8.17	8.23	8.29	8.34	8.40	8.46	8.51	8.57	8.63	8.69	8.74	8.80	8.86	8.91	8.97	9.03	9.09	9.14	9.20	9.26	9.31	9.37	9.43	9.49
2.72	7.94	8.00	8.06	8.11	8.17	8.23	8.29	8.34	8.40	8.46	8.51	8.57	8.63	8.69	8.74	8.80	8.86	8.91	8.97	9.03	9.09	9.14	9.20	9.26	9.31	9.37	9.43	9.49	9.54
2.74	8.00	8.06	8.11	8.17	8.23	8.29	8.34	8.40	8.46	8.51	8.57	8.63	8.69	8.74	8.80	8.86	8.91	8.97	9.03	9.09	9.14	9.20	9.26	9.31	9.37	9.43	9.49	9.54	9.60
2.76	8.06	8.11	8.17	8.23	8.29	8.34	8.40	8.46	8.51	8.57	8.63	8.69	8.74	8.80	8.86	8.91	8.97	9.03	9.09	9.14	9.20	9.26	9.31	9.37	9.43	9.49	9.54	9.60	9.66
2.78	8.11	8.17	8.23	8.29	8.34	8.40	8.46	8.51	8.57	8.63	8.69	8.74	8.80	8.86	8.91	8.97	9.03	9.09	9.14	9.20	9.26	9.31	9.37	9.43	9.49	9.54	9.60	9.66	9.71
2.80	8.17	8.23	8.29	8.34	8.40	8.46	8.51	8.57	8.63	8.69	8.74	8.80	8.86	8.91	8.97	9.03	9.09	9.14	9.20	9.26	9.31	9.37	9.43	9.49	9.54	9.60	9.66	9.71	9.77
2.82	8.23	8.29	8.34	8.40	8.46	8.51	8.57	8.63	8.69	8.74	8.80	8.86	8.91	8.97	9.03	9.09	9.14	9.20	9.26	9.31	9.37	9.43	9.49	9.54	9.60	9.66	9.71	9.77	9.83
2.84	8.29	8.34	8.40	8.46	8.51	8.57	8.63	8.69	8.74	8.80	8.86	8.91	8.97	9.03	9.09	9.14	9.20	9.26	9.31	9.37	9.43	9.49	9.54	9.60	9.66	9.71	9.77	9.83	9.89
2.86	8.34	8.40	8.46	8.51	8.57	8.63	8.69	8.74	8.80	8.86	8.91	8.97	9.03	9.09	9.14	9.20	9.26	9.31	9.37	9.43	9.49	9.54	9.60	9.66	9.71	9.77	9.83	9.89	9.94
2.88	8.40	8.46	8.51	8.57	8.63	8.69	8.74	8.80	8.86	8.91	8.97	9.03	9.09	9.14	9.20	9.26	9.31	9.37	9.43	9.49	9.54	9.60	9.66	9.71	9.77	9.83	9.89	9.94	10.00
2.90	8.46	8.51	8.57	8.63	8.69	8.74	8.80	8.86	8.91	8.97	9.03	9.09	9.14	9.20	9.26	9.31	9.37	9.43	9.49	9.54	9.60	9.66	9.71	9.77	9.83	9.89	9.94	10.00	10.06
2.92	8.51	8.57	8.63	8.69	8.74	8.80	8.86	8.91	8.97	9.03	9.09	9.14	9.20	9.26	9.31	9.37	9.43	9.49	9.54	9.60	9.66	9.71	9.77	9.83	9.89	9.94	10.00	10.06	10.11
2.94	8.57	8.63	8.69	8.74	8.80	8.86	8.91	8.97	9.03	9.09	9.14	9.20	9.26	9.31	9.37	9.43	9.49	9.54	9.60	9.66	9.71	9.77	9.83	9.89	9.94	10.00	10.06	10.11	10.17
2.96	8.63	8.69	8.74	8.80	8.86	8.91	8.97	9.03	9.09	9.14	9.20	9.26	9.31	9.37	9.43	9.49	9.54	9.60	9.66	9.71	9.77	9.83	9.89	9.94	10.00	10.06	10.11	10.17	10.23
2.98	8.69	8.74	8.80	8.86	8.91	8.97	9.03	9.09	9.14	9.20	9.26	9.31	9.37	9.43	9.49	9.54	9.60	9.66	9.71	9.77	9.83	9.89	9.94	10.00	10.06	10.11	10.17	10.23	10.29
3.00	8.74	8.80	8.86	8.91	8.97	9.03	9.09	9.14	9.20	9.26	9.31	9.37	9.43	9.49	9.54	9.60	9.66	9.71	9.77	9.83	9.89	9.94	10.00	10.06	10.11	10.17	10.23	10.29	10.34
3.02	8.80	8.86	8.91	8.97	9.03	9.09	9.14	9.20	9.26	9.31	9.37	9.43	9.49	9.54	9.60	9.66	9.71	9.77	9.83	9.89	9.94	10.00	10.06	10.11	10.17	10.23	10.29	10.34	10.40
3.04	8.86	8.91	8.97	9.03	9.09	9.14	9.20	9.26	9.31	9.37	9.43	9.49	9.54	9.60	9.66	9.71	9.77	9.83	9.89	9.94	10.00	10.06	10.11	10.17	10.23	10.29	10.34	10.40	10.46

40% FOOD COST CHART

COST OF TRIMMINGS

COST OF ENTREE	.06	.08	.10	.12	.14	.16	.18	.20	.22	.24	.26	.28	.30	.32	.34	.36	.38	.40	.42	.44	.46	.48	.50	.52	.54	.56	.58	.60	.62
.10	.40	.45	.50	.55	.60	.65	.70	.75	.80	.85	.90	.95	1.00	1.05	1.10	1.15	1.20	1.25	1.30	1.35	1.40	1.45	1.50	1.55	1.60	1.65	1.70	1.75	1.80
.12	.45	.50	.55	.60	.65	.70	.75	.80	.85	.90	.95	1.00	1.05	1.10	1.15	1.20	1.25	1.30	1.35	1.40	1.45	1.50	1.55	1.60	1.65	1.70	1.75	1.80	1.85
.14	.50	.55	.60	.65	.70	.75	.80	.85	.90	.95	1.00	1.05	1.10	1.15	1.20	1.25	1.30	1.35	1.40	1.45	1.50	1.55	1.60	1.65	1.70	1.75	1.80	1.85	1.90
.16	.55	.60	.65	.70	.75	.80	.85	.90	.95	1.00	1.05	1.10	1.15	1.20	1.25	1.30	1.35	1.40	1.45	1.50	1.55	1.60	1.65	1.70	1.75	1.80	1.85	1.90	1.95
.18	.60	.65	.70	.75	.80	.85	.90	.95	1.00	1.05	1.10	1.15	1.20	1.25	1.30	1.35	1.40	1.45	1.50	1.55	1.60	1.65	1.70	1.75	1.80	1.85	1.90	1.95	2.00
.20	.65	.70	.75	.80	.85	.90	.95	1.00	1.05	1.10	1.15	1.20	1.25	1.30	1.35	1.40	1.45	1.50	1.55	1.60	1.65	1.70	1.75	1.80	1.85	1.90	1.95	2.00	2.05
.22	.70	.75	.80	.85	.90	.95	1.00	1.05	1.10	1.15	1.20	1.25	1.30	1.35	1.40	1.45	1.50	1.55	1.60	1.65	1.70	1.75	1.80	1.85	1.90	1.95	2.00	2.05	2.10
.24	.75	.80	.85	.90	.95	1.00	1.05	1.10	1.15	1.20	1.25	1.30	1.35	1.40	1.45	1.50	1.55	1.60	1.65	1.70	1.75	1.80	1.85	1.90	1.95	2.00	2.05	2.10	2.15
.26	.80	.85	.90	.95	1.00	1.05	1.10	1.15	1.20	1.25	1.30	1.35	1.40	1.45	1.50	1.55	1.60	1.65	1.70	1.75	1.80	1.85	1.90	1.95	2.00	2.05	2.10	2.15	2.20
.28	.85	.90	.95	1.00	1.05	1.10	1.15	1.20	1.25	1.30	1.35	1.40	1.45	1.50	1.55	1.60	1.65	1.70	1.75	1.80	1.85	1.90	1.95	2.00	2.05	2.10	2.15	2.20	2.25
.30	.90	.95	1.00	1.05	1.10	1.15	1.20	1.25	1.30	1.35	1.40	1.45	1.50	1.55	1.60	1.65	1.70	1.75	1.80	1.85	1.90	1.95	2.00	2.05	2.10	2.15	2.20	2.25	2.30
.32	.95	1.00	1.05	1.10	1.15	1.20	1.25	1.30	1.35	1.40	1.45	1.50	1.55	1.60	1.65	1.70	1.75	1.80	1.85	1.90	1.95	2.00	2.05	2.10	2.15	2.20	2.25	2.30	2.35
.34	1.00	1.05	1.10	1.15	1.20	1.25	1.30	1.35	1.40	1.45	1.50	1.55	1.60	1.65	1.70	1.75	1.80	1.85	1.90	1.95	2.00	2.05	2.10	2.15	2.20	2.25	2.30	2.35	2.40
.36	1.05	1.10	1.15	1.20	1.25	1.30	1.35	1.40	1.45	1.50	1.55	1.60	1.65	1.70	1.75	1.80	1.85	1.90	1.95	2.00	2.05	2.10	2.15	2.20	2.25	2.30	2.35	2.40	2.45
.38	1.10	1.15	1.20	1.25	1.30	1.35	1.40	1.45	1.50	1.55	1.60	1.65	1.70	1.75	1.80	1.85	1.90	1.95	2.00	2.05	2.10	2.15	2.20	2.25	2.30	2.35	2.40	2.45	2.50
.40	1.15	1.20	1.25	1.30	1.35	1.40	1.45	1.50	1.55	1.60	1.65	1.70	1.75	1.80	1.85	1.90	1.95	2.00	2.05	2.10	2.15	2.20	2.25	2.30	2.35	2.40	2.45	2.50	2.55
.42	1.20	1.25	1.30	1.35	1.40	1.45	1.50	1.55	1.60	1.65	1.70	1.75	1.80	1.85	1.90	1.95	2.00	2.05	2.10	2.15	2.20	2.25	2.30	2.35	2.40	2.45	2.50	2.55	2.60
.44	1.25	1.30	1.35	1.40	1.45	1.50	1.55	1.60	1.65	1.70	1.75	1.80	1.85	1.90	1.95	2.00	2.05	2.10	2.15	2.20	2.25	2.30	2.35	2.40	2.45	2.50	2.55	2.60	2.65
.46	1.30	1.35	1.40	1.45	1.50	1.55	1.60	1.65	1.70	1.75	1.80	1.85	1.90	1.95	2.00	2.05	2.10	2.15	2.20	2.25	2.30	2.35	2.40	2.45	2.50	2.55	2.60	2.65	2.70
.48	1.35	1.40	1.45	1.50	1.55	1.60	1.65	1.70	1.75	1.80	1.85	1.90	1.95	2.00	2.05	2.10	2.15	2.20	2.25	2.30	2.35	2.40	2.45	2.50	2.55	2.60	2.65	2.70	2.75
.50	1.40	1.45	1.50	1.55	1.60	1.65	1.70	1.75	1.80	1.85	1.90	1.95	2.00	2.05	2.10	2.15	2.20	2.25	2.30	2.35	2.40	2.45	2.50	2.55	2.60	2.65	2.70	2.75	2.80
.52	1.45	1.50	1.55	1.60	1.65	1.70	1.75	1.80	1.85	1.90	1.95	2.00	2.05	2.10	2.15	2.20	2.25	2.30	2.35	2.40	2.45	2.50	2.55	2.60	2.65	2.70	2.75	2.80	2.85
.54	1.50	1.55	1.60	1.65	1.70	1.75	1.80	1.85	1.90	1.95	2.00	2.05	2.10	2.15	2.20	2.25	2.30	2.35	2.40	2.45	2.50	2.55	2.60	2.65	2.70	2.75	2.80	2.85	2.90
.56	1.55	1.60	1.65	1.70	1.75	1.80	1.85	1.90	1.95	2.00	2.05	2.10	2.15	2.20	2.25	2.30	2.35	2.40	2.45	2.50	2.55	2.60	2.65	2.70	2.75	2.80	2.85	2.90	2.95
.58	1.60	1.65	1.70	1.75	1.80	1.85	1.90	1.95	2.00	2.05	2.10	2.15	2.20	2.25	2.30	2.35	2.40	2.45	2.50	2.55	2.60	2.65	2.70	2.75	2.80	2.85	2.90	2.95	3.00
.60	1.65	1.70	1.75	1.80	1.85	1.90	1.95	2.00	2.05	2.10	2.15	2.20	2.25	2.30	2.35	2.40	2.45	2.50	2.55	2.60	2.65	2.70	2.75	2.80	2.85	2.90	2.95	3.00	3.05
.62	1.70	1.75	1.80	1.85	1.90	1.95	2.00	2.05	2.10	2.15	2.20	2.25	2.30	2.35	2.40	2.45	2.50	2.55	2.60	2.65	2.70	2.75	2.80	2.85	2.90	2.95	3.00	3.05	3.10
.64	1.75	1.80	1.85	1.90	1.95	2.00	2.05	2.10	2.15	2.20	2.25	2.30	2.35	2.40	2.45	2.50	2.55	2.60	2.65	2.70	2.75	2.80	2.85	2.90	2.95	3.00	3.05	3.10	3.15
.66	1.80	1.85	1.90	1.95	2.00	2.05	2.10	2.15	2.20	2.25	2.30	2.35	2.40	2.45	2.50	2.55	2.60	2.65	2.70	2.75	2.80	2.85	2.90	2.95	3.00	3.05	3.10	3.15	3.20
.68	1.85	1.90	1.95	2.00	2.05	2.10	2.15	2.20	2.25	2.30	2.35	2.40	2.45	2.50	2.55	2.60	2.65	2.70	2.75	2.80	2.85	2.90	2.95	3.00	3.05	3.10	3.15	3.20	3.25
.70	1.90	1.95	2.00	2.05	2.10	2.15	2.20	2.25	2.30	2.35	2.40	2.45	2.50	2.55	2.60	2.65	2.70	2.75	2.80	2.85	2.90	2.95	3.00	3.05	3.10	3.15	3.20	3.25	3.30
.72	1.95	2.00	2.05	2.10	2.15	2.20	2.25	2.30	2.35	2.40	2.45	2.50	2.55	2.60	2.65	2.70	2.75	2.80	2.85	2.90	2.95	3.00	3.05	3.10	3.15	3.20	3.25	3.30	3.35
.74	2.00	2.05	2.10	2.15	2.20	2.25	2.30	2.35	2.40	2.45	2.50	2.55	2.60	2.65	2.70	2.75	2.80	2.85	2.90	2.95	3.00	3.05	3.10	3.15	3.20	3.25	3.30	3.35	3.40
.76	2.05	2.10	2.15	2.20	2.25	2.30	2.35	2.40	2.45	2.50	2.55	2.60	2.65	2.70	2.75	2.80	2.85	2.90	2.95	3.00	3.05	3.10	3.15	3.20	3.25	3.30	3.35	3.40	3.45
.78	2.10	2.15	2.20	2.25	2.30	2.35	2.40	2.45	2.50	2.55	2.60	2.65	2.70	2.75	2.80	2.85	2.90	2.95	3.00	3.05	3.10	3.15	3.20	3.25	3.30	3.35	3.40	3.45	3.50
.80	2.15	2.20	2.25	2.30	2.35	2.40	2.45	2.50	2.55	2.60	2.65	2.70	2.75	2.80	2.85	2.90	2.95	3.00	3.05	3.10	3.15	3.20	3.25	3.30	3.35	3.40	3.45	3.50	3.55
.82	2.20	2.25	2.30	2.35	2.40	2.45	2.50	2.55	2.60	2.65	2.70	2.75	2.80	2.85	2.90	2.95	3.00	3.05	3.10	3.15	3.20	3.25	3.30	3.35	3.40	3.45	3.50	3.55	3.60

40% FOOD COST CHART

COST OF TRIMMINGS

COST OF ENTREE	.06	.08	.10	.12	.14	.16	.18	.20	.22	.24	.26	.28	.30	.32	.34	.36	.38	.40	.42	.44	.46	.48	.50	.52	.54	.56	.58	.60	.62
.84	2.25	2.30	2.35	2.40	2.45	2.50	2.55	2.60	2.65	2.70	2.75	2.80	2.85	2.90	2.95	3.00	3.05	3.10	3.15	3.20	3.25	3.30	3.35	3.40	3.45	3.50	3.55	3.60	3.65
.86	2.30	2.35	2.40	2.45	2.50	2.55	2.60	2.65	2.70	2.75	2.80	2.85	2.90	2.95	3.00	3.05	3.10	3.15	3.20	3.25	3.30	3.35	3.40	3.45	3.50	3.55	3.60	3.65	3.70
.88	2.35	2.40	2.45	2.50	2.55	2.60	2.65	2.70	2.75	2.80	2.85	2.90	2.95	3.00	3.05	3.10	3.15	3.20	3.25	3.30	3.35	3.40	3.45	3.50	3.55	3.60	3.65	3.70	3.75
.90	2.40	2.45	2.50	2.55	2.60	2.65	2.70	2.75	2.80	2.85	2.90	2.95	3.00	3.05	3.10	3.15	3.20	3.25	3.30	3.35	3.40	3.45	3.50	3.55	3.60	3.65	3.70	3.75	3.80
.92	2.45	2.50	2.55	2.60	2.65	2.70	2.75	2.80	2.85	2.90	2.95	3.00	3.05	3.10	3.15	3.20	3.25	3.30	3.35	3.40	3.45	3.50	3.55	3.60	3.65	3.70	3.75	3.80	3.85
.94	2.50	2.55	2.60	2.65	2.70	2.75	2.80	2.85	2.90	2.95	3.00	3.05	3.10	3.15	3.20	3.25	3.30	3.35	3.40	3.45	3.50	3.55	3.60	3.65	3.70	3.75	3.80	3.85	3.90
.96	2.55	2.60	2.65	2.70	2.75	2.80	2.85	2.90	2.95	3.00	3.05	3.10	3.15	3.20	3.25	3.30	3.35	3.40	3.45	3.50	3.55	3.60	3.65	3.70	3.75	3.80	3.85	3.90	3.95
.98	2.60	2.65	2.70	2.75	2.80	2.85	2.90	2.95	3.00	3.05	3.10	3.15	3.20	3.25	3.30	3.35	3.40	3.45	3.50	3.55	3.60	3.65	3.70	3.75	3.80	3.85	3.90	3.95	4.00
1.00	2.65	2.70	2.75	2.80	2.85	2.90	2.95	3.00	3.05	3.10	3.15	3.20	3.25	3.30	3.35	3.40	3.45	3.50	3.55	3.60	3.65	3.70	3.75	3.80	3.85	3.90	3.95	4.00	4.05
1.02	2.70	2.75	2.80	2.85	2.90	2.95	3.00	3.05	3.10	3.15	3.20	3.25	3.30	3.35	3.40	3.45	3.50	3.55	3.60	3.65	3.70	3.75	3.80	3.85	3.90	3.95	4.00	4.05	4.10
1.04	2.75	2.80	2.85	2.90	2.95	3.00	3.05	3.10	3.15	3.20	3.25	3.30	3.35	3.40	3.45	3.50	3.55	3.60	3.65	3.70	3.75	3.80	3.85	3.90	3.95	4.00	4.05	4.10	4.15
1.06	2.80	2.85	2.90	2.95	3.00	3.05	3.10	3.15	3.20	3.25	3.30	3.35	3.40	3.45	3.50	3.55	3.60	3.65	3.70	3.75	3.80	3.85	3.90	3.95	4.00	4.05	4.10	4.15	4.20
1.08	2.85	2.90	2.95	3.00	3.05	3.10	3.15	3.20	3.25	3.30	3.35	3.40	3.45	3.50	3.55	3.60	3.65	3.70	3.75	3.80	3.85	3.90	3.95	4.00	4.05	4.10	4.15	4.20	4.25
1.10	2.90	2.95	3.00	3.05	3.10	3.15	3.20	3.25	3.30	3.35	3.40	3.45	3.50	3.55	3.60	3.65	3.70	3.75	3.80	3.85	3.90	3.95	4.00	4.05	4.10	4.15	4.20	4.25	4.30
1.12	2.95	3.00	3.05	3.10	3.15	3.20	3.25	3.30	3.35	3.40	3.45	3.50	3.55	3.60	3.65	3.70	3.75	3.80	3.85	3.90	3.95	4.00	4.05	4.10	4.15	4.20	4.25	4.30	4.35
1.14	3.00	3.05	3.10	3.15	3.20	3.25	3.30	3.35	3.40	3.45	3.50	3.55	3.60	3.65	3.70	3.75	3.80	3.85	3.90	3.95	4.00	4.05	4.10	4.15	4.20	4.25	4.30	4.35	4.40
1.16	3.05	3.10	3.15	3.20	3.25	3.30	3.35	3.40	3.45	3.50	3.55	3.60	3.65	3.70	3.75	3.80	3.85	3.90	3.95	4.00	4.05	4.10	4.15	4.20	4.25	4.30	4.35	4.40	4.45
1.18	3.10	3.15	3.20	3.25	3.30	3.35	3.40	3.45	3.50	3.55	3.60	3.65	3.70	3.75	3.80	3.85	3.90	3.95	4.00	4.05	4.10	4.15	4.20	4.25	4.30	4.35	4.40	4.45	4.50
1.20	3.15	3.20	3.25	3.30	3.35	3.40	3.45	3.50	3.55	3.60	3.65	3.70	3.75	3.80	3.85	3.90	3.95	4.00	4.05	4.10	4.15	4.20	4.25	4.30	4.35	4.40	4.45	4.50	4.55
1.22	3.20	3.25	3.30	3.35	3.40	3.45	3.50	3.55	3.60	3.65	3.70	3.75	3.80	3.85	3.90	3.95	4.00	4.05	4.10	4.15	4.20	4.25	4.30	4.35	4.40	4.45	4.50	4.55	4.60
1.24	3.25	3.30	3.35	3.40	3.45	3.50	3.55	3.60	3.65	3.70	3.75	3.80	3.85	3.90	3.95	4.00	4.05	4.10	4.15	4.20	4.25	4.30	4.35	4.40	4.45	4.50	4.55	4.60	4.65
1.26	3.30	3.35	3.40	3.45	3.50	3.55	3.60	3.65	3.70	3.75	3.80	3.85	3.90	3.95	4.00	4.05	4.10	4.15	4.20	4.25	4.30	4.35	4.40	4.45	4.50	4.55	4.60	4.65	4.70
1.28	3.35	3.40	3.45	3.50	3.55	3.60	3.65	3.70	3.75	3.80	3.85	3.90	3.95	4.00	4.05	4.10	4.15	4.20	4.25	4.30	4.35	4.40	4.45	4.50	4.55	4.60	4.65	4.70	4.75
1.30	3.40	3.45	3.50	3.55	3.60	3.65	3.70	3.75	3.80	3.85	3.90	3.95	4.00	4.05	4.10	4.15	4.20	4.25	4.30	4.35	4.40	4.45	4.50	4.55	4.60	4.65	4.70	4.75	4.80
1.32	3.45	3.50	3.55	3.60	3.65	3.70	3.75	3.80	3.85	3.90	3.95	4.00	4.05	4.10	4.15	4.20	4.25	4.30	4.35	4.40	4.45	4.50	4.55	4.60	4.65	4.70	4.75	4.80	4.85
1.34	3.50	3.55	3.60	3.65	3.70	3.75	3.80	3.85	3.90	3.95	4.00	4.05	4.10	4.15	4.20	4.25	4.30	4.35	4.40	4.45	4.50	4.55	4.60	4.65	4.70	4.75	4.80	4.85	4.90
1.36	3.55	3.60	3.65	3.70	3.75	3.80	3.85	3.90	3.95	4.00	4.05	4.10	4.15	4.20	4.25	4.30	4.35	4.40	4.45	4.50	4.55	4.60	4.65	4.70	4.75	4.80	4.85	4.90	4.95
1.38	3.60	3.65	3.70	3.75	3.80	3.85	3.90	3.95	4.00	4.05	4.10	4.15	4.20	4.25	4.30	4.35	4.40	4.45	4.50	4.55	4.60	4.65	4.70	4.75	4.80	4.85	4.90	4.95	5.00
1.40	3.65	3.70	3.75	3.80	3.85	3.90	3.95	4.00	4.05	4.10	4.15	4.20	4.25	4.30	4.35	4.40	4.45	4.50	4.55	4.60	4.65	4.70	4.75	4.80	4.85	4.90	4.95	5.00	5.05
1.42	3.70	3.75	3.80	3.85	3.90	3.95	4.00	4.05	4.10	4.15	4.20	4.25	4.30	4.35	4.40	4.45	4.50	4.55	4.60	4.65	4.70	4.75	4.80	4.85	4.90	4.95	5.00	5.05	5.10
1.44	3.75	3.80	3.85	3.90	3.95	4.00	4.05	4.10	4.15	4.20	4.25	4.30	4.35	4.40	4.45	4.50	4.55	4.60	4.65	4.70	4.75	4.80	4.85	4.90	4.95	5.00	5.05	5.10	5.15
1.46	3.80	3.85	3.90	3.95	4.00	4.05	4.10	4.15	4.20	4.25	4.30	4.35	4.40	4.45	4.50	4.55	4.60	4.65	4.70	4.75	4.80	4.85	4.90	4.95	5.00	5.05	5.10	5.15	5.20
1.48	3.85	3.90	3.95	4.00	4.05	4.10	4.15	4.20	4.25	4.30	4.35	4.40	4.45	4.50	4.55	4.60	4.65	4.70	4.75	4.80	4.85	4.90	4.95	5.00	5.05	5.10	5.15	5.20	5.25
1.50	3.90	3.95	4.00	4.05	4.10	4.15	4.20	4.25	4.30	4.35	4.40	4.45	4.50	4.55	4.60	4.65	4.70	4.75	4.80	4.85	4.90	4.95	5.00	5.05	5.10	5.15	5.20	5.25	5.30
1.52	3.95	4.00	4.05	4.10	4.15	4.20	4.25	4.30	4.35	4.40	4.45	4.50	4.55	4.60	4.65	4.70	4.75	4.80	4.85	4.90	4.95	5.00	5.05	5.10	5.15	5.20	5.25	5.30	5.35
1.54	4.00	4.05	4.10	4.15	4.20	4.25	4.30	4.35	4.40	4.45	4.50	4.55	4.60	4.65	4.70	4.75	4.80	4.85	4.90	4.95	5.00	5.05	5.10	5.15	5.20	5.25	5.30	5.35	5.40
1.56	4.05	4.10	4.15	4.20	4.25	4.30	4.35	4.40	4.45	4.50	4.55	4.60	4.65	4.70	4.75	4.80	4.85	4.90	4.95	5.00	5.05	5.10	5.15	5.20	5.25	5.30	5.35	5.40	5.45

40% FOOD COST CHART

COST OF TRIMMINGS

COST OF ENTREE	.06	.08	.10	.12	.14	.16	.18	.20	.22	.24	.26	.28	.30	.32	.34	.36	.38	.40	.42	.44	.46	.48	.50	.52	.54	.56	.58	.60	.62
1.58	4.10	4.15	4.20	4.25	4.30	4.35	4.40	4.45	4.50	4.55	4.60	4.65	4.70	4.75	4.80	4.85	4.90	4.95	5.00	5.05	5.10	5.15	5.20	5.25	5.30	5.35	5.40	5.45	5.50
1.60	4.15	4.20	4.25	4.30	4.35	4.40	4.45	4.50	4.55	4.60	4.65	4.70	4.75	4.80	4.85	4.90	4.95	5.00	5.05	5.10	5.15	5.20	5.25	5.30	5.35	5.40	5.45	5.50	5.55
1.62	4.20	4.25	4.30	4.35	4.40	4.45	4.50	4.55	4.60	4.65	4.70	4.75	4.80	4.85	4.90	4.95	5.00	5.05	5.10	5.15	5.20	5.25	5.30	5.35	5.40	5.45	5.50	5.55	5.60
1.64	4.25	4.30	4.35	4.40	4.45	4.50	4.55	4.60	4.65	4.70	4.75	4.80	4.85	4.90	4.95	5.00	5.05	5.10	5.15	5.20	5.25	5.30	5.35	5.40	5.45	5.50	5.55	5.60	5.65
1.66	4.30	4.35	4.40	4.45	4.50	4.55	4.60	4.65	4.70	4.75	4.80	4.85	4.90	4.95	5.00	5.05	5.10	5.15	5.20	5.25	5.30	5.35	5.40	5.45	5.50	5.55	5.60	5.65	5.70
1.68	4.35	4.40	4.45	4.50	4.55	4.60	4.65	4.70	4.75	4.80	4.85	4.90	4.95	5.00	5.05	5.10	5.15	5.20	5.25	5.30	5.35	5.40	5.45	5.50	5.55	5.60	5.65	5.70	5.75
1.70	4.40	4.45	4.50	4.55	4.60	4.65	4.70	4.75	4.80	4.85	4.90	4.95	5.00	5.05	5.10	5.15	5.20	5.25	5.30	5.35	5.40	5.45	5.50	5.55	5.60	5.65	5.70	5.75	5.80
1.72	4.45	4.50	4.55	4.60	4.65	4.70	4.75	4.80	4.85	4.90	4.95	5.00	5.05	5.10	5.15	5.20	5.25	5.30	5.35	5.40	5.45	5.50	5.55	5.60	5.65	5.70	5.75	5.80	5.85
1.74	4.50	4.55	4.60	4.65	4.70	4.75	4.80	4.85	4.90	4.95	5.00	5.05	5.10	5.15	5.20	5.25	5.30	5.35	5.40	5.45	5.50	5.55	5.60	5.65	5.70	5.75	5.80	5.85	5.90
1.76	4.55	4.60	4.65	4.70	4.75	4.80	4.85	4.90	4.95	5.00	5.05	5.10	5.15	5.20	5.25	5.30	5.35	5.40	5.45	5.50	5.55	5.60	5.65	5.70	5.75	5.80	5.85	5.90	5.95
1.78	4.60	4.65	4.70	4.75	4.80	4.85	4.90	4.95	5.00	5.05	5.10	5.15	5.20	5.25	5.30	5.35	5.40	5.45	5.50	5.55	5.60	5.65	5.70	5.75	5.80	5.85	5.90	5.95	6.00
1.80	4.65	4.70	4.75	4.80	4.85	4.90	4.95	5.00	5.05	5.10	5.15	5.20	5.25	5.30	5.35	5.40	5.45	5.50	5.55	5.60	5.65	5.70	5.75	5.80	5.85	5.90	5.95	6.00	6.05
1.82	4.70	4.75	4.80	4.85	4.90	4.95	5.00	5.05	5.10	5.15	5.20	5.25	5.30	5.35	5.40	5.45	5.50	5.55	5.60	5.65	5.70	5.75	5.80	5.85	5.90	5.95	6.00	6.05	6.10
1.84	4.75	4.80	4.85	4.90	4.95	5.00	5.05	5.10	5.15	5.20	5.25	5.30	5.35	5.40	5.45	5.50	5.55	5.60	5.65	5.70	5.75	5.80	5.85	5.90	5.95	6.00	6.05	6.10	6.15
1.86	4.80	4.85	4.90	4.95	5.00	5.05	5.10	5.15	5.20	5.25	5.30	5.35	5.40	5.45	5.50	5.55	5.60	5.65	5.70	5.75	5.80	5.85	5.90	5.95	6.00	6.05	6.10	6.15	6.20
1.88	4.85	4.90	4.95	5.00	5.05	5.10	5.15	5.20	5.25	5.30	5.35	5.40	5.45	5.50	5.55	5.60	5.65	5.70	5.75	5.80	5.85	5.90	5.95	6.00	6.05	6.10	6.15	6.20	6.25
1.90	4.90	4.95	5.00	5.05	5.10	5.15	5.20	5.25	5.30	5.35	5.40	5.45	5.50	5.55	5.60	5.65	5.70	5.75	5.80	5.85	5.90	5.95	6.00	6.05	6.10	6.15	6.20	6.25	6.30
1.92	4.95	5.00	5.05	5.10	5.15	5.20	5.25	5.30	5.35	5.40	5.45	5.50	5.55	5.60	5.65	5.70	5.75	5.80	5.85	5.90	5.95	6.00	6.05	6.10	6.15	6.20	6.25	6.30	6.35
1.94	5.00	5.05	5.10	5.15	5.20	5.25	5.30	5.35	5.40	5.45	5.50	5.55	5.60	5.65	5.70	5.75	5.80	5.85	5.90	5.95	6.00	6.05	6.10	6.15	6.20	6.25	6.30	6.35	6.40
1.96	5.05	5.10	5.15	5.20	5.25	5.30	5.35	5.40	5.45	5.50	5.55	5.60	5.65	5.70	5.75	5.80	5.85	5.90	5.95	6.00	6.05	6.10	6.15	6.20	6.25	6.30	6.35	6.40	6.45
1.98	5.10	5.15	5.20	5.25	5.30	5.35	5.40	5.45	5.50	5.55	5.60	5.65	5.70	5.75	5.80	5.85	5.90	5.95	6.00	6.05	6.10	6.15	6.20	6.25	6.30	6.35	6.40	6.45	6.50
2.00	5.15	5.20	5.25	5.30	5.35	5.40	5.45	5.50	5.55	5.60	5.65	5.70	5.75	5.80	5.85	5.90	5.95	6.00	6.05	6.10	6.15	6.20	6.25	6.30	6.35	6.40	6.45	6.50	6.55
2.02	5.20	5.25	5.30	5.35	5.40	5.45	5.50	5.55	5.60	5.65	5.70	5.75	5.80	5.85	5.90	5.95	6.00	6.05	6.10	6.15	6.20	6.25	6.30	6.35	6.40	6.45	6.50	6.55	6.60
2.04	5.25	5.30	5.35	5.40	5.45	5.50	5.55	5.60	5.65	5.70	5.75	5.80	5.85	5.90	5.95	6.00	6.05	6.10	6.15	6.20	6.25	6.30	6.35	6.40	6.45	6.50	6.55	6.60	6.65
2.06	5.30	5.35	5.40	5.45	5.50	5.55	5.60	5.65	5.70	5.75	5.80	5.85	5.90	5.95	6.00	6.05	6.10	6.15	6.20	6.25	6.30	6.35	6.40	6.45	6.50	6.55	6.60	6.65	6.70
2.08	5.35	5.40	5.45	5.50	5.55	5.60	5.65	5.70	5.75	5.80	5.85	5.90	5.95	6.00	6.05	6.10	6.15	6.20	6.25	6.30	6.35	6.40	6.45	6.50	6.55	6.60	6.65	6.70	6.75
2.10	5.40	5.45	5.50	5.55	5.60	5.65	5.70	5.75	5.80	5.85	5.90	5.95	6.00	6.05	6.10	6.15	6.20	6.25	6.30	6.35	6.40	6.45	6.50	6.55	6.60	6.65	6.70	6.75	6.80
2.12	5.45	5.50	5.55	5.60	5.65	5.70	5.75	5.80	5.85	5.90	5.95	6.00	6.05	6.10	6.15	6.20	6.25	6.30	6.35	6.40	6.45	6.50	6.55	6.60	6.65	6.70	6.75	6.80	6.85
2.14	5.50	5.55	5.60	5.65	5.70	5.75	5.80	5.85	5.90	5.95	6.00	6.05	6.10	6.15	6.20	6.25	6.30	6.35	6.40	6.45	6.50	6.55	6.60	6.65	6.70	6.75	6.80	6.85	6.90
2.16	5.55	5.60	5.65	5.70	5.75	5.80	5.85	5.90	5.95	6.00	6.05	6.10	6.15	6.20	6.25	6.30	6.35	6.40	6.45	6.50	6.55	6.60	6.65	6.70	6.75	6.80	6.85	6.90	6.95
2.18	5.60	5.65	5.70	5.75	5.80	5.85	5.90	5.95	6.00	6.05	6.10	6.15	6.20	6.25	6.30	6.35	6.40	6.45	6.50	6.55	6.60	6.65	6.70	6.75	6.80	6.85	6.90	6.95	7.00
2.20	5.65	5.70	5.75	5.80	5.85	5.90	5.95	6.00	6.05	6.10	6.15	6.20	6.25	6.30	6.35	6.40	6.45	6.50	6.55	6.60	6.65	6.70	6.75	6.80	6.85	6.90	6.95	7.00	7.05
2.22	5.70	5.75	5.80	5.85	5.90	5.95	6.00	6.05	6.10	6.15	6.20	6.25	6.30	6.35	6.40	6.45	6.50	6.55	6.60	6.65	6.70	6.75	6.80	6.85	6.90	6.95	7.00	7.05	7.10
2.24	5.75	5.80	5.85	5.90	5.95	6.00	6.05	6.10	6.15	6.20	6.25	6.30	6.35	6.40	6.45	6.50	6.55	6.60	6.65	6.70	6.75	6.80	6.85	6.90	6.95	7.00	7.05	7.10	7.15
2.26	5.80	5.85	5.90	5.95	6.00	6.05	6.10	6.15	6.20	6.25	6.30	6.35	6.40	6.45	6.50	6.55	6.60	6.65	6.70	6.75	6.80	6.85	6.90	6.95	7.00	7.05	7.10	7.15	7.20
2.28	5.85	5.90	5.95	6.00	6.05	6.10	6.15	6.20	6.25	6.30	6.35	6.40	6.45	6.50	6.55	6.60	6.65	6.70	6.75	6.80	6.85	6.90	6.95	7.00	7.05	7.10	7.15	7.20	7.25
2.30	5.90	5.95	6.00	6.05	6.10	6.15	6.20	6.25	6.30	6.35	6.40	6.45	6.50	6.55	6.60	6.65	6.70	6.75	6.80	6.85	6.90	6.95	7.00	7.05	7.10	7.15	7.20	7.25	7.30

40% FOOD COST CHART

COST OF TRIMMINGS

COST OF ENTREE	.06	.08	.10	.12	.14	.16	.18	.20	.22	.24	.26	.28	.30	.32	.34	.36	.38	.40	.42	.44	.46	.48	.50	.52	.54	.56	.58	.60	.62
2.32	5.95	6.00	6.05	6.10	6.15	6.20	6.25	6.30	6.35	6.40	6.45	6.50	6.55	6.60	6.65	6.70	6.75	6.80	6.85	6.90	6.95	7.00	7.05	7.10	7.15	7.20	7.25	7.30	7.35
2.34	6.00	6.05	6.10	6.15	6.20	6.25	6.30	6.35	6.40	6.45	6.50	6.55	6.60	6.65	6.70	6.75	6.80	6.85	6.90	6.95	7.00	7.05	7.10	7.15	7.20	7.25	7.30	7.35	7.40
2.36	6.05	6.10	6.15	6.20	6.25	6.30	6.35	6.40	6.45	6.50	6.55	6.60	6.65	6.70	6.75	6.80	6.85	6.90	6.95	7.00	7.05	7.10	7.15	7.20	7.25	7.30	7.35	7.40	7.45
2.38	6.10	6.15	6.20	6.25	6.30	6.35	6.40	6.45	6.50	6.55	6.60	6.65	6.70	6.75	6.80	6.85	6.90	6.95	7.00	7.05	7.10	7.15	7.20	7.25	7.30	7.35	7.40	7.45	7.50
2.40	6.15	6.20	6.25	6.30	6.35	6.40	6.45	6.50	6.55	6.60	6.65	6.70	6.75	6.80	6.85	6.90	6.95	7.00	7.05	7.10	7.15	7.20	7.25	7.30	7.35	7.40	7.45	7.50	7.55
2.42	6.20	6.25	6.30	6.35	6.40	6.45	6.50	6.55	6.60	6.65	6.70	6.75	6.80	6.85	6.90	6.95	7.00	7.05	7.10	7.15	7.20	7.25	7.30	7.35	7.40	7.45	7.50	7.55	7.60
2.44	6.25	6.30	6.35	6.40	6.45	6.50	6.55	6.60	6.65	6.70	6.75	6.80	6.85	6.90	6.95	7.00	7.05	7.10	7.15	7.20	7.25	7.30	7.35	7.40	7.45	7.50	7.55	7.60	7.65
2.46	6.30	6.35	6.40	6.45	6.50	6.55	6.60	6.65	6.70	6.75	6.80	6.85	6.90	6.95	7.00	7.05	7.10	7.15	7.20	7.25	7.30	7.35	7.40	7.45	7.50	7.55	7.60	7.65	7.70
2.48	6.35	6.40	6.45	6.50	6.55	6.60	6.65	6.70	6.75	6.80	6.85	6.90	6.95	7.00	7.05	7.10	7.15	7.20	7.25	7.30	7.35	7.40	7.45	7.50	7.55	7.60	7.65	7.70	7.75
2.50	6.40	6.45	6.50	6.55	6.60	6.65	6.70	6.75	6.80	6.85	6.90	6.95	7.00	7.05	7.10	7.15	7.20	7.25	7.30	7.35	7.40	7.45	7.50	7.55	7.60	7.65	7.70	7.75	7.80
2.52	6.45	6.50	6.55	6.60	6.65	6.70	6.75	6.80	6.85	6.90	6.95	7.00	7.05	7.10	7.15	7.20	7.25	7.30	7.35	7.40	7.45	7.50	7.55	7.60	7.65	7.70	7.75	7.80	7.85
2.54	6.50	6.55	6.60	6.65	6.70	6.75	6.80	6.85	6.90	6.95	7.00	7.05	7.10	7.15	7.20	7.25	7.30	7.35	7.40	7.45	7.50	7.55	7.60	7.65	7.70	7.75	7.80	7.85	7.90
2.56	6.55	6.60	6.65	6.70	6.75	6.80	6.85	6.90	6.95	7.00	7.05	7.10	7.15	7.20	7.25	7.30	7.35	7.40	7.45	7.50	7.55	7.60	7.65	7.70	7.75	7.80	7.85	7.90	7.95
2.58	6.60	6.65	6.70	6.75	6.80	6.85	6.90	6.95	7.00	7.05	7.10	7.15	7.20	7.25	7.30	7.35	7.40	7.45	7.50	7.55	7.60	7.65	7.70	7.75	7.80	7.85	7.90	7.95	8.00
2.60	6.65	6.70	6.75	6.80	6.85	6.90	6.95	7.00	7.05	7.10	7.15	7.20	7.25	7.30	7.35	7.40	7.45	7.50	7.55	7.60	7.65	7.70	7.75	7.80	7.85	7.90	7.95	8.00	8.05
2.62	6.70	6.75	6.80	6.85	6.90	6.95	7.00	7.05	7.10	7.15	7.20	7.25	7.30	7.35	7.40	7.45	7.50	7.55	7.60	7.65	7.70	7.75	7.80	7.85	7.90	7.95	8.00	8.05	8.10
2.64	6.75	6.80	6.85	6.90	6.95	7.00	7.05	7.10	7.15	7.20	7.25	7.30	7.35	7.40	7.45	7.50	7.55	7.60	7.65	7.70	7.75	7.80	7.85	7.90	7.95	8.00	8.05	8.10	8.15
2.66	6.80	6.85	6.90	6.95	7.00	7.05	7.10	7.15	7.20	7.25	7.30	7.35	7.40	7.45	7.50	7.55	7.60	7.65	7.70	7.75	7.80	7.85	7.90	7.95	8.00	8.05	8.10	8.15	8.20
2.68	6.85	6.90	6.95	7.00	7.05	7.10	7.15	7.20	7.25	7.30	7.35	7.40	7.45	7.50	7.55	7.60	7.65	7.70	7.75	7.80	7.85	7.90	7.95	8.00	8.05	8.10	8.15	8.20	8.25
2.70	6.90	6.95	7.00	7.05	7.10	7.15	7.20	7.25	7.30	7.35	7.40	7.45	7.50	7.55	7.60	7.65	7.70	7.75	7.80	7.85	7.90	7.95	8.00	8.05	8.10	8.15	8.20	8.25	8.30
2.72	6.95	7.00	7.05	7.10	7.15	7.20	7.25	7.30	7.35	7.40	7.45	7.50	7.55	7.60	7.65	7.70	7.75	7.80	7.85	7.90	7.95	8.00	8.05	8.10	8.15	8.20	8.25	8.30	8.35
2.74	7.00	7.05	7.10	7.15	7.20	7.25	7.30	7.35	7.40	7.45	7.50	7.55	7.60	7.65	7.70	7.75	7.80	7.85	7.90	7.95	8.00	8.05	8.10	8.15	8.20	8.25	8.30	8.35	8.40
2.76	7.05	7.10	7.15	7.20	7.25	7.30	7.35	7.40	7.45	7.50	7.55	7.60	7.65	7.70	7.75	7.80	7.85	7.90	7.95	8.00	8.05	8.10	8.15	8.20	8.25	8.30	8.35	8.40	8.45
2.78	7.10	7.15	7.20	7.25	7.30	7.35	7.40	7.45	7.50	7.55	7.60	7.65	7.70	7.75	7.80	7.85	7.90	7.95	8.00	8.05	8.10	8.15	8.20	8.25	8.30	8.35	8.40	8.45	8.50
2.80	7.15	7.20	7.25	7.30	7.35	7.40	7.45	7.50	7.55	7.60	7.65	7.70	7.75	7.80	7.85	7.90	7.95	8.00	8.05	8.10	8.15	8.20	8.25	8.30	8.35	8.40	8.45	8.50	8.55
2.82	7.20	7.25	7.30	7.35	7.40	7.45	7.50	7.55	7.60	7.65	7.70	7.75	7.80	7.85	7.90	7.95	8.00	8.05	8.10	8.15	8.20	8.25	8.30	8.35	8.40	8.45	8.50	8.55	8.60
2.84	7.25	7.30	7.35	7.40	7.45	7.50	7.55	7.60	7.65	7.70	7.75	7.80	7.85	7.90	7.95	8.00	8.05	8.10	8.15	8.20	8.25	8.30	8.35	8.40	8.45	8.50	8.55	8.60	8.65
2.86	7.30	7.35	7.40	7.45	7.50	7.55	7.60	7.65	7.70	7.75	7.80	7.85	7.90	7.95	8.00	8.05	8.10	8.15	8.20	8.25	8.30	8.35	8.40	8.45	8.50	8.55	8.60	8.65	8.70
2.88	7.35	7.40	7.45	7.50	7.55	7.60	7.65	7.70	7.75	7.80	7.85	7.90	7.95	8.00	8.05	8.10	8.15	8.20	8.25	8.30	8.35	8.40	8.45	8.50	8.55	8.60	8.65	8.70	8.75
2.90	7.40	7.45	7.50	7.55	7.60	7.65	7.70	7.75	7.80	7.85	7.90	7.95	8.00	8.05	8.10	8.15	8.20	8.25	8.30	8.35	8.40	8.45	8.50	8.55	8.60	8.65	8.70	8.75	8.80
2.92	7.45	7.50	7.55	7.60	7.65	7.70	7.75	7.80	7.85	7.90	7.95	8.00	8.05	8.10	8.15	8.20	8.25	8.30	8.35	8.40	8.45	8.50	8.55	8.60	8.65	8.70	8.75	8.80	8.85
2.94	7.50	7.55	7.60	7.65	7.70	7.75	7.80	7.85	7.90	7.95	8.00	8.05	8.10	8.15	8.20	8.25	8.30	8.35	8.40	8.45	8.50	8.55	8.60	8.65	8.70	8.75	8.80	8.85	8.90
2.96	7.55	7.60	7.65	7.70	7.75	7.80	7.85	7.90	7.95	8.00	8.05	8.10	8.15	8.20	8.25	8.30	8.35	8.40	8.45	8.50	8.55	8.60	8.65	8.70	8.75	8.80	8.85	8.90	8.95
2.98	7.60	7.65	7.70	7.75	7.80	7.85	7.90	7.95	8.00	8.05	8.10	8.15	8.20	8.25	8.30	8.35	8.40	8.45	8.50	8.55	8.60	8.65	8.70	8.75	8.80	8.85	8.90	8.95	9.00
3.00	7.65	7.70	7.75	7.80	7.85	7.90	7.95	8.00	8.05	8.10	8.15	8.20	8.25	8.30	8.35	8.40	8.45	8.50	8.55	8.60	8.65	8.70	8.75	8.80	8.85	8.90	8.95	9.00	9.05
3.02	7.70	7.75	7.80	7.85	7.90	7.95	8.00	8.05	8.10	8.15	8.20	8.25	8.30	8.35	8.40	8.45	8.50	8.55	8.60	8.65	8.70	8.75	8.80	8.85	8.90	8.95	9.00	9.05	9.10
3.04	7.75	7.80	7.85	7.90	7.95	8.00	8.05	8.10	8.15	8.20	8.25	8.30	8.35	8.40	8.45	8.50	8.55	8.60	8.65	8.70	8.75	8.80	8.85	8.90	8.95	9.00	9.05	9.10	9.15

45% FOOD COST CHART

COST OF TRIMMINGS

COST OF ENTREE	.06	.08	.10	.12	.14	.16	.18	.20	.22	.24	.26	.28	.30	.32	.34	.36	.38	.40	.42	.44	.46	.48	.50	.52	.54	.56	.58	.60	.62
.10	.36	.40	.44	.49	.53	.58	.62	.67	.71	.76	.80	.85	.89	.94	.98	1.02	1.07	1.11	1.16	1.20	1.25	1.29	1.34	1.38	1.42	1.47	1.51	1.56	1.60
.12	.40	.44	.49	.53	.58	.62	.67	.71	.76	.80	.85	.89	.94	.98	1.02	1.07	1.11	1.16	1.20	1.25	1.29	1.34	1.38	1.42	1.47	1.51	1.56	1.60	1.65
.14	.44	.49	.53	.58	.62	.67	.71	.76	.80	.85	.89	.94	.98	1.02	1.07	1.11	1.16	1.20	1.25	1.29	1.34	1.38	1.42	1.47	1.51	1.56	1.60	1.65	1.69
.16	.49	.53	.58	.62	.67	.71	.76	.80	.85	.89	.94	.98	1.02	1.07	1.11	1.16	1.20	1.25	1.29	1.34	1.38	1.42	1.47	1.51	1.56	1.60	1.65	1.69	1.73
.18	.53	.58	.62	.67	.71	.76	.80	.85	.89	.94	.98	1.02	1.07	1.11	1.16	1.20	1.25	1.29	1.34	1.38	1.42	1.47	1.51	1.56	1.60	1.65	1.69	1.73	1.78
.20	.58	.62	.67	.71	.76	.80	.85	.89	.94	.98	1.02	1.07	1.11	1.16	1.20	1.25	1.29	1.34	1.38	1.42	1.47	1.51	1.56	1.60	1.65	1.69	1.73	1.78	1.82
.22	.62	.67	.71	.76	.80	.85	.89	.94	.98	1.02	1.07	1.11	1.16	1.20	1.25	1.29	1.34	1.38	1.42	1.47	1.51	1.56	1.60	1.65	1.69	1.73	1.78	1.82	1.87
.24	.67	.71	.76	.80	.85	.89	.94	.98	1.02	1.07	1.11	1.16	1.20	1.25	1.29	1.34	1.38	1.42	1.47	1.51	1.56	1.60	1.65	1.69	1.73	1.78	1.82	1.87	1.91
.26	.71	.76	.80	.85	.89	.94	.98	1.02	1.07	1.11	1.16	1.20	1.25	1.29	1.34	1.38	1.42	1.47	1.51	1.56	1.60	1.65	1.69	1.73	1.78	1.82	1.87	1.91	1.96
.28	.76	.80	.85	.89	.94	.98	1.02	1.07	1.11	1.16	1.20	1.25	1.29	1.34	1.38	1.42	1.47	1.51	1.56	1.60	1.65	1.69	1.73	1.78	1.82	1.87	1.91	1.96	2.00
.30	.80	.85	.89	.94	.98	1.02	1.07	1.11	1.16	1.20	1.25	1.29	1.34	1.38	1.42	1.47	1.51	1.56	1.60	1.65	1.69	1.73	1.78	1.82	1.87	1.91	1.96	2.00	2.05
.32	.85	.89	.94	.98	1.02	1.07	1.11	1.16	1.20	1.25	1.29	1.34	1.38	1.42	1.47	1.51	1.56	1.60	1.65	1.69	1.73	1.78	1.82	1.87	1.91	1.96	2.00	2.05	2.09
.34	.89	.94	.98	1.02	1.07	1.11	1.16	1.20	1.25	1.29	1.34	1.38	1.42	1.47	1.51	1.56	1.60	1.65	1.69	1.73	1.78	1.82	1.87	1.91	1.96	2.00	2.05	2.09	2.13
.36	.94	.98	1.02	1.07	1.11	1.16	1.20	1.25	1.29	1.34	1.38	1.42	1.47	1.51	1.56	1.60	1.65	1.69	1.73	1.78	1.82	1.87	1.91	1.96	2.00	2.05	2.09	2.13	2.18
.38	.98	1.02	1.07	1.11	1.16	1.20	1.25	1.29	1.34	1.38	1.42	1.47	1.51	1.56	1.60	1.65	1.69	1.73	1.78	1.82	1.87	1.91	1.96	2.00	2.05	2.09	2.13	2.18	2.22
.40	1.02	1.07	1.11	1.16	1.20	1.25	1.29	1.34	1.38	1.42	1.47	1.51	1.56	1.60	1.65	1.69	1.73	1.78	1.82	1.87	1.91	1.96	2.00	2.05	2.09	2.13	2.18	2.22	2.27
.42	1.07	1.11	1.16	1.20	1.25	1.29	1.34	1.38	1.42	1.47	1.51	1.56	1.60	1.65	1.69	1.73	1.78	1.82	1.87	1.91	1.96	2.00	2.05	2.09	2.13	2.18	2.22	2.27	2.31
.44	1.11	1.16	1.20	1.25	1.29	1.34	1.38	1.42	1.47	1.51	1.56	1.60	1.65	1.69	1.73	1.78	1.82	1.87	1.91	1.96	2.00	2.05	2.09	2.13	2.18	2.22	2.27	2.31	2.36
.46	1.16	1.20	1.25	1.29	1.34	1.38	1.42	1.47	1.51	1.56	1.60	1.65	1.69	1.73	1.78	1.82	1.87	1.91	1.96	2.00	2.05	2.09	2.13	2.18	2.22	2.27	2.31	2.36	2.40
.48	1.20	1.25	1.29	1.34	1.38	1.42	1.47	1.51	1.56	1.60	1.65	1.69	1.73	1.78	1.82	1.87	1.91	1.96	2.00	2.05	2.09	2.13	2.18	2.22	2.27	2.31	2.36	2.40	2.45
.50	1.25	1.29	1.34	1.38	1.42	1.47	1.51	1.56	1.60	1.65	1.69	1.73	1.78	1.82	1.87	1.91	1.96	2.00	2.05	2.09	2.13	2.18	2.22	2.27	2.31	2.36	2.40	2.45	2.49
.52	1.29	1.34	1.38	1.42	1.47	1.51	1.56	1.60	1.65	1.69	1.73	1.78	1.82	1.87	1.91	1.96	2.00	2.05	2.09	2.13	2.18	2.22	2.27	2.31	2.36	2.40	2.45	2.49	2.53
.54	1.34	1.38	1.42	1.47	1.51	1.56	1.60	1.65	1.69	1.73	1.78	1.82	1.87	1.91	1.96	2.00	2.05	2.09	2.13	2.18	2.22	2.27	2.31	2.36	2.40	2.45	2.49	2.53	2.57
.56	1.38	1.42	1.47	1.51	1.56	1.60	1.65	1.69	1.73	1.78	1.82	1.87	1.91	1.96	2.00	2.05	2.09	2.13	2.18	2.22	2.27	2.31	2.36	2.40	2.45	2.49	2.53	2.57	2.62
.58	1.42	1.47	1.51	1.56	1.60	1.65	1.69	1.73	1.78	1.82	1.87	1.91	1.96	2.00	2.05	2.09	2.13	2.18	2.22	2.27	2.31	2.36	2.40	2.45	2.49	2.53	2.57	2.62	2.66
.60	1.47	1.51	1.56	1.60	1.65	1.69	1.73	1.78	1.82	1.87	1.91	1.96	2.00	2.05	2.09	2.13	2.18	2.22	2.27	2.31	2.36	2.40	2.45	2.49	2.53	2.57	2.62	2.66	2.70
.62	1.51	1.56	1.60	1.65	1.69	1.73	1.78	1.82	1.87	1.91	1.96	2.00	2.05	2.09	2.13	2.18	2.22	2.27	2.31	2.36	2.40	2.45	2.49	2.53	2.57	2.62	2.66	2.70	2.76
.64	1.56	1.60	1.65	1.69	1.73	1.78	1.82	1.87	1.91	1.96	2.00	2.05	2.09	2.13	2.18	2.22	2.27	2.31	2.36	2.40	2.45	2.49	2.53	2.57	2.62	2.66	2.70	2.76	2.80
.66	1.60	1.65	1.69	1.73	1.78	1.82	1.87	1.91	1.96	2.00	2.05	2.09	2.13	2.18	2.22	2.27	2.31	2.36	2.40	2.45	2.49	2.53	2.57	2.62	2.66	2.70	2.76	2.80	2.85
.68	1.65	1.69	1.73	1.78	1.82	1.87	1.91	1.96	2.00	2.05	2.09	2.13	2.18	2.22	2.27	2.31	2.36	2.40	2.45	2.49	2.53	2.57	2.62	2.66	2.70	2.76	2.80	2.85	2.90
.70	1.69	1.73	1.78	1.82	1.87	1.91	1.96	2.00	2.05	2.09	2.13	2.18	2.22	2.27	2.31	2.36	2.40	2.45	2.49	2.53	2.57	2.62	2.66	2.70	2.76	2.80	2.85	2.90	2.93
.72	1.73	1.78	1.82	1.87	1.91	1.96	2.00	2.05	2.09	2.13	2.18	2.22	2.27	2.31	2.36	2.40	2.45	2.49	2.53	2.57	2.62	2.66	2.70	2.76	2.80	2.85	2.90	2.93	2.98
.74	1.78	1.82	1.87	1.91	1.96	2.00	2.05	2.09	2.13	2.18	2.22	2.27	2.31	2.36	2.40	2.45	2.49	2.53	2.57	2.62	2.66	2.70	2.76	2.80	2.85	2.90	2.93	2.98	3.02
.76	1.82	1.87	1.91	1.96	2.00	2.05	2.09	2.13	2.18	2.22	2.27	2.31	2.36	2.40	2.45	2.49	2.53	2.57	2.62	2.66	2.70	2.76	2.80	2.85	2.90	2.93	2.98	3.02	3.07
.78	1.87	1.91	1.96	2.00	2.05	2.09	2.13	2.18	2.22	2.27	2.31	2.36	2.40	2.45	2.49	2.53	2.57	2.62	2.66	2.70	2.76	2.80	2.85	2.90	2.93	2.98	3.02	3.07	3.11
.80	1.91	1.96	2.00	2.05	2.09	2.13	2.18	2.22	2.27	2.31	2.36	2.40	2.45	2.49	2.53	2.57	2.62	2.66	2.70	2.76	2.80	2.85	2.90	2.93	2.98	3.02	3.07	3.11	3.15
.82	1.96	2.00	2.05	2.09	2.13	2.18																					3.11	3.15	3.20

45% FOOD COST CHART

COST OF TRIMMINGS

COST OF ENTREE	.06	.08	.10	.12	.14	.16	.18	.20	.22	.24	.26	.28	.30	.32	.34	.36	.38	.40	.42	.44	.46	.48	.50	.52	.54	.56	.58	.60	.62
.84	2.00	2.04	2.09	2.13	2.18	2.22	2.27	2.31	2.36	2.40	2.44	2.49	2.53	2.58	2.62	2.67	2.71	2.76	2.80	2.84	2.89	2.93	2.98	3.02	3.07	3.11	3.16	3.20	3.24
.86	2.04	2.09	2.13	2.18	2.22	2.27	2.31	2.36	2.40	2.44	2.49	2.53	2.58	2.62	2.67	2.71	2.76	2.80	2.84	2.89	2.93	2.98	3.02	3.07	3.11	3.16	3.20	3.24	3.29
.88	2.09	2.13	2.18	2.22	2.27	2.31	2.36	2.40	2.44	2.49	2.53	2.58	2.62	2.67	2.71	2.76	2.80	2.84	2.89	2.93	2.98	3.02	3.07	3.11	3.16	3.20	3.24	3.29	3.33
.90	2.13	2.18	2.22	2.27	2.31	2.36	2.40	2.44	2.49	2.53	2.58	2.62	2.67	2.71	2.76	2.80	2.84	2.89	2.93	2.98	3.02	3.07	3.11	3.16	3.20	3.24	3.29	3.33	3.38
.92	2.18	2.22	2.27	2.31	2.36	2.40	2.44	2.49	2.53	2.58	2.62	2.67	2.71	2.76	2.80	2.84	2.89	2.93	2.98	3.02	3.07	3.11	3.16	3.20	3.24	3.29	3.33	3.38	3.42
.94	2.22	2.27	2.31	2.36	2.40	2.44	2.49	2.53	2.58	2.62	2.67	2.71	2.76	2.80	2.84	2.89	2.93	2.98	3.02	3.07	3.11	3.16	3.20	3.24	3.29	3.33	3.38	3.42	3.47
.96	2.27	2.31	2.36	2.40	2.44	2.49	2.53	2.58	2.62	2.67	2.71	2.76	2.80	2.84	2.89	2.93	2.98	3.02	3.07	3.11	3.16	3.20	3.24	3.29	3.33	3.38	3.42	3.47	3.51
.98	2.31	2.36	2.40	2.44	2.49	2.53	2.58	2.62	2.67	2.71	2.76	2.80	2.84	2.89	2.93	2.98	3.02	3.07	3.11	3.16	3.20	3.24	3.29	3.33	3.38	3.42	3.47	3.51	3.56
1.00	2.36	2.40	2.44	2.49	2.53	2.58	2.62	2.67	2.71	2.76	2.80	2.84	2.89	2.93	2.98	3.02	3.07	3.11	3.16	3.20	3.24	3.29	3.33	3.38	3.42	3.47	3.51	3.56	3.60
1.02	2.40	2.44	2.49	2.53	2.58	2.62	2.67	2.71	2.76	2.80	2.84	2.89	2.93	2.98	3.02	3.07	3.11	3.16	3.20	3.24	3.29	3.33	3.38	3.42	3.47	3.51	3.56	3.60	3.64
1.04	2.44	2.49	2.53	2.58	2.62	2.67	2.71	2.76	2.80	2.84	2.89	2.93	2.98	3.02	3.07	3.11	3.16	3.20	3.24	3.29	3.33	3.38	3.42	3.47	3.51	3.56	3.60	3.64	3.69
1.06	2.49	2.53	2.58	2.62	2.67	2.71	2.76	2.80	2.84	2.89	2.93	2.98	3.02	3.07	3.11	3.16	3.20	3.24	3.29	3.33	3.38	3.42	3.47	3.51	3.56	3.60	3.64	3.69	3.73
1.08	2.53	2.58	2.62	2.67	2.71	2.76	2.80	2.84	2.89	2.93	2.98	3.02	3.07	3.11	3.16	3.20	3.24	3.29	3.33	3.38	3.42	3.47	3.51	3.56	3.60	3.64	3.69	3.73	3.78
1.10	2.58	2.62	2.67	2.71	2.76	2.80	2.84	2.89	2.93	2.98	3.02	3.07	3.11	3.16	3.20	3.24	3.29	3.33	3.38	3.42	3.47	3.51	3.56	3.60	3.64	3.69	3.73	3.78	3.82
1.12	2.62	2.67	2.71	2.76	2.80	2.84	2.89	2.93	2.98	3.02	3.07	3.11	3.16	3.20	3.24	3.29	3.33	3.38	3.42	3.47	3.51	3.56	3.60	3.64	3.69	3.73	3.78	3.82	3.87
1.14	2.67	2.71	2.76	2.80	2.84	2.89	2.93	2.98	3.02	3.07	3.11	3.16	3.20	3.24	3.29	3.33	3.38	3.42	3.47	3.51	3.56	3.60	3.64	3.69	3.73	3.78	3.82	3.87	3.91
1.16	2.71	2.76	2.80	2.84	2.89	2.93	2.98	3.02	3.07	3.11	3.16	3.20	3.24	3.29	3.33	3.38	3.42	3.47	3.51	3.56	3.60	3.64	3.69	3.73	3.78	3.82	3.87	3.91	3.96
1.18	2.76	2.80	2.84	2.89	2.93	2.98	3.02	3.07	3.11	3.16	3.20	3.24	3.29	3.33	3.38	3.42	3.47	3.51	3.56	3.60	3.64	3.69	3.73	3.78	3.82	3.87	3.91	3.96	4.00
1.20	2.80	2.84	2.89	2.93	2.98	3.02	3.07	3.11	3.16	3.20	3.24	3.29	3.33	3.38	3.42	3.47	3.51	3.56	3.60	3.64	3.69	3.73	3.78	3.82	3.87	3.91	3.96	4.00	4.04
1.22	2.84	2.89	2.93	2.98	3.02	3.07	3.11	3.16	3.20	3.24	3.29	3.33	3.38	3.42	3.47	3.51	3.56	3.60	3.64	3.69	3.73	3.78	3.82	3.87	3.91	3.96	4.00	4.04	4.09
1.24	2.89	2.93	2.98	3.02	3.07	3.11	3.16	3.20	3.24	3.29	3.33	3.38	3.42	3.47	3.51	3.56	3.60	3.64	3.69	3.73	3.78	3.82	3.87	3.91	3.96	4.00	4.04	4.09	4.13
1.26	2.93	2.98	3.02	3.07	3.11	3.16	3.20	3.24	3.29	3.33	3.38	3.42	3.47	3.51	3.56	3.60	3.64	3.69	3.73	3.78	3.82	3.87	3.91	3.96	4.00	4.04	4.09	4.13	4.18
1.28	2.98	3.02	3.07	3.11	3.16	3.20	3.24	3.29	3.33	3.38	3.42	3.47	3.51	3.56	3.60	3.64	3.69	3.73	3.78	3.82	3.87	3.91	3.96	4.00	4.04	4.09	4.13	4.18	4.22
1.30	3.02	3.07	3.11	3.16	3.20	3.24	3.29	3.33	3.38	3.42	3.47	3.51	3.56	3.60	3.64	3.69	3.73	3.78	3.82	3.87	3.91	3.96	4.00	4.04	4.09	4.13	4.18	4.22	4.27
1.32	3.07	3.11	3.16	3.20	3.24	3.29	3.33	3.38	3.42	3.47	3.51	3.56	3.60	3.64	3.69	3.73	3.78	3.82	3.87	3.91	3.96	4.00	4.04	4.09	4.13	4.18	4.22	4.27	4.31
1.34	3.11	3.16	3.20	3.24	3.29	3.33	3.38	3.42	3.47	3.51	3.56	3.60	3.64	3.69	3.73	3.78	3.82	3.87	3.91	3.96	4.00	4.04	4.09	4.13	4.18	4.22	4.27	4.31	4.36
1.36	3.16	3.20	3.24	3.29	3.33	3.38	3.42	3.47	3.51	3.56	3.60	3.64	3.69	3.73	3.78	3.82	3.87	3.91	3.96	4.00	4.04	4.09	4.13	4.18	4.22	4.27	4.31	4.36	4.40
1.38	3.20	3.24	3.29	3.33	3.38	3.42	3.47	3.51	3.56	3.60	3.64	3.69	3.73	3.78	3.82	3.87	3.91	3.96	4.00	4.04	4.09	4.13	4.18	4.22	4.27	4.31	4.36	4.40	4.44
1.40	3.24	3.29	3.33	3.38	3.42	3.47	3.51	3.56	3.60	3.64	3.69	3.73	3.78	3.82	3.87	3.91	3.96	4.00	4.04	4.09	4.13	4.18	4.22	4.27	4.31	4.36	4.40	4.44	4.49
1.42	3.29	3.33	3.38	3.42	3.47	3.51	3.56	3.60	3.64	3.69	3.73	3.78	3.82	3.87	3.91	3.96	4.00	4.04	4.09	4.13	4.18	4.22	4.27	4.31	4.36	4.40	4.44	4.49	4.53
1.44	3.33	3.38	3.42	3.47	3.51	3.56	3.60	3.64	3.69	3.73	3.78	3.82	3.87	3.91	3.96	4.00	4.04	4.09	4.13	4.18	4.22	4.27	4.31	4.36	4.40	4.44	4.49	4.53	4.58
1.46	3.38	3.42	3.47	3.51	3.56	3.60	3.64	3.69	3.73	3.78	3.82	3.87	3.91	3.96	4.00	4.04	4.09	4.13	4.18	4.22	4.27	4.31	4.36	4.40	4.44	4.49	4.53	4.58	4.62
1.48	3.42	3.47	3.51	3.56	3.60	3.64	3.69	3.73	3.78	3.82	3.87	3.91	3.96	4.00	4.04	4.09	4.13	4.18	4.22	4.27	4.31	4.36	4.40	4.44	4.49	4.53	4.58	4.62	4.67
1.50	3.47	3.51	3.56	3.60	3.64	3.69	3.73	3.78	3.82	3.87	3.91	3.96	4.00	4.04	4.09	4.13	4.18	4.22	4.27	4.31	4.36	4.40	4.44	4.49	4.53	4.58	4.62	4.67	4.71
1.52	3.51	3.56	3.60	3.64	3.69	3.73	3.78	3.82	3.87	3.91	3.96	4.00	4.04	4.09	4.13	4.18	4.22	4.27	4.31	4.36	4.40	4.44	4.49	4.53	4.58	4.62	4.67	4.71	4.76
1.54	3.56	3.60	3.64	3.69	3.73	3.78	3.82	3.87	3.91	3.96	4.00	4.04	4.09	4.13	4.18	4.22	4.27	4.31	4.36	4.40	4.44	4.49	4.53	4.58	4.62	4.67	4.71	4.76	4.80
1.56	3.60	3.64	3.69	3.73	3.78	3.82	3.87	3.91	3.96	4.00	4.04	4.09	4.13	4.18	4.22	4.27	4.31	4.36	4.40	4.44	4.49	4.53	4.58	4.62	4.67	4.71	4.76	4.80	4.84

45% FOOD COST CHART

COST OF TRIMMINGS

COST OF ENTREE	.06	.08	.10	.12	.14	.16	.18	.20	.22	.24	.26	.28	.30	.32	.34	.36	.38	.40	.42	.44	.46	.48	.50	.52	.54	.56	.58	.60	.62
1.58	3.64	3.69	3.73	3.78	3.82	3.87	3.91	3.96	4.00	4.04	4.09	4.13	4.18	4.22	4.27	4.31	4.36	4.40	4.44	4.49	4.53	4.58	4.62	4.67	4.71	4.76	4.80	4.84	4.89
1.60	3.69	3.73	3.78	3.82	3.87	3.91	3.96	4.00	4.04	4.09	4.13	4.18	4.22	4.27	4.31	4.36	4.40	4.44	4.49	4.53	4.58	4.62	4.67	4.71	4.76	4.80	4.84	4.89	4.93
1.62	3.73	3.78	3.82	3.87	3.91	3.96	4.00	4.04	4.09	4.13	4.18	4.22	4.27	4.31	4.36	4.40	4.44	4.49	4.53	4.58	4.62	4.67	4.71	4.76	4.80	4.84	4.89	4.93	4.98
1.64	3.78	3.82	3.87	3.91	3.96	4.00	4.04	4.09	4.13	4.18	4.22	4.27	4.31	4.36	4.40	4.44	4.49	4.53	4.58	4.62	4.67	4.71	4.76	4.80	4.84	4.89	4.93	4.98	5.02
1.66	3.82	3.87	3.91	3.96	4.00	4.04	4.09	4.13	4.18	4.22	4.27	4.31	4.36	4.40	4.44	4.49	4.53	4.58	4.62	4.67	4.71	4.76	4.80	4.84	4.89	4.93	4.98	5.02	5.07
1.68	3.87	3.91	3.96	4.00	4.04	4.09	4.13	4.18	4.22	4.27	4.31	4.36	4.40	4.44	4.49	4.53	4.58	4.62	4.67	4.71	4.76	4.80	4.84	4.89	4.93	4.98	5.02	5.07	5.11
1.70	3.91	3.96	4.00	4.04	4.09	4.13	4.18	4.22	4.27	4.31	4.36	4.40	4.44	4.49	4.53	4.58	4.62	4.67	4.71	4.76	4.80	4.84	4.89	4.93	4.98	5.02	5.07	5.11	5.15
1.72	3.96	4.00	4.04	4.09	4.13	4.18	4.22	4.27	4.31	4.36	4.40	4.44	4.49	4.53	4.58	4.62	4.67	4.71	4.76	4.80	4.84	4.89	4.93	4.98	5.02	5.07	5.11	5.15	5.20
1.74	4.00	4.04	4.09	4.13	4.18	4.22	4.27	4.31	4.36	4.40	4.44	4.49	4.53	4.58	4.62	4.67	4.71	4.76	4.80	4.84	4.89	4.93	4.98	5.02	5.07	5.11	5.15	5.20	5.24
1.76	4.04	4.09	4.13	4.18	4.22	4.27	4.31	4.36	4.40	4.44	4.49	4.53	4.58	4.62	4.67	4.71	4.76	4.80	4.84	4.89	4.93	4.98	5.02	5.07	5.11	5.15	5.20	5.24	5.29
1.78	4.09	4.13	4.18	4.22	4.27	4.31	4.36	4.40	4.44	4.49	4.53	4.58	4.62	4.67	4.71	4.76	4.80	4.84	4.89	4.93	4.98	5.02	5.07	5.11	5.15	5.20	5.24	5.29	5.33
1.80	4.13	4.18	4.22	4.27	4.31	4.36	4.40	4.44	4.49	4.53	4.58	4.62	4.67	4.71	4.76	4.80	4.84	4.89	4.93	4.98	5.02	5.07	5.11	5.15	5.20	5.24	5.29	5.33	5.38
1.82	4.18	4.22	4.27	4.31	4.36	4.40	4.44	4.49	4.53	4.58	4.62	4.67	4.71	4.76	4.80	4.84	4.89	4.93	4.98	5.02	5.07	5.11	5.15	5.20	5.24	5.29	5.33	5.38	5.42
1.84	4.22	4.27	4.31	4.36	4.40	4.44	4.49	4.53	4.58	4.62	4.67	4.71	4.76	4.80	4.84	4.89	4.93	4.98	5.02	5.07	5.11	5.15	5.20	5.24	5.29	5.33	5.38	5.42	5.47
1.86	4.27	4.31	4.36	4.40	4.44	4.49	4.53	4.58	4.62	4.67	4.71	4.76	4.80	4.84	4.89	4.93	4.98	5.02	5.07	5.11	5.15	5.20	5.24	5.29	5.33	5.38	5.42	5.47	5.51
1.88	4.31	4.36	4.40	4.44	4.49	4.53	4.58	4.62	4.67	4.71	4.76	4.80	4.84	4.89	4.93	4.98	5.02	5.07	5.11	5.15	5.20	5.24	5.29	5.33	5.38	5.42	5.47	5.51	5.56
1.90	4.36	4.40	4.44	4.49	4.53	4.58	4.62	4.67	4.71	4.76	4.80	4.84	4.89	4.93	4.98	5.02	5.07	5.11	5.15	5.20	5.24	5.29	5.33	5.38	5.42	5.47	5.51	5.56	5.60
1.92	4.40	4.44	4.49	4.53	4.58	4.62	4.67	4.71	4.76	4.80	4.84	4.89	4.93	4.98	5.02	5.07	5.11	5.15	5.20	5.24	5.29	5.33	5.38	5.42	5.47	5.51	5.56	5.60	5.64
1.94	4.44	4.49	4.53	4.58	4.62	4.67	4.71	4.76	4.80	4.84	4.89	4.93	4.98	5.02	5.07	5.11	5.15	5.20	5.24	5.29	5.33	5.38	5.42	5.47	5.51	5.56	5.60	5.64	5.69
1.96	4.49	4.53	4.58	4.62	4.67	4.71	4.76	4.80	4.84	4.89	4.93	4.98	5.02	5.07	5.11	5.15	5.20	5.24	5.29	5.33	5.38	5.42	5.47	5.51	5.56	5.60	5.64	5.69	5.73
1.98	4.53	4.58	4.62	4.67	4.71	4.76	4.80	4.84	4.89	4.93	4.98	5.02	5.07	5.11	5.15	5.20	5.24	5.29	5.33	5.38	5.42	5.47	5.51	5.56	5.60	5.64	5.69	5.73	5.78
2.00	4.58	4.62	4.67	4.71	4.76	4.80	4.84	4.89	4.93	4.98	5.02	5.07	5.11	5.15	5.20	5.24	5.29	5.33	5.38	5.42	5.47	5.51	5.56	5.60	5.64	5.69	5.73	5.78	5.82
2.02	4.62	4.67	4.71	4.76	4.80	4.84	4.89	4.93	4.98	5.02	5.07	5.11	5.15	5.20	5.24	5.29	5.33	5.38	5.42	5.47	5.51	5.56	5.60	5.64	5.69	5.73	5.78	5.82	5.87
2.04	4.67	4.71	4.76	4.80	4.84	4.89	4.93	4.98	5.02	5.07	5.11	5.15	5.20	5.24	5.29	5.33	5.38	5.42	5.47	5.51	5.56	5.60	5.64	5.69	5.73	5.78	5.82	5.87	5.91
2.06	4.71	4.76	4.80	4.84	4.89	4.93	4.98	5.02	5.07	5.11	5.15	5.20	5.24	5.29	5.33	5.38	5.42	5.47	5.51	5.56	5.60	5.64	5.69	5.73	5.78	5.82	5.87	5.91	5.96
2.08	4.76	4.80	4.84	4.89	4.93	4.98	5.02	5.07	5.11	5.15	5.20	5.24	5.29	5.33	5.38	5.42	5.47	5.51	5.56	5.60	5.64	5.69	5.73	5.78	5.82	5.87	5.91	5.96	6.00
2.10	4.80	4.84	4.89	4.93	4.98	5.02	5.07	5.11	5.15	5.20	5.24	5.29	5.33	5.38	5.42	5.47	5.51	5.56	5.60	5.64	5.69	5.73	5.78	5.82	5.87	5.91	5.96	6.00	6.04
2.12	4.84	4.89	4.93	4.98	5.02	5.07	5.11	5.15	5.20	5.24	5.29	5.33	5.38	5.42	5.47	5.51	5.56	5.60	5.64	5.69	5.73	5.78	5.82	5.87	5.91	5.96	6.00	6.04	6.09
2.14	4.89	4.93	4.98	5.02	5.07	5.11	5.15	5.20	5.24	5.29	5.33	5.38	5.42	5.47	5.51	5.56	5.60	5.64	5.69	5.73	5.78	5.82	5.87	5.91	5.96	6.00	6.04	6.09	6.13
2.16	4.93	4.98	5.02	5.07	5.11	5.15	5.20	5.24	5.29	5.33	5.38	5.42	5.47	5.51	5.56	5.60	5.64	5.69	5.73	5.78	5.82	5.87	5.91	5.96	6.00	6.04	6.09	6.13	6.18
2.18	4.98	5.02	5.07	5.11	5.15	5.20	5.24	5.29	5.33	5.38	5.42	5.47	5.51	5.56	5.60	5.64	5.69	5.73	5.78	5.82	5.87	5.91	5.96	6.00	6.04	6.09	6.13	6.18	6.22
2.20	5.02	5.07	5.11	5.15	5.20	5.24	5.29	5.33	5.38	5.42	5.47	5.51	5.56	5.60	5.64	5.69	5.73	5.78	5.82	5.87	5.91	5.96	6.00	6.04	6.09	6.13	6.18	6.22	6.27
2.22	5.07	5.11	5.15	5.20	5.24	5.29	5.33	5.38	5.42	5.47	5.51	5.56	5.60	5.64	5.69	5.73	5.78	5.82	5.87	5.91	5.96	6.00	6.04	6.09	6.13	6.18	6.22	6.27	6.31
2.24	5.11	5.15	5.20	5.24	5.29	5.33	5.38	5.42	5.47	5.51	5.56	5.60	5.64	5.69	5.73	5.78	5.82	5.87	5.91	5.96	6.00	6.04	6.09	6.13	6.18	6.22	6.27	6.31	6.36
2.26	5.15	5.20	5.24	5.29	5.33	5.38	5.42	5.47	5.51	5.56	5.60	5.64	5.69	5.73	5.78	5.82	5.87	5.91	5.96	6.00	6.04	6.09	6.13	6.18	6.22	6.27	6.31	6.36	6.40
2.28	5.20	5.24	5.29	5.33	5.38	5.42	5.47	5.51	5.56	5.60	5.64	5.69	5.73	5.78	5.82	5.87	5.91	5.96	6.00	6.04	6.09	6.13	6.18	6.22	6.27	6.31	6.36	6.40	6.44
2.30	5.24	5.29	5.33	5.38	5.42	5.47	5.51	5.56	5.60	5.64	5.69	5.73	5.78	5.82	5.87	5.91	5.96	6.00	6.04	6.09	6.13	6.18	6.22	6.27	6.31	6.36	6.40	6.44	6.49

45% FOOD COST CHART

COST OF TRIMMINGS

COST OF ENTREE	.06	.08	.10	.12	.14	.16	.18	.20	.22	.24	.26	.28	.30	.32	.34	.36	.38	.40	.42	.44	.46	.48	.50	.52	.54	.56	.58	.60	.62
2.32	5.29	5.33	5.38	5.42	5.47	5.51	5.56	5.60	5.64	5.69	5.73	5.78	5.82	5.87	5.91	5.96	6.00	6.04	6.09	6.13	6.18	6.22	6.27	6.31	6.36	6.40	6.44	6.49	6.53
2.34	5.33	5.38	5.42	5.47	5.51	5.56	5.60	5.64	5.69	5.73	5.78	5.82	5.87	5.91	5.96	6.00	6.04	6.09	6.13	6.18	6.22	6.27	6.31	6.36	6.40	6.44	6.49	6.53	6.58
2.36	5.38	5.42	5.47	5.51	5.56	5.60	5.64	5.69	5.73	5.78	5.82	5.87	5.91	5.96	6.00	6.04	6.09	6.13	6.18	6.22	6.27	6.31	6.36	6.40	6.44	6.49	6.53	6.58	6.62
2.38	5.42	5.47	5.51	5.56	5.60	5.64	5.69	5.73	5.78	5.82	5.87	5.91	5.96	6.00	6.04	6.09	6.13	6.18	6.22	6.27	6.31	6.36	6.40	6.44	6.49	6.53	6.58	6.62	6.67
2.40	5.47	5.51	5.56	5.60	5.64	5.69	5.73	5.78	5.82	5.87	5.91	5.96	6.00	6.04	6.09	6.13	6.18	6.22	6.27	6.31	6.36	6.40	6.44	6.49	6.53	6.58	6.62	6.67	6.71
2.42	5.51	5.56	5.60	5.64	5.69	5.73	5.78	5.82	5.87	5.91	5.96	6.00	6.04	6.09	6.13	6.18	6.22	6.27	6.31	6.36	6.40	6.44	6.49	6.53	6.58	6.62	6.67	6.71	6.76
2.44	5.56	5.60	5.64	5.69	5.73	5.78	5.82	5.87	5.91	5.96	6.00	6.04	6.09	6.13	6.18	6.22	6.27	6.31	6.36	6.40	6.44	6.49	6.53	6.58	6.62	6.67	6.71	6.76	6.80
2.46	5.60	5.64	5.69	5.73	5.78	5.82	5.87	5.91	5.96	6.00	6.04	6.09	6.13	6.18	6.22	6.27	6.31	6.36	6.40	6.44	6.49	6.53	6.58	6.62	6.67	6.71	6.76	6.80	6.84
2.48	5.64	5.69	5.73	5.78	5.82	5.87	5.91	5.96	6.00	6.04	6.09	6.13	6.18	6.22	6.27	6.31	6.36	6.40	6.44	6.49	6.53	6.58	6.62	6.67	6.71	6.76	6.80	6.84	6.89
2.50	5.69	5.73	5.78	5.82	5.87	5.91	5.96	6.00	6.04	6.09	6.13	6.18	6.22	6.27	6.31	6.36	6.40	6.44	6.49	6.53	6.58	6.62	6.67	6.71	6.76	6.80	6.84	6.89	6.93
2.52	5.73	5.78	5.82	5.87	5.91	5.96	6.00	6.04	6.09	6.13	6.18	6.22	6.27	6.31	6.36	6.40	6.44	6.49	6.53	6.58	6.62	6.67	6.71	6.76	6.80	6.84	6.89	6.93	6.98
2.54	5.78	5.82	5.87	5.91	5.96	6.00	6.04	6.09	6.13	6.18	6.22	6.27	6.31	6.36	6.40	6.44	6.49	6.53	6.58	6.62	6.67	6.71	6.76	6.80	6.84	6.89	6.93	6.98	7.02
2.56	5.82	5.87	5.91	5.96	6.00	6.04	6.09	6.13	6.18	6.22	6.27	6.31	6.36	6.40	6.44	6.49	6.53	6.58	6.62	6.67	6.71	6.76	6.80	6.84	6.89	6.93	6.98	7.02	7.07
2.58	5.87	5.91	5.96	6.00	6.04	6.09	6.13	6.18	6.22	6.27	6.31	6.36	6.40	6.44	6.49	6.53	6.58	6.62	6.67	6.71	6.76	6.80	6.84	6.89	6.93	6.98	7.02	7.07	7.11
2.60	5.91	5.96	6.00	6.04	6.09	6.13	6.18	6.22	6.27	6.31	6.36	6.40	6.44	6.49	6.53	6.58	6.62	6.67	6.71	6.76	6.80	6.84	6.89	6.93	6.98	7.02	7.07	7.11	7.16
2.62	5.96	6.00	6.04	6.09	6.13	6.18	6.22	6.27	6.31	6.36	6.40	6.44	6.49	6.53	6.58	6.62	6.67	6.71	6.76	6.80	6.84	6.89	6.93	6.98	7.02	7.07	7.11	7.16	7.20
2.64	6.00	6.04	6.09	6.13	6.18	6.22	6.27	6.31	6.36	6.40	6.44	6.49	6.53	6.58	6.62	6.67	6.71	6.76	6.80	6.84	6.89	6.93	6.98	7.02	7.07	7.11	7.16	7.20	7.24
2.66	6.04	6.09	6.13	6.18	6.22	6.27	6.31	6.36	6.40	6.44	6.49	6.53	6.58	6.62	6.67	6.71	6.76	6.80	6.84	6.89	6.93	6.98	7.02	7.07	7.11	7.16	7.20	7.24	7.29
2.68	6.09	6.13	6.18	6.22	6.27	6.31	6.36	6.40	6.44	6.49	6.53	6.58	6.62	6.67	6.71	6.76	6.80	6.84	6.89	6.93	6.98	7.02	7.07	7.11	7.16	7.20	7.24	7.29	7.33
2.70	6.13	6.18	6.22	6.27	6.31	6.36	6.40	6.44	6.49	6.53	6.58	6.62	6.67	6.71	6.76	6.80	6.84	6.89	6.93	6.98	7.02	7.07	7.11	7.16	7.20	7.24	7.29	7.33	7.38
2.72	6.18	6.22	6.27	6.31	6.36	6.40	6.44	6.49	6.53	6.58	6.62	6.67	6.71	6.76	6.80	6.84	6.89	6.93	6.98	7.02	7.07	7.11	7.16	7.20	7.24	7.29	7.33	7.38	7.42
2.74	6.22	6.27	6.31	6.36	6.40	6.44	6.49	6.53	6.58	6.62	6.67	6.71	6.76	6.80	6.84	6.89	6.93	6.98	7.02	7.07	7.11	7.16	7.20	7.24	7.29	7.33	7.38	7.42	7.47
2.76	6.27	6.31	6.36	6.40	6.44	6.49	6.53	6.58	6.62	6.67	6.71	6.76	6.80	6.84	6.89	6.93	6.98	7.02	7.07	7.11	7.16	7.20	7.24	7.29	7.33	7.38	7.42	7.47	7.51
2.78	6.31	6.36	6.40	6.44	6.49	6.53	6.58	6.62	6.67	6.71	6.76	6.80	6.84	6.89	6.93	6.98	7.02	7.07	7.11	7.16	7.20	7.24	7.29	7.33	7.38	7.42	7.47	7.51	7.56
2.80	6.36	6.40	6.44	6.49	6.53	6.58	6.62	6.67	6.71	6.76	6.80	6.84	6.89	6.93	6.98	7.02	7.07	7.11	7.16	7.20	7.24	7.29	7.33	7.38	7.42	7.47	7.51	7.56	7.60
2.82	6.40	6.44	6.49	6.53	6.58	6.62	6.67	6.71	6.76	6.80	6.84	6.89	6.93	6.98	7.02	7.07	7.11	7.16	7.20	7.24	7.29	7.33	7.38	7.42	7.47	7.51	7.56	7.60	7.64
2.84	6.44	6.49	6.53	6.58	6.62	6.67	6.71	6.76	6.80	6.84	6.89	6.93	6.98	7.02	7.07	7.11	7.16	7.20	7.24	7.29	7.33	7.38	7.42	7.47	7.51	7.56	7.60	7.64	7.69
2.86	6.49	6.53	6.58	6.62	6.67	6.71	6.76	6.80	6.84	6.89	6.93	6.98	7.02	7.07	7.11	7.16	7.20	7.24	7.29	7.33	7.38	7.42	7.47	7.51	7.56	7.60	7.64	7.69	7.73
2.88	6.53	6.58	6.62	6.67	6.71	6.76	6.80	6.84	6.89	6.93	6.98	7.02	7.07	7.11	7.16	7.20	7.24	7.29	7.33	7.38	7.42	7.47	7.51	7.56	7.60	7.64	7.69	7.73	7.78
2.90	6.58	6.62	6.67	6.71	6.76	6.80	6.84	6.89	6.93	6.98	7.02	7.07	7.11	7.16	7.20	7.24	7.29	7.33	7.38	7.42	7.47	7.51	7.56	7.60	7.64	7.69	7.73	7.78	7.82
2.92	6.62	6.67	6.71	6.76	6.80	6.84	6.89	6.93	6.98	7.02	7.07	7.11	7.16	7.20	7.24	7.29	7.33	7.38	7.42	7.47	7.51	7.56	7.60	7.64	7.69	7.73	7.78	7.82	7.87
2.94	6.67	6.71	6.76	6.80	6.84	6.89	6.93	6.98	7.02	7.07	7.11	7.16	7.20	7.24	7.29	7.33	7.38	7.42	7.47	7.51	7.56	7.60	7.64	7.69	7.73	7.78	7.82	7.87	7.91
2.96	6.71	6.76	6.80	6.84	6.89	6.93	6.98	7.02	7.07	7.11	7.16	7.20	7.24	7.29	7.33	7.38	7.42	7.47	7.51	7.56	7.60	7.64	7.69	7.73	7.78	7.82	7.87	7.91	7.96
2.98	6.76	6.80	6.84	6.89	6.93	6.98	7.02	7.07	7.11	7.16	7.20	7.24	7.29	7.33	7.38	7.42	7.47	7.51	7.56	7.60	7.64	7.69	7.73	7.78	7.82	7.87	7.91	7.96	8.00
3.00	6.80	6.84	6.89	6.93	6.98	7.02	7.07	7.11	7.16	7.20	7.24	7.29	7.33	7.38	7.42	7.47	7.51	7.56	7.60	7.64	7.69	7.73	7.78	7.82	7.87	7.91	7.96	8.00	8.04
3.02	6.84	6.89	6.93	6.98	7.02	7.07	7.11	7.16	7.20	7.24	7.29	7.33	7.38	7.42	7.47	7.51	7.56	7.60	7.64	7.69	7.73	7.78	7.82	7.87	7.91	7.96	8.00	8.04	8.09
3.04	6.89	6.93	6.98	7.02	7.07	7.11	7.16	7.20	7.24	7.29	7.33	7.38	7.42	7.47	7.51	7.56	7.60	7.64	7.69	7.73	7.78	7.82	7.87	7.91	7.96	8.00	8.04	8.09	8.13

CHAPTER 6

Menu Mechanics

Certain mechanical factors must be considered in menu planning. No matter how well it is planned and priced, it must also be properly presented so that it is quickly understood and leads to satisfactory sales. Proper observance of mechanical factors can enhance a menu's appearance, make a favorable impression on patrons and advance the aims of management.

Some printing enterprises make a specialty of setting up menu cards and it is frequently wise to secure their services to make the original design, establish wording and set up the format.

Menu Presentation

While most menus are printed, some may not be. A cafeteria menu board may show items for sale and list prices. A menu can appear on closed circuit TV. A drive-in may have menu cards or menu signs near speakers or somewhere inside or outside the building where patrons can see what is available and know the price. Some operations have handwritten menus purposely done to give a homey and personal touch. A menu may be made to resemble a small newspaper and list the latest news along with menu items. A take-out or drive-in may have its menu printed on its paper goods or take-out cartons. Frontier Town, in Montana on the Continental Divide, has its menu burned on a small tanned animal skin that is strung between wooden branches. An oriental type foodservice may have its menu rolled as a silken scroll. A menu may be a placemat or napkin or a child's menu may be found in a puzzle or comic book. A fast food operation may print its menu card as a sale's ticket. The guest checks the foods desired and this is used for order placement. When the foods are brought to the guest, this check comes totaled so that it can be taken to the cashier at the end of the meal and used for payment.

Regardless of how a menu is presented, there are certain rules in format all of which should be observed. Wording and its arrangement should be such that the reader quickly understands what is offered. If foods are offered in groups, it should be clear what foods are in-

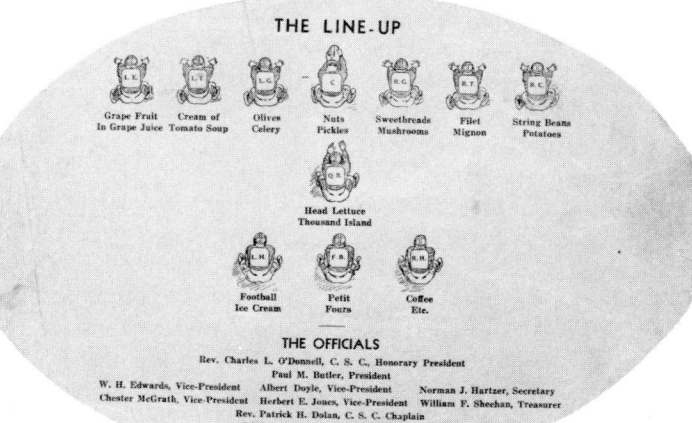

THE LINE-UP

Grape Fruit In Grape Juice — Cream of Tomato Soup — Olives Celery — Nuts Pickles — Sweetbreads Mushrooms — Filet Mignon — String Beans Potatoes

Head Lettuce Thousand Island

Football Ice Cream — Petit Fours — Coffee Etc.

THE OFFICIALS

Rev. Charles L. O'Donnell, C. S. C., Honorary President

Paul M. Butler, President

W. H. Edwards, Vice-President   Albert Doyle, Vice-President   Norman J. Hartzer, Secretary

Chester McGrath, Vice-President   Herbert E. Jones, Vice-President   William F. Sheehan, Treasurer

Rev. Patrick H. Dolan, C. S. C. Chaplain

Edward J. Meehan, Banquet Chairman

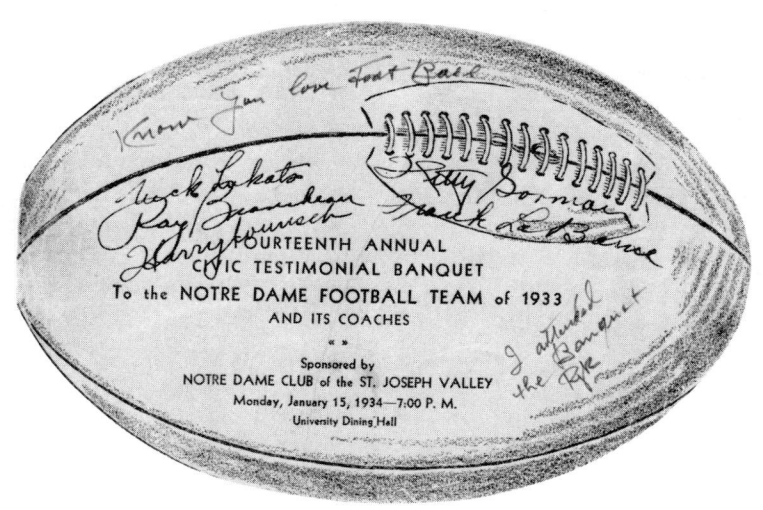

FOURTEENTH ANNUAL CIVIC TESTIMONIAL BANQUET

To the NOTRE DAME FOOTBALL TEAM of 1933

AND ITS COACHES

« »

Sponsored by

NOTRE DAME CLUB of the ST. JOSEPH VALLEY

Monday, January 15, 1934—7:00 P. M.

University Dining Hall

FIG. 6-1   Menus can take interesting shapes tying in with the theme of the occasion. This old menu was used at the awards banquet for the famous 1933 football team of the University of Notre Dame. The eleven items on the menu were placed in the positions of the players.

cluded. Clarity is promoted by making menu items stand out. Simplicity helps avoid clutter. Foods usually should be on the menu in the order in which they are eaten. An exception might be a cafeteria menu board, listing items as they appear in the counter—some offer cold foods first and hot foods last. This avoids having the hot foods cool off while a customer selects the cold ones. Some menus also indicate the location of foods, such as in a drive-in or take-out, where different counters offer different foods, or a shopping center type cafeteria where patrons move from a separate section to another in order to get different foods. In this case, the menu board can be helpful by indicating counter number, or by diagram or chart to show where foods are found.

Some menus may never be seen by patrons. They are written principally for the back-of-the-house people to enable them to know what must be produced. This requires a different form and terminology. Menus of this type are more like production schedules than menu cards. Selling words and fancy descriptions are not required. The term "carrot pennies," which sounds good on a menu read by patrons, instead will be "sliced carrots." Production information is included such as the amount to prepare, the recipe number to use, preparation time, distribution to service units, designation of the worker to prepare items, portion sizes and other information. Service instructions such as the dishing tool to use, portioning instructions, dishes to use, may also be added.

A cycle menu is usually seen by the production department only and thus may have features also found in production schedules. Some operations find that a three-day cycle is enough. Airlines often use a six-day cycle. The Las Vegas Hilton hotel finds a seven-day cycle satisfactory. Other operations may find it is better not to repeat a cycle on the same day of the week. Where an institution serves the same individuals over a long period of time, a cycle menu of less than 18 days is usually undesirable because patrons quickly learn the cycle. Some institutions of this type use four 28-day cycle menus, using one of the four for each season of the year, each menu being changed after it is used 13 weeks.

The manner in which menu items are presented should be selected to best meet the needs of the operation. A hospital may have selected menus printed on colored paper, each color indicating a different diet. On some, special instructions concerning selections by patients may be required. The sales department of a hotel or a catering department may need a special menu to give to people interested in arranging special functions at the hotel. This can list foods offered at weddings, receptions, banquets, buffets, etc., along with cost.

Some operations need a number of different menus. It is possible for an enterprise to need a breakfast, a brunch, a lunch, a matinée, a dinner and an evening menu. A hotel or motel may need a special room service menu. Another enterprise may need all of these for several service areas. A club may need menus for its bar where steaks, sandwiches and snack foods are served, another for the "19th hole" area, another for a coffee shop or gaming room, a small snack and beverage menu for the swimming pool, and another for the main dining room. And as these menus vary in their purpose and requirements so must they vary in the manner in which menu items are presented and the format of the menu.

The most common menu is one which is printed on a firm, hard, shiny-finish cover, the front being used for some logo design or motif. Inside, on the left and right sides of the fold, à la carte offerings (items selected and paid for individually) are listed. The back may also contain à la carte items and alcoholic beverages or give information on hours of operation and short notes of interest on the operation, the locale or some of the foods served. The items on this heavy, shiny-finish paper are permanent.

MONDAY Spring/Summer Week 1	GENERAL	SOFT-BLAND	ADA MEAL PLAN NO. 2 (1500 Calories) DIABETIC	RESTRICTED SODIUM (1 gram Sodium)

MORNING	Orange Juice
	Malt-O-Meal or
	   Ready-to-eat Cereal
	Scrambled Eggs
	Crisp Bacon
	Raisin Toast — Jelly
	Butter[1]
	Coffee — Milk
		Orange Juice
		Malt-O-Meal or
		   Ready-to-eat Cereal
		Scrambled Eggs
		Crisp Bacon
		Toast — Jelly
		Butter[1]
		Coffee — Milk
		(Decaffeinated for bland)
			Orange Juice (1/2 cup)
			Malt-O-Meal (1/2 cup) or
			   Ready-to-eat Cereal
			Scrambled Egg (1)
			Crisp Bacon (1 strip)
			Toast (1 slice)
			Coffee — Tea
				Orange Juice
				SF Malt-O-Meal or
				   Shredded Wheat
				SF Scrambled Egg (1)
				SF Toast — Jelly
				SF Butter[1]
				Coffee — Milk

NOON	Meat Balls in Buttermilk Sauce*
	Buttered Fordhook Lima Beans
	Tossed Green Salad with
	   French Dressing
	Corn Bread
	Butter[1]
	Chess Pie
	Milk, Coffee, or Tea
		Meat Balls in Buttermilk Sauce*
		Green Asparagus
		Pear-Lime Gelatin Salad
		Bread
		Butter[1]
		Baked Custard
		Milk
			Meat Balls (2 ozs.)
			Buttered Fordhook Lima Beans
			   (1/2 cup)
			Diet Pear Halves (2) Salad
			Cornbread (2-inch square)
			Butter[1] (1 pat)
			Special Baked Custard[2] (1/2 cup)
			Milk[3] (1/2 cup)
				SF Meat Balls
				SF Fordhook Lima Beans
				Tossed Green Salad with
				   Oil and Vinegar
				SF Bread
				SF Butter[1]
				SF Baked Custard
				Coffee — Tea

EVENING	Baked Liver with Onions
	Mashed Potatoes
	Green Peas with Pimiento
	Bread
	Butter[1]
	Fresh Frozen Peaches with
	   Whipped Topping
	Milk or Cocoa
		Baked Liver
		Mashed Potatoes
		Buttered Green Peas
		Bread
		Butter[1]
		Sliced Peaches with
		   Whipped Topping
		Milk or Cocoa
			Baked Liver (2 ozs.)
			Mashed Potatoes (1/2 cup)
			Green Peas with Pimiento (1/2 cup)
			Diet Sliced Peaches (1/2 cup)
			Coffee — Tea
				SF Baked Liver with Onions
				SF Mashed Potatoes
				SF Buttered Green Peas
				SF Bread
				SF Butter[1]
				Fresh Frozen Peaches with
				   Whipped Topping
				Milk

	[1] Or margarine
	[2] Special Baked Custard equals: 1 Meat Exchange
	                            1/2 Milk Exchange
	                            Sugar Substitute
	[3] Part of milk may be used for coffee, tea, or cereal
	* Rice Council Recipe
			BEDTIME:
			Milk[3] (1 cup)
			Bread (1 slice)
			Butter[1] (1 pat)	

FIG. 6-2 An example of a cyclic menu used in a hospital. This sheet is for Monday of the first week of the Spring-Summer cycle. (Courtesy Rice Council)

Often the menu items that change, including the table d'hôte listings which are foods or meals sold all together at one price and not individually as in à la carte, are printed in lighter paper and attached to this more rigid folder or card. Table d'hôte listings may vary. At one time it meant a complete meal offered at one price but today it may also mean a group of foods offered together at a price for all of them. Thus, a table d'hôte listing may offer entrées served with a salad, potato and bread and butter, with no appetizer or dessert included. Even the beverage may be à la carte.

Sometimes menus may list two prices for an item, one including the entrée as the main dish in a table d'hôte meal, the other offering it à la carte. Even as an à la carte item, it may be served with foods such as bread and butter. Thus, a menu might list items with two prices as follows:

	A la carte	Table d'hote
Southern Fried Chicken with Country Gravy and Corn Fritter	$2.25	$3.75
Crab Flakes Mornay in Coquille with Steamed Rice	2.60	4.10
Fillet of Cod en Paillote, French Fried Zucchini	1.80	3.35
Ham Steak Hawaiian, with Mashed Sweet Potatoes	2.50	4.00
New York Strip Steak, French Fried Potatoes	4.75	6.25
Breaded Veal Cutlet, Sauteed Mushrooms and Baked Potato	2.70	4.20

(With the table d'hote dinner you have a choice of salad or vegetable, beverage and dessert. Roll and butter are served with à la carte and table d'hote orders.)

While this listing shows a $1.50 differences between table d'hôte and à la carte items, it is not unusual to see that the difference between table d'hôte and à la carte is often not a set price but will vary.

Some menus may offer specials. These can be attached as clip-one or inserts. If they are used, the menu should provide space for them. They should not cover other material and make it difficult to read what is underneath.

Typefaces

The format and printing have much to do with the legibility and comprehension of the menu. Menus, like individuals, should have a personality. They should reflect the atmosphere and feeling of the operation. The eye should be pleased with what it sees and quickly grasp what is offered and the price. The presentation should blend in with the logo of the operation. The menu should be what a program is to a play or opera, indicating what is to come. It should be a prelude to a pleasing experience. It should not over promise. Patrons should clearly understand what they are to get and the price they are to pay for it.

One of the most important factors in accomplishing a menu's purpose is the style of type used. There are many different kinds but some are more easily read than others. The type most often used for menus is the Roman face, regular plain Bodoni, which investigations show is one of the easiest types to read. The following kinds of type are shown in order of their legibility rank:

Cheltenham

Braised in butter and then simmered in red wine with shallots and other herbs, this dish has been for centuries one of the most typical of the Bretony area. Braised in butter and then simmered in red wine with shallots and other herbs, this dish has

Antique

Braised in butter and then simmered in red wine with shallots and other herbs, this dish has been for centuries one of the most typical of the Bretony area. Braised in butter and then simmered in red wine with shallots and other herbs, this dish has

Bodoni

Braised in butter and then simmered in red wine with shallots and other herbs, this dish has been for centuries one of the most typical of the Bretony area. Braised in butter and then simmered in red wine with shallots and other herbs, this dish has been for centuries

Old Style

Braised in butter and then simmered in red wine with shallots and other herbs, this dish has been for centuries one of the most typical of the Bretony area. Braised in butter and then simmered in red wine with shallots and other herbs, this dish has been for centuries

Garamond

Braised in butter and then simmered in red wine with shallots and other herbs, this dish has been for centuries one of the most typical of the Bretony area. Braised in butter and then simmered in red wine with shallots and other herbs, this dish has been for centuries one of the most

American Typewriter

Braised in butter and then simmered in red wine with shallots and other herbs, this dish has been for centuries one of the most typical of the Bretony area. Braised in butter and then simmered in red wine with

Scotch Roman

Braised in butter and then simmered in red wine with shallots and other herbs, this dish has been for centuries one of the most typical of the Bretony area. Braised in butter and then simmered in red wine with shallots and other herbs, this dish has been for centuries one of

Caslon Old Style

Braised in butter and then simmered in red wine with shallots and other herbs, this dish has been for centuries one of the most typical of the Bretony area. Braised in butter and then simmered in red wine with shallots and other herbs, this dish has been for centuries

Kabel

Braised in butter and then simmered in red wine with shallots and other herbs, this dish has been for centuries one of the most typical of the Bretony area. Braised in butter and then simmered in red wine with shallots and other herbs, this dish has been for centuries one of

Black Letter

Braised in butter and then simmered in red wine with shallots and other herbs, this dish has been for centuries one of the most typical of the Bretony area. Braised in butter and then simmered in red wine with shallots and other herbs, this dish has been for centuries

It has been found that legibility does not always correlate with reading speed. Thus, while Cheltenham type has the best legibility rating, it ranks eighth among these 10 type faces in reading speed. Scotch Roman ranks first in reading speed but seventh in legibility. Antique, Bodoni and Old Style have fair correlation between their legibility and reading speed.

Investigators have also found that readers prefer bold-faced type, such as Antique, Cheltenham or Bodoni. Putting type into all capitals retards reading speed and legibility. Mixed type does the same. Arabic numerals in modern type are preferred over ornate type styles or script, and over Roman numerals.

Type will come plain (regular), bold (heavy print), italics and script. Any kind of italic or script print is more difficult to read than regular plain type.

Italic, script or specialty types develop reading fatigue quite rapidly.

The size of the type is also important to understanding and speed of reading. Too small a type face makes reading difficult but too large a type takes up too much space and may not give good comprehension because it spreads the words out too much. Type size is indicated by points. There are 72 points to the inch. Thus, 18-point is nearly a fourth of an inch high. This text is printed in 11-point Baskerville type. Most menu designers use 10- or 12-point type for listing menu items. They vary this for headings or for descriptions, etc. There is a difference in type size depending upon whether it is cast or cold type. A 24-point cast type usually has a face of about 20 points because shoulders are provided to keep the face itself from being battered in printing. In cold type, 24 points means 24-point size.

EL CORTEZ
HOTEL & CASINO

WEDNESDAY, FEBRUARY 13, 1974

ALL ENTREES INCLUDE

SOUP DU JOUR
or
TOSSED GREEN SALAD

WHIPPED POTATOES
and
BUTTERED VEGETABLES

CHOICE OF DRESSING
COFFEE OR TEA

BREAD & BUTTER

SHRIMP ALA NEWBURGH, White Rice	$1.65
CHICKEN FRIED STEAK, Cream Gravy	$1.85
BAKED MEAT LOAF, Pan Gravy	$1.65
BRAISED PORK TIPS, Steamed Rice	$1.50
ROAST SIRLOIN OF BEEF, Natural Gravy	$2.10
GRILLED NORTHERN HALIBUT STEAK, Lemon Butter	$1.95
ONE HALF PAN FRIED SPRING CHICKEN, Country Gravy	$1.95
CHOPPED TENDERLOIN STEAK, Sauteed Onions	$1.95
GRILLED BABY BEEF LIVER, Crisp Bacon or Onions	$2.30
BREADED VEAL CUTLET, Served with Cream Sauce	$1.85

Ice Cream, Sherbet, Jello or Pudding 30¢
Milk or Buttermilk 10¢ Extra

LOW CALORIE PLATE SPECIAL

Cold Roast Beef	Cooked Vegetable
Sliced Tomatoes	Cottage Cheese

Coffee or Tea
$1.95

Grilled Cubed Steak
with Mushroom Sauce
French Fried Potatoes
TossedGreen Salad
$1.75

Cup of Soup
Grilled Ham & Cheese Sand.
Potato Chips
$1.65

Underlying permanent menu card

ROAST SIRLOIN C
Slices of Cho

HONEY FRIED HA
Served with

GRILLED NORTHER
Eight Ounces

GRILLED BABY BE
Rasher of Ba

ROAST TOM TURI
Dressing, Gib

PORK CHOPS (We
Served with

CHOPPED TENDER
Served with

SCALOPPINI OF V

INC

TOSSED GREE

WHIPPED PO

ROLLS AN

ICE

COL

SHR

Sliced Tom
Ripe Oli
Quartered Egg

Rolls and Butter

2.50

DICED CHICKEN OR TUNA FISH
Served with
Quartered Egg   Ripe Olives   Crisp Celery
Sliced Tomato   Asparagus Tips
Rolls and Butter

1.95

— Olives

ian Spaghetti
h Meat Sauce
armesan Cheese
Garlic Bread
1.75

NER SALADS

reens	.35
Cottage Cheese	.45
Lettuce	.50
nd Tomatoes	.60
Cottage Cheese	.70

Carte Soups

Jour—Cup .25 Bowl	.35
Potato with Leek..	.60
Fresh Tomato	.60
nion au Croutons ..	.60

ES

		ermilk	.20
Iced Coffee	.15	Milk	.20
Pot of Tea	.15	Hot Chocolate	.25
Coca-Cola	.15	Orange Juice .30 &	.50
Sanka	.25	Postum	.25

DESSERTS

CHEESE CAKE	.75	with Fruit	.85
Fresh Strawberry Pie (In Season)			.65
Layer Cake	.50	Pan Pudding	.40
All Pies	.50	Ice Cream	.40
Fruit Jello	.40	Sherbet	.40
Sundaes — .15 extra		a la Mode — .40 extra	

FIG. 6-3 A shiny, hard-back menu card carrying permanent menu items, overlaid with a lightweight sheet giving daily items. A very common, versatile arrangement. The re-used panel or folder is easily kept clean. A daily sheet compatible in format makes for best appearance (Courtesy El Cortez Hotel and Casino)

Although printers nowadays usually prefer to designate type size by points, there are traditional names for sizes of type, as follows:

Point Size	Name
3½ point	Brilliant
4 or 4½ point	Diamond
5 point	Pearl
5½ point	Agate
6 point	Nonpareil
7 point	Minion
8 point	Brevier
9 point	Bourgeois
10 point	Long Primer
11 point	Small Pica
12 point	Pica
14 point	English
16 point	Columbian
18 point	Great Primer

Headings may be in caps in bolder and larger type. Different type sometimes may be used, but some mixtures may give an undesirable effect. If Figure 6-10 has a fault, it is that the mixture of type gives a somewhat cluttered appearance.

The use of Colonial, Antique or other type may give special effects. To give an oriental flavor, Japanese, Javanese, Chinese or Thai script can be used in the menu corners or elsewhere. The menu items and descriptions also can be written in a language arrangement typical of the foreign area one wishes to depict. If a Greek menu is presented, the use of some ancient Greek letters might be desirable.

Descriptions should be in keeping with the menu theme and set in a typeface compatible with other type on the page. All elements should blend together if a maximum effect is to be achieved. Type, color and other factors designed to achieve harmony must not be mixed together haphazardly. A few foreign words or special type at the corners, sides, top or elsewhere can be used effectively, without contributing to disharmony.

Another factor leading to ease of reading and comprehension is the spacing between letters in a word, and between words. If letters and words are set too close together, reading is difficult. Likewise, if too far apart reading is hampered. Associated with this horizontal dimension in typography is the width of the individual characters in a particular style of type. They may be *condensed* (narrow), *regular,* or *extended* (wide), and this quality has its effect on readability and scanning rate.

Vertical spacing, between *lines* of type, is also important to reading facility. This is called leading (pronounced "ledding") because thin strips of metal known as leads are used between lines of cast type to give them "air." If no leading is used, the type is said to be set "solid." The thickness of these "ledds" is also measured in points. Normally a three-point lead separation is

GRISWOLD'S
...more than just a restaurant

Bakeries

Bakers work the clock around in the Griswold's Claremont and Redlands bakeries to produce the finest quality and variety of breads and pastries. The slogan "made with butter 'n love" is a reality. More than 30 varieties of bread are baked daily. Danish, cookies, our famous bran muffins, many varieties of cakes, pastries, pies — holiday specialties and made-to-order goodies are available. One recent order was for a 50 pound loaf of bread. What a party that must have been!

Smorgasbords

Care to guess how many guests enjoyed our family style meals in Claremont and Redlands SMORGASBORDS during 1972? Over 1 million! Though the numbers are staggering, the calm, efficient staff members continue the same care with the same quality foods as in the past. Food orders for 16,000 pounds of fresh salmon are common...and astronomical quantities of chicken. How would you like to make out the weekly shopping list?

Gift Shops

Imaginative gifts are awaiting you at both Smorgasbord gift shops. As one guest said, "What a great place to get lost in!" Toys . . . collectors' items . . . gourmet food packs . . . chunks of old fashioned fudge cut to your request . . . . It's all here!

The Inn

Claremont's award winning Inn is the perfect place for the weekend. Deluxe accommodations offer comfort for visitors and for conventions or other groups.

With spacious grounds and a charming courtyard reminiscent of the Spanish Haciendas, an atmosphere of Early California pervades the entire hotel.

Away from the noise of freeways and big cities, the Inn specializes in an atmosphere of quiet ease and relaxation with emphasis on the personal touch. This is particularly reflected in the personal planning of each conference meeting or social occasion. The Indian Hill Restaurant offers lounge entertainment and finest dining – plus award winning banquets for groups large and small.

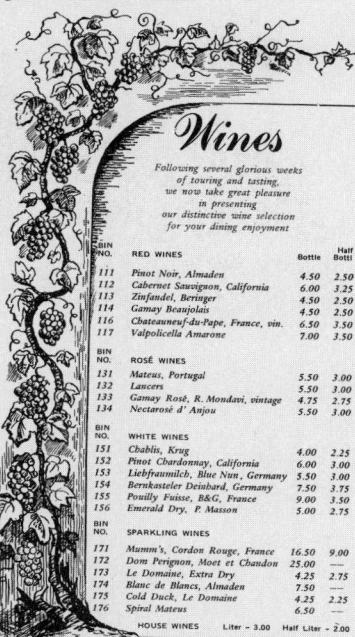

Wines

Following several glorious weeks of touring and tasting, we now take great pleasure in presenting our distinctive wine selection for your dining enjoyment

BIN NO.	RED WINES	Bottle	Half Bottl
111	Pinot Noir, Almaden	4.50	2.50
112	Cabernet Sauvignon, California	6.00	3.25
113	Zinfandel, Beringer	4.50	2.50
114	Gamay Beaujolais	4.50	2.50
116	Chateauneuf-du-Pape, France, vin.	6.50	3.50
117	Valpolicella Amarone	7.00	3.50

BIN NO.	ROSÉ WINES		
131	Mateus, Portugal	5.50	3.00
132	Lancers	5.50	3.00
133	Gamay Rosé, R. Mondavi, vintage	4.75	2.75
134	Nectarose d' Anjou	5.50	3.00

BIN NO.	WHITE WINES		
151	Chablis, Krug	4.00	2.25
152	Pinot Chardonnay, California	6.00	3.00
153	Liebfraumilch, Blue Nun, Germany	5.50	3.00
154	Bernkasteler Deinhard, Germany	7.50	3.75
155	Pouilly Fuisse, B&G, France	9.00	3.50
156	Emerald Dry, P. Masson	5.00	2.75

BIN NO.	SPARKLING WINES		
171	Mumm's, Cordon Rouge, France	16.50	9.00
172	Dom Perignon, Moet et Chandon	25.00	—
173	Le Domaine, Extra Dry	4.25	2.75
174	Blanc de Blancs, Almaden	7.50	—
175	Cold Duck, Le Domaine	4.25	2.25
176	Spiral Mateus	6.50	—

HOUSE WINES — Liter - 3.00   Half Liter - 2.00

DID YOU KNOW?

GRISWOLD'S OLD SCHOOL HOUSE — (GOSH) — in Claremont has made a beautiful old center of learning into a fascinating new center of enjoyment! The learning is still present as you visit GRISWOLD'S FOOTHILL ART GALLERY or take lessons or seminars from the professional artists-in-residence. Everything from textile design to ceramics, jewelry, painting and metal sculpture is present for lookers or learners.

Special shows by distinguished artists are scheduled frequently and gallery displays follow changing themes.

The OLD SCHOOL HOUSE is a beautiful shopping place for the newest look. The unusual in gifts, apparel, and ideas for home and family are displayed in exciting new shops. A bright new Mexican restaurant as well as a cozy spot for a cup of coffee and a place for snacks complete the opening phase of this spectacular outstanding shopping experience.

The GOSH PAVILION is a handsome place for meetings, exhibits, banquets, parties, concerts — or any reason for a gathering of 300 – 1,000.

GRISWOLD'S

the Country House
Dinner Menu

Dinners are served with Soup or Salad, Potatoes Maison, Vegetable du jour and Country House bread

Tournedos Rossini 650
Filet Mignon topped with pate de fois gras

Prime Rib à l'anglaise 525

Mignon de Boeuf aux Champignons 750
Filet Mignon - charcoal broiled & smothered in mushrooms

New York Strip Sirloin 695

Lobster Thermidor 525

Rack of Lamb 525
Griswold's famous feast

Veal Provençale 425
Sauteed in butter with special wine sauce

Coq au Vin 395
Chicken & mushrooms simmered in wine

Broiled Lobster Tail - Drawn Butter 725

Broiled Mahi Mahi - Polynesian Sauce 450

Coquilles St. Jacques 525
Scallops in wine and Cheese Sauce

Char-Broiled Shrimp a la Brittany 525
Large Shrimp marinated in teriyaki sauce

Menu du Jour 395
Chef's Blackboard Special

The Plentiful Plank 395
Broiled chopped sirloin garnished with potatoes & vegetables

~Patisserie~   ~Children's dinners 250~

Special Griswold's French Pastries .. 75

Ice Cream and Sherbet ... 40

Beverages 25

Menu du Jour

Our chef goes to the market each morning to make his du jour selections . . . and only then will he proclaim his special creation for the day. Too new to be in print, too vital to miss! See the blackboard for today's special or ask waitress.

FIG. 6-4   A menu printed as a newspaper, with folksy news items and articles of interest, as well as a rather select list of food and wine offerings for dinner. The script typeface is large enough and set in sufficient space to make it readable, as well as attractive. (Courtesy The Country House, Redlands, California)

Dinner in the *Ohioan Room*

Appetizers And Soups

Deviled Backfin of Crab 1.95
Jumbo Shrimp Cocktail 2.25
Herring Filet, Marinated in
Sour Cream 1.50

Chopped Liver Pate' 1.50
California Fruit Cup .95
Chilled Juices .50

French Onion Brown-Crock Soup
Cup .60 Bowl .85
Chicken Spaetzle Soup
Cup .60 Bowl .85
Soup du Jour Cup .50 Bowl .65

Salad Suggestions

The Spinning Salad Bowl 1.50
A delightful combination of iceberg lettuce,
romaine, endive and select garden vegetables
with hard-cooked egg. Served with our special
blended creamy garlic dressing.

Three Dimension Seafood Treat 4.75
King crab, Louisiana shrimp and Maine lobster
combined with our own special sauce. Served
on freshly shredded lettuce bed with
golden garlic toast.

California Fruit Plate Supreme 3.25
A selection of fresh fruits from around the
world with whole curd cottage cheese center.
Served with cinnamon toast.

Sliced Tomatoes Vinaigrette .75
Whole Curd Cottage Cheese .50

Hearts of Iceberg Lettuce .75
Fruited Gelatin Salad .50

Beverage Selections

Milk .30   Buttermilk .30

Coffee, freshly brewed .25
Weight Watcher's Milk .30

Tea, hot or iced .25
Sanka .25

Hot Chocolate .30
Soft Drinks .25

Dessert Suggestions

Our Special Southern Pecan Pie .55

Our own Cheese Cake .50

Broiled Cinnamon Peach Halves .70

Ice Cream Sundae (Strawberry, Pineapple, Chocolate) .65

Assorted Fruit Pies from our own ovens .50

With Fresh Strawberries .85

Ice Cream or Sherbet .50

The State of Ohio Requires Us to Collect 4% Sales Tax

← Cocktails

From the Hearth

New York Cut Sirloin Steak 7.95
Heavy cut, succulent prime beef broiled
to your satisfaction.

Spring Lamb Chops 5.75
Lancelot, served with mint jelly.

Chopped Tenderloin of Beef 4.25
With crisp onions.

Broiled Filet of English Dover Sole 4.75
Almondine.

Baked Sugar Cured Ham Steak 4.25
Pineapple glaze.

Filet Mignon, Bouquetiere 7.50
Succulent tenderloin of beef with broiled tomato,
parmesan. Bouquet of fresh garden vegetables.

Veal Steak, Panfried 4.50
With butter cream sauce.

Pork Chops 4.95
Thick, center cuts only. With
spiced apple sauce.

Jumbo Size Shrimp 5.50
Steamed in beer. Served hot, with our
special sauce.

Chicken Livers 3.75
Braised with mushrooms in wine.

Fisherman Wharf 4.95
A delightful selection of delicacies of the sea,
gathered from around the world.

Ohioan Room Favorites

Roast Rib of Prime Beef 7.50
Prepared in rock salt cask. Served as you like,
au jus. With yorkshire pudding.

Spare Ribs, Chinese Style 4.50
Served barbecued or sweet and sour

Chicken A la Maryland 3.95
Disjointed and delicately prepared in cream
sauce. (Please allow 25 minutes.)

All Dinner Selections Served With Your Choice Of Potato, Hot Rolls and Butter,
Plus Your Selection From Our Salad Bar.

For Your Pleasure and Convenience We Feature 24-Hour Coffee Room Service.

Sandwich Fare →

FIG. 6-5 A menu which makes it easy for the guest to find selections. Note how well the listings stand out, and that the guest is also shown where he can find, on other pages, selections he might like. (Courtesy Holiday Inn, Ohio State University, Columbus, Ohio)

used. The following shows lines set solid, and lines with one-, two-, three- and five-point leading:

SOLID

A treat to the palate sends taste buds soaring. A treat to the palate sends taste buds soaring. A treat to the palate sends taste

1-POINT LEADING

soaring. A treat to the palate sends taste A treat to the palate sends taste buds soaring. A treat to the palate sends taste buds

2-POINT LEADING

A treat to the palate sends taste buds soaring. A treat to the palate sends taste buds soaring. A treat to the palate sends taste

3-POINT LEADING

A treat to the palate sends taste buds soaring. A treat to the palate sends taste buds soaring. A treat to the palate sends taste

5-POINT LEADING

A treat to the palate sends taste buds soaring. A treat to the palate sends taste buds soaring. A treat to the palate sends taste

Emphasis can be given and items made to stand out by the wise use of light and bold type. This intensity of print is called "weight" or "lightness or grayness." Bold print is called "heavy", "thick" or "black." A medium weight is called "normal weight" and a light weight is called "light" or gray. The lighter types will not give good emphasis and are sometimes difficult to read. Extra bold type is extremely dark and black. Bold or heavy may be desirable to bring attention but should be used sparingly. Too bold a type face is not suitable for the menu of a refined, quiet

FIG. 6-7 This menu shows a rather good use of varied sizes and styles of type. The descriptions also help bring attention to the food items listed.

dining room. Sometimes a printer may refer to the weight of the type as its "color", but this is a term mostly used by professionals.

Another factor influencing ease of reading and comprehension is the use of capitals (upper case) or small letters (lower case). Capitals give emphasis and can set words out more clearly. Lower case is easier to read. Capitals are used with lower case to begin sentences, for proper nouns, etc. It is usually desirable to capitalize *all* first letters of proper names and item titles on the menu. For instance, the following would be normal: "Top Sirloin Steak Sandwich." Words such as "or", "the", "à la", "in", "and" or "with" are usually not

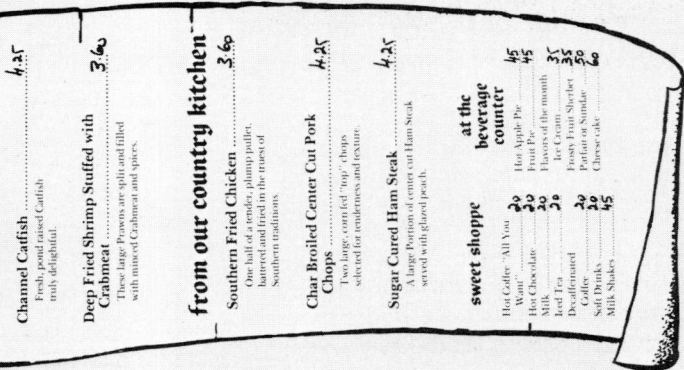

from the fisherman's net

Shrimp-A-Rama 3.60
An extravaganza that will satisfy the seafood lover. Tender meaty shrimp.

Pan Fried Rainbow Trout 4.25
From icy mountain streams served without the bone.

Broiled Filet of Red Snapper 4.25
We broil to perfection served with lemon butter.

Channel Catfish 4.25
Fresh, pond raised Catfish truly delightful.

Deep Fried Shrimp Stuffed with Crabmeat 3.60
These large Prawns are split and filled with minced Crabmeat and spices.

from our country kitchen

Southern Fried Chicken 3.60
One half of a tender, plump pullet, battered and fried in the truest of Southern traditions.

Char Broiled Center Cut Pork Chops 4.25
Two large, corn fed "top" chops selected for tenderness and texture.

Sugar Cured Ham Steak 4.25
A large Portion of center cut Ham Steak served with glazed peach.

sweet shoppe

Hot Coffee "All You Want"	.20
Milk	.20
Hot Chocolate	.20

at the beverage counter

Hot Apple Pie	.45
Fruit Pie	.45
Flavors of the month	
Ice Cream	.35
Decaffeinated Coffee	.50
Soft Drinks	.25
Milk Shakes	.45
Parfait or Sundae	.50
Cheese cake	.60

WELCOME
TO THE

CAPTAIN'S TABLE DINING ROOM

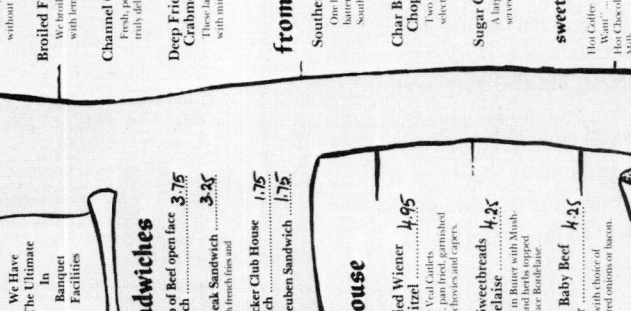

**We Have
The Ultimate
In
Banquet
Facilities**

**Be Sure And
Visit Our
Admiral's
Cocktail
Lounge**

salads

Ocean Cooler 2.95
Iced Jumbo Shrimp, Salmon Herring filets, garnished.

Chilled Stuffed Tomato 2.25
With Tuna salad, garnished with egg slices, relishes.

Holiday Salad Bowl 1.95
Julienne of Ham, Turkey, cheeses, garnished, choice of dressing.

sandwiches

Prime Rib of Beef open face 3.75
Sandwich.

Grilled Steak Sandwich 3.25
Served with french fries and cole slaw.

Three Decker Club House 1.75
Sandwich.

Grilled Reuben Sandwich 1.75

specials of the house

**Standing Rib Roast
of Prime Beef**
The finest aged beef roasted as succulently rare or tenderly well done as may please the most discriminate palate. Medium rare at its best.
Ladies cut 5.25
Regular cut 6.50

Kabob of Beef 4.50
Choice morsels of beef with bacon, onion, peppers on skewer.

**Barbecued Pork
Back Ribs** 4.50
Finger lickin good.

**Pan Fried Wiener
Schnitzel** 4.95
2 tender Veal Cutlets breaded, pan fried, garnished with anchovies and capers.

**Calf's Sweetbreads
Bordelaise** 4.25
Sauteed in Butter with Mushrooms and herbs topped with sauce Bordelaise.

**Grilled Baby Beef
Liver** 4.25
Served with choice of smothered onions or bacon.

All entrees include choice of potato or vegetable, crisp, green salad, complemented with bread basket and butter.

Please ask waitress for children's menu.

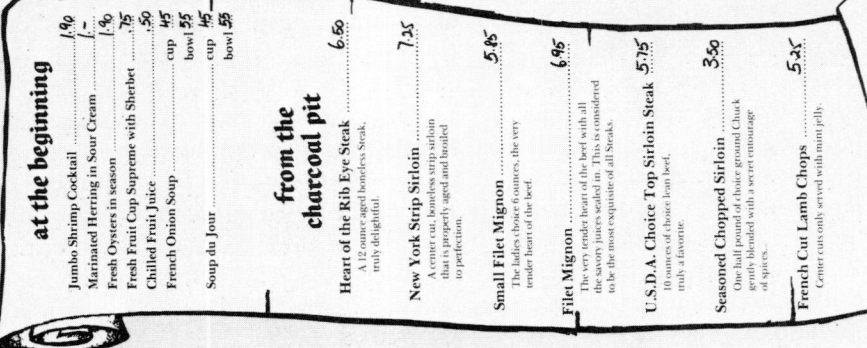

at the beginning

Jumbo Shrimp Cocktail	1.90
Marinated Herring in Sour Cream	1.—
Fresh Oysters in season	1.90
Fresh Fruit Cup Supreme with Sherbet	.75
Chilled Fruit Juice	.50
French Onion Soup	cup .45 bowl .55
Soup du Jour	cup .55 bowl .55

from the
charcoal pit

Heart of the Rib Eye Steak 6.50
A 12 ounce aged boneless Steak, truly delightful.

New York Strip Sirloin 7.25
A center cut, boneless strip sirloin that is properly aged and broiled to perfection.

Small Filet Mignon 5.95
The ladies choice 6 ounces, the very tender heart of the beef.

Filet Mignon 6.95
The very tender heart of the beef with all the savory juices sealed in. This is considered to be the most exquisite of all Steaks.

U.S.D.A. Choice Top Sirloin Steak 5.75
16 ounces of choice lean beef, truly a favorite.

Seasoned Chopped Sirloin 3.50
One half pound of choice ground Chuck gently blended with a secret entourage of spices.

French Cut Lamb Chops 5.25
Center cuts only served with mint jelly.

FIG. 6-6 A menu that has excellent spacing and a design which is eye-catching. Note that the prices are neatly written in — a very desirable feature at a time when food prices are subject to frequent change. (Courtesy **Captain's Table Dining Rooms, Holiday Inns**)

capitalized. Descriptive information such as "A combination of shrimp, scallops, halibut and oysters in Newburg Sauce" will not have capitalized letters except for the title of the sauce. "Newburg" is capitalized also because it is a proper noun. Capitals may be used to emphasize words, as in: *Includes French Fries, Tossed Green Salad with your Favorite Dressing and Choice of Beverage and Dessert.*

Often menu items will stand out when put in large, bold caps using lower case type for descriptive material below, capitalizing only those words that must be in the descriptive material. Special effects can be obtained at times by leaving all words in small caps.

Readers have ranked their preferences for size in print and leading. Liked from best to least were 11 point, 10 point and 12 point ranked together, 9 point, 8 point and then 6 point. In leading for 10 point type, they liked best to least: 2-point leading, 1-point leading, 4-point leading, and solid type. For column arrangements 60.5 per cent preferred a double column to a single one on a page. However, for length of line it was found that 22 picas* (about 3¾ in.) was most preferred, a finding somewhat contradictory to the preference noted for two columns on a page because, if two columns are on a page, the column must be narrower than 22 picas unless the page is quite broad. It was found, however, that in practice most books were printed in line lengths somewhere around 25 picas (about 4-3/16 in.) As indicated previously, italic type was more difficult to read than regular type,

*A pica is about .17 in.

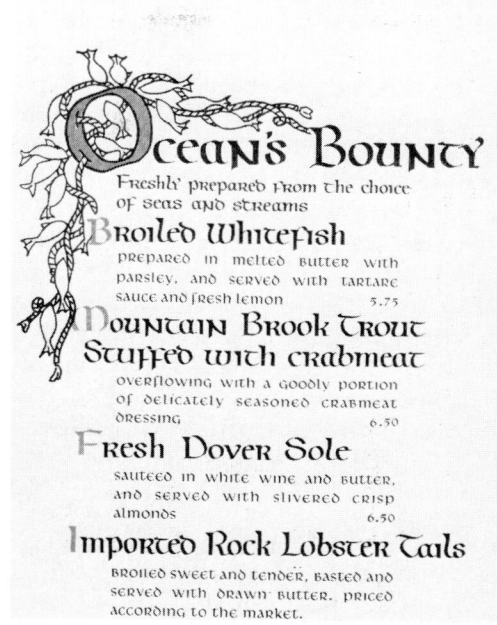

FIG. 6-8   The use of a special typeface here gives the feeling of old England which fits both the style of the menu and the dining area décor.

about five per cent more regular copy being read in 30 minutes over italics.

Readers also indicated they wanted margins and disliked copy that ran too close to the edge of the paper. (This could carry a message to menu planners who overcrowd areas.) Normally, just slightly more than 52 per cent of the space on a printed page has print on it and slightly over 47 per cent of the space is in margins. Figure 6-12 shows a page filled with black in the center and a margin around it. One would not suspect in looking at the black area that the white margin area is almost half the page. Readers indicated they preferred this in their page copy. Perhaps in menu copy slightly more than this could be covered but not much more. The fact that, of the space used, from a third to a fourth should be blank reduces considerably the space available for listing the menu. Nevertheless, there is a message here if one wishes to design the most effective menu.

Perhaps the best thing a novice can do in deciding both the kind and size of type is to call in a printer with a good reputation and have him set the menu and then look at proofs before decid-ing on the final makeup. However, menu designers who understand what is available and what the effect can be are more apt to design a better menu than one who may leave the job to a printer.

Menus printed in a single size of type are very monotonous. The size is therefore varied to give relief. Thus, menu items may be listed in 12-point type, with a 9- or 10-point type used for the description just below it. This also might be in italics to give further emphasis, as shown here.

Special Texas Sirloin Steak, Char-broiled $6.50
(Served with Baked or French Fried Potatoes and a Tossed Green Salad with your choice of French, Thousand Island or Blue Cheese Dressing.)

At times, to draw attention to a special menu item, larger type may be used than for regular items. For instance, the menu may list regular items in a 12-point face, normal weight, and then change to 14-point bold to give emphasis to the special. Additional emphasis can be given to the special item by enclosing it in a box.

FRUITS OF THE SEA

Sauteed English Sole, Almandine with Spinach Souffle $4.00
(With Cole Slaw and French Fried Potatoes)

New England Crab Cakes with Braised Fresh Garden Vegetables $3.50
(With Sliced Tomatoes and French or Thousand Island Dressing)

Curry of Shrimp on a Bed of Rice, Chutney Sauce $3.75
(With Fresh Fruit Salad and Creamy French Dressing)

Cold Boiled Salmon with Mayonnaise and Potato Salad $3.85
(With Sliced Cucumbers in Vinegrette Sauce)

Poached Sanddab Rolls on a Bed of Spinach with Hollandaise Sauce

Served with a light, mealy Idaho Baked Potato and Sour Cream topped with Bacon Bits and grated American Cheese

---

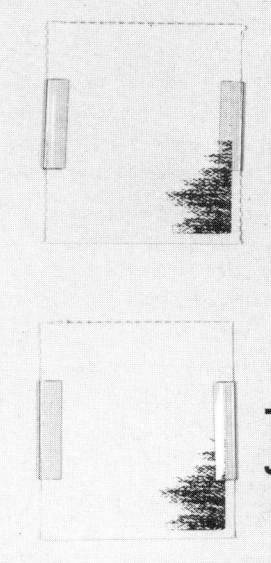

prime beef

CHARCOAL BROILED SIRLOIN STEAK
A thick and sizzling New York cut sirloin, broiled the way you like it and served with sauteed fresh mushroom caps   **9.95**

ROAST PRIME STEER RIBS OF BEEF
A thick hearty carving, or the English cut (the same, carved a bit thinner) served in its natural juices   **7.95**

LONDON BROIL
Tender beef marinated in herbed sauce and broiled to a turn. Served in its natural juices or add mushroom sauce if you like   **5.95**

CHOPPED SIRLOIN STEAK
Our fine steer beef, chopped, seasoned and charcoal broiled to just the right moment. Served plain or with onions and melted Vermont Cheddar Cheese   **4.50**

meats and poultry

A BRACE OF DOUBLE THICK LAMB CHOPS
Two Tenderly broiled chops, served with Vermont apple mint jelly to accent their flavor   **7.95**

YANKEE CHICKEN PIE
Beneath its flaky pastry crust you'll find tender chicken, fresh carrots, mushrooms and celery. Served with baked potato and vegetable   **4.50**

MEDALLIONS OF VEAL, CORTINA
Tender morsels of thinly sliced veal sauteed in butter. Served with spicy Vermont cream sauce and fluffy rice pilaf   **6.50**

salads included with all dinners. Ask your server about our salads for the day

seafoods

LIVE MAINE LOBSTER
Boiled or broiled to your order   *Price on request*

FANCY JUMBO SHRIMP
Ocean fresh shrimp, sauteed in a white wine and garlic butter sauce, served with rice   **6.25**

FILLET OF SOLE, CORTINA
Choice fresh fillet of sole sauteed in butter, served with fluffy rice pilaf   **5.25**

TENDER BAY SCALLOPS
Sauteed in white wine sauce with chopped parsley, and served with baked potato   **5.95**

We serve the fresh
vegetables
of the season whenever possible.
Cooked to order   .50

children's menu available

From our own ovens
comes an assortment of fruit and nutbreads baked fresh daily.

FIG. 6-9   This page carries little printed matter and yet it very effectively presents the menu items listed. Note the space reserved for specials. Such an arrangement gives neatness to the menu page and also avoids masking other listings the customer should see. (Courtesy Cortina Inn)

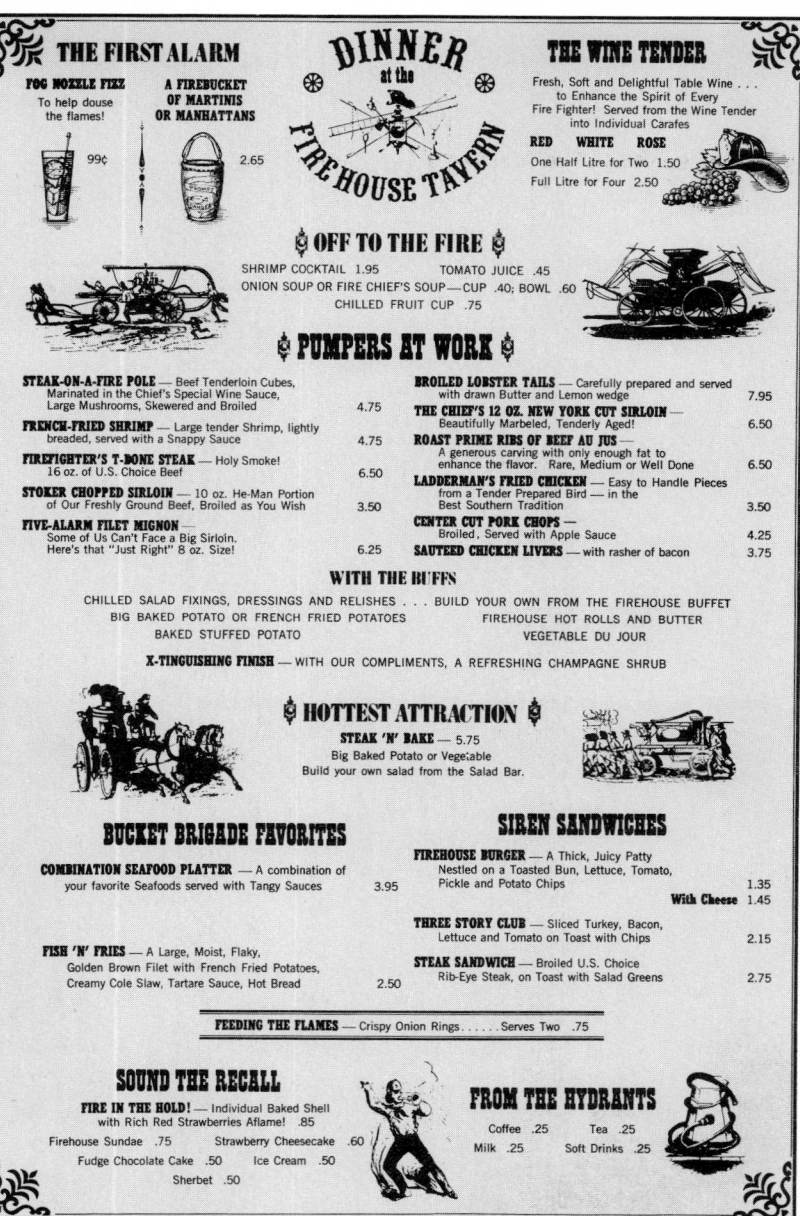

THE FIRST ALARM

FOG NOZZLE FIZZ
To help douse the flames!
99¢

A FIREBUCKET OF MARTINIS OR MANHATTANS
2.65

DINNER at the FIRE HOUSE TAVERN

THE WINE TENDER

Fresh, Soft and Delightful Table Wine . . . to Enhance the Spirit of Every Fire Fighter! Served from the Wine Tender into Individual Carafes

RED   WHITE   ROSE

One Half Litre for Two 1.50
Full Litre for Four 2.50

OFF TO THE FIRE

SHRIMP COCKTAIL 1.95   TOMATO JUICE .45
ONION SOUP OR FIRE CHIEF'S SOUP—CUP .40; BOWL .60
CHILLED FRUIT CUP .75

PUMPERS AT WORK

STEAK-ON-A-FIRE POLE — Beef Tenderloin Cubes, Marinated in the Chief's Special Wine Sauce, Large Mushrooms, Skewered and Broiled   4.75

FRENCH-FRIED SHRIMP — Large tender Shrimp, lightly breaded, served with a Snappy Sauce   4.75

FIREFIGHTER'S T-BONE STEAK — Holy Smoke!
16 oz. of U.S. Choice Beef   6.50

STOKER CHOPPED SIRLOIN — 10 oz. He-Man Portion of Our Freshly Ground Beef, Broiled as You Wish   3.50

FIVE-ALARM FILET MIGNON —
Some of Us Can't Face a Big Sirloin.
Here's that "Just Right" 8 oz. Size!   6.25

BROILED LOBSTER TAILS — Carefully prepared and served with drawn Butter and Lemon wedge   7.95

THE CHIEF'S 12 OZ. NEW YORK CUT SIRLOIN —
Beautifully Marbeled, Tenderly Aged!   6.50

ROAST PRIME RIBS OF BEEF AU JUS —
A generous carving with only enough fat to enhance the flavor. Rare, Medium or Well Done   6.50

LADDERMAN'S FRIED CHICKEN — Easy to Handle Pieces from a Tender Prepared Bird — in the Best Southern Tradition   3.50

CENTER CUT PORK CHOPS —
Broiled, Served with Apple Sauce   4.25

SAUTEED CHICKEN LIVERS — with rasher of bacon   3.75

WITH THE BUFFS

CHILLED SALAD FIXINGS, DRESSINGS AND RELISHES . . . BUILD YOUR OWN FROM THE FIREHOUSE BUFFET
BIG BAKED POTATO OR FRENCH FRIED POTATOES   FIREHOUSE HOT ROLLS AND BUTTER
BAKED STUFFED POTATO   VEGETABLE DU JOUR

X-TINGUISHING FINISH — WITH OUR COMPLIMENTS, A REFRESHING CHAMPAGNE SHRUB

HOTTEST ATTRACTION

STEAK 'N' BAKE — 5.75
Big Baked Potato or Vegetable
Build your own salad from the Salad Bar.

BUCKET BRIGADE FAVORITES

COMBINATION SEAFOOD PLATTER — A combination of your favorite Seafoods served with Tangy Sauces   3.95

FISH 'N' FRIES — A Large, Moist, Flaky, Golden Brown Filet with French Fried Potatoes, Creamy Cole Slaw, Tartare Sauce, Hot Bread   2.50

SIREN SANDWICHES

FIREHOUSE BURGER — A Thick, Juicy Patty Nestled on a Toasted Bun, Lettuce, Tomato, Pickle and Potato Chips   1.35
With Cheese 1.45

THREE STORY CLUB — Sliced Turkey, Bacon, Lettuce and Tomato on Toast with Chips   2.15

STEAK SANDWICH — Broiled U.S. Choice Rib-Eye Steak, on Toast with Salad Greens   2.75

FEEDING THE FLAMES — Crispy Onion Rings . . . . . Serves Two .75

SOUND THE RECALL

FIRE IN THE HOLD! — Individual Baked Shell with Rich Red Strawberries Aflame!   .85

Firehouse Sundae .75   Strawberry Cheesecake .60
Fudge Chocolate Cake .50   Ice Cream .50
Sherbet .50

FROM THE HYDRANTS

Coffee .25   Tea .25
Milk .25   Soft Drinks .25

FIG. 6-10   A menu which carries the theme of the firehouse into its menu offerings. Cover and main headings are fire-engine red. Clever wording in the presentations contributes to good merchandising. (Courtesy Firehouse Tavern, Louisville, Kentucky)

Color and Design

Color is also important in presenting a menu. Besides making an artistic contribution, color can affect legibility and speed of reading. The use of white print on a black background gets more attention than black print on a white background, but individuals read the former more slowly than the latter.

Black on white is read 42 per cent more rapidly than white on dark gray. Black type on light tints is read less easily than black on white. However, black on some light tints is about equal to black on white. The results of a test with various colors of paper stock are summarized below. The order is from easiest to least easy in each of the three classifications.

Quite Easy to Read	Fairly Easy to Read	Poorly Read
Black on slight cream	Black on light yellowish green	Black on fairly saturated yellowish red
Black on slight sepia cream	Black on light blue green	Black on reddish orange
Black on deep cream	Black on yellowish red	
Black on very light buff	Black on reddish orange	
Black on fairly saturated yellow		

In another test, to ascertain how well different colored inks stood out against various tints, the following results were obtained. (It is surprising that black on white did not turn out to be judged the most legible and most rapidly read.) Again the order is from easiest to least easy:

Black print on yellow	Blue print on white	White print on black
Green print on white	Yellow print on blue	Red print on yellow
Red print on white	White print on red	Green print on red
Black print on white	White print on green	Red print on green
White print on blue		

The range of difference in legibility and speed of reading was not indicated in either of these tests, but perhaps any of those "quite easy to read" in the first test and any of the first five in the second test could be considered adequate for use on menus.

Color and design can enhance a menu and make it a better merchandising tool. Color and design are to menus as they are to chinaware. A large amount can run into a sizable cost. Yet, as with china, considerable decorative effect can be obtained with only a *small* amount of color and design. Similarly, plain colored paper for menus can achieve good effect and is not too expensive. Some paper has color on one side and white, or another color, on the reverse. As special effects are added, costs increase. Silver and gold on china must be added after the china is baked and glazed and is usually put on by hand. Adding silver or gold to a menu card can also be expensive.

Too much color and design can give a disagreeable effect. Colors that are intense should be avoided unless some special effect is desired. Perhaps a shocking pink could be used in a club wishing to have a somewhat psychydelic effect, but the color would not be too appro-

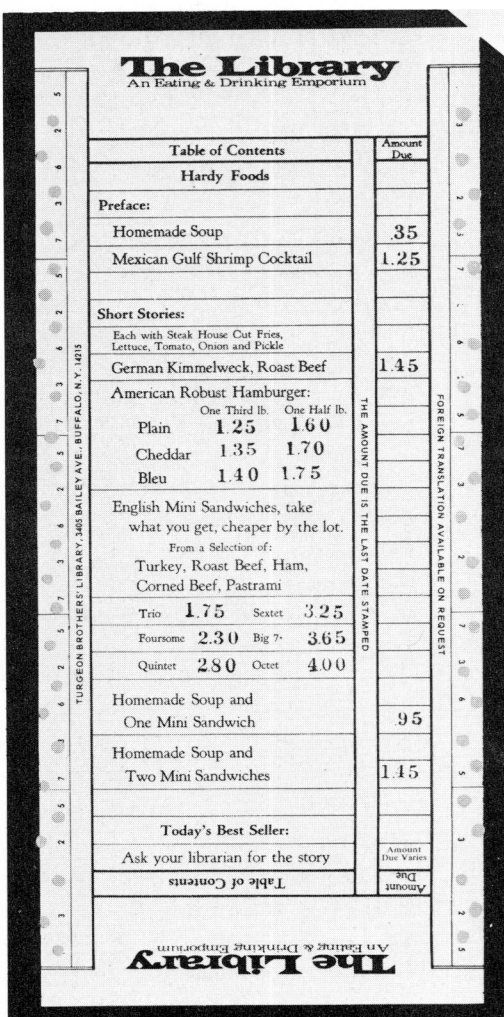

FIG. 6-11   This is a good example of a menu which also serves as an excellent accounting form for pricing and for tabulating later menu selections. (Courtesy The Library)

priate in most foodservices.

Clip-ons can be used to give a different design and color. Some menus may be given additional color by using ribbons, silken cords or tassels but these are usually restricted to menus for special dining areas. Color can be added by using different colored inks. This is not too expensive. Colored type should be limited to only a few hues, however, since too much can be confusing and give an undesirable effect. Different colors are usually most acceptable for section headings or to indicate separations.

The variety of colors in paper suitable for menus is wide, including almost every shade of ink and even metallic papers. Since the basic color must serve as a background for the print that describes menu items, lists prices, etc., it should be such that the print stands out very clearly. Dark browns, blacks, reds and other colors can be used if a light type is imprinted on them, but not with a dark type. Light print should not be used with light backings because of the lack of contrast.

Color can be used to give special meaning. Mandarin red with black print is most suitable to express a happy Chinese event. This red indicates a celebration. A halloween menu needs an orange and black combination. Black type on emerald green is suitable for a Tavern on the Green or for St. Patrick's Day. Black with soft tans and browns, with a typical design, would indicate a Hawaiian theme.

All colors and design on the menu should blend with the basic décor. They also can be contrasted with good effect. Thus, a rather outstanding color may be used to give a vivid color splash just as an interior decorator might use a vividly colored vase to give a highlight to a more subtle color scheme.

The colors selected on a menu should complement each other—that is blend well together. Complementary colors are usually those that come from the same primary ones but some contrasts between colors coming from different primaries also can be pleasing. For instance, some hues of red and green go well together. While some greens and blues clash, others do not. Color sense is something that is inherent in some individuals, while others lack it. The services of an expert can do much to produce a menu with striking color effects that are in good taste. The federal Bureau of Standards has developed a series of color samples for science, art and industry. These colors vary in hue, intensity and saturation, and can be used as a guide for almost any color that one would want.

Menu planners in working with printers may hear words such as "hue", or "saturation." Some understanding of what is meant may make it easier to communicate. Hues are usually defined as gradations in color. They may differ in lightness or brightness which is the amount of color transmitted to the viewer or the intensity of a color. Saturation refers to the vividness of the hue. Words used with hue such as "light", "medium", and "dark" indicate degrees of color intensity. The word "very" used with these teams indicates extremes at either end of the color range. To describe degrees of saturation, the words "grayish", "moderate", "strong" and "vivid" may be used. Other words are used to indicate combinations of lightness and saturation, such as "brilliant" for light and strong, "pale" for light and grayish, and "deep" for dark and strong.

Some menus may seek to achieve a desirable color effect by using a color in strips, squares, triangles or circles in some unique pattern. Obtaining a judicious balance takes an ability to blend hues, lightness and saturation. Frequently the help of an expert gives a more happy combination when trying to blend design with color.

Color in pictures results from the use of a relatively few colors combined in different hues, lightness and saturation. By using only two colors in a colored picture a great deal of color variation can be obtained. Four colors will give almost any combination of color desired in printing. Four colors must be used to give the complete color reproduction needed for color photographs. The color is added one at a time and so some pictures must be printed a number of times to get all the hues in them. The more colors used to produce a color, and the more printings, the higher the cost. Thus, the cost of colored photographs on menus can be quite expensive although a good merchandising tool. A good picture can indeed paint a thousand words.

There frequently are other costs other than reproducing a picture and printing it. A professional photographer may have to take the picture to get one that duplicates properly. Not all foods photograph as they appear, and specific techniques must be used to get a good picture that will reproduce well. The cost of taking a picture and setting it up for use in printing may be saved by finding in stock (in the "morgue") a picture that has already been put into positive color separations and plates. A "positive" is a unit that adds color. Color separations are needed so colors can be added in different printings to give the necessary hues, lightness and saturation.

Color plates may be so expensive that unless they have high merchandising value, their use will be prohibitive. However, a few may have enough effect to make the investment worth while.

A simpler color picture can be made if tint blocks are used. These are color reproductions that require an additional press run. Outline pictures, which may or may not have a background, can be used and be effective in line drawings. It is possible to add a color within a line picture to help give color contrast rather than have the line drawing appear filled with the basic color of the paper. Further emphasis can be obtained by putting the picture in a box. Additional color and design can be obtained by glueing items onto the menu. As noted, clip-ons can be used to assist in giving color.

The Printing

Most printing today is done by what is called offset or lithograph. This is a method of transferring a duplicate onto the printed page from a master. Type is not used on the press as in letter-press printing; rather, the method is some-

what akin to photography and requires a specially coated paper. However, the old-fashioned method of printing from cast type is still used and sometimes can give a more effective result than the off-set process. For extra special effects, block type or unusual type can be used. Both methods have their advantages and consultation with an expert may indicate the best method to use.

Silk screening is not usually used for printing but can be used to produce decorative effects on covers, etc. This is a method using a stencil to transfer a design on a screen of silk, other fabric or even certain kinds of paper. It is an expensive process but may be worth the cost. Block design printing is used also for covers. Block printing is imposing a design or print on paper by engraved wooden blocks or plastic material cut to transfer a design.

Menu Paper

Two types of paper usually are used for menus. Cover stock is used for covers. This is a paper stiff enough to be held in the hands without bending. It is frequently coated with materials such as plastic, enamel, varnish, clay, barite or other soil-resisting material. The surface is frequently shiny and smooth but different textures may be given these cover materials. Such papers last for a longer time than untreated ones. They can be easily wiped free of soil.

FIG. 6-12   Nearly half (about 45%) of the area outlined here is given to margins, the amount generally found to be most desirable for the printed page. The margin space may not appear to represent that much of the total space. While menus do not always need to commit half the page to margins, a much better designed menu results when printed matter is not run to the edge of the page, as is often done.

Textures can range from a slight rise on the paper, such as is seen in a wood grain, to a rough, coarse surface. Rough textures have less utility since soil is more difficult to remove from them. They also show wear more quickly. It is possible today to give paper almost any texture desired, even that of velvet or suede.

The need for a smooth, soil-resisting cover may be obviated by putting the menu in a plastic cover or some other transparent overwrap. Some of these can be quite effective, expecially if they are tinted with a color to give a decorative effect.

The weight of cover stock should be in heavy Cover, Bristol or Tag stock, at least .006 inch thick. The paper weight for inside leaves can be a lighter weight. Usually, strong heavy book paper is used. Its finish should be such that it resists soil and is smooth and somewhat shiny but not too much so. Book paper can be given different finishes to make them more suitable for menu use. If novelty or striking effects are desired, some specialty papers can be found.

Shape and Form

The shape and form of the menu can also help to create interest and sales appeal. A wine menu may be in the shape of a bottle, while one featuring seafood can be in the shape of a crab, lobster or fish. A steak house bill of fare may feature a Black Angus steer. A child's menu can be in the shape of a clown whose picture is on the front cover. A pancake house can have its menu shaped like a pancake or waffle.

The fold given the menu may also create an effect. Thus, instead of having a right and left side to a cover, a fold may be used which gives a half page on the right and a half page on the left so that the menu opens up like a gate. If different folds are given, the ability of the paper to take them should be investigated because some highly treated papers crack easily at the fold.

If a special fold or shape is required, a special die may have to be made. This costs money and should be the property of the one who pays for its making. (Also, the plates used for the menu should become the property of the individual paying for them. This should be clearly understood in making the original agreement. In some instances, printers may not wish to give up plates and may not be required to give them up.)

Menu Makeup

Menu space is very valuable and maximum achievement should be obtained in its use. From a fourth to a third of the printed space should be blank, in addition to margin space. To cover more than this leads to clutter and difficulty in reading. Type size should also be varied to emphasize main items and accompanying print should be smaller in size. Headings and other items indicating separations can appear in larger print. A reader is helped to understand a menu by varying the inset of menu items. To run items in a straight column makes is difficult to see all items readily, but if the margin on the left is varied with items appearing with different indentations, each entry can be more quickly identified. Items appearing first or last in a group are the most quickly seen. Also, items farthest out on the left margin are seen more quickly. Some operations may seek to give menu items having less gross profit the least desirable places.

If space is a problem, extra pages should be added rather than crowding the page. A good margin should remain on the left and right sides and on the top and bottom. Dividing a menu into separate sheet offerings of the same size may make it difficult to find items but if the sheets are sized so that each has a margin clearly identifying the items found on the particular page, the reader can be helped to find quickly what he wants. Figures 6-5 and 6-6 are good examples of advantageous use of space.

Making a menu so large that a patron has difficulty in holding it, and covering all the space with items are things to avoid. Some operations make menus very large to give the feeling of ostentation, but many guests find them extremely difficult to handle. An operation should give strong consideration to the menu size before deciding on a large one. If a large menu must be used, extra panels that fold open from the inside should be considered. Separate menus may also be used. For instance, if desserts are not given with the table d'hôte dinner, or if there is an additional group of à la carte desserts wanted, a special dessert menu may be set up, thus saving space on the main menu. Likewise, alcoholic beverages and wines can be on separate menus. A special fountain menu may be placed on tables and counters where customers may find them, leaving the main menu free to offer a more standard list of items.

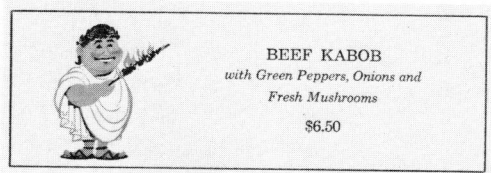

A simple illustration can be an effective, inexpensive device for giving a menu page some "color" in black and white.

CHAPTER 7

The Liquor Menu

Liquor menus may be written in many ways. Some establishments keep them separate from the food menu. A number of separate liquor menus may be used. One may cover drinks such as cocktails, highballs and similar beverages, another will present the wine list, another offers after-dinner drinks, and another afternoon beverages including cocktails, mixed drinks, tall, cooling drinks and dessert-type wines such as port, Madeira and muscat. The sales department may have still another, *banquet* wine and drink list for use in planning large dining events with patrons.

It is also not uncommon to see liquor items listed on the regular menu. This is done when only a few beverages are offered. Some institutional menus, such as those used in a hospital, may offer cocktails and wines to patients whose physicians give permission. These may be offered on separate lists or on the regular menu.

No matter what the procedure, it is very desirable that the regular menu merchandise alcoholic beverages so that guests are aware of their availability. A considerable amount of revenue and profit can be lost by failure to communicate this fact properly. It is also desirable that service personnel be prompt to ask guests after being seated, "What kind of cocktail can I bring you?"— putting the question in a positive way rather than saying, "May I?" or "Can I?" This should also be done with a wine at the proper time. In suggesting wine it is often a good idea to put the question near the final stage of order-taking, in words like: "And what kind of wine may I bring you?" If the waiter is alert to what has been ordered, a suitable wine may be proposed.

Some liquor menus can be quite elaborate and contain a vast number of items. If the establishment has a very fine wine cellar, the wine list will naturally be extensive and may run several pages. If it does, the pages should be so marked that patrons can quickly find the beverage desired. Usually, tabulations on the margins indicate what each page offers, to enable the guest to turn immediately to the correct page. An index is not as suitable.

Sometimes it is not necessary for a liquor menu to offer a wide assortment of drinks or wines in order to meet patrons' needs. A simpler one may suffice. Just as food menus should be analyzed to see what items move, so also should liquor menus be analyzed to see that the drinks or wines are moving. Those items that do not move should be eliminated. A sizable amount of money can be tied up in a liquor inventory, and unless these inventories are turned over fairly often they can be a hidden expense. One club found that an enterprising manager had tied up so much money in its wine cellar that it took more than 10 years to work off the inventory built up during his tenure!

Thus, the rule in planning beverage menus is to "keep them simple." However, this is not as easy to do as to state. There are a certain number of cocktails, highballs and other mixed drinks that patrons will want. If one also wishes to have a wine list which covers dry white wines and red wines (both domestics and imports), sparkling wines, apéritif wines and dessert wines, the list must necessarily be extensive. However, it is best not to offer too much—only those that meet the requirements. A simple list may do a better job of selling than an elaborate one.

Since menu planning for alcoholic beverages is a highly specialized one, it is often advisable to have an expert's advice. The presentation of some exotic drinks popular with women may take skill to set up and merchandise properly. Color may be necessary to enhance the menu and this again may take expert advice. Some of the references cited in the bibliography can also be helpful in indicating how to set up a liquor menu. The California Wine Advisory Board, in San Francisco, can be especially helpful. Furthermore, some of the better wine merchants and agents have individuals on their staffs who are experts in planning liquor menus. Some of the big brewers, distillers and liquor distributors can also give assistance. Each will have a considerable amount of written material for use in designing an attractive menu.

If only one liquor menu is used, careful consideration must be given to presentation of the various kinds of spirits. If a beverage list is to be made up of a folded unit, some designers advise that the front cover be used for the logo, and the back or the first inside page be set in four columns: the two center columns for mixed drinks and the two outer columns for specialty items; on the other inside page various wines can be offered. If necessary, the back panel can present liqueurs and other beverages.

If only a single hardback card is offered, the logo can appear on the front with perhaps a presentation of drinks that the establishment especially wishes to merchandise; on the back in the center columns the cocktails and mixed drinks can be offered. Wines can be in the fourth column and spirits and liqueurs in the first.

Usually, a liquor menu follows the order indicated in the ruled panel following.

Main Classification	Order within the Classification
Cocktails	Martinis, Manhattans, Daquiris, Gimlets, Old Fashioneds, Whiskey Sours, etc. (The order here is not especially important; merchandising may dictate which order is best.)
Mixed Drinks	Scotch, Bourbon, Rye, Vodka, Gin and other spirits in mixed drinks, such as with water, gingerale, tonic water, etc., along with tall drinks such as Tom Collins, etc. (Again the order is not too important, but since most people prefer Scotch, Bourbon or Gin drinks, perhaps these could head the list).
Beers, ales, etc.	Listing those available in draft or in bottles. Imports are usually listed separately from domestic items.
Wines	Usually the order of consumption is the order of listing: apéritifs; dry dinner wines, red or white; rosés; sparkling wines; and dessert wines.
After-dinner drinks	Frequently brandies and some other liqueurs are listed, followed by mixed drinks.

Beverage lists should be specifically designed for the particular enterprise because the requirements vary greatly. A German restaurant needs a very different list of wines from those offered by a French or Italian restaurant. It must also offer a number of beers. A menu featuring Mexican foods may present Margaritas prominently and perhaps make a specialty of them. The familiar Tequila with the lime slice and salt is also commonly featured. Some rich Spanish red wines such as the full-bodied Marques del Lagar from the Rioja hills or the Sangre de Toro (blood of the bull) can be offered along with one or more of the soft, luscious white wines of northern Spain. Cerveza (beer) may also be served, preferably in pitchers or attractive pottery mugs.

Follow-through is important in a liquor menu, and some research is necessary to make sure that an item is authentic when it is put on a menu meant to be typical of a culture. Follow-through should also include offering the drinks in traditional glasses or other drinking vessels.

Prices should be set forth plainly for each item or group. To obtain clarity and legibility, the information, descriptions, print, colors, etc., previously discussed under food menus should also be followed here. Merchandising is most important.

The Wine List

Eight to 10 wines may be sufficient to satisfy all needs on a wine list except perhaps for the most fastidious connoisseur who may wish to have a longer list. Some operations find that up to four listings are enough. One expert has said that if a wine list is well compiled a list of 24 to 30 wines should satisfy the most discriminating individual selecting wines for a meal.

It is becoming more and more common for restaurants to offer a house wine, filling a decanter from bulk stock. Such wines should be of the highest quality. Frequently when red and white dinner wines of the house are offered, no other choices are presented. Sometimes a house wine *plus* a list of bottled wines may be offered.

Wine lists are difficult to design. Certain wines *must* be on the menu, such as white or red dinner wines. These dry wines may have to be from both foreign and domestic sources. There is a very large variety of them, such as those from the Rheingau and Rheinhesse in Ger-

many, the Alsace and Moselle areas nearby, from the Burgundy, Bordeaux and other wine districts of France, and from many other countries. A complete list can be very extensive, and the individual making up the list should know how to reduce it as much as possible.

Wines are distinctive in numerous ways: they are produced from different varieties of grapes, from different vineyards or growths (crus) in particular vintage years; they come from various districts, parishes, chateaux or schlosses (castles), and are shipped by many different vintners. Most wines have a story behind them, and good merchandising

WINE SELECTIONS

		FULL BOTTLE	HALF BOTTLE
	RED WINES OF CALIFORNIA		
113	Zinfandel 1969/70 Napa Valley — Inglenook Vineyards	$ 5.00	$ 2.75
115	Gamay Beaujolais, 1970 San Jose — Mirassou Vineyards	5.50	3.00
122	Cabernet Sauvignon Private Reserve 1967/68 Napa Valley — Beaulieu Vineyard	10.50	5.50
	WHITE WINES OF CALIFORNIA		
133	Grey Riesling Livermore — Wente Brothers	$ 4.50	$ 2.50
140	Fumé Blanc San Jose — Mondavi Vineyards	6.50	3.50
145	Beaufort Pinot Chardonnay 1969 Napa Valley — Beaulieu Vineyard	7.50	
	RED WINES OF BORDEAUX		
170	St. Emilion, A. Roux 1969/70 Appellation St. Emilion Controlée	$ 6.50	$ 3.50
173	Pomerol Rothschild, 1966/67 Appellation Pomerol Controlée	8.50	
177	Château Mouton-Baron-Philippe 1967 5ème Cru, Pauillac Mis en Bouteilles au Château	11.50	6.00
	WINES OF BURGUNDY		
200	Beaujolais Villages, J. Drouhin 1970	$ 6.50	$ 3.50
203	Côte-de-Beaune Villages, L. Jadot 1970	8.75	4.75
208	Gevrey Chambertin, Thorin 1969 Côte-de-Nuits	12.75	6.75

Our complete vintage wine cellar selections are at your disposal.
Please request our Fournou's Ovens Wine List.

FIG. 7-1

A well-balanced list of wines that is part of the regular menu. Note that a larger wine list is also available.

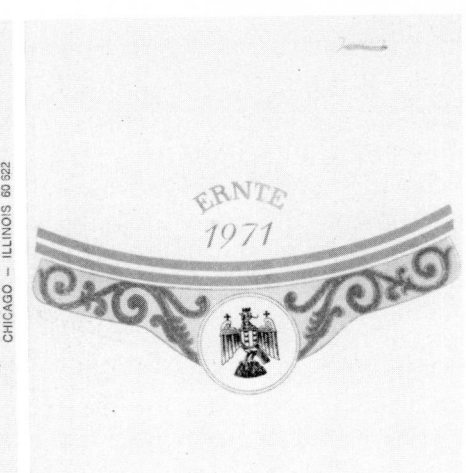

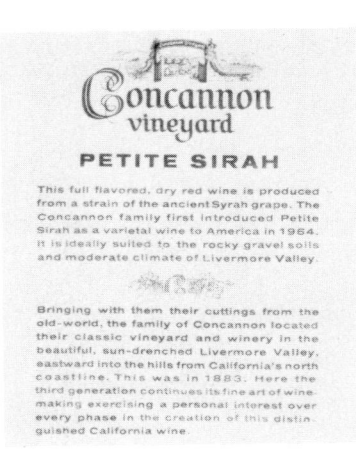

FIG. 7-2　At top is shown the label of an Austrian trockenbeeren (dry berry) auslese (select grapes) wine which is extremely sweet and is used frequently as a dessert wine. German wines of this type are very expensive, but this wine, of equivalent quality, can be purchased for much less. The label at bottom is that used by the Concannon vineyards for a new fine wine, estate bottled and made from grapes of a specified vintage year. More and more California and other American vineyards are showing the vintage years of their better wines.

should make use of interesting wine lore. An individual making up a wine list needs to be well informed. He should know, for example, the 1855 classification of Bordeaux wines. To call a Chateau Margaux wine a second cru and a Chateau Mouton Rothschild a premier cru causes the knowledgeable patron to lose faith in the list. To offer a Sauternes or a Barsac as a dinner wine

can also show that the individual making up the list does not know his wines. Attention must also be paid to the year or vintage. Certain years in Europe have produced better wines than others. Thus, Burgundies and red Bordeaux for the years 1959 and 1963 are known to be better than those produced in some other years. More California wines each year are being marked with a vintage

FIG. 7-3   Labels are subject to interpretation, and the discriminating buyer will examine them with much interest. At top, left, is the label on a bottle of champagne produced in Australia. It proved to be a product of high merit when tested against other champagnes of good quality. The label for the cognac at lower left is one known by connoisseurs of good brandy the world over. However, while an excellent brandy, it is not necessarily one one of the top brandies. Brandies can be tremendously expensive, especially those that are aged for a considerable period of time, produced from superb materials and made by celebrated manufacturers. The label at upper right was on a special selection of Alexis Lichine, a well known wine authority. His name attached to a product indicates it has a quality that he approves. Many patrons may feel that the approval of such an authority is desirable, and therefore will order the wine if offered on the menu. The label at lower right is for a Concannon Chateau haut (high) sauterne, a sweet wine from grapes of the Semillon variety that have been left to ripen until they have developed considerable sugar. The method is similar to that used with these grapes in their native Bordeaux area where the famous sweet Sauternes wine is produced.

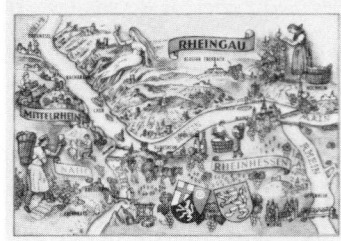

HAVEMEYER

1 Pt. 7,5 Fl. Oz.

RHEINHESSEN
RHINE-WINE

Rüdesheim a. Rh.
Alcohol 10% by Vol.

1970 Liebfraumilch

A full-flavored, mild appealing Rhine wine · Serve chilled

PRODUCED AND BOTTLED IN GERMANY
„HAVEMEYER"-Weine GmbH BINGEN/RHEIN

Sole U. S. Agents
BERCUT-VANDERVOORT & CO., SAN FRANCISCO, CALIF. 94111

HAVEMEYER'S LIEBFRAUMILCH

is a soft delicate wine of the Rhine Hessen district,
growing between Worms and Bingen. The original
wine was called after the Liebfraumilch monastery
in Worms, where the monks were the first wine
growers and produced an unusually pleasing wine.
Rhine Hesse's excellent wines are noted for their
aroma, their well balanced harmony and fragrance.
Havemeyer Liebfraumilch, as all white wines, is best
when served well chilled.

PRODUCE
OF HUNGARY

NET CONTENTS 17.6 OZ   Kb. 0,5 l

TOKAJI ASZU

HUNGARIAN TOKAJI WINE

Alc. CONTENTS
CCA. 14 % BY VOL.

SHIPPED BY

MAGYAR ÁLLAMI EXPORT PINCEGAZDASÁG – BUDAFOK

EXPORT MONIMPEX – BUDAPEST HUNGARY

ANNO 1967
3
PUTTONOS

FIG. 7-4   The labels at top are those used on a Liebfraumilch wine from Germany. As indicated by the label on the back of the bottle (appearing here on the right), the original wines were produced in a monastery in Worms; these vineyards still produce this famous wine but do not label it "liebfraumilch". Buyers should watch to see that the quality of some wines bearing generic names are truly of high quality. There are some on the market which are not of high quality but coast on the traditional name. The labels at bottom are from a bottle of the famous sweet dessert wine from Hungary, the Tokay Aszu. The numeral three in the label at right, which is found on the back of the bottle, indicates the relative degree of sweetness of the particular wine. This wine is frequently ranked in quality with the very sweet Sauternes of Bordeaux, the trockenbeeren auslese of Germany and some other sweet natural grape wines.

year. It is proper to show the vintage year on the wine list. The pricing of wines must be logical and justified. Ignorance here too can cause patrons to become negative about the wine list.

It is important that the proper spelling be used. The best assurance of correctness is to take the name and other information from a label. Mistakes like spelling the name of the sweet, white French wine "Sauterne" instead of "Sauternes" (it is from the celebrated Sauternes district of Bordeaux) * or to use

*We spell the California white wine "Sauterne", however.

the spelling "whiskey" for grain spirits from the British Isles and Canada are quickly caught by the knowing reader. (It is proper, however, to spell it "whiskey" when referring to American spirits made from corn, rye and the like.)

The individual designing the wine list should know how wines are used with foods and also which are which. Apéritif or appetizer wines may be a dry sherry such as Manzanillo, Fino, Amantillado or Dry Sack, etc., or a sweet wine such as Madeira, Marsala or cream (brown) sherry, a dry American sherry or cream sherry, Dubonnet, Byrrh, varieties of white, dry vermouth (French) or sweet

Bourgogne   Champagne   Bordeaux   Loire Valley   Alsace   Côtes du Rhone   Provence
                                        Anjou
                                       Touraine

FIG. 7-5   The major shapes of bottles for French wines are shown here. Most Rhone and Loire bottles have essentially the Burgundy shape; so does the Provence bottle shown here, but Provence shapes vary rather widely. Note also the slender, Alsatian bottle, similar to that used for Rhine wines (and Moselles) on the other side of the river in Germany.

Italian vermouth or white Lillet, among others.

Dinner wines should be divided between dry reds, whites and less dry rosés. Most patrons will prefer dry wines but some may like the small degree of sweetness in a rosé. (It is important that the word "dry" be used to describe a lack of sweetness, rather than sourness, in a wine.)

The waiter should know his wines and be able to suggest the correct one and know the reason for it. For instance, if lamb is selected as the dinner meat, a red Bordeaux is an excellent accompaniment; for a steak, a Burgundy is excellent; for a lobster or other seafood, a Chablis or a good German white wine is is order.

Some domestic wines are named after imports which they resemble. One may find on a list of domestic wines such names as Burgundy, Beaujolais and Chablis. These may or may not be good representations of the European wines they are supposed to imitate. It may depend upon the type of grape used. A domestic wine bearing a generic name such as Burgundy may or may not come from the grape used for the true Burgundy in France—the Pinot Noir grape. If one wishes to get a wine which would more nearly resemble the foreign generic wine, he should order a domestic wine bearing the name of the varietal grape used for that wine. Thus, if one orders a domestic wine named "Pinot Noir", a varietal name rather than generic such as Burgundy, the wine will more nearly resemble a French Burgundy because regulations require that, when the varietal name is used, the wine must be made from 51 per cent or more or that type of grape. Similarly, if one wishes to get a domestic wine resembling a true Chablis, he should order one labeled "Pinot Chardonany", the grape used to produce this wine in France. The price of a domestic varietal wine should be higher than the generic one, other factors being equal.

Use of the proper terminology is again stressed. To call a Moselle wine, which comes in tall green bottles, a Rheingau or Rheinhesse wine, which come in tall brown bottles, is quickly noted by knowing patrons. Similarly, labeling a German Sekt or an Italian Asti Spumante as "champagne" is a mistake the menu maker should avoid. Wine descriptions should be accurate. Good descriptions can help sell but they must truly represent the qualities and other factors found in the wine.

Normally, red dinner wines are served at room temperature (about 60 to 65° F) with red meats; white dinner wines are served chilled (about 45° F) with fish or poultry. The custom of serving red wines with red meats and white wines with white meats is, however, beginning to pass as a tradition, and many authorities today say the patron should select the wine he likes. If there is a doubt, a rosé can be offered since it is suitable for use in place of either a red or white wine. Normally, patrons who know very little about wines find that a rosé with just a touch of sweetness is highly acceptable. White wines usually have less body and less full flavor than the reds. The reds will also be slightly more astringent. Some whites have a flinty, harsh quality as evident in a Graves from Bordeaux or in some German dry white wines. This in no way

WENTE
PETITE SIRAH

This red table wine, made from grapes grown under the warm California sun in gravelly soils, has the excellence of quality so long associated with Wente wines.

It is a fragrant, rich Petite Sirah - born of grapes picked at the exact moment of maturity. Its round, ripe flavor is the result of careful tending of the juice - storing in small casks and a final aging for many months in the bottle.

You will find this Wente Petite Sirah adds immeasurably to your enjoyment of prime roast, sizzling steak or a fragrant stew.

WENTE PINOT NOIR

Years of aging produced this satisfying, robust red wine. First, quiet mellowing in small oak casks; then, the final maturing in this bottle, where the richness and fragrance of a fine Pinot Noir reaches its full development.

Try this wine with red meat . . . rib or pot roast of beef, steak or broiled ground chuck. You will revel in the perfect combination . . . and so will your most discriminating dinner guests. For a leisurely last course, serve a rich cheese, such as blue or Camembert, and a glass of Wente Pinot Noir.

FIG. 7-6 Note in these labels how the California wineries are beginning to show vintage and also to indicate that a wine is estate bottled, following some of the practices found in the labeling of European wines.

detracts from their quality. In fact, it may enhance it for the purpose intended. But some patrons, not appreciating these qualities, may prefer a softer more delicate wine.

Sweet wines such as Muscatel, Tokay or an imported Barsac or Trockenbeeren Auslese can be used with desserts. Port and some other quite sweet, fortified wines are proper after dinner but most Americans select brandy or a sweet liqueur.

If the house knows its wines, it can often feature a wine that is not well known but which is fine in quality and has characteristics making it a delightful wine to serve in place of a higher priced one. Thus, an Egri Bakiver, a Hungarian dry, red wine of considerable richness, bouquet and body (Egri Bakiver means "blood of the ox") can be used instead of a Bordeaux or Burgundy wine. Or, an Aszu Tokay from Hungary can be offered without apology as a sweet dessert wine in place of some others. An Italian Barbera from the Piedmont district in Italy is an excellent wine to offer instead of the higher-priced French red dinner varieties. It may have to be decanted before serving because of its tendency to cast out considerable lees (sediment).

With respect to using the romantic stories behind wines for merchandising, a good example can be seen in the famous remark of Dom Pérignon when he first tasted champagne, which he had made accidentally. "I am tasting stars!" he exclaimed. The fact that the Aszu Tokay wine from Hungary has been called the "king of wines and the wine of kings" also makes good copy. The famous wine from Italy—Est! Est! Est!—

derives its name from the exclamation made by the servant of a famous bishop sent on ahead to sample the wine before his master came. The servant, who had heard of the wine's fame, said when he had tasted it: "It is! It is! It is!". The fact that one of Napoleon's colonels thought so highly of the wines of the famous Clos de Vougeot vineyards that he ordered his soldiers to salute when they marched by the vineyard, also

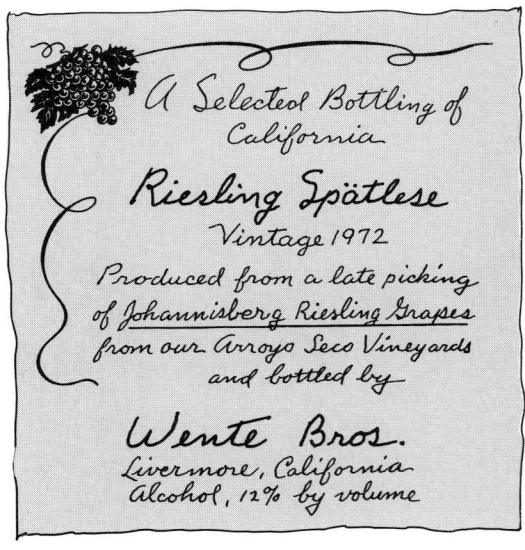

FIG. 7-7   Example of a special bottling. Frequently the quantity of wine bottled is limited, and the wine will be sought after by many who appreciate finer wines. Undoubtedly California producers will continue to market their more superior wines in this manner.

makes for interesting reading. The fact that Zinfandel, a red dinner wine somewhat resembling a Chianti, or an Emerald Dry, a luscious, dry white wine resembling a Moselle with a bit of "spritz" (a term meaning small bubbles or effervescence) come only from grapes grown in California, and are not duplicated anywhere else in the world, can be used to romance these wines.

A menu for a meal served with accompanying wines can be writen in three ways. A separate wine menu can be written along with a separate menu for the foods, or the wines and foods can both be on the same menu. Some list the wine adjacent to the foods to be served with it. Others list the wine directly under these foods. An earlier illustration indicated how the White House does this. A common method of writing the wine on the menu with foods is shown here:

Lobster Canapé
Small Cheese Puffs

Dubonnet

Double Consommé, Celestine
Cheese Straws

Amontillado, Dom Pedro

Celery   Olives   Salted Almonds
Poached Fillet of Turbot, Caper Sauce

Pouilly Fuisse 1955

Spooned Leg of Lamb
Mixed Spring Vegetables
Potatoes Anna

Egri Bikaver 1964

Fresh Asparagus, Vinegrette*
Camembert Cheese
Wafers

Chateau Margaux 1952

Schaum Torte

Schloss Johannisberger, Trockenbeeren Auslese, 1953

Coffee

Courvoisier, V.S.O.P.

Nuts   Mints   Bon Bons

*A wine is seldom served with the salad because of the tartness of the salad dressing. This tartness must be watched carefully and modified so as not to disturb the taste of the other wines.

Take care also that Brillat-Savarin's rule is followed: "The order of drinking is from the mildest to the fuller-bodied and to the richest in bouquet."

It is also necessary to couple good foods with the proper wine and its service. As indicated, some wines should be served at specific temperatures. Some guests may desire the wine at a different temperature, and service personnel may ask, when the wine is ordered, if any specific temperature is desired. If the guest prefers that a red dinner wine be chilled the waiter should show no evidence that this is not the usual service but go ahead and serve it that way. (Chilling a red wine harms some of the flavor and bouquet.) It is proper for the individual ordering a red wine to ask the waiter to pull the cork ahead of time so that "the wine can breathe". This allows the wine to oxidize slightly, giving it a fuller flavor and a better bouquet. Older, high priced wines should not be allowed to oxidize as much as newer reds.

The proper presentation and pouring must follow. It is customary for the patron ordering the wine to be shown the label on the bottle before the cork is pulled to allow him to see that it is the right wine. There is a proper way to remove the foil around the cork and to pull the cork, and the waiter should know this. After the cork is pulled, white wine may be put back into the wine holder to continue chilling. Red wine may be stood on the table, the label to the host, or it may be put into a basket. It is correct for the waiter to smell the cork to see that the wine is good in the bottle. He may set the cork down at the host's right so that he too can smell it.

The waiter may taste the wine in his silver *tastevin* if there is any doubt about the quality. This should be only a tiny sip. The wine is then poured in a small quantity into the host's glass so that he may taste it and judge if it is a suitable wine to serve with the food. The host should nod or indicate his approval. When this occurs, the service of the wine is, first to the ladies and often to the hostess first so that she will get any cork fragments in the bottle if the host has not already received these. Then the service of the wine continues to the other ladies. The gentlemen are next served and the host last. Only a part of the wine glass should be filled "to leave room for the nose."

The proper glass should be used. Using small glasses that are completely or nearly filled with wine is a mistake. A Burgundy wine requires a large tulip-shaped glass, a claret needs a narrower one, a Rhine or Moselle should have a glass with a tall stem. If these are not used, then the all-purpose wine glass should be used. Champagne is best served in the tall, narrow tulip glass rather than the flat open champagne glass. Brandy should be served in a proper snifter and not in a small liqueur glass.

The reason a wine glass is turned in at the top is to concentrate the wine odor so that it is fuller as the wine is consumed. Wine before tasting may be swirled in the glass, especially a red wine, to give it some oxidation and assist in building flavor and bouquet. It is proper to hold the wine up to the light to check its clarity and color, or to look at it through the glass against the white tablecloth to note these visual qualities. About two ounces of wine should be poured into the taster's glass so that plenty of space is left for sensing its bou-

WHITE BURGUNDY RED BURGUNDY RED BORDEAUX WHITE BORDEAUX

ALL-PURPOSE CHAMPAGNE ANJOU ALSACE

FIG. 7-8 Here are the various types of wine glasses used for the wines of France. The all-purpose glass shown at lower left is being used more and more. The Anjou glass is similar in shape to the tall-stemmed German wine glass but has a shorter stem. Usually a rosé is served in the Anjou glass.

quet. It is not improper to leave the bottle on the table for the host to pour more wine for his guests should the waiter not be there to do it.

The Drink List

The list of menu spirits is rather traditional and less variation is found in it than in a wine list. Only a few drinks may be on the menu, it being understood that the bar can furnish others if desired. Thus, a menu might list only those drinks that management wishes to push, as in the panel below.

dies, gins and, possibly, a rum are stocked, most requests can be filled. Often, if a patron orders one high-quality spirit which is not in stock, but is offered another of equal popularity, the patron will accept it. If bartenders and service personnel keep track of how many call items are *not* filled and what they are, a better list can be built.

Beers and Ales

On the liquor menu the list of beers, ales and similar drinks should be limited. Perhaps a sufficiently elaborate list will

---

**Special Decanter of Beefeater Martini on the Rocks
or Manhattan on the Rocks
$1.75**

**Old Fashioned   Gimlet   Whiskey Sour   Side Car
$1.65**

Various highballs, cocktails and mixed drinks can be listed along with Scotch, Bourbon, rye, vodka and gin. Rum drinks should also appear. The offerings should be balanced to what management feels will satisfy the need of clients. Normally, individuals ordering highballs, cocktails or similar drinks know what they want and a list is not required. In this case, the purpose of a menu is more to inform the patron about price rather than to spell out what is available. Most operations will find that they need a good list of "call" liquors; the number of these should be limited as much as possible. Checks should be kept on how frequently requests are made for call items. Those that move slowly should be eliminated. If a couple of good call Scotches, Bourbons, ryes, bran-

feature three or four domestic beers and ales and about three imports. Of course, if the operation is a beer garden or a German or Bavarian restaurant, more of these may have to be offered. But, if several good draft beers are served as house beverages, the need for a bigger list, even in one of these restaurants, will not be necessary. On some beverage menus, one or two draft beers *must* be offered.

Liqueurs and Cordials

The list of after-dinner drinks on a beverage menu should also be limited to what the trade requires and no more. Several domestic and imported brandies can be featured. Crème de Menthe, Crème de Cacao, a few fruit brandies,

Curacao, Cointreau, Benedictine, Chartreuse and, perahps, a few other popular ones might be sufficient to meet demands. Often the menu can feature some *mixed* after-dinner drinks which the establishments feels can be sold at a good profit and which will please patrons. These can be listed as clip-ons or boxed entries on the beverage menu to call special attention to them, in a way similar to that described for food menu items the managements wants to feature.

LIQUOR PRICING

Liquor is priced differently from food. A higher markup is taken and there is a tendency to average out prices more by groups of similar drinks than by individual cost. Food items frequently show more individual pricing. Thus, a large group of mixed cocktails may be priced at $1.50 each even though the cost of producing them may differ somewhat. If this were food, individual pricing likely would be used. Many operations attempt to have an average material cost for liquor items of around 20 per cent, while at the time time they may be attempting to operate the foodservices on a food cost of 30 to 40 per cent.

As in all menu pricing, a knowledge of cost is frequently desirable before establishing a menu price.

Pricing of Wines

It is common practice to price wines at 200 per cent of their bottle cost the equivalent of marking them up 100%. However, this may increase the price of some rather expensive wines above what the market will bear. Or it may bring in less total profit when only one bottle

is sold where two could be. Service personnel working on a wine-selling commission also are happier if more wine is sold because it not only increases their commission,[1] it also increases the amount of tips from the customer because of a larger bill. Furthermore, it is very desirable to have wines appear on tables because there is a great tendency for patrons at adjacent tables to purchase wine if they see others having it. Therefore, some operations may price higher costing wines at a lower markup to move them. Usually, the lowest limit used for markup on wines is 50 per cent. The reason for this is that costs on wine are usually calculated on the following cost percentages:

Interest on Inventory[2]	8%
Storage and other space cost	5%
Cooling and handling	3%
Labor	15%
Glassware	5%
Breakage	2%
Total	38%

The margin of 12 per cent on a 50 per cent markup (50% − 38% = 12%) must go for profit, variable and fixed costs, etc. Because 12 per cent may be insufficient, the markup may have to be higher.

A variation in the pricing method for wines may occur, and this will depend upon whether the price is based on fixed percentages of cost per bottle. Thus, costs such as those for space, cooling, service and glassware may be considered as the same for any bottle of wine and

---

[1] Commissions range from around 10 to 20 per cent, or a "cork" price may be given such at 25¢ for each bottle of wine (cork) sold.
[2] Wine inventories usually do not turn over more than four times a year.

therefore be priced *per bottle* rather than on the purchase price. However, some items such as interest and breakage should be based on cost since they are directly related to the item's cost. When the price is based on percentage of purchase price entirely, it is called the "percentage method," and when some costs are calculated per bottle, the method is called the "unit method."* The following indicates how these two methods may be used for a low-cost wine ($1.25 per bottle) and another higher priced one ($4.50 per bottle).

and the *actual* gross profit are going to be the same regardless of the cost method used. These are mathematical calculations, or estimates and whether one says the cost is going to be calculated on the basis of a bottle unit or a percentage of the purchase price will not dictate what the actual cost is going to be.

Pricing of Spirits

The cost of drinks made from spirits such as highballs, cocktails and so forth depends upon the quantity of spirits

	LOW-PRICED WINE		HIGH-PRICED WINE	
	Percentage Method	Unit Method	Percentage Method	Unit Method
Bottle cost	$1.250[1]	$1.250	$4.500[2]	$4.500[2]
Interest, 8%	.100	.100	.360	.360
Space cost 5% or 10¢	.063	.100	.270	.100
Cooling, etc. 3% or 5¢	.038	.050	.135	.050
Labor, 15% or 30¢	.188	.300	.675	.300
Glassware, 5% or 8¢	.063	.080	.360	.080
Breakage, 2%	.025	.025	.090	.090
Total cost	$1.727 (69.1%)	$1.905 (76.2%)	$6.390 (85.2%)	$5.480 (73.1%)
Selling price	2.500 (100%)	2.500 (100%)	7.500 (100%)	7.500 (100%)
Net profit	$ .773 (30.9%)	$ .595 (23.8%)	$1.11 (14.8%)	$2.020 (26.9%)

[1] Selling price is 10 per cent of bottle cost.
[2] Selling price is 60 per cent of bottle cost.

There is no clear-cut benefit in using either method. A higher gross profit is shown on a low cost wine with the percentage method and just opposite is true on a higher priced wine. One should realize, however, that the *actual* costs

used plus its cost and the cost of other ingredients in the drink such as carbonated beverage, ice, fruit, vermouth, etc. To control costs, an enterprise should establish exact quantities to be used for all drinks and see that these limits are followed. Bar manuals should list these quantities and procedures for making the drinks. Management should have follow-through to see that service personnel observe these di-

*For a fuller explanation of these methods see "Beverage Profits Through Controls," Professor Henry Ogden Barbour, *The Cornell Quarterly*, School of Hotel Administration, Cornell University, Ithaca, New York, Reprint 21.

rections. One national chain has established a strong reputation with patrons for its drinks because it has worked out excellent recipes and then sees to it that they are followed.

The quantity in a fifth is 25.6 volume ounces, in a quart 32 and in a half gallon 64. If 1½ ounce is poured for a drink, then a fifth gives about 17.3 drinks, a quart 21.3 drinks and a half gallon 42.6 drinks. However, this is seldom achieved because of a loss from spillage, overpouring or leaving a small quantity in the bottle. For this reason, some operations may allow a pouring loss of five per cent. The normal allowance for spillage in dispensing tap beer is 7 to 10 per cent.

Most operations price spiritous drinks on the cost of the basic ingredient only, adding a general markup to cover the cost of carbonated beverages, mixes, olives, vermouths, lemon twists, ice, limes, etc. They usually make a survey to find out what the sales mix is on drinks and then derive an average cost per drink. For instance, if a one-day survey indicated that an eight-hour shift had bar business and basic ingredient costs as shown in the panel below, the necessary information for pricing would be available.

DRINKS, PLAIN

	Oz. per drink	Cost per oz.	Cost per drink	Total cost
102 Scotch	1½	14¾¢	22⅛¢	$22.568
84 Bourbon	1½	13¼¢	19⅞¢	16.695
23 Gin	1½	12¼¢	18⅜¢	4.226
28 Vodka	1½	12¼¢	18⅜¢	5.145
6 Rye	1½	13½¢	20¼¢	1.215
4 Rum	1½	12¼¢	18⅜¢	.735

COCKTAILS, MIXED

86 Gin or vodka	2	11¼¢	22½¢	19.350
25 Manhattans	1½	12½¢	18⅜¢	4.593
66 Other Bourbon	1½	12½¢	18⅜¢	12.128
424 Total				$86.653
		Add 20% other material costs		17.331
				$103.984

In this example management decides to ascertain the per cent materials cost if Scotch drinks are sold for $1.50 and all other drinks for $1.30. Thus, 102 Scotch drinks, at $1.50 each, and 323 other drinks, at $1.30 each, will give a revenue of $572.90, and $103.984 as in the previous table is 18.2 per cent of this. Since management desires a material cost below 20 per cent, it may feel that this pricing structure is adequate, justifying the establishment of pricing based on the basic ingredient method. However, the assumptions that the sales mix will be this total, and that the other costs will not go over 20 per cent of the cost of spirits must prevail in order to achieve the desired goal. Also, tight bar control must be practiced so that the basic ingredient is not added in amounts other than those listed.

Some operations have just one price, regardless of what the drink is, such as the Playboy Clubs. They must see to it that the price is sufficient to cover all costs under the sales mix of drinks they produce. If they must make any adjustment in drinks, they can pour a slightly higher amount of basic ingredient, such as using two ounces of gin or vodka for a Martini, instead of 1½ ounces which is used for a gin or vodka tonic.

Other operations attempt to break drinks into certain categories such as highballs and other drinks blended with water and carbonated beverages, mixed cocktails such as Manhattans, Martinis, Daquiris, Old Fashioneds, etc., while grouping drinks such as Bloody Marys. Screwdrivers, etc. in another. Apéritif wines will be in another group and some cordials and liqueurs in still another. There is then a group price for each separate category.

Call brands must be priced out, and this may be done by individual drink, but again a study may be made as indicated previously and a general price established for call drinks of a specific kind. Thus, if it is found that 1½ ounces of Scotch costs 37½¢ and the average cost of call ryes and Bourbons is 25¢, the price for Scotch may be set at $2.00 and for other call drinks $1.75.

If an operation wishes to charge for each drink according to its cost, one would have to calculate the price of a vodka or gin Martini as follows:

Gin or vodka	2 oz	22.5¢
Vermouth	½ oz	2.5¢
Other		1.2¢
Total		26.2¢

which, at a 20 per cent material cost, would establish a selling price of slightly more than $1.30. Similarly, a Manhattan would have to be calculated as follows:

Bourbon	1½ oz	18.4¢
Vermouth	½ oz	2.5¢
Other		1.2¢
		22.1¢

which, at a 20 per cent material cost, would establish a selling price of about $1.10. It would be the same for a Bourbon and ginger ale as follows:

Bourbon	1½ oz	18.4¢
Gingerale and other		2.0¢
		20.4¢

which, at a 20 per cent material cost, would establish a selling price of something above $1.02. Because of the awkwardness of having a number of prices to keep track of, most operations prefer to average out prices and establish a pricing system based largely on the basic ingredient-cost method and set a price for a group of drinks.

For special drinks, individual costs and individual prices may be established. For instance, for exotic drinks one might find on a menu card various prices such as:

Paradise Cocktail	$1.75
Mai-Tai Swizzle	$1.50
Four Queens Pearl Diver	$1.80
Pimm's Cup O' Grog	$2.00
Coco Princess	$1.75

In this case, the price has been established on the basic cost of each drink and then rounded out to a selling price. Usually, the markup on such special drinks can be higher than on regular drinks.

When bottled goods are sold, a common procedure is to multiply the cost of the item by four. This usually gives a very high price compared with the price of the item as sold in retail stores. It is becoming more and more common to price such goods with a markup of two to three. This makes the price lower and covers the cost of ice, etc. It also tends to stop patrons from going out to the nearest liquor store and bringing their own liquor in a brown bag. It is common, however, to sell beers and ales with a markup of four times the cost price.

Pricing Tap Products

A barrel of beer is 31 gallons or 3968 ounces. This gives about 460 8-oz glasses, after allowing seven per cent for spillage. This is about the equivalent of 25 cases of 12-ounce bottles.

If a barrel of beer costs $34, the cost per ounce is 0.92¢, after allowing for spillage, and if an 8-ounce serving is given in a 12-ounce glass, allowing four ounces for foam collar, the cost per glass is 7.36¢ per glass. If a markup is desired with a material cost of 25 per cent (a factor of four can be used), the selling price is 30¢ for the beer (4 × 7.36¢ = 29.44¢).

BEVERAGE CONTROL

The control of assets applying to liquor frequently is emphasized more than the control of food. Perhaps this is because liquor can quickly run into considerable sums of money and the risk of pilferage may be greater.

Only a few authorized individuals should be allowed to make up requisitions or purchase orders for alcoholic beverages. None should be issued without proper authorization and the presentation of the proper slips. It is best to establish set times for the issuing of these items. The individual receiving the items should sign for them and should be responsible for seeing that they receive adequate security. Only authorized individuals should be permitted in areas where alcoholic beverages are stored, and the keys to such areas should be carefully controlled and safeguarded. Liquors issued for banquet or party use should also have separate and adequate storage. Bar checks should be numbered and issued by number. Individuals receiving them should sign for them and missing checks should be accounted for. Any checks not used should be returned and records maintained. Bartenders should not take their own cash register readings.

If different prices are charged for drinks during different times of the day or night, some record of checks issued

HYATT HOTELS
COMPLIMENTARY FOOD & LIQUOR ORDER

Liquor	Food
Gift Pack #1 _____	Fruit Basket #1 _____
Gift Pack #2 _____	Fruit Basket #2 _____
Other _____	Other _____
_____	_____
_____	_____

Deliver to: _____

    Room: _____

    Date: _____

Special Instructions: _____

_____

Ordered by: _____ Date: _____

Enclose Card of _____

F & B   NO. 10   H-2381   6-72

FIG. 7-9   All charges sent out from the kitchen, bar or pantry should be recorded. This is an example of how a complimentary food or beverage charge is recorded. A duplicate can be sent to the accounting department for making the necessary entries in the advertising or other appropriate account. (Courtesy Hyatt Corporation)

F & B   NO. 4   H-2316   6-72

HYATT HOTELS
WINE SALES

_____

DATE: _____

BRAND: _____

PRICE: _____

CAPTAIN:

APPROVED: _____

CAPTAIN NO.	TABLE NO.	CUSTOMER NO.	CHECK NO.

FIG. 7-10   Wine sales must be recorded not only because wine is merchandise that can easily disappear but because a cork price or a percentage price may be paid to the waiter selling the wine. Some operations pay a cork price of 25¢ or a percentage of the bottle's selling price. If wine is kept in an area outside the bar, the slip shown here is filled out and given to the bartender to record. He then indicates on the guest check presented with this slip that the transaction has been recorded. An approval slip is given to the individual controlling the wine issues who then supplies the wine. This approval slips can then be turned in to the storeroom to return stocks up to par. (Courtesy Hyatt Corporation)

DAILY BEVERAGE REQUISITION COST AND POTENTIAL

Date _____

Name of Bar _____

BRAND	NO. ISSUED	UNIT COST $	TOTAL COST $	POTENTIAL SALES $	ACTUAL SALES $	OV	SH	BAR COST %	POTENTIAL BAR COST %	DIFF
TOTALS										

FIG. 7-11 A daily requisition and potential sales sheet can be combined as shown here. The individual bottles are listed by brand, size and number. The purchase cost per bottle is entered in the adjacent column and the total cost of those issued is entered in the next. The potential sales figure is the number of drinks calculated as available from the bottles issued, times the selling price of the drink. Assuming a fifth contains 26 ounces, it will yield sixteen and one half $1\frac{1}{2}$-ounce drinks (95% of 26 oz ÷ $1\frac{1}{2}$ oz = $6\frac{1}{2}$). If each drink is sold for $1.35 the sales potential value is $22.27 (16.5 × $1.35 = $22.275). If the selling price fluctuates and drinks of two or more prices are sold from the same bottle, a cash register reading must be taken for several weeks to determine the sales mix. For instance, if a quart bottle showed that 60 per cent of the drinks from it were one-ounce drinks selling for $1.50 each, and 40 per cent were one-ounce drinks selling for $1.25, the sales potential would be calculated:

60% × 30½ oz* @ $1.50 = $27.45
40% × 30½ oz* @ 1.35 = 15.25
                TOTAL sales potential $42.70

Liquors such as white creme de cacao, white creme de menthe, and dry or sweet vermouth may show no sales potential since they are usually mixed with something else. Some operations calculate a minus potential for vermouths and credit this against the sales potential of the gin or vodka used. Partial bottles may throw the calculations off for a short time but eventually they even out. Overages (OV) or shortages (SH) of potential sales over actual sales are recorded on this sheet. The bar cost percentage is calculated on total cost of liquor to actual sales. Thus, if a bar were issued liquor valued at $124, potential sales were calculated as $620, and actual sales were $609.20, the bar cost percentage would be 20.35 ($124 ÷ $609.20 = 20.35%) and the potential bar cost would be 20 per cent ($124 ÷ $620 = 20%). Therefore, bar cost percentage would show a plus 0.35% over potential bar cost percentage. The actual dollar shortage would be $10.80 ($620 − $609.20 = $10.80). The daily beverage requisition cost and potential sales sheet can be totaled and this total transferred to the sheet shown in Figure 7-9. (Courtesy Hyatt Corporation)

*A 5% allowance is made for spillage and inaccuracies in pouring. Thus, a 26-oz fifth gives 16½ portions of 1½ ounces instead of 17.3 portions, and a 32-oz quart gives 30½ one-ounce portions instead of 32.

			BEVERAGE COST AND POTENTIAL TO DATE						
DATE	BAR COST $	POTENTIAL SALES $	ACTUAL SALES	OV	SH	BAR COST %	POTENTIAL BAR COST %	DIFF
1								
2								
3								
4								
5								
6								
7								
8								
9								
10								
11								
12								
13								
14								
15								
16								
17								
18								
19								
20								
21								
22								
23								
24								
25								
26								
27								
28								
29								
30								
31								
TOTAL								

Hyatt Press 2004 3/72

FIG. 7-12   This sheet accompanies the one shown in Figure 7-11 and is a recap to date of liquor issues, costs, sales potentials and actual sales. (Courtesy Hyatt Corporation)

and used during these times should be kept. Perhaps cash register readings should be taken at the beginning and end of such periods. The requisitioning of wine by waiters should be systematized so that adequate records are maintained. Room service sales should also conform to an adequate system. Separate analyses should be made of the profitability of party and room service sales.

Par stocks for the main storeroom, other storerooms and bars should be established and checks made to see that these are maintained.* No issue should be made on requisitions unless an empty bottle is returned for it. Frequent checks should be made to see that service personnel and bartenders are not bringing in their own bottles, selling

---

*A par stock is established to maintain a proper amount of liquor. Once this level is set, the stock should be in the bar, or elsewhere, either filled, partially filled or empty. A par stock list should be at hand at all times so that it can be checked. When extra heavy demands are to be made, it may be advisable to allow more than the par stock level. Changes in par stock levels should be made only after experience shows them to be nceessary.

drinks from them and pocketing the money. It is frequently desirable to time-stamp checks indicating when they go out for sales and when they are presented back with the money. A locked box method may be used. The method for voiding checks should be studied and complimentary issues of liquors should be accounted for.

It may be difficult at times to check on whether liqueurs and other miscellaneous drinks are being handled correctly. A system should be established which allows for checking this. The specific method for mixing drinks and amounts should be detailed and checks should be made to see that these are followed. Figures 7-9 through 7-12 are examples of some forms used to maintain adequate control of liquor stocks.

CHAPTER 8

Nutrition

Americans today are more concerned with nutrition than ever before. Some of this may be because of attention given to food fads and interest in "organic" foods. Whatever the cause, the increasing awareness by the public of the need for a balanced diet is causing many foodservices to pay more attention to nutritional principles in the preparation of food and in planning menus.

America is a well fed nation for the most part as compared with other nations of the world, but there are shortcomings in our dietary habits. Some other nations actually eat better than we do. This is not because they can afford to eat better; we have more money for food than they do. It is because these other populations select their foods more wisely than we. In 1955 a national survey showed that the average American lacked some important nutrients in the diet such as ascorbic acid

(vitamin C), thiamine, riboflavin, iron, etc. The average caloric consumption was adequate but with some people it was too low. However, for many there was a larger intake of calories than necessary, so much so that many nutritionists said the No. 1 problem in nutrition was not under-nutrition but over-nutrition. In the second nutritional survey in 1965, in spite of higher incomes and more abundant food, the results indicated that we ate more poorly as a nation than we did in 1955. In many instances lack of income was not the cause of a failure to consume a good diet. Many families with high incomes were found to eat more poorly than those with much less money. Furthermore, there was an increase in the consumption of fats and sugars—foods with fewer nutrients but more calories. The average excess consumption of calories again showed up but some individuals still lacked enough. Recent data published in late 1973 indicated that obesity is still a national problem, approximately 30 per cent of our population being overweight.

Nutritional Responsibility

The responsibility of a foodservice in providing adequate nutrition can vary. As noted previously, commercial operations should see that nutrients in food are preserved as much as possible in storage, pre-preparation, preparation and service. They should not be responsible for seeing to it that individuals who dine there select an adequate diet. They do have the responsibility for making it possible to select an adequate diet within their sphere of operation. Should the operation be a drive-in offering only hamburgers, carbonated beverages, French fries, etc., it cannot do much to see that an adequate diet is consumed, since even with the best selection from the menu an individual could not get a balanced meal. There are some people who would restrict the sale of some foods considered to contribute to an unbalanced diet, such as carbonated beverages, but such restriction would hardly fit in with the traditions of American life.

However, if a foodservice provides individuals with most of their food, such as a nursing home, a prison, a school, etc., then there is a responsibility to see that the meals are nutritionally balanced. Some may have to go so far as to provide special diets for individuals in the institution. Such diets may have to be provided in hospitals and, perhaps to a lesser extent, in nursing homes. Schools that participate in the federal School Lunch Program must serve a meal that meets specific requirements for quantity and must contain certain kinds of foods so that a child receives about a third of his daily nutritional requirements in the meal.

Many commercial operations are finding that patrons are asking for foods which meet their dietary needs. Menus offering attractive meals low in calories have good popularity. Attempts to provide special diets should be controlled, however; only a qualified dietitian or nutritionist should plan diets. Furthermore, most commercial operations are only qualified to prepare and serve some of the simplest diets. It is dangerous to permit personnel to prepare diets supposed to meet dietary requirements if such personnel do not know what these requirements really are, or are not supervised by someone who does know. For instance, if a 1,500-milligram low-sodium diet contains foods as they are normally salted in cooking plus certain kinds of foods like beets, carrots, potato chips, dill pickles and sauerkraut, serious breaches in the diet are being made.

However, the offering of a low-calorie (weight reduction) meal has proven popular, and many operations can offer meals that could be adequate for one on a low-calorie, diabetic or restricted-sodium diet, if they have only a limited understanding of nutritional principles. The following might represent three meals which give about 1,600 calories a day. It could also be made available to a diabetic who can consume around 150 grams of carbohydrates (starches and sugars) a day.

Breakfast	Approx. calories	Luncheon	Approx. calories	Dinner	Approx. calories
Orange juice	60	Chicken broth, cup	30	Broiled grapefruit	35
Cornflakes or cooked		Two Melba toasts	30	Broiled chicken	
oatmeal (½ c)	70	6 oz low-fat cottage		leg (5 oz)	250
½ c low-fat milk	50	cheese on low-cal		Broiled lean ground	
Poached egg on dry		peach	190	round (4 oz)	250
toast or	120	Toasted raisin bread	60	Mashed Hubbard	
Scrambled egg* with a		Sherbet, low-cal	120	squash, ½ c	35
slice of dry toast	120	Milk, low-fat, 1 c	70	Hard or soft roll	50
Coffee or tea	0	or, for the salad		Mixed green salad,	
		substitute:		low-cal French	
				dressing	35
		Poached cod (4 oz)		1/16 angel cake	100
		with lemon butter	125	Tea or coffee	0
		Sliced tomatoes	35		

*For a low cholesterol diet the egg should be prepared from the low cholesterol type of egg substitute and the poached egg or scrambled egg omitted. The chicken leg should also be used on such a diet and not the ground round. No butter should be served unless the calories allowed are higher. Fat restriction is usual in a low-cholesterol diet.

If such a diet were used for a moderately bland or soft diet, some slight modification might have to be made. The diet could be used, as noted, for a restricted-fat diet. The diet could also be used for a 2,500-milligram-per-day restricted-sodium diet if the foods were only lightly salted.

Most individuals who must diet know usually what they can or cannot eat. If a foodservice's menu contains salads, fruits, vegetables, cottage cheese, eggs, low-fat milk or buttermilk, and some plainly prepared fish, meat or poultry, there should not be too much trouble in selecting some of the more simple diets from it. In hospitals, nursing homes and other institutions where modified diets must be provided, a general menu is written and from this the modified diets are taken. The principle in working from a general diet into modified diets is to make as few changes as possible while observing the necessary modifications. Often only a few minor changes are required. In this way, diets do not become "denial programs" which make people feel sorry for themselves and make them think they are deprived.

If foodservices desire, they can retain the services of dietitians to plan a few diets which can be easily prepared. These can be put on the menu or a special diet menu, or attached to the menu as clip-ons. The dietitian can also provide good instructions on how to prepare some of these diets from the regular menu. For instance, a small portion of meat, fish or poultry without gravy or sauce; a vegetable; a salad with low-calorie dressing; bread or a roll; a glass of low-calorie milk or buttermilk; tea or coffee; and some low-calorie canned fruit or sauce, low-calorie sherbet or ice cream, angel cake, low-calorie gelatin or fresh fruit—these can satisfy people on a low-calorie diet or other simple, modified diets. Individuals requiring highly specialized diets might not be satisfied with this, but by and large the greater number of people on diets could be. The dietitian also could indicate that a vegetable plate served with a poached egg in the center or a small broiled beef patty, etc., would be satisfactory. Usually a large salad without too much dressing is a suitable meal, with a roll and perhaps a simple dessert. There are many ways to satisfy a number of dietary needs without changing menu offerings too much. If desired, a few dietary canned foods can be carried, plus items like low-calorie milk and low-calorie cottage cheese in a limited supply.

A foodservice should be sure that the foods it serves are bonafide representations and not fakes of dietary foods. It is dishonest to say that a broiled beef patty is from lean beef and have it made from ordinary hamburger that is 25 per cent fat, or that low-calorie French dressing is used when it is not. It is unethical to say a sherbet or gelatin dessert is made from low-calorie products when it is not. The portions listed on the menu should be observed in serving. If a patron orders a special meal for dietary reasons and then requests additions, such as cream for coffee or tea, butter for bread, or a scoop of vanilla ice cream (140 calories per one-eighth quart) service personnel should not argue about it. The professional obligation is only to make it possible to select an adequate diet—not to force patrons to eat one. One of the sad problems about diets is that more people talk about them than follow them.

NUTRITIONAL CONSIDERATIONS IN MENU PLANNING

Nutrition is a complex biological science which some individuals spend their entire lives studying. It is involved with an understanding of how food is utilized in the body. While our knowledge of nutrition has grown rapidly in the last 50 years or so, it is a dynamic discipline on which we are still seeking many answers.

Dietetics is the practical application of nutrition. It seeks to interpret for the nutritionist the way to apply his knowledge. Thus, while nutrition is the science, dietetics is the art. One does not need to know all the complexities of nutrition science to apply it, but the more one knows, the better off she or he is. Thus, it is possible to understand a limited area and be able to apply dietary principles. When we attempt to teach the average individual something about a diet he should follow, we try to stress only that area he needs to know and give enough of the complexities behind the restrictions so that he will understand why and how the diet should be applied. Therefore, in this chapter, there is no attempt to cover any area deeply, but only to give enough information so that one concerned with the administration of simple diets, or who must prepare simple ones, can have some background of understanding on why and how things are done the way they are. In no way does it cover what a dietitian must know to perform in that profession, nor even what a dietary aide might know—one who works in a dietary department. Only basic, simple information is presented. For those who would learn more, some of the references given in the bibliography may be helpful.

Food as Fuel

Our bodies can be considered as machines that utilize food as the fuel they need for proper operation. A car uses gasoline, oil, water, grease and electrical energy to run. Our bodies run on food and water, but from these they must get a number of different substances for the body if we wish them to run well. If one of the many compounds which our body needs to operate is missing in the food, the body does not do too well and death can occur if the omission is major or persists for too long a time.

Certain food substances give heat to warm the body or energy to move and run it. Other substances are needed to give growth and to maintain essential body functions. Some substances in food are called regulatory; that is, they help to regulate body functions. Much of what we need to do as driver of a car, to regulate speed, steering, braking, etc., is done automatically for us in our bodies by these substances. Thus, to run faster, we don't have to step on a pedal to obtain more energy. Automatic mechanisms in the body do this for us. These automatic mechanisms are usually regulatory substances found in our food supply.

We divide the substances we get from food into groups according to what they do in the body. We usually say there are five of these substances: (1) carbohydrates, (2) proteins, (3) fats, (4) vitamins and (5) minerals. In addition, the body requires water and a substance frequently referred to as bulk, residue or roughage Alcohol can be utilized in the body. Since it is used much as a carbohydrate, this text considers it under this group.

Carbohydrates

Carbohydrates, the substances that furnish heat or energy, are found in plentiful supply in starchy or sweet foods such as potatoes, syrup, honey, bread, macaroni products, corn, rice, dried legumes, cake, or sweet potatoes. The body can break carbohydrates into a simple sugar called glucose. If the more complex carbohydrates are not broken down into glucose, the body cannot use them. The body always maintains a supply of glucose in the blood for immediate needs for heating the body or running it. We call this supply "blood sugar" and usually we have enough to run us for about eight hours. We also keep a reserve energy substance called glycogen stored in our liver. We can quickly convert this to glucose if we need it. If we need more energy than we hold as glucose or glycogen, we must break down fat or protein, converting these to glucose, or eat something which we can change to glucose.

Foods high in starch or sugar, as named here, can furnish a considerable amount of glucose. Other foods can also furnish it, in lesser amounts. We need more carbohydrates to operate the body than any other kind of food, and it is usually recommended that 50 to 60 per cent of the total calories consumed in food be carbohydrates. It is usually considered better if the carbohydrates come from starchy foods rather than sweet ones. Too much carbohydrate in the body is not good because it may lead to the elimination of other foods we need to supply the body's requirements. As indicated, the body also can use fat or protein for heat or energy. When this is done we raise the cost of our diet and may not be doing the best for the body. Thus, most of the time, it is better to get the fuel we need from carbohydrates.

Many people think that starches and sweets are fattening, and they may try to eliminate them from the diet. This is wrong. They are not fattening. A gram of carbohydrate contains four calories; so does a gram of protein. A gram of fat is more than twice as fattening as these, since it contains nine calories; and a gram of alcohol is almost as much—it contains seven calories. Thus, anyone who believes that carbohydrate calories are more fattening than other calories, or that carbohydrates are more fattening than other food substances, just doesn't know his nutrition. Calories do count as fatteners—that's the only reason we get fat—and to lose weight we need to reduce our caloric intake. However, when we do this, we should see to it that we consume enough food to keep up the essential functions in our bodies.

Knowing where calories come from is important. For instance, a four-ounce baked potato (20 per cent starch) has 85 calories in it. The same amount of lean, cooked chicken breast, which some might think not fattening, has 166 calories or twice as many as the baked potato. If we put a pat of butter on this baked potato, we increase the calories to 164. One of the problems with some carbohydrate foods is that we may eat them in too concentrated a form, as in candies, a rich pasta dish, or one dressed with a lot of butter and other rich ingredients. A tablespoon of sugar contains 50 calories—it is almost pure carbohydrate—while a tablespoon of cooked rice has 17. A tablespoon of butter or oil contains almost 100 calories.

We can eat a considerable amount of some foods and not get many calories. Thus, we have to eat almost five pounds of lettuce to get the same number of calories that we get in a tablespoon of oil. If we add just 100 calories per day more than our bodies need, in a year we can gain more than 10 pounds. We can pile in the calories quickly by consuming alcoholic beverages. An ounce of spirits contains just about the same number of calories as its proof. Thus, if one drinks a Martini made with two ounces of 86-proof gin, there are about 175 calories without considering the vermouth and the olive. This is the equivalent of three slices of bread. Few individuals would think of eating six slices of bread at a meal, but some may go to a cocktail party and drink two Martinis and eat a lot of nuts, rich foods and other things besides. Therefore, individuals who think they will lose weight if they cut out starches and sweets may be mistaken if they do not also cut down on calories from other foods. Some plans allow a person to eat all the fat or protein or all the calories desired so long as these are not from carbohydrates. These plans don't work, as many authorities can attest. While it is true that a diet high in protein or fat takes more calories to digest and utilize in the body, this higher caloric requirement is not enough to make much difference.

Those who know nutrition agree that to lose weight there must be a restriction in the number of calories. Along with this, there also must be a permanent change in eating patterns. Weight increases because people eat too much over a fairly long period of time. To stop this gain requires that the pattern of overeating be changed and that a pattern of undereating be introduced until the desired loss in weight is achieved. Then a balanced pattern of eating can be established. If one knows how to eat, one can consume a tremendous amount, get all the other nutrients required in abundant supply and still cut down on calories. Such a diet also can be quite gourmet. This is the true way to lose weight. It is the only one subscribed to by those who know nutrition and diet. The other diets that appear from time to time are just plain bunk and often are extremely dangerous to remain on for too long a time.

Authorities are beginning to find that the tendency toward obesity can be built into the cells of one's body at an early age in life. A child that is overfed by a loving parent may be permanently encouraged to be obese because the body's cells are built to demand extra food. Therefore, building good food habits early in life, and practicing the dictum of eating limited amounts rather than huge amounts, is important.

Individuals usually reach their normal weight between their 25th and 30th years. After this they should gain very little. After 55 the body slows down and the number of calories consumed should be fewer although the same amount of other nutrients will be required. Elderly people who have very low caloric needs still require the same amount of nutrients as they did when they were young. If fewer than 1,200 calories are consumed in a day, it is extremely difficult to get all the other nutrients into the diet. At this time a vitamin pill or dietary supplement may be added to the diet. Normally, if one eats a balanced diet there is little need for these, and they may just be thrown off by the body as an excess. Some vitamins, like vitamin A, vitamin D and vitamin E, can harm an individual if taken in too great a quantity.

An individual 10 per cent heavier than he should be, according to standard weight tables for his height, is considered overweight; one 20 per cent heavier is considered obese. Overweight and obese people have more health problems than those who maintain their proper weight or keep slightly underweight.

Eating foods high in other nutrients but low in calories can be one way of eating a lot and still not getting fat while maintaining adequate nutrition. Thus, many fruits and vegetables, lean meats, fish or poultry and low-fat dairy products can pack a terrific wallop in essential nutrients without adding excess calories that go into fat. Many foods contain what are called "empty calories". This means the food has calories but not many other items the body needs. Thus, when one eats them they add calories but little else. Eating a candy bar can add a number of calories but not much else. This makes it necessary for the other foods consumed to carry a double load and make up for the other nutrients the candy bar did not provide. If we consume too many empty-calorie foods, we can get fat and still be under-nourished. Teenagers are not the only ones who do this. Young people may do it by consuming too many cokes and other empty-calorie foods, but older people can also do it by consuming too much alcohol!

To have an adequate diet, we say an individual should consume foods each day from four main groups: (1) dairy foods (the equivalent of a pint of milk a day), (2) meat, eggs, fish and poultry (one or two good servings a day—which can include cheese), (3) green and yellow vegetables and fruits (at least five servings a day, with oranges or other citrus fruit or tomatoes as one kind, and a leafy green or yellow vegetable every other day), and (4) cereals such as bread, rice, macaroni, oatmeal, corn-meal, etc. (whole grain or enriched cereals should be preferred.) The additional calories can come from sugars, fats, syrups, etc. If one neglects foods from these groups, he will not have good health and may have a poor appearance, stature, etc.

DIABETES. A person lacking insulin cannot burn glucose in the body. Such a person is a diabetic. Insulin is a hormone manufactured in the pancreas. Some people manufacture very little or none at all and have to take insulin either in shots or orally. About two per cent of the population is diabetic. Overweight individuals develop it to a greater degree than underweight ones, and diabetes is more common in individuals over 40.

A diabetic usually can handle only a limited amount of carbohydrate in his food and frequently it must be measured. Some others can consume a normal amount because the insulin they take is effective in burning up the carbohydrate. Some diabetics may have to limit carbohydrate in the diet and then expect to get the other calories they need to run the body from proteins and fats. Some diabetics may need more frequent feedings, each feeding containing a small amount of carbohydrate, to give a small quantity of glucose slowly and consistently into the bloodstream. If a diabetic eats too much carbohydrate, his body throws it off as glucose in the urine. Since a diabetic cannot carry too much sugar in his blood, care must be taken to see that he does not run out of it. If he does, he can go into a coma and die. Some diabetics needing quick energy may be given sugar or even have glucose introduced directly into the bloodstream intravenously. Normally it is best that they get what they need from starchy foods rather than from sweet ones.

Most diabetic diets are calculated on the exchange method. This method considers the total amount of carbohydrate allowed in the diet and then exchanges this for foods in the diet. Total calories are also considered and exchanges can be arranged with these in mind. Sometimes one food can be exchanged for another so long as the calories and carbohydrates are not exceeded. It is a flexible method and allows most diabetics to have a very liberal diet.

Protein

Meat, milk, cheese, eggs, fish, shellfish and poultry are foods that yield a high amount of protein. Protein is needed to promote growth and also to regulate the body. Individuals who have ceased to grow still need protein to replace worn-out body tissues. Most foods that come from animal sources are good sources of protein but there are exceptions such as gelatine. A fair amount of protein can also be obtained from cereals, nuts, legumes such as dried peas, dried beans or chick peas, and from seeds. Vegetables and fruits also contain some protein.

Some protein substances are better than others. Proteins are composed of chemical substances called amino acids. There is a fairly large number of these but there are eight needed by adults and 10 needed by children found only in animal foods such as meat, poultry, milk, cheese, eggs, fish and a few non-animal products. These are needed to maintain life. (Thus, a certain amount of the protein we eat should be animal protein, or come from those few non-animal products such as, soy, cottonseed and rape seed.) These amino acids are called *essential* amino acids because without them human life cannot exist. Some of the other amino acids we need can be manufactured from protein by the body. If in selecting a diet we have one or two servings of high quality protein a day, plus several glasses of milk and additional protein obtained in cereals and other foods, we do well, multiply and grow.

It is possible to combine legumes such as beans, peas, nuts and seeds with cereals and get a protein mixture that has all the essential amino acids in adequate supply. What the legumes or seeds do not have, cereals do have in good supply. Thus, a meal of Boston brown bread and baked beans gives a complete supply of protein. This ability to combine cereal and legumes to make good protein is why some civilizations, such as the ancient Egyptians, could do so well on legumes and rice; the Indians and Pakistanis so well on the legume dahl and the wheat bread called chapati; or the Chinese on rice and soy. The legume and the cereal must be eaten in the same meal to furnish the essential amino acids; eating one at one meal and another later doesn't work.

Today we are able to process soy and other proteins from plants and make them into products that are very similar to meat. Thus, we have baco-bits, made from soy, that taste just like bacon bits, and hamburger granules that taste exactly like hamburger. We also process these soy products into items that taste like sausage, ham, chicken, turkey or beef. Besides soy, we can use other plant proteins, and more and more analogs such as these are appearing on the market. The new product called "Hamburger Helper" is a soy analog. Since they are nutritionally complete, the USDA now allows the School Food Service Program to use a certain amount of these analogs with meats. Individuals who must carefully watch the quantity of animal fats consumed find that meat substitutes made from these products can be eaten in normal amounts like meat and still will not contribute the undesirable fat that meats would.

Fats

Fat is used in the body to promote essential body functions, to provide heat and energy and to put a protective padding around body organs and the body itself. Fats stay in the stomach longer than carbohydrates and somewhat longer than protein and so some fat in the diet helps to stay hunger.

We consume too much fat in this country. Not more than 35 per cent of our calories should come from fats, but we average more than this.

We can separate diets that restrict fats into three broad categories: (1) general restriction of all kinds of fats, (2) restriction of saturated fats and (3) restriction of fats and foods that contribute cholesterol to the diet. By using the first, one can also get the other two, and often by restricting saturated fats in the diet a low cholesterol diet is also achieved.

Some individuals with gall bladder problems and other digestive problems may have to reduce any type of fat in the diet. This will mean that salad dressings, fat meats, nuts high in oil, butter or margarine and other foods with fat in them, will be restricted. Cooking in a Teflon pan and boiling or broiling may be recommended for foods that must not contain fat.

Some individuals with high blood pressure or heart disease may be permitted some kinds of fats but not others. Thus, a diet restricting saturated fats may be prescribed. Foods such as dairy products, meat and a few oils may be high in saturated fats. Fish oil, a number of vegetable seed oils and poultry fat are less highly saturated. In fact they may contain fats that are called unsaturated and may be permitted in the diet. Sometimes we can take unsaturated fats and subject them to a process called "hydrogenation", which is adding hydrogen to the fat molecule making it more solid and firm, and turn the unsaturated fat into a saturated one. Thus, if we see on a package of margarine that a vegetable oil has been used but has been hydrogenated, this oil which may have been an unsaturated fat before hydrogenation is not so any more. Not all oils or fats from vegetables are unsaturated. For instance, coconut oil is highly saturated. Some oils like fish oils are so highly unsaturated that we call them polyunsaturated fats. Thus, a diet that should have few saturated fats can contain a fairly large quantity of fish. There are as many calories in a gram of saturated fat as in the same quantity of unsaturated and so, by using unsaturated fats, one does not reduce caloric intake.

Cholesterol is a substance found in fats. It is also a large part of a substance found deposited in the arteries of individuals having high blood pressure, heart problems, etc. It can contribute to senility in elderly people. Cholesterol is found in animal fats, egg yolks, shellfish and some other foods and these should be restricted in a low cholesterol diet. Even though individuals may eat a low cholesterol diet and very few fats, if they consume an excess of calories, their bodies may still manufacture cholesterol. Thus calorie restriction is also a part of the diet. There is some evidence to show that unsaturated fats can help to carry cholesterol out of the bloodstream.

The complete story on cholesterol is still to be told, but authorities feel that we have enough evidence at this time to restrict butter and other dairy products, eggs, meats and some other items in diets when cholesterol is a functional problem.

Vitamins

The word "vita" means life and the word "amine" means protein. So the term vitamin originally meant "a life-giving protein." Now we know that not all vitamins are proteins so the word is used to indicate a substance that is needed to control certain body functions so that life can go on.

The body uses vitamins in extremely small amounts but they have a big effect on essential body processes. For instance, the vitamin thiamin must be present if the body is to utilize glucose. For this reason, an individual's carbohydrate and thiamin intakes should be somewhat correlated. Vitamins usually do not work alone but together. Thus, even though the body may be plentifully supplied with some, if one or more are lacking, some vital body functions may not be able to take place.

When vitamins were first discovered, they were named after the letters of the alphabet. Thus, we have vitamins A, B, C and D. About the time we discovered D, we knew we were in trouble because what we thought was one vitamin in B was actually a group, and so we started to break the B's down into B_1 (thiamin), B_2 (riboflavin) and we reached vitamin B_{12} before we stopped. Today the new vitamins are called by their chemical names, such as choline, folic acid, pantothenic acid. It is becoming common to call the other B

vitamins by their chemical names, and to refer to vitamin C as ascorbic acid.

Vitamins are measured in very small quantities because that is the way they are found in food and the way the body uses them. Thus, we may say that an individual needs only 60 milligrams of ascorbic acid a day. This is a very small quantity since a milligram is only a thousandth of a gram. Some vitamins are measured in micrograms—one millionth of a gram. Other vitamins are measured in International Units (I. U's.) This came about because some of the early investigations to ascertain quantities required were performed with animals, so we called the number needed *units,* which varied with different vitamins. The word "international" was used because investigators wanted to indicate that this was the international standard that had been established rather than some individual or national one.

VITAMIN A. Leafy green vegetables, yellow or orange fruits and vegetables, cod liver oil, cream and egg yolks are good sources of vitamin A. A lack of this vitamin may cause night blindness, faulty vision or even blindness. In the body it helps to utilize proteins, to build tissues and to maintain other functions and growth. A very dry, scaly skin can indicate a lack of vitamin A. Xerophthalmia, a dryness of the eye, is usually the result of a low level of vitamin A.

Vitamin A is soluble in fat and will be found in butter, egg yolks or cod liver oil. The body can make vitamin A from the substance called carotene, found in leafy green vegetables or yellow or orange fruits such as canteloupe or apricots, squash, sweet potatoes, etc. Liver contains a good supply of vitamin A.

It is a fairly stable vitamin and is not much affected by cooking or other chemicals.

VITAMIN D. Vitamin D is closely related to Vitamin A in that both are relatively stable and both are oil soluble. However, vitamin D is very closely associated with the hormone structure of the body and there are some who consider it as a hormone and not a vitamin. The vitamin is needed to convert calcium and phosphorus into bones and teeth. Children lacking it develop rickets, a malformation of the bone structure.

It is found in fish liver oils, cream, butter and eggs but it can be manufactured by irradiating fats with ultraviolet light. Thus, we may irradiate evaporated milk or other dairy products with ultra-violet rays and make vitamin D. The sun's rays contain ultra-violet light and so sunlight shining on the skin can convert body fat immediately below the surface into vitamin D. Dark skinned individuals will not develop as much vitamin D as light-skinned people. Thus, the black race has less chance to develop vitamin D in this way than the white race.

Butter, cream and egg yolk are natural sources of vitamin D. Milk, margarine and some other foods may be fortified with this vitamin to supply it in the diet. No definite amount of vitamin D is known to be required by adults, a normal diet usually supplying enough, but children do require it for growth.

VITAMIN E. The need for vitamin E is limited. We know it is used to help the muscles function smoothly and that it acts as an anti-oxidant to fat in the body.

It may be helpful also in circulatory problems and in the body's utilization of amino acids. Claims that vitamin E may be effective in reducing problems of sclerosis, nephritis, diabetes, hypertension or heart problems have not been substantiated. In spite of this lack of evidence, some nutrition quacks are recommending high quantities of vitamin E in the diet. Many medical authorities feel that a large administration of the vitamin can be harmful and that only what is found in a good, normal diet should be recommended. Vitamin E is plentiful in the germ of cereals and in cod liver and some other liver oils as well as in liver. It is also found in small supply in some other foods and this may be enough to supply the body's needs.

VITAMIN K. Another fairly stable and oil soluble vitamin is Vitamin K, found usually in good supply in fresh fruits and vegetables, especially green vegetables. Probably it is also manufactured in the intestines by micro-organisms. Vitamin K helps the blood coagulate and may have other functions in the body. It is destroyed by "ergot" which can develop in mildewed rye or other grains. An excess of aspirin or sulfa drugs can also interfere with its action in the body.

B-VITAMIN COMPLEX. All the B-vitamins are water soluble. Some are not very stable. Thiamin and vitamin B_6 (pyridoxine) are easily destroyed by heat and by alkalies. Therefore, putting soda in cooking water is very harmful to them. Most B-vitamins are easily leached from vegetables as they soak in water. The quantity of B-vitamins required should be consumed daily since the body does not store them as well as it does the oil-soluble vitamins.

Thiamin or vitamin B₁ is needed to promote the appetite, burn carbohydrates and develop a stable nervous system. A lack of it can promote a disease called beriberi which is evidenced by severe constipation and a soreness of the leg muscles, causing lameness or even inability to walk. It is plentiful in whole-grain creals, fortified flours, yeast, meats—especially pork and liver—legumes and milk. Most individuals should consume some cereal products each day to assure that thiamin will be in adequate supply in the diet. Fortified flours and meals have B vitamins added to them.

Riboflavin, or vitamin B₂, is important in developing body energy. A lack of it may show up as tiny sores in the skin, especially at the corner of the mouth. The eyelids also become inflaméd and sore. It is plentiful in milk, cheese, eggs, meats and whole-grain or enriched cereals. The vitamin is easily destroyed by sunlight and this is why milk delivered in glass bottles often comes in colored glass.

Niacin is rather stable to heat but is very soluble in water. It is plentiful in nuts, especially peanuts, seeds, brewer's yeast, meats and enriched or whole-grain cereals. If we consume the amino acid tryptophane in adequate amounts, the body changes it into niacin. A lack of niacin causes pellagra, a disease evidenced by skin sores in the same place on the left and right sides of the body, accompanied by diarrhea and mental deterioration. It can even cause a falling off in body functions until death occurs. Niacin works with thiamin and riboflavin to develop energy in the body.

Required quantities of thiamin, riboflavin and niacin have been established, but not for some of the other B-vitamins. We know that we need them but not how much.

Pyridoxine (B₆) is important in metabolizing protein and fat and in changing the amino acid tryptophane into niacin. Vitamin B₁₂ is found in most foods but is most plentiful in fish, poultry, meat, cereals, dairy products, soy beans, yeast, nuts and organ meats. It is important in preventing anemia and is generating a good supply of blood in the body. Folic acid (folacin) is found in liberal supply in leafy (foliage) vegetables as well as liver, legumes, yeast, asparagus and broccoli. It is important for the proper functioning of the body cells and in forming blood. A lack of it affects the oxygen-carrying power of the blood. It is helpful in some anemias. Pantothenic acid is found in plentiful supply in foods high in pyridoxine. It is important in promoting metabolic processes. It also supports the nervous system and is involved in the function of the adrenal glands and body oxidations. Claims that it prevents hair from turning gray have not been proved. Vitamins choline and biotin are involved in promoting growth and in regulating and promoting body functions. They are usually found in good supply in foods supplying adequate quantities of other B-vitamins.

VITAMIN C. Vitamin C (ascorbic acid) is important for the formation and maintenance of body tissue, bones, blood and teeth. Individuals lacking the vitamin heal slowly. Vitamins A and C work closely together and a lack of one may cause the other not to function in their joint processes.

Scurvy is caused by a lack of vitamin C. It may be first evidenced by bleeding gums, lesions in the skin and, later, by skin hemorrhages. This disease was common among sailors who lacked fresh fruit and vegetables for long periods of time. Magellan died of scurvy, and his men, many ill of the same disease, finally brought his ship back home after circling the globe.

Ascorbic acid is plentiful in citrus fruits, tomato juice, cabbage, many fresh berries and in bean sprouts, broccoli, cauliflower, fresh leafy greens, melons, turnips, rutabagas, kohlrabi, okra, onions, parsnips, fresh peas, peppers, persimmons, pimientos, fresh pineapple, potatoes, rhubarb and spinach. We should have at least one good source of this vitamin every day.

Vitamin C is easily oxidized and is otherwise quite perishable. Mincing vegetables and letting them stand will encourage a rapid oxidation loss. Cooking or soaking in lots of water encourages a high leaching loss. Heat destroys ascorbic acid and foods containing it which are cooked in an alkaline medium suffer its destruction even faster. Acid protects it and thus the ascorbic acid in tomatoes can stand more heat than the ascorbic acid in blueberries contained in a muffin leavened by soda—an alkali.

Minerals

Minerals help to regulate our bodies and are important substances in body tissues, body fluids and other body components. They also regulate the acid-base balance of the body, regulate fluid pressure (osmotic pressure), help the blood to clot, and promote nerve impulse transfer. We know the body needs some minerals in specific amounts. We know it needs some other minerals but not how much. There are trace showings of minerals in the body but we are not sure if these are there by accident or because the body requires them.

CALCIUM AND PHOSPHORUS. Calcium and phosphorus frequently work together in the body. They are important in the formation of bones and teeth and also in many vital functions. Together they can help to maintain a good acid-base ratio.

Independently, calcium maintains good muscle tone, helps the blood to clot, the heart to beat rhythmically and the nerves to function. Phosphorus independently maintains normal muscle functions, is vital to the metabolism of carbohydrates, fats and proteins and is a part of some important enzyme activity. It is also an important substance in some vitamins and in the brain and nerve cells.

Most rapidly growing children should have a quart of milk a day to furnish them with the calcium and phosphorus they need. Adults need a pint (two glasses) a day. The milkfat in milk carries vitamins A and D but can be omitted from milk that is consumed largely for its phosphorus and calcium content.

Calcium can also be obtained from cereals, leafy vegetables and other foods but never as well as from milk. Phosphorus is found in good supply in meat and other protein-rich foods and in cereals and legumes.

IRON AND COPPER. Iron and copper work together in generating blood. A lack of either can cause anemia. If there is a loss of blood, the demand for these minerals is increased. Thus, women who menstruate, or any individual losing considerable blood, should have a larger supply of iron and copper.

Green leafy vegetables, meat, egg yolk, molasses, prunes and other dark dried fruits, whole-grain or enriched cereals or flours and legumes, organ meats, and a few fruits such as dark plums or grapes are good sources of iron. An adult needs about 10 milligrams of iron per day which could be obtained from an egg, four servings of whole grain or enriched cereals, a pint of milk and a serving of meat such as beef. Other foods in the diet would make up the balance. Copper is seldom lacking in diets since it is contained in many foods in good supply.

SODIUM. Table salt is one of our main sources of sodium. This mineral helps maintain a proper acid-alkaline base in the body, promotes good muscle tone and contraction and is associated with important tissue and fluid functions. A sodium deficiency may cause severe fatigue and even illness. Where there is a heavy loss of moisture, such as occurs in sweating, a doctor may recommend the taking of salt tablets.

Individuals with edema, high blood pressure or kidney diseases may have to restrict their sodium and therefore their salt intake. Most foodservices can provide a slightly restricted sodium diet within limits.

POTASSIUM. There is seldom a lack of potassium in most diets, but some individuals who take medications for high blood pressure which eliminate salts from the body may lose a considerable quantity of potassium. This must be replaced by potassium-rich foods such as dried apricots, orange juice and bananas.

OTHER MINERALS. Numerous other minerals are found in the body tissues but we do not know their function completely nor what quantity we may need. Some found in minute amounts are called "trace" minerals.

We know magnesium is important in regulating some functions, in forming bone and in the utilization of protein. Sulfur is a significant substance in many tissues, but whether or not it plays a part in regulating body functions we do not know. Zinc is important in maintaining metabolic functions and is found in substantial amounts in the pancreas gland, which may indicate a role in the formation of insulin. Fluorine is important for teeth formation and, perhaps, for their maintenance. If children have small amounts of fluorine in their drinking water—often added by the municipal agency supplying the drinking water—their teeth are stronger and more durable. Some other minerals are known to be important in the functioning of the enzyme structure of the body. Most of the minerals mentioned in this section can be considered to be liberally supplied by a good normal diet.

WATER. An individual should consume six to eight glasses of fluid a day—1½ to two quarts. This can come from drinking water, milk, soups, juices, semi-liquid foods, etc. Fluids are vital for numerous body functions and to flush out undesirable or toxic substances. They usually are passed off in the urine. We lose water when we sweat, work hard or pant, and to replace the liquid lost we must consume more water.

RESIDUE. Another non-food item the body needs is roughage or residue. This is largely cellulose which is a carbohydrate but cannot be digested by man. It is the fiber material in fruits and vegetables that make up their internal structure. Horses, cows, rabbits and other ruminants can digest it. Cellulose furnishes bulk, or fiber, which helps to separate foods in the digestive system and move them along. If it is lacking, poor absorption of the nutrients occurs. A lack of it can cause constipation. On the other hand, too much residue can be undesirable and result in irritation of the digestive system, especially the colon. Individuals with digestive problems and colitis must watch the amount of fiber in their diets. Usually a normal, well-balanced diet will have enough fiber in it to furnish the bulk needed.

Acid-Base Balance

Some individuals may talk a great deal about maintaining a good acid-base balance in the body. This text has mentioned that minerals can be helpful in maintaining it. The trouble with maintaining a good acid-base balance is like the weather: A lot of people talk about it, but nobody ever does anything about it. Most individuals consuming a normal diet will maintain a very well balanced acid-base ratio and there is little to be done in diet to change it. The body is able to take any excess acid and neutralize is quickly with alkaline reserves. It can do the same with alkaline substances by calling upon acid reserves to neutralize them. The body does this automatically without any help from us,

and the foods we eat cannot materially do much to change the balance. The body must maintain an almost perfect acid-base equilibrium for us to survive. Some diabetics may destroy the acid-base balance by creating too many metabolic substances from fats. If the kidneys do not work properly, too much uric acid and other substances can be left, causing the body to become too acid.

The body builds up large reserves to use in maintaining a good acid-base balance. Furthermore, there are substances in the body, such as proteins and others, that can absorb acids or alkalis and prevent them from being effective. Most of the time our bodies do a splendid job of maintaining the right balance and we should not try to "get into the act" and disturb it. If we do, we can cause harm.

Meat and other proteins, when digested, are acid in reaction. As are some minerals such as phosphorus, chlorine, etc. Other minerals like sodium and potassium are alkaline. Still others, such as phosphates, can be put into compounds that will neutralize an acid or do the same for an alkaline substance. Most vegetables and fruits are alkaline in reaction when utilized in the body.

Nutrient Retention in Quantity Food Preparation

The preparation of foods in quantity can take a heavy toll of nutrients. Some of this loss can be avoided or minimized. Knowing what nutrients are in which foods and how they can be destroyed can help to protect them. Thus, one should know that a long soaking period for cubed potatoes will leave very little ascorbic acid in them. Cooking vegetables in water that has soda added destroys the thiamin and ascorbic acid.

It is not as easy to preserve the nutrients in foods in quantity cooking as it is in small cooking. Often there are necessary procedures that will destroy nutrients. Thus, in mass operations there must be a longer time period between the pre-preparation of some foods and their service. At home, potatoes can be pared, cooked and mashed in close sequence. In an institution, this may take several hours or more because it is not possible to take the chance of delays and other imponderables.

A foodservice should try to reduce the holding time on foods. Purchasing high quality fresh foods and utilizing them as soon as possible helps to preserve nutrients. Steaming, broiling, baking or other methods can reduce some of the nutrient losses which occur when foods are boiled.

Vegetables cooked in smaller batches and sent more frequently to the service area are much better in quality and more nutritious. Vegetables should not be held more than 20 to 30 minutes in the steam table. After that, they should be replaced with a new batch. For this reason, it is recommended that foodservices cook their vegetables by "batch cooking". This means that they should be cooked in batches only large enough to last for about 20 minutes of service. Cooks should watch to see how fast a batch goes and have others ready when the last bit of the first one is gone. The use of a small high-pressure steamer— 17 pounds per square inch of steam— will process most small batches of vegetables in seconds.

To summarize the rules for the best preparation of foods from the standpoint of nutrition (not to mention quality):

1. Prepare foods for cooking as close to serving time as possible.
2. Reduce chances for nutrient losses: keep foods in larger pieces, avoid soaking, etc.
3. Cook foods as quickly as possible at the lowest possible temperatures by the cooking method least harmful to the nutrients.
4. Cook only in small batches.
5. Avoid using compounds which can destroy nutrients (e.g., using soda to keep vegetables green).

Some foods do not lose many nutrients when they are cooked. Vitamin A is fairly stable in carrots. The protein in meat, the carbohydrate in cereals, and the fat in pie crust are little harmed by cooking. However, there can be a high quality loss by cooking too far in advance. Other undesirable effects also can occur. Therefore, although some foods may not be harmed nutritionally, the same rules used to preserve nutrients in other foods should be applied to these.

In quantity food preparation many more nutrients are lost than in small quantity cooking. In many cases this cannot be avoided. Because of this, we frequently advise individuals who eat food prepared in quantity cookery to eat somewhat differently than they would if they ate at home. Since it is possible in quantity cooking to have a rather high loss of ascorbic acid, we no longer feel that we should depend upon some foods to supply this vitamin. Instead, we recommend that individuals who eat out a lot have one good source of vitamin C a day, such as a glass of orange juice, and then not worry about whether or not they are getting ascorbic acid in the other foods they eat. The same can be true of the nutrient iron. If an individual will see that one good source giving much of the day's needs is consumed each day or every other day, one need not worry about getting it from foods from which the nutrient may be lost in quantity preparation. Most foods do retain most of their nutrients, even in quantity cooking, and so, if an individual just watches to see that a balanced diet is consumed plus a few other foods which are high in nutrients that might be missing, an adequate diet will usually result.

Part II Bibliography

Barbour, Henry O., "Beverage Profits through Controls," *Cornell Quarterly,* School of Hotel Administration, Cornell University, Ithaca, New York.

Fay, G. T.; Rhoads, R. C., and Rosenblatt, R. L., *Managerial Accounting,* Wm. C. Brown Co., Dubuque, Iowa, 1971.

Grossman, H., *Guide to Wines' Spirits and Beers,* Scribners, New York City, 1955.

Hoke, Ann, *Menus,* John Willy, Inc., Evanston, Illinois, 1964.

Pedderson, R. B.; Avery, Arthur C.; Richard, R.; Ostenton, J. R., and Pope, Harry, *Increasing Productivity in Foodservice,* Cahners Books, Boston, Massachusetts, 1973.

Tinker, Miles A., *Legibility of Print,* Iowa State University Press, Ames, Iowa, 1964.

Updike, Daniel, *Printing Types,* Vol. II, Belknap Press, Harvard University, Cambridge, Massachusetts, 1966.

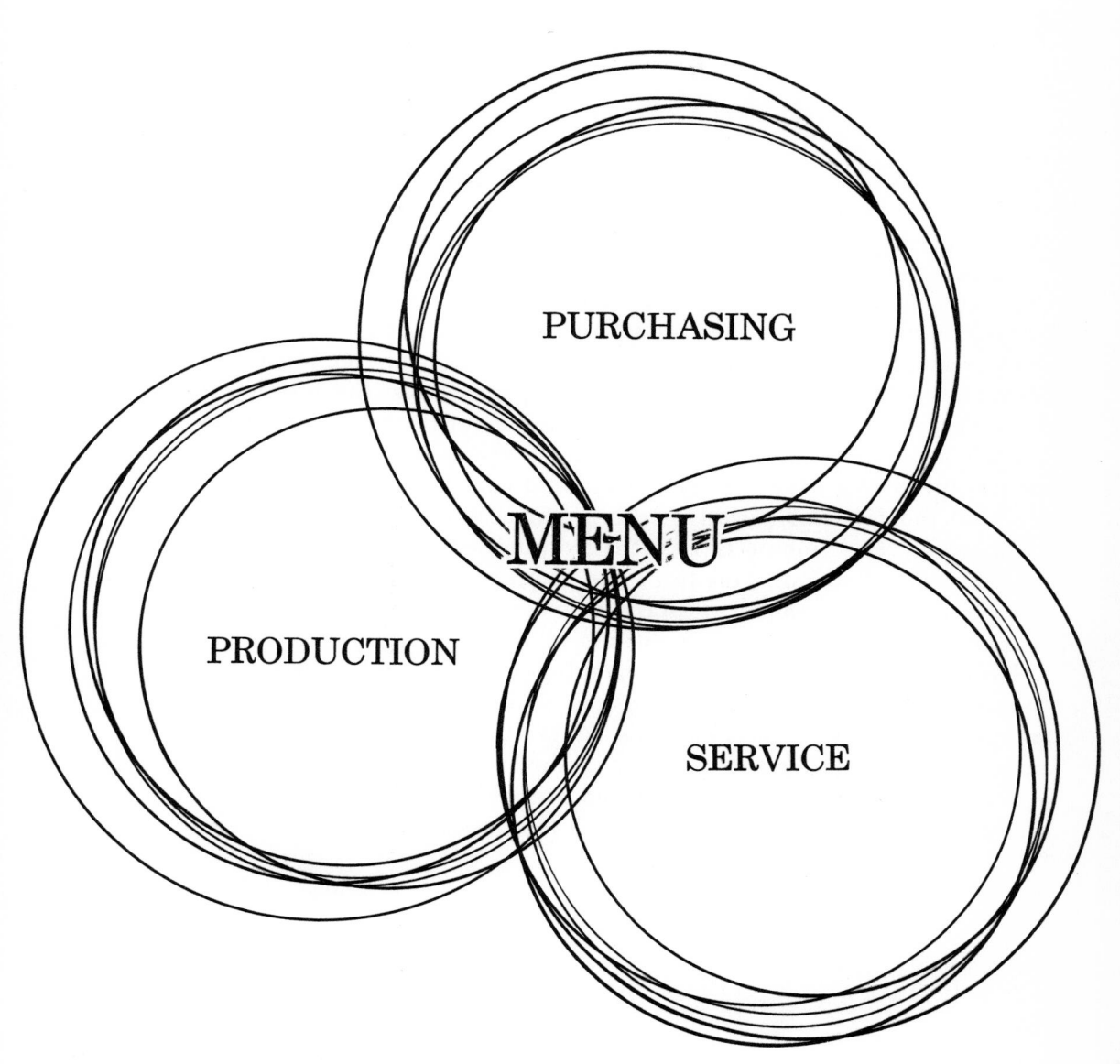

PURCHASING

MENU

PRODUCTION

SERVICE

THE menu cannot stand alone. While it is the central document which dictates what is to be done in almost every operating department of a foodservice, it is completely dependent on these departments for its fulfillment. It controls and directs, but it cannot act. In this respect the menu is somewhat like the staff member in an organization who originates directives but has no authority to take action. Instead, he must make recommendations to a line member who then translates these into action. Similarly, the menu depends upon the purchasing, production and service departments to implement its recommendations.

Failure to understand the line-staff relationship, and the fundamental difference between originating and executing a plan of action, is an all too familiar pitfall in the organization and management of a foodservice: A menu is beautifully planned and designed, is an excellent merchandising medium and is properly priced, but fails because it must rely upon voluntary, or vaguely defined, departmental cooperation to deliver what it promises.

How well a system functions depends upon how well its parts function and how well they are integrated. Thus, an automobile engine composed of many sub-systems and parts must have every component in good working order and precisely meshed so that each of them works at the right time to develop power and propel the car. In the same way, menu planning is a sub-system, albeit a most essential one, and if some other element is not working well, or is not well integrated, the whole system malfunctions.

In systems analysis it is frequently found that where two subsystems come together they do not interact smoothly — as when jurisdictions of two departments overlap — or do not operate in synchronism. Thus, the purchasing department must interpret correctly what the menu calls for and procure the necessary raw materials in time for the menu items to be produced. Production, in its turn, must prepare the food required by the menu in a timely manner and with due regard for quality and quantity. The service department, likewise, should see that the menu's expectations are met by serving the food promptly and properly. Purchasing, production and service, then, may be seen as three rings, each a vital part of the menu plan, interacting with each other.

Our purpose in the following chapters is to detail some of the essential things that must be done in the operating departments of a foodservice to ensure that the menu plan is carried out in a well-coordinated way. From this point of view we will look again at procedures in Purchasing, in Production, and in Service. When each of these departments turns in a heads-up performance, the menu writer's carefully drawn script can produce a real hit.

CHAPTER 9

The Menu and Purchasing

What is Purchasing?

The job of purchasing is to interpret properly what is needed to produce the items listed on the menu and to procure them at prices within constraints imposed by the menu. This is not easy, and many buyers fail because they do not understand these requirements or do not know how to satisfy them. Some buyers may lack sufficient background to search out the required products on the market. Others may lack knowledge of what is required to produce the menu item called out. Many buyers are merely "order givers" and not specialists, and often what the menu promises is not fulfilled because they do not take the time, nor the pains, to get the right ingredients. This is an easy way out but can lead to very poor performance of the system. Some purchasers may know the market and know food production and service very well, but fail to produce because they are market-oriented and not establishment-oriented; that is, they fail to follow through and see that their own operation receives products that it

can use to good advantage. Some buyers may also be misled by price, and obtain materials which do not fulfill the menu's promise. A part of the value in a menu must be quality and merchandising appeal, and if these two are lacking the price paid may be extremely high.

To purchase well takes a lot of know-how about the production, processing and marketing of foodstuffs, their use in the foodservice establishment and their pricing on the menu. The buyer thus needs to know a lot about how the market operates, about mark-ups, seasonal factors and where to procure specific items of the best quality for the best price. A good buyer is constantly in search of products which will simplify preparation and handling, improve quality and facilitate service. He should also be active in analyzing cost and performance factors, and in sorting out any and all facts which will improve his purchasing procedures.

Markets can change quickly and a buyer must be prepared to move with the changes. A rich background of information and knowledge about the market is needed if a buyer is to function adequately in it. A buyer must be sure to safeguard the interests of the enterprise for which he buys. He must not waste resources and he must not involve the enterprise in legal problems because of his action. The policies of the enterprise must be followed. Purchasing is a management function and, if delegated, must be given only to those who will protect the interests of the operation. Buying requires high ethical principles.

Purchasing is a complex task. A good definition would be: "Purchasing is (1) the determination of a need for an item along with the quality and other factors required to satisfy that need, (2) the search for the item on the market, (3) negotiation between the buyer and seller ending in a transfer of ownership, (4) receiving and inspection, ending with acceptance or rejection of the item, and (5) finally when the item is used, evaluating the efficiency with which these tasks were done as judged by the performance of the product and the economy with which all results were achieved.

In almost every purchasing task, these five steps must occur and only in rare instances can any be circumvented or omitted. The fifth step is a most important one and is frequently left out. Unless it takes place, the purchasing task may never be improved. Mistakes are constantly made over and over again and a less satisfactory job is done than if this important step were not omitted. Very frequently this fifth step is known as "value analysis."

Value analysis is an attempt to see if the best possible purchasing job has been done and whether or not it can be improved. After purchase, the items are analyzed to see if they can be improved in any way to better meet the needs for which they were purchased. Unessential factors are isolated and, if possible, eliminated. Thus, an operation purchasing No. 189 tenderloins may eliminate all the trim and labor necessary to bring them to a usable condition by purchasing No. 190 tenderloins which come well trimmed. Or prepared grapefruit sections may be purchased instead of fresh ones which require labor to section. The Armed Forces obtain most of their beef packaged deboned, with most fat removed, divided into quantities based on the methods required to cook it. This removes the necessity to cut the meat out after shipment where unskilled butchers do a much poorer job and higher waste occurs. In addition, the shipment of bones and fat, which are usually waste products, is eliminated. Working out things like this helps to simplify many procedures and reduce costs.

Value analysis is the observation of items as they are processed in the foodservice to see if they can be improved and to ascertain what the actual cost is. Quality should not be measured by price alone but by performance and satisfaction. Service must also be evaluated. Some purveyors perform more services and thus should be entitled to a higher price. Some value analysts say that value is quality divided by price, $V = \dfrac{Q}{P}$. If quality can be increased and price held stable, value is increased. If quality drops and price remains stable, value is lost. If price drops but quality remains the same, value increases. If price rises but quality remains the same, value is lost. Thus, if $V = \dfrac{4}{2}$, $V = 2$. If the value of 4 rises to 6, $V = 3$ instead of 2; if it drops to 2, $V = 1$ instead of 2. Similarly, changing the value of P will also cause a change in the value of V. Buyers should constantly attempt to increase the value of V.

There are numerous variables in the quality or price of items purchased on the market and buyers must seek constantly to equate one with the other. One of the requisites for doing this is to know what the yield is on items purchased. The Win Schuler Restaurants in Michigan weigh every rib before roasting and keep accurate track of all servings that are obtained from each rib. They can look over a year's record of yields and see what the portions cost. They can also evaluate the method they use to purchase ribs and see if this can be improved to get a better product at a lower cost.

Good value analysis is a constant search for ways to improve the purchasing task, and, if consistently practiced, can lead to most worthwhile savings. It is the search for facts, their analysis and then action on the basis of the information gained. It is usual for buyers and purveyors to work together to improve purchasing methods and reduce costs. It may be possible to have some foodservices consolidate their orders with one purveyor so that he can have a greater number of deliveries in a given area which would reduce his costs and enable him to give a more favorable price. It may be possible to work out arrangements such as cost plus, guaranteeing to

a purveyor a specific amount of business during a period, in return for his seeking out the best possible products for the enterprise, adding only a specific amount for this service above his costs. Orders may be placed more in advance so that purveyors can do a better job of searching the market and making the most favorable buys. Groups of foodservices may join together and purchase co-operatively. Some foodservices are slow in paying bills. As a result, those who pay promptly must help to defray the cost burden this places on the purveyor. By guaranteeing payment in a specified period, some enterprises may work out lower charges from purveyors. Simplifying purchasing procedures and reducing paper work can do much to assist in reducing costs, as can improving the purchase task to reduce inventories. In fact, there are many things that can be done by buyers, if value analysis is practiced, to bring lower costs and improve procedures.

Purchasing Procedures

There are many purchasing methods, varying with different organizations and needs. Operations joined together as chains or franchises may have similar specifications and even purveyors. As a result, they have little freedom in deciding many factors which an independent operator might settle himself, and therefore they have more parallel buying practices. In others, the purchasing procedures may vary from informal telephone buying to formalized bidding. Some of the most common buying procedures used are:

1. CALL SHEET PURCHASING. This is a method whereby the purchase needs are

PANTRY REQUISITION

DATE: _____   ORDERED BY: _____

Quantity	Size		Quantity	Size	
		MILK			**PICKLES—OLIVES—SEAFOOD**
	½ pt.	White		Gal.	Dill Pickles
	½ pt.	Chocolate		Gal.	Sliced Pickles
	½ pt.	Skim		Gal.	Olives
	½ pt.	Buttermilk		Qt.	Olives Ripe
	Gal.	Milk		Gal.	Sweet Relish
	Qt.	Buttermilk		Case	Anchovies
	Each	Yogourt			Caviar
		CREAM		Can	Tunafish
	Qt.	Whipping Cream		Lb.	Crabmeat
	Gal.	Sour Cream			
					CONDIMENTS
	Case	**EGGS**		#10	Catsup
				#10	Chili Sauce
		CHEESE		14 oz.	Catsup-bottles
	Case	Bleu		Gal.	Horseradish
	Case	Cream		Pt.	Lemon Juice-bottle
	Box	Bar		Gal.	Vinegar Cider
		Cottage		Gal.	Vinegar White
	Box	Camembert		Gal.	Vinegar Red Wine
	Box	Liederkranz		Gal.	Wesson Oil
				Drum	Mayonnaise
		VEGETABLES			Apple Sauce
	Case	Cabbage		Can	Mint Jelly
	Case	Cherry Tomatoes		Can	Currant Jelly
	Case	Tomatoes		Case	Blackhawk Dressing
	Each	Cucumbers		Case	Blackhawk Dressing with
	Each	Green Peppers			Bleu Cheese
	Case	Lettuce-Boston		Qt.	Low Calorie Dressing
	Bskt.	Radishes		Pt.	Peanut Butter
	Each	Red Cabbage			
	Bag	Chives			**SEASONINGS**
	Bunch	Leaves Galax		Box	Paprika
	Bunch	Celery Hearts		Can	Garlic Powder
	Bunch	Green Onions		Box	White Pepper
				Box	Salt
		FRUITS		Box	Lawry Seasoning Salt
	Pts.	Blueberries		Box	Dry Mustard
	Pts.	Strawberries		Box	Celery Seed
	Each	Peaches			
	Lb.	Grapes			**JUICES**
	Each	Apples		Case	Tomato
	Each	Oranges		Can	Grapefruit
	Each	Grapefruit		Can	Pineapple
	Each	Watermelon			
	DOZ.	Lemons			**MISCELLANEOUS**
	#10	Fruit Cocktail		Lb.	Sugar
	#10	Pears		Box	Ice Cream Cones
	#10	Peaches		Can	Raspberry Jello
	Qt.	Cherries w/stems		#10	Chocolate Sauce
	Can	Cherries Bing		#10	Butterscotch Sauce
	#2½ tin	Pineapple sliced		Box	Potato Chips
	Each	Melons			
					PAPER SUPPLIES
				Box	Wax Paper
				Each	Doggie Bags
				Box	Frill Tooth Picks
				Box	Doilies for Pastry Tray
				Box	Doilies Blackhawk under-
					liner
				Box	Souffle Cups
				Roll	Saran Wrap
				Box	Whippet Bombs

FIG. 9-1
A simple requisition form which can be prepared and sent to the purchasing department. Similar sheets can be set up for other foods and supplies. (Courtesy Don Roth, Blackhawk Restaurants, Chicago)

listed with brief quality specifications shown. The buyer then calls a number of purveyors, discusses his needs with them, the quantity required, and obtains a price which is placed on the "call sheet" opposite the item or items. After talking to various purveyors and listing the price each gives, a study of the prices

is made, evaluated against the purveyors' service and other factors and then a decision is made as to which items will be purchased from which purveyors. A buyer should attempt to lump orders together so that it is worthwhile for the purveyor to make the delivery. Spreading orders out simply because of a very

PAGE 1			TOWN & COUNTRY ORDERING SHEET				
DAY:			DATE:	DELIVERY			
ON HAND	ORDER	PAR STOCK	SPECIFICATION AND DESCRIPTION	PURVEYOR	UNIT PRICE	EXTENSION TOTAL	
		12pcs	Canadian Bacon, 12/8lb. Stick				
		100lb.	Corned Beef, Ch., Deckle-Off 7-8lb.				
		25pcs	Choice Top Butts 12/14				
		8pcs	Choice Strips 17-18lb.				
		300lb.	Commercial Chuck				
		20lb.	Beef Liver				
		15pcs	Knuckles Choice 8-9lb.				
		8pcs	Choice Insides 16/20				
		4pcs	Hams, Round, VC 10/12lb.				
		3pcs	Hams, Pullman Canned 6/7				
		40lb.	Lamb Breast				
		12pcs	Pork Loins, 10/12lb.				
		12pcs	Choice Beef Ribs, 28/32lb.				
		30lb	Spareribs				
		70lb.	Pork Sausage, 5lb.				
		10lb.	Salt Pork				
		24lb.	Fresh Brisket, Ch., Deckle-Off				
		10lb.	Pork Tenderloins				
		30lb.	Veal Stew				
		100lb.	Beef Bones				
		12lb.	Weiners 8/lb.				
			TOTAL MEAT				
			- - POULTRY ORDER - -				
		8cs	Turkeys, 24/26lb. Toms				
		4cs	Chicken, 2¼/lb. p.c. 65lb./cs.				
		40lb.	Chicken Livers, Fresh				
			Fowl Livers - Frozen				
		12cs	Eggs, grade A Extra Large, 30 doz/cs.				
			TOTAL POULTRY				
			- - FISH ORDER - -				
		100lb.	Halibut, 40lb.				
		75lb.	Shrimp, Green, 15/20 ct., 10/5lb.				
		140lb.	Whitefish - 3/3½lb.				
		4pcs	Herring, 10lb., Sour Cream				
		40lb.	Lobster Tails, African 10lb., 31-35 ct.				
		150lb.	Filet of Sole, 50lb.				
		60lb.	King Crabmeat, 6/5lb.				
		5lb.	Scallops, 5lb.				
			Smelts, 25lb.				
		20cs	Head Lettuce 24's				
		12cs	Tomatoes, 20lb. flat, 5x6				
		8	Potatoes, bakers, 100 ct., 50lb. bag				
		6	Onions, Spanish, 50lb.				
		1	Onions, Red, 25lb.				
		2	Cabbage, New Green cs				
		1	Cabbage, Red				
		2	Celery Cabbage				
		2	Celery Pascal, Cal., 30/cs				
		2	Cucumbers, 1lb. Med.				
		2	Carrots, 50 loose				
		2	Romaine, 24's				

FIG. 9-2

An order sheet that lists amounts on hand and amounts to order as well as the purveyor from whom to order. A copy can be sent to the receiving department for verification of orders. (Courtesy Town & Country Restaurants, Chicago)

QUOTATIONS FOR DAIRY PRODUCTS   DATE _____

Item & Specification:	Quan.	Unit	HH	HM	Vendor Bid	Vendor Bid	Vendor Bid	Remarks
EGG PRODUCTS								
Butter prints								
Margarine								
Fresh eggs								
Fresh med. shell								
Frozen shell-less								
Frozen egg white								
Frozen whole								
Frozen sugar yolk								
CHEESE PRODUCTS								
Cream cheese								
Dan. bleu cheese								
Grated Italian								
Swiss cheese								
Past. Swiss								
MISC. ITEMS								
Rich whip top.								
Butter pats								

FIG. 9-3   A quotation sheet used to survey the offerings and prices of various vendors. The vendor is told what is required, the amount, and something about the quality required. The vendor then quotes a price. Other vendors are queried in the same manner. After all have responded, the buyer indicates which vendor to select by circling his price on the sheet. A secretary or clerk can then place the orders. A copy of this completed sheet is sent to receiving. (Courtesy United Air Lines)

small saving eventually drives the costs of delivery and billing to a point where the original purpose may be defeated. The cost to the enterprise in handling bills from a number of purveyors may alone be enough to wipe out the savings made. Usually, the buyer circles the price, indicating that he has decided to purchase that item from the purveyor giving that price. A clerk or stenographer can then call in the orders. A copy of the call sheet should then be given to the receiving department to check in the orders and see that they conform to the data on the call sheet.

2. COST PLUS. In some cases, it works well to arrange with the purveyor to bill the enterprise for the cost of the items plus an agreed markup. An operation, for instance, agrees with a fresh produce purveyor to give him all their orders in return for seeking out the best quality and price on the market, plus a markup for this service. Such an ar-

rangement may be limited to the purchase of specified categories.

3. BLANK CHECK. At times there is a need to obtain an item without an agreed-on price. The operation must have the item and is willing to pay any reasonable price for it. In such cases, a purveyor may be instructed to purchase at the best possible price and bill the enterprise for it. Such an arrangement is made only in special instances and the reliability of the purveyor should be known before it is done.

4. BIDDING. There are different levels of formality in bidding. A rather informal way may be for a buyer to contact a limited number of purveyors and obtain from them a price for a given quality and quantity of merchandise. Usually no fewer than three are contacted. This information can then be evaluated and a purveyor selected. Sometimes this evaluation is made by another office. This procedure is much

		BLACKHAWK RESTAURANT			
		DAILY PURCHASE AND RECEIVING RECORD			
		FOR GROCERIES, FROZEN FRUITS AND VEGETABLES			
DATE _____				DAY _____	
Item	Amount To Be Purchased	Purveyor Quotations	Amount Received	Specification Check	Remarks

FIG. 9-4　A purchase form that serves both as call sheet and receiving sheet. (Courtesy Don Roth, Blackhawk Restaurants, Chicago)

the same as call sheet buying except that it is usually more formalized.

Formal bidding is a procedure in which specifications for items are written and published, indicating quantity desired, quality, packaging and other factors, such as billing, deliveries, general conditions of performance and re-

sponsibility on the part of purveyors and buyers, etc. Then, in writing, purveyors offer items based on these requirements. Sometimes "reference samples" may have to be submitted along with the offer to sell at a stated price. These samples will be examined before a decision is made as to which pur-

Sambo's		FOOD INVENTORY CONTROL ❸										
LOCATION	DATE▶	BUILD TO										
SAMBO REGULAR PANCAKE MIX 25#	ON HAND											
	ORDERED											
SAMBO WAFFLE MIX 25#	ON HAND											
	ORDERED											
	ON HAND											
	ORDERED											
SAMBO BUCKWHEAT MIX 6/5#	ON HAND											
	ORDERED											
SAMBO REG. PANCAKE (RE-SALE) 6/5#	ON HAND											
	ORDERED											
ALL PURPOSE FLOUR 2/25#	ON HAND											
	ORDERED											
KELLOGG CORN FLAKES 50/IND.	ON HAND											
	ORDERED											
KELLOGG BRAN FLAKES 50/IND.	ON HAND											
	ORDERED											
KELLOGG RICE KRISPIES 50/IND.	ON HAND											
	ORDERED											
KELLOGG FROSTED FLAKES 50/IND.	ON HAND											
	ORDERED											
KELLOGG SPECIAL K 50/IND.	ON HAND											
	ORDERED											
QUICK OATS 12/42 OZ.	ON HAND											
	ORDERED											
INSTANT CREAM OF WHEAT 12/28 OZ.	ON HAND											
	ORDERED											
TABLE SALT 24/26 OZ	ON HAND											
	ORDERED											
GRANULATED SUGAR 50# SK.	ON HAND											
	ORDERED											
POWDERED SUGAR 24/1#	ON HAND											
	ORDERED											
CHOICE SLICED PEACHES 24/2½	ON HAND											
	ORDERED											
SLICED PINEAPPLE 24/2	ON HAND											
	ORDERED											
PRUNES IN SYRUP 24/2½	ON HAND											
	ORDERED											

SAM-302-C-2 KEEP A BALANCED INVENTORY!

FIG. 9-5
This form combines a requisition sheet and inventory control sheet. Note that it indicates a maximum limit to which purchases should build. Similar sheets would be used for other foods and supplies. (Courtesy Sambo's, Inc.)

veyor's bid to accept. Some of the samples may be retained to compare with the goods delivered to see that they are the equivalent of what was offered.

Such bidding can be quite formal and purveyors may have deadlines at which bids must be received. Bids may be publicly opened and the awards made publicly. Bidders may be notified in writing of acceptance of bids and they will then have a specified time in which to perform. In many cases, a bid bond is required which guarantees that if an award is made to a purveyor, he will perform as agreed. If he does not, the bonding company must see that he does or pay the bond forfeit. Usually bidding of this kind involves a rather large volume of business and is done by state, federal or other governmental agencies and large enterprises. A hospital or other unit that uses a considerable amount of food may use such a system of buying. Unless the volume is large, the cost of setting up the program and administering it is not worth while.

Specification Writing

The heart and soul of purchasing is the specification, which is a delineation of what the buyer wants in an item. It should cover all characteristics and factors needed to get the right product at the right price. Some specifications can be extremely simple and brief. They may only indicate what is wanted, how much, the brand and packaging size. Involved specifications are needed when the item required is not well known and there have been few quality or other purchase factors established for it. For instance, the purchase of vacuum dried apricot nuggets may require a buyer to write up a detailed list of quality factors needed in the item. Or if an enterprise wishes something special that differs from the commonly marketed item, it may be necessary to set up a detailed specification.

Buying should not be done unless the buyer completely understands what he wants. Even though briefly written (including call sheet buying), a few factors should be listed so that the right item can be obtained. Purveyors also need this information so that they can do a better job of supplying the required items. In bid buying, a complete specification is needed. It is a demonstrable fact that when well written specifications are used, better quality is obtained at a lower price.

Usually, a specification should have the following:

a. The name of the item
b. The quantity
c. The grade of the item, brand or other quality information
d. The packaging method, size package, etc.
e. The basis for price—by the pound, case, piece, dozen, etc.
f. Miscellaneous factors required to get the right item, such as the number of days beef should be aged, the area in which the item is produced, the requirement that all items be inspected and passed for wholesomeness

In the writing of specifications, much detail can be eliminated if factors which apply to all items are detailed together in what is called the "general specification" section. This section can carry instructions for delivery, methods of billing, acceptance bid requirements, etc. Buyers should learn the common procedures in marketing so that they can use market terms and other factors that are commonly known. These terms are definitive enough to eliminate the need for further detail. For instance, if a buyer indicates that he wants a No. 109 rib roast, by just mentioning this he indicates the preparation of the rib, the trim, the distance from the plate and from the ribeye of the meat, etc. All meat purveyors understand the meaning of the federal government's Institutional Meat Purchase Specifications, for they are commonly used on the market. The mention of any number for an item as outlined in these specifications eliminates a great deal of detail which otherwise would have to be written. The accompanying examples indicate how a buyer might set up specifications for some market items.

Where a considerable amount of market information exists on merchandise, the writing of the specification is not difficult. However, when items are not well known, the writing becomes much more difficult. Buyers have been especially hampered in the writing of specifications for many of the new "convenience foods" because there are few factors extant in the market which delineate what these items are and the quality and other elements needed for their purchase. However, many federal and state agencies have begun to develop specifications for these items which can be of considerable assistance to enterprises writing similar specifications. Others may take a recipe for a product and from this fashion a specification indicating the ingredients that must be in it. The federal government and other agencies may have rather good specifications or information on the quality factors for some items which are very much like the one to be purchased. For instance, there are some good standards and purchase criteria for canned meats. If these are studied, perhaps the necessary standards for a frozen equivalent can be developed.

Examples of specifications:

Hamburger*

Name:	Hamburger, IMPS No.
Amt Needed:	150 lb (1200 patties)
Grade:	From U. S. Good (top)
Packaging:	2-oz patties, frozen; packed in 25 lb lots, layer packed with wax paper separators
Price:	price per lb net
Misc:	Conform to all IMPS requirements; only from chucks, rounds, flanks or shanks; deliver at 0° F or lower internal temperature.

Turkeys*

Turkeys, Beltsville, fresh-killed

80 lb

U. S. Grade A, ready-to-cook, young toms

Wrapped in polyethylene and air exhausted, two to a carton, delivered at 40° F or less but not frozen

Price per lb net

Minnesota grain-fed birds each between 24 and 26 lb, no tolerance permitted over or under.

*Institutional Meat Purchase Specifications of the USDA.

Fish

Name:	Cod fillets, boneless, no skin
Amt Needed:	40 lb (about 60 to 70 fillets)
Grade:	Strictly fresh caught cod processed in plants meeting federal sanitary standards
Packaging:	Dry layer packed in 20 lb lots
Price:	Per lb
Misc:	Shall be treated with no preservatives or seasonings; from Boston docked cod, hake, pollock, cusk or haddock 1½ to 3 lb size (scrod)

Tomatoes

Tomatoes, canned

10 cases

U. S. Grade B or Choice

6/10's

Per dozen 6/10's

Shall be tomatoes with no added juice or other liquid, California pack

Pears

Name:	Pears, halves, Bartlett
Amt Needed:	2 cases
Grade:	U. S. Grade A or Fancy
Packaging:	24/2½'s
Misc:	7 to 9 count per can; minimum drained weight 17 oz; heavy sirup (18 to 22° Brix).

Shrimp

Shrimp, headless, frozen, in shell (raw green)

120 lb (24 5-lb packages)

Highest quality, pink shrimp

In 5-lb blocks with no added moisture in wax paper wraps and in cardboard boxes, 8 boxes to the carton

Shall be large size, 21 to 25 per lb.

Eggs

Name:	Eggs, fresh, in shell
Amt Needed:	Two cases (1 lot)
Grade:	U. S. AA
Packaging:	30 doz paper cartons
Price:	Per dozen
Misc:	Size large, min. wt. net per case 45 lb; no dozen shall weigh more than 25 oz nor less than 23 oz.

Butter

Butter, sweet cream

400 lb

U. S. Grade A (93 score)

5-lb packs, 72 pats per lb

Per pound

Pats shall be individually separated by wax paper and layer packed; deliver over two-month period in lots not under 40 lb each

Apples

		Milk
Name:	Apples, fresh, Rome Beauty	Milk, fresh, homogenized, $3\frac{1}{2}\%$
Amt Needed:	20 Washington cases	60,300 half pints
Grade:	U. S. Extra Fancy or Washington Extra Fancy	U. S. Grade A, pasteurized
Packaging:	100 size, minimum net weight per box 45 lb	In sealed $\frac{1}{2}$ pt paper containers; 64 containers per carton
Misc:	Paper cartons; apples shall have been stored in federally supervised environment controlled warehouses.	Flash pasteurized; milk shall not be over two days old from milking time; shall conform in all respects to local and state ordinances.

PURCHASE STANDARDS

Buyers and sellers use a language peculiar to purchasing. Terms such as "California lug", "No. 10", "18°Brix", "5 × 5 tomato", etc., have precise meanings which both understand. This code shortens and simplifies buying, and makes for better communication between buyers and sellers.

Quality can be defined in buying in different ways. Many buyers use a brand to assure quality and this is often a very good method of assuring a consistent quality. Brands, however, are only as good as the manufacturer makes them. Their quality is not based on any standard other than that observed by the manufacturer.

Quality definition can also be established by grade. Many grades for foods exist. Grading is the separation of a product into different quality levels. Thus, for canned fruits there may be three quality levels: Grade A (highest), Grade B and Grade C (lowest). Buyers and sellers know what quality levels these grades represent. Grades are usually established on known quality factors and do not change. Trade grades may be used which have recognition only on specific markets. Thus, trade grades may have been established for fresh fruits and vegetables, dried fruits, eggs and poultry, but many of these are rapidly losing out in market use as federal grades take over. For instance, very few markets now use the trade grades for eggs because federal grades are more universally used.

At times the federal government may adopt a trade grade and copy it. This has happened with meat and canned items. A federal grade is first established after consulting industry and is issued as a tentative grade. It is tested for a time to see how it works, and industry can suggest changes. After a period of testing, the grade may be revised and then be made official. Federal grades are usually established for different levels of the market—the consumer level, the wholesale level and the manufacturing level. A food buyer may use all three. However, consumer or retail grades often dominate the food market because this is where most of the food is sold and processors and producers tend to follow these standards more than any others. Thus, eggs today move in institutions almost totally on the basis of consumer grades and not on wholesale ones.

The federal government's grading system is based on the development of scores for certain factors and then, based on the total score of a product, a grade is assigned to it. Thus, an item scoring anywhere from 90 to 100 may be Grade A, another from 80 to 89, Grade B and another from 70 to 79, Grade C. Anything below a score of 70 is said to be "below standard". This does not mean that the food is inedible or not suitable for some uses. It only means that it is below standard in quality. Various methods of scoring have been developed for different kinds of foods. The scoring for meat varies considerably from the scoring for fruits and vegetables. Buyers must learn the basis for scoring different products, the value given different quality factors and what the scores mean in quality.

We also use other standards in purchasing. A very important one is called "standards of identity." This is a statement by the government that defines exactly what an item is. Thus, no manufacturer of egg noodles can use the term "egg" with noodles unless the noodles contain 5½ per cent dry egg solids. Unless a product comes from a specific species and variety recognized in the standard of identity, it may not be called by the name of the product that does come from that particular species and variety. Thus, a juice from anything other than *citrus paradisi* cannot be called grapefruit juice. Standards of identity also indicate what is meant by terms such as "diced", "salt free", "shoestring," "cream", etc. When a standard of iden-

REQUISITION ON PURCHASING DEPARTMENT (NOT A PURCHASE ORDER)				
TO	Date 19	No. 1690		
Suggested Supplier		Date Required		
QUANTITY	PLEASE ORDER ITEMS LISTED BELOW		PRICE	AMOUNT
1.				
2.				
3.				
4.				
5.				
6.				
7.				
8.				
9.				
10.				
11.				
12.				
13.				
14.				
15.				
16.				
17.				
ORDERED BY:	APPROVED BY:			
STD. FORM 1H MOORE BUSINESS FORMS, INC.—M	HYATT HOUSE HOTELS			

FIG. 9-6
Some operations follow a procedure requiring departments to send requisitions to the purchasing department which in turn completes a purchase order and sends it to a purveyor or purveyors. This form serves the requisitioning purpose. (Courtesy Hyatt Corporation)

tity is established, it is a legal description of what the item is. The buyer and seller can negotiate more easily when such terms are defined in this manner.

Other standards that assist in promoting buying and selling on the market are those of fill or weight. Thus, canned items must be filled to a specific level in the can. Standard size barrels, hampers, bushels, crates and other package units have been established—and also their fractions. For instance, a barrel must hold 7,056 cubic inches or two 98-lb sacks of flour. However, market practices had so firmly established that a barrel of cranberries held 100 lb or 5,826 cubic inches of cranberries, this was allowed to stand as an exception when the standard barrel was established legally.

There are also laws to control markets and establish procedures. Some laws such as the Pure Food, Drug and Cosmetic Act provide for standards of sanitation in foods. Others, such as the Federal Trade Commission Act, the Agricultural Marketing Act, and the Perishable Commodities Act, deal with how the market is to function and what constitutes legal actions on the market. These acts protect both buyers and sellers. They also give order, reliability and stability to the market.

GRADES FOR MAJOR FOOD ITEMS. If the right item is to be obtained for the menu, the buyer should know the various grades for products. These vary, hence he must know a great number. Some of the most commonly used grading standards follow.

Table 9-1
Purchase Factors for Fresh Fruits and Vegetables

Item	Season	Grades	Comments
		Fresh Fruits	
Apples (3,890)*	Year around; summer varieties are over in late Sept. Fall and winter varieties available almost the year around. Low peak in June to Sept.	Federal: U. S. Extra Fancy, Fancy, No. 1, Utility and Combination. Washington: Ex Fancy, Fancy and C. Buy 100's or 113's for general use and 88's for large baking apples.	Some varieties are only suitable for specific uses such as salads or eating, sauce, pies or baking. Other varieties are known as all-purpose and are suitable for all these needs. A box should weigh 40-45 lb, bushels 42 to 52 lb and cartons vary with size.
Apricots	June and July	U. S. No. 1 and No. 2. If row packed, size is indicated by rows of 5, 6, 7 or 8.	Royal, Tilton or Moorpak varieties. Store 36°F at 90% humidity. A lug weighs 24 to 25 lb net.
Avocados (166)	Year around.	U. S. No. 1 and No. 2.	The smaller pear-shaped Calavo comes from California, the larger round Lula from Florida.

*The number in parentheses indicates the millions of pounds produced per year, according to USDA records.

Table 9-1 cont'd.

Item	Season	Grades	Comments
Bananas (3,623)	Year around; Gros Michel and Cavendish are the two main varieties.	No official grades but may be locally graded as No. 1 or No. 2. Usually sold in 40-lb cartons.	Specify as *full ripe, hard ripe* or *turning ripe*. The first is ready to use; hard ripe is ready to use in 2 to 3 days if held at 68-72°F.
Berries (4)	June through Aug. Local strawberries usually in May.	U. S. No. 1 and No. 2 blueberries, which only indicates size.	Store at 36°F and 90% humidity. A 16-qt crate should hold, net, about 20 to 24 lb. Cranberries come in 1-lb packages or 25-lb boxes or cartons, Sept. through Dec.
Cantaloupe (1,394)	Mar. to Nov.; peak is June through Sept.	Federal: U. S. Fancy, No. 1, Combination and No. 2; There may be local grading; *full slip* indicates picked when ripe and is a smooth, round depressed scar where the stem is detached.	Order 45's for a good half cantaloupe portion; jumbo crates 80-89 lb and standards 70 to 80 lb net of fruit.
Cherries sweet (124)	May to Aug.; Royal Annes are pink-yellow; Black Tartarian, Bing, Lambert and Republican are dark. The first ships poorly.	U. S. No. 1 and Commercial; specify fill equal to facing. Sour cherries usually purchased canned or frozen.	Lug weighs 18-20 lb; some lugs may contain only 15 lb on some markets; store 36°F at 90% humidity.
Grapefruit (1,677)	Year around but best Oct. to early May. Low peaks July through Sept.	U. S. Fancy, No. 1, No. 2 and No. 3; 4/5 bushel weighs 38-40 lb in carton or crate. Also graded according to amount of tarnish on skin; 32's are best size for half portion.	Marsh are seedless; Thompson may be called Pink Marsh. Duncan has seeds but is an excellent fruit. Foster is sometimes called Pink Duncan. Burgundy is quite red.
Grapes (487)	Perlettes—June; Thompson Seedless—fall; Ribiers—Aug. to Jan.; Tokays—Sept. through Mar.; Emperors—Nov. through Mar.	U. S. Fancy and No. 1.	Lugs or cartons 24 to 28 lb; store 32°F, 90% humidity.
Honeydew melon (315)	June-Oct.; imports at other times may be available.	U. S. No. 1, Combination, and No. 2; like canteloupe a slip skin on the stem end indicates picking at maturity.	Standard jumbo flat crate 45-50 lb; a melon usually is about 5 to 6 lb. Store at 50°F at 80 to 85% humidity.

Item	Season	Grades	Comments
Lemons (373)	Year around; peak in summer.	U. S. No. 1, Combination, and No. 2. Eureka and Lisbon are main varieties.	Lug or carton usually weighs 38 to 40 lb; picked 105 to 294 size.
Limes (40)	Year around; peak June-Aug.	U. S. No. 1, Combination, and No. 2; Persian or Tahiti usually comes from Florida, and Bearis from California.	Flat cartons contain 11 to 13 lb; store at 50°F at 80 to 85% humidity.
Nectarines (124)	June through Sept.	U. S. No. 1 and No. 2.	Treat as oranges.
Oranges (3,250)	Valancias Feb. through Oct.; Navels Nov. through May; Florida Temples Nov. through Mar.	U. S. Fancy, No. 1, No. 2 and No. 3; also graded on the basis of tarnish showing on the skin.	4/5 bushel carton weighs 38-40 lb. Hamlin (seedless), Parson Brown (seedy), Pineapple and Homosassa are other varieties that come on the market largely from Florida.
Peaches (1,139)	July through Sept.	U. S. Extra No. 1, No. 1, and No. 2.	Calif. lug 20 lb; bushel 45-48 lb; many eastern packs are ¾ bushel.
Pears (393)	Aug. through May; Bartletts are summer pears; Anjous, Bosc, Nellis, Comice and Easter are winter.	U. S. Extra No. 1, No. 1, Combination, and No. 2; store at 32°F but ripen at 60 to 65°F at 85 to 95% humidity.	Western box weighs 45 to 48 lb; sizes are 70 to 245 per box; best institutional sizes are 110, 120 and 135.
Pineapple (145)	Year around; peak Mar. through June	U. S. Fancy, No. 1, and No. 2. A fresh sweet odor indicates ripeness; a sour smell spoilage.	½ crates weigh 35 lb and usually hold 15 pineapple; *hard ripe* are not ready; *yellow ripe* are. Ripen at 40 to 45°F, 85 to 90% humidity.
Plums, Fresh prunes (290)	June-Sept.	U. S. Fancy, No. 1, Combination, and No. 2.	Lug 20 lb; 4 basket crate 22-29 lb; ½ bushel 27-30 lb.
Tangerines (228)	Nov. through Jan.	U. S. Fancy, No. 1, No 2 and No. 3.	4/5 bushel carton 38-40 lb; store 36°F, 90% humidity.
Watermelons	May through summer.	U. S. No. 1, Commercial and No. 2.	25-30 lb size cut best; store 50°F, 80-85% humidity.

The number in parentheses indicates the millions of pounds produced per year, according to USDA records.

Table 9-1 cont'd.

Item	Season	Grades	Comments
		Fresh Vegetables	
Asparagus	Feb. through June; may be available off season.	U. S. No. 1, and No. 2. Store 35-40°F, 85-90% humidity; should show some white at base resting in wet moss or paper.	Crate 12 2½-lb bundles; 30 lb serves 100 3-oz portions.
Lima Beans	June-Sept.; some all year.	U. S. No. 1 and No. 2. Purchase frozen or canned because of the labor cost of shelling.	Bushel weighs 35 lb; store 40-50°F; 1 bushel yields about 13½ lb which gives slightly over 100 3-oz portions.
Beans, snap, wax green or (331)	May through Oct. are peaks; year around.	U. S. Fancy, No. 1, Combination and No. 2.	Bushel is 30 lb; 22½ lb should give 100 3-oz portions. Store 45 to 50°F at 85-90% humidity.
Beets (83)	June through Nov. peak; all year.	U. S. No. 1 and No. 2. Bunched or topped.	Topped in 50 lb bags; 23 lb should give 100 3-oz portions. Store 45-50°F with good air circulation.
Broccoli (62)	Low peaks June through Oct.; all year.	U. S. Fancy, No. 1 and No. 2; Italian or sprouting varieties are most popular.	Crate 22 lb (14 bunches), 31 lb should give 100 3-oz portions.
Cabbage (1,718)	All year; green is an early spring type; domestic summer and Danish a winter cabbage.	U. S. No. 1 and Commercial; other varieties are red, Savoy (curly type) and Chinese. Store at 34°F, 90-95% humidity.	50 lb crates or sacks; 16 lb AP for cole slaw (100 2-oz portions); 24 lb AP cooked, 100 3-oz portions as a wedge and 25 lb AP when sliced or diced.
Carrots (1,366)	All year; peak June through Sept.	U. S. Extra, No. 1, Jumbo, and No. 2. Store 32-34°F.	50 lb bags topped; 25 lb AP gives 100 3-oz portions; 15 lb AP 100 2-oz portions grated, strips or diced raw.
Cauliflower (145)	June through Nov. peak; all year.	U. S. No. 1; store 34°F 85-90% humidity.	Eastern crate weighs 45 lb; pony crate of 12 to 15 heads, 42 lb; 43 lb 100 3-oz portions.
Celery (1,346)	Year around; peak Sept. through Nov.	U. S. Extra No. 1, No. 1 and No. 2; store 32-34°F, 90-95% humidity.	Standard crate 60-65 lb; may be packed otherwise; 100 3-oz portions raw 25 lb AP; cooked 27 lb AP for 100 3-oz portions; 100 2-oz portions raw strips, 17 lb.

Item	Season	Grades	Comments
Corn (1,470)	May through Sept.	U. S. Fancy, No. 1 and No. 2; store 32-34°F, 85-90% humidity.	50-lb bags containing about 5 doz ears; doz ears weigh 7 lb.
Cucumbers (620)	May through Oct.; year around.	U. S. Fancy, Extra No. 1, No. 1 large or small, No. 2; 45-50°F best storage; storage under 40°F causes rapid breakdown after refrigerated removal.	A bushel contains about 2 doz cucumbers and should weigh 50 lb; 100 3-oz portions sliced 26 lb.
Eggplant (83)	July through Oct.; year around.	U. S. No. 1; store 40-50° F; humidity 85-90%.	Bushel holds 30 lb; 33 lb yields 100 4-oz portions.
Endive Escarole Chicory	May through Dec. but also all year.	U. S. No. 1; store 35-40° F, 90-95% humidity.	A doz heads should weigh about 8 lb; 100 portions 1 oz raw requires 8 lb AP.
Garlic	All year.	U. S. No. 1.	Store in dry cool place.
Greens (237)	All year except for lesser used varieties.	U. S. No. 1.	Minimum net weight per bushel should be specified as 20 lb; hold 34°F, 90-95% humidity.
Lettuce (4,264)	All year; peak July-Sept.	Iceberg: U. S. Fancy, No. 1 and No. 2; Leaf: U. S. Fancy and No. 1; Boston, Limestone, etc. lettuce is graded as Iceberg.	Iceberg 40 lb/24 head carton. Leaf usually packed in 10 lb baskets. 17 lb AP = 100 2-oz portions. Hold 34°F, 90-95% humidity.
Mushrooms (59)	Year around.	U. S. No. 1 and No. 2; small under 1 in., medium 1 to 1⅛ in., large 1⅝ to 3 in., and specials over 3 in. in diameter.	4 qt basket equals 3 lb; 28 lb AP = 100 3 oz portions; store at 34°F, 85 to 90% humidity.
Onions dry (2,400)	Year around.	U. S. No. 1, Commercial, No. 2; store 34°F, 70 to 75% humidity.	25 lb AP = 100 3-oz cooked portions; 7 lb AP = 1-oz portions served raw. Use Globes, Granos, Browns, etc., for general cooking, and Spanish or Bermuda for use raw.

The number in parentheses indicates the millions of pounds produced per year, according to USDA records.

Table 9-1 cont'd.

Item	Season	Grades	Comments
Onions green (193)	All year; peak is April to Aug.	U. S. No. 1 and No. 2. Leeks are large with slight bulb and broad, flat leaves; shallots are like green onions but do not develop bulbs.	Dozen bunches equals about 5 lb; 31 lb AP equals 100 portions of raw onions.
Parsley (73)	All year.	U. S. No. 1.	Sold by bushel or crate; 1 dozen bunches equals about 3 lb; a 4-oz bunch gives about 20 sprigs; store at 34°F, 95% humidity.
Peas green (40)	All year; peak is May to Sept.	U. S. Fancy and No. 1. Because of labor cost in shelling use canned or frozen.	Specify 30 lb minimum per bushel; 52 lb AP gives 100 3-oz cooked portions; store at 34°F, 85-90% humidity.
Peppers (455)	All year; peak is June to Sept.	U. S. Fancy, No. 1, and No. 2; specify minimum 35 lb per bushel or bushel crate.	Store 40 to 45°F; 85 to 90% humidity; 21 lb AP gives 100 ½-c portions raw and 19 lb AP gives 100 1½-oz portions cooked.
Potatoes, Irish (12,150)	All year.	U. S. Fancy, No. 1, Commercial, and No. 2; store at 50 to 60°F.	Boiled: 35 lb AP gives 100 5-oz portions; french fried: 24 lb AP gives 100 2-oz portions; diced: 25 lb AP gives 100 3-oz portions; mashed: 33 lb AP gives 100 4-oz portions.
Potatoes sweet (766)	All year; peak is Sept. to April.	U. S. Fancy, No. 1, Commercial, and No. 2; store at 55°F and keep only two weeks.	50 lb AP gives 100 medium potatoes; 31 lb AP gives 100 4-oz portions mashed and 23 lb AP gives 100 3-oz portions sliced.
Pumpkins (43)	Year around; 74% are marketed in Oct.	U. S. No. 1 and Commercial.	Most institutions use the canned product.
Radishes (227)	All year.	U. S. No. 1.	9 lb AP gives 100 portions of 4 small radishes; 7 lb AP gives 100 1-oz portions sliced; store at 34°F, 85 to 95% humidity.
Rhubarb (17)	Feb. to June is the peak but some is available all year.	U. S. Fancy, No. 1, and No. 2.	Store 34°F, 90 to 95% humidity; usually sold in 20 lb boxes; 18 lb AP gives 100 3-oz cooked portions.

Item	Season	Grades	Comments
Spinach (83)	Year around.	U. S. No. 1 and Commercial.	Minimum weight per bushel 20 lb; store 34°F, 90 to 95% humidity; 28 lb AP gives 100 3-oz portions; 9 lb AP gives 100 1-oz raw portions.
Squash (339)	Year around for both summer and hard-shell types.	U. S. No. 1 and No. 2.	Store hardshell squash at 50 to 55°F, 70 to 75% humidity, and summer squash at 32°F at 85 to 95% humidity; 23 lb AP gives 100 portions 3-oz of summer squash and 30 lb AP gives 100 4-oz portions of mashed hardshell type; use 45 to 50 lb hardshell for 100 portions baked.
Tomatoes (2,153)	Year around.	U. S. No. 1, Combination, No. 2, and No. 3.	20 lb AP gives 100 portions of 3 slices each; 8 lb gives 100 portions of 1 wedge each; if ripe, store at 50°F, 85 to 90% humidity.
Turnips, Rutabagas (198)	Year around.	U. S. No. 1 and No. 2.	Store at 34°F, 90 to 95% humidity; 24 lb AP gives 100 3-oz portions cubed; 32 lb AP gives 100 4-oz portions mashed.

The number in parentheses indicates the millions of pounds produced per year, according to USDA records.

Fruit and Vegetable Grades

The fresh fruit and vegetable market is one of the most variable markets in which buyers deal. Grading standards vary among consumer, wholesale and manufacturing grades, and a buyer must be acutely aware of their differences. Grades also vary with the market. Washington apples must have more red on them to make a particular grade than apples grown elsewhere. Oranges and and grapefruit raised in California and Arizona are graded differently from Florida and Texas oranges and grapefruit.

Brand buying is very common on the fruit and vegetable market, and grades are not as important as they are in meats, butter, etc. A buyer may specify that only Orchid Brand grapefruit from Florida is acceptable, or he may specify only Bud brand lettuce because he knows that these brands give him exactly what he needs. Purchasing experience and good evaluation of brands is required before buyers can purchase by brand effectively.

The fresh fruit and vegetable market is highly dynamic, changing rapidly and with large price movement. A market can be flooded with items and then, in a few days, have a scarcity. Seasonal changes are great and prices can vary considerably in a short time. Buyers must watch market and weather reports to note factors indicating a market change. For instance, a May freeze in Idaho, Washington and Oregon in 1971

Table 9-2

Quantities Required in Fresh Fruits and Vegetables

Item	Purchase Unit	Wt (lbs)	Yield AS (%)	Portion Size	Amount (lbs) for 100 Portions
Asparagus	Crate	28	49	3 oz (4 spears)	29¼
Beans, lima (in pod)	Bu	32	40	3 oz	47
Beans, lima (shelled)	Lb		102	3 oz	18½
Beans, snap	Bu	30	84	3 oz	22½
Beet greens	Bu	20	44	3 oz	43
Beets, topped	Sack	50	76	3 oz	25
Beets, tops	Lb		43	3 oz	44
Blackeyed peas, shelled	Lb		93	3 oz	20¼
Broccoli	Crate	40	62	3 oz (2 or 3 spears)	30¼
Cabbage	Sack	50	75	3 oz.	25
Cabbage	Sack	50	75	2 oz as slaw	16
Cabbage, Chinese	Lb		88	2 oz raw	14¼
Carrots, no tops	Sack	50	75	3 oz	25
Cauliflower	Crate	37 or 50	44	3 oz	43
Celery	Crate	60	70	2 oz raw	17
Celery	Crate	60	70	3 oz cooked	27
Chard	Bu	20	56	3 oz	33½
Collards	Bu	20	81	3 oz	23¼
Corn, in husks	Crate or bag	40		1 ear	60/crate or bag
Cucumber	Bu	48	95	3 oz raw	25
Eggplant	Bu	33	75	4 oz	33½
Endive, escarole, chicory	Bu	25	75	1 oz raw	8½
Kale	Bu	18	81	3 oz	23¼
Kohlrabi	Lb		50	3 oz	37½
Lettuce, iceberg	Carton	40	74	2 oz raw	17
Lettuce, romaine	Lb		64	2 oz raw	20
Mushrooms	Basket	9	67	3 oz	9½
Mustard greens	Bu	20	59	3 oz	32
Okra	Bu	30	96	3 oz	20
Onions, green	Crate	50	60	3 oz raw	31¼
Onions, mature	Sack	50	76	1 oz raw	7¼
Onions, mature	Sack	50	76	3 oz cooked	25
Parsley	Crate	19		(1 bu = 19 sprigs	6½
Parsnips	Bu	50	84	3 oz	22½
Peas, green, in pod	Bu	28	36	3 oz	52¼
Peas, green shelled	Lb		96	3 oz	20

Item	Purchase Unit	Wt (lbs)	Yield AS (%)	Portion Size	Amount (lbs) for 100 Portions
Peppers, green	Bu	25	82	1 oz raw	7¾
Peppers, green	Carton	30	82	2 oz cooked	17
Potatoes, pared	Sack	100	52	1 med	33½
Potatoes, pared	Sack	100	52	2 oz french fried	24¼
Potatoes, pared	Sack	100	52	3 oz cubed or diced	25
Potatoes, pared	Sack	100	52	4 oz mashed	28
Pumpkin	Lb		63	4 oz	40
Radishes, no tops	Lb		90	1 oz raw	7
Radishes, no tops	Lb		90	4 small	6
Radishes, tops	Lb		63	4 small	9
Spinach	Bu	20	70	1 oz raw	9
Spinach	Bu	20	70	3 oz	28¼
Squash, summer	Bu	35	83	3 oz	23
Squash, winter					
Acorn	Lb			½ baked	50
Hubbard, etc.	Lb		58	4 oz	43¼
Sweet potatoes					
or yams	Bu	50	81	4 oz	44
Tomatoes, medium	Lug	32	91	2 slices, raw	13½
Tomatoes, medium	Bu	53	91	1 wedge, raw	8½
Turnip greens	Bu	20	48	3 oz	39¼
Turnips, no tops	Bu	50	73	3 oz	34½
Watercress	Bunch		92	½ c	
Apples	Bu	40		1 med (100 or 113)	33½
Apples	Box	45	76	2 oz raw	16½
Apples	Box	45	87	4 oz applesauce	29
Apples	Box	45	63	2.12 lb per pie	35½
Apricots	Lug	24	75	2 medium	17
Avocados	Lug	12	75	2 oz raw	17
Bananas	Box	25		1 medium	33½
Bananas	Box	25	68	2 oz	18½
Blackberries	Crate	34	95	3 oz	14 qt
Blueberries	Crate	47	92	3 oz	10½ qt
Blueberries	Crate	47	92	.6 qt per pie	10 qt
Cantaloupe	Crate (36 size)	80	50	½ medium	140 (3 crates)
Cantaloupe	Crate	80	50	3 oz raw	37
Cherries, sweet	Lug	16	89	3 oz raw pitted	21¼
Cranberries	Box	25	239	2 oz cooked sauce	5¼
Cranberries	Box	25	96	1 oz raw as relish	7
Figs	Box	6		3 medium	25
Grapefruit	Carton 32 size	40	44	4 oz juice	62¼
Grapefruit	Carton	40	47	4 oz segments	53¼
Grapefruit	Carton	40		½	3 cartons
Grapefruit					
segments	Gal	8½	100	4 oz	3 gal

Table 9-2 cont'd.

Quantities Required in Fresh Fruits and Vegetables

Item	Purchase Unit	Wt (lbs)	Yield AS (%)	Portion Size	Amount (lbs) for 100 Portions
Grapes	Lug	24	94	4 oz	27
Honeydew melon	1 melon	4	60	3 oz	31¼
Lemons	Carton	36		1 slice	12½ lemons
Lemons	Carton	36	43	2 oz juice	32
Limes	Carton	20		¼ lime	25
Limes	Carton	20	48	2 oz juice	28½
Mangoes	Lug	24	67	3 oz raw	28¼
Oranges					
California	Carton	38	70	4 oz segments	55
Florida	Carton	47½	50	4 oz juice	30
Medium					
No. 176's	Carton			1 medium	
Orange segments	Gal	8½	100	4 oz	3 gal
Peaches	Bu	48	76	3 oz raw	25
Peaches	Bu	48		1 medium	25
Peaches	Bu	48	76	1.9 lb per pie	31½
Pears	Bu	46	78	3 oz raw	24¼
Pineapple	½ crate	35	52	3 oz cubed	36¼
Pineapple, 18 size	½ crate	35	85	1/6 wedge	17 pineapple
Pineapple chunks	Gal	8½	100	4 oz	3 gal
Plums	4-basket crate	28	94	3 oz pitted	20
Plums	Crate	28		3 medium	37½
Raspberries	24-qt crate	35	97	3 oz raw	13¼ qt
Raspberries	24-qt crate	35	97	.7 qt per pie	11½ qt
Rhubarb, trimmed	Lb		103	3 oz cooked	18¼
Rhubarb, trimmed	Lb			1½ lb per pie	26 lb
Strawberries	24 pt crate	35	87	3 oz raw	15 qt
Tangerines	Box, 180 size	45		1 medium	
Watermelon	1 melon	18 to 30		1/16 melon	6¼ melons

(Source: USDA, Agr. Handbook 284)

badly damaged potato crops. Alert buyers bought dehydrated and frozen potatoes heavily to avoid having to pay the very high price for fresh potatoes later in that fall and winter. A heavy freeze in Florida, a year later, meant that fresh citrus prices jumped overnight. However, later prices on canned and frozen citrus juices were found to be lower because much of the damaged crop was salvaged by rushing it to processing plants.

Many markets have developed their own unique methods of grading, packaging and other practices. Buyers therefore must learn these. There are few standard procedures nationally in the fruit and vegetable markets of this country except for highly stable items such as potatoes, onions, etc., that store and

Table 9-3

Equivalent in Fresh, Frozen and Canned Vegetables and Fruits

Item	Amount	Yield in No. 10 cans	Yield in Frozen (Lbs)
Asparagus	8 to 9 lb	1	
Asparagus	Crate (28 lb)	3 to 4	15
Beans, lima	5 lb	1	
Beans, lima	Bu (32 lb)	6	29
Beans, snap	4 to 5 lb	1	
Beans, snap	Bu (30 lb)	6 to 8	24
Broccoli	Crate 40		23
Carrots, no tops	8 lb	1	
Carrots, no tops	25 lb	6 to 7	18½
Corn, in husks	17 to 18 lb	1	
Corn, in husks	Crate (40 lb)	2¼	8
Peas, green	4 to 5 lb shelled	1	
Peas, green	Bu (28) in pod	2½	10
Pumpkin or winter squash	17 to 18 lb	1	
Pumpkin or winter squash	Lb		10 oz
Spinach and other greens	8 lb	1	
Spinach and other greens	Bu (20 lb)	2 to 3	10 to 11
Sweetpotatoes	7 lb	1	
Sweetpotatoes	1 bu (50 lb)	7	
Tomatoes	12 lb	1	
Tomato catsup	19 lb	1	
Tomato paste	40 to 41 lb	1	
Tomato sauce	21 lb	1	
Apples	10 lb	1	
Apples	Bu (40 lb)	4 to 5	28 (5:1)*
Berries, except strawberries	5 lb	1	
Berries, except strawberries	Crate (24 qt)	7	34 (4:1)*
Cherries, sour	7 lb	1	
Cherries, sour	1 bu	8	53 (4:1)*
Peaches	7 lb	1	
Peaches	Bu (48 lb)	6 to 7	43 (3:1)*
Plums	6 lb	1	
Strawberries	6 lb	1	
Strawberries	24-qt crate	6	42 (3:1)*

*Refers to the fruit-sugar ratio.

AVAILABILITY OF FRESH FRUIT

G=Good Supply   **F=Fair Supply**   **S=Small Supply**

	January	February	March	April	May	June	July	August	September	October	November	December
Apples	G	G	G	G	F	S	S	S	G	G	G	G
Apricots					S	G	G	S				
Avocados	G	G	G	G	G	F	F	F	F	F	G	G
Bananas	G	G	G	G	G	G	G	G	G	G	G	G
Berries (misc.)					S	G	G	G	S	S	S	
Blueberries					S	G	G	G	S			
Cantaloupes		S	S	S	F	G	G	G	G	S	S	
Cherries				S	G	G	S	S				
Cranberries	S								F	F	G	G
Dates	G	F	F	S	S	S	S	S	S	S	G	G
Figs						F	G	G	F			
Grapefruit	G	G	G	G	G	F	S	S	S	G	G	G
Grapes	S	S	S	S	S	F	G	G	G	G	G	F
Honeydews		F	G	F	F	G	G	G	G	G	S	S
Lemons	G	G	G	G	G	G	G	G	G	G	G	G
Limes	S	S	S	S	G	G	G	F	F	F	S	G
Mangoes			S	F	G	G	G	F	S			
Nectarines	S	S				F	G	G	G	S		
Oranges	G	G	G	G	G	F	S	S	S	F	G	G
Papayas	S	S	S	S	F	S	S	S	S	F	S	S
Peaches					S	G	G	G	G	S		
Pears	F	F	F	F	F	S	S	G	G	G	G	F
Pineapples	S	F	G	G	G	G	F	F	S	F	F	F
Plums-Prunes							G	G	G	S		
Strawberries	S	S	F	G	G	G	G	S	S	S	S	S
Tangelos	F	S							S	F	G	G
Tangerines	G	S	S	S	S	S				S	G	G
Watermelons	S	S	S	S	F	G	G	G	S	S	S	S

NOTE: Each year's production will vary. This chart is an estimate of probable availability.

FIG. 9-7
A seasonal fruit availability chart compiled by the U. S. Department of Agriculture.

ship well. Wide variability in packaging, grading and marketing will be found in highly perishable items such as berries or fresh peaches.

The wholesale grades for fresh fruit and vegetables are usually U. S. No. 1 and No. 2. A Combination grade exists which combines these two grades. A Commercial grade, better or below No. 2 in quality, may also be available. Higher grades than No. 1 exist. These were developed to give a place for items which may be superior in a particular year and should not sell for the normal top grade. This gives market stability and provides a standard for better than the average produce in years when it exists. It also assures that a good standard U. S. No. 1 will usually be available. Products above No. 1 in quality will usually be called Extra No. 1, Fancy or Extra Fancy.

Consumer grades usually are U. S. Grade A, B and sometimes C, but buyers may find that grades such as "AA", "Extra No. 1", etc., exist. A buyer should learn what a grade term means on his individual market. It is quite possible that a grade called "Fancy" could be a second or a third grade product.

The grade of fresh fruits and vegetables will be decided by different factors. Outward appearance, freedom from defects, shape, damage, rot, blemishes, freedom from soil or dirt, color, crispness, maturity and other factors will be evaluated, depending upon the item. Buyers must learn which of these apply to specific items and what they mean in grading. Some qualities cannot be evaluated as easily as others, and buyers develop their own techniques in judging quality.

Some tests are:

Shaking a bag of onions to hear if there is a dry rustle which indicates freedom from decay; noting whether the onions have moist stems at the neck can also indicate this.

Dropping cranberries on a hard surface to see if they bounce; a good bounce indicates freshness and freedom from decay.

Cutting a beet with a knife, holding it close to the ear; if a grating sound is heard, fibers are being cut indicating toughness; this is also a good quality test for some other root vegetables.

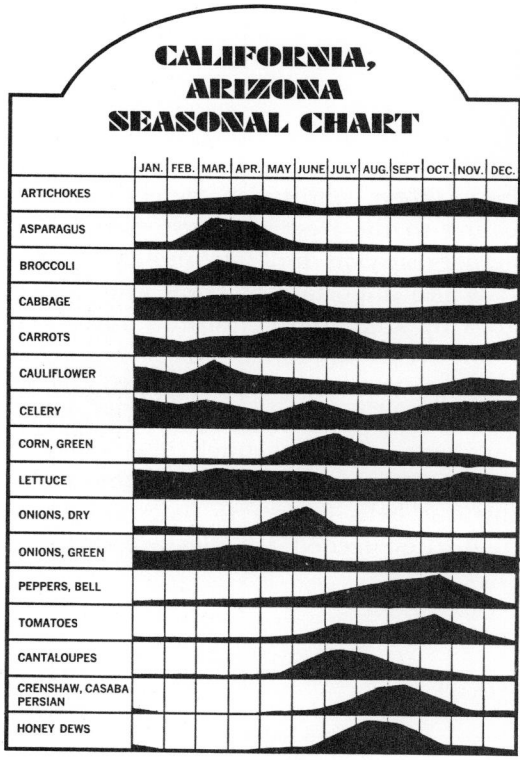

FIG. 9-8   California is one of our largest fruit and vegetable producers, and its seasons for there items dominate the market. Shown here are production times for some California produce. (Courtesy USDA)

Cutting an apple, orange or other fruit in two and tasting it.

Lifting fruit or vegetables to see how heavy they feel in the hand.

Noting how tight the buds are on broccoli or cauliflower.

Noting the high, soft sheen on eggplant or cucumbers.

Cutting summer squash to note if the seeds are immature and not hard.

Putting the thumbnail into a cucumber, or other item, to see how crisp it is.

Snapping string beans.

Smelling a pineapple; a rich smell indicates ripeness.

Examining cauliflower or cabbage for evidence of worm or mite damage.

Noting the tassels on fresh corn on the cob; a brown silky tassel is desirable.

There are many others and buyers need to learn all they can to improve their ability to detect quality. Going to the fresh produce market can help greatly in judging quality factors. It is also important to know a lot about growing areas and conditions and when items are or are not in season.

Quantities required are difficult to determine because preparation losses can vary. Keeping track of these and the ones that occur in serving and cooking can help buyers to ascertain exact quantities needed. Tables presented in this chapter can be helpful but should be modified to suit local factors and individual needs. It is difficult to get bids for items over long periods because of the great market variability. Usually, purchase of fruits and vegetables is by direct negotiation, and call sheet buying is common.

Processed Fruits and Vegetables

Fruits and vegetables subjected to some processing, even though slight, are usually classified as processed and not fresh items. Thus, fresh peeled potatoes are considered processed and cleaned, as are salad greens. Most processed fruits and vegetables are canned or frozen. Besides fresh and canned, other processed forms are pasteurized and chilled, dried or pickled.

A specification for canned or frozen fruits and vegetables should contain (1) grade, (2) fill, (3) size or count, (4) drained weight, (5) style, and (6) packaging. Information specific to the product, such as density of syrup on canned fruits or fruit-to-sugar ratio in frozen fruit, is also important.

(1) GRADES. Grades for canned and frozen fruits and vegetables are as shown in the panel below.

	FRUITS		VEGETABLES	
GRADE LEVEL	U.S. GRADE	TRADE GRADE	U.S. GRADE	TRADE GRADE
First	Grade A or Fancy	Fancy	Grade A or Fancy	Fancy
Second	Grade B or Choice	Choice	Grade B or Extra-Standard	Extra-Standard
Third	Grade C or Standard	Standard	Grade C or Standard	Standard

Items below standard must be so labeled and the reason given. It is edible food and suitable for some food production needs.

The federal grades are obtained by scoring various factors such as character, maturity, clarity of liquor or syrup, color, defects, etc., and adding up the factor scores to get a total score that indicates the grade.

In some instances. if a factor fails to attain a certain score, the product cannot be rated higher than the score for this factor regardless of its total score. Thus, even though canned asparagus may have a total score of 90 making it a grade A product, it cannot attain this grade unless it scores above 24 in the factor of defects or 33 in the factor of character. This, in grading, is called a "limiting" rule. A "partially limiting rule" is the same, except that the grader may or may not at his discretion apply the rule.

There is an increasing tendency today to use more statistical sampling methods in establishing grades. Also, instead of estimating defects, they are counted and weighted variously to establish scores. For instance, for leafy greens to meet U. S. Grade A, the average sample may not have more than 0.75 severe defects, nor over 4.5 major ones. Defects are also more precisely defined and are not left so much to the judgment of the grader.

(2) FILL. In the new standard being published there is also a tendency, especially in canned fruits, to establish standards of fill as well as drained weights.

(3) SIZE. In writing specifications for canned vegetables, it may be important to give a sieve size, such as a No. 2, for peas, or a count such as 125 to 175 for whole beets in a No. 10 can. Asparagus may be sized small, medium, large, extra large or mammoth, colossal and giant or supercolossal. Beet slices also will be sized and the buyer should state the size he wants. Sizing is important for many other food items.

(4) WEIGHT. Every specification should indicate the minimum acceptable drained weight. This is obtained by draining the items thoroughly on a mesh screen for two minutes. Certain mesh sizes are specified for different foods. About two-thirds of a can should be drained weight. Thus, a No. 10 can holding net 103 ounces should drain to around 70 ounces and if a three ounce portion is given, a No. 10 should yield around 25 portions.

(5) STYLE. Vegetables and fruits should also be specified by style. String beans are classified short cut, long cut, julienne, whole, whole vertical, French, or mixed. Peaches might be whole, sliced, half, diced, etc. Variety may also be important, e.g., White or Golden corn or Early (Alaska) or Sweet (Sugar) peas.

(6) PACK. The packaging size also must be stated. Canned items come in many sizes. Vegetables and fruits usually will be found in No. 303, No. 2, No. 2½ and No. 10 cans holding, respectively 15.6, 19.9, 28.5 and 103.7 ounces by volume. Cans go by numbers, the first number being the diameter and the second the height. Thus, a No. 303 can is also called a 303 x 406 which means it is three and three-sixteenth inches in diameter and four and six-sixteenth inches high. A No. 10 is called a 603 x 700, which means it is six and three-sixteenth inches in diameter and seven

inches tall. (A can with a number such as 512 would be five and twelve-sixteenth inches tall, the first number being the inches and the second two numbers indicating sixteenths of an inch.) Buyers should know the can sizes for canned items and the number of cans per case, and should be able to make price comparisons on the basis of the can size. For instance, if a case of 6/10 tomatoes costs $5.20, and a case of 24/2* peas sells for $4.00, the cost per ounce is 0.849¢ for the 6/10 peas and 0.838¢ for the 24/2 peas. Each of the 24 No. 2 cans in a case holds 19.9 ounces, and each of the six No. 10 cans in a case holds 103.7 ounces. Thus, $24 \times 19.9 = 477.6$ and $6 \times 103.7 = 622.2$ ounces. $5.20 ÷ 622.2 ounces $= 0.849¢$ and $4.00 ÷ 477.6 = 0.838¢$. However, it might be well to know the drained weight to see how much the cost of the servable product is. If the 6/10 cans drain out 70 percent and the 24/2 cans drain 65 percent, then .70 $\times$ 622.2 = 435.5 ounces of drained peas in the case of 6/10's, and .65 $\times$ 477.6 = 310.4 ounces in the case of 24/2's. Therefore, $5.20 ÷ 428.5 ounces = 1.192¢ per ounce and $4.00 ÷ 310.4 ounces = 1.289¢ per ounce. Hence, because of better drainage, the 6/10 product is less expensive per ounce. Buyers constantly have to make such comparisons and relate price to quality. Thus, if the 24/2 peas were of better quality, it might be worthwhile to pay the slight difference to obtain a better quality item.

Many operations may purchase most of their needs in 6/10 cans but purchase a few cases of No. 2's or 2½'s to use when a full No. 10 can is not required.

Specifications for canned fruits should list count or size, density of syrup, style, type or variety, and size of can.

Counts are important and the buyer should know what size is desired for the menu need. Most fruits are packed in syrup and the buyer should specify which is desired. Packing mediums are water, juice, light syrup, medium syrup, heavy syrup and extra heavy syrup. Syrups are frequently specified in Brix densities rather than as light, medium, heavy or extra heavy. Thus, if a buyer wanted peaches in a light syrup, he would order them in a 14 to 19° Brix, heavy 19 to 24° Brix, and extra heavy 24 to 35° Brix. The same Brix density is not used for different fruits. If a buyer wanted to purchase sweet cherries in a light syrup, the specification would call for a Brix density between 16 and 19°, for heavy, a density of 20 to 25°, and for extra heavy 25 to 35°. Drained weight should also be specified. Styles are also required for some items. For instance, styles of pineapple will be whole slices, half or broken slices, chunks, cubes, spears or tidbits. The statement of types may or may not be required. For instance, if plums are ordered the buyer must indicate whether purple, Green Gage, Yellow Egg or other type is desired. Prunes would be either French (sweet) or Italian (tart). The pack or size of can and number in the case must also be indicated.

A review of the few requirements mentioned here for writing an adequate specification for canned vegetables or fruits will indicate the vast amount of information a buyer must have to do an ade-

---

*There are six No. 10 cans in a case and 24 No. 2. There are also 24 No. 2½'s and 12 46-oz cans per case.

quate job of establishing a good specification.

Frozen vegetables are pre-blanched to destroy enzymes that might cause deterioration in frozen storage. They are also lightly salted — about 1 per cent salt — and should be frozen without additional liquid. The drained weight after thawing should be 100 per cent. Styles, varieties, size of pack, and other factors closely follow those for canned vegetables. Packaging will be in 2½ or five pound lots packed approximately 30 pounds per case. Purchase is usually on the basis of price per pound.

Frozen fruits are frequently packed with some sugar and a ratio figure of "1:4" means that the fruit is packed one part sugar to four parts fruit. Most berries will be packed at this ratio, but apples and rhubarb may be packed as 1:7. The addition of sugar aids in preserving color and flavor and, to a small extent, texture. The sugar, however, pulls juice from the fruit. There are no recommended drained weights for frozen fruits but the total pack sometimes may be less than 50 per cent fruit.

Canned fruit and vegetable juices are usually used in institutions in 46-oz cans although they are also canned in No. 2's, No. 10's and some other sizes. Frozen juices are usually concentrated and reconstituted by adding three parts water. Thus, a 12-oz can of frozen juice will make 48 ounces of finished juice (1½ quarts). Fresh juice pasteurized and chilled is also on the market. Because most juices are high in acid, they have a long shelf-life. This chilled juice is served just as received (with no added water).

The grades for juices usually are U. S. Grade A or Fancy, and U. S. Grade C or Standard. Occasionally there may be a Grade B or Choice available. Scores for grades usually are 85 or above for Grade A and 70 to 84 for Grade C.

Fruits and vegetables are dried by various methods. Some which are seeds, such as nuts, beans, split peas and lentils, may be *air-dried*. Others may be preserved by *Freeze-drying,* a process in which the product is frozen and then put in a heavy vacuum in which its moisture is "boiled" off at a temperature below freezing. *Vacuum-drying* is a method of extracting moisture with moving warm gas, usually nitrogen. If oxygen in the air is excluded, a better product is obtained, oxidation giving a hay-like flavor. *Sun-drying* is usually used only on fruits such as apricots, peaches, apples, pears, raisins and prunes. These can also be dried with warm air. Apples, apricots, pears or peaches may be treated with sulfur dioxide fumes to prevent them from tarnishing during the drying process.

Nuts, beans and peas, are graded U. S. No. 1, No. 2, etc. Some dried vegetables are not graded and some dried fruits may not be. Most dried fruits move on the market under either trade or federal grades. Trade grades are largely based on size, while federal grades will rate quality factors such as freedom from defects, shape, etc. The size of prunes and a few other dried fruits may affect federal grading but size is not as influential here as in the trade grades. Buyers must learn the various sizing terms.

Specifications for dried fruits should indicate the grade, the type, the style such as nugget, slab, flakes, pieces and slices; color variety, etc. The maximum moisture content permitted should also be indicated.

The following yields are usually obtained from dried fruit:

ONE POUND DRIED FRUIT	COOKED YIELD	PORTION	PORTIONS PER POUND
Apples	4 lb 8 oz	1/2 c	17
Apricots	2 lb 15 oz	4 halves	10
Figs	2 lb 7 oz	3 figs	10
Peaches	2 lb 10 oz	3 halves	11
Pears	2 lb 10 oz	2 halves	14
Prunes	2 lb 3 oz	4 prunes	12
Raisins	3 lb 4 oz	1/3 c	17

A pound of dried beans, split peas, black-eyed peas, etc., gives about 2-1/2 to 2-2/3 lbs of cooked product; low-moisture vacuum-dried cabbage, carrots, celery, onions, potatoes and tomatoes increase about five times in weight during cooking. Vacuum-dried fruits will increase as much as 12 times in weight.

Egg Grades

Eggs are graded AA, A and B. Grade C eggs are no longer on the wholesale market for sale to institutions. They can now only be used by processors who must pasteurize them in the processing. Some large buyers may purchase Procurement I or II eggs which are slightly lower in quality than these consumer grades.

The grade of an egg is decided by outside factors, such as cleanliness of the shell, shape and soundness. Inside factors deciding grade include the size of the air cell, the condition of the white —blood spots, etc., are noted— the condition of the white and yolk, and the position of the yolk.

About 10 years ago the federal government introduced a new method of grading eggs and included the grades Fancy Quality, Fancy, Grade A, etc. However, because the cost of the program has been more than expected, this grading method is slowly disappearing from the market. Eggs used for breakfast should be either AA or A. Eggs can lose quality rapidly at room temperature and should therefore be refrigerated. If AA eggs become warm and stand awhile they can easily drop to A quality or lower.

Eggs are sold by size but size does not affect grade. The size of the egg, weight per dozen, and net weight per case of 30 dozen eggs are tabulated:

Size	Wt/Doz	Wt/Case
Jumbo[1]	30 oz	56 1/4 lb
Extra-large	27 oz	50 1/2 lb
Large	24 oz	45 lb
Medium	21 oz	39 1/2 lb
Small	18 oz	34 lb
Peewee[2]	15 oz	37 1/2 lb

[1] Usually not available on the foodservice market.
[2] Seldom available.

Institutional recipes are usually set for large eggs and this is the size that is usually purchased. Some buyers use the rule that when the price difference between two adjoining sizes is 11 per cent or more, a price comparison should be made. For instance, if large eggs are selling for 67¢ per dozen and medium eggs for 64¢ per dozen, the best buy is the large eggs. [The cost per ounce for large eggs is 2.79¢ (67¢ ÷ 24 oz = 2.79¢) and the cost per ounce for medium eggs is 3.05¢ (64¢ ÷ 21 oz = 3.05¢)] However because a standard size egg must be used for breakfast eggs, it is seldom possible to purchase by best bargain according to size.

Processed eggs are freeze-dried, dried or frozen. All must be pasteurized. Some high-quality frozen whole eggs on the market can be used at breakfast time for omelets, scrambled eggs, French toast, etc. Bakeshops may use either dried or frozen eggs.

Dairy Product Standards

The U. S. Public Health Service Milk code has been used as a model by many states in establishing their milk regulations. Under this code, milk must come from cows and contain not less than $8\frac{1}{4}$ per cent non-fat milk solids and $3\frac{1}{4}$ per cent milkfat. Grade A milk must come from the pasteurizer with not more than 20,000 bacteria per milliliter and not more than 10 coliform bacteria per milliliter. It may be fortified with vitamins such as vitamin D, vitamin A, riboflavin, thiamin and niacin. Iron may also be added. If any of these are added, the label must note it.

MILK

Milk is evaluated on the basis of taste but this will not affect grade. Factors such as freshness, off-flavors, cooked flavor, flatness, oxidation and acidity are checked. Federal standards of identity have also been established for milk.

A recent article by *Consumers Union* (January 1974) was very critical of both the bacterial level and quality level of milk. Its study showed that 44 per cent of the samples tested failed to meet the state standard.

Cream should not be less than 18 per cent milkfat. Sour cream should be at this level, and also measure 0.2 per cent acidity (lactic acid content). Light whipping cream should be not less than 30 per cent milkfat, and heavy whipping cream not less than 35 per cent milkfat. Buttermilk is usually made of non-fat milk soured by a special bacterial culture. It may contain small globules of butter. These are added to simulate real buttermilk, traditionally the result of churning most of the butter from soured whole milk. Skim or non-fat milk must not have more than one-half per cent milkfat. It must have $8\frac{1}{4}$ per cent non-fat milk solids but many may be fortified to contain around 10 per cent non-fat milk solids. Low-fat milks may contain various amounts of milkfat, some as little as one-half per cent and others as much as two per cent.

BUTTER

Butter must come from cream and be at least 80 per cent milkfat (it is usually slightly higher than this). The remainder will be salt, milk solids and liquid. It is scored on much the same factor as those listed for evaluating the flavor of milk. However, salt, packaging and other factors are also considered. The best butter will be scored 93, second grade is 92. There is no 91-score butter. Third grade scores 90 and the lowest score is 89. A cooking-grade butter is sometimes available. Sweet cream butter is usually not salted. Butter is sold in 64-lb cubes or tubs, unwrapped. Prints may be in pound or quarter-pound wraps. Pats are available in five-pound lots cut 70 to 90 pats per pound.

Margarine is made from either vegetable or animal fats, or a combination of these, colored by annato and flavored with milk solids and other items to make it resemble butter. Salt will be added. As with butter, margarine must not be less than 80 per cent milk fat. Vitamins A and D may be added. There are a number of margarines made for special foodservice use such as deep-frying, for rolled-in doughs or puff paste. For dietary reasons, some individuals may desire margarines made from only vegetable oils. Such oils are more unsaturated than butter. However, if they are hydrogenated or hardened, they will lose much of their unsaturated quality. Margarine is packaged the same as butter. Some states require that if it is made into pats it must be in the shape of triangles and not squares so as to differentiate it from butter.

ICE CREAM

Ice cream must be not less than eight per cent milkfat if it is a so-called "heavy" flavor, such as chocolate, strawberry, nut or other flavor. If it is vanilla, it must be not less than 10 per cent milkfat. The reason for the difference between eight per cent for heavy flavors and 10 per cent for vanilla is that the heavy flavors have about two per cent of added ingredients, bringing them up to a combined 10 per cent level in milkfat and added ingredients. Standards of identity for ice cream also require that it weigh not less than 4½ pounds per gallon, contain not less than 20 per cent total milk solids (16 per cent for heavy flavors) and have a total of 1.6 pounds of total food solids per gallon. Frozen desserts may contain a one-half per cent of stabilizer such as gelatin, agar agar, etc. The better ice creams contain more than the minimum of milkfat, and some other ingredients.

When a frozen dessert is made, freezing causes a swelling or increase in volume. The whipping process also creates a foam which increases the volume. Such an increase in volume is desirable to give a quality of lightness. This volume increase is called overrun. The maximum overrun allowed for ice cream is 100 per cent (that means a half-gallon of liquid mix makes a gallon of ice cream). Some of the better ice creams have about 80 per cent overrun. If the overrun is less than 80 per cent, the flavor is somewhat flat and pasty. Sherbets have up to a 40 per cent overrun and ices 25 per cent.

Sherbets usually contain about four per cent milkfat. They may vary in total milk solids. An ice is water plus fruit juice or flavoring, sugar, stabilizer and perhaps coloring. A gallon of sherbet or ice should weigh approximately six pounds.

CHEESE

Cheese is usually made from milk casein. Milk when subjected to acid will set into a gel. It will also do this when the enzyme rennet is added to it. After setting, it can be cubed and then worked to remove about half of the moisture or whey. This rubbery solid that remains, which is largely casein, fat and moisture, can be made into cheese by various treatments.

Cheese improves in flavor and texture with aging or ripening. A cheddar or American cheese that is aged less than 30 days is called "current", a "medium" cheese is aged 30 to 150 days, and a "cured" or "aged" cheese is aged over 150 days. A "current" Swiss cheese is aged less than 60 days, "medium" 60 to 180 days and "aged" or "cured" over

180 days. Some cheeses must have bacteria or molds added to them in their making to give the desired cheese. Thus, Roquefort cheese made from ewe's milk in France is innoculated with a mold. Swiss cheese is innoculated with bacteria.

Domestic cheeses are usually aged less and have slightly less pronounced flavor than foreign varieties. There are literally hundreds of different cheeses, and buyers will perhaps purchase only a few of these.

The federal government has grades for some cheese such as cheddar and Swiss. These are U. S. Grades A, B and C. Grade is decided on the basis of flavor, appearance, texture, etc. Other factors specific to the cheese may also decide grade, as, for instance, a Swiss cheese with holes too small will be downgraded. If the eyes of the holes are also dull, the grade may be dropped further. Too many holes, called "sweet holes", "gas holes" or "fine holes" can be another cause for downgrading. Swiss cheese that shows lines in it something like shattered glass will be lowered in grade.

Cheese can be purchased in various sized units, and buyers should check to see what is available on the local market. Some types keep better than others. Quantities purchased should be watched. Cheese, like butter, can absorb odors easily and should therefore be stored in an area where this cannot happen. Unprocessed cheese—that is, natural cheese —will continue to cure in storage and this may cause a change in the nature of the cheese. Thus, a well-cured Camembert that is delightfully flavorful, soft and creamy at time of purchase can become hard and flavorless in two weeks of storage.

Standards of identity for cheese require that it contain not less than a specified amount of milkfat and not more than a certain percentage of moisture. Thus, cheddar cheese must not be over 39 per cent moisture and must on a dry basis contain at least 50 per cent milkfat. This on a moist basis is 31 per cent or more of milkfat. Colby, Washed Curd and some other cheeses can be higher than 39 per cent in moisture content and lower in milkfat content on a moist basis.

A "processed cheese" is regular cheese which is pasteurized. It contains emulsifiers which give it a very smooth texture. Processed cheese originated as a method of utilizing natural cheeses that did not cure properly. By heating this cheese, the undesirable reactions could be stopped. However, the method produced such an acceptable cheese that today only a small quantity of the cheese used in processed cheese comes from cheese that failed to cure properly. In processing, the manufacturer can produce a cheese consistent in flavor and texture, something extremely difficult to do in natural cheese. Pasteurized processed cheese must be 27 per cent or more milkfat on a moist basis. It can contain up to 43 per cent moisture.

A "cheese food" is made of natural cheese but may contain whey or milk solids, etc. It must be 23 per cent milkfat on a moist basis and can contain up to 44 per cent moisture. A "cheese spread" must be 20 per cent milkfat and can contain up to 60 per cent moisture. Items such as imitation cheese spread or a processed cheese product will not have a legal minimum for milkfat nor a legal maximum for moisture. Thus, when a

Federal – State Graded

Metal Wing Clips

Wing Tags

FIG. 9-9 Poultry grade and inspection indicia may appear together or separately. Metal wing clips, wing tags and other devices are used to indicate the grade and show that the bird has passed inspection for wholesomeness. The number appearing in the circular stamp identifies the inspecting office. (Courtesy USDA)

buyer purchases cheese or cheese-like items he should know what some of the standards for these are. In a market test in August 1973,* some of the imitation cheese spreads or cheese products were found to cost more than regular cheese.

Poultry

In 1956 all poultry shipped interstate had to be inspected and passed for wholesomeness. This approval is indicated by the same circular stamp used to indicate inspected and passed meat. Since later regulations have brought many poultry processing operations (even those doing business within a state) under these regulations, almost all poultry nowadays is inspected. Buyers should require that their poultry purchases have the benefit of such certification.

A specification for poultry should list (1) class of poultry, (2) kind, (3) condition, (4) style, (5) size, (6) grade, and perhaps (7) breed and (8) type of pluck.

(1) and (2) CLASS AND KIND. Classes of poultry are chicken, turkey, duck, etc., while kind is a type under class such as Rock Cornish Hen, broilers, fryers, roasters, hens, stags and cocks under chickens. Frequently the kind for a class will be either "mature" or "young", such as a "mature hen turkey" or "young goose".

(3) CONDITION. Poultry may come onto the market in a condition described as "fresh-killed" which means that fewer than three days have elapsed since slaughter. Storage chickens are those held unfrozen up to 30 days. "Frozen storage" usually means that the birds have been

held a long time—poultry should not be held more than nine months to a year. "Fresh-storage" means the birds have been recently slaughtered and frozen. Buyers should examine frozen birds for evidence of freezer-burn, a condition in which the birds first show a whitish pock mark and then later show wide patches of a dull, white covering.

(4) STYLE. Since 1956, "New York dressed" birds have disappeared from the market. In the inspection for wholesomeness, the bird must be eviscerated to allow examination of the intestines and inner parts. Thus, "New York dressed" which meant a bird undrawn and with the head and feet on, is a style term no longer used. Instead, birds are now called ready-to-cook. This means they come with the head and feet off, and with the giblets cleaned, wrapped in paper and stored in the neck. In other words, the bird is actually ready to cook. Other styles in which poultry may be purchased include parts and boneless parts. Cooked poultry, now increasingly available on the market, is another.

(5) SIZE. The size of the bird is important for yield and also for best portioning. If a whole half chicken is to be given as a portion, the bird should not have a ready-to-cook weight much over $1\frac{3}{4}$ to two pounds in order to give a portion that is adequate to fit onto a regular dinner plate. If the fowl is larger than this, it cannot very well be served as a half but must be divided into parts. A duckling that weighs about $3\frac{1}{2}$ pounds divides very well into four equal parts for good portions. A turkey that weighs 18 pounds and another that weighs 30 pounds have about the same size skeletal

---

*Consumers Union, January 1974.

Table 9-4
Classes of Poultry*

Chickens

ROCK CORNISH GAME HEN

A Rock Cornish game hen or Cornish game hen is a young immature chicken (usually 5 to 7 weeks of age) weighing not more than 2 pounds ready-to-cook weight. It may be a Cornish chicken or the progeny of a Cornish chicken crossed with another breed of chicken.

BROILER OR FRYER

A broiler or fryer is a young chicken (usually 9 to 12 weeks of age), of either sex, that is tender-meated with soft, pliable, smooth-textured skin and flexible breastbone cartilage.

ROASTER

A roaster is a young chicken (usually 3 to 5 months of age), of either sex, that is tender-meated with soft, pliable, smooth-textured skin and breastbone cartilage that may be somewhat less flexible than that of a broiler or fryer.

CAPON

A capon is a surgically unsexed male chicken (usually under 8 months of age) that is tender-meated with soft, pliable, smooth-textured skin.

STAG

A stag is a male chicken (usually under 10 months of age) with coarse skin, somewhat toughened and darkened flesh, and considerable hardening of the breastbone cartilage. Stags show a condition of fleshing and a degree of maturity intermediate between that of a roaster and a cock or old rooster.

HEN, STEWING CHICKEN OR FOWL

A hen or stewing chicken or fowl is a mature female chicken (usually more than 10 months old) with meat less tender than that of a roaster, and non-flexible breastbone.

COCK OR OLD ROOSTER

A cock or old rooster is a mature male chicken with coarse skin, toughened and darkened meat, and hardened breastbone.

Turkeys

FRYER-ROASTER TURKEY

A fryer-roaster turkey is a young immature turkey (usually under 16 weeks of age), of either sex, that is tender-meated with soft, pliable, smooth-textured skin, and flexible breastbone cartilage.

YOUNG HEN TURKEY

A young hen turkey is a young female turkey (usually 5 to 7 months of age) that is tender-meated with soft, pliable, smooth-textured skin, and breastbone cartilage that is somewhat less flexible than a fryer-roaster turkey.

YOUNG TOM TURKEY

A young tom turkey is a young male turkey (usually 5 to 7 months of age) that is tender-meated with soft, pliable, smooth-textured skin, and breastbone cartilage that is somewhat less flexible than in a fryer-roaster turkey.

YEARLING HEN TURKEY

A yearling hen turkey is a fully matured female turkey (usually under 15 months of age) that is reasonably tender-meated and with reasonably smooth-textured skin.

YEARLING TOM TURKEY

A yearling tom turkey is a fully matured male turkey (usually under 15 months of age) that is reasonably tender-meated and with reasonably smooth-textured skin.

---

*Prepared from USDA's "Grading and Inspection of Poultry and Edible Products Thereof; and United States Classes, Standards, and Grades with Respect Thereto," July 1, 1960.

Mature Turkey (Hen or Tom)

A mature or old turkey is an old turkey of either sex (usually in excess of 15 months of age) with coarse skin and toughened flesh.

For labeling purposes, the designation of sex within the class name is optional and the three classes of young turkeys may be grouped and designated as "young turkeys."

Ducks

Broiler or Fryer Duckling

A broiler duckling or fryer duckling is a young duck (usually under 8 weeks of age), of either sex, that is tender-meated and has a soft bill and soft windpipe.

Roaster Duckling

A roaster duckling is a young duck (usually under 16 weeks of age), of either sex, that is tender-meated and has a bill that is not completely hardened and a windpipe that is easily dented.

Mature Duck

A mature duck or an old duck is a duck (usually over 6 months of age), of either sex, with toughened flesh, hardened bill, and hardened windpipe.

Geese

Young Goose

A young goose may be of either sex, is tender-meated, and has a windpipe that is easily dented.

Mature Goose

A mature goose or old goose may be of either sex and has toughened flesh and hardened windpipe.

Guineas

Young Guinea

A young guinea may be of either sex and is tender-meated.

Mature Guinea

A mature guinea or an old guinea may be of either sex and has toughened flesh.

Pigeons

Squab

A squab is a young, immature pigeon of either sex, and is extra tender-meated.

Pigeon

A pigeon is a mature pigeon of either sex, with coarse skin and toughened flesh.

---

structure, so purchasing larger birds gives a far greater yield. The accompanying table indicates the quantity of poultry to purchase for a specified number of portions.

(6) GRADE. Poultry is graded U. S. Grade A, B and C. Procurement grades are sometimes used by large quantity purchasers. These are Procurement I and II. Procurement grade standards are somewhat lower than the regular grades. These standards are based on conformation, fleshing, fat coverage, freedom from pinfeathers and vestigial feathers (that is, hair and down), freedom from cuts and tears, freedom from blemishes and bruises of the skin and flesh, freedom from broken or disjointed bones and the degree of freedom from freezer burn.

(7) BREED. Sometimes a buyer may wish to specify a breed of poultry. For instance, heavy chickens are best for meat purposes. Egg-laying breeds yield much less meat per pound of purchased weight. Beltsville turkeys are the broad-breasted type and give a much better yield than other types. Many buyers prefer the Emden or Chinese goose because of its

better appearance, although after cooking the Toulouse (gray) goose is as good and perhaps gives a slightly larger yield. Most ducks on the market are of the Peking breed, a white duck that grows rapidly and has a good yield of meat. A Rock Cornish hen may be a cross between a Cornish rooster and a white Plymouth Rock hen. The meat is quite light and tender.

(8) Pluck. Most poultry today is given a semi-scald and plucked by machine. However, some may be dry picked or wax picked. These methods give a superior appearance but do little to improve the eating quality.

Rabbits are classed as poultry and are sold under the same purchase factors.

Table 9-5

Quantities of Poultry Required per 100 Portions

Type	Type Cooking	Quantity/ 100
Chicken, broiler	Fry or broil	60-75 lb
Chicken, fryer	Fry or broil	60-75 lb
Chicken, stewing	Stew*	35-60 lb
Turkey	Roasting	50-75 lb
Turkey	Stewing*	35-60 lb
Duck or Goose	Roasting	75-100 lb

*The lower amounts would be used for chicken and noodles, turkey and noodles, creamed chicken or turkey, and chicken or turkey a la king, etc.

Fish Quality Controls

Unlike meat and poultry, fish is not required to be inspected and passed for wholesomeness. There are also no grades for fresh or frozen fish and shellfish except for a few processed items such as halibut steaks and fish sticks. Buyers must therefore be alert to note the quality and condition of products they purchase. Shellfish beds are required to be inspected by the U. S. Public Health Service before any shellfish can be taken from them. However, only original shipping containers must carry the approval number. Buyers should be sure that purveyors are selling products either in the original containers or that they come from beds that have been approved.

The fish markets are quite variable just as fresh produce markets are. The reason is that fish is not a product easily shipped, and markets have therefore tended to be set up for local use rather than for industry or national use. Also, the types of fish caught in various areas are quite different, and special marketing practices are used depending upon the type of fish offered. Thus, Chicago, the big fresh water market, has developed special marketing practices for fresh water fish. Seattle has specific practices for salmon and Boston for cod and sole. Seattle oyster sizes are not the same as those used in East Coast markets. Scrod, a small cod, will have various market sizes depending upon the variety of cod and the market in which it is docked.

The main fish markets which establish local practices are Boston, New York, Gulf ports (largely New Orleans and the shrimp ports), Chicago and Seattle. Other extremely important ones are Norfolk, Savannah, San Francisco, and Portland, Oregon. Anyone who wishes to do an adequate job of buying must learn the practices of the particular market in which he purchases.

Quality in fish is based largely on freshness. Fresh fish should have a firm flesh, scales should not loosen easily, the eyes should be bright and not sunken, the gills should have a bright appearance and the odor should be fresh and not smell of ammonia. Frozen fish should show no evidence of having thawed and then been refrozen. A slight brown edge may indicate this. Fish and shellfish can deteriorate rapidly under frozen storage, especially if the temperatures are not low enough and/or if they fluctuate too much.

LIVE SEAFOOD

Shellfish such as oysters, clams or mussels in the shell, crab, conches, lobsters, etc., may be purchased alive. Buyers should look for evidence of vitality or life such as the snap of a live lobster, tightly closed shells on clams or oysters, etc. Odor may also be an evidence of deterioration. A sharp ammonia smell is a rejection signal. Open shells of mollusks indicate death. Signs of life in a lobster—a moving eye, antenna, or claw—are simple to detect.

Shucked or shelled seafood items may be available. Oysters are frequently shucked. They should not be soaked in non-salted water—federal regulations frown on this—since oysters and other mollusks imbibe large amounts of fresh water and gain weight. Evidence of considerable moisture on shucked products should be cause for rejection. An acid smell indicates over age in shucked bivalves.

Shrimp may be sold shelled. These should have a white, translucent greenish cast. Buyers may specify that they be deveined and cooked. The odor should be sweet—not that of acid or ammonia. If shrimp is sold deveined, inspect it to see that an adequate job has been done.

Some shellfish are sold cooked, either in or out of the shell. Buyers should be sure these products had not deteriorated and been cooked in order to salvage them. The odor should be sweet and the taste of the flesh good. The fill of the flesh in the shell should be good. Some shellfish can be held so long that they starve, consuming their own flesh and becoming just fragments of the harvested product.

Cooked crab is frequently marketed as picked meat either fresh or frozen. Examine for odor, freedom from shells, etc. Also, examine cooked lobster, shrimp or crayfish in the same manner.

MERCHANDISE UNITS

Fish are sold on the market as whole or round (as they come from the sea), drawn (eviscerated), dressed (drawn with the head, tail, scales and fins removed)—trout may only be drawn and is called pan-dressed—as fillet (which may be boneless or not), sticks, steak (cross-section cuts), chunks or pieces.

The quantity of fish required for a portion varies considerably depending on how it is purchased. It takes around 30 pounds of fillet to give 100 portions of about four- to five-ounces each, 35 to 50 pounds of dressed fish to give 100 five- to six-ounce steaks, 50 to 75 pounds, if drawn, to give 100 five- to six-ounce steaks, and from 60 to 100 pounds if the fish is whole or round for the same number of five- to six-ounce steaks. To obtain 100 five-ounce portions of catfish in the round, one must have 165 pounds AP. Knowing the yield AS will help considerably in indicating what the real menu cost of a fish item is.

When shellfish are served by the count, a buyer can estimate fairly well how much to purchase. There are about 300 to 325 cherrystone clams per bushel and about 350 medium-size Bluepoint oysters.

Meat Purchasing Standards

Most meat today is inspected for wholesomeness. Approval by a state or federal inspector is shown as a round, red or other colored, stamp in which one will find imprinted "U. S. Insp'd & P'S'D" or U. S. Inspected and Passed by Department of Agriculture". A number in the circle indicates the official number of the establishment where the inspection occurred. Some boxes of meat may be labeled differently; for example, a tag may be attached indicating that the meat has been inspected and passed. Poultry and animals must pass an inspection before and after death to receive this approval. Unfit ones are condemned. Such meat may have to be destroyed but sometimes the meat can be sold if it is cooked.

Meat is also graded by federal and state inspectors. Conformation and quality are the two factors considered in grading. Finish, the amount of fat on a carcass, is no longer a factor in grading. Conformation relates to the amount of meat obtained in the major cuts. A bulky, blocky animal will usually rate high. Rangy, thin animals have a low yield and therefore are downgraded in conformation. Quality relates to the color of the flesh, the amount of marbling (the amount of flecks of fat in the flesh), the firmness of the flesh, condition of the bones, age of the animal, etc. Graders are allowed to trade off quality points to raise up the points given a carcass on conformation and

vice versa. Thus, if a carcass is a third of a grade off Choice grade in conformation but is a third higher than it needs to be otherwise, the extra points for quality can be added to the conformation points to make the carcass finally grade Choice. There are limits to such trade-offs.

The grading method for quality has changed considerably. Age is much less a factor than it was, and it is possible for an animal not meeting age standards still to be graded higher or lower if the flesh has specific quality characteristics. For instance, a calf just over a veal in age can be classed as a veal if its flesh has veal characteristics. Similarly, if an animal is in the age of veal but lacks flesh characteristics of veal, it must be classed as a calf.

Age and sex may be factors in grading. Thus, bulls, stags (males castrated after sexual maturity), and cows cannot qualify for Prime grade. However, heifers, steers and young bulls (bullocks) can. As these animals age, they may be discriminated against in grading. Usually a beef over 36 months old cannot qualify for Prime; similarly one over 42 months usually cannot qualify for Choice.

Separate grading standards may also be used for different sexes. A sow is not graded against the same standards as barrows (young or desexed male hogs) and gilts (young female hogs). Mature bulls have a separate grading standard from other beef. If young animals show definite sex characteristics, they may be dropped in grading.

Grades used in grading carcasses are shown in the panel on the facing page.

CLASS OR KIND	GRADES
Steers, heifers, bullocks	Prime, Choice, Good, Standard*, Commercial, Utility, Cutter, Canner
Bulls, stags and cows	Choice, Good, Commercial, Utility, Cutter, Canner
Calf and veal	Prime, Choice, Good, Standard, Utility, Cull
Lamb or yearling mutton	Prime, Choice, Good, Utility, Cull
Mutton (over a year old)	Choice, Good, Utility, Cull
Pork (barrows and gilts)	U. S. No. 1, 2 and 3

*Standard is usually reserved for young animals of Commercial grade. Thus, cows will never grade Standard because they are over age for this grade.

Weight of the carcass is sometimes considered in grading. A carcass must weigh a specific amount to qualify for a specific grade. Because cattle do not grow quite as large in our southern states as in our northern ones, graders may al low slightly lighter carcasses to qualify for a grade in the South than they would in the North.

QUANTITY & QUALITY

The amount of meat required to fill menu needs may be easy or difficult to calculate depending upon whether the items purchased are portion cut or are processed from wholesale or carcass units. Wide variability occurs in yields from wholesale or carcass meat as has been previously noted in the discussion of cost calculations.

The portion size times the number of portions gives the total quantity required. Thus, if a six-ounce hamburger patty is to be served and 65 are needed, the amount required is 24½ pounds (65 × 6 = 390 ÷ 16 = 24.375). Standardized recipes also are helpful in indicating quantities required. Standard lists of portions commonly served will indicate proper portion sizes. Good forecasting will be required. In addition, a buyer should know that meat shrinks in cooking. Thus, a roast may lose 35 per cent of its total weight in being cooked. It can lose five per cent more being cut into portions. Considering the loss in bones and fat, a final yield of only 40 per cent or less of the original weight can be expected.

Deciding what quality of meat to buy may also be a challenge. This must be decided by the production need. For some purposes a lower quality may be better than a higher one. U. S. Good or U. S. Standard gives leaner ground beef of better flavor than U. S. Choice. If meat is to be cooked by moist heat methods such as in pot roasting or stewing, it can be of a lower grade than if it is to be cooked by dry heat methods such as broiling or roasting. Thus, the preparation of the menu item decides the quality needed. Price and quality standards desired by the enterprise must also be considered in deciding quality.

After deciding the cut, the amount

Table 9-6

Market Terms for Meat Animals

BEEF

Steer	Male beef castrated before sexual maturity.
Stag	Male beef castrated after sexual maturity.
Bullock	Very young bull.
Bull	Mature beef of the male sex.
Cow	Female beef animal that has borne young.
Heifer	Female beef animal that has not borne young.
Calf	Beef of either sex that is older than three or five months.
Baby beef	Young beef of either sex about a year old or under—not officially recognized as a class in federal classifications.
Veal	Young beef of either sex under three to five months old.

PORK

Sow	Mature female hog, usually has borne young.
Boar	Mature male hog.
Stag	Mature male hog desexed after sexual maturity.
Barrow	Male hog that has not reached sexual maturity or has been castrated before reaching it.
Gilt	Young female hog that has not borne young.

LAMB & MUTTON

Lamb	Young sheep of either sex, usually under a year.
Yearling mutton	Young sheep of either sex about a year old.
Mutton	Sheep over a year old.
Ewe	Female sheep that has borne young.
Ram	Male sheep that has matured sexually.

and the quality, a buyer can enter the market and seek out his product. It is also highly important to see that what has been specified, has been received. Good receiving methods require that the weight of the meat delivered be verified and that the quality and the cut be as specified. All meat should be weighed in and the weight recorded on the receiving sheet. The recever should be able to recognize quality and type of cut. This takes experience and knowledge and a janitor, cook or someone else without experience cannot do this. There are narrow demarcations between the grades of meat and only a knowledgeable person will know them. Meat cuts are best recognized when one knows the bone and muscle structure and the shape of the basic cuts.

MEAT SPECIFICATIONS

Most meat is purchased on the basis of the USDA's Institutional Meat Purchase Specifications. These have the approval and strong sponsorship of the National Institute of Meat Purveyors. The IMPS is a detailed list of specifications indicating precisely how various wholesale and portion cuts are to be made. Each specification carries a number. For instance, beef wholesale cuts are all in the 100 numbers and portion cuts in the 1100 numbers. Lamb and mutton are in the 200 and 1200 series, etc. Besides these, fresh and frozen pork (400), cured, cooked and smoked pork (500) calf and veal (300), sausages, cured, dried and smoked beef (800), and edible by-products such as liver, tongue and sweetbreads (700) are covered. Buyers can quickly and simply specify a meat cut without writing a great deal in the specifications by just giving the specification number. For instance, a No. 109 rib will come ready to be put into the oven, with the scapula blade, the muscle over it and the tendinous portion below it removed and the fat cover taken off and then tied back on. Similarly, stating that No. 1180 is desired, a buyer indicates that a shortcut strip steak must be delivered processed in the manner outlined in the IMPS.

In addition to listing the number, it is desirable that a buyer indicate the range or the weight classification of the carcass. For instance, beef has five ranges, Range A for carcasses from 500 to 600 pounds, Range B for carcasses 600 to 700 pounds, Range C for carcasses from 700 to 800 pounds, Range D for carcasses from 800 to 900 pounds and Range E for carcasses over 900 pounds. The weight of the individual cuts coming from animals within these ranges will vary as do the carcasses. No tolerance should be allowed over or under these weights. For portion cuts, the exact weight in ounces or pounds should be specified. There is usually some tolerance permitted over and under the specified weight. Buyers should know what ranges of weight and tolerances are permitted over or under for portion, wholesale and carcass units.

A buyer should specify what aging the meat should have. Some buyers also indicate that only steer beef is acceptable or that the beef must be Black Angus, etc. The specification must also list whether the meat is to be frozen or unfrozen.

Because a buyer uses an IMPS does not mean that he cannot write in a special requirement. Thus, on a No. 109

rib a buyer may wish a shorter cut (less distance from the plate end to the eye of the meat in the rib) and he can specify this. Otherwise, the remainder of the requirements stay the same as in the IMPS.

Copies of the Institutional Meat Purchase Specifications can be obtained by writing to the Superintendent of Public Documents, Washington, D. C. The National Meat Purveyors Association in Chicago has published brochures summarizing these specifications along with colored prints of the cuts themselves so that buyers will know what they are getting. Probably no greater change has occurred in quantity buying, nor standardization been better advanced than through the use of these IMPS.

Another type of federal grading has been established. This is grade by yield. Meat that has a high yield may be graded Yield 1; if the yield is good but not excellent, the grade is Yield 2. Yield 3 is a fair yield, Yield 4 is lacking in yield, and Yield 5 is a poor yield. However, it is largely employed in the retail trade for which it was originally established, and not significantly in institutional purchasing since buyers in the latter category can specify the depth and range of fat, etc., in their meat procurement.

PURCHASING PROCEDURES

Purchasing is not simply a matter of deciding what, when and how much to buy; it entails further effort in accounting for the food and supplies purchased, and this means considerable record-keeping. The required item must first be *requested* by the using unit. If it is not available from stores on hand, additional steps must be taken: the item must be *purchased;* it must be *received,* and, finally, it must be *delivered,* directly to the user, or placed in inventory. The interaction amongst these functions should be well organized, and simplified as much as possible. Management should scrutinize the system to see if any procedure can be streamlined or eliminated. However, control must not be lost in simplification. The system has to provide an adequate flow of information for good accountability. These four steps in the classical procurement process—requisitioning, purchasing, receiving and delivery—can be divided for study into internal and external transactions.

REQUISITION

Internal transactions revolve around the original ordering of needs, and the receiving and delivery which can be either direct or to storage areas. Some forms used for these transactions are shown in the preceding figures. Original orders are usually closed by requisition, which is a list of needs. Requisitions can be prepared for withdrawal of items from inventory. They may also be used for inter-departmental or section transactions. Dining areas may have to inform the main production kitchen of their requirements and, in turn, the kitchen may have to prepare requisitions to storage units to meet these needs. At times there may be a return

HYATT HOUSE HOTELS

PURCHASE ORDER NO. 45845

REQ. NO. ____________

DATE ____________ 19 ____

SHIP TO

FOR	DATE REQUIRED	HOW SHIP	F.O.B.

	QUANTITY	PLEASE SUPPLY ITEMS LISTED BELOW	PRICE	UNIT
1				
2				
3		VOID		
4		SAMPLE ONLY		
5				
6				
7				
8				

☐ CAPITAL EXPENDITURE ☐ OTHER ____________

☐ CONFIRMING ORDER – DO NOT DUPLICATE

IMPORTANT
OUR ORDER NUMBER MUST APPEAR ON ALL INVOICES, PACKAGES, ETC.
PLEASE NOTIFY US IMMEDIATELY IF YOU ARE UNABLE TO SHIP COMPLETE ORDER BY DATE SPECIFIED.

PLEASE SEND COPIES OF YOUR INVOICE WITH ORIGINAL BILL OF LADING

PURCHASE AGENT

1780 Hyatt Press - Form 106 Rev. 2/72

FIG. 9-10
Example of a purchase order indicating the account to which a charge is made. Copies of the order sent to a vendor go to the originating department, the general manager, storeroom, receiving, and to file. (Courtesy the Hyatt Corporation)

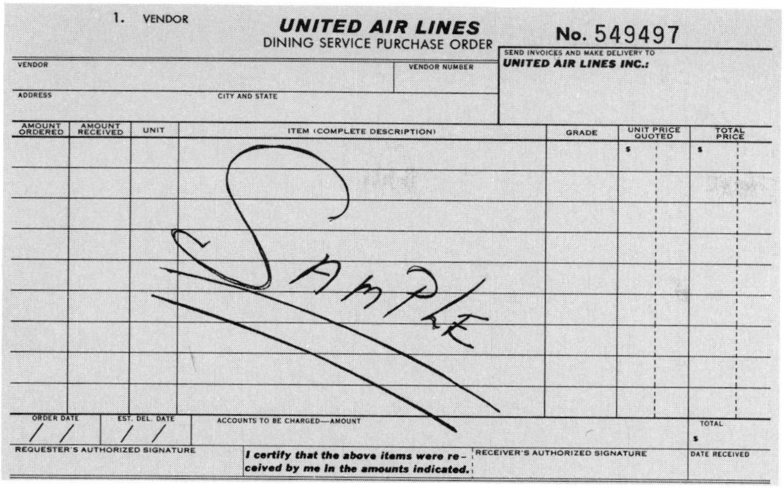

1. VENDOR

UNITED AIR LINES
DINING SERVICE PURCHASE ORDER

No. 549497

SEND INVOICES AND MAKE DELIVERY TO
UNITED AIR LINES INC.:

VENDOR		VENDOR NUMBER
ADDRESS	CITY AND STATE	

AMOUNT ORDERED	AMOUNT RECEIVED	UNIT	ITEM (COMPLETE DESCRIPTION)	GRADE	UNIT PRICE QUOTED	TOTAL PRICE
					$	$

SAMPLE

ORDER DATE	EST. DEL. DATE	ACCOUNTS TO BE CHARGED—AMOUNT	TOTAL
/ /	/ /		$

REQUESTER'S AUTHORIZED SIGNATURE

I certify that the above items were received by me in the amounts indicated.

RECEIVER'S AUTHORIZED SIGNATURE

DATE RECEIVED

FIG. 9-11
Note that purchase orders carry their own number, and this must usually appear on all invoices, packages and shipping papers so they can be readily identified with the order. (Courtesy United Air Lines)

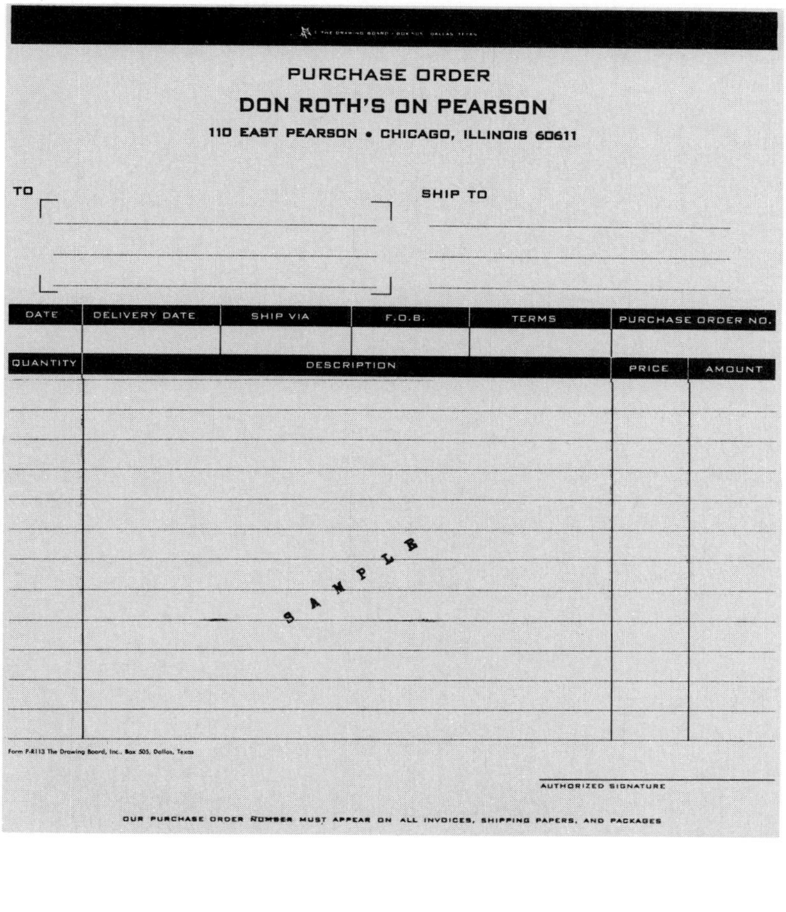

PURCHASE ORDER
DON ROTH'S ON PEARSON
110 EAST PEARSON • CHICAGO, ILLINOIS 60611

TO

SHIP TO

DATE	DELIVERY DATE	SHIP VIA	F.O.B.	TERMS	PURCHASE ORDER NO.

QUANTITY	DESCRIPTION	PRICE	AMOUNT
	SAMPLE		

Form P-8113 The Drawing Board, Inc., Box 505, Dallas, Texas

AUTHORIZED SIGNATURE

OUR PURCHASE ORDER NUMBER MUST APPEAR ON ALL INVOICES, SHIPPING PAPERS, AND PACKAGES

FIG. 9-12
A purchase order used for ordering supplies and foods. Note the amount of information given to the purveyor. Some purchase orders require that a copy be returned to the buyer signed by a responsible person in the purveyor's office. (Courtesy Don Roth, Blackhawk Restaurants, Chicago)

CANTEEN CORPORATION

DAILY ORDER AND RECEIVING RECORD

FOR THE _____ PERIOD _____

(OPERATION STAMP)

QUOTE FROM AND PRICE				ITEM DESCRIPTION	SUPPLIER ITEM CODE	DATE ORDERED	QUAN. ON HAND	QUAN. ORDERED	PERIOD REFERENCE NUMBER	RECEIVED		DATE INVOICE PROC.	REMARKS
FROM	UNIT PRICE	FROM	UNIT PRICE							DATE	QUAN.		

FORM NO. 1858 (REV. 2-68) PRINTED IN U.S.A.

FIG. 9-13 A purchase record that provides quote information and serves as a receiving document. (Courtesy Canteen Corporation)

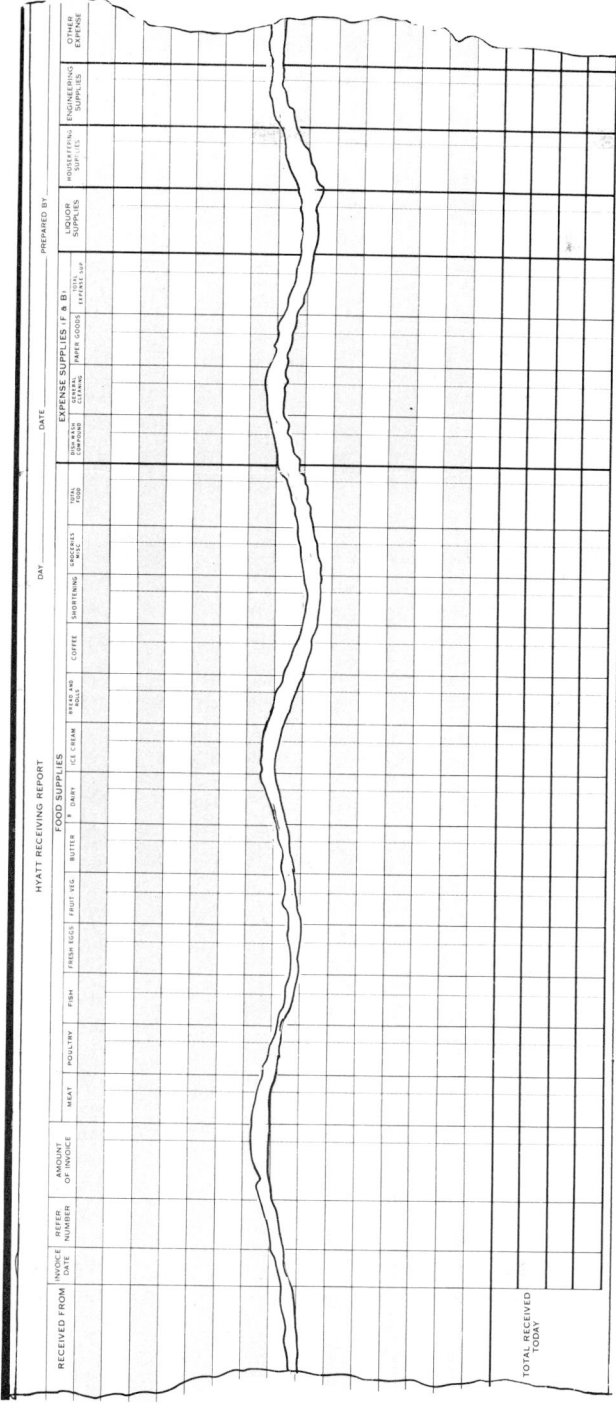

FIG. 9-14 A form (shown in part) that serves as a receiving record for various categories of purchases: foods, supplies, liquors, etc. (Courtesy Hyatt Corporation)

of items, and some system should be devised to show the credit. Many satellite operations today must order from central commissaries. These as well as other requisitions should be prepared sufficiently in advance to make it possible to deliver the items on time.

Some systems use automatic data processing to organize and simplify the internal transactions. For instance, a satellite may mark on a card with a sensitizing pencil the items and amounts required. This is transferred to the central commissary where the order goes into the data process. It is now a simple procedure to consolidate orders, calculate ingredients and other items required, set up orders, establish production and delivery schedules, prepare billings, etc.

It is desirable to establish some system by which the receipt of items asked for by requisition be acknowledged by the receiving activity. This can be a signed copy of the original requisition. Some provision for substitutions, shortages, etc., should also be set up if the delivery varies from the original requisition. The accounting department will use requisitions to record internal transfers and other accounting data.

PURCHASE & RECEIPT

Requisitions may be the basis for setting up a purchase order, that is, a request from the establishment to a purveyor. Or they may be the basis for informal purchasing, such as calling various purveyors for quotations and then deciding which one gets the order. Frequently a call sheet or quotation and order sheet is used for this. A formal system of purchasing may involve bids. In this case, the list of requirements is prepared, specifications are written and purveyors prepare quotations for examination at a set time. Awards are made on the basis of these quotations. Ordering is considered an external transaction for at this point, the transaction moves outside the establishment.

Only responsible individuals of the enterprise should be allowed to sign requisitions and purchase orders. A pur-

---

HYATT HOTELS

RETURNED MERCHANDISE OR SHORTAGE REPORT

Name of Supplier _____ Invoice # _____

Amount of Correction _____

Reason _____

_____

_____

_____

Date _____ Deliveryman's Signature _____

By _____ Company _____

FIG. 9-15
Returned items and items short on delivery should be recorded. Forms such as this should be issued in multiple copies — one retained by the receiving department, one by accounting, and one sent to the purveyor. Additional copies may be required for kitchen records or other purposes. (Courtesy Hyatt Corporation)

L I N E	SUPPLIER		PERIOD REFERENCE NUMBER	INVOICE DATA			Meat Fish Fowl 4110714	Dairy 4110722
	NAME	CODE		DATE	NUMBER	AMOUNT		
1								
2								
3								
4								
5								
6								
7								
8								
9								
10								
11								
12								
13								
14								
15								
16								
17								
18								
19								
20								
21								
22								
23								

DATE PREPARED

CANTEEN CORPORATION
DAILY PURCHASE RECORD

PERIOD   OPERATION   PAGE

FINAL FOR PERIOD ☐ _____ MANAGER'S SIGNATURE _____   **TOTAL**

FORM NO. 1861 (REV. 6—73) PRINTED IN U.S.A.

FIG. 9-16   A daily purchase and receiving record which also can serve as a quotation sheet. Combining control forms in this manner simplifies the system and also reduces the amount of copying from one sheet to another. (Courtesy Canteen Corporation)

chase order may not be a legal document unless the person signing it has significant authority in the operation, and again it may not be legal unless some equally responsible person signs the purchase order indicating acceptance by the supplier. Many purchase orders include a copy which is to be used for this purpose. This copy is returned to the originator.

Receiving is both an internal and external transaction. Goods are delivered by the various purveyors to the establishment ordering them. They should be accompanied by proper invoices, shipping papers, etc. The purpose of receiving is to acknowledge receipt of the items and to check to see that they meet specifications. Any discrepancies should be noted. It is important that the records prepared by the receiver give the accounting department the desired information. The security of items until they are delivered may also be the responsibility of the receiving department. The system should also provide for acknowledgement of items by the receiving unit or individual when the delivery is made.

INVENTORY CONTROL

The last step, inventorying, is an internal transaction. Keeping inventories has a two-fold purpose. The first is to provide information about what is on hand, and the second is to provide information on its value. Usually, minimum and maximum inventory quantities are established. When the quantities reach the minimum amount, a purchase order is prepared to bring inventory up to the desired level. Requisitions usually withdraw items from inventory. This completes a full circle of functions and starts the purchasing cycle all over again.

Some inventories must be taken daily, as of quantities of food on hand in the kitchen, or bar supplies available. This inventory form may also be used as a requisition to bring items up to a par level. It is important that management establish good policies and procedures for the taking of inventories. Often, two individuals are assigned to participate, one of whom comes from the accounting department. The inventories must be signed by those taking them.

There are two main kinds of inventories: perpetual and physical. A perpetual inventory is derived solely from records, such as delivery reports indicating what items have been received and put into storage, and from requisitions indicating what items have been withdrawn from storage. Some operations use a slightly different system for meats. When a meat order is received, it is tagged with the proper receiving information indicating the weight, the value and the name of the item. A copy of this record is used to indicate on the perpetual inventory that this item is on hand. When the item is withdrawn from storage for use, the tag is taken off and sent through proper channels, and the item deducted from the perpetual inventory. The food and beverage department or the accounting division may maintain perpetual inventories.

A physical inventory is an actual count of items on hand. It is not made up from records. Normally, the value of items on inventories is an average cost. Some operations may use the last price in; others may use an established price. Discrepancies between the perpetual in-

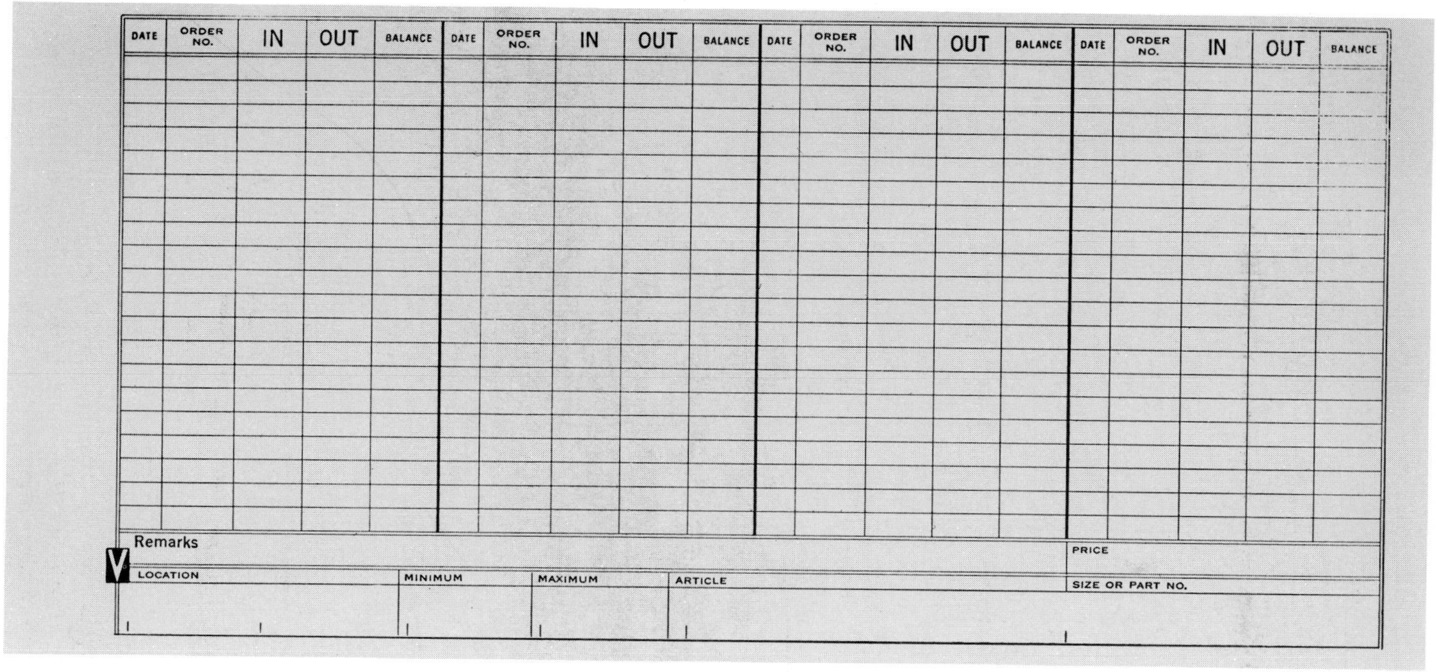

DATE	ORDER NO.	IN	OUT	BALANCE	DATE	ORDER NO.	IN	OUT	BALANCE	DATE	ORDER NO.	IN	OUT	BALANCE	DATE	ORDER NO.	IN	OUT	BALANCE

Remarks

PRICE

LOCATION

MINIMUM

MAXIMUM

ARTICLE

SIZE OR PART NO.

FIG. 9-17 A perpetual inventory is a record of items in inventory less those requisitioned out. Thus, if there are 534 of an item on hand and 124 are requisitioned out, the balance will show 410. If 50 more on order come in, the balance will then be 460. The perpetual inventory is maintained usually in the accounting office from information on purchase orders, receiving sheets, invoices, etc., for incoming items; and from requisitions or withdrawal slips for outgoing items.

ITEM NO.	DATE: DAY:	KITCHEN	COOLER	TOTAL	ISSUES
1	Sirloin Steaks − 16 oz				
2	Sirloin Steaks − 12 oz				
3	Sirloin − Bone in − 12 oz				
4	Filet Mignon − 9 oz				
5	Filet Mignon − 6 oz				
6	Butt Steaks − 10 oz				
7	Sirloin Steaks − 8 oz				
8	Ribs − Heavy Each				
9	Top Rounds Each				
10	Beef Strips Each				
11	Corned Beef Briskets Each				
12	Beef Rounds Each				
13	Chopped Beef Lb.				
14	Chopped Beef Patties Box				
15	Lamb Chops − 8 oz				
16	Pork Chops − 8 oz				
17	Salt Pork Lb.				
18	Calves Liver Lb.				
19	Chickens Halves				
20	Bacon Lb.				
21	Bacon, Canadian Lb.				
22	Knuckles				
23	Frankfurters 4/1 lb.				
24	Beef Tongues Each				
25	Hams, Smoked Each				
26	Hams, Boiled Each				
27	Turkey Rolls Each				
28	Chicken Livers Lb.				
29	Herring				
30	Lobster Tails − 16 oz				
31	Lobster Tails − 8 oz				
32	Shrimps Lb.				
33	Shrimps − Breaded Lb.				
34	White Fish Lb.				
35	Scallops Lb.				
36	London Broil				
37	Halibut Lb.				
38	Crabmeat				
39	Fowl Breasts				
40	Dover Sole				

FIG. 9-18 This sheet provides useful inventory information plus data on the amount of issues. (Courtesy Blackhawk Restaurants, Chicago)

HYATT HOTELS BAR REQUISITION

5311 Central Printing 10/73

ITEM	Unit	ORDER	SHIP	UNIT COST PRICE	AMOUNT	ITEM	Unit	ORDER	SHIP	UNIT COST PRICE	AMOUNT
STRAIGHT						**SCOTCH (Continued)**					
Ancient Age	Q					Peter Dawson	Q				
Ancient Age						Peter Dawson					
Jim Beam	Q					Teacher's	Q				
Jim Beam						White Horse	Q				
Jack Daniel's Black	Q										
Jack Daniel's Black											
Jack Daniel's Green	Q										
Early Times	Q										
Early Times											
I. W. Harper	Q										
I. W. Harper											
Old Charter	Q										
Old Crow	Q										
Old Fitzgerald	Q										
Old Forester	Q					**GIN**					
Old Grand Dad	Q					Beefeater	Q				
Old Taylor	Q					Beefeater					
Walker Deluxe	Q					Bombay	Q				
Wild Turkey	Q					Calvert's	Q				
Yellowstone	Q					Fleishmann's	Q				
						Gilbey's	Q				
						Gordon's	Q				
						Gordon's					
						Plymouth	Q				
						Schenley	Q				
						Schenley					
						Tanqueray	Q				
						Tanqueray					
BOTTLED IN BOND											
I. W. Harper	Q										
Old Forester	Q										
						VODKA					
						Gordon's	Q				
RYE						Schenley	Q				
Old Overholt	Q					Schenley					
						Smirnoff	Q				
						Smirnoff					
						Wolfschmidt	Q				
BLENDED						Wolfschmidt					
Schenley Reserve	Q										
Seagram's 7 Crown	Q										
CANADIAN						**COGNAC**					
Canadian Club	Q					Courvoisier V.S.	5				
Canadian Club						Hennessey	Q				
Seagram's Crown Royal	Q					Martel	Q				
Seagram's V.O.	Q					Martel Cordon Blue	5				
Seagram's V.O.						Remy Martin VSOP	5				
Schenley O.F.C.	Q					Metaxa	5				
						Otard Special	Q				
IRISH											
Bushmill	5					**BRANDY**					
John Jameson	5					Christian Brothers	Q				
						Korbel	Q				
						Paul Masson	Q				
SCOTCH						Speas Apple	5				
Ballantine	Q					Apricot	Q				
Black & White	Q					Blackberry	Q				
Chivas Regal	Q					Cherry	Q				
Chivas Regal						Peach	Q				
Cutty Sark	Q										
Cutty Sark											
Dewar's White Label	Q										
Dewar's White Label											
Grant's 8	Q					**RUM**					
Haig	Q					Bacardi Dark	Q				
Haig Pinch	Q					Bacardi Dark					
J & B	Q					Bacardi Light	Q				
J & B						Bacardi Light					
Johnny Walker Black	Q					Meyers	Q				
Johnny Walker Black						Ron Rico Dark	Q				
Johnny Walker Red	Q					Ron Rico Dark					
Johnny Walker Red						Ron Rico Light	Q				

Req. by	Filled by		Del. by	Rec'd by	Ext. Ck. by	Unit No.	Day	Date

FIG. 9-19

First of a two-sheet inventory and requisition form for alcoholic beverages. (Courtesy Hyatt Corporation)

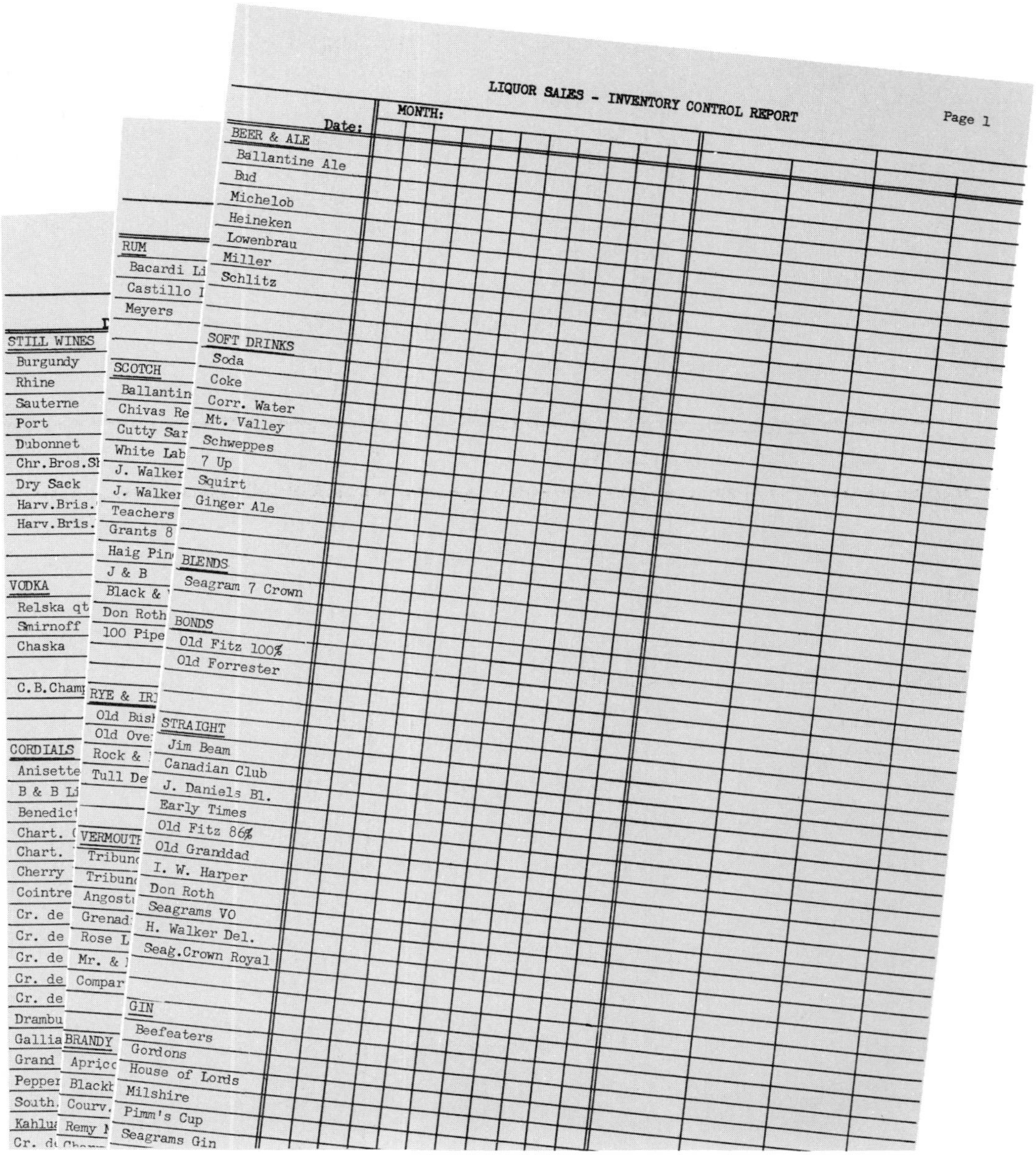

LIQUOR SALES - INVENTORY CONTROL REPORT   Page 1

MONTH:

Date:

BEER & ALE
Ballantine Ale
Bud
Michelob
Heineken
Lowenbrau
Miller
Schlitz

SOFT DRINKS
Soda
Coke
Corr. Water
Mt. Valley
Schweppes
7 Up
Squirt
Ginger Ale

BLENDS
Seagram 7 Crown

BONDS
Old Fitz 100%
Old Forrester

STRAIGHT
Jim Beam
Canadian Club
J. Daniels Bl.
Early Times
Old Fitz 86%
Old Grandad
I. W. Harper
Don Roth
Seagrams VO
H. Walker Del.
Seag.Crown Royal

GIN
Beefeaters
Gordons
House of Lords
Milshire
Pimm's Cup
Seagrams Gin

RUM
Bacardi Li
Castillo
Meyers

SCOTCH
Ballantin
Chivas Re
Cutty Sar
White Lab
J. Walker
J. Walker
Teachers
Grants 8
Haig Pin
J & B
Black &
Don Roth
100 Pipe

RYE & IR
Old Bus
Old Ove
Rock &
Tull De

VERMOUTH
Tribun
Tribun
Angost
Grenad
Rose I
Mr. &
Compar

BRANDY
Apric
Black
Courv.
Remy

STILL WINES
Burgundy
Rhine
Sauterne
Port
Dubonnet
Chr.Bros.S
Dry Sack
Harv.Bris.
Harv.Bris.

VODKA
Relska qt
Smirnoff
Chaska

C.B.Champ

CORDIALS
Anisette
B & B Li
Benedict
Chart.
Chart.
Cherry
Cointre
Cr. de
Cr. de
Cr. de
Cr. de
Cr. de
Drambu
Gallia
Grand
Pepper
South.
Kahlu
Cr. d

FIG. 9-20 Liquor inventories must be taken frequently, usually daily. This form, in three pages, is simple but gives a continuous inventory record. Some operations require that the individual or individuals preparing the record sign it. (Courtesy Don Roth Blackhawk Restaurants, Chicago)

ventory and the physical inventory should be checked. The amount on hand indicated by the perpetual inventory should tally with the actual physical count. The security of inventory spaces should be sufficient to protect these assets.

To facilitate the taking of the physical inventory, the order of items on the inventory sheet follows that of the location of items in the storeroom. Systems can be devised so that counts can be taken rapidly and accurately. Some experience and knowledge are required to take a good inventory. Those taking the inventory must, for example, know the various can sizes and package quantities to obtain accurate data.

CHAPTER 10

The Menu and Production

Menu writing and food production are mutually dependent. The success of the menu depends very much upon how well the production system interprets what the menu offers. Conversely, successful production depends upon how completely and accurately the menu itself is prepared, just as it depends upon the performance of the purchasing system in providing the right materials at the right time.

If the menu properly considers the limitations and assets of the production department in layout, equipment and personnel, there should be adequate performance to achieve what is desired. Additionally, adequate forecasts, recipe preparation and portioning information must be provided so that the production department knows quantities, methods and times to prepare the items. Co-ordination between service, management, purchasing and other departments of the operation is essential. A failure to co-ordinate properly can cause the production department to fail to meet the menu's needs. It is necessary for management to study the system of production

used and develop the flow of information required. Forecasts must be accompanied by proper purchase quantities, and the production department needs to know how much and when foods are to come. For itself, the production department should also be advised of menu requirements so that personnel can be properly scheduled. The department must also establish planned procedures so that items are produced in the proper quantity and proper quality when they are required.

Management should see to it that the production department knows precisely what is meant when items are put on the menu. A menu item should be worked out in precise detail as to ingredients required, their amounts and the procedures used to produce the item. Too frequently, management puts an item on the menu and then allows employees free rein on the interpretation. Recipes should be used and controls established to produce exactly the same item each time it is offered to a guest. Costs should be accurately known. The most successful enterprises are those which establish good information flow so the production department knows what is to be done and how to do it. A failure of management to see that the production department is informed, and is able to perform as expected, brings about a menu failure. Too often management puts items on a menu without adequate planning as to what should result, the cost of the item, and also customer acceptance. Management may leave the performance up to others who are not adequately informed. Because of this, the work may be haphazard and the product frequently disappointing.

It is sometimes said that a menu promises and the production department reneges. There should be a complete understanding between the planner, the patron and the food production department on what is promised in the menu. A toasted sandwich should be made with toast, not bread that is browned on a griddle on both sides—this latter is a "grilled" sandwich. A consommé is not a bouillon or rich broth but a special soup produced by specific methods from specific ingredients. When a menu says the steaks come from prime beef, this means the beef grades prime and not some other grade. A bisque is a cream soup flavored with shellfish, yet one national company producing canned soups says it has a "tomato bisque," which is a false declaration. Every menu planner should be sure of the terms he uses and what they mean when they are put on the menu. Too much license in the use of terms is frequently taken in writing menus. Selecting words to describe a food and give it glamour must be done carefully. To try to make a curry sound more exotic by calling it

"Curry of Chicken, Bombay" without undertaking to use the typical ingredients that a curry from Bombay, India, would have, is to be discouraged. The right curry seasoning, accompaniments (especially the small dried fish called Bombay duck) and other factors should be there. Today too much ignorance exists on what menu terms mean, and menu planners would do well to consult an authoritative menu dictionary and use the proper terms to describe items on the menu. Certain terms mean *specific* things and their misuse is to be condemned.

Each item on the menu should be thoroughly tested and standardized so the food production department can produce the item desired. Recipes must be complete, precise and carefully followed. Figures 10-1 and 10-2 show examples of recipe forms used. A wide variance in quality, portion size or appearance can bring about dissatisfied customers. Service personnel should check foods they receive and, if they are not correct, call the attention of food production supervisors to this fact.

Foods should be prepared at the proper time. Some can be prepared ahead and often are better if they are. Others should be prepared as close to service as possible. Foods that stand too long lose culinary and nutritional quality, and may become unsafe. Production schedules can help to indicate the amount of food required and the times it should be ready for service. Checks should be made to see how much is left over after the service period. Run-out times should be noted.

Good organization is required of supporting units. Thus, the butcher shop

STANDARD RECIPE CARD

Number_____

Recipe For_____ Restaurant_____ Date_____

Portion Size_____ Meal Period_____ Number Portions_____

| INGREDIENT | WEIGHT | COST PRICE | | | INGREDIENT | WEIGHT | COST PRICE | | |
		Pur. Unit	Per Unit	Ingredient			Pur. Unit	Per Unit	Ingredient

Cost Per Portion _____

Menu Price _____

Food Cost _____

FORM 312

FIG. 10-1 This menu card is designed to indicate production information considered important to management and supervisors in the food production department. It gives a quick check on the cost of an item but it lacks directions which some foodservice personnel may need to produce the item. (Courtesy Hyatt Corporation)

CARROT TIMBALES

Q. VEGETABLES No. 57
Issue 5

YIELD: 2 Roasting Pans 17 by 26 Inches or 100 Portions   EACH PORTION: ½ Cup

INGREDIENTS	WEIGHTS	MEASURES	PORTIONS	METHOD
Carrots, chopped, E.P.	8 lb.			1. Cook carrots in boiling salted water about 15 minutes. Drain.
Water, hot		½ gal.		
Salt	1½ oz.	3 tbsp.		
Milk, liquid		3 qt.		2. Mix all ingredients. Pour into 2 roasting pans.
Eggs, beaten, whole	3½ lb.	35 eggs (1¾ qt.)		3. Bake (325° F.) 40 minutes or until soft.
Onion, minced	1½ oz.	4 tbsp.		4. Take out about 10 minutes before serving. Serve with 1 gallon medium white sauce (Recipe Card O–13), or bechamel sauce (Recipe Card O–14), and crisp fried bacon.
Pepper, red		¼ tsp.		
Crumbs, bread, soft	6 oz.	1 qt.		

NOTE: 10½ lb. of carrots A.P. will yield 8 lb. E.P.

FIG. 10-2 A form often used by institutions for a standardized recipe. It gives precise information to operating personnel producing the item. It is designed to serve 100 portions, and the portion size is indicated as well as the total yield. (Courtesy U. S. Navy Recipe Service)

LEFTOVER REPORT

DATE: _____

EXECUTIVE SUITE		OLD FRONTIER		MAIN KITCHEN	
Item	Quantity	Item	Quantity	Item	Quantity
Prime Rib		B		Prime Rib	
Corned Beef		Corned Beef		Corned Beef	
Cooked Burgers		A		Cooked Burgers	
Schrod		Special		Schrod	
Special		B-B-Q. Beef		Special	
Veg. ( )		Mashed Pot.		Special	
Veg. ( )		Schrod		Veg. ( )	
Boiled Pot.		French Fries		Veg. ( )	
Mashed Pot.		Cole Slaw		Boiled Pot.	
French Fries		Chef's Salad		Mashed Pot.	
B.H. Sauce		Cottage Cheese		French Fries	
Cole Slaw		35		B.H. Sauce	
Cottage Cheese		34A: 1) Ham		Chef's Salad	
Chef's Salad		2) Turkey		Cottage Cheese	
		3) Salami		Cole Slaw	
		4) Cheese		Hollywood	
		Fruit Plate		New Orleans	
				Symphony	
COMMENTS:		COMMENTS:		COMMENTS:	

Time: _____   Time: _____   Time: _____

FIG. 10-3   Overproduction can be a significant factor in increasing food costs. It also can result in lowered quality, since it is often difficult to maintain as high a quality in reworked foods as in fresh products. Regularly kept, a record like the one shown here can provide valuable help to production personnel in estimating the quantities that will be needed. (Courtesy Don Roth Black Hawk Restaurants, Chicago)

should have items on hand as they are needed. The vegetable preparation section should be informed as to the amounts of vegetables required and have these ready at proper times. Purchasing obviously must be sufficiently in advance to allow proper preparation. Guests dislike to select an item from the menu and then find that it is "out". There is also a certain amount of get-ready or *mise en place* work to be done in the production operation. Stocks need to be made in advance as well as sauces and other preparations. Long before service begins a check should be made to see that supplies and foods required are on hand for customer demand. Good organization in these matters will make the meal time rush go a lot smoother and promote high-quality production.

Workers should completely understand what the menu indicates will be served, and the food production department should attempt to achieve this goal. Some time spent with the food production staff, showing what is intended by the menu as written, may help them to give patrons the feeling that they have been well served—a desirable situation.

Food Production Personnel

The personnel working in food production should be capable of producing what the menu lists. If not, the menu should be changed. Wide variety is found in menu items. If the operation is a drive-in serving only a limited menu, the skill, abilities and knowledge of the food production personnel may be limited to the making of a few simple items. Nevertheless, they should all have the ability to produce high-quality items. If

they do not, management should replace them with capable personnel or else establish a training program to bring the level of competency up to that required.

It is essential that food production people know enough about production principles to understand what is happening when they prepare foods. A worker may know from experience that a steak or hamburger changes color when subjected to heat, and that it becomes slightly more firm and less moist. However, if he understands further the reasons for these phenomena—how in the food production task some of the more desirable changes can be encouraged and some of the less desirable ones retarded—better-quality items will be produced because the employee now understands what is happening. Teaching employees the "why" is frequently required to have adequate performance. A manager who tries to discourage an employee from cooking hamburgers too far in advance of service may not be able to prevent the practice until the employee learns how heat and extended holding affect the shrink and moisture loss in meat. Knowing this, he then knows why management might wish to have hamburgers cooked as close to service time as possible. An employee might think that egg cookery is a simple procedure and therefore produce breakfast egg orders of indifferent or even poor quality. However, if he knows something about the complex chemical and physical reactions in the cooking of an egg, he will have a far greater respect for the work he is doing and produce better results. Often the reason employees produce foods of poor quality is that they have

PRODUCTION SHEET

DAY _____ DATE _____

AMOUNT	• ITEM •	LOCATION	TEMP.	TIME	REMARKS
	• REHEATS •				
					EMPLOYEES' CAFETERIA
	• VEGETABLES •				
	CASES OF SPINACH				
	PANS OF BAK-ING POTATOES				

AMOUNT OF RIBS LEFT: _____ • OUT AT • _____

BAKED POTATOES LEFT: _____

AMOUNT GREENS LEFT: _____

AMOUNT OF SPINACH LEFT: _____

GREENS IN WALK-IN ICED: _____

FISH PROPERLY ICED: _____

STOCKPOTS CHECKED (SIMMER): _____

TOTAL NUMBER OF DINNERS: _____

GENERAL REMARKS: _____

_____

_____

FIG. 10-4   The above tally provides production guidance as well as a record of quantities on hand. It also gives information on run-outs. With such data, management can make better estimations of quantities to be produced. (Courtesy Don Roth Blackhawk Restaurants, Chicago)

little knowledge of what they are doing and lack a respect for the task of preparing that food. Excellent courses of study exist which will give employees the basic information required to produce high-quality foods and help them develop skills on the job.

Personnel organization should be highly functional and lead to good management practices. In many operations, a chef may be in charge, with assistants—called *chefs du partie* in continental kitchen organizations—working under him. In other institutions, a food production manager may be in charge, with head cooks taking direction from him. Whatever the organization, it should lead to efficient, smooth production of high-quality menu items. Those in charge should constantly seek to develop high standards of performance in staff members. "Building pictures in the minds of employees" of what good food looks like is one way of having employees know what they should be producing. The organization should ensure that workers are adequately supervised and are assisted when they need help from their superiors. Adequate pre-planning should occur so that the work progresses smoothly and employees know what they are to do, how much food to produce and when.

Food Production Systems

For many years the foodservice industry has consisted of operations that produce food on the premises upon the demand of customers. This is changing. Service units are still located at the point where customers are most likely to require food, and service still caters to the customers' demand, but the foods are now often produced in food production centers a considerable distance away from the service point. In such cases, menu items may have to be those that will permit preparation ahead of time and be of high quality upon reconditioning or rethermalization. Where items cannot be produced in such a center and then transported to and later prepared at the satellite unit, a dual type menu may be prepared with some items still prepared on the premises from "scratch" while others which respond to centralized handling and treatment are prepared at the production center.

The reasons for producing food in a central unit may vary. In some cases, the scarcity of skilled employees required to produce items on the premises makes it necessary to establish central production centers and then staff the satellite service areas with workers who do not need to have a high degree of skill to serve the food. In other instances, the reason may be reduction of costs, the control of production, etc.

Convenience Foods

There are many new market forms of foods available that are almost ready for service except for some slight processing. These can reduce labor; and where labor cost is high or there is a lack of skilled labor or production facilities, these foods can solve some of the problems. These foods are commonly referred to as "convenience foods." These items have not always had complete acceptance, because they lacked adequate quality, were too high in cost, or had not overcome the prejudice against them. At times, management has favored their introduction but resistance and even sabotage by employees has negated their use. Since they are higher in material cost than foods made on the premises, management should be sure that the labor saved by their use more than pays for the extra cost. Management at times may be willing to have them on a par in total cost or even slightly higher if they solve problems.

The introduction and use of new foods is not a novelty of today. Since earliest times man has used new foods and these were probably the convenience foods of the day. Thus, at one time, salted, cured or dried foods were convenience foods. Later came canned foods, and then, just a short time ago, frozen foods. Ice cream is a convenience food widely used today.

Once, only fresh foods were available and these lasted only a short time. Any excess became a waste because it could not be held. Then methods were found by which many foods could be preserved. This made it possible for them to be held over from times when there was plenty to times of scarcity. For a long time this was the purpose of preservation. Even canning and freezing at one time had this as their prime purpose.

For a number of reasons, such as the high cost of labor, the lack of skilled labor, etc., the reason for using preservation methods changed in the processing of some foods. Instead of holding foods over for periods of scarcity, preservation was used to capture labor in foods so that it could be eliminated later, and this was the beginning of convenience foods.

Undoubtedly, future foodservices will be using more of these foods and perhaps we can look to the time when it will not be unusual to see a foodservice functioning completely with them. Kitchens may be merely assembly points, rather than processing units, and the emphasis of management may be less on the back of the house but more on the front where merchandising and selling will be emphasized.

Many new technological developments hold promise of being able to preserve foods more efficiently and to retain quality better. Freeze-drying is a method in which foods are frozen and their moisture extracted in a vacuum. In doing this, ice crystals change to vapor without ever becoming water. The resultant product is spongy and exhibits a remarkably fresh flavor and appearance once it is rehydrated. Dehydro-freezing is a process in which foods are partially dehydrated and then frozen. The quality is high because the freezing process does not harm the cellular structure since there is less moisture in the cells. One of the problems of freezing has been that many food cells are fragile and cannot withstand the expansion occurring in freezing. This expansion, plus the fact that ice crystals can pierce the cells, causes them to collapse when the item is thawed. By extracting a part of the moisture as is done in dehydro-freezing, the cell rupture is avoided. Similarly, foods frozen under very low temperatures do not develop large ice crystals nor swell, and this again avoids destroying the cells. Because of this, we can use freezing agents like liquid nitrogen or Freon which reach very low temperatures. The quick freezing produces a product which upon thawing does not sustain damage to its cellular structure. Thus, we could freeze tomato slices, thaw them and have them much like fresh slices when these low-temperature freezing methods are perfected.

We are also developing some sophisticated methods of drying, such as high-temperature steam drying, or osmotic drying. Radiation can also be used to preserve foods, and experimentation continues on the use of irradiated particles from such substances such as cobalt-60.

We are also beginning to develop synthesized foods. The use of soy protein to make meat, nut, milk and other substitute products has already gone a long way. Many foodservices today use coffee cream substitutes that have little or no dairy products in them. They often use these materials also in place of whipping cream. Recently the use of soy products instead of meat has grown considerably. School foodservices are now permitted to add up to 30 per cent of these products with ground meat, for example. Experiments have shown that using as much as 20 per cent of these substitutes yields a product that cannot be distinguished from the unmodified original. Today we are also able to produce synthetic fruit juices and other food substitutes. Undoubtedly the development of synthesized foods will continue and eventually change our food supply. With the expected world food shortages foreseen for the near future, such developments will be welcomed.

As noted before, many foodservices are today operating their own central commissaries, in which foods are prepared and then shipped to satellite units where they are served. Thus, the Marriott Corporation, from its Fairfield Farms near Washington, D.C. ships many products to its foodservices as far away as Florida and the Twin Cities in Minnesota. The Hilton Hotels have begun central processing in Chicago on an experimental basis. Many companies have found that central commissary operations can make a contribution. The Ford in-plant feeding units, Win Schuler restaurants (which yearly are listed by *Fortune* as some of the outstanding restaurants in the country), the Bill Knapp restaurants, Howard Johnsons, the Horn restaurants and many, many others operate with foods produced in their own central production centers. As experience and knowledge are gained in central commissary operations, we can expect this trend to continue. Certainly, the very definite trend in the school foodservice systems of this country toward centralized production has become significant.

An operation wishing to use these new forms of food and new production methods should carefully investigate their quality aspects, their cost, their acceptance by the public and the problems inherent in using them. While they may reduce some production problems, they may create other problems which would make their use debatable. Service requirements, presentation and suitability for the operation must be considered. If investigation shows they have promise, they can be tested as menu items. This should give good data for judging their suitability.

Production Forms

To accomplish the production task, many control documents must be used. The personnel forms required are alone numerous, including time cards, payroll records, training records, health records, ad infinitum. Labor must be properly scheduled to see that the work is done.

Information must be compiled on menu selections, costs, etc. Requisitions for supplies must be prepared and filled. Amounts prepared compared with amounts sold can give valuable information and reduce waste. Recipes must be compiled and constantly revised. As in purchasing, management should study its system to see that it is efficient and gives the information desired. It should be simple. Insofar as possible, one form should do the work of many, to reduce the amount of copying and to eliminate errors. Some forms in use have previously been presented, and a few more are presented here. However, each operation should design its own system to meet its own needs. There is less uniformity here than in purchasing, and one will find that the number and kind of forms used will not be consistent.

FOOD PREPARATION PRINCIPLES

A knowledge of cooking principles and techniques is required to produce menu items of a high standard. Preparation personnel must know these.

Salads

The pantry should be able to produce a wide variety of salads based on menu requirements. However, the menu should not list too many salads that require a wide variety of ingredients making it necessary to have a large number of different perishable items on hand. The menu should attempt to provide variety with a limited number of basic salads. Labor costs can also be lowered by such planning. Pantry work must be fast, including proper pre-planning and lining up of ingredients for last-minute assembly. *"Mise en place"* is most important in this work.

The pantry must be sure that all salads are fresh appearing, colorful and attractive. Greens should be pre-crisped by moistening them lightly and then chilling. Pulling greens apart rather than cutting them is recommended.

Many salads require underliners, made from iceberg or leaf lettuce leaves or other leafy greens. They should be prepared in advance and crisped. Fruit and vegetables also should be prepared in advance and be ready for use. If the workers have to stop to make radish roses and other garnishings, too much time will be required and service demands will not be met. Items prepared ahead should be placed in separate containers and kept chilled. Except for hot salads, salads should be cold, and plates for them should be refrigerated. Insofar as possible, to ensure a fresh, crisp salad, final assembly should wait until the last moment before service time as orders come in.

If experience shows that a certain number of salads will be sold during a meal, some can be prepared in advance and placed under refrigeration or in refrigerated pass-throughs so that service personnel can get them quickly. Then, during service, pantry workers can observe when items are running out and prepare more as needed. Likewise, some pre-preparation of cocktails, juices, etc., can save valuable time later when the service rush is on.

Salads and other items required from the pantry for special parties, banquets, and buffets can be prepared in advance and left under refrigeration. Advance preparation, however, should not be so far ahead of service that the products deteriorate.

Salad dressings will be required and these should be prepared in advance. If small containers of dressings are to be sent out with salads, these can be dished ahead. Most operations today purchase their dressings already prepared although some specialty items may have to be made in house—a special fruit French dressing, for instance. An operation may wish to have its own boiled dressing or mayonnaise, and these will have to be available. Workers should understand something about the theory of emulsions, if they make salad dressings. Every work shift should set aside slow times for making up salad dressings and other pre-prepared constituents. For instance, if a potato salad is to be used for cold plates, the potatoes should be cooked, allowed to cool and then cut into cubes or slices, as desired, and held for use. Eggs, poultry, meat and fish should be cooked in advance, cooled, prepared for use and then refrigerated.

Gelatin salads must be made up at least four to six hours in advance of need. A gelatin mixture can be encouraged to gel more rapidly if only a part of the liquid is used to bring the gelatin into solution and the remainder of the liquid required is added chilled with flake ice in it.

If a salad is to be made from a gelatin dessert, one and one half pounds of dessert powder will be required per gallon of liquid. A half cup of this salad is served. For 100 portions, three and one eighth gallons of mixture will be required. If pure gelatin is used, two and two thirds ounces will be needed to set a gallon of liquid. Pure gelatin must be pre-soaked in cold water; the water used

to put the gelatin or dessert powder into solution should be 170°F. If a considerable amount of acidic ingredient such as lemon juice, vinegar or other tart substance is used, the gel will be weaker. Sugar strengthens a gel; sugar and acid may therefore counteract each other in a molded salad. Adding a considerable quantity of chopped ingredients, or whipping a gelatin mixture to a foam also weakens the gel, as does speeding the setting of gelatin with ice water. Therefore, the quantity of dessert powder or pure gelatin used may at times have to be varied according to the product.

Frozen salads are best made eight to 24 hours in advance of need. Usually these are fruit, and since some fruits do not freeze well, the fruit added should be of a kind that withstands freezing.

Hot tossed salads with greens must be made to order and should be served on hot plates. They should be made by tossing the greens and other materials in hot vinegar, liquid, and oil or fat. Service should be made immediately after preparation and the timing must be exact. Hot potato, cauliflower, bean or other salads which do not deteriorate quickly from heat can be prepared in advance and held ready for service. The plates for these should also be hot.

Quantities required should be calculated on the basis of standardized recipes or experience.

Sandwiches

Some operations may derive a considerable amount of their revenue from sandwiches, especially at lunch and snack times. Sandwiches, like salads and many other pantry items, take a considerable amount of labor so efficient work patterns, organization and pre-preparation work must be established to promote efficiency and high quality products. As for salads, meat items, chopped egg salad and other salad mixtures, these should be prepared in advance, stored in good containers and properly refrigerated. Cross stacking of meats, cheese, etc., may help workers to grasp portions quickly. Bread and other items should be sliced and ready for use within reach. Butter and other spreads should be softened and in containers near at hand. Garnishes, pickles, potato chips, etc., should also be nearby.

Unless a dry, firm bread that does not contain either sodium or calcium pantothenate is used, many salad fillings quickly soak the sandwich bread. Such sandwiches may therefore have to be made up as ordered. Some sandwich fillings freeze well and can be made up in advance and frozen. Sandwiches made in advance should be tightly sealed in moisture-vapor-proof wrapping. Labels should be used to indicate the kind of sandwich. Certain kinds of crayons write easily on plastic wraps. Some sandwiches may be cut in half and the filling left exposed for easy identification.

The kinds of bread needed for sandwiches vary. Day-old or older bread may be desirable for some sandwiches so that a firmer product is obtained, such as for a Monte Cristo sandwich. Some breads may be sliced transversely for making fancy sandwiches. These will have the crusts trimmed and will be cut the long way about a fourth of an inch thick. Such bread may also be used in preparing canapés, rolled sandwiches, etc. It may need some rolling with a rolling pin before use to give it even greater firmness. Hard-crusted breads should

be fresh each day. These should be sliced and ready for the filling. Many breads need to be wrapped and stored in dry, cool, well-ventilated drawers or storage areas.

While spreads are added to give enrichment and flavor, butter and margarine well spread over bread can also prevent soaking from fillings. Mayonnaise and other dressings that contain considerable moisture can be used with fillings which do not tend to get soaked, such as cheese or meat.

Quantities required should be well calculated and controlled. Half an ounce of meat or cheese can change the expected food cost percentage considerably. For instance, if a beef sandwich filling is calculated to cost 22 cents for a two-ounce portion giving a 35 per cent food cost, but a two and one half ounce portion is served, a food cost of 44 per cent can result. Too many sandwiches served at this food cost can raise havoc with the cost projection.

Vegetables

The preparation and cooking of vegetables is important not only from the standpoint of quality but for nutritional considerations. Many important minerals and vitamins are water soluble or can be destroyed by heat. If these are left soaking too long, especially if cut up fine, the leaching loss can be significant. Some nutrients can be lost by oxidation. Thus, aerating a fruit juice encourages some loss of ascorbic acid. Riboflavin is lost when sunlight strikes it. An alkaline medium destroys thiamin and ascorbic acid quickly, especially if heat is present. Vegetables (and fruits) should be cooked for as short a time as possible and never have soda or other alkaline products added to the cooking medium. Alkalizers can destroy the texture of many vegetables and make them too mushy to eat. Alkaline products attack the cellulose structure of fruits and vegetables; adding a bit of soda to beans and other legumes causes them to cook to a soft stage more quickly. Sugar strengthens cellulose; if a firm result is desired, fruit should be cooked in heavy syrup. If it is desirable to have fruit break up, it should be cooked in water first and the sugar added after cooking.

COLOR AND FLAVOR

The color of vegetables and fruits is affected by heat and chemical substances. There are five basic color substances: (1) green contributed by the pigments in chlorophyll, (2) orange or yellow contributed by the pigments in carotenes, (3) red contributed by pigments in anthocyanins, (4) red contributed by pigments in lycopenes and (5) white contributed by pigments in flavones. Heat can destroy the chlorophyll pigments, changing them from a bright green to an olive green. Acid does the same. Alkalies tend to retard the destruction of chlorophyll pigments by heat, but because they destroy vitamins and also make the product sloughy their use is not recommended. A small amount of salt helps to retain a green color and protect vitamin C. Carotenes and lycopenes are not harmed by heat, nor by alkalies and acids. They are quite durable pigments. (Carotenes in the body are changed to vitamin A.) Anthocyanins are blue in an alkaline medium and red in an acid one. Thus, in making blueberry muffins we would not use soda

as the leavening agent because the berries would be turned to a dirty purple. We frequently see recipes for beets, red cabbage and other vegetables that call for the addition of acids such as contained in vinegar, tart fruits, lemon juice, etc. Flavones are found in white vegetables such as onions. In an alkaline medium these pigments turn yellow and in an acid one they turn white. A bit of cream of tartar added to mashed potatoes gives them a nice white color.

The flavors in vegetables are also affected by cooking. Mild flavored vegetables are put into a small quantity of boiling, salted water and cooked as quickly as possible. If they are green, the pan should not be covered until the vegetables have boiled for about five minutes. The reason for this is that vegetables contain a bit of volatile acid which boils off in the early stages of cooking. If the lid is on, this acid is dropped back into the cooking water where it more quickly destroys the chlorophyll. Some cooks use a lot of water for boiling mild-flavored vegetables. They bring the water to a vigorous boil, drop the vegetables in and cook them barely to doneness and then remove them and blanch in cold water. The reason for using a lot of water is that the cooking time is shorter after the addition of the vegetables than if a large quantity of vegetables were added to a smaller amount of water. Steaming is also a good way to preserve the flavor of mild vegetables but some vegetables, such as spinach and peas, do not steam well. They pack and overcook on the outside layers before the inside is done. Sometimes these vegetables are put into water to get more even cooking during the steaming. However, carrots, potatoes, turnips, cauliflower, broccoli and other vegetables that keep a space between them can be steamed successfully. Some steamers cook at around five to seven pounds pressure while others cook at 17 psi (pounds per square inch). In either case, the cooking time is much less than in boiling. However, cooking times may be only 30 seconds for vegetables in the 17 psi steamer. In cooking vegetables it is advisable to achieve just a *slight* underdoneness. Then they finish cooking while they are in the steam table. This gives the best color, texture and flavor. It is also advisable to use batch cooking for vegetables since very few of them should be in the steam table more than 20 minutes. Batches should be timed for this kind of turnover. Old and new batches should never be mixed.

Strong-flavored vegetables of the cabbage and turnip families should be cooked as rapidly as possible with the cover off. A short cooking time helps to reduce the build-up of strong flavors. Acids tend to develop strong flavors and this is the reason for leaving the cover off, at least in the early stages of cooking. These vegetables may be divided finely to make them yield some of their strong flavor in cooking. Old vegetables are stronger in flavor than young ones.

Strong-flavored vegetables of the onion family should be cooked a long time. This is because the pungent flavor is volatile and boils off. Thus, it is a good idea to put onions into a stew a bit early or precook them before adding them to a bread dressing. Dividing finely and using young vegetables also helps to reduce unwanted flavor strength.

Very often one may see a cook sauté onions or garlic. This is done because many of the flavoring substances are soluble in the fat and the cooking also dissipates the strong flavors, which are volatile. Some cooks add a bit of salad oil to mild-flavored vegetables that are to be boiled. This oil helps to hold in some of the flavor.

RECONSTITUTION

Dried vegetables should be pre-soaked and then slowly cooked until tender. This produces a better product than putting them into cold water, bringing them to a boil and cooking them. Legumes such as split peas, lentils or beans should be sorted to remove stones and dirt, washed well and then soaked over night. They should then be cooked in the water in which they soaked.

Frozen vegetables that have been blanched, giving them a partial cooking, should have a reduced cooking time in comparison with fresh products. They should usually be cooked from the frozen state. However, it may be better to cook spinach and other greens slightly thawed. Corn on the cob should be thawed before being cooked; otherwise the ear of corn may cook with a frozen core and cool too quickly.

Canned vegetables are completely cooked and require only rewarming. Some recommend a boiling or simmering period of 20 minutes to destroy *Clostridium botulinum* toxin, should it be present, but this is very rarely found in commercially canned vegetables. It is important that canned vegetables be given some treatment to make them as palatable as possible before service. Simply warming them many times leaves a poor vegetable, but if canned Blue Lake string beans, for example, are cooked with a small quantity of bacon, salt pork or diced ham, they are much more flavorful. Peas flavored with a bit of mint can take on a heightened flavor.

If vegetables are cooked and then blanched in cold water to prevent them from cooking further, and are then held for service, it is advisable to save some of the cooking water to reheat them. This reduces flavor and nutrient losses.

Eggs

Some individuals may think it is not difficult to cook an egg but it takes knowledge and skill to do it properly. A good egg is dependent, first of all, on its goodness, upon its own quality, and for proper handling after that.

For breakfast eggs, either Grade AA or A should be used. They should also be refrigerated until the time of use, and large quantities should not be allowed to stand outside of refrigeration for long periods.

When an egg cooks, it coagulates or becomes firm. It also changes color. Coagulation is an endothermic action; that is, it absorbs heat. Thus, while an egg custard is thickening, the temperature of the mass does not rise since heat is being absorbed. However, as soon as coagulation ceases, the temperature starts to rise again. If a thermometer is used, this second rise can be taken as a signal that the custard is done. If an egg is mixed with additional moisture and then overcooked, the egg will separate from the moisture into a curdled product or an open, cheesy, watery mass. This is called syneresis. Thus, custards should be baked at low heat and only to the point of doneness. A cheese rarebit is an extremely difficult product to cook because of this tendency of the eggs to curdle at high heat.

Too high heat or overcooking can also cause an egg to develop an undesirable flavor. The white of an egg contains sulfur and the yolk contains iron. These can combine to develop a blackish or greenish color and a strong flavor—the odor often associated with hot springs. If the egg is quite fresh or if it is shelled and mixed with an acid such as lemon juice, vinegar or cream of tartar, the development of the off-flavor is retarded. Eggs should not be left too long in the steam table or under other high heat. Hard-cooked eggs should be cooked to doneness and then plunged into cold water to stop the cooking. A dark circle around the yolk of an egg means a poor flavored egg as well as one of poor appearance. Hard-cooked eggs are best shelled immediately after they have been plunged into cold water. Holding them under running water and cracking at the large air sac side helps in the shelling.

The amount of heat an egg receives in cooking can cause toughness, thus, scrambled eggs are better flavored and creamier in texture if they are just slightly undercooked. If an egg is to be hard cooked and then stuffed or sliced, it should be boiled; but if it is to be served as a breakfast egg, either soft-cooked or medium-cooked, the temperature should be at simmering level rather than at boiling. While the cooking time is longer, the egg is more tender. A coddled egg is one that has a pint or more of boiling water poured over it. A cover is then put on the pan and left for five to seven minutes to cook. The resultant product is very tender. A shirred egg is a baked egg, and if the egg is baked at too high a heat, such as a very hot over or under a broiler, it will become tough and rubbery. However, if eggs are to be shirred in hash and served, the hash should be very hot; otherwise, the eggs will not cook underneath, near the hash, but only on the top.

Eggs should be poached in simmering salted water about two to two-and-one-half inches deep. A very small amount of vinegar—about two tablespoons per gallon—gives a whiter, more tender egg that is slightly bunched. If an egg is old, the yolk tends to break when it is shelled and the egg when poached has its white spread throughout the water. The egg should be slid into the water or dropped gently, since the impact of hitting the water surface can tend to spread the egg out.

Eggs for frying should be put into a pan of hot grease about one eighth of an inch deep. The heat should be reduced immediately to prevent the development of a crisp bottom and edge, and a strong sulfury flavor. (The reason for adding the egg to quite hot fat is to try, as much as possible, to keep it from spreading and hold it bunched up.) An egg "sunny side up" is not turned over. An egg "over easy" is turned over and cooked just enough to coat it. A basted or "country style" egg may be spooned with hot fat to give a white covering to the egg, or a small quantity of water may be added to the pan as the egg is almost done. The pan is then covered and the steam cooks the top of the egg.

EGG MIXTURES

French omelets are usually made by fairly rapid cooking since some browning is desired on the outside. If the omelet is filled with sweet preserves such as apricot jam, the top may be dusted with powdered sugar and slightly browned with a hot poker to give a caramelized flavor. A foamy omelet is one made by whipping the egg yolks and whites separately to a soft foam and then blending these and baking the product. It is somewhat like a soufflé but is not often made in foodservices because of the labor involved and the difficulty in getting a light product out in time to suit the customer.

Fondues and timbales are actually custard-like mixtures made from eggs and milk. There are other kinds of fondues, one made of Swiss and Gruyere cheese with kirsch and white wine as added ingredients. Another is made by frying small pieces of meat in hot oil and then dipping the meat into tangy sauces. A fondue made with eggs and milk is a strong custard poured over bread cubes and diced cheese, diced chicken, or diced mushrooms, etc., and then baked. A sauce is served over it. A timbale is a strong egg custard mixture used to bind vegetables such as spinach and corn.

A soufflé is made by adding yolks and a flavoring ingredient such as cheese, chicken, mushrooms, ham, etc., to a heavy cream sauce or paste mixture. Softly beaten egg whites are then folded into the mixture and the product is baked into a light, fluffy mass. A sauce is served over it. A soufflé is difficult to make and only skilled workers can make one that does not fall when held for service. The best soufflé recipe in the experience of your author is the one that appears on the large package of General Foods instant tapioca. It is an extremely reliable recipe and holds up well in the steam table.

Eggs can be beaten to a foam better if

they are around 110°F rather than cold. A slight bit of acid as from lemon juice, cream of tartar or vinegar also helps to extend the eggs and gives a more stable foam of greater volume. Salt also seems to assist in giving extensibility. Old eggs will beat up to a better foam than quite fresh eggs.

There are four stages of foam in eggs. Eggs barely mixed together are called Stage 1 and this is the type that will be used for making French toast, custards, scrambled eggs, etc. A soft foam, Stage 2, is used for sponge cake, angel cake, soufflés and foamy omelets. A stiff foam of small air cells with the mixture no longer fluid and the peaks standing is called a Stage 3 foam and is used for frostings, divinity fudge, soft or hard meringues, etc. Only the whites can be whipped to a final, Stage 4 foam, and when this occurs they are so over-extended that they collapse in cooking or baking. Thus, one should avoid whipping whites to this stage when heat is to be applied.

Processed eggs are eggs that are dried or frozen. All processed eggs must be pasteurized. Bakeshops use a considerable quantity of frozen eggs. These eggs should be thoroughly thawed and mixed before using. In freezing, the egg solids are driven into the center so that the egg mass is more concentrated in the center than on the outside edges. Thorough mixing redistributes the egg solids. Most bakeshop frozen eggs come from Grade B or Grade C and these are not of sufficiently high quality for use as breakfast eggs. However, a very high quality frozen whole egg is on the market and can be used for breakfast eggs. It comes from Grade AA eggs, of low bacterial content, and can be used for scrambled eggs, French toast, custards, etc. Frozen eggs are available whole, as yolks, whole eggs with added yolks, yolks with sugar, or egg whites. Dried eggs are available as whole, whites or yolks.

Dairy Products

One of the problems in handling dairy products in cooking is that they tend to curdle. Another is that they scorch easily.

Milk is nearly neutral when it is fresh. However, lactic acid-producing bacteria can attack the lactose (sugar) in the milk and produce lactic acid which sours the milk. Acids in foods can do the same thing. Tannins may be found in potatoes, asparagus, etc., in sufficient quantity to cause souring. Salting milk products or cooking for too long, or at too high heat, may encourage curdling. Binding milk with some flour and thickening it may help to prevent curdling. A cream soup or bisque should be made by adding the soup base mixture to the milk, giving vigorous agitation during the addition. Thus, a tomato mixture would be blended into hot milk to make a cream of tomato soup. Also, cream soups or bisques should be blended together in small quantities and put into the steam table. Old batches should not be mixed with fresh ones.

Milk tends to curdle easily in escalloped potatoes. If the milk is slightly thickened with a roux and then poured over the potatoes, there will be less danger of curdling. Not overcooking, and slightly undersalting also helps.

Cheese is a high-protein mixture that, like eggs, milk or meat, can be damaged by high heat. In cooking sauces, rarebits, soufflés, and other things containing a large amount of cheese, an attempt should be made to hold down the heat and avoid overcooking. Cheese put under a broiler quickly becomes tough and rubbery. Aged cheese blends into sauces better than younger cheese. Processed cheese blends into sauces better than any other type since it contains an emulsifier that helps to put it into solution.

Soups, Sauces and Gravies

Stock is the base for soups, sauces and gravies. A good stock may be used for other foods. There are two kinds of stock: meat stock and neutral stock. The latter contains no meat essences but may be a tomato sauce, milk, wine, etc.

A meat stock should be made from the shin or knuckle or joint bones of young animals having a good red marrow. The bones should be cracked or cut into small pieces. For a gallon of stock, five quarts of water are used to cover four pounds of meat and bones. A pound of mixed vegetables called a *mirepoix* is added. In addition, some spices in a small cloth—called a *sachet* or *bouquet garni*—may be added for additional seasoning. Beef should be simmered up to 10 hours or more but poultry and fish stocks need not be. Cooking too long may cause a stock to cloud. Many kitchens collect vegetable scraps, the juice from canned vegetables, bones and waste meat, etc., and add them to the stock pot to develop flavor. Ham, mutton or lamb meat or bones will give stock a flavor that may not be desired. Stock should be strained through several thicknesses of cheese cloth. Stock is highly perishable and should be cooled quickly at room temperature and then placed under refrigeration. Some stocks can be clarified by allowing them to chill and then decanting them, while others are clarified by using raw meat and eggs.

A brown stock results when the meat and bones and the *mirepoix* are well browned. Heavy onion rings may also be well browned to give an additional brown color and a somewhat caramelized flavor. White stock is made from unbrowned products. Today many operations find that using a soup base avoids the necessity of having a constant supply of stocks on hand.

Many soups are made from soup stocks. Some may be broths which result when poultry, meat or fish is cooked. To these may be added vegetables and starch products such as rice, noodles. etc. Other soups, such as bouillon or consommé, may require clarified stock using eggs and raw meat, seasonings and additional vegetables. It is possible to have several bouillons or consommés on the menu by varying the garnish. There are a large number of specialty soups such as Mulligatawny, Cocky-Leeky, Scotch Mutton Broth, Philadelphia Pepper Pot and Vichysoisse. The first is an Indian soup containing curry and grated apples. The second is a Scotch soup made of chicken and leeks. Scotch Mutton Broth is made with the stock from mutton bones and contains diced vegetables, particles of mutton and barley. A distinguishing ingredient in Philadelphia Pepper Pot is thinly sliced tripe. Vichysoisse is a cold cream of potato soup, usually garnished with chopped raw chives. Many others exist, are very popular on menus and will be good revenue makers.

Cream soups are best made by sautéing chopped vegetables in some fat until they are almost cooked, adding flour to make a roux and then working into this the flavoring ingredient for the soup, such as puréed asparagus, tomato purée, puréed potatoes, etc., plus stock, to make a thick sauce. If desired, the sautéed vegetables may be strained out of the soup by using a china cap. This mixture is kept warm and blended with hot milk as the soup is required for service. Some cream soups are made by using a cream sauce a béchamel sauce or a white sauce. They are not as stable as the one previously described.

'LIAISONING'

Bisques are cream soups flavored with shellfish such as oysters, crab or lobster. They are quite delicate. Cream soups and bisques may be finished with a product called a liaison, which is whipping cream and egg yolks in about equal parts. Some of the hot soup is put into a small quantity of the liaison and stirred well. This mixture is then worked into the main quantity of soup giving it good agitation. After a liaison is added, the soup is never boiled because it is apt to curdle. A liaison gives a smooth, creamy flavor to the soup. It also contributes some thickening, so the soup should not be too thick to start with.

There are many quite heavy soups that are not usually served as a meal accompaniment but as a complete meal. These would be the heavy vegetable soups, chicken soup thick with noodles, etc. Purées may also be quite heavy. However, some purées may be made sufficiently light to be used as a meal accompaniment for even a heavy meal. Chowders are also heavy soups made of some flavoring ingredient such as clams, lima beans, corn, diced bacon or salt pork, cubed potatoes or diced onions, and a stock either of milk (Boston or New England type) or fish stock (Manhattan, Coney Island or Philadelphia). The latter chowder will have tomatoes added.

A sauce is a stock which is a blend of subtle flavors, with no one flavor predominating, used to accompany a food product. Some sauces are neutral, such as hollandaise, cream or tomato, and have no meat in them. Some are thickened while others are not. Thus, an *au jus* is the unthickened brown drippings from a roast. In some respects it might be considered a gravy rather than a sauce.

There are about a dozen major or "mother" sauces. Brown or espagnole, velouté, béchamel, tomato, white, hollandaise and mayonnaise are some of the most important. From these mother sauces, small or secondary sauces are made. Thus, a velouté is a white stock thickened with a white roux. If cream is added we get a small sauce called Supreme, and if to this sauce we add a few chopped almonds, another small sauce called Reine (Queen) Sauce results. A béchamel sauce is made from rich chicken or veal stock and milk thickened with a white roux. If parmesan cheese is added, it becomes a Mornay sauce. A hollandaise sauce becomes a béarnaise sauce if a small bit of tarragon is added to it. Thus, chefs are able to produce a large number of sauces from a few basic ones just as they can produce a wide number of consommés or bouillons by simply changing the garnish.

THICKENING

The most common thickener used for sauces is a roux, which is equal parts of flour and fat, by weight. Using this item prevents the sauce from lumping and gives a smooth product. Using a slurry of water and flour will also thicken the sauce but the flavor is not as smooth or delicate. Other thickeners can be used. If the sauce is slightly acid, more thickener is required than if it is neutral.

There are three kinds of roux. A white roux is a mixture of flour and fat cooked until it has a bubbly appearance and the odor of hazelnuts. A blond (white) sauce is made with this roux. A browned roux is made from well browned flour and is used with brown sauces. More of this roux must be used to give the same thickness because the browning of the flour destroys some of its thickening power. A roux made of slightly browned flour is sometimes used. A dry roux is a flour that has been put into an oven and baked until it is slightly gritty.

A gravy may be similar to a sauce except that the flavor of one item will predominate. Thus, a beef gravy will have a pronounced flavor of beef. Gravies are thickened with roux, flour and other thickeners as are sauces.

Pasta, Rice, Grains, Cereals (Farinaceous)

Macaroni, spaghetti and other starch items such as rice and grains must be cooked in a considerable quantity of water. Usually a gallon of water is used to a pound of product, except for breakfast cereals which must be cooked into a thick paste. Macaroni products should be just barely cooked. As the Italian chef describes this state of cooking, it is "al dente" or "to the tooth," meaning that the item should still have some bite in it. These products are usually blanched after cooking, except breakfast cereals.

Breakfast cereals are dropped into boiling salted water and stirred gently until thickening begins. Stirring after this should be minimal because it tends to develop a pasty product.

Dressings or stuffings are sometimes classed as farinaceous items.

Deepfrying and Sautéing

Deepfrying means cooking in deep fat. The item is browned and given a delicate nutty flavor. Many foods respond well to it.

The ratio of food to fat is important to quality development. One part potatoes to six of fat is considered a desirable ratio for french fries but for other foods, such as breaded veal cutlets, breaded oysters or breaded eggplant, the ratio should be in the range of 1:7 to 1:8, food to fat. Thus, a fryer holding 15 pounds of fat should be filled with not more than two and one half pounds of potatoes, or about two pounds of other foods.

Fat is a temperamental substance and most be properly handled. It is combustible and if heated to around 550° to 600°F will spontaneously burst into flame. A grease fire is a terrible thing and all operations should see to it that filters over cooking units and air ducts above them are well cleaned. If a fire starts below, it will leap into these units and cause a general fire. (Such a fire is best controlled by using a cloth or blanket to smother it or by using the type of extinguishing material that creates a foam. A water-base extinguisher may spread such a fire.)

Fat can break down from either too high heat or from other factors. If a fat is raised above its smoking temperature, it smokes. This is a signal that the fat has lost its frying power or the frying temperature is too high. Fryers should not be left on when not in use. If necessary, the temperature can be dropped so that when the thermostat is turned up, heating takes only a few moments. Too much water in foods can cause breakdown of fat. Salts can also do this. Thus, foods should not be salted over the fryer. Frying cured meats in a deep fryer adds curing salts as well as the table salt contained in them.

The fryer and the fat should be kept clean. If they are not, the fat breaks down at a lower temperature. Each day a fat is used, it should be strained and the fryer cleaned. The remaining fat should be placed back in the fryer. If about 20 per cent of the fat that the fryer holds is used up in frying foods each day and fresh fat added in its place, no fat should ever have to be discarded. However, if the frying temperatures are too high or the fryer is used only infrequently, it may be necessary to throw out a complete container of frying fat and add fresh. Crumbs and sediment can break down fats quickly. When new fat is added to a fryer, the thermostat must be turned below 200°F so that the thin pool of melted fat around the heating elements is not charred. After a pool of fat forms around the elements, the temperature can be turned up.

Sautéing is frying in shallow fat. Some animal fats, and some vegetable fats such as olive oil, smoke at lower temperatures than other fats and oils. If the griddle or pan used for sautéing is well conditioned the quantity of fat required will be less. Usually about one eighth inch of fat is needed to fry items properly. Cooks should know how to condition pans and griddles.

Sautéing may be done prior to cooking by another method. Vegetables and fruits may be sautéed and then baked, steamed or broiled. The Chinese sauté tender vegetables very quickly and serve them with some bite still in them. When sautéing items, the fat must be hot enough to do the job quickly.

Coffee and Tea

The coffee served in a foodservice may be one of the most significant items establishing a quality image in the patron's mind. Good coffee is not easy to make. Much care must be taken. The difference in cost between the best and second or third best coffee is small and the cost difference per cup is usually insignificant. For first-rate coffee, a high-quality product must be used. Furthermore, the coffee should be fresh. After three days of standing at room temperature, freshly ground coffee has lost a significant amount of its flavor, because the coffee oils that give flavor and aroma are very volatile and escape easily. Some coffee companies today package their product in sealed plastic bags. This helps to hold flavors in, but not completely. Un-ground coffee in the bean holds flavor much longer than ground coffee and some foodservices purchase it this way and grind it fresh for use daily. The coffee should be one that has a grind suited to the equipment used. It should also be suited to commercial and institutional use. Some coffees prepared for home use do not stand up well in quantity production equipment.

Coffee oils are also easily oxidized and quickly become rancid. Therefore, equipment should be well cleaned every time it is used, and about twice a week should be given a "major overhaul." Some urns are soaked overnight with an urn cleaning compound. Coffee bags and filters should be kept clean and stored under water to prevent oxidation when not in use.

The importance of using the proper grind is emphasized. Urn or drip coffee is moderately coarse and is designed so that from four to six minutes in contact with the hot water will give a good coffee. Vacuum coffee is finer and is designed so that from two to four minutes in contact with the water gives a good brew. It is extremely important that the proper contact time be observed. If it is too short, a weak coffee results. If it is too long, an over-extracted coffee results. Water containing sodium bicarbonates (which can come from a sodium-exchange water softener) tends to remain too long on grounds and produces an over-extracted coffee.

The water for coffee can be slightly hard but not excessively so. Neutral or slightly acid water is also acceptable. The water should be boiling when it is poured over the grounds. When this water comes in contact with the grounds it is cooled slightly to an extracting temperature of about 205°F which is about right. If the water is too hot—if coffee is boiled—too much extraction occurs. If it is not hot enough, a weak brew results.

Coffee flavors are extracted from the coffee grounds at different times. The mild flavors come off first and the bitter ones last. Coffee should have some bitterness but not too much. Many coffee extractions should be mixed after making to blend these fractions together. For urn coffee, the bag should be removed and about a gallon of coffee taken out and dumped into the remaining brew to give a good mixing action.

Two to three gallons of water should be used per pound of coffee. The grounds of a pound of coffee absorb about a quart of water. A cup of coffee is about six ounces. Coffee should be held at about 190°F and should not be served to the customer below 160°F. Coffee can be held about one and one half hours. Shorter holding time is preferred.

Tea is also temperamental. It too must be made from a good quality product. There are three kinds of tea: green, oolong and black. The difference between them is a function of processing. Green tea is produced when no oxidation of the leaves (called fermentation) occurs in processing. A slight oxidation produces oolong. Black tea is fully fermented. There is less tannin in black tea than in green, the oxidation causing a loss of this compound.

Iced tea can cloud easily especially if a strong brew is refrigerated and then poured over ice. Tea will cloud less easily if it is slightly acid. It is best to make fresh tea in the morning, use it during the day and throw out what is left at night. Some operations make 50 portions of iced tea by pouring a quart of boiling water over two ounces of tea and allowing it to steep for about six minutes. The brew is then decanted and three quarts of cold water are poured into it. This is called the 1-2-3 method. Some operations find that instant tea is suitable for iced tea.

Hot tea should be made by heating the tea pot with very hot water, pouring this out, adding the tea and then pouring boiling water over the tea. A poor tea results usually when hot water is put into a cup or pot and the tea bag is served on the side. By the time the patron gets it the water is usually not hot enough to extract the full flavor from the tea. Pouring hot water over tea is called "wet service."

Meat, Fish and Poultry

Meat is an expensive item. Some restaurants and hotels find that it is 55 per cent of the total food bill. It is also difficult to prepare. Meat is mostly water, and one of the problems in cooking it is to retain enough moisture so that a moist, flavorful result is obtained. The solids in meat are protein, fat, bones and very small amounts of minerals and vitamins. Meat is important nutritionally—a good source of iron, the B-vitamins, and protein. Individuals who do not eat meat must get complete proteins from other sources such as milk products, eggs, or combinations of vegetables, nuts, cereals and a few fruits.

Cooking meat can develop flavor. It can also make it more tender or it can make it less so. If meat is cooked so that much of its moisture is retained, more servings will be obtained and the meat will be juicier and of better flavor. It also may be more tender, because overcooked meat is dry and pulpy and somewhat tough. High temperatures in cooking, or too long a cooking time, can cause a higher moisture loss in meat.

This moisture loss is often called "shrink". Thus, preparation procedures should call for meat to be cooked at low temperatures and only long enough to attain the desired doneness.

Meat fibers are held together by a substance called connective tissue. The amount of this tissue will largely determine whether meat is tough or not. There are two kinds of connective tissue. One is collagen, the white connective tissue. It can be dissolved by long, moist cooking; acid also seems to speed its breakdown. This is why a Swiss steak may be braised or a shoulder clod pot-roasted. By subjecting the meat to long, moist cooking the breakdown of collagen is encouraged. The technical name for the yellow connective tissue is elastin. Cooking does nothing to it. To use meat containing a fairly large quantity of elastin, the meat must be either ground, cubed, cut up or pounded, or the connective tissue otherwise mechanically broken down. Cutting meat across the grain may help to divide up the connective tissues if these have not been softened in cooking. Thus, cutting a rare flank steak into thin slices makes it tender enough to offer as a London broil. Both short-time cooking, which preserves moisture, and cutting thinly across the grain help to give a tender product.

Meat is red because it contains a pigment called *myoglobin*. Pork, veal, chicken and fish contain less myoglobin than beef or mutton. Myoglobin can be oxidized into a product called *oxymyoglobin* which is bright red in color. This can sometimes be noted on a steak which, when cut, it a bright red on the outside and a darker red inside. Hamburger that stands will show this as a bright red surface and a darker interior. Myoglobin can also join with nitrite or nitrate salts found in curing solutions. The product formed is called *nitrosomyoglobin,* a pigment which does not change color in cooking. (Myoglobin at about 160°F changes to *hematin* which gives meat its "done" appearance.) Thus, corned beef, ham and other cured products will be red after cooking and will not have the done appearance of fresh-cooked meat. Hence, if we add some trimmings of ham to a meat loaf, it may appear red and not look well done. Onions dried in nitrogen gas may also develop enough nitrogen compounds to give meat loaf a red color, as may vegetables grown in high-nitrogen soil. Customers judge the doneness of meat by its color and somewhat by its texture. Aged meat, meat cooked in an acid medium, or meat that is marinated in an acid mixture, will turn to a done color at a lower temperature than meat not so treated.

Doneness may be judged by cooking so many minutes per pound, by the interior temperature, by feel, or by appearance. The most certain way is to insert a thermometer in the meat. At 140°F meat is rare, at 160°F it is medium and around 170°F, or higher, it is well done. Except for beef and, perhaps, lamb and mutton and some game, most meats are cooked to well done. Pork should be well cooked to make certain that trichinae are destroyed. Some fowl are cooked rare. For instance, the famous pressed duck comes from a duck cooked to the rare stage. It takes experience and skill to tell when meat is done to the exact stage ordered by a patron, and those who work on the broilers or grills must develop adequate knowledge so as to produce items the way customers want them. Waiters and waitresses should work with production personnel so that orders can come out exactly at the time they are required. If guests come in and order steaks and eat slowly, service personnel should inform the production department of this fact and have it hold up cooking. At the right time, the service personnel should indicate when the orders can be started. Not only must production personnel know how to time meats and other flesh foods in cooking, but service personnel also must know this and be able to work with production people in timing orders.

TENDER MEATS

Tender meats will usually be cooked by dry-heat methods. This means that no moisture is introduced or allowed to form on the meat during cooking. Dry-heat methods are broiling, roasting, grilling (frying or sautéing), pan broiling, deep-frying and ovenizing.

BROILING. Broiling is cooking by radiant heat. Radiant heat must be developed by a glowing object to give a good broiling temperature. The size of the item and its thickness will decide how close the meat should be to the heat source. If the item is small and thin, it is cooked close to the heat. If it is thick and large, the distance is increased. Very fat items can be cooked close to the heat because there is moisture in fatty tissues which helps to reduce drying out. Thus, bacon can be broiled quite close to the heat source. Frozen meats should be put a considerable distance from the heat at first. After they have thawed or almost so, they should be moved close to the heat source. Some barbecueing utilizes broiling but is frequently accompanied by a basting of the meat with some type of barbecue sauce. Some items may be broiled and then put into an oven to finish cooking. Overcooking the outside of a product in broiling can develop a tough exterior and leave the inside underdone and cool.

ROASTING. Roasting is cooking meat in a pan in an oven. The roasting pan is not covered. Usually the meat is put on a screen or trivet to keep it up out of its juices. Meat should be roasted at low temperatures. High temperatures overbrown the outside and give a high shrink. The meat is also less palatable and tender. Meat is not salted if browning is desired, since salt delays browning. The penetration of salt in roasting is about one-fourth inch, and much meat that is roasted never gets the salt. Usually salt is added in a gravy or sauce.

It is advisable that doneness in roasted meat be judged by thermometer. A large roast, such as a seven-rib roast, will rise by 15 to 25°F after it comes from the oven. Thus, if one wants them rare at serving, the ribs must be taken from the oven around 115° to 125°F. Meat also can cook further in a hot steam table.

The size of the roasting pan should be suited to the quantity of meat roasted in it. If too much bottom space is left, the juices dry out and char. The roasting pan should be made of heavy metal although strapped black roasting pans are also satisfactory. Bright pans are not as good as black or dark ones: the bright surface reflects heat away from the meat. Browning also does not occur so well when bright pans are used.

Barbecueing in a closed pit is a form of oven roasting. The term "bake" is frequently used interchangeably to indicate roasting. Thus, we say we "bake" a ham but we "roast" ribs of beef. But the technique used is the same. Only in rare instances will roasting mean anything else but dry heat cooking. However, veal, which lacks fat and therefore can cook to a rather dry stage, may be roasted with the cover on in an attempt to reduce moisture loss. Meat, fish and poultry that lack some fat will not roast or broil very well. Thus, sole or a cut of veal should usually not be cooked by dry heat methods because the flesh is dry to begin with.

GRILLING. Cooking meat in shallow fat is called grilling, frying or sautéing. The depth of the fat is usually about an eighth of an inch. Some meat items may be floured or breaded and then sautéed. Some meat may be fried to pre-brown and then braised. The frying surface and fat should be hot enough to give a good cooking action but not so high as to overcook and toughen the meat.

PAN BROILING. Pan broiling is cooking meat in a pan without fat. Heat is therefore conducted through the pan surface and a sort of broiling action occurs. The meat will have an appearance somewhat between a fried and a broiled product. As fat accumulates in cooking, it is poured from the item being cooked. Any meat that can be broiled can be pan broiled.

DEEP-FRYING. Deep-frying is cooking food by immersing it in hot fat. As in sautéing, the fat is the conductor of heat into the food. Many breaded, batter-dipped or dough-coated items are deep-fried. In addition to cooking, deep-frying imparts a nutty flavor and a nice brown coating. It is usually best to deep-fry items that are not too fat. Thus, fat salmon, trout or other fat fish are not best deep-fried. Similarly, fat meats are better not treated in this manner. However, lean items are helped by deep-frying. Thus, a breaded veal cutlet, breaded oysters or breaded filet of sole respond well to deep-frying. Deep-frying is not a simple task and employees handling the deep-fried items should know a great deal about the subject. The knowledge and skills required are too extensive to be treated in a book of this type. Employees should be given special training to equip them to handle the deep-fry process with true expertise.

OVENIZING. Ovenizing is a method of cooking meat by placing portions on well greased baking sheets and drizzling fat over them, then baking them in a hot oven. Meat prepared in this manner appears as if it has been sautéed. It is a method whereby a quantity of meat can be cooked quickly for large numbers. For instance, breaded veal cutlets, chops, and floured chicken can be prepared in this manner, reducing the amount of labor and time required.

TOUGH MEATS

Tough cuts of meat and those lacking in fat are usually cooked with moist-heat methods. Simmering, steaming, poaching, braising, stewing, and blanching are usually classified as moist cooking.

SIMMERING. Few meats should be boiled. They are more tender, flavorful and juicy if simmered. Simmering is cooking in a lot of water just below boiling. The French chef describes simmering as "making the water smile, not laugh out loud."

STEAMING. There are two types of steaming: under pressure, and just over steam (often called free-vent steaming). Pressure cookers usually cook at around five to seven psi but some high pressure steamers can bring pressures up to 17 psi. At six psi the cooking temperature is about 230°F and at 17 psi it is around 255°F. These higher cooking temperatures speed cooking. They also break down connective tissue more rapidly. Steam is moist and therefore it helps to dissolve collagen.

POACHING. Poaching is cooking gently in a small quantity of water. Poaching is used for fish more than for any other type of flesh product. Some poultry may be poached. Poach-roasting is a method in which parts of poultry are placed in a pan and seasoned water is poured over them. Then the poultry is put into a moderate oven and cooked until done. The resultant product is moist and juicy, and the yield is greater than with regular roasting. It is usual to allow the products to cool down in the stock after removal from the oven. This assists in keeping the product plump.

BRAISING. Braising is cooking in a small quantity of liquid. Some products are allowed to produce their own juices. This can be done by covering the pan tightly and allowing the meat juices to collect, to furnish the required moisture. However, liquids such as water, wine, tomato juice, etc., also may be added.

A browned braised product is first sautéed to brown it and then it is cooked in a covered container with a small quantity of moisture. Browning is not merely a matter of caramelizing by heat. It is a chemical reaction between a protein and a carbohydrate. Dried fruits can slowly undergo a browning reaction causing them to change flavor, appearance and texture, which is not beneficial. Therefore, when meat is heated, not only are some of the products caramelized, but the reaction called browning is encouraged. (One can brown a pot roast or stew meat in a steam-jacketed kettle.) If the meat is not browned, the resultant product is called "blond" because of the lack of browning and the white appearance of the sauce.

There are other terms used for braising in cooking meat. A pot roast is a braised piece of meat. Swissing is braising. A fricassée is an unbrowned braised meat item. The requirement is that the product be cooked in a small quantity of liquid in a covered container.

STEWING. Stewing is similar to simmering but the quantity of water or liquid used is usually less.

BLANCHING. Blanching is a method in which meat items are dipped into very hot or boiling water, or boiling water is poured over them. This may be done to prepare sweetbreads or brains for the removal of membranes. It may also be done to liver to remove tendinous portions.

FISH

Fish cookery requires some special techniques and knowledge different from that used for the cooking of meat. The fat content of fish usually dictates how it will be cooked. Lean fish cannot be broiled nor does it bake well. It must be poached, breaded or batter-dipped and sautéed, deep-fried or floured and sautéed. On the other hand, fat fish is best broiled or baked but it can be sautéed or poached. It does not respond well to deep-frying. Since fish has little connective tissue in its flesh, there is little need to cook it for a long time. In fact, long cooking dries out the flesh and may toughen it. Shellfish, especially, toughen with extended cooking or at high cooking temperatures.

POULTRY

Poultry cookery differs little from meat. It has been found that poaching poultry gives a higher yield than roasting. Poach-roasting also gives a slightly higher yield than roasting, and only slightly less than poaching. The product is also more tender and juicy. Mature birds may be cooked better by moist-heat methods while young birds can usually be best cooked by dry-heat cooking methods. An exception to low temperature cookery may be made with small poultry or parts, and this can even apply to small pieces of meat. Low-temperature cooking may subject a small fowl to prolonged cooking, and because it has a large surface area in proportion to mass, it can dry out and lose palatability. Such items are therefore cooked at high heat for short periods of time.

BAKERY PRODUCTS

Many foodservices no longer operate bakeshops. Instead, they purchase all their breads, cakes, pies and other bakery items. They may make a few simple desserts such as gelatins, baked apples, cream puddings, etc., that take little skill and only a limited amount of equipment. In fact, most of these simple products can be made in the section where regular cooking occurs.

Breads

Very few operations will make their own loaf breads but some may wish to have hot yeast rolls and other products made on the premises. The requirements for doing so are not too great. Fresh, hot products can do much to draw favorable opinions from patrons. If the volume is not large, an upright mixer can be used to make the rolls. It is best to have a small proofer, but if one is not available the products can still be produced without much difficulty. A regular oven can bake off the items. Roll warmers can hold the products for service.

YEAST DOUGH. Yeast is a plant that grows by dividing. It feeds on sugars and starches. Once moistened, it grows best at from 74 to 84°F and this is the optimum temperature for fermenting the dough. Dry pellet active yeast can be put into solution in water as warm as 110°F but cake (compressed) yeast should be put into solution around 100°F. If temperatures go too far above 110°F yeast will not grow. Fermentation of the dough should take place in a warm area where there are no drafts.

Most small operations will use the straight-dough method, a procedure in which all of the ingredients are mixed together at one time and the dough fermented. A "no-time" dough also is mixed with all ingredients together but the amount of yeast and sugar is slightly increased and fermentation and proofing temperatures may be slightly higher than when bread is made by the straight-dough method. A no-time dough is made

when there is a lack of time and products must be produced quickly for service. The rolls are usually not as good as those made by the straight-dough method and are somewhat yeasty in flavor. However, when time is limited the method is a good one to use. A sponge-dough is made by withholding some of the flour in the first mixing. The dough is fermented and then the remaining flour is added and a second fermentation occurs. Usually about 60 per cent of the total flour is added to the sponge and then, in the second mixing, the remaining 40 per cent. When production is large, the sponge method may be used.

It is possible to ferment a dough and then refrigerate it so that it is available for make-up and proofing as needed. This method is called retarding. When it is used, slightly more yeast and sugar will be added to the dough. Products can also be made up after fermentation and then frozen. They can be taken from the freezer, allowed to thaw and then be proofed and baked. Again, slightly more yeast and sugar should be added to the dough when this is done.

Sweet doughs are rich yeast doughs that contain more fat, eggs and sugar than doughs used for regular rolls. They will be used to make breakfast products such as coffee cakes, cinnamon rolls and snails.

A rolled-in dough is one in which a layer of washed butter, margarine or fat is set between a yeast dough. The dough is folded and rolled out several times so that there is a thin layer of fat and a thin layer of dough. When the dough is subsequently baked a flaky product is obtained. The added fat also gives a much richer dough. When a regular dough is made into a rolled-in dough, it may be used for croissants, fan-tans, and the like. A sweet dough which is rolled-in may be used for rich, flaky breakfast pastries like bear claws and snails.

QUICK BREADS. Quick breads are those made with a leavening agent such as baking powder or soda. To be of best quality they should be made only a short time before service. Cornbread, biscuits, muffins, popovers, date and nut or banana breads, and some coffee cakes are quick breads. Some operations earn special reputations because they serve one of these products of high quality and patrons will go to the establishment just to obtain them. Many of these products can be made from mixes that are simple to make and bake.

If an operation makes its own hot breads, the menu card should make note of it and obtain merchandising benefit from it. The products should be of top quality, freshly prepared and served at a proper temperature. Hard rolls usually are not served hot. Breads should also be properly presented in baskets covered with a napkin. An unusual but attractive service might be to serve piping hot biscuits fresh from the oven in a hot iron skillet. Accompanied by butter and honey, they can be a conversation piece at the table, and a valuable good-eating story later on. Since their cost is not great, distinctive differentiation can be obtained for very little. They can also serve to satisfy a hungry patron at not too much cost.

Pastries and Desserts

If cakes, pies or other desserts are prepared on the premises, they should be top-quality products. It is also wise to offer items which are special and unique to the enterprise. It is not necessary to have a wide variety because patrons will tend to concentrate on only a few. These appealing menu items can be supplemented with ice cream or sherbet, a few puddings, etc. However, unless an operation can produce enough sales to keep a baker busy, purchase from an outside bakery is perhaps best. In some cases, a cook can also bake, or a baker can also cook, so even if the quantity sold is not large, it may still be worth while to produce them and offer them on the menu.

Frozen desserts are low labor-cost items. They are also not high in food cost if employees know how to dish them and if they are held at a proper dishing temperature—around 8°F to 15°F. If the temperature is too low, a good deal of pressure must be put on the product and packing occurs. If the temperature is too high, the products packs too much. Normal loss in packing is around 40 to 45 per cent. Thus, if a No. 10 scoop is used, which would give 10 scoops to the quart if no packing occurred, the average number of scoops obtained should be five and one half to six.

It is important that frozen desserts be attractively presented to patrons, and using attractive and different dishes can help to do this. Many frozen desserts gain in patron acceptance when they are served with good toppings and are well garnished. Complete instructions should be posted near areas where desserts of this type are dished up. Employees should be taught to follow these instructions carefully, not only to give products of a desirable standard but also to ensure that they are served at the right cost to the house.

CHANGING TO METRIC WEIGHTS & MEASURES

The United States may soon be converting to the metric system and when this occurs some confusion is certain to result for people long accustomed to dealing with ounces, pints and pounds in the preparation of food. However, in the end we will transfer to a far more simple system and one much easier to use.

Since this book will also be used by food production personnel already working in the metric system or converting to it, it might be well to have data readily available that will enable us to translate some of the values given in the text to metric values. Table 10-1 provides conversion factors for translating American weights and measures into metric values, and for converting metric to American values.

Table 10-1

Approximate Conversions from Customary to Metric, and Vice Versa

	When you know	You can find:	If you multiply by:
Length	Inches	Millimeters	25
	Feet	Centimeters	30
	Yards	Meters	0.9
	Miles	Kilometers	1.6
	Millimeters	Inches	0.04
	Centimeters	Inches	0.4
	Meters	Yards	1.1
	Kilometers	Miles	0.6
Area	Square inches	Square centimeters	6.5
	Square feet	Square meters	0.09
	Square yards	Square meters	0.8
	Square miles	Square kilometers	2.6
	Acres	Square hectometers (Hectares)	0.4
	Square centimeters	Square inches	0.16
	Square meters	Square yards	1.2
	Square kilometers	Square miles	0.4
	Square hectormeters (Hectares)	Acres	2.5
Mass	Ounces	Grams	28
	Pounds	Kilograms	0.45
	Short tons	Megagrams (Metric tons)	0.9
	Grams	Ounces	0.035
	Kilograms	Pounds	2.2
	Megagrams (Metric tons)	Short tons	1.1
Liquid (volume)	Ounces	Milliliters	30
	Pints	Liters	0.47
	Quarts	Liters	0.95
	Gallons	Liters	3.8
	Milliliters	Ounces	0.034
	Liters	Pints	2.1
	Liters	Quarts	1.06
	Liters	Gallons	0.26
Temperature	Degrees Fehrenheit	Degrees Celsius	5/9 (after subtracting 32)
	Degrees Celsius	Degrees Fahrenheit	9/5 (then add 32)

U.S. Dept. of Commerce

In the conversion tables provided, one will note the use of some terms that may not be familiar. Thus, the following may be helpful:

Liter   Basic unit of volume, 1,000 milliliters; slightly more than our quart, 946 milliliters. A liter of water weighs one kilogram.

Gram   Basic unit of mass; the weight of a milliliter (about one cubic centimeter) of water. A kilogram is about 2.2 pounds.

Meter   Basic unit of length, about 3.37 inches longer than our yard. A centimeter is approximately four tenths of an inch.

Deca-   Means 10 times.
Hecto-   Means 100 times.
Kilo-   Means 1,000 times.
Mega-   Means 1,000,000 times.
Giga-   Means a billion times.
Tera-   Means a trillion times.
Deci-   Means a tenth of.
Centi-   Means a hundredth of.

Milli-   Means a thousandth of.
Micro-   Means a millionth of.
Nano-   Means a billionth of.
Pico-   Means one trillionth of.

While these tabulations simplify considerably the calculations required in converting our weights and measures to metric values, the factors used in the multiplications sometimes give only approximate values. If more accurate values are desired, the additional information on accompanying pages (Tables 2, 3, 4, 5, and 6) will be of use.

The conversion data presented will help in translating American weights and measures into British weights and measures, but further information may be needed in making translations in the liquid volume area since the American and the British (Imperial) gallons differ, the former being 231 cubic inches, and the Imperial gallon being 277.4 cubic inches—1.2 times larger than ours. The following applies to British measures:

Table 10-2

Dry and Liquid Measure Equivalents

Dry			Liquid		
2 Pints	1 Quart	1.101 Liters	4 Gills	1 Pint	473.25 Cubic centimeters
8 Quarts	1 Peck	8.808 Liters			
4 Pecks	1 Bushel	35.24 Liters	2 Pints	1 Quart	0.9465 Liters
			4 Quarts	1 Gallon	3.786 Liters
			31½ Gallons	1 Barrel	
			2 Barrels	1 Hogshead	

Table 10-3

Liquid Measure Conversion

	United States Measure				Imperial Measure (British)				Metric Measure		Weight of Indicated Volume of Water	
	Gallon	Quart	Pint	Gill	Gallon	Quart	Pint	Gill	Liter	Cubic centimeter	Pound (avoirdupois)	Kilogram
1 Gallon	1	4	8	32	0.833	3.33	6.66	26.66	3.785	3,785.4	8.33	3.785
1 Quart............	.25	1	2	8	.208	.833	1.666	6.67	.946	946.4	2.08	.946
1 Pint	.125	.5	1	4	.104	.417	.833	3.33	.473	473.2	1.04	.473
1 Gill	.031	.125	.25	1	.026	.104	.208	.833	.118	118.3	.26	.118
Imperial measure (British)												
1 Gallon	1.2	4.8	9.6	38.4	1	4	8	32	4.543	4,543.5	10	4.543
1 Quart	.3	1.2	2.4	9.6	.25	1	2	8	1.136	1,135.9	2.5	1.136
1 Pint	.15	.6	1.2	4.8	.125	.5	1	4	.568	567.9	1.25	.568
1 Gill	.038	.15	.3	1.2	.031	.125	.25	1	.142	142.0	.312	.142
Metric measure												
1 Liter	.264	1.057	2.11	8.45	.220	.880	1.761	7.044	1	1,000	2.20	1
1 Cubic centimeter	.0003	.001	.002	.008	.0002	.0009	.002	.077	.001	1	.002	.001

Table 10-4

Conversion Table: Grams, Ounces, Pounds

Grams	Ounces	Pounds	Grams	Ounces	Pounds	Grams	Ounces	Pounds
28.35	1	.06	198.45	7	.44	340.20	12	.75
56.70	2	.13	226.80	8	.50	368.55	13	.81
85.05	3	.19	255.15	9	.56	396.90	14	.88
113.40	4	.25	283.50	10	.63	425.25	15	.94
141.75	5	.31	311.85	11	.69	453.60	16	1.00
170.10	6	.38						

Table 10-5

Volume Conversion Table
(Fluid Ounces to Milliliters)

Fl. Oz.	Ml.	Fl. Oz.	Ml.
1	29.6	17	502.8
2	59.1	18	532.3
3	88.7	19	561.9
4	118.3	20	591.7
5	147.9	21	621.0
6	177.4	22	650.6
7	207.0	23	680.2
8	236.6	24	709.8
9	266.2	25	739.3
10	295.7	26	768.9
11	325.3	27	798.5
12	354.9	28	828.1
13	384.5	29	857.7
14	414.0	30	887.2
15	443.6	31	916.8
16 (1 pint)	473.2	32 (1 quart)	946.4

Table 10-6

Equivalents of Household Food Measures

Quarts	Pints	Standard Cups	Fluid Ounces	Table-spoonfuls	Tea-spoonfuls	Milli-liters
1.0	2.0	4.0	32.0	64.0	192.0	946.4
0.5	1.0	2.0	16.0	32.0	96.0	473.2
0.25	0.5	1.0	8.0	16.0	48.0	236.6
0.125	0.25	0.5	4.0	8.0	24.0	118.3
....	0.125	0.25	2.0	4.0	12.0	59.2
....	....	1.125	1.0	2.0	6.0	29.6
....	....	....	0.5	1.0	3.0	14.8
....	....	....	......	0.33	1.0	4.9
....	....	....	......	......	0.2	1.0

British Liquid Measure (Volume)

Knowing	Multiply by	To find
Ounces*	28.400	Milliliters
Pints	0.568	Liters
Quarts	1.136	Liters
Gallons	4.544	Liters
Milliliters	0.035	Ounces*
Liters	1.760	Pints
Liters	0.833	Quarts
Liters	0.220	Gallons

*The British fluid ounce is not 1.2 times the American ounce as the British gallon, quart, pint, cup and gill are 1.2 times greater than the American units. The British pint is 568 milliliters and they divide this into 20 fluid ounces (not into 16 fluid ounces, as we do), so their fluid ounce is 28.4 cubic centimeters while ours is 29.6 cubic centimeters.

The cup used in this country is about one fourth of a liter (236 milliliters). There are 16 tablespoons in it and there are three teaspoons in a tablespoon. This makes our tablespoon 15 milliliters and our teaspoon five milliliters. (These values in British measures are, respectively, 284 milliliters, 18 milliliters and six milliliters.) If we wish to translate these values into grams, we can just replace the word "milliliter" by grams and have an approximate weight measure. However, an American cup holding molasses or honey which is heavier than water would weigh about 300 grams (British, 360). If it held flour, the American cup would hold 110 grams (British, 132 grams). It is much wiser, in working with foods, to weigh and not measure. Recipes should call for weights because this gives far more accuracy and more standard products.

Undoubtedly as we move into the metric system, we will change many of our recipes over to metric values and then not have to recalculate the recipe each time we use it. When this is done, perhaps some slightly different amounts may be specified for ingredients to round off values but such differences would not cause an appreciable difference in the product. Many of the present tables we use will also be revised. Also, our common kitchen measures may be changed slightly. A two-ounce ladle used to portion gravy may then hold 60 milliliters which is just about two ounces. A No. 12 ice cream scoop which holds level full two and a half ounces will probably be called a No. 75 (indicating it holds 75 milliliters). The size of the portion would probably be the same but would be called differently. Instead of a three-ounce portion of vegetables being given, we may give a 90- or 100-gram portion, etc.

Gradually, however, the names and labeling will change to metric terms and, while there may be some difficulty at the start, we will quickly get used to it and, when we do, we will find we have a universal and much simpler system.

CHAPTER 11

The Menu and Service

Service is the act of serving. In doing this, we perform tasks to satisfy the personal needs of others. That a foodservice renders service is evident from its name. We are classified among groups of industries as a "service industry." Today there are more people engaged in the service industries than in any other segment of the marketing structure.

As an industry we render a special service, one in which we not only take care of the sustenance and nutritional needs of individuals but also seek to please people in the manner in which we render our service. Because of this specialized task, some say we are a part of the "hospitality" industry. Brillat-Savarin has said, "When we invite someone, we make ourselves responsible for his happiness while he is under our roof." Patrons in a foodservice are invited guests and, while they are in our establishment, our management and employees have the responsibility for seeing to it that they are courteously treated and are made happy and satisfied.

The feeling of responsibility for a guest's comfort and pleasure has had a long tradition in many cultures. It used to be traditional that a guest should come

to no harm while under our roof. Macbeth's crime was much the greater because Duncan was murdered in his castle while there as a guest. The principal of sanctuary arose from this tradition that people must be cared for and not injured while in an establishment.

In many cultures guests are greeted at the door and special tokens of friendship are exchanged before they enter. Under an ancient Irish custom guests were offered wine and a pinch of salt as they came through the door. The Bible relates how Jesus was received as a guest in the house of Lazarus where his feet were first bathed and oil was put on them. Today, when a head waiter or hostess greets guests as they come into the dining area to be seated, the same spirit of hospitaltiy should prevail. We should be proud to maintain these traditions and see that guests are properly greeted. There is great satisfaction and reward in knowing we can please others with our food and service. When this pleasure is lost, we are losing something extra that comes with our jobs.

When the foodservice industry first came into being, the feeling was that guests were coming into an abode of the proprietor, and in many areas of the world a customer is still treated as if he were coming into a home rather than into a business establishment. The Arab merchant goes through a considerable ceremony to let you know how pleased he is that you are his guest. Guests should be made to feel they are friends whom we wish to serve and make happy. Doing this is not an act of servility but the performance of a skill which the server possesses and is proud to possess. In many of today's foodservices courtesy is lacking. This loss in service can be like the loss of rain to a fertile plain. If rain fails, the plain dies and becomes a desert.

Greeting the Guest

A maitre d'hôtel, headwaiter, host or hostess may greet patrons as they enter, take them to their places, seat them and give them menus. If some individual is not forward to do this, the first person encountered should give the greeting and make the guests feel welcome. Benjamin Franklin said, "The taste of the roast is often determined by the handshake of the host." Greetings should be warm but not so overly friendly that guests are embarrassed. Knowing exactly how to give a greeting takes training and practice. Guests should be made to feel that they are welcome and that their wants will be properly taken care of.

It is not easy to greet 200 guests during a meal and escort them to their places, but this idea should not be conveyed to guests. Every greeting should be distinctive and special so that guests feel they have been especially identified. It is much more important to have guests feel the warmth of the greeting rather than to have them be startled by an over-

done hair style and a daringly abbreviated costume on the hostess. An overdressed greeter with a frigid countenance and bored expression, who does not smile but mechanically grasps menu cards from a rack and, just as mechanically, takes guests to a table, does not meet the requirement of making guests feel at home. This may perform a function; it does not serve as a welcome.

The Food and Service

Poor service can ruin the best food. The success of the menu will depend not only on how well the food is prepared and appears but how it is served. Different foods require different kinds of service, and service personnel should know these requirements. There is also a proper sequence to be observed in giving good service. The server must time the service so that associated food—main dish and accompaniments—come to the table together. Water should be brought to the guest shortly after the menu is left at the table.

Personnel should not serve food that will displease the guest. A good motto is: "If you are not proud of it, don't serve it." Food must be at the right temperature. Poor service can cause food to be disappointing—to one who otherwise would have found it acceptable.

Service Personnel

Good service is not easy to give and takes a lot of skill, effort and knowledge. People who give good service work at it. They study their jobs to find our how they can make serving easier and better. They are constantly alert to make themselves more efficient and better able to please their guests. This pays off in personal satisfaction—and in tips; to say nothing of happier clientele and better business for the establishment. A person serving others should like people and have a pleasing personality. He should get along with his fellows and guests. He must want to do the best possible job. Often guests may try a server's patience and be difficult to serve. At times a lot of fast work must be done under pressure.

Serving is hard work and requires a strong person who can not only work under stress but do so for long hours requiring continuous effort. His health should be good. Full use of the hands, feet and body is required. The individual should have a good appearance, be neat, trim and clean. Hands and fingernails should be immaculate. The hair should be neat, well combed and dressed. The uniform should be well fitting, attractive and clean. He should be efficient in doing the work—quick and intelligent.

MISE EN PLACE IN SERVICE

Good service does not begin upon the arrival of the guest. It depends very much upon the preparations made for him ahead of time. *Mise en place* means getting ready for the job to be performed. Service personnel should see that the necessary preliminaries are done before guests arrive so that service can proceed smoothly and efficiently. Without it, the job may be poorly done and both the server and the guests will be dissatisfied with the results.

Before service begins, butter must be cut (unless pats are ordered) and arranged in bowls so that it can be iced. Ice, silver, napkins, water, condiments, juices, salads, dressings and other items

needed for service should be assembled and put in place where they can be obtained quickly. It is essential for service personnel to be briefed on how foods are prepared an how they are to be served. Sometimes this is the job of the head person in the dining room, and a short meeting just before service may be held to cover the menu and its items for the day.

The first requirement in getting ready for guests is to see that the area they will occupy is clean and in good order. Chairs, tables and other items in the area should be in good condition. Women object strenuously to chairs that snag stockings. The linen should be spread clean and neat, and the tables should be properly set with sparkling glassware and bright silverware. Menu cards should be bright and clean.

The manager or his assistant should walk through the dining area several times a day and ask himself, as he checks details, if he would want to dine there. Supervisory and other personnel should submit survey reports to management on the condition of the dining area, Management should promptly see to it that repairs, maintenance and other needs are taken care of. Outside areas should also be checked. A systematic plan should be followed for tending the shrubbery and seeing that the area is neat and clean. A poorly maintained operation may be expected to offer poor food and service.

The needs of guests should always be considered. People like enough room to be comfortable and not crowded while eating. In a fast turnover operation, a small hook on the table edge where a purse can hang is appreciated. Students like a shelf on which to leave books and papers. If a business man takes clients to dine with him he will appreciate a quiet place where they can discuss their affairs. Guests dislike cold air or drafts blowing on them. They also want enough light to be able to read the menu.

The Service System

A good serving system is needed so that orders are properly taken, properly given to the production department, properly prepared and properly served. It is wise to have a service manual that all service personnel and others can read to learn how service should go in the operation. This should cover rules of conduct and procedures for doing the job from greeting the guest to resetting the table in proper sequence. Service personnel should be informed where to place orders in the kitchen for different kinds of foods. They should be told the times required for preparation.

Servers need to have good organizational ability and be competent to follow the system used in the house. They should be instructed on how to present the menu card, how to pour water, how to take an order, concentrating on what the guest is saying, and writing an order so that production personnel can follow it in detail. The server must also know, when returning with the food to the table, which guest has ordered which food. This usually requires a set procedure for writing down the orders and numbering the guests, starting always in one specific place and going around the table clockwise or in some other systematic way.

A good system for placing orders in the kitchen is also needed. Usually they are given in written form. Some operations use a circular rack so that orders come in proper rotation as the rack is turned. Other methods can be used. Whatever the method, it should be simple and workable. Service personnel should develop a system for informing production workers when to start orders so that the orders are ready on time but are not prepared so far in advance that they lose quality. A good communication system is needed to inform service personnel when their orders are ready. This can be a quiet bell tone, lights, or other signalling arrangement.

A method needs to be worked out for keeping hot foods hot and cold foods cold after they are prepared and while awaiting pickup by service personnel. Infra-red lights over a table on which hot foods sit is efficient. A refrigerated shelf may be used for cold foods. The method should include storage areas where dishes can be properly warmed or chilled.

Some method for checking foods as service personnel pick them up should be devised so that the right foods are taken and course units come properly together. Sometimes checkers can help with this.

Tableware must be handled properly. Glassware should be handled so that the fingers do not go inside. Silverware should be held by the handles. A dish should be held with the four fingers under it and the thumb steadying it at the *edge*.

Serving should proceed from a selected spot at the table. It is usual to serve ladies first. Wherever the start is made, service goes to the server's left in a clockwise fashion. As the server moves to

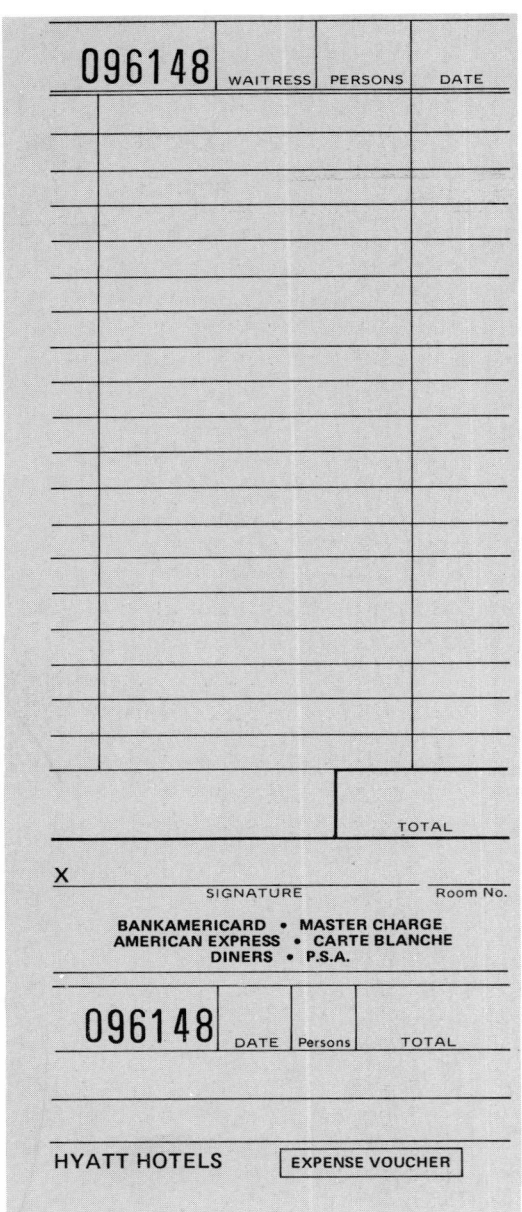

096148   WAITRESS | PERSONS | DATE

TOTAL

X
SIGNATURE   Room No.

BANKAMERICARD • MASTER CHARGE
AMERICAN EXPRESS • CARTE BLANCHE
DINERS • P.S.A.

096148   DATE | Persons | TOTAL

HYATT HOTELS   EXPENSE VOUCHER

FIG. 11-1   A standard check typically used in a coffee shop or similar foodservice. (Courtesy Hyatt Corporation)

the next guest to be served, the worker turns to the right, using the right hand on the guest's right to put down the main dishes and items served on the right. He will then turn and with the left hand put down the items to be served at the guest's left, such as a salad. He then moves to the next guest and goes through the same procedures. It should be understood, however, that while the procedure described here is usual, there it no reason why the service *has* to move clockwise, etc., as long as good service occurs.

It is proper, after guests have been served and have sampled their food, to ask if everything is satisfactory. Prompt attention should be given to complaints. Service personnel should not argue with patrons. If necessary, supervisory personnel should be called to the table to correct any deficiencies or smooth over difficulties. It is also wise after service to have some means for taking up problems that have arisen during a shift in the dining area. A problem can be reviewed and discussed, and perhaps a recurrence can be avoided. It is a grave error to allow the same mistakes to occur over and over again without making an attempt to correct the cause.

After guests have been served and they have finished eating, the check must be brought. If the service person knows who is to get the check, it can be placed upside down at the right of this individual. If not, it can be placed in the middle of the table. If there are to be separate checks this should be ascertained at the start, the correct check going to the proper guest. The check is usually totalled and presented on a tray to the proper person or persons. An expression of thanks should be given. It is proper for guests to check the accuracy of the check. Prompt attention should be given to questions about charges.

Some system for maintaining a record of service checks should be established. Each service person, at the start of a shift, should be given and sign for a set of checks which are consecutively numbered. Later, a consecutive count of checks turned in by guests to cashiers should be made by the accounting department—if the count is made by the service department, collusion can occur. Missing checks should be investigated. Some operations charge service personnel as much as $10 for each missing check. Rarely will guests walk out without paying, but this can occur and it may be necessary to make allowance for it. Some operations say that walkouts numbering one tenth of a percent is not unrealistic.

In addition to its own serial number, a service check should have space provided for identifying the waiter or waitress who used it and for showing the number of persons served, the date and, perhaps, the table number. Only one item should be put on a line on the check. Some checks provide a ticket which the service person can tear off and keep as a record. Many different kinds of checks are used. Each is designed to fit some special need of the operation.

Some operations use checkers, who usually take station at the kitchen entrance where they can review orders coming to the kitchen to ensure that only the foods ordered on the check are taken out. Portions are checked by this individual to see that they are adequate but not too large. The appearance and garnishing of the food can also be

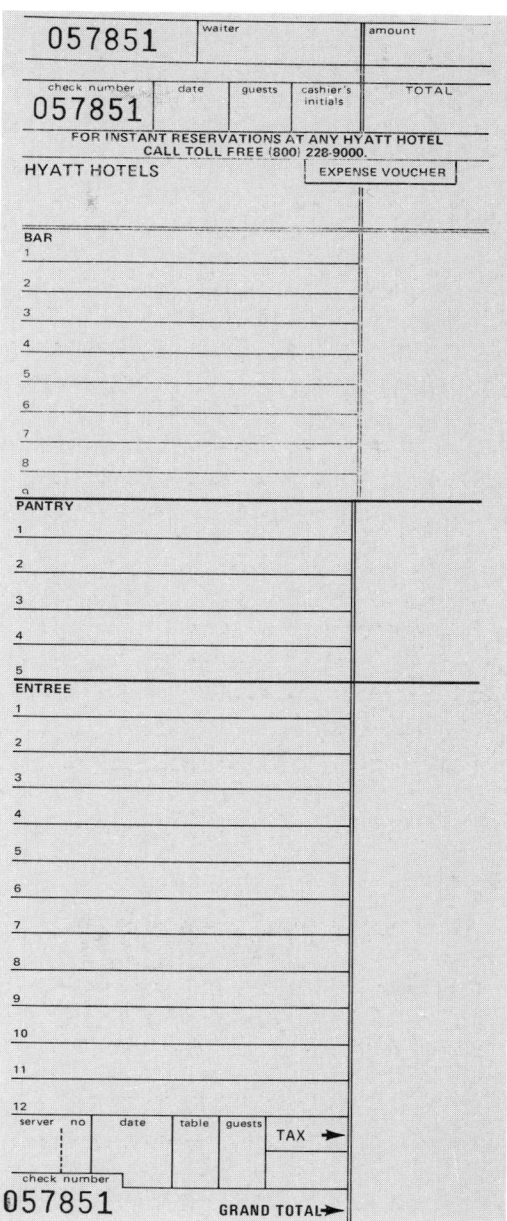

FIG. 11-2 A dining room check that provides for a division of charges amongst production departments — in this case grouping items from the bar, pantry and entrée kitchen. If a guest is to sign this check and have it added to his bill, the signature and other information would be put on the back.

inspected at the same time. For instance, if tea is on the tray, the checker may have the waiter get a slice of lemon to go with it. Checkers frequently price out individual items and total the bill. The checker should initial it so that the cashier will know it has been checked. Variations on what a checker may do will occur in different operations.

There are many occasions for mishandling of checks, especially when service personnel collect the money. In a bar, for instance, if the service check goes out at six in the evening and is still out by 10, one might suspect that the check is being held by the service person and being reused for orders and presentation to different guests. To

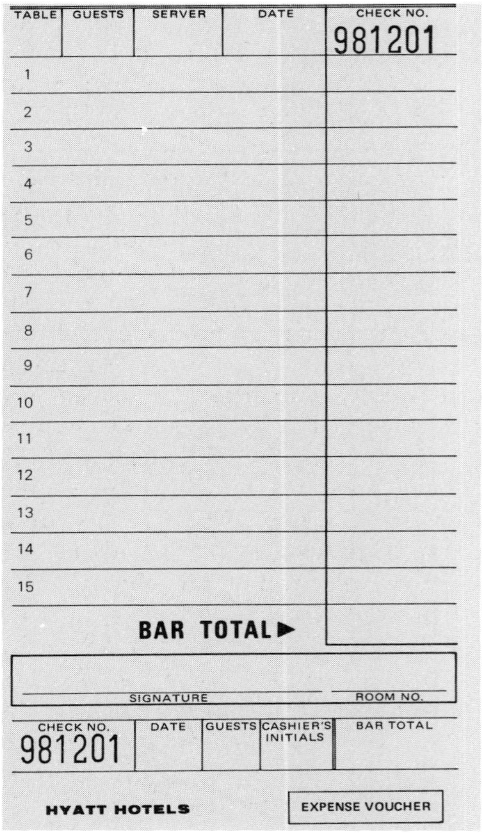

TABLE | GUESTS | SERVER | DATE | CHECK NO. 981201

1
2
3
4
5
6
7
8
9
10
11
12
13
14
15

BAR TOTAL ▶

SIGNATURE | ROOM NO.

CHECK NO. 981201 | DATE | GUESTS | CASHIER'S INITIALS | BAR TOTAL

HYATT HOTELS

EXPENSE VOUCHER

FIG. 11-3 A bar check which provides a tab that can be detached and retained by the service person. (Courtesy Hyatt Corporation)

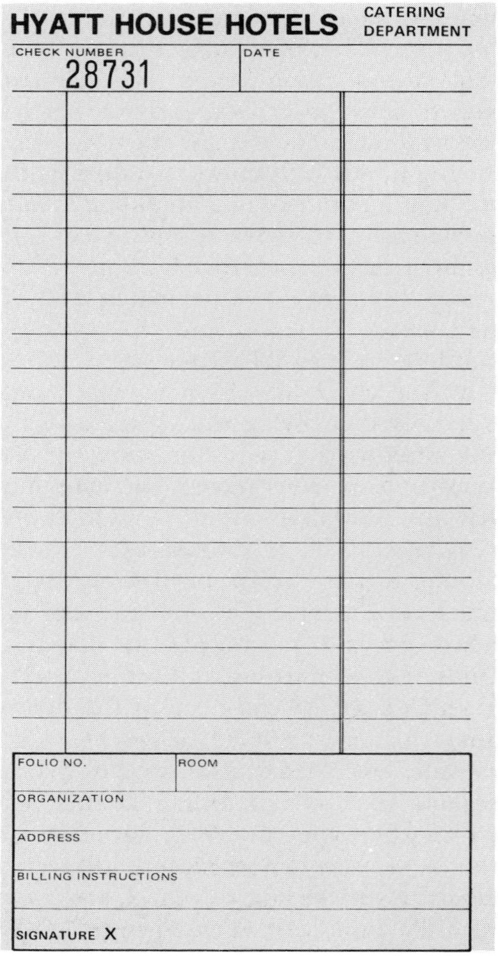

HYATT HOUSE HOTELS

CATERING DEPARTMENT

CHECK NUMBER 28731 | DATE

FOLIO NO. | ROOM

ORGANIZATION

ADDRESS

BILLING INSTRUCTIONS

SIGNATURE X

FIG. 11-4 A type of check used for recording catering charges. Note the information required on the bottom of the check for use by the accounting department.

avoid this and other abuses, an operation may establish the following procedures:

Checks are issued in consecutive numbers, either by management or by the bartender, and service personnel sign for the checks. Missing check reconciliation is done by the accounting office the next day not by service personnel. A locked box is provided into which checks can be inserted immediately after they have been rung up on the cash register. The accounting department or some authorized person should have the key to this box. Often the food and beverage director has an additional key. At night, usually the night auditor has the key. The box is emptied whenever cash register readings are taken. A time stamp is also provided which is used to stamp each check with the time the first drink is served and the time the check is finally paid. This indicates how long the check has been in use. Some operations allow service personnel to time-stamp the checks; others require the bartender or some other individual do it.

In this system, no paid checks can be on the bar, at the service area, or on the service person's tray or carried elsewhere by the service person. When a check is paid the check is picked up and a receipt is left with the guest. Thus, any customer at the bar or at a table should have either a guest check or a receipt in front of him. Checks must be in the locked box, in transit from the table to the locked box or service area, or on the guest's table. A reconciliation should be made of times stamped on checks to ascertain the length of time they have been out. Any variation from a norm should be investigated.

Where guests make charges to be put on their bills, as in a hotel, it is important that these charges be forwarded promptly to the accounting department. Some hotels and others today give a guest a code number that identifies his account. When a charge is given to a cashier by a guest, the total of the charge, the department where the charge is being made, and the guest's code number are put into the cash register. The register is connected to the accounting department so it is immediately notified of a charge by that guest. This prevents guests from checking out before all charges are on their bills.

Some guests indicate on a sales check that a tip is to be given an employee. The amount of the tip is noted by the accounting department and added to the employee's wage check. However, some operations pay the employee each day the amount of these tips. For this it is necessary to maintain a charge summary sheet. The information required on this sheet is compiled before checks are sent to the accounting department for posting. Usually this information includes the check number, room number, tip, and total charge. Tax and miscellaneous information may not be recorded. The service person getting the tip should sign for it in the "tip received" column to substantiate the paid-out-tips reading on the register or to reconcile the cash. This is proof that the service person received the tip. The total column is also a cross-reference to balance guest charges. The sheet is turned in to the food and beverage department daily.

Unless an operation has some way to keep a record of checks, money and other items, it may find that while the menu is doing an excellent job of getting sales and pleasing customers it is not generating the right amount of revenue.

Tipping varies from 10 to 20 per cent of the total bill; 15 per cent is very common. TIP means "to insure promptness" and is given as a token of appreciation for service above the ordinary. There is no reason to tip if the service is mediocre or poor. In fact, it is wrong to do so since this encourages continued poor service. A more judicious use of tipping on the part of patrons would do much to improve service. It is usual for service personnel to give about 15 per cent of the tips received to bus boys or others who might assist in the service. Tips should not be counted in the dining area.

As guests leave they should receive an expression of appreciation for their patronage.

In the more formal seated-service es-

ROOM SERVICE CONTROL SHEET
Coffee Shop

PERSON RECEIVING ORDER	ROOM NUMBER	No.of Guests	WAITER'S NAME	TIME ORDER PLACED	TIME ORDER LEAVES	TIME TRAY PICKED UP	CHECK NUMBER

DAY OF WEEK _____ DATE _____ HOTEL _____

FIG. 11-5
The method for recording and controlling room service orders must be carefully established. This sheet gives good information on room service charges and times of service.

tablishments it is not proper to pick up items from the table until guests have left the room. However, a soiled table is not attractive and the soiled items should be removed and the table or space reset, or prepared for resetting, as quickly as possible. Bus boys and others who clear and set tables should be trained to do the job quickly and efficiently with the least possible disturbance. Dishes should be properly stacked into tote boxes or trays. Glassware is usually handled separately from dishes. Flatware may also be separated. Heavy dishes can wreak havoc on lighter ones and should be given special handling. The process of clearing and setting should be as unobtrusive and quiet as possible.

To reset a table, all accessories—sugars, salts, peppers, ashtrays, etc.—should be moved to one side of the table. (They should not be set on chairs. They can be removed to a tray sitting on a tray stand.) The table cloth should then be put on the opposite, empty side and the accessories placed on the half that will cover this side. The other half is then pulled over the table so that the cloth covers the complete table. The accessories are then moved into the middle. In setting the table, the silver and dishes should be about half an inch from the table edge. Silver should be straight and properly spaced in correct order.

TYPES OF SERVICE

Counter Service

Counter service is fast and usually has a high rate of customer turnover. In such service patrons can be quickly seated, order and eat without much loss of time. Contrary to some thinking, it does not save space. The space needed for the backbar, service area, counter and seats, plus aisle space for traffic, is rather large. In some cases seated service requires less space than counter service.

A waitress may have from eight to 20 stools to serve at the counter. Everything possible should be within reach so that the server has little need to move about. The counter should also be close to the production area to permit orders to be placed, picked up and served quickly. Some training in work simplification is desirable. Work center arrangement should be studied. The use of a communication system that gets orders into the kitchen without service personnel having to go there to place them speeds service and allows servers more time to wait on guests.

In some counter service, places may be pre-set for guests. A place mat may be set down and the required silver placed upon it, the knife and spoon to the guest's right, the forks and napkin to the left. The server should therefore pick up knife and spoon with his left hand as he faces the counter setting them down, and the forks and napkin with his right hand so they will be in the proper place. Only water and a menu then need to be handed the guest when he is seated. Menus and napkins may also be available on the counter for self-service. Water should be placed on the guest's right just above the tip of the knife. The blade of the knife should face in toward the center. If other silverware is needed, it is put in proper postion after the guest has ordered.

Good counter service is not easy. It is fast-moving hard work. The individual doing it must have excellent organization and be deft and quick in the work. While the mind must be constantly on orders and details of service, the service person must also manage to be pleasant and make guests feel welcome. Good team work is required with other counter servers and with production personnel. When not serving, it is usually necessary to keep busy cleaning up the backbar, replenishing supplies and otherwise organizing the station. Salts, peppers and sugar bowls will need filling, as will napkin holders. Failure to do these things in slack moments can mean that service goes slowly at peak times and confusion results. Getting behind in one's counter work can make the job harder and frustrating. Learning how to keep ahead is essential.

After a guest has been given a check with a "thank you" and leaves, the soiled dishes should be removed quickly. Some sorting of items is usually desirable. Counters should be arranged so that tote boxes are handy and workers do not have to walk long distances to get to them with used tableware. Bus boys or others who remove tote boxes should see that they are removed when full, and that new boxes are put into place.

Cafeteria Service

When guests go to a counter where service personnel serve them the foods they select, and the guests take these foods to a table they select, the service is called cafeteria. There may be modified types such as in some family cafeteria operations where service personnel stand at the end of the line and pick up the tray and take it to a table for the guest. Furthermore, water, silver and beverages may also be served by service personnel. Good cafeteria service should put about six people per minute through the cafeteria line. A cafeteria line over 50 feet long is usually not as efficient as one shorter than this.

A shopping center or "scramble" cafeteria system is one in which guests go to specific locations to get certain types of foods. For instance, beverages may be obtainable at an island in the center, salads and first courses at a counter where one enters the service area, and desserts at another counter. Hot entrées may be obtainable at a central location and vegetables at a separate bay. None of these locations is connected to another and guests must pick up their trays and move to the next, without sliding them along in a line. This prevents the formation of long lines and allows the individual who wants only a few items to get them quickly and leave the service area. Such an individual does not wait in line while someone else wanting more takes time to make the selections. The patron pays as he leaves the service region before proceeding to a table. Some cafeteria lines have a checker who adds up the cost of the foods on the tray and hands the guest a slip with the total on it. The guest then moves to the cashier and pays the check. Instead, the guest may pay the check at the door after finishing his meal. If this second method is used, some system needs to be worked out so that a guest does not go through the line and get food and a check, eat this food, go through the line again for only one or two items and then use this smaller check for payment, pocketing and walking out with the larger one. If every patron picks up a check when he enters and all charges are entered on only this one check and *every* person leaving must give up a check, a fairly secure system exists. If a guest in this system goes through the line a second time, getting food, the second charge can also be put on the check and the original total wiped out.

Some cafeteria lines can be moved more quickly by having special lines where certain foods only are obtainable. Thus, some cafeterias have cold-food lines or snack-food lines which relieve the hot-food line of patrons who want only a limited amount of food and who would delay service.

Self-bussing may be used. If this is done, the station where guests carry their used dishes should be located on the way out. If this is not done, most guests will walk out and leave their dishes on the table. It has been found most satisfactory for cafeterias to have floor personnel who bus dishes, clean tables, replenish salt, pepper, sugar and condiments, see that napkins and glasses are available, and do other general dining area work. It is important that they work diligently, establish good procedures for clearing tables, separating dishes and putting them properly into tote boxes. They themselves should be neat and clean and dressed in clean, well-fitting uniforms.

Buffet Service

Buffet service has the advantage of reducing service personnel, but the disadvantage that it can be quite wasteful of food. In times of high food cost, the cost of the food may outweigh the advantage of lower labor cost with the result that the final cost is higher. Normally, a buffet is served at a set price with guests taking what and as much as they desire. Sometimes food portions may be controlled, as when service personnel serve guests or a service person carves the meat. Second helpings are frequently allowed, however.

Buffets make it possible to display food attractively and to merchandise in this manner. They are being used more and more to give simple, fast service for continental and other breakfasts, light lunches or meals where service must be fast and guests wish to come and go quickly. They are also good for handling large numbers of people who may wish to eat at different times. When seated service cannot handle the numbers to be served, a buffet line may work out. For instance, the Regent Hotel of Honolulu found that, with large tours in the hotel, the seated-service restaurants could not handle the demand. Therefore, for a set price to tour groups, the guests were invited to go to the banquet room of the hotel in which a buffet was set up. This enabled the hotel to accommodate them adequately with good guest satisfaction. Likewise, stag dinners, receptions, luncheons, and other special occasions can be nicely handled with buffet service.

A smorgasbord is a Swedish buffet popular in this country. It includes a large assortment of cold foods after which hot foods and then a dessert and beverage are offered. To be a true smorgasbord, pickled herring, rye bread and myost or gjetost cheese must be among the cold foods. Similarly, a Russian buffet must have caviar in a beautfiul glass bowl (or in an ice carving bowl), rye bread and sweet butter, to be properly called a Russian buffet. Other foods will, of course, be served.

It is possible for a buffet to be combined with certain kinds of other service. For instance, guests may pick up only cold foods and order the remainder of the meal. Or they may eat the cold and hot foods and then be served a dessert and beverage or just a beverage alone, the foods previous to this having been picked up at the buffet. Butter and rolls may or may not be served. Usually, water is poured by service personnel.

The table setting used for buffets is frequently American. The dishware and flatware required, plus the napkin, are usually set on the table for each cover. Normally, plates and other dishes needed for the buffet are set at the start of the line where guests can pick them up. Silver, napkins, water, etc., (picked up by guests), are usually placed at the end of the line or in another area. Desserts may be set on a separate table. Using separate tables speeds service but it is necessary to watch the flow to avoid cross traffic. It is also faster to have service personnel serve guests than to have guests serve themselves. It is best to have meat carved at a separate station.

Foods served at buffets should be colorful and attractively arranged. It is artistically desirable to have different shapes and sizes of dishes. Rechauds, bains-marie and other units can be used to keep foods hot. The height of the foods and the dishes should be varied to give an interesting pattern. Foods from the garde manger section used

for decoration, for example, can be placed behind other foods that are to be used. They should be arrayed with candles, flowers and other decorative pieces to give an attractive display. It is not desirable to have one food in back of another—making guests reach over the food in front—unless the food to the rear is tiered up so that it is easy to reach.

The buffet table should be neatly spread and have a cover on the front that completely closes the underside and table legs from view. A white table cloth can cover the top. Table linen in other colors can be used to achieve an interesting effect. The table shape can vary, but consideration should be given to flow, since some shapes will not speed service and may even hinder it.

A good system for replenishing the buffet should be worked out. Some buffets have service from both sides and these are difficult to replenish. The table should be as close as possible to the food preparation point, but this convenience factor will be influenced by service considerations. Some operations may have a rule that when a dish is about two thirds or half gone, it is removed from the table, and another, full one put in its place. The one removed is returned to the preparation area to be refilled. Vessels containing food should be about two to three inches back from the table edge.

Food served at a buffet should be of a kind that lends itself to self-service. A dish requiring a thin sauce and others that are not easy to handle should be avoided. It is usual to put cold foods and less expensive ones first in line.

However, the proper sequence may be dictated by the type of food and the time it should be eaten during the course of a meal.

Seated Service

The restaurant or other foodservice that seats its guests and serves them at their table in the familiar way is classified as a "seated-service" establishment. This is the basic, traditional method of serving food and drink. The term is used to distinguish it from other, more or less specialized methods.

TYPES OF SEATED SERVICE

There are three distinct types of table service used in this country although others may be seen occasionally. These three are: American, Russian, and French.

American Service

The simplest and least expensive type of seated service is American service. It is also fast and does not require a large amount of labor. The table setting for this service places the knife (blade side in) at the right, the soup spoon next and the teaspoon next on the outside. Normally settings are made so that the first utensil on the outside, on either the left or right, is used first, then the next utensil to it, moving in as the courses progress. Placing the soup spoon inboard of the teaspoon violates this rule but is a more common way of positioning the soup spoon. However, it is not improper to put the soup spoon on the outside where it is used

first with the first course, the teaspoon next, and the knife on the inside.

The dinner fork and then the salad fork are placed on the left. In the center a service or hors d'oeuvre plate will be set. The water glass is set at the tip of the knife and about an inch away. The coffee cup and saucer are usually placed on the table next to the teaspoon bowl. The ashtray and salt and pepper will be in the center.

If a wine glass is used, it is placed to the right of the water glass. The bread and butter plate should be above the forks and perhaps a bit to the left of them. The butter knife should be parallel to the forks on the right side of the butter plate with the blade turned in toward the center. The table may be covered first with a silence cloth and then a table cloth. However, place mats alone may be used. In more formal meals, the silencer and table cloth would be used. Silverware and dishes should not be any closer than a half inch from the edge of the table. Chairs should be out from the table, away from the cloth, and not completely under the table.

In American service, food is dished onto plates in the kitchen. The waiter takes the food on this plate to the dining area. This differs from French service, in which food is prepared and dished in front of guests from a cart near the guests' table in the dining room; and from Russian service, wherein food is dished onto serving dishes in the kitchen and then taken to the dining room where portions are removed and placed on the plates sitting in front of the guests. Coffee is often served with the meal in American service but not in other services. The coffee cup and saucer may be on the table to speed service.

American service is usually followed in fast turnover operations, coffee shops and other places where quick service is essential and the needs are not too formal. If well done, it is also adequate for seated-service operations where good service is required. Frequently, if it is used with the better type of dining operation, the coffee cup and saucer are not on the table when the guest is seated and the beverage will be served later with the dessert instead of with the meal. The procedures vary with different operations.

It is usual to serve solid foods from the left and liquids from the right, moving around the table from right to left.*

---

*Much variation occurs. Some say serve all food from the guest's left with the left hand but all beverages from the guest's right with the right hand. All clearing may be done from the right using the right hand.

Soiled dishes are removed from the table as follows: items to the left, from the left-hand side using the left hand; central items and items to the right, from the right-hand side using the right hand. The general rule in all service is that when serving at the guest's right use the right hand, and when serving at his left use the left hand. There are many variations; a fixed rule is hard to establish. Most rules should be based on what is easiest to do most efficiently and quickly for the guest. The guest's comfort should always be considered.

It is not proper to remove dishes or to start a new course, in American service or any other, until everyone at the table has finished eating the present course. Often ladies are served first completely around the table and then the men. If there is a host and hostess, the host is usually served last or next to last, and the hostess is served either last or next to last depending upon ser-

An American service setting as seen from above. (1) Ashtray, (2) salt and pepper, (3) napkin on service or hors d'oeuvre plate, (3a) an alternate position for the napkin, (4) dinner knife, (5) soup spoon, (6) teaspoon, (7) water glass, (8) cup and saucer, (9) wine glass, (10) bread and butter plate with butter knife, (11) salad and dinner fork. (The salad usually will be served where the napkin is, at 3a, after the napkin is picked up by the guest.)

vice to the host. It is usually considered improper to eat before the hostess has tasted her food or, at least, touched it with her fork. However, many times guests are urged to eat before the hostess has had an opportunity to touch the food on her plate, the reason being that eating the food while hot is most desirable.

American service is used frequently at banquets because a large number of guests can be handled qiuckly by a limited number of service personnel. Russian service is slower and takes slightly more labor but is more elegant.

The banquet head waiter is responsible for all dining room service. He directs the service personnel in how the tables should be set up, in arrangements for the head table, for setting of the silver, for decorations, and, in general, how the service is to go. If wine is served, he will plan this service, indicate the proper glass, etc. On the average, about 15 guests will be assigned per waiter. Bus boys may assist, but at the most a waiter should not be responsible for more than 25 guests.

Russian Service

Russian service has great elegance and showmanship and is frequently used for very nice meals. It is also efficient and relatively fast. It, like American service, takes less labor than French and is also suitable for rather elaborate banquet service. It takes more labor than American service but less than French and therefore may be seen more often. It also takes less skill than French service. Some individuals confuse French and Russian service. The two are, in fact, quite different.

The table setting for Russian service

follows what is common for French service, but a water glass may be on the table just above the tip of the knife, and an ash tray may be on the table. A bread and butter plate and butter knife are also used. Since Russian service is considered slightly less formal than French, the rules for setting the cover are not quite as strict.

In Russian service the plates for the course to follow are put down in their proper places before the guests. If the food is to be served hot, the plates should be hot. Likewise, cold food should be served on chilled plates. Sometimes, salads are brought to the table already dished onto cold plates.

To put the plates down for a course, a waiter or waitress uses the right hand to place the item on the right side of the guest. The movement is then to the next guest, on the left, and proceeds clockwise. When all plates are in position, the serving dish is picked up by the waiter and held in the palm of the left hand, or by the left arm and palm if it be a tray or a large platter. The right hand serves the food from the serving dish to the guest's plate at the right. Soup may be ladled into soup dishes from a tureen or it may be brought to the table in small (individual) serving dishes on a tray. Then serving personnel take these, one by one, and pour the hot soup from them into the guest's soup bowl or cup.

Considerable dexterity is required to perform good Russian service. The silver tray on which the portions of food have been dished can be heavy and very hot. Some waiters wrap a towel tightly around their left arm before putting on the jacket. This protects the arm from being burned by the hot dish.

The serving dish must be securely held and nicely balanced while the right hand manipulates a large spoon and fork, grasping the portion and then moving it without spillage to the bowl or plate of the guest. Skill and dexterity are required to pick the foods up, holding them securely during the transfer. The right hand holds the serving spoon with its bowl facing up. Directly over this, with the tongs up, is the fork. The spoon is used to scoop up the item while the fork, with some pressure on the top, holds the item on the spoon as it is being transferred to the guest's plate. The spoon can be used alone to pick up a bit of sauce from the platter and pour it over the item on the plate. The spoon is also used alone to serve some vegetables and sauces.

Coffee is served after the main meal. Coffee cups and saucers are not on the table; coffee may be poured from a buffet and served. Cream is not on the table as it may be with American service.

French Service

The most elegant service is French service but it is also slower and more expensive. At one time it was even more elaborate than it is today. It might have consisted of three or four settings of the table with each setting accommodating a number of courses. Guests would sit down and eat all the courses planned for a given setting. Then they would leave the table while it was being cleared and reset. They would then sit down again and eat another series of courses. As many as 48 or more foods might be served at one meal. Guests were not supposed to eat much of any one thing but only to taste. To a large

extent, the purpose of all the food was to make for a lavish display.

French service reached its peak in the court of Louis XIV. At that time it was called the grand cover *(le grand couvert)*. A good part of the service was the ceremony that accompanied each setting and the serving of the courses. The French service of today is descended from this service but has been considerably simplified.

Basically, French service is done from a cart called a *gueridon* which has a *rechaud* or heating unit on it. This *rechaud* is usually heated by an alcohol lamp but some *gueridons* may be equipped with a small bottle of butane or propane which fires a gas burner. The food for the guests is brought raw, or partially prepared, to the cart where it is prepared next to the table of the guests. Meats, poultry and fish may be cooked in the kitchen but will be carved or deboned on the cart. Sometimes food preparation must occur in the kitchen and only service is done at the cart. Salads, deserts and other foods may be prepared completely at the *gueridon* from raw foods.

While Russian service requires a skilled waiter, perhaps assisted by an apprentice, the personnel used for French service will be more numerous and much more skilled. A dining room using French service has a *maitre d'hôtel* in charge. In Europe, he will exercise much more authority than in this country. In America he is in charge of making reservations and assigning tables as well as determining service procedures. He may greet guests, and some *maitre d's* may even take guests to their tables and give them menus.

In foreign countries a Chef de la Salle (in this country "headwaiter") may take guests to the table and provide them with menus. In other cases, the menu is not presented by these individuals but by the captain or waiter (*Chef du Rang*). Captains are in charge of about four waiters. The *Chef du Rang* has charge of a table and is assisted by an apprentice called the *Commis du Rang*. In foreign countries another more highly trained individual may help the *Chef du Rang* and is called the *Demi-Chef*.

The dress is usually black tie, and service personnel will wear white knit cotton gloves. Large napkins will be carried *on the arm,* not under it. The *Commis* frequently is in a white waiter's jacket with white shirt, black bow tie and dark trousers.

The *Chef du Rang* usually takes the orders, gives them to the *Commis* who takes the orders to the kitchen. He gives the orders to the *Abboyeur* (announcer) who in a loud, clear voice calls them out. (The *Abboyeur* is said to have been introduced by Escoffier who wanted to reduce loud talking in the kitchen between cooks and service personnel.) When the foods are ready, the *Commis* takes them to the *Chef du Rang* who waits at the *gueridon*. The *Commis* must also bring the plates, dishes and other items required for the service.

As the *Chef du Rang* prepares the foods on the *rechaud* or in other equipment and then dishes them onto the service dishes for guests, the *Commis* serves. Service is from the right, with the right hand, except for items to be placed on the left. If the waiter is left-handed, the service may differ. Removal of plates and dishes is usually from the right with the right hand, but this too can vary. Plates and items should not be removed until all individuals have finished eating. Second servings are not given in French service.

Fingerbowls are proper after each course, at the end of the meal, or at any other time required. Fresh napkins also may be given at any time during the meal. In the most formal French service, rolls and butter are not served, and salts and peppers are not on the table. Water is not served—only wine— and, at the most, only three wine glasses are in place at a setting. More are placed on the table as needed. Ash trays are not on the table since guests are not supposed to smoke until the meal is completed. However, if guests request them, they are brought to the table.

If guests want alcoholic beverages before the meal, the *Chef du Rang* will take the orders and serve them. However, today some dining rooms allow a cocktail waitress to do this. A wine steward, the *Chef du Sommelier,* should bring the wine list and take the wine order and then later serve the wine. In some dining rooms an assistant or *Commis Sommelier* may be used. Glasses should be on the table in such position that the first wine to be consumed has its glass on the right. The progression will be inward as it is with the silverware. Some variation in wine glass placement may occur, however. No one rule will apply. It is not proper to have wine glasses inverted on the table when guests come into the dining room. This indicates that the room is not ready for them.

The *Chef du Rang* usually presents the check and collects the money. The *Commis* clears. In some large dining rooms, the man who comes around with the cart of attractive French pastries or other foods may be called the *Chef du Trancheur*. Curry boys are those who serve certain condiments and other food accompaniments.

All the silverware needed may not be on the table in French service, but will be put down as required. It is not considered proper to have more than three or four pieces of silver on either side at one time. No gross display of silver is considered proper.

A service (show) plate is usually in the center when the guest is seated and an hors d'oeuvre plate may be on this if required. The napkin can be put on this latter plate with the fold to the left. This makes it possible to pick it up with the right hand so that it opens as it is lifted. It is likewise proper for the service person seating guests to pick the napkin up, open it and give it to the guest.

The dinner fork and other forks should be on the left of the service plate. The cocktail fork for a crab, shrimp or other cocktail can be on the plate on which the cocktail is served, or placed in position on the service plate so that the right hand can pick it up conveniently. The dinner knife is to the right of the service plate with the cutting edge toward the plate. The soup spoon is usually to the right of the knife. The dessert fork and spoon are placed lengthwise across the top of the service plate. If a bread and butter plate is used, it is above and to the left of the dinner fork with the butter knife parallel to the dinner fork and the blade facing the service plate.

The number of courses in a French meal will be limited today. A dinner can consist of a soup, main course, salad and dessert served in that order. The salad is served as a separate course after the main course. If there are more courses, an hors d'oeuvre may start the meal, a fish course may then follow with a poul-

A simple French cover. (1) Dessert spoon and fork, (2) bread and butter knife (omitted in formal French service) (3) forks, (4) service plate, (5) napkin, (6) dinner knife, (7) soup spoon, (8) teaspoon, (9) wine glasses.

try course next. The main course should then be served. A salad course may also be followed by a cheese course. Coffee in demi-tasse is usually proper after the meal.

The service plate is left on until the main course is to be served. It is replaced when the salad course is to be served and remains until the end of the meal. Soup is brought from the kitchen in a tureen or other container, placed on the *rechaud* and ladled from there into cups or bowls and served to the guests.

Different foods require different eating utensils and dishes plus an appropriate method of service. The knowledge of what is correct and proper takes considerable study and training. The skill required of the *Chef du Rang* is considerable and must be coupled with a lot of showmanship. Sometimes it may be necessary for the captain or the *maitre d'hotel* to do some of the more intricate manipulations if the *Chef du Rang* is not sufficiently skilled.

French service usually requires more equipment and space than American or Russian service. However, Russian service may require extensive silver service. French service is designed for the operation that specializes in emphasizing fine dining, décor, good service, good food, good conversation and wine. It connotes leisurely dining.

French service has many traditions but modern practice may vary these, and so can ignorance. Russian service may use a platter service and then incorporate some French service procedures. This is not wrong and may introduce a desirable service. Purity for the purist's sake is not necessarily the most desirable procedure to bring about good service; some license may be permitted, providing it leads to better service. However, tradition and some of the finer points of French service should be preserved because they help us maintain some of the things that give much grace and elegance to eating.

English Service

At some clubs and, on some occasions in other foodservices, a service called English may be used. In this, foods are brought from the kitchen on platters and in serving dishes. The host carves the meat while the hostess serves the vegetables, the salad, the dessert and the beverage. The host will first place the meat portion on a hot plate and then have this passed down to the hostess who puts on the other foods and then passes it on to a guest. The first plate usually goes to the hostess because this will be the coldest food and should not go to a guest. The host is served last because there is no room for his plate until the meat being carved is removed. The meat should be in front of the host, with plates used for service immediately in front of him and between the meat and the host. In passing the plates, it is desirable to work out a passing pattern that requires the least handling of the plates. Sometimes service personnel may take plates and carry them to guests instead of having them passed.

In English service, just as in other types, the male guest of honor is seated at the right of the hostess and the second male guest of honor is seated at her left. Also, the honored lady is seated at the host's right while the second lady of honor is at his left.

It is proper to have the first course placed on the table when guests come into the dining room. Water can be poured and butter can be placed on the butter plates. Coffee cups and saucers will not be on the table but brought at the conclusion of the meal or when dessert is served. Small tables may be placed to the right and left of the host and hostess where service dishes can be placed when the service is ended. However, service personnel may remove these.

The setting of the silverware on the table may follow that used in American service but this can vary. Knives and spoons are to the right and forks are to the left. The order of placement is from the outside in as the courses occur. Wine glasses will be placed to the right of the water glass which sits just above the tip of the knife.

In English service it may be proper for guests to fold their napkins and put them back in place. This is also proper at family service because the napkin is expected to be used again by a particular member of the family, and napkins may be put in napkin rings for this purpose. It is usually not considered proper to fold the napkin after its use in other types of service. Sometimes English service is called formal family service.

Room Service

Room service represents an important source of revenue for the food and beverage department as well as a significant factor in the satisfaction of guests. Hotels and motels may wish to offer the service of food or beverages in the rooms of guests. If so, a special organization may be required to give such service.

Some hotels even have special room service production kitchens where the foods and beverages ordered are prepared.

Considerable space must be available so that small mobile tables can be preset and ready to be moved with the items ordered to guests' rooms. *Mise en place* is extremely important since distances are usually great and hot foods can quickly cool down and cool foods can warm up. A special service elevator is desirable if the amount of service is large.

Normally a hotel or motel will have a special number for guests to call for room service. The order will be taken and transferred to the proper personnel so beverages and foods can be readied. Timing is important so items come out together. Service personnel must also be trained to assemble all of the tableware required, butter, rolls, etc., as required. A recheck should be made to see that everything is on hand since, as may be the case in a dining room, items are not quickly available if they are forgotten.

Many operations follow the practice of having the check time-stamped when the order is received, when it leaves for the guest's room and when the signed check is brought back.

Oriental Dining

There are three major types of Chinese food—the Peking, or north food; the Shanghai, or middle area food; and the Cantonese, or southern food. Peking food is spicier; some dishes can be downright hot with seasonings. Instead of rice, wheat products such as noodles and buns are served. The food varies somewhat even within the area, depending upon local sources of food. Meat is more common and seafood less so in the interior areas. The Shanghai food resembles the northern cuisine more than the Cantonese and will depend upon wheat and other grains more than rice. Cantonese food features rice, much seafood and much more fruit. It is more delicate than the others. A wider variety of foods will also be served.

Chinese dining and food customs are quite traditional and eating may be accompanied by rites indicating the meaning behind the service and the kinds of foods being eaten. The wheat bun eaten in northern and middle cuisines is often said to be the symbol of longevity. Rice is consumed in the Cantonese meal at the end, not only to satisfy a lusty appetite, but to indicate that "You have deigned to eat my poor meal, which must end with the most common of food, rice." Research may well show that the Chinese developed a level of cuisine with no equal in history, in excellence of food and ceremony of eating, long before the French established their continental or haute cuisine.

Japanese food is quite different from Chinese, but there are some parallels. Rice is common but so are noodles (udon). Seafood is common. The Japanese are fond of raw fish which is served commonly and is delicious. The Japanese believe that food must be pictorial as well as flavorful, and they will show remarkable plastic likenesses of the different foods they serve—in show cases or windows—so that customers can view the offerings before they enter the restaurant. Japanese tradition holds that food and dining, as every human activity, should be made as beautiful as possible. Foods therefore will be presented on extremely attractive dishware very aritstically arranged. It is of interest to note that soup can be served at a Japanese meal at almost any time. Foods can be prepared on charcoal broilers or on gas-heated griddles in front of guests. Guests are often seated on the floor and served from a very low table. Some operations in this country provide a sunken floor beneath the table to accommodate the legs of guests.

Much of the success of foods from the Orient depends upon the service, the dishware, the dress of the service personnel, the décor and atmosphere. Much food called Polynesian is a polyglot of Eastern foods from as far apart as India and Japan. It is frequently more Cantonese and Hawaiian than typical of the South Sea Islands. Since much of the success of these Oriental foods will depend upon service, the details of this function should be carefully established.

Organization for Table Service

The organization for the dining area may vary considerably with different operations. The organization used in continental types of foodservices has been explained, in which the maitre d'hôtel is in charge with a large number of individuals working under him. Some foodservices may have no head of services but the task is handled by an assistant manager. Some may use a host or hostess who, in addition to being in charge, will greet and seat guests. Sometimes this individual in charge may be a head waiter or head waitress. Whatever form of organization is established should be effective and made to work.

The number of hours usually clocked in a foodservice is substantial and, unless they are managed properly, costs higher than required can be incurred. Usually, the ratio of hours used for service, or front of the house, to the hours used for food production, or back of the house, is 10 to 7.

The individual in charge should see to it that service proceeds properly and that service personnel are neat, clean and follow established policy. This person should discipline and, perhaps, may be responsible for hiring and firing, although management may reserve this right for itself or some other person higher in authority. The scheduling of the service personnel should be under this person as well as assignment of work stations and days off. Work assignments should be made on an impartial and balanced basis. Schedules should be posted sufficiently in advance so that members of the service staff can make personal plans. A rotation system should be used in allocating days off and the stations at which personnel will work. In this manner, the same day off will not always fall to the same person and, from time to time, the days off will fall on a weekend. Of course, this can be varied if personnel wish to have the same days off. However, the system devised should be fair to all. Some stations in the dining area are better than others because they are easier to work or provide more tips. Unless there is a policy which says that the service personnel longest on the payroll get these stations, or for some other reason, the working at stations should be rotated.

A policy should be established to set up time for breaks and for eating meals. Some type of rotation system usually works well. A policy should exist on what can and cannot be eaten by the help and the head of the service department, or the production department, may have to check this. Some type of record should be maintained on what service personnel eat so that its cost can be calculated.

Part III Bibliography

Anon., *Meat Manual,* 6th ed., National Livestock and Meat Board, Chicago, 1961.

American Meat Institute, *Science of Meat and Meat Products,* W. H. Freeman, San Francisco, 1960.

Bull, S., *Meat for the Table,* McGraw Hill Co., New York City, 1951.

Cornell Quarterly, "Essentials of Table Service," School of Hotel Administration, Cornell University, Ithaca, N. Y., 1971.

Hedrick, Floyd D., *Purchasing Management in the Small Company,* American Management Association, Inc., New York City, 1971.

Kotschevar, Lendal H., *Quantity Food Production,* 3rd edition, Cahners Books, Boston, 1974.

Kotschevar, Lendal H., *Quantity Food Purchasing,* 2nd ed., John Wiley & Sons, New York City, 1975.

Lundberg, D., and Kotschevar, L., *Understanding Cooking,* Avi Press, Newport, Conn., 1965.

Miles, Lawrence D., *Value Analysis Technology,* McGraw Hill Co., New York City, 1966.

West, B., Wood, LaVelle, and Harger, G., *Foodservice in Institutions,* John Wiley & Sons, New York City, 1965.

THE
INVESTMENT
VENTURE

A summing up

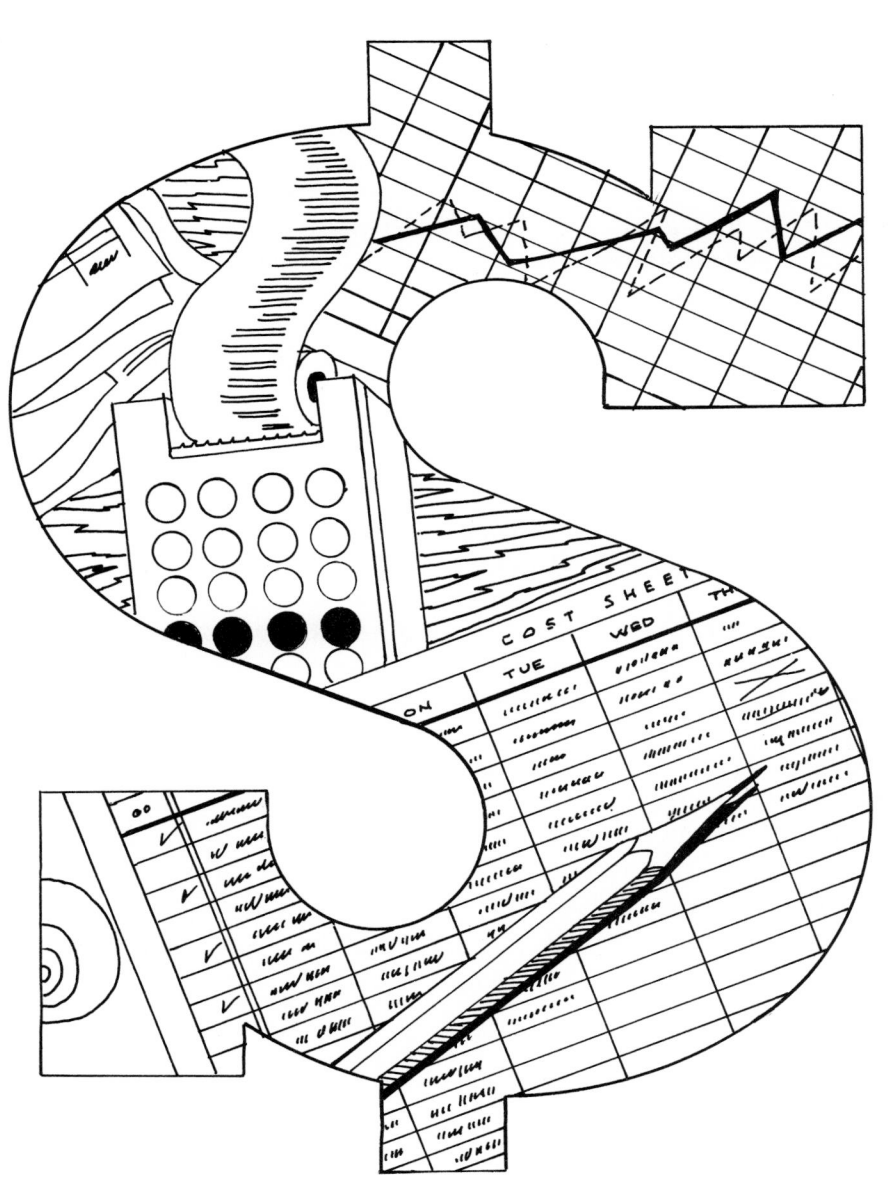

IN the preceding chapters we have studied foodservice management with the menu at the center of all planning and operations. In doing this we moved from a simple definition to a rather complex one. It was early noted that the menu is a device for communicating to the patron the food and drink offered and the price to be paid. We saw the menu as a merchandising tool. As our discussions proceeded we expanded our concept of the menu. We began to see it as a working plan as well as a published bill of fare. Ultimately we identified the menu as a management tool of the first importance, used in initiating and controlling almost all work activity.

From the beginning we accepted the thesis that competent menu making requires knowledge of the industry as a whole, and special acquaintance with the type of foodservice operation in which we are engaged, as well as experience in a particular establishment. We reviewed the history of foodservice and surveyed the industry as it stands today.

In the second part of our study we examined the task of constructing a menu and found that it involves two kinds of effort: (1) research and analysis for laying a firm foundation, and (2) the actual planning and writing of the menu. Too frequently, we observed, menu writers neglect the first phase or do a poor job of it.

In Part III we recognized the inherent problems faced by management in making the menu work. It was clear that, standing alone, the menu is only a plan; that its provisions can be realized only by integrating them into the operation of the three major departments — Purchasing, Production and Service.

We have now arrived at the point of planning a foodservice enterprise. How do all these operating principles apply in a concrete situation? This we may well ask if our propositions are to meet the rigorous test of justifying our investment.

Although our discussions have not always emphasized the profit principle, we have consistently had at least a "third eye" on the bottom line of the ledger. In this final part of the text, special attention is given to the financial aspects of menu planning. We will see that the menu must inevitably fit into the financial structure of the enterprise — for more reasons than one. Whether his foodservice is profit-oriented or not, the menu planner must concern himself with costs and budgets, if only to allow his plan to operate in an atmosphere of financial stability.

When the commercial menu does not produce enough revenue, or when the institutional menu does not keep within reasonable budgetary limits, financial failure is certain to result. It may often be necessary to strike a fine balance in either kind of operation. What must be avoided are the two extremes: expecting unrealistic revenues from a menu, and giving the menu free rein to demand resources it does not need.

Ordinarily a commercial menu must generate enough revenue to cover capital costs in addition to paying direct operational costs and producing a profit. The non-profit menu is usually expected to show at least enough return to cover operational costs, if not some capital costs as well. We shall now address ourselves to these aspects of sound management policy.

CHAPTER 12

Planning a Foodservice Enterprise

Controlling costs is frequently one of the biggest management problems regardless of whether a profit or a budget constraint must be met. Margins over cost in most foodservices are small and, since it is extremely difficult to control some costs such as those for labor, food or supplies, one can quickly get into trouble. Banks frequently label foodservices as "an easy to enter, low skill, high risk and low profit" industry, which means that banks use a lot of discretion in making loans to them.

Many individuals seek to go into business in this industry because they believe it to be profitable and not too difficult to operate a foodservice. Some foodservices do not require a high capital investment, as in franchises, and individuals who otherwise could not go into business find this one within their reach. Recent data, however, show that investment costs are rising. For instance, in 1971 foodservice corporations had to invest $43 for every $100 they gained in sales. It could easily be higher in 1975.

Most foodservices can be started with from 25 to 50 per cent of their total capital costs. Some franchises can be started with only $10,000 to $20,000 put up by the franchisee. A new seated-service restaurant of any consequence will cost more than $4,000 per seat. Thus, if an individual wanted to have a restaurant of 100 seats, he would need a half million dollars or more. If he put up 20 per cent in cash, he would have to borrow or owe to creditors $400,000. Going into foodservice today is big business and usually requires more capital than an individual has. This is one of the reasons the foodservice industry is becoming more and more a corporate-type industry and less and less an individually or family owned industry.

Because of ease of entry, believed profitability and easy management, the industry has many who enter it only to find they have been mistaken. Anyone planning to go into this business should examine the venture carefully and seek the advice and counsel of experienced operators. A large number of favorable characteristics must be identified before taking the leap. A menu and its potential may be a highly desirable item to study at this time.

Location and Market

One of the most important success factors in a foodservice is location, which indeed may be decisive in determining whether the operation has a market. Some have put it more emphatically, as witness Mr. Statler's famous remark on the subject. When asked what three things a hotel had to have for success, he replied: "Location, location, location."

Some operations get 95 per cent of their patrons within a relatively close area, while others may have to seek them from a considerable distance away. It is important to know how many potential customers go by the door. It is also important to know whether or not they might come in. For instance, an operation may be successful on one side of the street and unsuccessful on the other side. On the Ohio State Turnpike patronage is good at the eastern entrance for westbound traffic, but poor at the western exit for that traffic. Contrariwise, east-moving traffic patronizes the restaurant at the west entrance well, but the one at the east exit poorly. The reason given for this difference in units opposite each other on the turnpike is that people seem to set a goal, which in this case is to reach a state border. Only after achieving it do they plan to stop.

The speed of traffic may be important. Signs must be strategically set to coincide with speed so that people see them ahead and can make plans to stop, but not so far ahead that they forget they wanted to stop. Suddenly, they come upon the unit going at high speed and thus pass by. The orange roof of Howard Johnson's or the golden arches of McDonald's have been purposely designed to show up some distance away so that motorists can identify the unit before they come upon it.

Parking can be important to some locations and not to others. Often the location may lack desirability because it is in a deteriorating neighborhood or it may be desirable because it is a growing neighborhood.

Competition should also be checked. The effect of it can vary. Competition may be harmful if the new operation is to be in direct competition with existing services. However, it may not be harmful if it is a complementary type of operation. Many foodservices may be in close proximity to each other but each, by emphasizing a different product, does well. Thus, within a block one may find a McDonald's, a Red Barn, a Colonel Sanders, a Pancake House, an Arbys and all doing well. However, if two operations in the same area offer identical or similar products, one or the other seems to fade away.

A market can be known to exist for a certain location or there may be a market potential that must be built. Even with an existing market, it should be well researched because it may not be durable. A very popular owner may sell and the buyer may think he has inherited the clientele, only to find that they have followed the former owner who has set up in a new location. Unless a market is well established and is well defined and can be held, it is best to interpret market projections conservatively. Studies show there is a marked tendency to overestimate, rather than underestimate, markets.

It is important to get an estimate of the number of potential customers but a definition of their characteristics is also necessary. Their income, social habits, eating patterns, ethnic background, age levels, sex and many other factors must be known as precisely as possible when designing an operation and a product for the market. Locating a drive-in for teenagers in a community where a large number of retired individuals live would obviously be a poor marketing decision.

Good market studies ask questions like these:

Who are the customers or the potential customers? Can they be well defined?

What do they want? Can it be produced for them at a price they want to pay?

Why will they come to this establishment?

What are their incomes? When do they get paid?

What is their age level? What is their background?

How many potential customers are there in the area?

What percentage of these will probably come in on a single day?

Where does the market eat now? What do they eat?

What is the competition for this market? Is the market durable?

The Feasibility Study

Any planning for the installation of a foodservice should include a feasibility study designed to answer the question: "Will the business pay?" This question, if applied to a commercial operation, should read ". . . pay a profit." If it is

an institution, a better question would be, "Can it be operated within budgeted cost restraints?"

The feasibility study should be far reaching and cover all expected costs, conditions and income. It must be realistic and built upon the best obtainable facts. If it is not, it is a waste of time. There are many guides and broad estimates that can be used to help in estimating costs, but in the final figures actual costs should be given. Thus, while one might in preliminary planning use the standard of $35 per square foot for equipping a kitchen, the final feasibility study should list the equipment needed and the cost installed.

CAPITAL INVESTMENT

One of the first things to determine in a feasibility study is what the capital costs are. There are a number of ways in which a foodservice can be established. A new building can be erected on a site by the owner of the foodservice, with land, equipment and furnishings belonging to him. Or, the land can be leased and the owner puts up the building, equips it and furnishes it. Or, the site and building can be built by someone else and leased; the owner of the building then furnishes and equips it. Sometimes the furnishings and equipment are leased. Where everything is furnished and the place is ready to operate, the operation is called a "turn-key" facility.*

---

*A "one party" business is one with a single owner of the land, building, equipment and furnishings. "In a "two party" business the landowner puts the building on the land as a shell and the business owner equips and furnishes it. "Three party" indicates that the landowner leases the land to the building owner who in turn leases it to the business operator.

Costs may run a third of the total cost each for (1) building, (2) equipment and furnishings and (3) mechanical—plumbing, ventilation, wiring, ductwork, heating and air-conditioning. There is evidence, however, that mechanical is beginning to cost more than the other two.

An architect's fee normally is eight to 15 per cent of total costs. It is important in planning that all details be incorporated by the architect in the original plans. Changes in plans cost a great deal more than original designs.

A minimum of three months is usually required for the architect to draft the plans after management gives him final details. After this, bidding must take place. A month or more may elapse before a bid is accepted and a bonded contractor awarded the bid. Another eight to 12 months may be required to complete the building.

Parking frequently is an important consideration in planning. A foodservice in an urban area in which patrons come in cars should have parking spaces for a fourth of the house seats. An establishment on a highway should have one space for every two seats. Site work for a new area usually runs two per cent of total costs.* This includes parking lot preparation and paving, landscaping, lawn, trees, outdoor shrubbery and outside lighting. A 40 square foot sign installed can cost from $400 to $1,200. It can also be leased. Whether owned or leased, it is best to include a maintenance

contract in the arrangements. Maintenance contracts may also be desirable for other equipment.

BUILDING COSTS

Costs vary considerably in different areas. Some planners figure on spending $25 to $35 a square foot for building space alone. In 1968 the cost of furnishing a kitchen with equipment, pots and pans, etc., ran from $25 to $40 per square foot. Dining room furniture with equipment such as dishware, silverware, etc., cost $15 to $18 per square foot. In 1968 the cost of a good seated-service restaurant ran $1,200 to $3,000 per seat.

If a building shell—a conventional finished building—is used, the cost of adding the mechanical equipment can be from 20 to 25 per cent of total additional costs. In 1968, the cost of changing the open space of a shell into an acceptable dining area ran around $10 per square foot, with furnishings and equipment to be added to this.

The minimum space for a seat in a dining area is 12 square feet but usually 15 to 18 square feet is better. The ratio of dining to back-of-the-house space usually is 50-50 but the tendency today is to have the latter less. Some back-of-the-house areas now run only 25 per cent to 35 per cent of total space.

If a central commissary is used, the space needs can be less for the kitchen but not for refrigeration or freezer space. One satellite cafeteria of Howard Johnson's operating on central commissary production can serve over 1,000 meals a day from a 12x12-foot kitchen. The use of space today, because of its high cost, should be carefully analyzed, especially in high-rent areas.

---

*In 1968 the Bank of America reported that parking lot improvement costs ran:

Gravel parking	15¢ per square foot
Asphalt paving	25¢ per square foot
Concrete curbs and gutters	$2.25 per linear foot

If a new operation is planned to be set up in a building that needs renovation, four months or more will be required to complete the unit. Present equipment and furnishings should be carefully evaluated. Furnishing life is usually considered as about five years. Some equipment has the same life span. Normally, equipment is considered as having a 10-year life but some units can last 20 years. Buildings can be depreciated in 15 to 40 years, depending upon conditions. Interior décor may have to be changed every three to five years to keep up with competition and to offer needed novelty and newness. Thus, in any renovation project or installation of new units, the life of carpeting, decorations, etc., should be carefully evaluated. It is possible to add too much life to kitchens and furnishings. Some kitchen stainless steel ware will be there long after the building has collapsed from old age!

Trade-in value of old operating equipment is usually 10 to 15 per cent of original cost. If reconditioned, the value may be as high as 40 to 50 per cent of original cost.

Examine buildings over 30 to 40 years old very carefully. They may not be worth renovating. About $1.50 to $2.00 per square foot may be needed to gut an existing interior, plus an additional $7 to $10 per square foot to complete the reconstruction. This does not include costs per square foot of $3 to $4 for electrical, $3 to $5 for plumbing and air-conditioning, and 75¢ for a fire-sprinkling system. To add interior finishing such as booths, counters, bar, and floor covering—not including equipment and furnishings—costs an additional $16

to $20 per square foot. Equipment costs can run from $15 to $35 per square foot. Thus, to renovate a building of 4,000 square feet could cost nearly half a million dollars.

RENT OR LEASE

There are various ways to make arrangements to rent or lease a building and its furnishings. A straight rental of so much per year, per month or other period, may be arranged. This may be two per cent to 20 per cent of gross sales depending upon what is included. The highest rent would be for a turn-key operation, called a Grade 4 lease, with everything ready to go. Even some utilities may be paid by the landlord. A "net, net, net" lease is one in which the business owner pays taxes and insurance in addition to a rental. In a "net, net" lease the operator pays only the taxes and rental. A "net" lease means that only a rental is paid and the owner of the building pays taxes and insurance on the property. The owner of the business, and not the landlord, must usually carry insurance on equipment and furnishings if he owns them. When the landlord owns them, the procedure will vary.

The length of the lease is also variable. If the operator has a good track record in business, the lease may be written for 10 years. Because of the instability of many foodservices, leases often run for only five years or less. The lessee must usually guarantee the lease. This guarantee may require that two to four months rent be applied on the final months of the lease. Options to renew the lease may be included. Transfer of the lease may be allowed only with the property owner's approval. The seller of the lease may be able to get his lease guarantee back from the new buyer.

A Grade 3 lease is one covering an improved building shell with food preparation equipment in it. New furnishings and some décor and other changes may be required. Rent is lower than for a Grade 4 or turn-key operation. A Grade 2 lease is for a slightly improved shell. It should include partitions, finished floor (carpet, tile, hardwood, etc.), finished coiling, heating, ventilation, electrical wiring and outlets, air-conditioning run-outs, finished plumbing with fixtures and drains, etc. The rental cost for this may run six to eight per cent of gross sales.

The lowest rental is a Grade 1 lease which is an unimproved shell. It is completed with exterior and interior walls and has basic floors. Almost any business could go into it. The rent per square foot per year for the following types of units might be:

Luxury restaurant $2.50
Coffee shop ....$3.00 to $4.00
Cafeteria $2.25
Snack bar or Carry-out $5.00
Drive-in ....$5.00 to $6.00

Thus, if a 2,000-square-foot shell had a luxury restaurant put in it with 75 seats, and did $225,000 in gross sales per year, the rental cost would be about 2¼ per cent of gross sales. A drive-in occupying the same building and doing double the amount of business would pay 2½ per cent of gross sales as lease rent.

A rental agreement can also be set up as a percentage of gross sales, which means that a variable rental is paid. Another method is to have a minimum rental plus a percentage of gross sales.

Or rent can be set at a sliding percentage on gross sales with the per cent figure declining as sales increase. Usually, there is not much difference in the final amount; the owner has to get a certain amount to pay an adequate return. A return on the investment of eight per cent is normal and a profit for the individual leasing the property is around two to five per cent of sales.

It is important in negotiating a lease to establish when the lease is to start. If rent is paid for a period before the business opens, the property may have to be operated for some time to erase the rental deficit, before it begins to show a profit.

OTHER BUILDING COSTS

It takes a down payment of 25 to 30 per cent to purchase equipment and furnishings with three to five years to pay, interest being paid on the balance. Equipment and furnishings can also be leased.

If a business already operating is purchased, from 25 to 30 per cent down is the minimum, although an individual having good credit might get the business with a lower down-payment.

The amount paid for goodwill should be analyzed. Goodwill is the value of obtaining an operating business, representing the money, effort and time in building a profitable operation. Some say it is the earning power of a business. But it should not be over-valued. It is necessary to estimate how long goodwill can be kept.

In purchasing any foodservice, the buyer should look at the books for past profitability, going back at least three to five years. Many indirect factors can be examined for operating clues, such as taxes paid on employee wages (for labor cost), maintenance and repair charges, accounts payable and how long they existed, and similar indicators.

There is a value in getting a good labor force but an evaluation should be made to determine exactly how good it is. Check absenteeism, turnover rate, etc. Check the condition of equipment and furnishings and the building. Examine the lease. Some authorities say that if a going business is purchased, approximately one to three days' gross sales can be paid as rent or approximately three to nine per cent gross sales. It is wise also to check with past owners to gain past performance data rather than data that applies only to the present ownership.

OTHER CAPITAL COSTS

More capital is necessary than that required to get a business into turn-key condition. Working capital sufficient for pre-opening expenses, payroll, supplies, advertising, menus, operating expenses for three to six months, and a contingency fund for emergencies, will be needed.

Some costs may be taken from cash flow but this should not be overestimated. Cash flow is money from income derived from sales, reserves for depreciation or capital reduction held until payment is needed, etc. Capital needs for inventories may also be substantial. Payment for purchases may be C.O.D. or weekly. With good credit rating, credit for 30 days may be obtained.

Normally, a good inventory should turn over 26 times a year. Thus, if an inventory of $4,000 is maintained in food, food purchases will run around $104,000 per year. Some operators say the storage facilities should be like a checking account with items moving in and out fast rather than being held as money in a savings account. Liquor inventories may turn over four or five times a year if wines are stocked because these may be held. However, some operators check the turnover of beers and spirits separately and require that they have a turnover every two weeks (unless spirits are purchased in large quantities to gain discounts and are held).

There will also be the cost of licenses, bonds for taxes, performance bonds, etc., plus other capital requirements. Liquor licenses can be costly; a transfer usually takes one to two months. The license usually is in the name of the business owner even though someone else operates the business for him.

Health and sanitation regulations should be checked at the very start of planning. Approval by public health authorities of layout and equipment is frequently required. If a foodservice ships food across state lines or serves food on a public transportation system crossing state lines, federal health regulations must be observed. Most public health licenses are non-transferable.

Setting up the Feasibility Study

There are various ways to set up a feasibility study. One might set up a hypothetical profit and loss statement, or a budget (for a non-profit type of operation), and then analyze these figures. Sometimes the yield desired on the investment, plus the amount of expected profit, may be the base used to set up operating figures. For instance, consider a seated-service restaurant including a catering service and bar, serving only lunches and dinners. If the following data is applied, the analysis might appear as shown below.

Operating Data

Lunch: Turnover 2½ times   Occupancy average 75%   Check average $1.50
Dinner: Turnover 2 times   Occupancy average 80%   Check average $3.15
Bar and special catering income per day: $100
Closed Mondays except holidays; average number of days of operation per year 312
Yield on investment desired 8%
Profit before taxes desired 5%

Feasibility Data

Amount invested	$200,000
Return on investment	$200,000 × 8% = $16,000
Sales needed at 5% profit to gives $16,000 return per year	$16,000 ÷ 5% = $320,000
Average check*	$2.50
Checks needed per year to produce $320,000 in sales	$320,000 ÷ $2.50 = 128,000 checks
Checks per day needed	128,000 ÷ 312 days = 410 checks per day
Income needed per day	$2.50 average check × 410 = $1,025.

Estimated Income per Day

Lunch: 120 seats × .75 occupancy × 2½ turnovers × $1.50 check average	= $ 337.50
Dinner: 120 seats × .80 occupancy × 2 turnovers × $3.15 check average	= $ 604.80
Bar and catering income per day	= $ 100.00
Income per day	$1,042.30
Income needed per day	1,025.00
Expected income over income needed per day	$ 17.30

*Average check is derived as follows:
(120 × .75 × 2½) + (120 × .80 × 2) = 417 served per day and $1,042.30 income per day ÷ 417 = $2.499.

Thus, this operation should be successful if the basic data on occupancy, check average, etc. are corerct or approximately so.

In addition to checking for feasibility, location and market, other factors are needed to produce a successful operation. Management must be competent to operate the business, having good capability in finance and accounting, food production and service, merchandising, personnel management, sanitation, hosting, etc. The foodservice business is a personality business and a manager must be able to meet people and have them like him at the first meeting. Stamina and good health are needed because hours of work are long and there may be few days away from the job.

Evaluating Performance

Profit is not the sole criterion in evaluating the satisfactory performance of a business. Many foodservice operators want other things besides profit and some of these may be satisfaction in pleasing customers and winning recognition as a leader in the industry and as a valued citizen of the community. Frequently an individual who can operate a business successfully is also able to accomplish these other things he thinks are the mark of success. The measurement of these non-dollar factors as success indicators is difficult and perhaps such measurement must be made by the individual himself.

However, all businesses must function "in the black" and most standards of evaluation will be based on dollar evaluations and can be obtained either from the balance sheet or from the profit and loss statement. Some of these dollar standards follow.

To determine whether a business is liquid or not, a factor called the "current ratio" may be used. This is a comparison of current assets to current liabilities. Assets should be greater than liabilities. A ratio of 1:1 is barely satisfactory and a 2:1 or 3:1 ratio better. This means that current assets such as accounts receivable, inventory, cash and other quickly convertible assets must exceed liabilities such as capital payments due within a current operating period, accounts payable, etc.

Another standard method of evalua-

tion is to calculate the ratio between dollar sales and working capital. This can indicate satisfactory operation and good financial achievement. A high ratio of sales to working capital such as $40:1 to $50:1 is desirable. Thus, if an operation has $320,000 in gross sales per year, the working capital should be between $8,000 and $6,400. This shows a low ratio of working capital requirement to sales, and a quick turnover of working capital.

Another ratio called the "solvency ratio" may be used to indicate worth with respect to debt. This is a ratio of the dollars an owner has in the business to the dollars creditors have in it. A 1:1 ratio is considered adequate but the more dollars an owner has in the business as compared to the ones he owes, the stronger will be his business. A ratio of less than 1:1 such as 1:4 indicates the foodservice is operating more on the money of creditors than on that of ownership, a condition that might be desirable but could be quite dangerous if creditors pressed for payment.

Certain indicators of profitability are used to evaluate the performance of a business. Net profit has been mentioned as a measure. This is usually stated as a percentage of gross sales. Net profit represents the amount remaining after all expenses have been deducted. A net profit before taxes of $1\frac{1}{4}$ to five per cent is not unusual.

Another way to measure profitability is to calculate the percentage of the rate of return, or yield, on capital invested, sometimes called the ratio of net profit to net worth. (Net worth is the amount the owner actually has in the business.) From five to 12 per cent is usually considered satisfactory. This means that a profit of $1 should be earned for every $8 to $20 the owner has in the business.

A third percentage in this group used as an evaluating factor is the ratio of net profit to total assets. From three to six per cent is considered a fair return when comparing net profit and total assets. It is a measure of the ability of the operation to get a fair return on the total assets used.

Another measure can be based on the return on investment. We saw this done in the feasibility study. For instance, if an owner makes $15,000 profit in a year and has $200,000 invested in the business, he has a 7½ per cent return ($15,000 ÷ $200,000 = .075). It can also be calculated using these three steps:

1. Calculate the sales turn using gross sales divided by investment.

2. Calculate how much profit is in every sales dollar.

3. From these, get the per cent return on investment by multiplying the per cent of profit times the sales turn.

For instance, if the profit is $15,000 the investment is $200,000 and sales are $400,000, we would calculate:

1. $\dfrac{\$400,000 \text{ sales}}{\$200,000 \text{ investment}} = 2$ (sales turn)

2. $\dfrac{\$15,000 \text{ profit}}{\$400,000 \text{ sales}} = 3.75\%$ profit

3. 2 (sales turn) × .0375 (profit) = 7½% return on investment.

A measurement of the operating efficiency of a non-commercial operation is often simpler. The most usual check is to see if operating costs are below budgeted amounts or income. Many institutional foodservices are operated for reasons other than dollars and it may be important to compare other factors as well as performance in dollars. However, a satisfactory performance must be achieved in dollars, or an operation cannot last very long in achieving these other factors.

Part IV Bibliography

Dukas, P., and Lundberg, D., *How to Operate a Restaurant,* Ahrens, New York City, 1960.

Fairbrook, Paul, *Starting and Managing a Small Restaurant,* Small Business Administration, U. S. Government Printing Office, Washington, D. C., 1964.

Fay, G. T., Rhoads, R. C., and Rosenblatt, R. L., *Managerial Accounting,* Wm. C. Brown Co., Dubuque, Iowa, 1971.

Fitzgerald, Jean, *The Foodservice Business,* Bank of America, San Francisco, 1968.

National Restaurant Association, *Washington Report,* Vols. 16 through 22, Chicago, Ill.

National Restaurant Association, *Uniform System of Accounts for Restaurants,* Chicago, Illinois, 1967.

Index